THE PATH OF PURIFICATION

To my Upajjhāya, the late venerable Paeḷāēnē Siri Vajirañāṇa Mahānāyakathera of Vajirārāma, Colombo, Ceylon.

FOREWORD

The spiritual path is based on working with and training the mind. The example of this is the Buddha himself. Persevering in the practise of meditation, he attained full, complete enlightenment. Enlightenment cannot be attained by magic. It requires exertion and dedication to the path of buddhadharma, the essence and process of which is meditation.

The simplicity and richness of the Theravadin tradition provides the foundation for all Buddhist practise. Therefore I would like to welcome this new edition of the Visuddhimagga, which has been the foremost guide to Theravadin discipline for more than a thousand years. It should enable Western students to share Buddhaghosa's insights into reality and into the essentials of Buddhist practise. The publication of a text such as this is an important step towards making the entire wealth of the teachings of enlightenment accessible and should inspire many to follow the Buddha's way of meditation.

Chögyam Trungpa

TRANSLATOR'S PREFACE

Originally I made this translation for my own instruction because the only published version was then no longer obtainable. So it was not done with any intention at all of publication; but rather it grew together out of notes made on some of the book's passages. By the end of 1953 it had been completed, more or less, and put aside. Early in the following year a suggestion to publish it was put to me, and I eventually agreed, though not without a good deal of hesitation. Reasons for agreeing, however, seemed not entirely lacking. The only previous English version of this remarkable work had long been out of print. Justification too could in some degree be founded on the rather different angle from which this version is made.

Over a year was then spent in typing out the MS. during which time, and since, a good deal of revision has taken place, the intention of the revision being always to propitiate the demon of inaccuracy and at the same time to make the translation perspicuous and the translator inconspicuous. Had publication been delayed, it might well have been more polished. Nevertheless the work of polishing is probably endless. Somewhere a halt must be made.

A guiding principle—the foremost, in fact—has throughout been avoidance of misrepresentation or distortion; for the ideal translation (which has yet to be made) should, like a looking-glass, not discolour or blur or warp the original which it reflects. Literalness, however, on the one hand and considerations of clarity and style on the other make irreconcilable claims on a translator, who has to choose and to compromise. Vindication of his choice is sometimes difficult.

I have dealt at the end of the Introduction with some particular problems. Not, however, with all of them or completely; for the space allotted to an introduction is limited.

Much that is circumstantial has now changed since the Buddha discovered and made known his liberating doctrine 2,500 years ago, and likewise since this work was composed some 9 centuries later. On the other hand, the Truth he discovered has remained untouched by all that circumstantial change. Old cosmologies give place to new; but the questions of consciousness, of pain and death, of responsibility for acts, and of what should be looked to in the scale of values as the highest of all, remain. Reasons for the perennial freshness of the Buddha's teaching—of his handling of these questions—are several, but not least among them is its independence of any particular cosmology. Established as it is for its foundation on the self-evident insecurity of the human situation (the Truth of Suffering), the structure of the Four Truths provides an unfailing standard of value, unique in its simplicity, its completeness and its ethical purity, by means of which any situation can be assessed and a profitable choice made.

Now I should like to make acknowledgements, as follows, to all those without whose help this translation would never have been begun, persisted with or completed.

To the venerable Nyanatiloka Mahathera (from whom I first learned Pali) for his most kind consent to check the draft MS. However, although he had actually read through the first two chapters, a long spell of illness unfortunately prevented him from continuing with this himself.

To the venerable Soma Thera for his unfailing assistance both in helping me to gain familiarity with the often difficult Pali idiom of the commentaries and to get something of the feel—as it were, 'from inside' — of Pali literature against its Indian background. Failing that, no translation would ever have been made: I cannot tell how far I have been able to express any of it in the rendering.

To the venerable Nyanaponika Thera, German pupil of the venerable Nyanatiloka Mahathera, for very kindly undertaking to check the whole MS. in detail with the venerable Nyanatiloka Mahathera's German translation (I knowing no German).

To all those with whom I have had discussions on the *Dhamma*, which have been many and have contributed to the clearing up not a few unclear points.

Lastly, and what is mentioned last bears its own special emphasis, it has been an act of singular merit on the part of Mr. A. Semage, of Colombo, to undertake to publish this translation.

The Printers must also be thanked for the excellence of their work.

Island Hermitage,
Dodanduwa, Ceylon.

Ñāṇamoli Bhikkhu,
Vesākha-māse, 2499: May, 1956.

INTRODUCTION

The *Visuddhimagga*—here rendered 'Path of Purification'—is perhaps unique in the literature of the world. It systematically summarizes and interprets the teaching of the Buddha contained in the Pali *Tipiṭaka*, which is now recognized in Europe as the oldest and most authentic record of the Buddha's words. As the principal non-canonical authority of the *theravāda*, it forms the hub of a complete and coherent method of exegesis of the Tipitaka, using the 'Abhidhamma Method' as it is called. And it sets out detailed practical instructions for developing purification.

Background and main facts

The works of Bhadantăcariya Buddhaghosa fill more than thirty volumes in the Pali Text Society's Latin-Script edition; but what is known of the writer himself is meagre enough for a page or two to contain the bare facts.

Before dealing with those facts, however, and in order that they may appear oriented, it is worth while first to digress a little by noting how Pali literature falls naturally into three main historical periods. The early or classical period, which may be called the First period, begins with the *tipiṭaka* itself in the 6th century B.C. and ends with the *Milinda-pañhā* about five (?) centuries later. These works, composed in India, were brought to Ceylon where they were maintained in Pali but written about in Sinhalese. By the 1st century A.C. Sanskrit (independently of the rise of Mahayana) or a vernacular had probably quite displaced Pali as the medium of study in all the Buddhist 'schools' on the Indian mainland. Literary activity in Ceylon declined and, it seems, fell into virtual abeyance between A.C. 150 and 350, as will appear below. The first Pali renascence was under way in Ceylon and S. India by about 400 and was made viable by Bhadantăcariya Buddhaghosa. This can be called the Middle Period. Many of its principal figures were Indian. It developed in several centuries in the S. Indian mainland and spread to Burma, and it can be said to have lasted till about the 12th century. Meanwhile the renewed literary activity again declined in Ceylon till it was eclipsed by the disastrous invasion of the 11th century. The second renascenee, or the Third Period as it may be termed, begins in the following century with Ceylon's recovery, coinciding more or less with major political changes in Burma. In Ceylon it lasted for several centuries and in Burma for much longer, though India about that time or soon after lost all forms of Buddhism. But this period does not concern the present purpose and is only sketched in for the sake of perspective.

INTRODUCTION

The recorded facts relating from the standpoint of Ceylon to the rise of the middle Period are very few, and it is worth while tabling them.[1]

Principal events in centuries preceding Bh. Buddhaghosa

KINGS OF CEYLON	RELEVANT EVENTS	REFS.
Devānampiya-Tissa: B.C. 307-267	-Arrival in Ceylon of the Arahant Mahinda bringing Pali Tipitaka with Commentaries; Commentaries translated into Sinhalese; Great Monastery founded.	Mahāvamsa, Ch. 13
Duṭṭhagāmani 161-137	-Expulsion of invaders after 76 years of foreign occupation of capital; restoration of unity and independence.	Mv. Chs. 25-32
	-Many names of Gt. M. elders, noted in Commentaries for virtuous behaviour, traceable to this and following reign.	Adikaram, Early Hist. of Buddhism in Ceylon, pp. 65-70
Vaṭṭagāmani 104-88	-Reign interrupted after 5 months by rebellion of Brahman Tissa, famine, invasion, and king's exile.	Mv. 33, 33f.
	-Bhikkhus all disperse from Great Monastery to South and to India.	A.A.i,92
	-Restoration of king after 14 years and return of bhikkhus.	Mv.33,78
	-Foundation of Abhayagiri Monastery by king.	Mv.33,81
	-Abh. M. secedes from Gt. M. and becomes schismatic.	Mv.33,96
	-Committal by Gt. M. of Pali Tipitaka to writing for 1st time (away from royal capital).	Mv.33,100; Nikāya-saṅgraha (trsl.),pp.10-11
	-Abh. M. adopts 'Dhammaruci Nikāya of Vajjiputtaka Sect' of India.	Ns.,p.11

1. Exact dates are not agreed. The Ceylon Chronicles give the lengths of reigns of kings of Ceylon back to the time of the Buddha and also of kings of Magadha from Asoka back to the same time. Calculated backwards the list gives 543 B.C. as the year of the Buddha's *parinibbāna* (see list of kings in Codrington's *Short History of Ceylon,* Macmillan 1947, p.xvf.). For adjustments to this calculation that bring the date of the *parinibbāna* forward to 483 B.C. (the date most generally accepted in Europe), see e.g. Geiger *Mahāvaṁsa* Translation (introduction); Epigraphia Zeylanica i, 156; E. J. Thomas, *Life of the Buddha,* Kegan Paul, p.26, n.1. It seems certain, however, that Mahānāma was reigning in the year 428 because of a letter sent by him to the Chinese court (Codrington p.29; E.Z. III, 12). If the adjusted date is accepted then 60 extra years have somehow to be squeezed out without displacing Mahānāma's reign. Here the older date has been used.

	-Meeting of Gt. M. bhikkhus decides that care of texts and preaching comes before practice of their contents.	AA.i,92f.; EHBC,p.78
	-Many Gt. M. elders' names noted in Commentaries for learning and contributions to decision of textual problems, traceable to this reign	EHBC,p.76
Kuṭakaṇṇa-Tissa 42-20	-Many elders as last stated traceable to this reign too.	EHBC,p.80
	-Last Ceylon elders' names in *Vinaya Parivāra* (p.2) traceable to this reign; *Parivāra* can thus have been completed by Gt. M. any time later, before 5th cent.	EHBC,p.86
Bhātikābhaya B.C. 20-A.C. 9	-Dispute between Gt. M. and Abh. M. over Vinaya adjudged by Brahman Dīghakārāyana in favour of Gt. M.	Vn.A.532; EHBC,p.99
Khaṇirājānu Tissa30-33	-60 bhikkhus punished for treason.	Mv.35,10
Vasabha 66-110	-Last reign to be mentioned in body of Commentaries.	EHBC,pp.3, 86-7
	-Sinhalese Commentaries can have been closed at any time after this reign.	EHBC,pp.3, 86-7
Gajabāhu I 113-135	-Abh. M. supported by king and enlarged.	Mv.35, 119
6 kings 135-215	-Mentions of royal support for Gt. M. and Abh. M.	Mv.35, 1, 7, 24, 33, 65
Vohārika-Tissa 215-237	-King supports both monasteries.	
	-Abh. M. has adopted Vetulya (Mahayana?) Pitaka.	Ns.p.12
	-King suppresses Vetulya doctrines.	Mv.36,41
	-Vetulya books burnt and heretic bhikkhus disgraced.	Ns.p.12
	-Corruption of bhikkhus by *Vitaṇḍa-vādins* (heretics or destructive critics).	Dīpavamsa Ch.22,33
Goṭhābhaya 254-267	-Gt. M. supported by king.	Mv.36,102
	-60 bhikkhus in Abh. M. banished by king for upholding Vetulya doctrines.	Mv.36,111
	-Secession from Abh. M.; new sect formed.	Ns.p.13
	-Indian bhikkhu Sanghamitta supports Abh. M.	Mv.36,112
Jeṭṭha-Tissa 267-277	-King favours Gt. M.; Saṇghamitta flees to India.	Mv.36,123

Mahāsena 277-304	-King protects Saṅghamitta, who returns. Persecution of Gt. M.; its bhikkhus driven from capital for 9 years.	Mv.37, 1-50
	-Saṅghamitta assassinated.	Mv.37,27
	-Restoration of Gt. M.	EHBC,p.92
	-Vetulya books burnt again.	EHBC,p.92
	-Dispute over Gt. M. boundary; bhikkhus again absent from Gt. M. for 9 months.	Mv.37,32
Siri Meghavaṇṇa 304-332	-King favours Gt. M.	EHBC,p.92 Mv.37,51f.
	-Sinhalese monastery established at Buddha Gayā in India.	Malalasekera P.L.C.,p.68; Epigraphia Zeylanica iii, 11
Jeṭṭha-Tissa II 332-34 Buddhadāsa 341-70 Upatissa 370-412	-Dīpavaṁsa composed in this period	Quoted in VinA.
	-Also perhaps Mūlasikkhā and Khuddasikkhā (Vinaya Summaries) and some of Buddhadatta Thera's works.	PLC,p.77
Mahānāma 412-434	-Bh. Buddhaghosa arrives in Ceylon	Mv.37,215-46
	-Samantapāsādikā (Vinaya commentary) begun in 20th and finished in 21st year of this king's reign.	VinA. Epilogue

Why did Bhadantācariya Buddhaghosa come to Ceylon? And why did his work become famous beyond the island's shores? The bare facts without some interpretation will hardly answer these questions. Certainly any interpretation must be speculative; but if this is borne in mind, some attempt (without claim for originality) may perhaps be made on the following lines.

Up till the reign of king Vaṭṭagāmani Abhaya in the first century B. C. the Great Monastery, founded by Asoka's son, the Arahant Mahinda, and hitherto without a rival for the royal favour, had preserved a reputation for the saintlines of its bhikkhus. The violent upsets in his reign followed by his founding of the Abhayagiri Monastery, its secession and schism, changed the whole situation at home. Sensing insecurity, the Great Monastery took the precaution to commit the Tipitaka for the first time to writing, doing so in the provinces away from the king's presence. Now by about the end of the first century B.C. (dates are very vague), with Sanskrit Buddhist literature just launching out upon its long era of magnificence, Sanskrit was on its way to become a language of international culture. In Ceylon the Great Monastery, already committed by tradition to strict othodoxy based on Pali, had been confirmed in that attitude by the schism of its rival, which now began publicly to study the new ideas from India. In the first century B.C. probably the influx of Sanskrit thought was still quite small, so that the Great Monastery could well maintain its name in Anurādhapura as the principal centre of learning by developing its ancient Tipitaka commentaries in Sinhalese. This might account for the shift of emphasis from Practice to Scholarship in king Vaṭṭagāmani's reign. Evidence shows great activity in this latter field throughout the first century B.C., and all this material was doubtless written down too. In the first century A.C. Sanskrit Buddhism ('Hinayana', and perhaps by then Mahayana) was growing rapidly and spreading abroad. The Abhayagiri Monastery would naturally have been busy studying and advocating some of these weighty developments while the Great Monastery had nothing new to offer: the rival was thus able, at some risk, to appear go-ahead and up-to-date while the old institution perhaps began to fall behind for want of new material, new inspiration, and international connexions, because, its studies being restricted to the orthodox presentation in the Sinhalese language, it had already done what it could in developing Tipitaka learning (on the mainland Theravada was doubtless deeper in the same predicament). Anyway we find that from the first century onwards its constructive scholarship dries up, and instead, with the reign of king Bhātika Abhaya (B.C.20-A.C.9), public wrangles begin to break out between the two monasteries. This scene indeed drags on, gradually worsening through the next three centuries, almost bare as they are of illuminating information. King Vasabha's reign (A.C.66-110) seems to be the last mentioned in the Commentaries as we have them now, from which it may lie assumed that soon afterwards they were closed (or no longer kept up), nothing further being added. Perhaps the Great Monastery, now living only on its past, was itself getting infected with heresies. But without speculating on the immediate reasons that induced it to let its chain of teachers lapse and to cease adding to its body of Sinhalese learning, it is enough to note that the situation went on deteriorating, further complicated by intrigues, till in Mahāsena's reign (A.C. 277-304) things came to a head. With the persecution of the Great Monastery given royal assent and the expulsion of its bhikkhus from the capital the Abhayagiri Monastery enjoyed nine years of triumph. But the ancient institution rallied its supporters in the southern provinces and the king repented. The bhikkhus returned and the king restored the buildings, which had been stripped to adorn the rival. Still, the Great Monastery must have foreseen, after this affair, that unless it could successfully compete with Sanskrit it had small hope of holding its position. With that the only course open was to launch a drive for the rehabilitation of Pali—a drive to bring the study of that language up to a standard fit to compete with the 'modern' Sanskrit in the field of international Buddhist culture: by cultivating Pali at home and abroad it could assure its position at home. It was a revolutionary project, involving the displacement of Sinhalese by Pali as the language for the study and discussion of Buddhist teachings, and the founding of a school of Pali literary composition. Earlier it would doubtless have been impracticable; but the atmosphere had changed. Though various Sanskrit non-Mahayana sects are well known to have continued to flourish all over India, there is almost nothing to show the status of the Pali language there by now. Only the *Mahāvaṁsa* [Ch.37, vv.215f. quoted below] suggests that the Theravada sect there had not only put aside but lost perhaps all of its old non-Pitaka material dating from Asoka's time.[2] One may guess that the pattern of things in Ceylon only echoed a process that had gone much further in India. But in the Island of Ceylon the ancient body of learning, much of it pre-Asokan, had been kept lying by, as it were maturing in its two and a half centuries of neglect, and it had by now acquired a new and great potential value due to the purity of its pedigree in contrast with the welter of new original thinking. Theravada centres of learning on the mainland were also doubtless much interested and themselves anxious for help in a repristinization.[3] Without such cooperation there was little hope of success. It is not known what was the first original Pali composition in this period; but the *Dīpavaṁsa* (dealing with historical evidence) belongs here (for it ends with Mahāsena's reign and is quoted in the (*Samantapāsādikā*), and quite possibly the *Vimuttimagga* (dealing with practice—see below) was another early attempt by the Great Monastery in this period (4th cent.) to reassert its supremacy through original Pali literary composition: there will have been others too.[4] Of course, much of this is very conjectural. Still it is plain enough that by 400 A.C. a movement had begun, not confined to Ceylon, and that the time was ripe for the crucial work, for a Pali recension of the Sinhalese Commentaries with their unique tradition. Only the right personality, able to handle it competently, was yet lacking. That personality appeared in the first quarter of the fifth century.

2. See also *A Record of Buddhist Religion* by I-tsing trsl. J. Takakusu, Clarendon Press 1896, p. xxiii, where a geographical distribution of various Schools gives Mūlasarvāstivāda mainly in the North and Ariyasthavira mainly in the South of India. I-tsing who did not visit Ceylon, was in India at the end of the 7th cent. ; but he does not mention whether the Ariyasthavira (Theravāda) Nikāya in India pursued its studies in the Pali of its Tipitaka or in Sanskrit or in a local vernacular.

3. In the epilogues and prologues of various works between the 5th and 12th centuries there is mention of *e.g.*, Padaratittha (VisA. prol. : near Madras,) Kañcipura (AA. epil. : =Conjevaram near Madras), and other places where different teachers accepting the Great-Monastery tradition lived and worked. See also Malalasekera *Pali Literature in Ceylon*, p. 13 ; E.Z., IV, 69-71 ; Journal of Oriental Research, Madras, Vol. XIX, pp. 278f.

4. Possibly the *Vinaya* summarises, *Mūlasikkhā* and *Khuddasikkhā* (though Geiger places these much later), as well as some works of Buddhadatta Thera. It has not been satisfactorily explained why the *Mahāvaṁsa*, composed in the late 4th or early 5th cent., ends abruptly in the middle of Chapter 37 with Mahāsena's reign (the Chronicle being only resumed eight centuries later).

INTRODUCTION

The Visuddhimagga and its author

Sources of information about that person fall into three groups. There are firstly the scraps contained in the prologues and epilogues to the works ascribed to him. Then there is the account given in the second part of the Ceylon Chronicle, the *Mahāvaṁsa* (or *Cūlavaṁsa* as the part of it is often called), written in about the 13th century, describing occurrences placed by it in the 5th century. And lastly the still later *Buddhaghosuppatti* (15th cent.?) and other later works. It seems still uncertain how to evaluate the old Talaing records of Burma, which may not refer to the same person (see below). India herself tells us nothing at all.

It seems worth while, therefore, to give a rendering here of the principal passage from the prologues and epilogues of the works ascribed to him by name; for they are few and short, and they have special authentic value as evidence. The *Mahāvaṁsa* account will be reproduced in full, too, since it is held to have been composed from evidence and records before its author, and to have the ring of truth behind the legends it contains. But the later works (which European scholars hold to be legendary rather than historical in what they add to the accounts already mentioned) can only be dealt with very summarily here.

The books actually ascribed to Bhadantācariya Buddhaghosa have each a 'postscript' identical in form with that at the end of Chapter XXIII of the present work, mentioning the title and author by name. This can be taken to have been appended, presumably contemporaneously, by the Great Monastery (the *Mahāvihāra*) at Anurādhapura in Ceylon as their official seal of approval. Here is a list of the works (also listed in the modern *Gandhavaṁsa* and *Sāsanavaṁsa* with one or two discrepancies):[5]

Commentaries to the Vinaya Piṭaka

Samantapāsādikā ...	... Commentary to		Vinaya
Kaṅkhāvitaraṇī ...	...	,, ,,	Pāṭimokkha

Commentaries to the Sutta Piṭaka

Sumaṅgalavilāsinī...	...	,, ,,	Dīgha-nikāya
Pāpañcasūdanī ...	...	,, ,,	Majjhima - nikāya
Sāratthappakāsini ...	...		Samyutta - nikāya
Manorathapūraṇī ...	...	,, ,,	Aṅguttara - nikāya
Paramatthajotikā ...	...	,- ,,	Khuddakapāṭha, Suttanipāta
Dhammapadatthakathā	...	,, ,,	Dhammapada
Jātakatthakathā ...	...	,, ,,	Jātaka

5. The *Gandhavaṁsa* also gives the *Apadāna* Commentary as by him.

Commentaries to the Abhidhamma Piṭaka

Atthasālinī	,,	,,	Dhammasaṅgaṇī
Sammohavinodanī... ...	,,	,,	Vibhaṅga
Pañcapakaraṇatthakathā ...	,,	,,	Remaining 5 books

Beyond the bare hint that he came to Ceylon from India his actual works tell nothing about his origins or background. He mentions 'The Elder Buddhamitta, with whom I formerly lived at Mayūrasuttapaṭṭana' (MA. epil.),[6] and 'The well-known Elder Jotipāla, with whom I once lived at Kañcipura and elsewhere' (AA. epil.)[7] Also the 'postscript' attached to the *Visuddhimagga* says, besides mentioning his name, that he 'should be called "of Moraṇḍacetaka" '.[8] And that is all.

On coming to Ceylon, he went to Anurādhapura, the royal capital, and set himself to study. He seems to have lived and worked there during the whole of his stay in the Island, though we do not know how long that stay lasted. To render his own words: 'I learned three Sinhalese commentaries—the *Mahā-Attha-*[*katha*], *Mahā-Paccarī*, *Kuruṇḍi*—from the famed Elder known by the name of Buddhamitta, who has expert knowledge of the Vinaya. Set in the grounds of the Mahā-Meghavana Park [in Anurādhapura] there is the Great Monastery graced by the [sapling from the] Master's Enlightenment Tree. A constant supporter of the Community, trusting with unwavering faith in the Three Jewels, belonging to an illustrious family and known by the name of Mahanigamasāmi (Lord of the Great City), had an excellent work-room built there on its southern side accessible to the ever virtuously conducted Community of Bhikkhus. The building was beautifully appointed, aggreeably endowed with cool shade and had a

---

6. Other readings are : Mayūrarūpapaṭṭana, Mayūradūtapaṭṭana. Identified with Mylapore near Madras (J.O.R., Madras, Vol. XIX, p. 281).

7. Identified with Conjevaram near Madras. P.L.C., p. 113. Ācariya Ānanda, author of the Sub-commentary to the Abhidhamma Pitaka (Mūla-Ṭīkā) also lived there, perhaps any time after the middle of the 5th century. The Elder Dhammapāla sometimes refers to the old Sinhalese commentaries as if they were still available to him.

8. Other readings are : Moraṇḍakheṭaka, Mudantakhedaka, Muraṇḍakheṭaka, etc. ; not yet identified. Refers more probably to his birth-place than to his place of *pabbajā*. See also J.O.R., Madras, Vol. XIX, p. 282, article *Buddhaghosa—his Place of Birth* by R. Subramaniam and S. P. Nainar, where a certain coincidence of names is mentioned that might suggest a possible identification of Moraṇḍakheṭaka (*mor-aṇda* being Pali for ' peacock egg ' and *khedaka* Skr. for ' village '—see Vis. Harvard ed., p. xv) with two adjacent villages, 51 miles from Nāgārjunakoṇḍa and 58 m. from Amarāvatī, called Kotanemalipuri and Gundlapalli (*nemali* and *gundla* being Telegu respectively for ' peacock ' and ' egg '). However, more specific information will be needed in support before it can be accepted as an indication that the *Mahāvaṁsa* is wrong about his birth-place. More information about any connexion between Ceylon and those Great South-Indian Buddhist centres is badly needed.

lavish water supply. The Vinaya Commentary was begun by me for the sake of the Elder Buddhasiri of pure virtuous behaviour while I was living there in Mahānigamasāmi's building, and it is now complete. It was begun by me in the twentieth year of the reign of peace of the King Sirinivāsa (Of Glorious Life), the renowned and glorious guardian who has kept the whole of Lanka's (Ceylon's) island free from trouble. It was finished in the twenty-first year. And just as this was finished in one year without mishap in a world beset by mishaps, so may all beings attain...' (Vin A.epil.).

Mostly it is assumed that he wrote and 'published' his works one by one as authors do today. The assumption may not be correct. There is an unerring consistency throughout the system of explanation he adopts, and there are cross-references between works. This suggests that while the *Visuddhimagga* itself may perhaps have been composed and produced first, the others as they exist now were more likely worked over contemporaneously and all more or less finished before any one of them was given out. They may well have been given out then following the order of the books in the Tipitaka which they explain. So in that way it may be taken that the *Vinaya* Commentary came next to the *Visuddhimagga*; then the Commentaries on the four *Nikāyas* (Collections of Suttas), and after them the Abhidhamma Commentaries. Though it is not said that the Vinaya Commentary was given out first of these, still the prologue and epilogue contain the most information. The four *Nikāya* Commentaries all have the same basic prologue; but the *Saṁyutta Nikāya* Commentary inserts in its prologue a stanza referring the reader to 'the two previous Collections' (i.e. the *Digha* and *Majjhima Nikāyas*) for explanations of the names of towns and for illustrative stories, while the *Aṅguttara Nikāya* Commentary replaces this stanza with another referring to 'the Dīgha and Majjhima' by name for the same purpose. The point may seem laboured and even trivial, but it is not irrelevant; for if it is assumed that these works were written and 'published' in some historical order of composition, one expects to find some corresponding development of thought and perhaps discovers what one's assumption has projected upon them. The more likely assumption, based on consideration of the actual contents, is that their form and content was settled before any one of them was given out.

Sometimes it is argued that the commentaries to the *Dhammapada* and the *Jātaka* may not be by the same author because the style is different. But that fact could be accounted for by the difference in the subject matter; for these two commentaries consist mainly of popular stories, which play only a very minor role in the other works. Besides, while this author is quite inexorably consistent throughout his works in his explanations of Dhamma, he by no means always maintains that consistency in different versions of the same story in, say, different *Nikāya* Commentaries (compare for instance, the version of the story of the Elder Tissabhūti given in the Commentary to A. *Ekanipāta* II, 6 with that at MA. i, 66; also the version of the story of the Elder Mahā-Tissa in the AA., same ref., with that at MA. i, 185). Perhaps less need for strictness was felt with such story material. And there is also another possibility. It may not unreasonably be supposed that he did not work alone, without help, and that he had competent assistants. If so, he might well have delegated the drafting of the *Khuddaka Nikāya* commentaries—those of the *Khuddakapāṭha* and *Suttanipāta*, *Dhammapada*, and the *Jātaka*—, or part of them, supervising and completing them himself, after which the official 'Postscript' was appended. This assumption seems not implausible and involves less difficulties than its alternatives.[9] These secondary commentaries may well have been composed after the others.

The full early history of the Pali Tipitaka and its Commentaries in Sinhalese is given in the Ceylon Chronicle, the *Dīpavaṁsa* and *Mahāvaṁsa*, and also in the introduction to the Vinaya Commentary. In the prologue to each of the four *Nikāya* Commentaries it is conveniently summarized by Bhadantācariya Buddhaghosa himself as follows: '[I shall now take] the commentary, whose object is to clarify the meaning of the *subtle and most excellent Long Collection* (*Dīgha Nikāya*) ... set forth in detail by the Buddha and by his like [i.e. the Elder Sāriputta and other expounders of discourses in the *Sutta Piṭaka*]—the commentary that in the beginning was chanted [at the First Council] and later rechanted [at the Second and Third], and was brought to the Sīhala Island (Ceylon) by the Arahant Mahinda the Great and rendered into the Sīhala tongue for the benefit of the Islanders—, and from that commentary I shall remove the Sīhala tongue, replacing it by the graceful language that conforms with Scripture and is purified and free from flaws. Not diverging from the standpoint of the Elders residing in the Great Monastery [in Anurādhapura], who illumine the Elders' Heritage and are all well versed in exposition, and rejecting subject matter needlessly repeated, I shall make the meaning clear for the purpose of bringing contentment to good people and contributing to the long endurance of the Dhamma'.

There are references in these works to 'the Ancients (*Porāṇā*)' or 'Former Teachers (*Pubbācariyā*)' as well as to a number of Sinhalese Commentaries additional to the three referred to in the quotation given earlier. The fact is plain enough that a complete body of commentary had been built up during the nine centuries or so that separate Bhadantācariya Buddhaghosa from the Buddha. A good proportion of it dated no doubt from the actual time of the Buddha himself, and this core had been added to in India (probably in Pali), and later by learned Elders in Ceylon (in Sinhalese) as references to their pronouncements show (e.g. Vis. Ch. XII 105 and 117).

---

9. A definite statement that the DhA. was written later by someone else can hardly avoid the inference that the 'postscript' was a fraud, or at least misleading.

This body of material—one may guess that its volume was enormous—Bhadantācariya Buddhaghosa set himself to edit and render into Pali (the Tipitaka itself had been left in the original Pali). For this he had approval and express invitation (see, e.g., the epilogue to the present work, which the Elder Saṅghapāla invited him to compose). Modern critics have reproached him with lack of originality: but if we are to judge by his declared aims, originality, or to use his own phrase 'advertizing his own standpoint' (Vis.Ch. XVII 25), seems likely to have been one of the things he would have wished to avoid. He says, for instance, 'I shall expound the comforting Path of Purification, pure in expositions, relying on the teaching of the dwellers in the Great Monastery' (Vis. Ch. I 4: see also epilogue), and again 'Now as to the entire trustworthiness (*samantapāsādikatta*) of this Samantapāsādikā: the wise see nothing untrustworthy here when they look—in the chain of teachers, in the citations of circumstance, instance and category [in each case], in the avoidance of others' standpoints, in the purity of [our] own standpoint, in the correctness of details, in the word-meanings, in the order of construing the text, in the exposition of the training precepts, in the use of classification by the analytical method—, which is why this detailed commentary on the Vinaya ... is called Samantapāsādikā' (VinA. epilogue). And then: 'The Commentary on the *Pāṭimokkha*, which I began at the request of the Elder Soṇa for the purpose of removing doubts in those uncertain of the Vinaya, and which covers the whole Sinhalese Commentarial system based upon the arrangement adopted by the dwellers in the Great Monastery, is finished. The whole essence of the Commentary and the entire meaning of the text has been extracted and there is no sentence here that might conflict with the text or with the commentaries of the dwellers in the Great Monastery or those of the Ancients (*Pāṭimokkha* Commentary epilogue). Such examples could be multiplied (see especially also Vis. Ch. XVII 25). There is only one instance in the *Visuddhimagga* where he openly advances an opinion of his own, with the words 'our preference here is this' (Ch. XIII, 123). He does so once in the *Majjhima Nikāya* Commentary, too, saying 'the point is not dealt with by the Ancients, but this is my opinion' (MA. i, 28). The rarity of such instances and the caution expressed in them imply that he himself was disinclined to speculate and felt the need to point the fact out when he did. He actually says 'one's own opinion is the weakest authority of all and should only be accepted if it accords with the Suttas' (DA. 567-8). So it is likely that he regarded what we should call original thinking as the province of the Buddha, and his own task as the fortification of that thought by coordinating the explanations of it. However, not every detail that he edited can claim direct support in the Suttas.

The following considerations lend some support to the assumptions just made. It has been pointed out[10] that in describing in the *Vinaya* Commentary how the tradition had been 'maintained up to the present day by the chain of teachers and pupils' (VinA.61-2) the list of teachers' names that follows contains names only traceable down to about the middle of the 2nd century A.C., but not later. Again, there appear in his works numbers of illustrative stories, all of which are set either in India or Ceylon. However no single one of them can be pointed to as contemporary. Stories about India in every case where a date can be assigned are not later than Asoka (3rd cent. B.C.). Many stories about Ceylon cannot be dated, but of those that can none seems later than the 2nd century A.C. This suggests that the material which he had before him to edit and translate had been already completed and fixed more than two centuries earlier in Ceylon, and that the words 'present day' were not used by him to refer to his own time, but were already in the material he was coordinating. This final fixing, if it is a fact, might have been the aftermath of the decision taken in Ceylon in the 1st century B.C. to commit the Pali *Tipiṭaka* to writing.

Something now needs to be said about the relation of the *Visuddhiṁagga* to the other books. This author's work is characterized by relentless accuracy, consistency and fluency of erudition, and much dominated by formalism. Not only is this formalism evident in the elaborate pattern of the *Visuddhimagga* but also that work's relationship to the others is governed by it. The *Visuddhimagga* itself extracts from the *Tipiṭaka* all the central doctrines that pivot upon the Four Truths, presenting them as a coherent systematic whole by way of quotation and explanation interspersed with treatise on subjects of more or less relative importance, all being welded into an intricate edifice. The work can thus stand alone. But the aim of the Commentaries to the four main *Nikāyas* or Collections of Suttas is to explain the subject matter of individual discourses and, as well, certain topics and special doctrines not dealt with in the *Visuddhimagga* (many passages commenting on identical material in the Suttas in different *Nikāyas* are reproduced *verbatim* in each commentary, and elsewhere, e.g., M. Sutta 10, cf. D. Sutta 22, *Satipaṭṭhāna Vibhaṅga*, etc., etc., and respective commentaries). But these commentaries always refer the reader to the *Visuddhimagga* for explanations of the central doctrines. And though the *Vinaya* and *Abhidhamma* Commentaries are less closely bound to the *Visuddhimagga*, still they too either refer the reader to it or reproduce large blocks of it. The author himself says 'The treatises on Virtue and on the Ascetic's Rules, all the Meditation Subjects, the details of the attainments of the Jhanas, together with the directions for each Temperament, all the various kinds of Direct-knowledge, the exposition of the Definition of Understanding, the Aggregates, Elements, Bases, and Faculties, the Four

10. Adikaram *Early History of Buddhism in Ceylon*, pp. 3 and 86.

Noble Truths, the explanation of the Structure of Conditions (Dependent Origination), and lastly the Development of Insight, by methods that are purified and sure and not divergent from Scripture—since these things have already been quite clearly stated in the *Visuddhimagga* I shall no more dwell upon them here; for the *Visuddhimagga* stands between and in the midst of all four Collections (Nikāyas) and will clarify the meaning of such things stated therein. It was made in that way: take it therefore along with this same commentary and know the meaning of the *Long Collection* (*Dīgha Nikāya*)' (prologue to the four *Nikāyas*).

This is all that can, without unsafe inferences, be gleaned of Bhadantācariya Buddhaghosa himself from his own works (but see below).

Now there is the *Mahāvaṁsa* account. The composition of the second part (often called *Cūlavaṁsa*) of that historical poem is attributed to an Elder Dhammakitti, who lived in or about the thirteenth century, Here is a translation of the relevant passage:

10. Adikaram *Early History of Buddhism in Ceylon*, pp. 3 and 86.

'There was a Brahman student who was born near the Site of the Enlightenment Tree. He was acquainted with the arts and accomplishments of the Sciences and was qualified in the Vedas. He was well versed in what he knew and unhesitant over any phrase. Being interested in doctrines, he wandered over Jambudīpa (India) engaging in disputation.

'He came to a certain monastery, and there in the night he recited Pātañjali's system with each phrase complete and well rounded. The Senior Elder there, Revata by name, recognized "This is a being of great understanding who ought to be tamed." He said "Who is that braying the ass's bray ?". The other asked "What, then, do you know the meaning of the ass's bray ?". The Elder answered "I know it," and he then not only expounded it himself, but explained each statement in the proper way and also pointed out contradictions. The other then urged him "Now expound your own doctrine," and the Elder repeated a text from the Abhidhamma, but the visitor could not solve its meaning. He asked "Whose system is this ?", and the Elder replied "It is the Enlightened One's system." "Give it me" he said, but the Elder answered "You will have to take the Going Forth into Homelessness." So he took the Going Forth, since he was interested in the system, and he learnt the three Pitakas, after which he believed "This is the only way" (M. i. 55). Because his speech (*ghosa*) was profound (voice was deep)like that of the Enlightened One (*Buddha*) they called him Buddhaghosa, so that like the Enlightened One he might be voiced over the surface of the Earth. He prepared a treatise there called *Ñaṇodaya*, and then the *Atthasālinī*, a comment on the *Dhammasaṅgaṇī*. Next he began work on a commentary to the *Paritta*.[11] When the Elder Revata saw that, he said "Here only the text has been preserved. There is no commentary here, and likewise no Teachers' Doctrine ; for that has been allowed to go to pieces and is no longer known. However, a Sinhalese commentary still exists, which is pure. It was rendered into the Sinhalese tongue by the learned Mahinda with proper regard for the way of commenting that was handed down by the three Councils as taught by the Enlightened One and inculcated by Sāriputta and others. Go there, and after you have learnt it translate it into the language of the Magadhans. That will bring benefit to the whole world." As soon as this was said, he made up his mind to set out.

11. *Paritta* or 'protection'; a name for certain Suttas recited for that purpose. see MA. iv, 114.

'He came from there to this island in the reign of this king (Mahānāma). He came to the Great Monastery, the monastery of all true men. There he stayed in a large work room, and he learnt the whole Sinhalese Commentary of the Elders' Doctrine (*Theravāda*) under Saṅghapāla.[12] He decided "This alone is the intention of the Dhamma's Lord." So he assembled the Community there and asked "Give me all the books to make a commentary." Then in order to test him the Community gave him two stanzas, saying "Show your ability with these ; when we have seen that you have it, we will give you all the books." On that text alone he summarized the three Pitakas together with the Commentary as an epitome, which was named the *Path of Purification* (*Visuddhimagga*). Then, in the precincts of the (sapling of the) Enlightenment Tree (in Anurādhapura), he assembled the Community expert in the Fully Enlightened One's system, and he began to read it out. In order to demonstrate his skill to the multitude deities hid the book, and he was obliged to prepare it a second time, and again a third time. When the book was brought for the third time to be read out, the gods replaced the other two copies with it. Then the bhikkhus read out the three copies together, and it was found that there was no difference between the three in either the chapters or the meaning or the order of the material or the phrases and syllables of the Theravāda texts. With that the Community applauded in high delight, and again and again it was said "Surely this is (the Bodhisatta) Metteyya ". They gave him the books of the three Pitakas together with the Commentary. Then, while staying undisturbed in the Library Monastery, he translated the Sinhalese commentary into the Magadhan language, the Root-Speech of all, by which he brought benefit to beings of all tongues. The teachers of the Elders' Tradition accepted it as equal in authority with the texts themselves. Then, when the tasks to be done were finished, he went back to Jambudīpa to pay homage to the Great Enlightenment Tree.

'And when Mahānāma had enjoyed twenty-two years' reign upon earth and had performed a variety of meritorious works, he passed on according to his deeds'—(Mahāvāṃsa, ch. 37, vv. 215-47).

King Mahānāma is identified with the 'King Sirinivāsa' and the 'King Sirikudda' mentioned respectively in the epilogues to the *Vinaya* and *Dhammapada* Commentaries. There is no trace, and no other mention anywhere, of the 'Ñāṇodaya'. The 'Atthasālinī' described as composed in India could not be the version extant today, which cites the Ceylon Commentaries and refers to the *Visuddhimagga*; it will have been revised later.

The prologues and epilogues of this author's works are the only instances in which he can be sure that he is speaking of his own experience and not only simply editing; and while they point only to his residence in south India, they neither confute nor confirm the *Mahāvaṁsa* statement than he was born in Magadha (see note 8). The Ceylon Chronicles survived the historical criticism to which they were subjected in the last hundred years. The independent evidence that could be brought to bear supported them, and Western scholars ended by pronouncing them reliable in essentials. The account just quoted is considered to be based on historical fact even if it contains legendary matter.

It is not possible to make use of the body of Bhadantācariya Buddhaghosa's works to test the *Mahāvaṁsa's* claim that he was a learned Brahman from central India, and so on. It has been shown already how the presumption is always, where the contrary is not explicitly stated, that he is editing and translating material placed

12. See Vis. epil.

before him rather than displaying his own private knowledge, experience and opinoins. And so it would be a critical mistake to use any such passage in his work for assessing his personal traits; for in them it is, pretty certainly, not him we are dealing with at all but people who lived three or more centuries earlier. Those passages probably tell us merely that he was a scrupulously accurate and conscientious editor. His geographical descriptions are translations, not eye-witness accounts. Then such a Sutta passage as that commented on in Chapter I, §86-7 of the present work, which is a part of a Sutta used by bhikkhus for daily reflexion on the four requisites of the life of a bhikkhu, is certain to have been fully commented on from the earliest times, so that it would be just such a critical mistake to infer from this comment anything about his abilities as an original commentator, on anything else of a personal nature about him or his own past experience.[13] And again, the controversial subject of the origin of the Brahman caste (see MA.ii,418) must have been fully explained from the Buddhist standpoint from the very start. If then that account disagrees with Brahmanical lore—and it would be odd, all things considered, if it did not—, there is no justification for concluding on those grounds that the author of the *Visuddhimagga* was not of Brahman origin and that the *Mahāvaṁsa* is wrong. What does indeed seem improbable is that the authorities of the Great Monastery, resolutely committed to oppose unorthodoxy, would have given him a free hand to 'correct' their traditions to accord with Brahmanical texts or with other alien sources, even if he had so wished. Again, the fact that there are allusions to extraneous, non-Buddhist literature (e.g. Vis. Ch. VII, §58; XVI, §4 n.2; §85, etc.) hardly affects this issue because they too can have been already in the material he was editing or supplied to him by the Elders with whom he was working. What might repay careful study is perhaps those things, such as certain Mahayana teachings and names, as well as much Brahmanical philosophy, which he ignores though he must have known about them. This ignoring cannot safely be ascribed to ignorance unless we are sure it was not dictated by policy; and we are not sure at all. His silence (in

13. For instance, Prof. Kosambi, in his preface to the Vis. Harvard ed., overlooks these considerations when he says ' More positive evidence (that he was not a North-Indian Brahman) is in the passage " *Uṇhassa ti aggisantāpassa. Tassa vanadāhādisu sambhavo veditabbo* "—(Ch. I. -86). " Heat : the heat of fire, such as occurs at the time of forest fires, etc." This is a comment upon protection against heat given by a cīvara. His explanation is obviously ridiculous. It is not known to Indian southerners that a bare skin is sure to be sunburnt in the northern summer ' (p. xii). And Professor Kosambi has not only overlooked the fact that it is almost certainly translated material that he is criticizing as original composition, but he appears not to have even read the whole passage. The Sutta sentence (M. i, 10) commented on in the *Visuddhimagga* (Ch. i, §§86-7) contains *two* words *uṇha* and *ātapa*. If, before condemning the explanation as ' ridiculous,' he had read on, he would have found, a line or two below, the words *Ātapo ti suriyātapo*' (' " Burning " is burning of the sun '—Ch. I, §87).

contrast to the author of the *Paramatthamañjūsā*) are sometimes notable in this respect.

The 'popular novel' called *Buddhaghosuppatti*, which was composed in Burma by an Elder called Mahāmaṅgala, perhaps as early as the 15th century, is less dependable. But a survey without some account of it would be incomplete. So here is a *précis*:

Near the Bodhi Tree at Gayā there was a town called Ghosa. Its ruler had a Brahman chaplain called Kesi married to a wife called Kesinī. An Elder Bhikkhu, who was a friend of Kesi, used to wonder, when the Buddha's teaching was recited in Sinhalese and people did not therefore understand it, who would be able to translate it into Magadhan (Pali). He saw that there was the son of a deity living in the Tavatiṁsa Heaven, whose name was Ghosa and who was capable of doing it. This deity was persuaded to be reborn in the human world as the son of the Brahman Kesi. He learnt the Vedas. One day he sat down in a place sacred to Vishnu and ate peas. Brahmans angrily rebuked him, but he uttered a stanza, 'The pea itself is Vishnu ; who is there called Vishnu ? And how shall I know which is Vishnu ?', and no one could answer him. Then one day while Kesi was instructing the town's ruler in the Vedas a certain passage puzzled him ; but Ghosa wrote down the explanations on a palm leaf, which was found later by his father—(Ch. I).

Once when the Elder Bhikkhu was invited to Kesi's house for a meal Ghosas' mat was given him to sit on. Ghosa was furious and abused the Elder. Then he asked him if he knew the Vedas and any other system. The Elder gave a recitation from the Vedas. Then Ghosa asked him for his own system, whereupon the Elder expounded the first Triad of the Abhidhamma Schedule, on profitable unprofitable, and indeterminate, thought-arisings. Ghosa asked whose the system was. He was told that it was the Buddha's and that it could only be learnt after becoming a bhikkhu. He accordingly went forth into homelessness as a bhikkhu, and in one month he learnt the three Pitakas. After receiving the Full Admission he acquired the four Discriminations. The name given to him was Buddhaghosa—(Ch. II).

One day the question arose in his mind : 'Which has more understanding of the Buddha-word, I or my Preceptor ? ' His Preceptor, whose cankers were exhausted, read the thought in his mind and rebuked him, telling him to ask his forgiveness. The pupil was then very afraid, and after asking for forgiveness, he was told that in order to make amends he must go to Ceylon and translate the Buddha-word (*sic*) from Sinhalese into Magadhan. He agreed, but asked that he might first be allowed to convert his father from the Brahman religion to the Buddha's teaching. In order to achieve this he had a brick apartment fitted with locks and furnished with food and water. He set a contrivance so that when his father went inside he was trapped. He then preached to his father on the virtues of the Buddha, and on the pains of hell resulting from wrong belief. After three days his father was converted, and he took the Three Refuges. The son then opened the door and made amends to his father with flowers and such things for the offence done to him. Kesi became a Stream-Enterer—(Ch. III).

This done, he set sail in a ship for Ceylon. The Mahāthera Buddhadatta[14] had set sail that day from Ceylon for India. The two ships met by the intervention of Sakka Ruler of Gods. When the two Elders saw each other, the Elder Buddhaghosa told the other 'The Buddha's Dispensation has been put into Sinhalese ; I shall go and translate it and put it into Magadhan,' the other said 'I was sent to go and translate the Buddha-word and write it in Magadhan. I have only done the *Jinālaṅkāra*, the *Dantavaṁsa*, the *Dhātuvaṁsa* and the *Bodhivaṁsa*, not the commentaries and the sub-commentaries (*Ṭīkā*). If you, sir, are translating the Dispensation from Sinhalese into Magadhan, do the Commentaries to the Three Pitakas.' Then praising the Elder Buddhaghosa, he gave him the

14. The allusion is to the author of various Pali works including the Abhidhammāvatāra ; see n. 4.

gall-nut, the iron stylus and the stone given him by Sakka Ruler of Gods, adding 'If you have eye trouble or backache, rub the gall-nut on the stone and wet the place that hurts; then your ailment will vanish.' Then he recited a stanza from his *Jinālaṅkāka*. The other said 'Venerable sir, your book is written in very ornate style. Future clansmen will not be able to follow its meaning. It is hard for simple people to understand it.'—'Friend Buddhaghosa, I went to Ceylon before you to work on the Blessed One's Dispensation. But I have little time before me and shall not live long. So I cannot do it. Do it therefore yourself, and do it well.' Then the two ships separated. Soon after they had completed their voyages the Elder Buddhadatta died and was reborn in the *Tusita* Heaven —(Ch. IV).

The Elder Buddhaghosa stayed near the port of Dvijaṭhāna in Ceylon. While there he saw one woman water-carrier accidentally break another's jar, which led to a violent quarrel between them with foul abuse. Knowing that he might be called as a witness, he wrote down what they said in a book. When the case came before the king, the Elder was cited as a witness. He sent his notebook, which decided the case. The king then asked to see him—(Ch. V).

After this the Elder went to pay homage to the Saṅgharājā,[15] the Senior Elder of Ceylon. One day while the Senior Elder was teaching bhikkhus he came upon a difficult point of Abhidhamma that he could not explain. The Elder Buddhaghosa knew its meaning and wrote it on a board after the Senior Elder had left. Next day it was discovered and then the Senior Elder suggested that he should teach the Order of Bhikkhus. The reply was : 'I have come to translate the Buddha's Dispensation into Magadhan.' The Senior Elder told him 'If so, then construe the Three Pitakas upon the text beginning "When a wise man, established well in virtue............" ' He began the work that day, the stars being favourable, and wrote very quickly. When finished, he put it aside and went to sleep. Meanwhile Sakka Ruler of Gods abstracted the book. The Elder awoke, and missing it, he wrote another copy very fast by lamplight ; then he put it aside and slept. Sakka abstracted that too. The Elder awoke, and not seeing his book, he wrote a third copy very fast by lamplight and wrapped it in his robe. Then he slept again. While he was asleep Sakka put the other two books beside him, and when he awoke he found all three copies. He took them to the Senior Elder and told him what had happened. When they were read over there was no difference even in a single letter. Thereupon the Senior Elder gave permission for the translating of the Buddha's Dispensation. From then on the Elder was known to the people of Ceylon by the name of Buddhaghosa—(Ch. VI).

He was given apartments in the Brazen Palace, of whose seven floors he occupied the lowest. He observed the Ascetic Practices and was expert in all the Scriptures. It was during his stay there that he translated the Buddha's Dispensation. When on his alms round he saw fallen palm leaves he would pick them up ; this was a duty undertaken by him. One day a man who had climbed a palm tree saw him. He left some palm leaves on the ground, watched him pick them up, and then followed him. Afterwards he brought him a gift of food. The Elder concluded his writing of the Dispensation in three months. When the Rainy Season was over and he had completed the Pavarana Ceremony, he consigned the books to the Senior Elder, the Saṅgharājā. Then the Elder Buddhaghosa had the books written by the Elder Mahinda piled up and burnt near the Great Shrine, the pile was as high as seven elephants. Now that this work was done, and wanting to see his parents, he took his leave before going back to India. Before he left however, his knowledge of Sanskrit was queried by bhikkhus ; but he silenced, this by delivering a sermon in that language by the Great Shrine. Then he departed—(Ch. VII).

On his return he went to his Preceptor and cleared himself of his penance. His parents too forgave him his offences ; and when they died they were reborn in the *Tusita* Heaven. He himself, knowing that he would not live much longer,

15. *Saṅgharājā* ('Ruler of the Community'—a title existing in Thailand today): possibly a mistake for Saṅghapāla here (see Vis. epil.)

paid homage to his Preceptor and went to the Great Enlightenment Tree. Foreseeing his approaching death, he considered thus : 'There are three kinds of death : death as cutting off, momentary death, and conventional death. Death as cutting off belongs to those whose cankers are exhausted (and are Arahants.) Momentary death is that of each consciousness of the Cognitive Series beginning with life-continuum consciousness, which arise each immediately on the cessation of the one preceding. Conventional death is that of all (so-called) living beings.[16] Mine will be conventional death.' After his death he was reborn in the *Tusita* Heaven in a golden mansion seven leagues broad surrounded with divine nymphs. When the Bodhisatta Metteyya comes to this human world, he will be his disciple. After his cremation his relics were deposited near the Enlightenment Tree and shrines erected over them—(Ch. VIII).

It has already been remarked that the general opinion of European scholars is that where this imaginative tale differs from, or adds to, the *Mahāvaṁsa's* account it is in legend rather than history.

Finally there is the question of the Talaing Chronicles of Burma, which mention an Elder named Buddhaghosa, of Brahman stock, who went from Thaton (the ancient Buddhist stronghold in the Rāmaññadesa of Burma) to Ceylon (perhaps via India) to translate the Buddha-word into Talaing and bring it back. It is hard to evalute this tradition on the evidence available; but according to the opinion of the more reliable Western scholars another elder of the same name is involved here.[17]

What can be said of the *Visuddhimagga's* author without venturing into unfounded speculation is now exhausted, at least in so far as the restricted scope of this introduction permits. The facts are tantalizingly few. Indeed this, like many scenes in Indian history, has something of the enigmatic transparencies and uncommunicative shadows of a moonlit landscape—at the same time inescapable and ungraspable.

Some answer has, however, been furnished to the two questions: why did he come to Ceylon? and why did his work become famous beyond its shores? Trends such as have been outlined, working not quite parallel on the Theravada of India and Ceylon, had evolved a situation favouring a rehabilitation of Pali, and consequently the question was already one of interest not only to Ceylon, where the old material was preserved. Again the author possessed outstandingly just those personal qualities most fitted to the need—accuracy, an indefatigable mental orderliness and insight able to crystallize the vast unwieldy accumulated exegesis of Tipitaka into a coherent workable whole with a dignified vigorous style, respect for authenticity and dislike of speculation, and (in the circumstances not at all paradoxically) preference for self-effacement. The impetus given by him to Pali scholarship left an indelible

16. A learned allusion to Vis. Ch. VIII, §1.

17. Hastings' *Encyclopaedia of Religion, article* 'Buddhaghosa' by T. W. Rhys Davids. Note also that another elder of the same name invited the writing of the Sammohavinodani. The problem is discussed at some length by Prof. Niharranjan Ray, *Theravada Buddhism in Burma*, pp. 24ff.

mark on the centuries that followed, enabling it to survive from then on the Sanskrit seige as well as the continuing schism and the political difficulties and disasters that harassed Ceylon before 'Second Renascence'. A long epoch of culture stems from him. His successors in the Great Monastery tradition continued to write in various centres in S. India till 12th century or so while his own works spread to Burma and beyond. Today in Ceylon and South East Asia his authority is as weighty as it ever was and his name is venerated as before.

* * * *

The Vimuttimagga

Besides the books in Sinhalese that Bhadantācariya Buddhaghosa names as available to him (which have all disappeared) there was also a manual (existing now only in a Chinese translation of the 6th century A.C.), presumed to have been written in Pali. Bhadantācariya Buddhaghosa himself makes no mention of it; but his commentator, Bhadantācariya Dhammāpāla (writing perhaps within two centuries of him), mentions it by name (see Vis. Ch. III, n, 19). The *Visuddhimagga* refutes a certain method of classifying temperaments as unsound. The Elder Dhammapāla ascribes the theory refuted to the *Vimuttimagga*. The theory refuted is actually found in the Chinese version. Then other points rejected by the *Visuddhimagga* are found in the *Vimuttimagga*. Some of these are attributed by the Elder Dhammāpāla to the Abhayagiri Monastery. However the *Vimuttimagga* itself contains nothing at all of the Mahayana, its unorthodoxies being well within the 'Hinayana' field.

The book is much shorter than the *Visuddhimagga*. Though set out in the same three general divisions of Virtue, Concentration and Understanding, it does not superimpose the pattern of the Seven Purifications. Proportionately much less space is devoted to Understanding, and there are no stories. Though the appearance in both books of numbers of nearly identical passages suggests that they both drew a good deal from the same sources, the general style differs widely. The four Measureless States and the four Immaterial States are handled differently in the two books. Besides the 'material octads', 'enneads' and 'decads' it mentions 'endecads', etc., too. Its description of the 13 Ascetic Practices is quite different. Also Abhidhamma, which is the keystone of Bhadantācariya Buddhaghosa's exegesis, is not used at all in the *Vimuttimagga* (Aggregates, Truths, etc., do not *in themselves* constitute Abhidhamma in the sense of that Pitaka). There is for instance even in its description of the Consciousness Aggregate, no reference to the *Dhammasaṅgaṇī's* classification of 89 types, and nothing from the *Paṭṭhāna*; and though the 'Cognitive Series' is stated once in its full form (in Ch. 11) no use is made of it to explain conscious workings. This *Vimuttimagga* is in fact a book ofpractical instructions, not of exegesis.

Its authorship is ascribed to an Elder Upatissa. But the mere coincidence of names is insufficient to identify him with the Arahant Upatissa (prior to 3rd cent. A.C.) mentioned in the *Vinaya Parivāra*. A plausible theory puts its composition sometime before the *Visuddhimagga*, possibly in India. That is quite compatible with its being a product of the Great Monastery before the *Visuddhimagga* was written, though again evidence is needed to support the hypothesis. That it contains ome minor points accepted by the Abayagiri Monastery does not necessarily imply that it had any special connexion with that centre. The source may have been common to both. The disputed points are not schismatical. Bhadantācariya Buddhagosa himself never mentions it.

* * * *

Trends in the development of Theravāda Doctrine

The doctrines (Dhamma) of the Theravada Pali tradition can be conveniently traced in three main layers. (1) The first of these contains the main books of the Pali *Sutta Piṭaka*. (2) The second is the *Abhidamma Piṭaka*, notably the closely related books, the *Dhammasaṅgaṇī*, *Vibhaṅga Paṭṭhāna*. (3) The third is the system which the author of the *Visuddhimagga* completed, or found completed, and which he set himself to edit and translate back into Pali (some further minor developments took place subsequently, particularly with the 12th-century (?) *Abhidhammatthasangaha*, but they are outside the present scope). The point at issue here is not the much-debated historical question of how far the *Abhidhamma* books (leaving aside the *Kathāvatthu*) were contemporary with the *Vinaya* and *Suttas*, but rather what discernible direction they show in evolution of thought.

(1) The Suttas being taken as the original exposition of the Buddha's teaching, (2) the *Abhidamma Piṭaka* itself appears as a highly technical and specialized systematization, or complementary set of modifications built upon that. Its immediate purpose is, one may say, to describe and pin-point mental constituents and characteristics and relate them to their material basis and to each other (with the secondary object, perhaps, of providing an efficient defence in disputes with heretics and exponents of outsiders' doctrines). Its ultimate purpose is to furnish additional techniques for getting rid of unjustified assumptions that favour clinging and so obstruct the attainment of the extinction of clinging. Various instruments have been forged in it for sorting and re-sorting experience expressed as *dhammas* (see Ch. VII, n. 1). These instruments are new to the Suttas, though partly traceable to them. The principal instruments peculiar to it are three, that is to say: (a)

the strict treatment of experience (or the knowable and knowledge using the words in their widest possible sense) in terms of momentary cognizable states (*dhamma*) and the definition of these states, which is done in the *Dhammasaṅgaṇī* and *Vibhaṅga*; (b) the creation of a 'Schedule' (*mātikā*) consisting of a set of triple (*tika*) and double (*duka*) classifications for sorting these states; and (c) the enumeration of twenty-four kinds of conditioning relations (*paccaya*), which is done in the *Paṭṭhāna*. The states as defined are thus, as it were, momentary 'stills'; the structure of relations combines the stills into continuities; the Schedule classifications indicated the direction of the continuities.

The three Abhidhamma books already mentioned are the essential basis for what later came to be called the 'Abhidhamma Method': together they form an integral whole. The other four books, which may be said to support them in various technical fields, need not be discussed here. This, then, is a bare outline of what is in fact an enormous maze with many unexplored side-turnings.

(3) The system found in the Commentaries has moved on (perhaps slightly diverged) from the strict Abhidhamma-Pitaka standpoint. The Suttas offered descriptions of discovery; the Abhidhamma, map-making; but emphasis now is not on discovery, or even on mapping, so much as on consolidating, filling in and explaining. The material is worked over for consistency. Among the principal new developments here are these. The 'Cognitive Series' (*citta-vīthi*) in the occurrence of the conscious process is organized (see Ch. IV, n. 13 and Table V) and completed, and its association with three different kinds of kamma is laid down. The term *sabhāva* ('individual-essence', 'own-being' or 'it-ness', see Ch. VII, n. 68) is introduced to explain the key word *dhamma*, thereby submitting that term to ontological criticism, while the *samaya* ('event' or 'occasion') of the *Dhammasaṅgaṇī* is now termed a *khaṇa* ('moment') thus shifting the weight and balance a little in the treatment of time. Then there is the specific ascription of the three 'instants' (*khaṇa*, too) of Arising, Presence and Dissolution (*uppāda-ṭṭhiti-bhaṅga*), to each 'moment' (*Khaṇa*), one 'material moment' being calculated to last as long as sixteen 'mental moments' (Ch. XX, §24; DhsA. 60).[18] New to the Pitakas are also the rather unwieldy enumeration of concepts (*paññatti*, see Ch. VII, n. 11), and the handy defining-formula of Word-meaning, Characteristic, Function. Manifestation, and Proximate Cause (Locus); also many minor instances such as the substitution of the specific 'heart-basis' for the *Paṭṭhāna's* 'material basis of mind', the conception of 'material octads' etc., the detailed descriptions of the thirty-two parts of the body instead of the bare enumeration of the names in the Suttas

18. The legitimateness of the mental moment of 'presence' (*ṭhiti*) as deducible from A.i, 152 is questioned by Ācariya Ānanda (VbhAA.), who wrote early in the Middle Period, and he cites the Yamaka (refs.: ii, 13, ii, 14; and i, 216-7) against it.

(thirty-one in the Four *Nikāyas* and thirty-two in the *Khuddaka-pāṭha* and the *Paṭisambhidāmagga*), and many more. And the word *paramattha* acquires a new and slightly altered currency. The question of how much this process of development owes to post-Maurian evolution of Sanskrit thought on the Indian mainland (either through assimilation or opposition) still remains to be explored, like so many others in this field. The object of this sketch is only to point to a few landmarks.

* * * *

The Paramatthamañjūsā

The notes to this translation contain many quotations from the commentary to the *Visuddhimagga*, called the *Paramatthamañjūsā* or *Mahā-Ṭīkā*. It is regarded as an authoritative work. The quotations are included both for the light they shed on difficult passages in the *Visuddhimagga* and for the sake of rendering for the first time of the essays interspersed in it. The prologue and epilogue give its author as an elder named Dhammapāla, who lived at Padaratirtha (identified as near Madras). This author, himself also an Indian, is usually held to have lived within two centuries or so of Bhadantācariya Buddhaghosa. There is nothing to say that he ever came to Ceylon.

The *Visuddhimagga* quotes freely from the *Paṭisambhidāmagga*, the commentary to which was written by an elder named Mahānāma (date in the Middle Period and place of residence uncertain). Mostly but not quite always, he says the same thing, when commenting on these quoted passages, as the Elder Mahānāma but in more words[19] He relies much on syllogisms and logical arguments. Also there are several discussions of some of the systems of the 'Six Schools' of Brahmanical philosophy. There are no stories. This academic writer is difficult, formalistic and often involved, very careful and accurate. Various other works are attributed to him.

* * * *

Some main threads in the Visuddhimagga

Visuddhimagga is probably best regarded as a detailed manual for meditation masters, and as a work of reference. As to its

19. The Elder Dhammapāla, commenting on Vis. Ch. XXI, §77, takes the reading *phuṭṭhantam sacchikato* and explains that (cf. Mūla Ṭīkā Pug. AA. p. 32) but the Elder Mahānāma, commenting on the *Patisambhidāmagga* from which the passage is quoted, takes the reading *phuṭṭhattā sacchikato* and comments differently (PsA., p. 396 Hewavitarne ed.). Again, what is referred to as 'said by some (*keci*)' in the Elder Dhammapāla's comment on the *Vissuddhimagga* (see Vis. Ch. VIII, n.46) is put forward by the Elder Mahānāma with no such reservation (PsA., p.351). It is the usual standard of strict consistency that makes such very minor divergences noticeable. These two commentators, though, rarely reproduce each other

rather intricate construction. The List of Contents is given rather fully in order to serve as a guide to the often complicated form of the chapters and to the work as a whole in addition, the following consideration.

Chapters I and II, which deal with Virtue as the practice of restraint, or withdrawal, need present no difficulties. It can be remarked here, though, that when the Buddhist ascetic goes into seclusion (restrains the sense door), it would be incorrect to say of him that he 'leaves the *world*'; for where a man is, there is his world (*loka*), as appears in the Discourse quoted in Ch. VII, §36 (cf. also S. iv, 116 as well as many other Suttas on the same subject). So when he retreats from the clamour of society to the woods and rocks, he takes his world with him, as though withdrawing to his laboratory, in order the better to analyse it.

Chs. III to XI describe the process of concentration and give directions for attaining it by means of a choice of 40 meditation subjects for developing concentration. The account of each single meditation subject as given here is incomplete unless taken in conjunction with the whole of Part III (Understanding), which applies to all. Concentration is training in intensity and depth of focus and in single-mindedness. While Buddhism makes no exclusive claim to teach Jhana Concentration (*samatho=Samādhi*), it does claim that the development of Insight (*vipassanā*) culminating in penetration of the Four Truths is peculiar to it. The two have to be coupled together in order to attain the Truths[20] and the end of suffering. Insight is initially training to see experience as it occurs. without misperception, invalid assumptions or wrong inferences.

Chs. XII and XIII describe rewards of Concentration fully developed without insight.

Chs. XIV to XVII on Understanding are entirely *theoretical*. Experience in general is dissected, and the separated components are described and grouped in several alternative patterns in Chs. XIV. to XVI, §1-12. The rest of Ch. XVI expounds the Four noble Truths, the centre of the Buddha's teaching. After that, Dependent Origination, or the Structure of Conditionality, is dealt with in its aspect of *arising*, or the process of Being (Ch. XVII: as *cessation*, or nibbana, it is dealt with separately in Chs. XVI and XIX). The formula of Dependant Origination in its varying modes describes the working economics of the first two Truths (Suffering as object of Craving, and Craving itself—see also Ch. XVII, n. 48). Without an understanding of conditionality the Buddha's teaching cannot be grasped: 'He who sees dependent orgination sees the Dhamma' (M. i, 191), though not all details in this work are always necessary. Since the detailed part of this chapter is very

---

verbatim. Contrastingly, where the *Paramatthamañjūsā* and the *Mūla Ṭīkā* similarly overlap, the sentences are mostly *verbatim*, but the former, with extra material, looks like an expanded version of the latter, or the latter a cut version of the former.

20. See A. ii, 56; Ps. ii, 92f.

elaborate (§58-272), a first reading confined to §1-6, §20-57 and §273-314, might help to avoid losing the thread. These four chapters are 'theoretical' because they contain in detailed form what needs to be learnt, if only in outline, as 'book-learning' (*sotā-vadhāna-ñāṇa*). They furnish techniques for describing the total experience and the experienceable rather as the branches of arithmetic and double-entry book-keeping are to be learnt as techniques for keeping accurate business accounts.

Chs. XVIII to XXI, on the contrary are *practical* and give instructions for applying the book-knowledge learnt from Chs. XIV to XVII by analysing in its terms the meditator's individual experience, dealing also with what may be expected to happen in the course of development. Ch. XVIII as 'Defining of Mentality-materiality' (first application of Chs. XIV to XVI and Ch. XIX as 'Discerning Conditions' (first application of Ch. XVII) are preparatory to Insight proper, which begins in Ch. XX with Contemplation of Rise and Fall. After this, progress continues through the '8 Knowledges' with successive clarification—clarification of view of the Object and consequent alterations of Subjective Attitude towards it—till a point, called 'Conformity Knowledge'; is reached which through one of the 'Three Gateways to Liberation', heralds the attainment of the first Supramundane Path.

In Ch. XXII the attainment of the four successive Supramundane Paths (or successive stages in realization) is described, with the first of which nibbana (extinction of the craving which originates suffering) is 'seen' for the first time, having till then been only intellectually conceived. At that moment Suffering as a Noble Truth is fully understood, Craving, its origin, is abandoned, suffeing's Cessation is realized, and the Way to its cessation is developed.[21] The three remaining paths develop further and complete that vision.

Finally Ch. XXIII, as the counterpart of Chs. XII and XIII, describes the benefits of Understanding. The description of nibbana is given at Ch. VIII §245ff., and a discussion of it at Ch. XVI, §66ff.

* * * *

Concerning the translation

The pitfalls that await anyone translating from another European language into his own native English are familiar enough: there is no need for him to fall into them. But when he ventures upon rendering an Oriental language, he will often have to be his own guide

21. In the present work the development of Serenity (Concentration) is carried to its limit before Insight (Understanding) is dealt with. This is for clarity. But in the Commentary to the *Satipaṭṭhāna Suta* (D. Sutta 22, M. Sutta 10) either the two are developed contemporaneously or Insight is allowed to precede Jhana Concentration. According to the Suttas, concentration of jhana strength is necessary for the manifestation of the Path (see e.g. Vis. Ch. XIV, §127; XV, n. 7; D. ii, 313=M.iii, 252; A.ii, 156 quoted at Ps. ii, 92f).

INTRODUCTION

Naturally, a translator from Pali today owes a large debt to his predecessors and to the Pali Text Society's publications including in particular the Society's invaluable Pali-English Dictionary. A translator of the *Visuddhimagga*, too, must make due acknowledgement of its pioneer translation (now long out of print) by U Pe Maung Tin.

The word '*pāḷi*' is translatable by 'text' The *Pāḷi* Language (the 'text language', which the commentators call Magadhan) holds a special position, with no European parallel, being reserved to one field namely, the Buddha's teaching. So there are no alien echoes. In the Suttas the sanskrit is silent, and it is heavily muted in the later literature. This fact, coupled with the richness and integrity of the subject itself, gives it a singular limpidness and depth in its early form, as in a string quartet or the clear ocean, which attains in the style of the Suttas to an exquisite and unrivalled beauty unreflectable by any rendering. Traces seem to linger even in the intricate formalism preferred by the commentators.

This translation presents many formidable problems. Mainly either epistemological, and psychological, or else linguistic, they relate either to what idea and things are being discussed, or else to the manipulation of dictionary meaning of words used in discussion.

The first is perhaps dominant. As mentioned earlier, the *Visuddhimagga* can be properly studied only as part of the whole commentarial edifice, whose corner-stone it is. But while indexes of words and subjects to the P.T.S. edition of the *Visuddhimagga* exist, most of its author's works have only indexes of Pitaka words and names commented on but none for the mass of subject matter. So the student has to make his own. Of the Commentaries too, only the *Atthasālinī*, the *Dhammapada Commentary* and the *Jātaka Commentary* have so far been translated (and the latter two are rather in a separate class). But that is a minor aspect.

This book is largely technical and presents all the difficulties peculiar to technical translation: it deals, besides, with mental happenings. Now where many synonyms are used, as they often are in Pali, for public material objects—an elephant, say, or gold or the sun—the 'material objects' should be pointable to, if there is doubt about what is referred to. Again even such generally recognized private experiences as those referred to by the words 'consciousness' or 'pain' seem too obvious to introspection for uncertainty to arise (communication to fail), if they are given variant symbols. Here the English translator can forsake the Pali allotment of synonyms and indulge a liking for 'elegant variation', if he has it, without fear of *muddle*. But mind is fluid, as it were, and materially negative, and its analysis needs a different and a strict treatment. In the Suttas and still more in the Abhidhamma, charting by analysis and definition of pin-pointed mental states is carried far into unfamiliar waters. It was already recognized then that this is no more a solid landscape of 'things' to be pointed to when variation has resulted in vagueness. As an instance of disregard of this fact: a greater scholar with impeccable historical and philological judgement (perhaps the most eminent of the English translators) has in a single work rendered the *cattāro satipaṭṭhānā* (here represented by 'Four Foundations of Mindfulness') by Four Inceptions of Deliberation', 'Fourfold Setting Up of Mindfulness', 'Fourfold Setting Up of Starting', 'Four Applications of Mindfulness', and other variants. The P.T.S. Dict. Foreword observes 'No one needs now to use the one English word "desire" as a translation of sixteen distinct Pali words, no one of which means precisely desire. Yet this was done in Vol. X. of the Sacred Books of the East by Max Müller and Fausböll'. True; but need one go to the other extreme? How without looking up the Pali can one be sure if the same idea is referred to by all these variants and not some other such as those referred to by *cattāro iddhipādā* ('Four Roads to Power or Bases of Success'), *cattāro Sammappadhānā* ('Four Right Endeavours'), etc., or one of the many other 'fours'? It is customary not to vary, say, the 'Call for Categorical Imperative' in a new context by some such alternative as 'Uncomprising Order' or 'Plain-speaking Bidding' or 'Call for Unconditional Surrender,' which the dictionaries would justify, or 'faith' which the exegetists might recommend; that is to say, if it is hoped to avoid confusion. The choosing of an adequate rendering is however, a quite different problem.

But there is something more to be considered before coming to that. So far only the difficulty of isolating, symbolizing and describing individual mental states has been touched on. But here the whole mental structure with its temporal-dynamic process is dealt with too. Identified mental as well as material states, (none of which can arise independently) must be recognizable with their associations when encountered in new circumstances: for here arises the central question of thought-association and its manipulation. That is tacitly recognized in the Pali. If disregarded in the English rendering the tenuous structure with its inferences and negations—the flexible pattern of thought-associations—can no longer be communicated or followed, because the pattern of speech no longer reflects it, and whatever may be communicated is only fragmentary and perhaps deceptive. Renderings of words have to be distinguished, too, from renderings of words used to explain those words. From this aspect the Oriental system of word-by-word translation, which transliterates the sound of the principal substantive and verb stems and attaches to them local inflexions, has much to recommend it, though, of course, it is not readable as 'literature'. One is handling instead of pictures of isolated ideas or even groups of ideas a whole coherent chart system.

And besides, words, like maps and charts, are conventionally used to represent high dimensions.

What already identified states or currents are encountered from new angles, the new situation can be verbalized in one of two ways at least: either by using in a new appropriate verbal setting the words already allotted to these states, or by describing the whole situation afresh in different terminology chosen *ad hoc*. While the second may gain in individual brightness, connexion with other allied references can hardly fail to be lost. Aerial photographs must be taken from consistent altitudes, if they are to be used for making maps. And words serve the double purpose of recording ideas already formed and of arousing new ones.

Structural coherence between different parts in the Pali of the present work needs reflecting in the translation—especialy in the last ten chapter—if the thread is not soon to be lost. In fact, in the Pali (just as much in the Tipitaka as in its commentaries), when such subjects are being handled, one finds that a tacit rule. 'One term and one flexible definition for one idea (or state or event or situation) referred to' is adhered to pretty thoroughly. The reason has already been made clear. With no such rule ideas are apt to disintegrate or coalesce or fictitiously multiply (and, of course, any serious attempt at indexing in English is stultified).

One thing needs to be made clear, though; for there is confusion of thought on this whole subject (one so far only partly investigated).[22] This Rule of Parsimony in Variants has nothing to do with mechanical transliteration, which is a translator's refuge when he is unsure of himself. The guiding rule 'One recognizable idea, one word or phrase to symbolize it' in no sense implies any such rule as 'One Pali word, one English word,' which is neither desirable nor practicable. Nor in translating need the rule apply beyond the scope reviewed.

So much for the epistemological and psychological problems.

The linguistic problem is scarcely less formidable though much better recognized. While English is extremely analytic, Pali (another Indo-European language) is one of the group of tongues regarded as dominated by Sanskrit, strongly agglutinative, forming long compounds and heavily inflected. The vocabulary chosen occasioned much heart-searching but is still very imperfect. If a few of the words encountered seem a bit algebraical at first, contexts and definitions should make them clear. In the translation of an Oriental language, especially a classical one, the translator must recognize that such knowledge which the Oriental reader is taken for granted to possess is lacking in his European counterpart, who tends unawares to fill the gaps from his own foreign store: the result can be like taking two pictures on one film. Not only is the common background evoked by the words shadowy and patchy, but Euro-

22. See Prof. I. A. Richards' *Mencius on Mind*, Kegan Paul, 1932.

pean thought and Indian thought tend to approach the problems of human existence from opposite directions. This affects word-formations. And so double meanings (utraquisms, puns, and metaphors) and etymological links often follow quite different tracks, a fact which is particularly intrusive in describing mental events, where the terms employed are mainly 'material' ones used metaphorically. Unwanted contexts constantly creep in and wanted ones stay out. Then there are no well-defined techniques for recognizing and handling idioms, literal rendering of which misleads (while, say, one may not wonder whether to render *tour de force* by 'enforced tour' or 'tower of strength', one cannot always be so confident in Pali).

Then again in the *Visuddhimagga* alone the actual words and word-meanings not in the P.T.S. Dictionary come to more than 240. The Dictionary as its preface states, is 'essentially preliminary'; for when it was published many books had still not been collated; it leaves out many words even from the Sutta Pitaka, and the Sub-commentaries are not touched by it. Also—and most important here—in the making of that dictionary the study of Pali literature had for the most part not been tackled much from, shall one say, the philosophical or better, epistemological, angle,[23] work and interest having been concentrated till then almost exclusively on history and philology. For instance, the epistemologically unimportant word *vimāna* (divine mansion) is given more than twice the space allotted to the term *paṭicca-samuppāda* (dependent origination), a diffcult subject of central importance, the article on which is altogether inadequate and misleading (owing partly to misapplication of the Historical Method). Then *gala* (throat) has been found more glossarilly interesting than *paṭisandhi* ('rebirth-linking'], the original use of which word at M. iii, 230 is ignored. Under *nāma*, too, *nāma-rūpa* is confused with *nāma-kāya*. And so one might continue. By this, however, it is not intended al all to depreciate that great dictionary, but only to observe that in using it the Pali student has sometimes to be wary: if it is criticized in particular here (and it can well hold its own against criticism), tribute must also be paid to its own inestimable general value.

* * * * *

Now a few points to conclude.

Current standard English has been aimed at and preference given always to simplicity. This has often necessitated cutting up long involved sentences, omitting connecting particles (such as *pana*, *pan'etha*, *yasmā* when followed by *tasmā*, *hi*, *kho*, etc.), which serve simply as grammatical grease in long chains of subordinate periods.

23. Exceptions are certain early works of Mrs. C.A.F. Rhys Davids. See also discussions in appendixes to the translations of the *Kathāvatthu* (*Points of Controversy*, P.T.S.) and The *Abhidhammatthasaṅgaha* (*Compendium of Philosophy*, P.T.S.).

Conversely the author is sometimes extraordinarily elliptic (as in Chapter XIV, §46 and Ch. XVI, §68f.), and then the device of square brackets has been used to add supplementary matter, without which the sentence would be too enigmatically shorthand. Such additions (kept to the minimum) are in almost every case taken from elsewhere in the work itself or from the *Paramatthamañjūsā*. Round brackets have been reserved for reference and for alternative renderings (as, e.g., in Ch. I, §140) where there is a sense too wide for any appropriate English word to straddle.

A few words have been left untranslated (see individual notes). The choice is necessarily arbitrary. It includes kamma, dhamma (sometimes) jhana, Buddha (sometimes), bhikkhu, nibbana, patimokkha, kasina, Pitaka, and arahant. There seemed no advantage and much disadvantage in using the Sanskrit forms, *bhiksu*, *dharma*, *dhyāna*, *arhat*, etc., as is sometimes done (even though 'karma' and 'nirvana' are in the Concise Oxford Dictionary), and no reason against absorbing the Pali words into English as they are by dropping the diacritical marks. Proper names appear in their Pali spelling without italics and with diacritical marks. Wherever Pali words or names appear, the stem form has been used (e.g. *Buddha*, *kamma*) rather than the inflected nominative (*Buddho kammaṃ*), unless there were reasons against it.[24]

Accepted renderings have not been departed from nor earlier translators gone against capriciously. It seemed advisable to treat certain emotionally charged words such as 'real' especially with a capital R) with caution. Certain other words have been avoided altogether. For example, *vassa* ('rains') signifies a three-month period of residence in one place during the Rain Season, enjoined upon bhikkhus by the Buddha in order that they should not travel about trampling down crops and so annoy farmers. To translate it by 'Lent' as is sometimes done lets in a historical background and religious atmosphere of mourning and fasting quite alien to it (with no etymological support). 'Metempsychosis' for *paṭisandhi* is another notable instance.[25]

---

24. Pronounce letters as follows: a as in countryman, ā father, e whey, i chin, ī machine, u full, ū rule; ch church (always), g give (always); h always sounded separately, e.g. bh in cab-horse, c in catch him (not kitchen), ph in upholstery (not telephone), th in hot-house (not pathos), etc.; j joke; ṁ and ṅ as ng in singer, ñ as ni in onion; ḍ, ḷ, ṇ and ṭ are pronounced with tongue-tip on palate; d, l, n and t with tongue-tip on teeth; double consonants as in Italian, e.g. dd as in mad dog (not madder), gg as in big gun (not bigger); rest as in English.

25. Of the principal English value words, 'real', 'truth', 'beauty', 'good'. 'absolute', 'being', etc.: 'real' has been used for *tatha* (Ch. XVI, §24), 'truth' allotted to *sacca* (Ch. XVI, §25) and beauty to *subha* (Ch. IX, §119); 'good' has been used sometimes for the prefix *su-* and also for the adj. *kalyāṇa* and the subst. *attha*. "Absolute" has been not employed, though it might perhaps be used for the word *advaya*, which qualifies the word *kasiṇa* ('universality', 'totalization') at M. ii, 14, and then 'One (man) perceives earth as a Universality above, below, around, absolute, measureless' could be an alternative for the rendering given in

The handling of three words, *dhamma*, *citta* and *rupa* (see Glossary and relevant notes) is admittedly something of a makeshift. The only English word that might with some agility be used consistently for *dhamma* seems to be 'idea'; but it has been crippled by philosophers and would perhaps mislead. *Citta* might with advantage have been rendered throughout by 'cognizance', in order to preserve its independence, instead of rendering it sometimes by 'mind' (shared with *mano*) and sometimes by 'consciousness' (shared with *viññāṇa*) as has been done. But in many contexts all three Pali words are synonyms for the same general notion (see Ch. XIV, §82); and technically, the notion of 'cognition', referred to in its bare aspect by *viññāṇa*, is also referred to along with its concomitant affective colouring, thought and memory, etc., *by citta*. So the treatment accorded to *citta* here finds support to that extent. Lastly 'mentality-materiality' for *nāma-rūpa* is inadequate and 'name-and-form' in some ways preferable. 'Name' (see Ch. XVIII, n. 4) still suggests *nāma's* function of 'naming'; and 'form' for the *rūpa* of the *rūpa-kkhanda* ('materiality-aggregate') can preserve the link with the *rūpa* of the *rūp-āyatana*, ('visible-object base') by rendering them respectively with 'material form aggregate' and 'visible-form base'—a point not without philosophical importance. A compromise has been made at Ch. X, §13, 'Materiality' or 'matter' whereever used should not be taken implying any hypostasis, any 'permanent or semi-permanent substance behind appearances' (the objective counterpart of the subjective ego), which would find no support in the Pali.

The editions of Ceylon, Burma and Thailand have been consulted as well as the two Latin-script editions; and Sinhalese translations, besides. The paragraph numbers of the Harvard University Press edition will be found on the left of the pages and the page numbers of the Pali Text Society's edition in square brackets in the text (the latter, though sometimes appearing at the end of paragraphs mark the beginnings of the P.T.S. pages). Errors of readings and punctuation in the P.T.S. edition not in the Harvard edition have not been referred to in the notes.

For the quotations from the Tipitaka it was found impossible to make use of existing published translations because they lacked the kind of treatment sought. However, other translation work in hand served as the basis for all the Pitaka quotations.

Rhymes seemed unsuitable for the verses from the Tipitaka and the 'Ancients'; but they have been resorted to for the summarizing verses belonging to the *Vissuddhimagga* itself. The Engligh language is too weak in fixed stresses to lend itself to Pali rhythms, though one attempt to reproduce them was made in Chapter IV.

Where a passage from a Sutta is commented on, the order of the

Ch. V, §38. 'Being' (as abstract subst.) has sometimes been used for *bhava*, which is otherwise rendered by 'becoming.'

explanatory comments follows the Pali order of words in the original sentence, which is not always that of the translation of it.

In Indian books the titles and sub-titles are placed only at the end of the subject matter. In the translations they have been inserted at the beginning, and some sub-titles added for the sake of clarity. In this connexion the title at the end of Chapter XII 'Description of Concentration' is a 'heading' applying not only to that chapter but as far back as the beginning of Chapter III. Similarly, the title at the end of Chapter XIII refers back to the beginning of Chapter XII. The heading 'Description of the Soil in which Underestanding Grows' (*paññā-bhūmi-niddesa*) refers back from the end of Chapter XVII to the beginning of Chapter XIV.

The book abounds in 'shorthand' allusions to the Pitakas and to other parts of itself. They are often hard to recognize, and failure to do so results in a sentence with a half-meaning. It is hoped that most of them have been hunted down.

Criticism has been strictly confined to the application of Pali Buddhist standards in an attempt to produce a balanced and uncoloured English counterpart of the original. The use of words has been stricter in the translation itself than the Introduction to it.

The translator will, of course, have sometimes slipped or failed to follow his own rules; and there are many passages any rendering of which is bound to evoke query from some quarter where there is interest in the subject. As to the rules, however and the vocabulary chosen, it has not been intended to lay down laws, and when the methods, adopted are described above that is done simply to indicate the line taken: '*Janapada-niruttiṁ nābhiniveseyya, samaññaṁ nātidhāveyyā ti*' (see Ch. XVII, §24).

BIBLIOGRAPHY

PRINTED EDITIONS OF THE VISUDDHIMAGGA PALI TEXT

Sinhalese script:
Hewavitarne Bequest edition, Colombo.
Burmese script:
Hanthawaddy Press edition, Rangoon, 1900.
Siamese script:
Royal Siamese edition, Bankok.
Latin script:
Pali Text Society's edition, London.
Harvard University Press edition, Harvard Oriental Series, Vol. 41, Cambridge, Mass., 1950.

TRANSLATIONS OF THE VISUDDHIMAGGA

English: 'The Path of Purity' by Pe Maung Tin, P.T.S. 1922 (Vol. I), 1928 (Vol. II), 1931 (Vol. III), London.

German: 'Visuddhimagga (der Weg zur Reinheit)' by Nyanatiloka, Verlag Christiani, Konstanz, 1952.

Sinhalese: King Parakramabāhu's translation (13th cent. A.C.), Chs. I to XX, Colombo, 1948. 'Sinhala Visuddhimargaya' by Paṇḍita Mātara Sri Dharmavaṁsa Sthavira, Mātara, Ceylon, 1953 (Chs. I to IX). Etc.

OTHER WORKS

Ācariya Dhammapāla's *Paramatthamañjūsā*, commentary to the *Visuddhimagga* (*Visuddhimagga-mahā-ṭīkā*). Vidyodaya edition in Sinhalese script, Colombo (Chs. I to XVII only). P.C. Mundyne Pitaka Press edition in Burmese script, Rangoon, 1909 (Chs. I to XI), 1910 (Chs. XII to XXIII). Siamese edition in Siamese script, Bankok. No Latin-script edition. No English translation.

Mahāvaṁsa or Great Chronicle of Ceylon, English trsln. by W. Geiger, P.T.S. London.

Cūḷavaṁsa or Minor Chronicle of Ceylon (or *Mahāvaṁsa* Part II), English trsln. by W. Geiger, P.T.S. London.

Dīpavaṁsa (Chronicle of Ceylon), English trsln. by H. Oldenberg, London, 1879.

The Pali Text Society's Pali-English Dictionary, P.T.S. London.

Trenckner's Critical Pali Dictionary (Pali-English), Vol. 1 (letter a), Commissioner Ejnar Munkagaard, Copenhagen, 1924-48.

The Life and Work of Buddhaghosa, by B.C. Law, Thacker and Spink. Calcutta and Simla, 1923.

Vimuttimagga and Visuddhimagga—a Comparative Study, by P. V. Bapat, Poona, 1937.

History of Indian Literature, by M. Winternitz, English trsln. by Mrs. S. Ketkar and Miss H. Kohn, University of Calcutta, 1933.

Pali Literature and Language, by W. Geiger, English trsln. by Batakrishna Ghosh, University of Calcutta, 1943.

The Pali Literature of Ceylon, by G. P. Malalasekera, Royal Asiatic Society, London, 1928.

History of Pali Literature, by B. C. Law, London, 1933 (2 Vols.).

The Early History of Buddhism in Ceylon, by E. W. Adikaram, Ceylon, 1946.

Theravāda Buddhism in Burma, by Niharranjan Ray, Calcutta University, 1946 (pp. 24 ff.).

Buddhaghosuppatti, edited and translated into English, by J. Gray, Luzac and Co., London, 1892.

Vimuttimagga, Chinese text.

Vimuttimagga,privately circulated English translation from the Chinese by N. R. M. Ehara, V. E. P. Pulle and G. S. Prelis, new printed edition Colombo 1961.

LIST OF ABBREVIATIONS USED

All editions Pali Text Society unless otherwise stated

A.	Aṅguttara Nikāya	
AA.	Aṅguttara Nikāya Atthakathā (Commentary) = Manorathapūraṇī	
Cp.	Cariyāpiṭaka	
Dh.	Dhammapada	
DhA.	Dhammapada Atthakathā (Commentary)	
Dhs.	Dhammasaṅgaṇī	
DhsA.	Dhammasaṅgaṇī Atthakathā (Commentary) = Atthasālinī	
DhsAA.	Dhammasaṅgaṇī Tīkā (Sub-commentary) = Mūla Ṭīkā (pt. I)	
Dhk.	Dhātukathā	
D.	Dīgha Nikāya	
DA.	Dīgha Nikāya Atthakathā (Commentary) = Sumaṅgalavilāsinī	
Iti.	Itivuttaka	
Jā.	Jātaka (Fausböll's ed.)	
Kv.	Kathāvatthu	
Mv.	Mahāvaṁsa	
M.	Majjhima Nikāya	
MA.	Majjhima Nikāya Atthakathā (Commentary) = Papañcasūdanī	
Miln.	Milinda-pañhā	
Netti.	Netti-pakaraṇa	
Nd1.	Mahā Niddesa	
Nd2.	Cūḷa Niddesa (Siamese ed.)	
Ps.	Paṭisambhidāmagga	
PsA.	Paṭisambhidāmagga Atthakathā (Commentary) = Saddhammappakāsinī (Sinhalese Hewavitarne ed.).	
Ptn1.	Paṭṭhāna, Tika Paṭṭhāna	
Ptn2.	Paṭṭhāna, Duka Paṭṭhāna (Siamese and Burmese eds.)	
Pm.	Paramattha-mañjūsā, Visuddhimagga Aṭṭhakathā (Commentary) = Mahā Tīkā (Vis. Chs. I to XVII Sinhalese Vidyodaya ed.; Chs. XVIII to XXIII Burmese ed.)	
Pe.	Peṭakopadesa	
Pv.	Petavatthu	
S.	Samyutta Nikāya	
SA.	Samyutta Nikāya Atthakathā (Commentary) = Sāratthappakāsinī	
Sn.	Sutta-nipāta	
SnA.	Sutta-nipāta Atthakathā (Commentary) = Paramatthajotikā	
Thag.	Thera-gāthā	
Ud.	Udāna	
Vbh.	Vibhaṅga	
VbhA.	Vibhaṅga Atthakathā (Commentary) = Sammohavinodanī	
VbhAA.	Vibhaṅga Tīkā (Sub-commentary) = Mūla-Tīkā (pt. 2)	
Vv.	Vimāna-vatthu	
Vin. i.	Vinaya Piṭaka (3)—Mahāvagga	
Vin. ii.	Vinaya Piṭaka (4)—Cūlavagga	
Vin. iii.	Vinaya Piṭaka (1)—Suttavibhaṅga 1	(Oldenberg's ed.)
Vin. iv.	Vinaya Piṭaka (2)—Suttavibhaṅga 2	
Vin. v.	Vinaya Piṭaka (5)—Parivāra	
Vis.	Visuddhimagga (P.T.S. ed. and Harvard Oriental Series ed.)	

Numbers in square brackets in the text thus (25) refer to the page numbers of the Pali Text Society's edition of the Pali.

Paragraph numbers on the left correspond to the paragraph numbers of the Harvard ed. of the Pali.

Chapter and section headings and other numberings have been inserted for clarity.

CONTENTS

PART I. VIRTUE

1. Purification of Virtue

CHAPTER 1

DESCRIPTION OF VIRTUE

CHAPTER II

DESCRIPTION OF THE ASCETIC PRACTICES   ...59

PART II. CONCENTRATION

2. Purification of Consciousness

CHAPTER III

DESCRIPTION OF CONCENTRATION—TAKING A MEDITATION SUBJECT

CHAPTER IV
DESCRIPTION OF CONCENTRATION — THE EARTH KASINA

CHAPTER V
DESCRIPTION OF CONCENTRATION—THE REMAINING KASINAS

CHAPTER VI
DESCRIPTION OF CONCENTRATION—FOULNESS AS A MEDITATION SUBJECT

CHAPTER VII
DESCRIPTION OF CONCENTRATION—SIX RECOLLECTIONS

PART III. UNDERSTANDING

The Soil in which Understanding Grows

CHAPTER XIV

THE SOIL IN WHICH UNDERSTANDING GROWS—DESCRIPTION OF THE AGGREGATES

CHAPTER XV

THE SOIL IN WHICH UNDERSTANDING GROWS—DESCRIPTION OF THE BASES AND ELEMENTS

CHAPTER XVI

THE SOIL IN WHICH UNDERSTANDING GROWS—DESCRIPTION OF THE FACULTIES AND TRUTHS

CONTENTS

CHAPTER XVII

THE SOIL IN WHICH UNDERSTANDING GROWS—CONCLUSION

3 **Purification of View**

CHAPTER XVIII

4. Purification by Overcoming Doubt

CHAPTER XIX

5. Purification By Knowledge and Vision of What Is and What Is Not Path

CHAPTER XX

CONTENTS

6. Purification By Knowledge and Vision of the Way

CHAPTER XXI

7. Purification By Knowledge and Vision

CHAPTER XXII

CONTENTS

The Benefits of Understanding

CHAPTER XXIII

Namo tassa bhagavato arahato sammāsambuddhassa

THE PATH OF PURIFICATION

(*Visuddhi-magga*)

PART I. VIRTUE (*Sīla*)

CHAPTER I. DESCRIPTION OF VIRTUE

(*Sīla-niddesa*)

[1. INTRODUCTORY]

1. [1] 'When a wise man, established well in Virtue,
'Develops Consciousness and Understanding,
'Then as a bhikkhu ardent and sagacious
'He succeeds in disentangling this tangle' (S.i,13).

This was said. But why was it said? While the Blessed One was living at Sāvatthi, it seems, a certain deity came to him in the night, and in order to do away with his doubts he asked this question:

'The inner tangle and the outer tangle—
'This generation is entangled in a tangle.
'And so I ask of Gotama this question:
'Who succeeds in disentangling this tangle?' (S.i,13).

2. Here is the meaning in brief. *Tangle* is a term for the network of craving. For that is a tangle in the sense of lacing together, like the tangle called network of branches in bamboo thickets, etc., because it goes on arising again and again up and down[1] among the objects [of consciousness] beginning with what is visible. But it is called *the inner tangle and the outer tangle* because it arises [as craving] for one's own requisites and another's, for one's own person and another's, and for the internal and external bases [for consciousness]. Since it arises in this way, *this generation is entangled in a tangle*. As the bamboos, etc., are entangled by the bamboo tangle, etc., so too this generation, in other words, this order of living beings, is all entangled by the tangle of craving—the meaning is that it is intertwined, interlaced by it. [2] And because it is entangled like this, *so I ask of Gotama this question*, that is why I ask this. He addressed the Blessed One by his race name as *Gotama*. *Who succeeds in disentangling this tangle*: who may disentangle this tangle that keeps the three kinds of existence entangled in this way?—What he asks is, who is capable of disentangling it?

1. From a visible datum sometimes as far down as a mental datum, or vice versa, following the order of the six kinds of objects of consciousness as given in the teaching (Pm. 5, see Ch. XV, §1).

1024 – B

3. However, when questioned thus, the Blessed One, whose knowledge of all things is unimpeded, Deity of Deities, excelling Sakka [Ruler of Gods], excelling Brahmā, fearless in the possession of the four kinds of perfect confidence, Wielder of the Ten Powers, All-seer with unobstructed knowledge, uttered this stanza in reply to explain the meaning :

'When a wise man, established well in Virtue,
'Develops Consciousness and Understanding,
'Then as a bhikkhu ardent and sagacious
'He succeeds in disentangling this tangle'.

* * *

4. My task is now to set out the true sense,
Divided into virtue and the rest,
Of this same verse composed by the Great Sage.
There are here in the Victor's Dispensation
Seekers gone forth from home to homelessness,
And who although desiring purity
Have no right knowledge of the sure straight way
Comprising virtue and the other two,
Right hard to find, that leads to purity—
Who, though they strive, here gain no purity.
To them I shall expound the comforting Path
Of Purification, pure in expositions,
Relying on the teaching of the dwellers
In the Great Monastery;[2] let all those
Good men who do desire purity
Listen intently to my exposition.

5. Herein, *purification* should be understood as nibbana, which being devoid of all stains, is utterly pure. The *Path of Purification* is the path to that purification; it is the means of approach that is called the *path*. The meaning is, I shall expound that path of purification.

6. In some instances this path of purification is taught by insight alone,[3] according as it is said :

'Formations are all impermanent :
'When he sees thus with understanding

2. The Great Monastery (*Mahāvihāra*) at Anurādhapura in Ceylon.

3. 'The words "*insight alone*" are meant to exclude, not virtue, etc., but serenity (*i.e.* jhana), which is the opposite number in the pair, serenity and insight. This is for emphasis. But the word "alone" actually excludes only that concentration with distinction [of jhana]; for concentration is classed as both access and absorption (see Ch. IV,§32). Taking this stanza as the teaching for one whose vehicle is insight does not imply that there is no concentration; for no insight comes about without momentary concentration. And again, insight should be understood as the three contemplations of impermanence, pain, and not-self; not contemplation of impermanence alone' (Pm. 9-10).

'And turns away from what is ill,
'That is the path to purity' (Dh. 277). [3]

And in some instances by jhana and understanding according as it is said:

'He is near unto nibbana
'In whom are jhana and understanding' (Dh. 372).

And in some instances by deeds (kamma), etc., according as it is said:

'By deeds, vision and righteousness,
'By virtue, the sublimest life—
'By these are mortals purified,
'And not by lineage and wealth' (M.iii, 262)

And in some instances by virtue, etc., according as it is said:

'He who is possessed of constant virtue,
'Has understanding, and is concentrated,
'Is strenuous and diligent as well,
'Will cross the flood so difficult to cross' (S.i,53).

And in some instances by the Foundations of Mindfulness, etc., according as it is said: 'Bhikkhus, this path is the only 'way for the purification of beings,...for the realization of 'nibbana, that is to say, the four Foundations of Mindfulness' (D.ii,290); and similarly in the case of the Right Efforts, and so on. But in the answer to this question it is taught by virtue and the other two.

7. Here is a brief commentary [on the stanza]. *Established well in virtue*: standing on virtue. It is only one actually fulfilling virtue who is here said to 'stand on virtue'. So the meaning here is this: being established well in virtue by fulfilling virtue. *A man*: a living being. *Wise*: possessing the kind of understanding that is born of kamma by means of a rebirth-linking with triple root-cause. *Develops Consciousness and Understanding*: develops both concentration and insight. For it is concentration that is described here under the heading of 'consciousness', and insight under that of 'understanding'.[4] *Ardent* (*ātāpin*): possessing energy. For it is

4. '"*Develops*" applies to both "*Consciousness*" and "*Uuderstanding*". But are they mundane or supramundane? They are supramundane because the sublime goal is described; for one developing them is said to disentangle the tangle of craving by cutting it off at the path moment, and that is not mundane. But the mundane are included here too because they immediately precede, since supramundane (see Ch. III, note 5) concentration and insight are impossible without mundane concentration and insight to precede them; for without the access and absorption concentration in one whose vehicle is serenity, or without the momentary concentration in one whose vehicle is insight, and without the Gateways to Liberation (see Ch. XXI, §66f.), the supramudane can never in either case be reached' (Pm. 13). '*With triple root-cause*' means with non-greed, non-hate and non-delusion.

energy that is called 'ardour (*ātāpa*)' in the sense of burning up and consuming (*ātāpana-paritāpana*) defilements. He has that, thus he is ardent. *Sagacious* : it is understanding that is called 'sagacity'; possessing that, is the meaning. This word shows protective understanding. For understanding is mentioned three times in the reply to the question. Herein, the first is native understanding, the second is understanding consisting in insight, while the third is the protective understanding that guides all affairs. He sees fear (*bhayam ikkhati*) in the round of rebirths, thus he is a *bhikkhu*. *He succeeds in disentangling this tangle* : [4] Just as a man standing on the ground and taking up a well-sharpened knife might disentangle a great tangle of bamboos, so too, he—this bhikkhu who possesses the six things, namely, this virtue, and this concentration described under the heading of consciousness, and this threefold understanding, and this ardour —, standing on the ground of virtue and taking up with the hand of protective-understanding exerted by the power of energy the knife of insight-understanding well-sharpened on the stone of concentration, might disentangle, cut away and demolish all the tangle of craving that had overgrown his own life's continuity. But it is at the moment of the Path that he is said to be disentangling that tangle : at the moment of fruition he has disentangled the tangle and is worthy of the highest offerings in the world with its deities. That is why the Blessed One said :

'When a wise man, established well in Virtue,
'Develops Consciousness and Understanding,
'Then as a bhikkhu ardent and sagacious
'He succeeds in disentangling this tangle'.

8. Herein there is nothing for him to do about the [native] understanding on account of which he is called *wise* ; for that has been established in him simply by the influence of previous kamma. But the words *ardent and sagacious* mean that by persevering with energy of the kind here described and by acting in full awareness with understanding he should, having become well established in virtue, develop the serenity and insight that are described as *Concentration and Understanding.* This is how the Blessed One shows the path of purification under the headings of virtue, concentration and understanding there.

9. What has been shown so far is the three trainings, the dispensation that is good in three ways, the necessary condition for the threefold clear-vision, etc., the avoidance of the two extremes and the cultivation of the middle way, the means to surmounting the states of loss, etc., the abandoning of defilements in three aspects, prevention of transgression, etc.,

purification from the three kinds of defilements, and the reason for the states of Stream-entry and so on. How ?

10. Here the training of higher virtue is shown by *Virtue*; the training of higher consciousness, by *Concentration*; and the training of higher understanding, by *Understanding*.

The dispensation's goodness in the beginning is shown by *Virtue*. Because of the passage 'And what is the beginning 'of profitable things ? Virtue that is quite purified' (S.v,143), and because of the passage beginning 'The not doing of any 'evil' (Dh. 183), *Virtue* is the beginning of the dispensation. And that is good because it brings about the special qualities of non-remorse,[5] and so on. Its goodness in the middle is shown by *Concentration*. [5] Because of the passage beginning 'Entering upon the profitable' (Dh. 183), *Concentration* is the middle of the dispensation. And that is good because it brings about the special qualities of supernormal-power, and so on. Its goodness in the end is shown by *Understanding*. Because of the passage 'The purifying of One's own mind—this is the 'Buddhas' dispensation' (Dh. 183), and because understanding is its culmination, *Understanding* is the end of the dispensation. And that is good because it brings about equipoise with respect to the desired and the undesired. For this is said :

'Just as a solid massive rock
'Remains unshaken by the wind,
'So too, in face of blame and praise
'The wise remain immovable' (Dh. 81).

11. Likewise the necessary condition for the triple clear-vision is shown by Virtue. For with the support of perfected virtue one arrives at the three kinds of clear-vision, but nothing besides that. The necessary condition for the six kinds of direct-knowledge is shown by *Concentration*. For with the support of perfected concentration one arrives at the six kinds of direct-knowledge, but nothing besides that. The necessary condition for the categories of discrimination is shown by *Understanding*. For with the support of perfected understanding one arrives at the four kinds of discrimination, but not for any other reason.[6]

And the avoidance of the extreme called devotion to indulgence of sense-desires is shown by *Virtue*. The avoidance of

5. One who is virtuous has nothing to be remorseful about.

6. The three kinds of clear-vision are : Recollection of Past Life, Knowledge of the Passing Away and Reappearance of Beings (Divine Eye), and Knowledge of Destruction of Cankers (M. i, 22-3). The six kinds of direct-knowledge are : Knowledge of Supernormal Power, the Divine Ear Element, Penetration of Minds, Recollection of Past Life, Knowledge of the Passing Away and Reappearance of Beings, and Knowledge of Destruction of Cankers (M. i, 34-5). The four discriminations are those of meaning, law, language, and intelligence (A. ii, 160).

the extreme called devotion to mortification of self is shown by *Concentration*. The cultivation of the middle way is shown by *Understanding*.

12. Likewise the means for surmounting the states of loss is shown by *Virtue*; the means for surmounting the element of sense-desires, by *Concentration* ; and the means for surmounting all becoming, by *Understanding*.

And the abandoning of defilements by substitution of opposites is shown by *Virtue*; that by suppression is shown by *Concentration* ; and that by cutting off is shown by *Understanding*.

13. Likewise prevention of defilements' transgression is shown by *Virtue* ; prevention of obsession [by defilement] is shown by *Concentration*; prevention of inherent tendencies is shown by *Understanding*.

And purification from the defilement of misconduct is shown by *Virtue*; purification from the defilement of craving, by *Concentration* ; and purification from the defilement of [false] views, by *Understanding*. [6]

14. Likewise the reason for the states of Stream-entry and Once-return is shown by *Virtue;* that for the state of Non-return, by *Concentration;* that for Arahantship, by *Understanding*. For the Stream-enterer is called 'Perfected in the 'kinds of virtue'; and likewise the Once-returner. But the Non-returner is called 'Perfected in concentration'. And the Arahant is called 'Perfected in understanding' (See A.i, 233).

15. So thus far these nine and other like triads of special qualities have been shown, that is, the three trainings, the dispensation that is good in three ways, the necessary condition for the threefold clear-vision, the avoidance of the two extremes and the cultivation of the middle way, the means for surmounting the states of loss etc., the abandoning of defilements in three aspects, prevention of transgression, etc., purification from the three kinds of defilements, and the reason for the states of Stream-entry and so on.

[II. Virtue]

16. However, even when this path of purification is shown in this way under the headings of Virtue, Concentration and Understanding, each comprising various special qualities, it is still only shown extremely briefly. And so since that is insufficient to help all there is in order to show it in detail the following set of questions dealing in the first place with Virtue :

(i) What is virtue ?
(ii) In what sense is it virtue ?
(iii) What are its characteristic, function, manifestation, and proximate cause ?

(iv) What are the benefits of virtue ?
(v) How many kinds of virtue are there ?
(vi) What is the defiling of it ?
(vii) What is the cleansing of it ?

17. Here are the answers :

(i) WHAT IS VIRTUE ? It is the states beginning with volition present in one who abstains from killing living things, etc., or in one who fulfils the practice of the duties. For this is said in the Paṭisambhidā: What is virtue ? There is virtue 'as volition, virtue as consciousness-concomitant,[7] virtue as 'restraint, [7] virtue as non-transgression' (Ps. i, 44).

Herein, *Virtue as volition* is the volition present in one who abstains from killing living things, etc., or in one who fulfils the practice of the duties. *Virtue as consciousness-concomitant* is the abstinence in one who abstains from killing living things, and so on. Furthermore, *Virtue as volition* is the seven volitions [that accompany the first seven] of the [ten] courses of action (kamma) in one who abandons the killing of living things, and so on. *Virtue as consciousness-concomitant* is the [three remaining] states consisting of non-covetousness, non-ill-will, and right view, stated in the way beginning 'Abandoning covetousness, he dwells with mind 'free from covetousness' (D.i,71).

18. *Virtue as restraint* should be understood here as restraint in five ways : restraint by the Rules of the Community (*Pāṭimokkha*), restraint by mindfulness, restraint by knowledge, restraint by patience, and restraint by energy. Herein, 'restraint by the Patimokkha' is this : 'He is furnished, 'fully furnished, with this Patimokkha restraint' (Vbh. 246); 'Restraint by mindfulness' is this : 'He guards the eye 'faculty, enters upon restraint of the eye faculty' (D.I,70). 'Restraint by knowledge' is this :

' "The currents in the world that flow, Ajita,"
said the Blessed One,
' "Are stemmed by means of mindfulness ;
' "Restraint of currents I proclaim,
' "By understanding they are dammed" ' (Sn.1035);

and use of requisites is here combined with this. But what is called 'restraint by patience' is that given in the way beginning 'He is one who bears cold and heat' (M.i,10). And what is called 'restraint by energy' is that given in the way beginning 'He does not endure a thought of sense-desires 'when it arises' (M.i,11); purification of livelihood is here combined with this. So this five-fold restraint, and the

7. 'Consciousness-concomitants (*cetasika*)' is a collective term for feeling, perception, and formations, variously subdivided; in other words, aspects of mentality that arise together with consciousness.

abstinence, in clansmen who dread evil, from any chance of transgression met with, should all be understood to be 'virtue as restraint'.

Virtue as non-transgression is the non-transgression, by body or speech, of precepts of virtue that have been undertaken.

This in the first place is the answer to the question 'What is virtue ?'. [8] Now as to the rest.—

19. (ii) IN WHAT SENSE IS IT VIRTUE ? It is virtue (*sīla*) in the sense of composing (*sīlana*).[8] What is this composing ? It is either a coordinating (*samādhāna*), meaning non-inconsistency of bodily action, etc., due to virtuousness; or it is an upholding (*upadhārana*),[8] meaning a state of basis (*ādhāra*) owing to its serving as foundation for profitable states. For those who understand etymology admit only these two meanings. Others, however, comment on the meaning here in the way beginning 'The meaning of virtue (*sīla*) is the meaning of head (*siras*), the meaning of virtue is the meaning of cool (*sītala*).'

20. (iii) Now WHAT ARE ITS CHARACTERISTIC, FUNCTION, MANIFESTATION, AND PROXIMATE CAUSE ? Here

> The characteristic of it is composing
> Even when analysed in various ways,
> As visibility is of visible data
> Even when analysed in various ways.

Just as visibleness is the characteristic of the visible-data base even when analysed into the various categories of blue, yellow, etc., because even when analysed into these categories it does not exceed visibleness, so also this same composing, described above as the coordinating of bodily action, etc., and as the foundation of profitable states, is the characteristic of virtue even when analysed into the various categories of volition, etc., because even when analysed into these categories it does not exceed the state of coordination and foundation.

21. While such is its characteristic,

> Its *function* has a double sense :
> *Action* to stop misconduct, then
> *Achievement* as the quality
> Of blamelessness in virtuous men.

So what is called virtue should be understood to have the function (nature) of stopping misconduct as its function (nature) in the sense of action, and a blameless function

8. *Sīlana*, and *Upadhāraṇa* in this meaning (cf. Ch. I, §141 and *Sandhāraṇa* Ch. XIV, §61), are not in P.T.S. Dict.

(nature) as its function (nature) in the sense of achievement. For under [these headings of] characteristic, etc., it is action (*kicca*) or it is achievement (*sampatti*) that is called 'function (*rasa*—nature)'.

22. Now virtue, so say those who know,
Itself as purity will show;
And for its proximate cause they tell
The pair, conscience and shame, as well. [9]

This virtue is manifested as the kinds of purity stated thus: 'Bodily purity, verbal purity, mental purity' (A.i,271); it is manifested, comes to be apprehended, as a pure state. But conscience and shame are said by those who know to be its proximate cause; its near reason, is the meaning. For when conscience and shame are in existence, virtue arises and persists; and when they are not, it neither arises nor persists.

This is how virtue's characteristic, function, manifestation, and proximate cause, should be understood.

23. (iv) WHAT ARE THE BENEFITS OF VIRTUE? Its benefits are the acquisition of the several special qualities beginning with non-remorse. For this is said: 'Ānanda, 'profitable, habits (virtues) have non-remorse as their aim and, 'non-remorse as their benefit' (A.v,1). Also it is said further 'Householder, there are these five benefits for the virtuous 'in the perfecting of virtue. What five? Here, householder, 'one who is virtuous, possessed of virtue, comes into a large 'fortune as a consequence of diligence; this is the first benefit 'for the virtuous in the perfecting of virtue. Again, of one 'who is virtuous, possessed of virtue, a fair name is spread 'abroad; this is the second benefit for the virtuous in the 'perfecting of virtue. Again, whenever one who is virtuous, 'possessed of virtue, enters an assembly, whether of khattiyas '(warrior nobles) or brahmans or householders or ascetics, 'he does so without fear or hesitation; this is the third bene- 'fit for the virtuous in the perfecting of virtue. Again one who 'is virtuous, possessed of virtue, dies unconfused; this is the 'fourth benefit for the virtuous in the perfecting of virtue. 'Again, one who is virtuous, possessed of virtue, on the break 'up of the body, after death, reappears in a happy destiny, 'in the heavenly world; this is the fifth benefit for the 'virtuous in the perfecting of virtue' (D.ii, 86). There are also the many benefits of virtue beginning with being dear and loved and ending with destruction of cankers described in the passage beginning 'If a bhikkhu should wish "May I '"be dear to my fellows in the life of purity and loved by '"them, held in respect and honoured by them", let him perfect 'the virtues' (M.i.33). This is how virtue has as its benefits the several special qualities beginning with non-remorse. [10]

24. Furthermore,

Dare anyone a limit place
On benefits that virtue brings,
Without which virtue clansmen find
No footing in the dispensation ?
No Ganges, and no Yamunā,
No Sarabhū, Sarassatī,
Or flowing Aciravatī,
Or noble River of Mahī,
Is able to wash out the stain
In things that breathe here in the world ;
For only virtue's water can
Wash out the stain in living things.
No breezes that come bringing rain,
No balm of yellow sandalwood,
No necklaces beside, or gems,
Or soft effulgence of moonbeams,
Can here avail to calm and soothe
Men's fevers in this world; whereas
This noble, this supremely cool,
Well-guarded virtue quells the flame.
Where is there to be found the scent
That can with virtue's scent compare,
And that is borne against the wind
As easily as with it ? Where
Can such another stair be found
That climbs, as virtue does, to heaven ?
Or yet another door that gives
Onto the City of Nibbana ?
Shine as they may, there are no kings
Adorned with jewelry and pearls
That shine as does a man restrained
Adorned with virtue's ornament.
Virtue entirely does away
With dread of self-blame and the like ;
Their virtue to the virtuous
Gives gladness always by its fame.
From this brief sketch it may be known
How virtue brings reward, and how
This root of all good qualities
Robs of its power every fault.

25. (v) Now here is the answer to the question, HOW MANY KINDS OF VIRTUE ARE THERE ?

1. Firstly all this virtue is of one kind by reason of its own characteristic of composing.

2. It is of two kinds as keeping and avoiding.

3. Likewise as that of good behaviour and that of the beginning of the life of purity.

4. As abstinence and non-abstinence,

5. As dependent and independent,

6. As temporary and lifelong,

7. As limited and unlimited.

8. As mundane and supramundane. [11]

9. It is of three kinds as inferior, medium, and superior.

10. Likewise as giving precedence to self, giving precedence to the world, and giving precedence to the Dhamma (Law).

11. As adhered to, not adhered to, and tranquillized.

12. As purified, unpurified, and dubious.

13. As that of the Trainer, that of the Non-trainer, and that of the neither-trainer-nor-non-trainer.

14. It is of four kinds as partaking of diminution, of stagnation, of distinction, of penetration.

15. Likewise as that of bhikkhus, of bhikkhunis, of the not-fully-admitted, of the laity,

16. As natural, customary, necessary, due to previous causes,

17. As virtue of Patimokkha restraint, of restraint of sense faculties, of purification of livelihood, and that concerning requisites.

18. It is of five kinds as virtue consisting in limited purification, etc.; for this is said in the Paṭisambhidā: 'Five kinds 'of virtue: virtue consisting in limited purification, virtue 'consisting in unlimited purification, virtue consisting in 'fulfilled purification, virtue consisting in unadhered-to 'purification, virtue consisting in tranquillized purification' (Ps.1,42).

19. Likewise as abandoning, refraining, volition, restraint, and non-transgression.

26. 1. Herein, in the section dealing with that of one kind, the meaning should be understood as already stated.

2. In the section dealing with that of two kinds: fulfilling a training precept announced by the Blessed One thus 'This should be done' is *keeping*; not doing what is prohibited by him thus 'This should not be done' is *avoiding*. Herein, the word-meaning is this; they keep (*caranti*) within that, they proceed as people who fulfil the virtues, thus it is keeping (*cāritta*); they preserve, they protect, avoidance, thus it is *avoiding*. Herein, *keeping* is accomplished by faith and energy; *avoiding*, by faith and mindfulness. This is how it is of two kinds as keeping and avoiding.

27. 3. In the second dyad good behaviour is the best kind of behaviour. Good behaviour itself is *that of good behaviour;* or what is announced for the sake of good behaviour is *that*

of good behaviour. This is a term for virtue other than that which has livelihood as eighth.[9] It is the initial stage of the life of purity consisting in the path, thus it is *that of the beginning of the life of purity.* This is a term for the virtue that has livelihood as eighth. It is the initial stage of the path because it has actually to be purified in the prior stage too. Hence it is said 'But his bodily action, his verbal action, 'and his livelihood, have already been purified earlier' (M.iii,289). Or the training precepts called 'lesser and minor' (D.ii,154) [12] are *that of good behaviour*; the rest are *that of the beginning of the life of purity.* Or what is included in the Double Code (the Bhikkhus' and Bhikkhunis' *Pāṭimokkha*) is *that of the beginning of the life of purity* ; and that included in the duties set out in the Khandhakas [of the Vinaya] is *that of good behaviour.* Through its perfection *that of the beginning of the life of purity* comes to be perfected. Hence it is said also 'that this bhikkhu shall fulfil the state 'consisting in the beginning of the life of purity without 'having fulfilled the state consisting in good behaviour— 'that is not possible' (A.iii, 14-15). So it is of two kinds as that of good behaviour and that of the beginning of the life of purity.

28. 4. In the third dyad virtue as *abstinence* is simply abstention from killing living things etc.; the other kinds consisting in volition, etc., are virtue as *non-abstinence.* So it is of two kinds as abstinence and non-abstinence.

29. 5. In the fourth dyad there are two kinds of dependence: dependence through craving and dependence through [false] views. Herein, that produced by one who wishes for a fortunate kind of becoming thus 'Through this virtuous conduct '(rite) I shall become a [great] deity or some[minor] deity' (M.i,102) is *dependent* through craving. That produced through such [false] view about purification as 'Purification 'is through virtuous conduct (rites)' (Vbh. 374) is *dependent* through [false] view. But the supramundane, and the mundane that is the pre-requisite for the aforesaid supramundane, are *independent.* So it is of two kinds as dependent and independent.

30. 6. In the fifth dyad *temporary* virtue is that undertaken after deciding on a time limit. *Lifelong* virtue is that practised in the same way but undertaking it for as long as life lasts. So it is of two kinds as temporary and lifelong.

31. 7. In the sixth dyad the *limited* is that seen to be limited by gain, fame, relatives, limbs, or life. The opposite is

9. The three kinds of profitable bodily kamma or action (not killing or stealing or indulging in sexual misconduct), the four kinds of profitable verbal kamma or action (refraining from lying, malicious speech, harsh speech, and gossip), and right livelihood as the eighth.

unlimited. And this is said in the Paṭisambhidā. 'What is the 'virtue that has a limit? There is virtue that has gain as its 'limit, there is virtue that has fame as its limit, there is 'virtue that has relatives as its limit, there is virtue that 'has limbs as its limit, there is virtue that has life as its limit. 'What is virtue that has gain as its limit? Here someone with 'gain as cause, with gain as condition, with gain as reason, 'transgresses a training precept as undertaken: that 'virtue has gain as its limit' (Ps.i,43), [13] and the rest should be elaborated in the same way. Also in the answer dealing with the *unlimited* it is said 'What is virtue that does not 'have gain as its limit? Here someone does, not with gain 'as cause, with gain as condition with gain as reason, even 'arouse the thought of transgressing a training precept as 'undertaken, how then shall he actually transgress it? That 'virtue does not have gain as its limit' (Ps.i,44), and the rest should be elaborated in the same way. So it is of two kinds as limited and unlimited.

32. 8. In the seventh dyad all virtue subject to cankers is *mundane*; that not subject to cankers is *supramundane*. Herein, the *mundane* brings about improvement in future becoming and is a prerequisite for the escape from becoming, according as it is said: 'Discipline is for the purpose of 'restraint, restraint is for the purpose of non-remorse, non-'remorse is for the purpose of gladdening, gladdening is for 'the purpose of happiness, happiness is for the purpose of 'tranquillity, tranquillity is for the purpose of bliss, bliss is 'for the purpose of concentration, concentration is for the 'purpose of correct knowledge and vision, correct knowledge 'and vision is for the purpose of dispassion, dispassion is for 'the purpose of fading away [of greed], fading away is for the 'purpose of deliverance, deliverance is for the purpose of 'knowledge and vision of deliverance, knowledge and vision 'of deliverance is for the purpose of complete extinction '[of craving etc.] through not clinging. Talk has that purpose, 'counsel has that purpose, support has that purpose, giving 'ear has that purpose, that is to say, the liberation of the 'mind through not clinging' (Vin.v,164). The *supramundane* brings about the escape from becoming and is the plane of Reviewing Knowledge. So it is of two kinds as mundane and supramundane.

33. 9. In the first of the triads the *inferior* is produced by inferior zeal, [purity of] consciousness, energy, or inquiry; the *medium* is produced by medium zeal, etc.; the *superior*, by superior [zeal, and so on]. That undertaken out of desire for fame is *inferior*; that undertaken out of desire for the fruits of merit is *medium*; that undertaken for the sake of the noble state thus 'This has to be done' is *superior*. Or

again that defiled by self-praise and disparagement of others etc., thus 'I am possessed of virtue, but these other bhikkhus 'are ill-conducted and evil-natured' (M.i,193) is *inferior;* undefiled mundane virtue is *medium ;* supramundane is *superior.* Or again that motivated by craving, the purpose of which is to enjoy continued existence, is *inferior ;* that practised for the purpose of one's own deliverance is *medium ;* the virtue of the perfections practised for the deliverance of all beings is *superior.* So it is of three kinds as inferior, medium, and superior.

34. 10. In the second triad that practised out of self-regard by one who regards self and desires to abandon what is unbecoming to self [14] is virtue *giving precedence to self.* That practised out of regard for the world and out of desire to ward off the censure of the world is virtue *giving precedence to the world.* That practised out of regard for the Dhamma (Law) and out of desire to honour the majesty of the Dhamma is virtue *giving precedence to the Dhamma.* So it is of three kinds as giving precedence to self, and so on.

35. 11. In the third triad the virtue that in the dyads was called 'dependent' (no. 5) is *adhered-to* because it is adhered-to through craving and [false] view. That practised by the magnanimous ordinary man as the prerequisite of the path, and that associated with the path in Trainers, are *not-adhered-to.* That associated with trainers' and non-trainers' fruition is *tranquillized.* So it is of three kinds as adhered-to, and so on.

36. 12. In the fourth triad that fulfilled by one who has committed no offence or has made amends after committing one is *pure.* So long as he has not made amends after committing an offence it is *impure.* Virtue in one who is dubious about whether a thing constitutes an offence or about what grade of offence has been committed or about whether he has committed an offence is *dubious.* Herein, the meditator should purify impure virtue. If dubious, he should avoid cases about which he is doubtful and should get his doubts cleared up. In this way his mind will be kept at rest. So it is of three kinds as pure, and so on.

37. 13. In the fifth triad the virtue associated with the four paths and with the [first] three fruitions is *that of the trainer.* That associated with the fruition of Arahantship is *that of the non-trainer.* The remaining kinds are *that of the neither-trainer-nor-non-trainer.* So it is of three kinds as that of the Trainer, and so on.

38. But in the world the nature of such and such beings is called their 'habit (*sīla*)', of which they say 'This one is of happy habit (*sukha-sīla*), this one is of unhappy habit, this one is of quarrelsome habit, this one is of dandified habit'. Because of that it is said in the Patisambhidā figuratively

'Three kinds of virtue (habit); profitable virtue, unprofitable 'virtue, indeterminate virtue' (Ps.i,44). So it is also called of three kinds as profitable, and so on. Of these, the unprofitable is not included here since it has nothing whatever to do with the heads beginning with the characteristic, which define virtue in the sense intended in this [chapter]. So the threefoldness should be understood only in the way already stated.

39. 14. In the first of the tetrads:

The unvirtuous he cultivates,
He visits not the virtuous,
And in his ignorance he sees
No fault in a transgression here, [15]
With wrong thoughts often in his mind
His faculties he will not guard—
Virtue in such a constitution
Comes to *partake of diminution.*
But he whose mind is satisfied
With virtue that has been achieved,
Who never thinks to stir himself
And take a meditation subject up,
Contented with mere virtuousness,
Nor striving for a higher state—
His virtue bears the appellation
Of *that partaking of stagnation.*
But who, possessed of virtue, strives
With concentration for his aim—
That bhikkhu's virtue in its function
Is called *partaking of distinction.*
Who finds mere virtue not enough
But has dispassion for his goal—
His virtue through such aspiration
Comes to *partake of penetration.*

So it is of four kinds as partaking of diminution, and so on.

40. 15. In the second tetrad there are training precepts announced for bhikkhus to keep irrespective of what is announced for bhikkhunis. This is the virtue *of bhikkhus.* There are training precepts announced for bhikkhunis to keep irrespective of what is announced for bhikkhus. This is the virtue of *bhikkhunis.* The ten precepts of virtue for male and female novices are the virtue of the *not fully admitted.* The five training precepts—ten when possible—as a permanent undertaking, and eight as the factors of the Uposatha Day,[10] for male and female lay followers are the virtue *of the laity.* So it is of four kinds as the virtue of bhikkhus, and so on.

10. *Uposatha* (der. from *upavasati* to observe or to prepare) is the name for the day of 'fasting' or 'vigil' observed on the days of the newmoon,

41. 16. In the third tetrad the non-trangression on the part of Uttarakuru human beings is *natural virtue.* Each clan's or locality's, or sect's, own rules of conduct are *customary virtue.* The virtue of the Bodhisatta's mother described thus, 'It is the necessary rule, Ānanda, that when the Bodhisatta 'has descended into his mother's womb, no thought of men 'that is connected with the cords of sense desire comes to her' (D.ii,13) is *necessary virtue.* But the virtue of such pure beings as Mahā-Kassapa, etc., and of the Bodhisatta in his various births is virtue *due to previous causes.* So it is of four kinds as natural virtue, and so on.

42. 17, In the fourth tetrad :

(*a*) the virtue described by the Blessed One thus, 'Here a 'bhikkhu dwells restrained with the Pāṭimokkha restraint, 'possessed of the [proper] conduct and resort, and seeing 'fear in the slightest fault, he trains himself by undertaking 'the precepts of training' (Vbh. 244), is *virtue of Patimokkha restraint.*

(*b*) that described thus, 'On seeing a visible object with the 'eye, [16] he apprehends neither the signs nor the particulars 'through which, if he left the eye faculty unguarded, evil and 'unprofitable states of covetousness and grief might invade 'him, he enters upon the way of its restraint, he guards the 'eye faculty, undertakes the restraint of the eye faculty. 'On hearing a sound with the ear... On smelling an odour 'with the nose... On tasting a flavour with the tongue... 'On touching a tangible object with the body...On cogniz-'ing a mental object with the mind, he apprehends neither 'the signs nor the particulars through which, if he left the 'mind faculty unguarded, evil and unprofitable states of 'covetousness and grief might invade him, he enters upon 'the way of its restraint, he guards the mind faculty, under-'takes the restraint of the mind faculty (M.i,180), *is virtue of restraint of the sense faculties.*

(*c*) Abstinence from such wrong livelihood as entails transgression of the six training precepts announced with respect to livelihood and entails the evil states beginning with 'Scheming, talking, hinting, belittling, pursuing gain 'with gain' (M.iii,75) is *virtue of livelihood purification.*

---

waxing half-moon, full moon, and waning half moon. On these days it is customary for laymen to undertake the Eight Precepts (*sīla*) or Five Precepts. On the new-moon and full-moon days the *Pāṭimokkha* (see note 11) is recited by bhikkhus. The two quarter-moon days are called the 'Eighth of the Half-moon'. The full-moon day is called the 'Fifteenth' (*i.e.* 15 days from the new-moon) and is the last day of the lunar month. That of the new-moon is called the 'Fourteenth' when it is the second and fourth new-moon of the four-month season (*i.e.* 14 days from the full-moon), the other two are called the 'Fifteenth'. This compensates for the irregularities of the lunar period

(*d*) Use of the four requisites that is purified by the reflection stated in the way beginning 'Reflecting wisely, he 'uses the robe only for protection from cold'(M.i.10) is called *virtue concerning requisites*.

43. Here is an explanatory exposition together with a word-commentary, starting from the beginning.

(*a*) *Here* : in this dispensation. *A bhikkhu*: a clansman who has gone forth out of faith and is so styled because he sees fear in the round of rebirths (*saṁsāre bhayaṁ ikkhanatā*) or because he wears cloth garments that are torn and pieced together, and so on.

Restrained with the Pāṭimokkha restraint; here '*Pāṭimokkha* (Rule of the Community)'[11] is the virtue of the training precepts; for it frees (*mokkheti*) him who protects (*pāti*) it, guards it, it sets him free (*mocayati*) from the pains of the states of loss, etc., that is why it is called '*Pāṭimokkha*'. 'Restraint' is restraining; this is a term for bodily and verbal non-transgression. The Pāṭimokkha itself as restraint is 'Pāṭimokkha restraint'. 'Restrained with the Pāṭimokkha restraint' is restrained by means of the restraint consisting in that Pāṭimokkha; he has it, possesses it, is the meaning. *Dwells*: bears himself in one of the postures. [17]

44. The meaning of *possessed of* [*the proper*] *conduct and resort* etc., should be understood in the way in which it is given in the text. For this is said: 'Possessed of [the proper] conduct and 'resort: there is [proper] conduct and improper conduct. 'Herein, what is improper conduct ? Bodily transgression, 'verbal transgression, bodily and verbal transgression—'this is called improper conduct. Also all unvirtuousness is 'improper conduct. Here someone makes a livelihood by 'gifts of bamboos, or by gifts of leaves, or by gifts of flowers, 'fruits, bathing powder, and tooth sticks, or by flattery, 'or by bean-soupery, or by fondling, or by going on errands 'on foot, or by one or other of the sorts of wrong livelihood 'condemned by the Buddhas—this is called improper con-'duct. Herein, what is [proper] conduct ? Bodily non-'transgression, verbal non-transgression, bodily and verbal 'non-transgression—this is called [proper] conduct. Also all 'restraint through virtue is [proper] conduct. Here someone 'does not make a livelihood by gifts of bamboos, or by gifts

11. The Suttavibhanga, the first book of the Vinaya Piṭaka, contains in its two parts the 227 rules for bhikkhus and the rules for bhikkhunis, who have received the Admission (*upasampadā*), together with accounts of the incidents that led to the announcement of the rules, the modifications of the rules and the explanations of them. The bare rules themselves form the *Pāṭimokkha* for bhikkhus and that for bhikkhunis. They are also known as the 'Two Codes (*Dve Mātikā*)'. The *Pāṭimokkha* is recited by bhikkhus on the Uposatha days of the full-moon and new-moon.

'of leaves, or by gifts of flowers, fruits, bathing powder, and 'tooth sticks, or by flattery, or by bean-soupery, or by 'fondling, or by going on errands on foot, or by one or other 'of the sorts of wrong livelihood condemned by the Buddhas— 'this is called [proper] conduct.

45. '[Proper] resort: there is [proper] resort and improper 'resort. Herein, what is improper resort? Here someone has 'prostitutes as resort, or he has widows, old maids, eunuchs, 'bhikkhunis, or taverns as resort; or he dwells associated 'with kings, kings' ministers, sectarians, sectarians' disciples, 'in unbecoming association with laymen; or he cultivates, 'frequents, honours, such families as are faithless, untrusting, 'abusive and rude, who wish harm, wish ill, wish woe, wish 'no surcease of bondage, for bhikkhus and bhikkhunis, for 'male and female devotees [18]—this is called improper 'resort. Herein, what is [proper] resort? Here someone does 'not have prostitutes as resort...or taverns, as resort; he 'does not dwell associated with kings,...sectarians' disciples, 'in unbecoming association with laymen; he cultivates, 'frequents, honours, such families as are faithful and trusting, 'who are a solace, where the yellow cloth glows, where the 'breeze of sages blows, who wish good, wish well, wish joy, 'wish surcease of bondage, for bhikkhus and bhikkhunis, for 'male and female devotees—this is called [proper] resort. 'Thus he is furnished with, fully furnished with, provided 'with, fully provided with, supplied with, posssessed of, 'endowed with, this [proper] conduct and this [proper] 'resort. Hence it is said "Possessed of [the proper] conduct 'and resort"' (Vbh.246-7).

46. Furthermore [proper] conduct and resort should also be understood here in the following way; for improper conduct is twofold as bodily and verbal. Herein, what is bodily improper conduct? 'Here someone acts disrespectfully 'before the Community, and he stands jostling elder bhikkhus, 'sits jostling them, stands in front of them, sits in front of 'them, sits on high seat, sits with his head covered, talks 'standing up, talks waving his arms,... walks with sandals 'while elder bhikkhus walk without sandals, walks on a high 'walk while they walk on a low walk, walks on a walk while 'they walk on the ground,... stands pushing elder bhikkhus, 'sits pushing them, prevents new bhikkhus from getting a 'seat,... and in the bath house... without asking elder bhik'khus he puts wood on [the stove],...bolts the door,...and at 'the bathing place he enters the water jostling elder bhikkhus, 'enters it in front of them, bathes jostling them, bathes in 'front of them, comes out jostling them, comes out in front of 'them,... and entering inside a house he goes jostling elder 'bhikkhus, goes in front of them, pushing forward he goes

'in front of them,... and where families have inner private 'screened rooms in which the women of the family,...the girls 'of the family, sit, there he enters abruptly, and he strokes a 'a child's head' (Nd1.228–9). This is called bodily improper conduct.

47. Herein, what is verbal improper conduct ? 'Here some-'one acts disrespectfully before the Community. Without 'asking elder bhikkhus he talks on the Dhamma, answers 'questions, recites the Pāṭimokkha, talks standing up, (19) 'talks waving his arms,... having entered inside a house, he 'speaks to a woman or a girl thus "You, so-and-so of such-' "and-such a clan, what is there ? Is there rice gruel ? Is ' "there cooked rice ? Is there any hard food to eat ? What ' "shall we drink ? What hard food shall we eat ? What soft ' "food shall we eat ? Or what will you give me ?"—he 'chatters like this' (Nd1.230). This is called verbal improper conduct.

48. Proper conduct should be understood in the opposite sense to that. Furthermore, a bhikkhu is respectful, deferential, possessed of conscience and shame, wears his inner robe properly, wears his upper robe properly, his manner inspires confidence whether in moving forwards or backwards, looking ahead or aside, bending or stretching, his eyes are downcast, he has (a good) deportment, he guards the doors of his sense faculties, knows the right measure in eating, is devoted to wakefulness, possesses mindfulness and full-awareness, wants little, is contented, is strenuous, is a careful observer of good behaviour, and treats the teachers with great respect. This is called (proper) conduct.

This firstly is how (proper) conduct should be understood.

49. (Proper) resort is of three kinds: (proper) resort as support, (proper) resort as guarding, and (proper) resort as anchoring.

Herein, what is (proper) resort as support? A good friend who exhibits the ten instances of talk,[12] in whose presence one hears what has not been heard, corrects what has been heard, gets rid of doubt, rectifies one's view, and gains confidence: or by training under whom one grows in faith, virtue, learning, generosity and understanding—this is called *(proper) resort as support.*

50. What is (proper) resort as guarding ? Here 'A bhikkhu, 'having entered inside a house, having gone into a street, 'goes with downcast eyes, seeing the length of a plough yoke,

12. The 'ten instances of talk (*dasa kathāvatthūni*)' refer to the kinds of talk given in the Suttas thus 'Such talk as is concerned with effacement, as favours the heart's release, as leads to complete dispassion, fading, cessation, peace, direct knowledge, enlightenment, nibbana, that is to say: talk on wanting little, contentment, seclusion, aloofness from contact, strenuousness, virtue, concentration, understanding, deliverance, knowledge and vision of deliverance' (M. i, 145; iii, 113).

'restrained, not looking at an elephant, not looking at a horse, 'a carriage, a pedestrian, a woman, a man, not looking up, 'not looking down, not staring this way and that' (Nd 1. 474). This is called *(proper) resort as guarding.*

51. What is (proper) resort as anchoring? It is the four foundations of mindfulness on which the mind is anchored; for this is said by the Blessed One: 'Bhikkhus, what is a 'bhikkhu's resort, his own native place? It is these four 'foundations of mindfulness' (S. v, 148). This is called *(proper) resort as anchoring.*

Being thus furnished with... endowed with, this (proper) conduct and this (proper) resort, he is also on that account called 'one possessed of (proper) conduct and resort'. (20)

52. *Seeing fear in the slightest fault* (§42): one who has the habit (*sīla*) of seeing fear in faults of the minutest measure, of such kinds as unintentional contravening of a minor training rule of the Patimokkha, as an unprofitable thought. *He trains himself by undertaking* (*samādāya*) *the precepts of training*: whatever there is among the precepts of training to be trained in, in all that he trains by taking it up rightly (*sammā ādāya*). And here, as far as the words 'one restrained by the Patimokkha restraint', virtue of Patimokkha restraint is shown by Discourse in Terms of Persons.[13] But all that beginning with the words 'possessed of (proper) conduct and resort' should be understood as said in order to show the way of practice that perfects that virtue in him who so practises it.

53. (*b*) Now as regards the virtue of restraint of faculties shown next to that in the way beginning 'on seeing a visible object with the eye', herein, '*he*' is a bhikkhu established in the virtue of Patimokkha restraint. *On seeing a visible object with the eye*: on seeing a visible object with the eye-consciousness that is capable of seeing visible objects and has borrowed the name 'eye' from its instrument. But the Ancients (*Porāṇā*) said 'The eye does not see a visible object because it has no 'mind. The mind does not see because it has no eyes. But 'when there is the impingement of door and object he sees 'by means of the consciousness that has eye-sensitivity 'as its physical basis. Now (an idiom) such as this is called 'an "accessory locution (*sasambhārakathā*)", like "He shot '"him with his bow", and so on. So the meaning here is this: '"On seeing a visible object with eye-consciousness"'.[14]

---

13. See Ch. IV, note 27.
14. '"*On seeing a visible object with the eye*": if the eye were to see the visible object, then (organs) belonging to other kinds of consciousness would see too; but that is not so. Why? Because the eye has no thought (*acetanattā*). And then, were consciousness itself to see a visible object, it would see it even behind a wall because of being independent of sense-resistance (*appaṭighabhāvato*); but that is not so either because there

54. *Apprehends neither the signs:* he does not apprehend the sign of woman or man, or any sign that is a basis for defilement such as the sign of beauty, etc.: he stops at what is merely seen. *Nor the particulars:* he does not apprehend any aspect classed as hand, foot, smile, laughter, talk, looking ahead, looking aside, etc., which has acquired the name 'particular (*anubyañjana*)' because of its particularizing (*anu anu byañjanato*) defilements, because of its making them manifest themselves. He only apprehends what is really there. Like the Elder Mahā-Tissa who dwelt at Cetiyapabbata.

55. It seems that as the Elder was on his way from Cetiyapabbata to Anurādhapura for alms, a certain daughter-in-law of a clan, who had quarrelled with her husband and had set out early from Anurādhapura all dressed up and tricked

---

is no seeing in all kinds of consciousness. And herein, it is consciousness dependent on the eye that sees, not just any kind. And that does not arise with respect to what is enclosed by walls, etc., where light is excluded. But where there is no exclusion of light, as in the case of a crystal or a mass of cloud, there it does arise even with respect to what is enclosed by them. So it is as a basis of consciousness that the eye sees.

' "*When there is the impingement of door and object*": what is intended is: when a visible datum as object has come into the eye's focus. "*One sees*": one looks (*oloketi*); for when the consciousness that has eye-sensitivity as its material support is disclosing (*obhāsente*) by means of the special quality of its support a visible datum as object that is assisted by light (*āloka*), then it is said that a person possessed of that sees the visible datum. And here the illuminating is the revealing of the visible datum according to its individual essence, in other words the apprehending of it experientially (*paccakkhato*).

'Here it is the "*sign of woman*" because it is the cause of perceiving as "woman" all such things as the shape that is grasped under the heading of the visible data (materiality) invariably found in a female continuity, the un-clear-cut-ness (*avisadatā*) of the flesh of the breasts, the beardlessness of the face, the use of cloth to bind the hair, the un-clear-cut stance, walk, and so on—The "*sign of man*" is in the opposite sense.

' "*The sign of beauty*" here is the aspect of woman that is the cause for the arising of lust. By the word "etc." the sign of resentment (*paṭigha*), etc., are included, which should be understood as the undesired aspect that is the cause for the arising of hate. And here admittedly only covetousness and grief are specified in the text but the sign of equanimity needs to be included too; since there is non-restraint in the delusion that arises due to overlooking, or since "forgetfulness or unknowing" is said below (§57). And here the "sign of equanimity" should be understood as an object that is the basis for the kind of equanimity associated with unknowing through overlooking it. So "*the sign of beauty, etc.*" given in brief thus is actually the cause of greed, hate, and delusion.

' "*He stops at what is merely seen*": according to the Sutta method "The seen shall be merely seen" (Ud. 8). As soon as the colour basis has been apprehended by the consciousnesses of the cognitive series with eye-consciousness he stops; he does not fancy any aspect of beauty, etc., beyond that...In one who fancies as beautiful, etc., the limbs of the opposite sex defilements arisen with respect to them successively become particularized, which is why they are called "particulars".

out like a celestial nymph to go to her relatives' home, saw him on the road, and being low-minded, [21] she laughed a loud laugh. [Wondering] 'What is that?', the Elder looked up, and finding in the bones of her teeth the perception of foulness (ugliness), he reached Arahantship.[15] Hence it was said:

'He saw the bones that were her teeth,
'And kept in mind his first perception;
'And standing on that very spot
'The Elder became an Arahant'.

But her husband who was going after her saw the Elder and asked 'Venerable sir, did you by any chance see a woman?'. The Elder told him:

'Whether it was a man or woman
'That went by I noticed not;
'But only that on this high road
'There goes a group of bones'.

56. As to the words *through which*, etc., the meaning is: by reason of which, because of which non-restraint of the eye faculty, *if he*, if that person, *left the eye faculty unguarded*, remained with the eye door unclosed by the door-panel of mindfulness, these *states of covetousness*, etc., *might invade*, might pursue, might threaten, *him*. *He enters upon the way of its restraint*: he enters upon the way of closing that eye faculty by the door-panel of mindfulness. It is the same one of whom it is said *he guards the eye faculty, undertakes the restraint of the eye faculty*.

57. Herein, there is neither restraint nor non-restraint in the actual eye faculty, since neither mindfulness nor forgetfulness arises in dependence on eye-sensitivity. On the contrary when a visible datum as object comes into the eye's focus, then, after the life-continuum has arisen twice and ceased, the functional mind-element accomplishing the function of adverting arises and ceases. After that, eye-consciousness with the function of seeing; after that, resultant mind-element with the function of receiving; after that, resultant

---

But these are simply modes of interpreting (*sannivesākāra*) the kinds of materiality derived from the (four) primaries that are interpreted (*sanniviṭṭha*) in such and such wise; for apart from that there is in the ultimate sense no such thing as a hand and so on' (Pm. 40–1). See also Ch. III, note 31.

15. 'As the Elder was going along (occupied) only in keeping his meditation subject in mind, since noise is a thorn to that in the early stage, he looked up with the noise of the laughter (wondering) "What is that?". "*Perception of foulness*" is perception of bones; for the Elder was then making bones his meditation subject. The Elder, it seems, as soon as he saw her teeth-bones while she was laughing, got the counterpart-sign with access-jhana because he had developed the preliminary-work well. While he stood there he reached the first jhana. Then he made that the basis for insight, which he augmented until he attained the paths one after the other and reached destruction of cankers' (Pm. 41–2).

root-cause-less mind-consciousness-element with the function of investigating; after that, functional root-cause-less mind-consciousness-element accomplishing the function of determining arises and ceases. Next to that, impulsion impels.[16] Herein, there is neither restraint nor non-restraint on the occasion of the life-continuum, or on any of the occasions beginning with adverting. But there is non-restraint if unvirtuousness or forgetfulness or unknowing or impatience or idleness arises at the moment of impulsion. When this happens, it is called 'non-restraint in the eye faculty'. [22]

58. Why is that? Because when this happens, the door is not guarded, nor are the life-continuum and the consciousnesses of the cognitive series. Like what? Just as, when a city's four gates are not secured, although inside the city house doors, storehouses, rooms, etc., are secured, yet all property inside the city is unguarded and unprotected since robbers coming in by the city gates can do as they please, so too, when unvirtuousness, etc., arise in impulsion in which there is no restraint, then the door too is unguarded, and so also are the life-continuum and the consciousness of the cognitive series beginning with adverting. But when virtue, etc., has arisen in it, then the door too is guarded and so also are the life-continuum and the consciousnesses of the cognitive series beginning with adverting. Like what? Just as, when the city gates are secured, although inside the city the houses, etc., are not secured, yet all property inside the city is well guarded, well protected, since when the city gates are shut there is no ingress for robbers, so too, when virtue, etc., have arisen in impulsion, the door too is guarded and so also are the life-continuum and the consciousnesses of the cognitive series beginning with adverting. Thus although it actually arises at the moment of impulsion, it is nevertheless called 'restraint in the
59. eye faculty'. So also as regards the phrases *on hearing a sound with the ear* and so on. So it is this virtue, which in brief has the characteristic of avoiding apprehension of signs entailing

16. To expect to find in the Paramatthamañjūsā an exposition of the 'cognitive series (*citta-vīthi*)', and some explanation of the individual members in addition to what is to be found in the Visuddhi-magga itself, is to be disappointed. There are only fragmentary treatments. All that is said here is this;

'There is no unvirtuousness, in other words, bodily or verbal misconduct, in the five doors; consequently restraint of unvirtuousness happens through the mind door, and the remaining restraint happens through the six doors. For the arising of forgetfulness and the other three would be in the five doors since they are unprofitable states opposed to mindfulness, etc.; and there is no arising of unvirtuousness consisting in bodily and verbal transgression there because five-door impulsions do not give rise to intimation. And the five kinds of non-restraint beginning with unvirtuousness are stated here as the opposite of the five kinds of restraint beginning with restraint as virtue' (Pm. 42). See also Ch. IV, note 13.

defilement with respect to visible objects, etc., that should be understood as *Virtue of restraint of faculties.*

60. (*c*) Now as regards the virtue of livelihood purification mentioned above next to the virtue of restraint of the faculties (§42), the words *of the six precepts announced on account of livelihood* mean, of the following six training precepts announced thus: 'With livelihood as cause, with livelihood as 'reason, one of evil wishes, a prey to wishes, lays claim to a 'higher than human state that is non-existent, not a fact', the contravention of which is Defeat; 'With livelihood as 'cause, with livelihood as reason, he acts as go-between', the contravention of which is an offence entailing a Meeting of the Order; 'With livelihood as cause, with livelihood as reason, he 'says "A bhikkhu who lives in your monastery is an Arahant"', the contravention of which is a Serious Offence in one who is aware of it; 'With livelihood as cause, with livelihood as 'reason, a bhikkhu who is not sick eats superior food that he 'has ordered for his own use', the contravention of which is an offence Requiring Expiation; 'With livelihood as cause, with livelihood as reason, a bhikkhuni who is not sick eats 'superior food that she has ordered for her own use', the contravention of which is an Offence Requiring Confession; 'With livelihood as cause, with livelihood as reason, one who 'is not sick eats curry or boiled rice [23] that he has ordered 'for his own use', the contravention of which is an Offence of Wrongdoing (Vin.v,146). Of these six precepts.

61. As regards *scheming*, etc. (§42), this is the text: 'Herein, 'what is scheming? It is the grimacing, grimacery, scheming, 'schemery, schemedness,[17] by what is called rejection of 'requisites or by indirect talk, or it is the disposing, posing, 'composing, of the deportment on the part of one bent on gain, 'honour and renown, of one of evil wishes, a prey to wishes— 'this is called scheming.

62. 'Herein, what is talking? Talking at others, talking, talking 'round, talking up, continual talking up, persuading, con- 'tinual persuading, suggesting, continual suggesting, ingra- 'tiating chatter, flattery, bean-soupery, fondling, on the 'part of one bent on gain, honour and renown, of one of evil 'wishes, a prey to wishes—this is called talking.

63. 'Herein, what is hinting? A sign to others, giving a sign, 'indication, giving indication, indirect talk, roundabout 'talk, on the part of one bent on gain, honour and renown, 'of one of evil wishes, a prey to wishes—this is called hinting.

17. The formula '*kuhana kuhāyanā kuhitattaṃ*', *i.e.* verbal noun in two forms and abstract noun from pp., all from the same root, is common in Abhidhamma definitions. It is sometimes hard to produce a corresponding effect in English, yet to render such groups with words of different derivation obscures the meaning and confuses the effect.

64. 'Herein, what is belittling? Abusing of others, disparaging, 'reproaching, snubbing, continual snubbing, ridicule, con- 'tinual ridicule, denigration, continual denigration, tale- 'bearing, backbiting, on the part of one bent on gain, honour 'and renown, of one of evil wishes, a prey to wishes. This is 'called belittling.

65. 'Herein, what is pursuing gain with gain? Seeking, seeking 'for, seeking out, going in search of, searching for, searching 'out, material goods by means of material goods, such as 'carrying there goods that have been got from here, or carry- 'ing here goods that have been got from there, by one bent 'on gain, honour and renown, by one of evil wishes, a prey to 'wishes—this is called pursuing gain with gain' (Vbh. 352 –3).[18]

66. The meaning of this text should be understood as follows: Firstly, as regards description of *scheming*: *on the part of one bent on gain, honour and renown* is on the part of one who is bent on gain, on honour, and on reputation; on the part of one who longs for them, is the meaning. [24] *Of one of evil wishes*: of one who wants to show qualities that he has not got. *A prey to wishes*:[19] the meaning is, of one who is attacked by them. And after this the passage beginning *or by what is called rejection of requisites* is given in order to show the three instances of scheming given in the Mahā-Niddesa as rejection of requisites, indirect talk, and that based on deportment.

67. Herein, [a bhikkhu] is invited to accept robes, etc., and, precisely because he wants them, he refuses them out of evil wishes. And then, since he knows that those householders believe in him implicitly, when they think 'Oh, how few are our lord's wishes! He will not accept a thing! How lucky for us if he would accept just a little thing!' and they put fine robes, etc., before him by various means, he then accepts, making a show that he wants to be compassionate towards them—it is this hypocrisy of his, which becomes the cause of their subsequently bringing them even by cartloads, that should be understood as the instance of scheming called rejection of requisites.

68. For this is said in the Mahā-Niddesa: 'What is the instance 'of scheming called rejection of requisites? Here house- 'holders invite bhikkhus [to accept] robes, alms food, resting

18. The renderings, 'scheming' and so on in this context do not in all cases agree with the P.T.S. Dict. They have been chosen after careful consideration. The rendering 'rejection of requisites' takes the preferable reading *paṭisedhana* though the more common reading here is *paṭisevana* (cultivation).

19. The Pali is: '*Icchāpakatassā ti icchāya apakatassa*; *upaddutassā ti attho*'. *Icchāya apakatassa* simply resolves the compound *icchāpakatassa* and is therefore untranslatable into English. Such resolutions are therefore sometimes omitted in this translation.

'place, and the requisite of medicine as cure for the sick. 'One who is of evil wishes, a prey to wishes, wanting robes... 'alms food...resting place... the requisite of medicine as cure 'for the sick, refuses robes... alms food... resting place... 'the requisite of medicine as cure for the sick, because he 'wants more. He says "What has an ascetic to do with '"expensive robes? It is proper for an ascetic to gather rags '" from a charnel ground or from a rubbish heap or from a '"shop and make them into a patchwork cloak to wear. '"What has an ascetic to do with expensive alms food? It is '"proper for an ascetic to get his living by the dropping of '"lumps [of food into his bowl] while he wanders for gleanings. '"What has an ascetic to do with an expensive resting place? '"It is proper for an ascetic to be a tree-root-dweller or an '"open-air-dweller. What has an ascetic to do with an expen- '"sive requisite of medicine as cure for the sick? It is proper for '"an ascetic to cure himself with putrid urine[20] and broken '"gall nuts." Accordingly he wears a coarse robe, eats coarse 'alms food, [25] uses a coarse resting place, uses a coarse 'requisite of medicine as cure for the sick. Then householders 'think "This ascetic has few wishes, is content, is secluded, '"keeps aloof from company, is strenuous, is a preacher of '"ascetism", and they invite him more and more [to 'accept] robes, alms food, resting places, and the requisite 'of medicine as cure for the sick. He says "With three things '"present a faithful clansman produces much merit: with '"faith present a faithful clansman produces much merit, '"with goods to be given present a faithful clansman produces '"much merit, with those worthy to receive present a faith- '"ful clansman produces much merit. You have faith; the '"goods to be given are here; and I am here to accept. If '"I do not accept, then you will be deprived of the merit. '"That is no good to me. Rather will I accept out of com- '"passion for you". Accordingly he accepts many robes, 'he accepts much alms food, he accepts many resting places, 'he accepts many requisites of medicine as cure for the sick. 'Such grimacing, grimacery, scheming, schemery, schemed- 'ness, is known as the instance of scheming called rejection 'of requisites' (NdI,224–5).

69. It is hypocrisy on the part of one of evil wishes, who gives it to be understood verbally in some way or other that he has attained a higher than human state, that should be understood as the instance of scheming called indirect talk, according as it is said: 'What is the instance of scheming 'called indirect talk? Here someone of evil wishes, a prey 'to wishes, eager to be admired [thinking] "Thus people

20. '"*Purtid urine*" is the name for all kinds of cow's urine whether old or not' (Pm. 45). Fermented cow's urine with gall-nuts (myrobalan) is a common Indian medicine today.

' "will admire me" speaks words about the noble state. He 'says "He who wears such a robe is a very important ' "ascetic". He says "He who carries such a bowl, metal cup, ' "water filler, water strainer, key, wears such a waistband, ' "sandal, is a very important ascetic". He says "He who has ' "such a preceptor,... teacher,... who has the same pre- ' "ceptor, who has the same teacher, who has such a friend, ' "associate, intimate, companion; he who lives in such a ' "monastery, lean-to, mansion, villa,[21] cave, grotto, hut, ' "pavilion, watch tower, hall, barn, meeting hall, [26] room, ' "at such a tree root, is a very important ascetic". Or 'alternatively, all-gushing, all-grimacing, all-scheming, all- 'talkative, with an expression of admiration, he utters such 'deep, mysterious, cunning, obscure, supramundane talk 'suggestive of voidness as "This ascetic is an obtainer ' "peaceful abidings and attainments such as these". Such 'grimacing, grimacery, scheming, schemery, schemedness, 'is known as the instance of scheming called indirect talk' (Ndɪ, 226-7).

70. It is hypocrisy on the part of one of evil wishes, which takes the form of deportment influenced by eagerness to be admired, that should be understood as the instance of scheming dependent on deportment, according as it is said: 'What is the 'instance of scheming called deportment? Here someone 'of evil wishes, a prey to wishes, eager to be admired, [think- 'ing] "Thus people will admire me", composes his way of 'walking, composes his way of lying down; he walks stu- 'diedly, stands studiedly, sits studiedly, lies down studiedly; 'he walks as though concentrated, stands, sits, lies down as 'though concentrated; and he is one who meditates in pub- 'lic. Such disposing, posing, composing, of deportment, 'grimacing, grimacery, scheming, schemery, schemedness, is 'known as the instance of scheming called deportment' (Ndɪ, 225-6).

71. Herein, the words *by what is called rejection of requisites* (§ 61) mean: by what is called thus 'rejection of requisites'; or they mean: by means of the rejection of requisites that is so called. *By indirect talk* means: by talking near to the subject. *Of deportment* means: of the four modes of deportment (postures). *Disposing* is initial posing, or careful posing. *Posing* is the manner of posing. *Composing* is prearranging; assuming a trust-inspiring attitude, is what is meant. *Grimacing* is making grimaces by showing great intenseness; facial contraction is what is meant. One who has the habit of making grimaces is a grimacer. The grimacer's state is *grimacery. Scheming* is hypocrisy. The way (*āyanā*) of a schemer

21. It is not always certain now what kind of buildings these names refer to.

(*kuha*) is *schemery* (*kuhāyanā*). The state of what is schemed is *schemedness*.

72. In the description of *talking*: *talking at* is talking thus on seeing people coming to the monastery, 'What have you come for, good people? What, to invite bhikkhus? If it is that, then go along and I shall come later with [my bowl]', etc.; or alternatively, *talking at* is talking by advertising oneself thus 'I am Tissa, the king trusts me, such and such king's ministers trust me'. [27] *Talking* is the same kind of talking on being asked a question. *Talking round* is roundly talking by one who is afraid of householders' displeasure because he has given occasion for it. *Talking up* is talking by extolling people thus 'He is a great landowner, a great ship-owner, a great lord of giving'. *Continual talking up* is talking by extolling [people] in all ways.

73. *Persuading* is progressively involving[22] [people] thus 'Lay followers, formerly you used to give first-fruit alms at such a time; why do you not do so now?' until they say 'We shall give venerable sir, we have had no opportunity', etc.; entangling, is what is meant. Or alternatively, seeing someone with sugarcane in his hand, he asks 'Where are you coming from, lay follower?'—'From the sugarcane field, venerable sir.' —'Is the sugarcane sweet there?'—'One can find out by eating, venerable sir.'—'It is not allowed, lay follower, for bhikkhus to say "Give [me some] sugarcane."' Such entangling talk from such an entangler is *persuading*. Persuading again and again in all ways is *continual persuading*.

74. *Suggesting* is insinuating by specifying thus 'That family alone understands me; if there is anything to be given there, they give it to me only'; pointing to, is what is meant. And here the story of the Oil-seller should be told.[23] Suggesting in all ways again and again is *continual suggesting*.

75. *Ingratiating chatter* is endearing chatter repeated again and again without regard to whether it is in conformity with truth and Dhamma. *Flattery* is speaking humbly, always maintaining an attitude of inferiority. *Bean-soupery* is resemblance to bean soup; for just as when beans are being cooked only a few do not get cooked, the rest get cooked, so too the person in whose speech only a little is true, the rest being false, is called a 'bean soup'; his state is *bean-soupery*.

---

22. '*Nahanā*—tying' from *nayhati* (to tie). The noun is not in P.T.S. Dict.
23. The story of the Oil-seller is given in the Sammohavinodani (VbhA. 483), which reproduces this part of Vis. with some additions. 'Two bhikkhus, it seems, went into a village and sat down in the sitting hall. Seeing a girl, they called her. Then one asked the other "Whose girl is this, venerable sir?"—"She is the daughter of our supporter the Oil-seller, friend. When we go to her mother's house and she gives us ghee, she gives it in the pot. And this girl too gives it in the pot as her mother does."' Quoted at Pm. 46.

76. *Fondling* is the state of the act of fondling. [28] For when a man fondles children on his lap or on his shoulder like a nurse —he nurses, is the meaning—, that fondler's act is the act of fondling. The state of the act of fondling is *fondling*.

77. In the description of *hinting* (*nemittikatā*): a sign (*nimitta*) is any bodily or verbal act that gets others to give requisites. *Giving a sign* is making a sign such as 'What have you got to eat?', etc., on seeing [people] going along with food. *Indication* is talk that alludes to requisites. *Giving indication:* on seeing cowboys, he asks 'Are these milk cows' calves or buttermilk cows' calves?', and when it is said 'They are milk cows' calves, venerable sir', [he remarks] 'They are not milk cows' calves. If they were milk cows' calves the bhikkhus would be getting milk', etc.; and his getting it to the knowledge of the boys' parents in this way, and so making them give milk, is *giving indication*'.

78. *Indirect talk* is talk that keeps near [to the subject]. And here there should be told the story of the bhikkhu supported by a family. A bhikkhu, it seems, who was supported by a family went into the house wanting to eat and sat down. The mistress of the house was unwilling to give. On seeing him she said 'There is no rice', and she went to a neighbour's house as though to get rice. The bhikkhu went into the storeroom. Looking round, he saw sugarcane in the corner behind the door, sugar in a bowl, a string of salt fish in a basket, rice in a jar, and ghee in a pot. He came out and sat down. When the housewife came back, she said 'I did not get any rice'. The bhikkhu said 'Lay follower, I saw a sign just now that alms will not be easy to get today.' — 'What, venerable sir?' — 'I saw a snake that was like sugarcane put in the corner behind the door; looking for something to hit it with, I saw a stone like a lump of sugar in a bowl. When the snake had been hit with the clod, it spread out a hood like a string of salt fish in a basket, and its teeth as it tried to bite the clod were like rice grains in a jar. Then the saliva mixed with poison that came out to its mouth in its fury was like ghee put in a pot.' She thought 'There is no hoodwinking the shaveling', so she gave him the sugarcane [29] and she cooked the rice and gave it all to him with the ghee, the sugar and the fish.

79. Such talk that keeps near [to the subject] should be understood as indirect talk.

Roundabout talk is talking round and round [the subject] as much as is allowed.

80. In the description of *belittling: abusing* is abusing by means of the ten instances of abuse.[24] *Disparaging* is contemptuous

---

24. The 'ten instances of abuse (*akkosa-vatthu*)' are given in the Sammohavinodanī (VbhA. 340) as: 'You are a thief, you are a fool, you are an idiot, you are a camel (*oṭṭha*), you are an ox, you are

talk. *Reproaching* is enumeration of faults such as 'He is faithless, he is an unbeliever'. *Snubbing* is taking up verbally thus 'Don't say that here'. Snubbing in all ways, giving grounds and reason, is *continual snubbing*. Or alternatively, when someone does not give, taking him up thus 'Oh, the prince of givers!' is *snubbing*; and the thorough snubbing thus 'A mighty prince of givers!' is *continual snubbing*. *Ridicule* is making fun of someone thus 'What sort of a life has this man who eats up his seed [grain]?'. *Continual ridicule* is making fun of him more thoroughly thus 'What, you say this man is not a giver who always gives the words "There is
81. nothing" to everyone?'. *Denigration*[25] is denigrating someone by saying that he is not a giver, or by censuring him. All-round denigration is *continual denigration*. *Tale-bearing* is bearing tales from house to house, from village to village, from district to district, [thinking] 'So they will give to me out of fear of my bearing tales'. *Backbiting* is speaking censoriously behind another's back after speaking kindly to his face; for this is like biting the flesh of another's back, when he is not looking, on the part of one who is unable to look him in the face; therefore it is called *backbiting*. *This is called belittling* (*nippesikatā*) because it scrapes off[25] (*nippeseti*), wipes off,[25] the virtuous qualities of others as a bamboo scraper[25] (*veḷupesikā*) does unguent,[25] or because it is a pursuit of gain by grinding[25] (*nippiṁsitvā*) and pulverizing others' virtuous qualities, like the pursuit of perfume by grinding the kinds of perfumed substances; that is why it is called *belittling*.

82. In the description of *pursuing gain with gain*: *pursuing* is hunting after. *Got from here* is got from this house. *There* is into that house. *Seeking* is wanting. *Seeking for* is hunting after. *Seeking out* is hunting after again and again. [30] The story of the bhikkhu who went round giving away the alms he had got at first to children of families here and there and in the end got milk and gruel should be told here. *Searching*, etc., are synonyms for 'seeking' etc., and so the construction here should be understood thus: *going in search of* is seeking; *searching for* is seeking for; *searching out* is seeking out.

This is the meaning of *scheming*, and so on.

---

a donkey, you belong to the states of loss, you belong to hell, you are a beast, there is not even a happy or an unhappy destiny to be expected for you' (see also SnA. 364).

25. The following words are not in P.T.S. Dict.: *Pāpanā* (denigration), *pāpanaṁ* (nt. denigrating), *nippeseti* (scrapes off—from *piṁsati?* cf. *nippesikatā*—'belittling' §42, 64), *nippuñchati* (wipes off—only *puñchati* in Dict.), *pesikā* (scraper—not in this sense in Dict.: from same root as *nippeseti*), *nippimsitvā* (grinding, pounding), *abbhaṅga* (unguent =*abbhañjana* Pm. 47).

83. Now [as regards the words] *The evil states beginning with* (§42): here the words *beginning with* should be understood to include the many evil states given in the Brahmajāla Sutta in the way beginning 'Or just as some worthy ascetics, while 'eating the food given by the faithful, make a living by wrong 'livelihood by such low arts as these, that is to say, by palmis- 'try, by fortune-telling, by divining omens, by interpreting 'dream., marks on the body, holes gnawed by mice; by fire 'sacrifice, by spoon oblation,...' (D.i,9).

84. So this wrong livelihood entails the transgression of these six training precepts announced on account of livelihood, and it entails the evil states beginning with 'Scheming, talking, hinting, belittling, pursuing gain with gain'. And so it is the abstinence from all sorts of wrong livelihood that is *virtue of livelihood purification*, the word-meaning of which is this: on account of it they live, thus it is livelihood. What is that? It is the effort consisting in the search for requisites. 'Purification' is purifiedness. 'Livelihood purification' is purification of livelihood.

85. (*d*) As regards the next kind called *virtue concerning requisites*, [here is the text: 'Reflecting wisely, he uses the 'robe only for protection from cold, for protection from heat, 'for protection from contact with gadflies, flies, wind, burning 'and creeping things, and only for the purpose of concealing 'the private parts. Reflecting wisely, he uses alms food 'neither for amusement nor for intoxication nor for smarten- 'ing nor for embellishment, but only for the endurance and 'continuance of this body, for the ending of discomfort, and 'for assisting the life of purity: "Thus I shall put a stop to ' "old feelings and shall not arouse new feelings, and I shall ' "be healthy and blameless and live in comfort." Reflecting 'wisely, he uses the resting place only for the purpose of 'protection from cold, for protection from heat, for protection 'from contact with gadflies, flies, wind, burning and creeping 'things, and only for the purpose of warding off the perils of 'climate and enjoying retreat. Reflecting wisely, he uses the 'requisite of medicine as cure for the sick only for protection 'from arisen hurtful feelings and for complete immunity from 'affliction' (M.i,10).] Herein *reflecting wisely* is reflecting as the means and as the way;[26] by knowing, by reviewing, is the meaning. And here it is the reviewing stated in the way beginning 'For protection from cold' that should be understood as 'reflecting wisely'.

86. Herein, *The robe* is any one of those beginning with the inner cloth. *He uses*: he employs; dresses in [as inner cloth], or puts on [as upper garment]. *Only* [31] is a phrase signifying

26. For attention (*manasi-kāra*) as the means (*upāya*) and the way (*patha*) see MA. i, 64.

invariability in the definition of a limit[27] of a purpose; the purpose in the meditator's making use of the robes is that much only, namely, protection from cold, etc., not more than that. *From cold*: from any kind of cold arisen either through disturbance of elements internally or through change in temperature externally. *For protection*: for the purpose of warding off; for the purpose of eliminating it so that it may not arouse affliction in the body. For when the body is afflicted by cold, the distracted mind cannot be wisely exerted. That is why the Blessed One permitted the robe to be used for protection from cold. So in each instance. Except that *from heat* means from the heat of fire, the origin of which should be understood as forest fires, and so on.

87. *From contact with gadflies and flies, wind and burning and creeping things*: here *gadflies* are flies that bite; they are also called 'blind flies'. *Flies* are just flies. *Wind* is distinguished as that with dust and that without dust. *Burning* is burning of the sun. *Creeping things* are any long creatures such as snakes and so on that move by crawling. Contact with them is of two kinds: contact by being bitten and contact by being touched. And that does not worry him who sits with a robe on. So he uses it for the purpose of protection from such things.

88. *Only*: the word is repeated in order to define a subdivision of the invariable purpose; for the concealment of the private parts is an invariable purpose; the others are purposes, periodically. Herein, *private parts* are any parts of the pudendum. For when a member is disclosed, conscience (*hiri*) is disturbed (*kuppati*), offended. It is called 'private parts (*hirikopīna*)' because of the disturbance of conscience (*hiri-kopana*). *For the purpose of concealing the private parts*: for the purpose of the concealment of those private parts. [As well as the reading *hirikopīnapaṭicchādanatthaṁ*'] there is a reading '*hirikopīnaṁ paṭicchādanatthaṁ*'.

89. *Alms food* is any sort of food. For any sort of nutriment is called 'alms food (*piṇḍapāta*—lit. lump-dropping)' because of its having been dropped (*patitattā*) into a bhikkhu's bowl during his alms round (*piṇḍolya*). Or alms food (*piṇḍapāta*) is the dropping (*pāta*) of the lumps (*piṇḍa*); it is the concurrence (*sannipāta*), the collection, of alms (*bhikkhā*) obtained here and there, is what is meant.

Neither for amusement: neither for the purpose of amusement, as with village boys, etc.; for sake of sport, is what is meant. *Nor for intoxication*: not for the purpose of intoxication, as with boxers, etc.; for the sake of intoxication with strength and for the sake of intoxication with manhood, is

27. '*Avadhi*—limit'=*odhi*: this form is not in P.T.S. Dict. (see MA. ii, 292).

what is meant. [32] *Nor for smartening*: not for the purpose of smartening, as with royal concubines, courtesans, etc.; for the sake of plumpness in all the limbs, is what is meant. *Nor for embellishment*: not for the purpose of embellishment, as with actors, dancers, etc.; for the sake of a clear skin and complexion, is what is meant.

90. And here the clause *neither for amusement* is stated for the purpose of abandoning support for delusion; *nor for intoxication* is said for the purpose of abandoning support for hate; *nor for smartening nor for embellishment* is said for the purpose of abandoning support for greed. And *neither for amusement nor for intoxication* is said for the purpose of preventing the arising of fetters for oneself. *Nor for smartening nor for embellishment* is said for the purpose of preventing the arising of fetters for another. And the abandoning of both unwise practice and devotion to indulgence of sense pleasures should be understood as stated by these four. *Only* has the meaning already stated.

91. *Of this body*: of this material body consisting of the four great primaries. *For the endurance*: for the purpose of continued endurance. *And continuance*: for the purpose of not interrupting [life's continued] occurrence, or for the purpose of endurance for a long time. He makes use of the alms food for the purpose of the endurance, for the purpose of the continuance, of the body, as the owner of an old house uses props for his house, and as a carter uses axle grease, not for the purpose of amusement, intoxication, smartening, and embellishment. Furthermore, endurance is a term for the life faculty. So what has been said as far as the words *for the endurance and continuance of this body* can be understood to mean: for the purpose of maintaining the occurrence of the life faculty in this body.

92. *For the ending of discomfort*: hunger is called 'discomfort' in the sense of afflicting. He makes use of alms food for the purpose of ending that, like annointing a wound, like counteracting heat with cold, and so on. *For assisting the life of purity*: for the purpose of assisting the life of purity consisting in the whole dispensation and the life of purity consisting in the path. For while this [bhikkhu] is engaged in crossing the desert of existence by means of devotion to the Three Trainings depending on bodily strength whose necessary condition is the use of alms food, he makes use of it to assist the life of purity just as those seeking to cross the desert used their child's flesh,[28] just as those seeking to cross a river use a raft, and just as those seeking to cross the ocean use a ship.

---

28. *'Child's flesh (putta-maṁsa)'* is an allusion to the story (S. ii, 98) of the couple who set out to cross a desert with an insufficient food supply but got to the other side by eating the flesh of their child who

93. *Thus I shall put a stop to old feelings and shall not arouse new feelings*: [33] thus as a sick man uses medicine, he uses [alms food, thinking]: 'by use of this alms food I shall put a stop to the old feeling of hunger, and I shall not arouse a new feeling by immoderate eating, like one of the [proverbial] brahmans, that is, one who eats till he has to be helped up by hand, or till his clothes will not meet, or till he rolls there [on the ground], or till crows can peck from his mouth, or till he vomits what he has eaten. Or alternatively, there is that which is called "old feelings" because, being conditioned by former kamma, it arises now in dependence on unsuitable immoderate eating—I shall put a stop to that old feeling, forestalling its condition by suitable moderate eating. And there is that which is called "new feeling" because it will arise in the future in dependence on the accumulation of kamma consisting in making improper use [of the requisite of alms food] now—I shall also not arouse that new feeling, avoiding by means of proper use the production of its root'. This is how the meaning should be understood here. What has been shown so far can be understood to include proper use [of requisites], abandoning of devotion to self-mortification, and not giving up lawful bliss (pleasure).

94. *And I shall be healthy*: 'In this body, which exists in dependence on requisites, I shall, by moderate eating, have health called "long endurance" since there will be no danger of severing the life faculty or interrupting the [continuity of the] postures'. [Reflecting] in this way, he makes use [of the alms food] as a sufferer from a chronic disease does his medicine. *And blameless and live in comfort* (lit. and have blamelessness and a comfortable abiding): he makes use of them thinking 'I shall have blamelessness by avoiding improper search, acceptance and eating, and I shall have a comfortable abiding by moderate eating'. Or he does so thinking 'I shall have blamelessness due to absence of such faults as boredom, sloth, sleepiness, blame by the wise, etc., that have unseemly immoderate eating as their condition; and I shall have a comfortable abiding by producing bodily strength that has seemly moderate eating as its condition'. Or he does so thinking 'I shall have blamelessness by abandoning the pleasure of lying down, lolling and torpor through refraining from eating as much as possible to stuff the belly; and I shall have a comfortable abiding by controlling the four postures through eating four or five mouthfuls less than the maximum'. For this is said:

'With four or five lumps still to eat
'Let him then end by drinking water;

died on the way. The derivation given in the P.T.S. Dict. 'A metaphor probably distorted from *pūta-maṁsa*' has no justification. The reference to rafts might be to D. ii, 89.

'For energetic bhikkhus' needs
'This should suffice to live in comfort'
(Thag. 983).[29] [34]

Now what has been shown at this point can be understood as discernment of purpose and practice of the middle way.

95. *Resting place* (*senāsana*) : this is the bed (*sena*) and seat (*āsana*). For wherever one sleeps (*seti*), whether in a monastery or in a lean-to, etc., that is the bed (*sena*); wherever one seats oneself (*āsati*), sits (*nisīdati*), that is the seat (*āsana*). Both together are called 'resting-place (or abode—*senāsana*)'. *For the purpose of warding off the perils of climate and enjoying retreat*: the climate itself in the sense of imperilling (*parisahana*) is 'perils of climate (*utu-parissaya*)'. Unsuitable climatic conditions that cause mental distraction due to bodily affliction can be warded off by making use of the resting place ; it is for the purpose of warding off these and for the purpose of the pleasure of solitude, is what is meant. Of course, the warding off of the perils, of climate is stated by, [the phrase] 'protection from cold', etc., too; but, just as in the case of making use of the robes the concealment of the private parts is stated as an invariable purpose while the others are periodical [purposes], so here also this [last] should be understood as mentioned with reference to the invariable warding off of the perils of climate. Or alternatively, this 'climate' of the kind stated is just climate; but 'perils' are of two kinds: evident perils and concealed perils (see NdI.12). Herein, evident perils are lions, tigers, etc., while concealed perils are greed, hate, and so on. When a bhikkhu knows and reflects thus in making use of the kind of resting place where these [perils] do not, owing to unguarded doors and sight of unsuitable visible objects, etc., cause affliction, he can be understood as one who 'reflecting wisely makes use of the resting place for the purpose of warding off the perils of climate'.

96. *The requisite of medicine as cure for the sick*: here 'cure (*paccaya*=going against)' is in the sense of going against (*pati-ayana*) illness; in the sense of countering, is the meaning. This is a term for any suitable remedy. It is the medical man's work (*bhisakassa kammaṁ*) because it is permitted by him, thus it is medicine (*bhesajja*). Or the cure for the sick itself as medicine is 'medicine as cure for the sick'. Any work of a medical man such as oil, honey, ghee, etc., that is suitable for one who is sick, is what is meant. A 'requisite (*parikkhāra*)', however, in such passages as 'It is well supplied with the requisites of a city' (A.iv,106) is equipment; in such passages as 'The chariot has the requisite of virtue, the axle of jhana, the wheel of energy' (S.v,6) [35] it is an ornament; in such passages as 'The requisites for the life of

29. This verse has been misunderstood in 'Psalms of the Brethren.'

'one who has gone into homelessness that should be available' (M.i,104) it is an accessory. But here both equipment and accessory are applicable. For that medicine as a cure for the sick is equipment for maintaining life because it protects by preventing the arising of affliction destructive to life; and it is an accessory too because it is an instrument for prolonging life. That is why it is called 'requisite'. So it is medicine as cure for the sick and that is requisite, thus it is a 'requisite of medicine as cure for the sick'. [He makes use of] that requisite of medicine as cure for the sick; any requisite for life consisting of oil, honey, molasses, ghee, etc., that is allowed by a medical man as suitable for the sick, is what is meant.

97. *From arisen*: from born, become produced. *Hurtful*: here 'hurt (affliction)' is a disturbance of elements, and it is the leprosy, tumours, boils, etc., originated by that disturbance. *Hurtful* (*veyyābādhika*) because arisen in the form of hurt (*byābādha*). *Feelings*: painful feelings, feelings resulting from unprofitable kamma—from those hurtful feelings. *For complete immunity from affliction*: for complete freedom from pain; so that all that is painful is abandoned, is the meaning.

This is how this *virtue concerning requisites* should be understood. In brief its characteristic is the use of requisites after wise reflection. The word-meaning here is this: because breathing things go (*ayanti*), move, proceed, using [what they use] in dependence on these robes, etc., these robes, etc., are therefore called requisites (*paccaya*=ger. of *paṭi*+*ayati*); 'concerning requisites' is concerning those requisites.

98. (*a*) So, in this fourfold virtue, *Pātimokkha restraint* has to be undertaken by means of *faith*. For that is accomplished by faith, since the announcing of training precepts is outside the disciples' province; and the evidence here is the refusal of the request to [allow disciples to] announce training precepts (See Vin. iii, 9—10). Having therefore undertaken through faith the training precepts without exception as announced, one should completely perfect them without regard for life. For this is said: [36]

'As a hen guards her eggs,
'Or as a yak her tail,
'Or like a darling child,
'Or like an only eye—
'So you who are engaged
'Your virtue to protect,
'Be prudent at all times
'And ever scrupulous' ( ).

Also it is said further 'So too, Sire, when a training precept 'for disciples is announced by me, my disciples do not 'transgress it even for the sake of life' (A.iv,201).

99. And the story of the Elders bound by robbers in the forest should be understood in this sense.

It seems that robbers in the Mahāvaṭṭanī Forest bound an Elder with black creepers and made him lie down. While he lay there for seven days he augmented his insight, and after reaching the fruition of Non-return, he died there and was reborn in the Brahmā World.

Also they bound another Elder in Tambapaṇṇi Island (Ceylon) with string creepers and made him lie down. When a forest fire came and the creepers were not cut, he established insight and attained nibbana simultaneously with his death. When the Elder Abhaya, a preacher of the Dīgha Nikāya, passed by with five hundred bhikkhus, he saw [what had happened] and he had the Elder's body cremated and a shrine built. Therefore let other clansmen also

Maintain the Rules of Conduct pure,
Renouncing life if there be need,
Rather than break virtue's restraint
By the World's Saviour decreed.

100. (*b*) And as Patimokkha restraint is undertaken out of faith, so *restraint of the sense faculties* should be undertaken with *mindfulness*. For that is accomplished by mindfulness, because when the sense faculties' functions are founded on mindfulness, there is no liability to invasion by covetousness and the rest. So, recollecting the Fire Discourse, which begins thus, 'Better, bhikkhus, the extirpation of the eye ' faculty by a red-hot burning blazing glowing iron spike than ' the apprehension of signs in the particulars of visible objects ' cognizable by the eye' (S. iv, 168), this [restraint] should be properly undertaken by preventing with unremitting mindfulness any apprehension, in the objective fields consisting of visible data, etc., of any signs, etc., likely to encourage covetousness, etc., to invade consciousness occurring in connexion with the eye door, and so on.

101. [37] When not undertaken thus, virtue of Patimokkha restraint is unenduring: it does not last, like a crop not fenced in with branches. And it is raided by the robber defilements as a village with open gates is by thieves. And lust, leaks into his mind as rain does into a badly-roofed house. For this is said

' Among the visible objects, sounds, and smells,
' And tastes, and tangibles, guard the faculties ;
' For when these doors are open and unguarded,
' Then thieves will come and raid as 'twere a village'
( ).

' And just as with an ill-roofed house
' The rain comes leaking in, so too
' Will lust come leaking in for sure
' Upon an undeveloped mind' (Dh. 13).

102. When it is undertaken thus, virtue of Pātimokkha restraint is enduring: it lasts, like a crop well fenced in with branches. And it is not raided by the robber defilements, as a village with well-guarded gates is not by thieves. And lust does not leak into his mind, as rain does not into a well-roofed house. For this is said:

'Among the visible objects, sounds and smells,
'And tastes and tangibles, guard the faculties;
'For when these doors are closed and truly guarded,
'Thieves will not come and raid as 'twere a village'
( ).

'And just as with a well-roofed house
'No rain comes leaking in, so too
'No lust comes leaking in for sure
'Upon a well-developed mind' (Dh. 14).

103. This, however, is the teaching at its very highest.

This mind is called 'quickly transformed' (A. I,10), so restraint of the faculties should be undertaken by removing arisen lust with the contemplation of foulness, as was done by the Elder Vangīsa soon after he had gone forth. [38]

As the Elder was wandering for alms, it seems, soon after going forth, lust arose in him on seeing a woman. Thereupon he said to the venerable Ānanda:

'I am afire with sensual lust.
'And burning flames consume my mind ;
'In pity tell me, Gotama,
'How to extinguish it for good' (S.i,188).

The Elder said:

'You do perceive mistakenly,
'That burning flames consume your mind.
'Look for no sign of beauty there,
'For that it is which leads to lust.
'See foulness there and keep your mind
'Harmoniously concentrated ;
'Formations see as alien,
'As ill, not self, so this great lust
'May be extinguished, and no more
'Take fire thus ever and again' (S.i,188).

The Elder expelled his lust and then went on with his alms round.

104. Moreover a bhikkhu who is fulfilling restraint of the faculties should be like the elder Cittagutta resident in the Great Cave at Kuraṇḍaka, and like the Elder Mahā-Mitta resident at the Great Monastery of Coraka.

105. In the Great Cave of Kuraṇḍaka, it seems, there was a lovely painting of the Renunciation of the Seven Buddhas. A number of Bhikkhus wandering about among the

dwellings saw the painting and said 'What a lovely painting, venerable sir !'. The Elder said 'For more than sixty years, friends, I have lived in the cave, and I did not know whether there was any painting there or not. Now, today, I know it through those who have eyes'. The Elder, it seems, though he had lived there for so long, had never raised his eyes and looked up at the cave. And at the door of his cave there was a great ironwood tree. And the Elder had never looked up at that either. He knew it was in flower when he saw its petals on the ground each year.

106. The king heard of the Elder's great virtues, and he sent for him three times, desiring to pay homage to him. When the Elder did not go, he had the breasts of all the women with infants in the town bound and sealed off, [saying] 'As long as the Elder does not come let the children go without milk'. [39] Out of compassion for the children the Elder went to Mahāgāma. When the king heard [that he had come, he said] 'Go and bring the Elder in. I shall take the Precepts'. Having had him brought up into the inner palace, he paid homage to him and provided him with a meal. Then, saying 'Today, venerable sir, there is no opportunity. I shall take the Precepts tomorrow', he took the Elder's bowl. After following him for a little, he paid homage with the queen and turned back. As seven days went by thus, whether it was the king who paid homage or whether it was the queen, the Elder said 'May the king be happy'.

107. Bhikkhus asked 'Why is it, venerable sir, that whether it is the king who pays the homage or the queen you say "May the king be happy"?'. The Elder replied 'Friends, I do not notice whether it is the king or the queen'. At the end of seven days [when it was found that] the Elder was not happy living there, he was dismissed by the king. He went back to the Great Cave at Kurandaka. When it was night he went out onto his walk. A deity who dwelt in the ironwood tree stood by with a torch of sticks. Then his meditation subject became quite clear and plain. The Elder, [thinking] 'How clear my meditation subject is today !', was glad, and immediately after the middle watch he reached Arahantship, making the whole rock resound.[30]

108. So when another clansman seeks his own good,

Let him not be hungry-eyed,
Like a monkey in the groves,
Like a wild deer in the woods,
Like a nervous little child.
Let him go with eyes downcast

30. '"*Making the whole rock resound*": making the whole rock reverberate as one, doing so by means of an earth tremor. But some say that it was owing to the cheering of the deities who lived there' (Pm. 58).

Seeing a plough yoke's length before,
That he fall not in the power
Of the forest-monkey mind.

109. The Elder Mahā-Mitta's mother was sick with a poisoned tumour. She told her daughter, who as a bhikkhuni had also gone forth, 'Lady, go to your brother. Tell him my trouble and bring back some medicine'. She went and told him. The Elder said 'I do not know how to gather root medicines and such things and concoct a medicine from them. But rather I will tell you a medicine: since I went forth I have not broken [my virtue of restraint of] the sense faculties by looking at the bodily form of the opposite sex with a lustful mind. By this [40] declaration of truth may my mother get well. Go and tell the lay devotee and rub her body'. She went and told her what had happened and then did as she had been instructed. At that very moment the lay devotee's tumour vanished, shrinking away like a lump of froth. She got up and uttered a cry of joy: 'If the Fully Enlightened One were still alive, why should he not stroke with his net-adorned hand the head of a bhikkhu like my son?'. So

110. Let another noble clansman
Gone forth in the Dispensation
Keep, as did the Elder Mitta,
Perfect faculty restraint.

111. (*c*) As restraint of the faculties is to be undertaken by means of mindfulness, so *Livelihood purification* is to be undertaken by means of *energy*. For that is accomplished by energy, because the abandoning of wrong livelihood is effected in one who has rightly applied energy. Abandoning, therefore, unbefitting wrong search, this should be undertaken with energy by means of the right kind of search consisting in going on alms round, etc., avoiding what is of impure origin as though it were a poisonous snake, and using only requisites of pure origin.

112. Herein, for one who has not taken up the Ascetic Practices any requisites obtained from the Community, from a group of bhikkhus, or from laymen who have confidence in his special qualities of teaching the Dhamma, etc., are called 'of pure origin'. But those obtained on alms round, etc., are of extremely pure origin. For one who has taken up the Ascetic Practices those obtained on alms round, etc., and—as long as this is in accordance with the rules of the ascetic practices—from people who have confidence in his special qualities of ascetism, are called 'of pure origin'. And if he has got putrid urine with mixed gall nuts and 'four sweets'[31] for the purpose of curing a certain affliction, and he eats only

31. 'Four-sweets—*catumadhura*': a medicinal sweet made of four ingredients.

the broken gall nuts, thinking 'Other companions in the life of purity will eat the "four-sweets"', his undertaking of the ascetic practices is befitting, for he is then called a bhikkhu who is supreme in the Noble Ones' Heritages (See A. ii, 28).

113. As to the robe and the other requisites, no hint, indication, roundabout talk, or intimation, about robes and alms food is allowable for a bhikkhu who is purifying his livelihood. But a hint, indication, or roundabout talk, about a resting place is allowable for one who has not taken up the ascetic practices. [41].

114. Herein, a 'hint' is when one who is getting the preparing of the ground, etc., done for the purpose of [making] a resting place is asked 'What is being done, venerable sir? Who is having it done?' and he replies 'No one'; or any other such giving of hints. An 'indication' is saying 'Lay follower, where do you live?'—'In a mansion, venerable sir,'—'But, lay follower, a mansion is not allowed for bhikkhus.' Or any other such giving of indication. 'Roundabout talk' is saying 'The resting place for the Community of Bhikkhus is crowded'; or any other such oblique talk.

115. All, however, is allowed in the case of medicine. But when the disease is cured, is it or is it not allowed to use the medicine obtained in this way? Herein, the Vinaya specialists say that the opening has been given by the Blessed One, therefore it is allowable. But the Suttanta specialists say that though there is no offence, nevertheless the livelihood
116. is sullied, therefore it is not allowable. But one who does not use hints, indications, roundabout talk, or intimation, though these are permitted by the Blessed One, and who depends only on the special qualities of fewness of wishes, etc., and makes use only of requisites obtained otherwise than by indication, etc., even when he thus risks his life, is called supreme in living in effacement, like the venerable Sāriputta.

117. It seems that the venerable one was cultivating seclusion at one time, living in a certain forest with the Elder Mahā-Moggallāna. One day an affliction of colic arose in him, causing him great pain. In the evening the Elder Mahā-Moggallāna went to attend upon him. Seeing him lying down, he asked what the reason was. And then he asked 'What used to make you better formerly, friend?'. The Elder said 'When I was a layman, friend, my mother used to mix ghee, honey, sugar and so on, and give me rice gruel with pure milk. That used to make me better'. Then the other said 'So be it, friend. If either you or I have merit, perhaps
118. tomorrow we shall get some'. Now a deity who dwelt in a tree at the end of the walk overheard their conversation. [Thinking] 'I will find rice gruel for the lord tomorrow'

he went meanwhile to the family who was supporting the Elder [42] and entered into the body of the eldest son, causing him discomfort. Then he told the assembled relatives the price of the cure: 'If you prepare rice gruel of such a kind tomorrow for the Elder, I will set this one free'. They said 'Even without being told by you we regularly supply the Elder's needs', and on the following day they prepared rice gruel of the kind needed.

119. The Elder Mahā-Moggallāna came in the morning and said 'Stay here, friend, till I come back from the alms round'. Then he went into the village. Those people met him. They took his bowl, filled it with the stipulated kind of rice gruel, and gave it back to him. The Elder made as though to go, but they said 'Eat, venerable sir, we shall give you more'. When the Elder had eaten, they gave him another bowlful. The Elder left. Bringing the alms food to the venerable Sāriputta, he said 'Here, friend Sāriputta, eat'. When the Elder saw it, he thought 'The gruel is very nice. How was it got?', and seeing how it had been obtained, he said 'Friend, the alms food cannot be used'.

120. Instead of thinking 'He does not eat alms food brought by the likes of me', the other at once took the bowl by the rim and turned it over on one side. As the rice gruel fell on the ground the Elder's affliction vanished. From then on it did not appear again during forty-five years.

121. Then he said to the venerable Mahā-Moggallāna 'Friend, even if one's bowels come out and trail on the ground, it is not fitting to eat gruel got by verbal intimation', and he uttered this exclamation:

'My livelihood might well be blamed
'If I were to consent to eat
'The honey and the gruel obtained
'By influence of verbal hints.
'And even if my bowels obtrude
'And trail outside, and even though
'My life is to be jeopardized,
'I will not blot my livelihood (Miln. 370).
'For I will satisfy my heart
'By shunning all wrong kinds of search;
'And never will I undertake
'The search the Buddhas have condemned' ( ). [43]

122, And here too should be told the story of the Elder Mahā-Tissa the Mango-eater who lived at Cīragumba (see §132 below).[32] So in all respects

32. The Elder Mahā-Tissa, it seems, was going on a journey during a famine, and being tired in body and weak through lack of food and travel weariness, he lay down at the root of a mango tree covered with fruit. There were many fallen mangoes here and there' (Pm. 60). 'Though ownerless mangoes were lying fallen on the ground near him,

A man who has gone forth in faith
Should purify his livelihood
And, seeing clearly, give no thought
To any search that is not good.

123. (*d*) And as livelihood purification is to be undertaken by means of energy, so *virtue dependent on requisites* is to be undertaken by means of *understanding*. For that is accomplished by understanding, because one who possesses understanding is able to see the advantages and the dangers in requisites. So one should abandon greed for requisites and undertake that virtue by using requisites obtained lawfully and properly, after reviewing them with understanding in the way aforesaid.

124. Herein, reviewing is of two kinds: at the time of receiving requisites and at the time of using them. For use is blameless in one who at the time of receiving robes, etc., reviews them either as [mere] elements or as repulsive,[33] and puts them aside for later use, and in one who reviews them thus at the time of using them.

125. Here is an explanation to settle the matter. There are four kinds of use: use as theft,[34] use as debt, use as an inheritance, use as a master. Herein, use by one who is unvirtuous and makes use [of requisites], even sitting in the midst of the community, is called 'use as theft'. Use without reviewing by one who is virtuous is 'use as a debt'; therefore the robe should be reviewed every time it is used, and the alms food lump by lump. One who cannot do this [should review it] before the meal, after the meal, in the first watch, in the middle watch, and in the last watch. If dawn breaks on him without his having reviewed it, he finds himself in the position

---

he would not eat them in the absence of someone to accept them from' (Pm. 65). 'Then a lay devotee, who was older than he, went to the Elder, and learning of his exhaustion, gave him mango juice to drink. Then he mounted him on his back and took him to his home. Meanwhile the Elder admonished himself as follows:

"Nor your mother nor your father", etc. (See §133).

And beginning the comprehension [of formations], and augmenting insight, he realized Arahantship after the other paths in due succession while he was still mounted on his back' (Pm. 60).

33. '"*As elements*" in this way: "This robe, etc., consists merely of [the four] elements and occurs when its conditions are present; and the person who uses it [likewise]". "*As repulsive*" in this way: Firstly perception of repulsiveness in nutriment in the case of alms food; then as bringing repulsiveness to mind thus: "But all these robes, etc., which are not in themselves disgusting, become utterly disgusting on reaching this filthy body"' (Pm. 61).

34. '"*Use as theft*": use by one who is unworthy. And the requisites are allowed by the Blessed One to one in his own dispensation who is virtuous, not unvirtuous; and the generosity of the givers is towards one who is virtuous, not towards one who is not, since they expect great fruit from their actions' (Pm. 61; cf. M. Sutta 142 and commentary).

of one who has used it as a debt. Also the resting place should be reviewed each time it is used. Recourse to mindfulness both in the accepting and the use of medicine is proper; but while this is so, though there is an offence for one who uses it without mindfulness after mindful acceptance, there is no offence for one who is mindful in using after accepting without mindfulness.

126. Purification is of four kinds: purification by the Teaching, purification by restraint, purification by search, and purification by reviewing. Herein, *virtue of the Patimokkha restraint* is called 'purification by the Teaching'; [44] for that is so called because it purifies by means of teaching. *Virtue of restraint of faculties* is called 'purification by restraint'; for that is so called because it purifies by means of the restraint in the mental resolution 'I shall not do so again'. *Virtue of livelihood purification* is called 'purification by search'; for that is so called because search is purified in one who abandons wrong search and gets requisites lawfully and properly. *Virtue dependent on requisites* is called 'purification by reviewing'; for that is so called because it purifies by the reviewing of the kind already described. Hence it was said above (§125) 'There is no offence for one who is mindful in using after accepting without mindfulness'.

127. Use of the requisites by the seven kinds of Trainers is called 'use as an inheritance'; For they are the Buddha's sons, therefore they make use of the requisites as the heirs of requisites belonging to their father. But how then, is it the Blessed One's requisites or the laity's requisites that are used? Although given by the laity, they actually belong to the Blessed One, because it is by the Blessed One that they are permitted. That is why it should be understood that the Blessed One's requisites are used. The confirmation here is in the Dhammadāyāda Sutta (M. Sutta 3).

Use by those whose cankers are destroyed is called 'use as a master'; for they make use of them as masters because they have escaped the slavery of craving.

128. As regards these kinds of use, use as a master and use as an inheritance are allowable for all. Use as a debt is not allowable, to say nothing of use as theft. But this use of what is reviewed by one who is virtuous is use freed from debt because it is the opposite of use as a debt or is included in use as an inheritance too. For one possessed of virtue is called a Trainer too because of possessing this training.

129. As regards these three kinds of use, since use as a master is best, when a bhikkhu undertakes *virtue dependent on requisites,* he should aspire to that and use them after reviewing them in the way described. And this is said: [45]

'The truly wise disciple
'Who listens to the Dhamma
'As taught by the Sublime One
'Makes use, after reviewing,
'Of alms food, and of dwelling,
'And of a resting place,
'And also of the water
'For washing dirt from robes' (Sn. 391).
'So like a drop of water
'Lying on leaves of lotus,
'A bhikkhu is unsullied
'By any of these matters,
'By alms food, [and by dwelling,]
'And by a resting place,
'And also by the water
'For washing dirt from robes' (Sn. 392).
'Since aid it is and timely
'Procured from another
'The right amount he reckons,
'Mindful without remitting
'In chewing and in eating,
'In tasting food besides :
'He treats it as an ointment
'Applied upon a wound' ( ).
'So like the child's flesh in the desert
'Like the greasing for the axle,
'He should eat without delusion
'Nutriment to keep alive' ( ).

130. And in connexion with the fulfilling of this virtue dependent on requisites there should be told the story of the novice Saṅgharakkhita the Nephew. For he made use of requisites after reviewing, according as it is said:

'Seeing me eat a dish of rice
'Quite cold, my Preceptor observed:
'"Novice, if you are not restrained,
'"Be careful not to burn your tongue".
'On hearing my Preceptor's words,
'I then and there felt urged to act
'And, sitting in a single session,
'I reached the goal of Arahantship.
'Since I am now waxed full in thought
'Like the full moon of the Fifteenth (See M.iii, 277),
'And all my cankers are destroyed,
'There is no more becoming now'. [46]

And so should any other man
Aspiring to end suffering
Make use of all the requisites
Wisely after reviewing them.

So virtue is of four kinds as 'virtue of Patimokkha restraint', and so on.

131. 18. In the first pentad in the fivefold section the meaning should be understood in accordance with the virtue of those not fully admitted to the Order, and so on. For this is said in the Paṭisambhidā: '(*a*) What is virtue consisting in 'limited purification? That of the training precepts for those 'not fully admitted to the Order: such is virtue consisting in 'limited purification. (*b*) What is virtue consisting in 'unlimited purification? That of the training precepts for 'those fully admitted to the Order: such is virtue consisting 'in unlimited purification. (*c*) What is virtue consisting in 'fulfilled purification? That of Magnanimous Ordinary 'Men devoted to profitable things, who are perfecting [the 'course] that ends in Trainership, regardless of the physical 'body and life, having given up [attachment to] life: such is 'virtue of fulfilled purification. (*d*) What is virtue consisting 'in purification not adhered to? That of the seven kinds of 'Trainer: such is virtue consisting in purification not adhered 'to. (*e*) What is virtue consisting in tranquillized purification? 'That of the Perfect One's disciples with cankers des-'troyed, of the Undeclared Enlightened Ones, of the Perfect 'Ones, accomplished and fully enlightened: such is virtue 'consisting in tranquillized purification' (Ps. i, 42–3).

132. (*a*) Herein, the virtue of those not fully admitted to the Order should be understood as *virtue consisting in limited purification*, because it is limited by the number [of training precepts, that is, 5 or 8 or 10].

(*b*) That of those fully admitted to the Order is [describable] thus:

Nine thousand millions, and a hundred
And eighty millions then as well,
And fifty plus a hundred thousand,
And thirty-six again to swell
The total restraint disciplines:
These rules the Enlightened One explains
Told under heads for filling out,
Which the Discipline restraint contains.[35]

So although limited in number, [47] it should yet be understood as *virtue consisting in unlimited purification*, since it is undertaken without reserve and has no obvious limit such as gain, fame, relatives, limbs or life. Like the virtue of the Elder Mahā-Tissa the Mango-eater who lived at Cīragumba (see §122 above).

133. For that venerable one never abandoned the following Good Man's Recollection,

35. The figures depend on whether *koṭi* is taken as 1,000,000, 100,000, or 10,000.

'Wealth for a sound limb's sake should be renounced,
'And one who guards his life gives up his limbs;
'And wealth and limbs and life, each one of these,
'A man gives up who practices the Dhamma',

and never transgressed a training precept even when his life was in the balance, and in this way be reached Arahantship with that same virtue of unlimited purification as his support while he was being carried on a lay devotee's back. According as it is said:

'Nor your mother nor your father
'Nor your relatives and kin
'Have done as much as this for you
'Because you are possessed of virtue'.
So, stirred with urgency, and wisely
Comprehending[36] with insight,
While carried on his helper's back
He reached the goal of Arahantship.

134. (*c*) The Magnanimous Ordinary Man's virtue, which from the time of admission to the Order is devoid even of the stain of a [wrong] thought because of its extreme purity, like a gem of pures† water, like well-refined gold, becomes the proximate cause for Arahantship itself, which is why it is called *consisting of fulfilled purification;* like that of the Elders Saṅgharakkhita the Great and Saṅgharakkhita the Nephew.

135. The Elder Saṅgharakkhita the Great (*Mahā-Saṅgharakkhita*), aged over sixty, was lying, it seems, on his deathbed. The Order of Bhikkhus questioned him about attainment of the supramundane state. The Elder said 'I have no supramundane state'. Then the young bhikkhu who was attending on him said 'Venerable sir, people have come as much as twelve leagues, thinking that you have reached nibbana. It will be a disappointment for many if you die as an ordinary man'.—'Friend, thinking to see the Blessed One Metteyya, I did not try for insight; [48]. So help me to sit up and give me the chance.' He helped the elder to sit up and went out. As he went out the Elder reached Arahantship and he gave a sign by snapping his fingers. The Order assembled and said to him 'Venerable sir, you have done a difficult thing in achieving the supramundane state in the hour of death'.—'That was not difficult, friends. But rather I will tell you what is difficult. Friends, I see no action done [by me]

36. 'Comprehending (*sammasana*)' is a technical term that will become clear in Ch. XX. In short it is inference that generalizes the 'three characteristics' from one's own directly-known experience to all possible formed experience at all times (See S. ii, 107). Commenting on *He comprehended that same illness'* (138), Pm. says 'He exercised insight by discerning the feeling in the illness under the heading of the feeling [aggregate] and the remaining material dhammas as materiality' (Pm. 65).

without mindfulness and unknowingly since the time I went forth.' His nephew also reached Arahantship in the same way at the age of fifty years.

136. 'Now if a man has little learning
'And he is careless of his virtue,
'They censure him on both accounts,
'For lack of virtue and of learning.
'But if he is of little learning
'Yet he is careful of his virtue,
'They praise him for his virtue, so
'It is as though he too had learning.
'And if he is of ample learning
'Yet he is careless of his virtue,
'They blame him for his virtue, so
'It is as though he had no learning.
'But if he is of ample learning
'And he is careful of his virtue,
'They give him praise on both accounts
'For virtue and as well for learning.
'The Buddha's pupil of much learning
'Who keeps the Law with understanding—
'A jewel of Jambu River gold[37]—
'Who is here fit to censure him ?
'Deities praise him [constantly],
'By Brahmā also is he praised' (A.ii,7).

137. (*d*) What should be understood as *virtue consisting in purification not adhered to* is Trainers' virtue, because it is not adhered to by [false] views, and ordinary men's virtue when not adhered to by greed. Like the virtue of the Elder Tissa the Landowner's Son (*Kuṭumbiyaputta-Tissa-thera*).

Wanting to become established in Arahantship in dependence on such virtue, this venerable one told his enemies:
'I broke the bones of both my legs
'To give the pledge you asked from me.
'I am revolted and ashamed
'At death accompanied by greed. [49]
'And after I had thought on this,
'And wisely then applied insight,
'When the sun rose and shone on me,
'I had become an Arahant' (see MA.i,233).

138. Also there was a certain Senior Elder who was very ill and unable to eat with his own hand. He was writhing smeared with his own urine and excrement. Seeing him a certain young bhikkhu said 'Oh, what a painful process life is!'. The senior Elder told him 'If I were to die now, friend, I should obtain the bliss of heaven; I have no doubt of that.

37. A story of the Jambu River and its gold is given at MA. iv, 147.

But the bliss obtained by breaking this virtue would be like the lay state obtained by disavowing the training', and he added 'I shall die together with my virtue'. As he lay there, he comprehended that same illness [with insight],[36] and he reached Arahantship. Having done so, he pronounced these verses to the Order of Bhikkhus:

'I am victim of a sickening disease
'That racks me with its burden of cruel pain;
'As flowers in the dust burnt by the sun,
'So this my corpse will soon have withered up.
'Unbeautiful called beautiful,
'Unclean while reckoned as if clean,
'Though full of ordure seeming fair
'To him that cannot see it clear.
'So out upon this ailing rotting body,
'Fetid and filthy, punished with affliction,
'Doting on which this silly generation
'Has lost the way to be reborn in heaven!' (Jā.ii,437).

139. (*e*) It is the virtue of the Arahants, etc., that should be understood as *tranquillized purification*, because of tranquillization of all disturbance and because of purifiedness.

So it is of five kinds as 'consisting in limited purification', and so on.

140. 19. In the second pentad the meaning should be understood as the abandoning, etc., of killing living things, etc.; for this is said in the Paṭisambhidā:

Five kinds of virtue:

'(1) In the case of killing living things, (*a*) abandoning 'is virtue, (*b*) abstention is virtue, (*c*) volition is virtue, '(*d*) restraint is virtue, (*e*) non-transgression is virtue. '(2) In the case of taking what is not given,... (3) In the 'case of sexual misconduct,... (4) In the case of false speech,.. '(5) In the case of malicious speech,... (6) In the case of 'harsh speech,... (7) In the case of gossip,... [50] (8) In the 'case of covetousness,... (9) In the case of ill will,... (10) In 'the case of wrong view,...

'(11) Through renunciation in the case of lust, (*a*) aban- 'doning is virtue,... (12) Through non-ill-will in the case of 'ill-will,... (13) Through perception of light in the case of 'stiffness-and-torpor,... (14) Through non-distraction,... 'agitation,.. (15) Through definition of states (dhamma)... 'uncertainty,... (16) Through knowledge... ignorance,...(17) 'Through gladdening in the case of boredom,...

(18) Through the first jhana in the case of the hindrances, '(*a*) abandoning is virtue,... (19) Through the second jhana... 'applied and sustained thought,... (20) Through the third 'jhana... happiness... (21) Through the fourth jhana in the 'case of pleasure and pain, (*a*) abandoning is virtue,...

'(22) Through the attainment of the base consisting of 'boundless space in the case of perceptions of matter, per- 'ceptions of resistance, and perceptions of variety, (*a*) aban- 'doning is virtue,... (23) Through the attainment of the base 'consisting of boundless consciousness in the case of the per- 'ception of the base consisting of boundless space,... (24) 'Through the attainment of the base consisting of nothingness 'in the case of the perception of the base consisting of bound- 'less consciousness,... (25) Through the attainment of the 'base consisting of neither perception nor non-perception in 'the case of the perception of the base consisting of nothing- 'ness,...

'(26) Through the contemplation of impermanence in 'the case of the perception of permanence, (*a*) abandoning is 'virtue,... (27) Through the contemplation of pain in the case 'of the perception of pleasure.... (28) Through the contem- 'plation of not-self in the case of the perception of self,... '(29) Through the contemplation of dispassion in the case of 'the perception of delighting.... (30) Through the con- 'templation of fading away in the case of greed,... (31) 'Through the contemplation of cessation in the case of 'originating,... (32) Through the contemplation of relin- 'quishment in the case of grasping...

'(33) Through the contemplation of destruction in the case 'of the perception of compactness, (*a*) abandoning is virtue,... '(34) Through the contemplation of fall [of formations] 'in the case of accumulating [kamma],... (35) Through 'the contemplation of change in the case of the perception of 'lastingness,... (36) Through the contemplation of the 'signless in the case of a sign,... (37) Through the contem- 'plation of the desireless in the case of desire,... (38) Through 'the contemplation of voidness in the case of misinter- 'preting (insistence), (39) Through Insight into States 'that is Higher Understanding in the case of misinterpreting '(insistence) due to grasping,...(40) Through Correct Know- 'ledge and Vision in the case of misinterpreting (insistence) 'due to confusion,... (41) Through the contemplation of 'danger in the case of misinterpreting (insistence) due to 'reliance [on formations],... (42) Through reflexion in the 'case of non-reflexion,... (43) Through the contemplation 'of turning away in the case of misinterpreting (insistence) 'due to bondage,...

'(44) Through the path of Stream-entry in the case of 'defilements coefficient with [false] view, (*a*) abandoning 'is virtue,...(45) Through the path of Once-return in the 'case of gross defilements,... (46) Through the path of Non- 'return in the case of residual defilements,... (47) Through 'the path of Arahantship in the case of all defilements, (*a*) 'abandoning is virtue, (*b*) abstention is virtue, (*c*) volition 'is virtue (*d*) restraint is virtue, (*e*) non-transgression is 'virtue.

'Such virtues lead to non-remorse in the mind, to gladden-'ing, to happiness, to tranquillity, to joy, to repetition, to 'development, to cultivation, to embellishment, to the re-'quisite [for concentration], to the equipment [of concentra-'tion], to fulfilment, to complete dispassion, to fading away, 'to cessation, to peace, to direct-knowledge, to enlighten-'ment, to nibbana' (Ps.i,46-7).[38]

141. And here there is no state called abandoning other than the mere non-arising of the killing of living things, etc., as stated. But the abandoning of a given [unprofitable state] upholds [51] a given profitable state in the sense of providing a foundation for it, and concentrates it by preventing wavering, so it is called 'virtue (*sīla*)' in the sense of composing (*sīlana*), reckoned as upholding and concentrating as stated earlier (§19).

The other four things mentioned refer to the presence[39] of occurrence of will as abstention from such and such, as restraint of such and such, as the volition associated with both of these, and as non-transgression in one who does not transgress such and such. But their meaning of virtue has been explained already.

So it is of five kinds as 'virtue consisting in abandoning' and so on.

142. At this point the answers to the questions, 'What is virtue? In what sense is it virtue? What are its characteristic function, manifestation, and proximate cause? What are the benefits of virtue? How many kinds of virtue are there?', are complete.

---

38. This list describes, in terms of abandoning, etc., the stages in the normal progress from ignorance to Arahantship, and it falls into the following groups: I. VIRTUE: the abandoning of the 10 unprofitable courses of action (1)—(10). II. CONCENTRATION: A. abandoning the seven hindrances to concentration by means of their opposites (11) - (17); B. the 8 attainments of concentration, and what is abandoned by each (18)—(25). III. UNDERSTANDING: A. INSIGHT: the 18 Principal Insights beginning with the Seven Contemplations (26)—(43). B. PATHS: the 4 paths and what is abandoned by each (44)—(47).

Pm. comments here as follows on (26): 'The contemplation of what is impermanent, or contemplation as "impermanent", is "contemplation of impermanence"; this is insight. It is the name for the kind of insight that occurs in apprehending the impermanence in dhammas of the three [mundane] planes. "In the case of the perception of permanence" means in the case of wrong perception of formed dhammas that occurs thus "They are permanent, eternal". The same method applies below' (Pm. 67). For explanations of the other Principal Insights see Ch. XX, notes 3 and 28.

39. '*Sabbhāva*—presence' (=*sat*+*bhāva*): not in P.T.S. Dict. Not to be confused with '*sabhāva*—individual essence' (= *sa* (Skr. *sva*)+*bhāva*, or *saha*+*bhāva*).

143. However, it was also asked (vi) WHAT IS THE DEFILING OF IT ? and WHAT IS THE CLEANSING OF IT?

We answer that virtue's tornness, etc., is its defiling, and that its untornness, etc., is its cleansing. Now that tornness, etc., is comprised under the breach that has gain, fame, etc., as its cause, and under the seven bonds of sexuality. When a man has broken the training course at the beginning or at the end in any instance of the seven classes of offences,[40] his virtue is called torn, like a cloth that is cut at the edge. But when he has broken it in the middle, it is called rent, like a cloth that is rent in the middle. When he has broken it twice or thrice in succession, it is called blotched, like a cow whose body is some such colour as black or red with a discrepant colour appearing on the back or the belly. When he has broken it [all over] at intervals, it is called mottled, like a cow speckled [all over] with discrepant-coloured spots at intervals. This in the first place is how there comes to be tornness with the breach that has gain, etc., as its cause.

144. And likewise with the seven bonds of sexuality; for this is said by the Blessed One: 'Here, brahman, some ascetic or 'brahman claims to lead the life of purity rightly; for he does 'not [52] enter into actual sexual intercourse with women. 'Yet he agrees to massage, manipulation, bathing and rub- 'bing down by women. He enjoys it, desires it and takes satis- 'faction in it. This is what is torn, rent, blotched and mott- 'led in one who leads the life of purity. This man is said to 'lead a life of purity that is unclean. As one who is bound 'by the bond of sexuality, he will not be released from birth, 'ageing and death,... he will not be released from suffering,
145. 'I say. Furthermore, brahman,... while he does not agree to '[these things], yet he jokes, plays and amuses himself
146. 'with women ... Furthermore, brahman, ... while he does 'not agree to [these things], yet he gazes and stares at women
147. 'eye to eye ... Furthermore, brahman,...while he does not 'agree to [these things], yet he listens to the sound of women 'through a wall or through a fence as they laugh or talk or sing
148. 'or weep... Furthermore, brahman,... while he does not 'agree to [these things], yet he recalls laughs and talks and
149. 'games that he formerly had with women... Furthermore, 'brahman,... while he does not agree to [these things] [53] 'Yet he sees a householder or a householder's son possessed 'of, endowed with, and indulging, the five cords of sense
150. 'desire... Furthermore, brahman, while he does not agree to '[these things], yet he leads the life of purity aspiring to some 'order of deities, [thinking] "Through this rite (virtue) or '"this ritual (vow) or this asceticism I shall become a [great]

40. The seven consisting of *pārājikā, sanghādisesā, pācittiyā, pāṭidesaniyā, dukkaṭā, thullaccayā, dubbhāsitā* (mentioned at MA. ii, 33).

'deity or some [lesser] deity". He enjoys it, desires it, and 'takes satisfaction in it. This, brahman, is what is torn, 'rent, blotched and mottled in one who leads the life of 'purity. This man...will not be released from suffering, I say' (A.iv,54–6).

This is how tornness, etc., should be understood as included under the breach that has gain, etc., as its cause and under the seven bonds of sexuality.

151. Untornness, however, is accomplished by the complete non-breaking of the training precepts, by making amends for those broken for which amends should be made, by the absence of the seven bonds of sexuality, and, as well, by the non-arising of such evil things as anger, enmity, contempt, domineering, envy, avarice, deceit, fraud, obduracy, presumption, pride (conceit), haughtiness, conceit (vanity), and negligence (see M. Sutta 7), and by the arising of such qualities as fewness of wishes, contentment, and effacement (see M. Sutta 24).

152. Virtues not broken for the purpose of gain, etc., and rectified by making amends after being broken by the faults of negligence, etc., and not damaged by the bonds of sexuality and by such evil things as anger and enmity, are called entirely untorn, unrent, unblotched, and unmottled. And those same virtues are *liberating* since they bring about the state of a freeman, and *praised by the wise* since it is by the wise that they are praised, and *un-adhered-to* since they are not adhered to by means of craving and views, and *conducive to concentration* since they conduce to access concentration or to absorption concentration. That is why their untornness etc., should be understood as 'cleansing' (see also Ch. VII, §101f.).

153. This cleansing comes about in two ways: through seeing the danger of failure in virtue, and through seeing the benefit of perfected virtue. [54] Herein, the danger of failure in virtue can be seen in accordance with such suttas as that beginning 'Bhikkhus, there are these five dangers for the 'unvirtuous in the failure of virtue' (A.iii,252).

154. Furthermore, on account of his unvirtuousness an unvirtuous person is displeasing to deities and human beings, is uninstructable by his fellows in the life of purity, suffers when unvirtuousness is censured, and is remorseful when the virtuous are praised. Owing to that unvirtuousness he is as ugly as hemp cloth. Contact with him is painful because those who fall in with his views are brought to long-lasting suffering in the states of loss. He is worthless because he causes no great fruit [to accrue] to those who give him gifts. He is as hard to purify as a cesspit many years old. He is like a log from a pyre (see Iti. 99); for he is outside both [recluseship and the lay state]. Though claiming the bhikkhu

state he is no bhikkhu, so he is like a donkey following a herd of cattle. He is always nervous, like a man who is everyone's enemy. He is as unfit to live with as a dead carcase. Though he may have the qualities of learning, etc., he is an unfit for the homage of his fellows in the life of purity as a charnel-ground fire is for that of brahmans. He is as incapable of reaching the distinction of attainment as a blind man is of seeing a visible object. He is as careless of the Good Law as a guttersnipe is of a kingdom. Though he fancies he is happy, yet he suffers because he reaps suffering as told in the Discourse on the Mass of Fire (A.iv, 128–34).

155. Now the Blessed One has shown that when the unvirtuous have their minds captured by pleasure and satisfaction in the indulgence of the five cords of sense-desires, in [receiving] salutation, in being honoured, etc., the result of that kamma, directly visible in all ways, is very violent pain, with that [kamma] as its condition, capable of producing a gush of hot blood by causing agony of heart with the mere recollection of it. Here is the text:

'Bhikkhus, do you see that great mass of fire burning, 'blazing and glowing?—Yes, venerable sir.—What do you think, 'bhikkhus, which is better, that one [gone forth] should sit down 'or lie down embracing that mass of fire burning, blazing and 'glowing, or that he should sit down or lie down embrac- 'ing a warrior-noble maiden or a brahman maiden or a 'maiden of householder family, with soft, delicate hands and 'feet?—It would be better, venerable sir, that he should sit 'down or lie down embracing a warrior-noble maiden... '[55] It would be painful, venerable sir, if he sat down or lay 'down embracing that great mass of fire burning, blazing 'and glowing.

156. 'I say to you, bhikkhus, I declare to you, bhikkhus, that it 'would be better for one [gone forth] who is unvirtuous, who is 'evil-natured, of unclean and suspect habits, secretive of his 'acts, who is not an ascetic and claims to be one, who does not 'lead the life of purity and claims to do so, who is rotten within, 'lecherous, and full of corruption, to sit down or lie down 'embracing that great mass of fire burning, blazing and glow- 'ing. Why is that? By his doing so, bhikkhus, he might come 'to death or deadly suffering, yet he would not on that account, 'on the break up of the body, after death, reappear in states 'of loss, in any unhappy destiny, in perdition, in hell. But if 'one who is unvirtuous, evil-natured,...and full of corruption, 'should sit down or lie down embracing a warrior-noble 'maiden... that would be long for his harm and suffering: 'on the break up of the body, after death, he would reappear, 'in states of loss, in an unhappy destiny, in perdition, in hell' (A. iv, 128–9).

157. Having thus shown by means of the analogy of the mass of fire the suffering that is bound up with women and has as its condition the indulgence of the five cords of sense-desires [by the unvirtuous], to the same intent he showed, by the following similes of the horse-hair rope, the sharp spear, the iron sheet, the iron ball, the iron bed, the iron chair, and the iron cauldron, the pain that has as its condition [acceptance of] homage and reverential salutation, and the use of robes, alms food, bed and chair, and dwelling [by unvirtuous bhikkhus]:

'What do you think, bhikkhus, which is better, that 'one should have a strong horse-hair rope twisted round both 'legs by a strong man and tightened so that it cut through 'the outer skin, and having cut through the outer skin it cut 'through the inner skin, and having cut through the inner 'skin it cut through the flesh, and having cut through the 'flesh it cut through the sinews, and having cut through the 'sinews it cut through the bones, and having cut through the 'bones it remained crushing the bone-marrow—or that he 'should consent to the homage of great warrior nobles, great 'brahmans, great householders?' (A.iv,129), [56]

and 'What do you think, bhikkhus, which is better, that 'one should have a strong man wound one's breast with a sharp 'spear tempered in oil—or that he should consent to the 'reverential salutation of great warrior nobles, great brah'mans, great householders?' (A.iv,130),

and 'What do you think, bhikkhus, which is better, that 'one's body should be wrapped by a strong man in a red-hot 'iron sheet burning, blazing, and glowing—or that he should 'use robes given out of faith by great warrior nobles, great 'brahmans, great householders? (A.iv,130–1),

and 'What do you think, bhikkhus, which is better, that 'one's mouth should be prized open by a strong man with 'red-hot iron tongs burning, blazing and glowing, and that 'into his mouth should be put a red-hot iron ball burning, 'blazing and glowing, which burns his lips and burns his 'mouth and tongue and throat and belly and passes 'out below carrying with it his bowels and entrails—or that 'he should use alms food given out of faith by great warrior 'nobles,... (A.iv,131–2),

and 'What do you think bhikkhus, which is better, 'that one should have a strong man seize him by the 'head or seize him by the shoulders and seat him or lay him 'on a red-hot iron bed or iron chair, burning, blazing and 'glowing—or that he should use a bed or chair given out 'of faith by great warrior nobles,...?' (A.iv,132–3),

and 'What do you think, bhikkhus, which is better, 'that one should have a strong man take him feet up 'and head down and plunge him into a red-hot metal 'cauldron burning, blazing and glowing, to be boiled there in a 'swirl of froth, and as he boils in the swirl of froth to be 'swept now up, now down, and now across—or that he should 'use a dwelling given out of faith by great warrior nobles... ?, (A.iv.133–4).

158. What pleasure has a man of broken virtue
Forsaking not sense pleasures, which bear fruit
Of pain more violent even than the pain
In the embracing of a mass of fire?

What pleasure has he in accepting homage
Who, having failed in virtue, must partake
Of pain that will excel in agony
The crushing of his legs with horse-hair ropes? [57]

What pleasure has a man devoid of virtue
Accepting salutations of the faithful,
Which is the cause of pain acuter still
Than pain produced by stabbing with a spear ?

What is the pleasure in the use of garments
For one without restraint, whereby in hell
He will for long be forced to undergo
The contact of the blazing iron sheet ?

Although to him his alms food may seem tasty,
Who has no virtue, it is direst poison,
Because of which he surely will be made
For long to swallow burning iron balls.

And when the virtueless make use of couches
And chairs, though reckoned pleasing, it is pain
Because they will be tortured long indeed
On red-hot blazing iron beds and chairs.

Then what delight is there for one unvirtuous
Inhabiting a dwelling given in faith,
Since for that reason he will have to dwell
Shut up inside a blazing iron pan?

The Teacher of the world, in him condemning,
Described him in these terms: 'Of suspect habits,
Full of corruption, lecherous as well,
By nature evil, rotten too within'.

So out upon the life of him abiding
Without restraint, of him that wears the guise
Of the ascetic that he will not be,
And damages and undermines himself !

What is the life he leads, since any person,
No matter who, with virtue to his credit
Avoids it here, as those that would look well
Keep far away from dung or from a corpse?

He is not free from any sort of terror,
Though free enough from pleasure of attainment;
While heaven's door is bolted fast against him,
He is well set upon the road to hell.

Who else if not one destitute of virtue
More fit to be the object of compassion?
Many indeed and grave are the defects
That brand a man neglectful of his virtue.

Seeing danger in the failure of virtue should be understood as reviewing in such ways as these. And seeing benefits in perfected virtue should be understood in the opposite sense.

159. Furthermore, [58]

His virtue is immaculate,
His wearing of the bowl and robes
Gives pleasure and inspires trust,
His Going Forth will bear its fruit.

A bhikkhu in his virtue pure
Has never fear that self-reproach
Will enter in his heart: indeed
There is no darkness in the sun.

A Bhikkhu in his virtue bright
Shines forth in the Ascetics' Wood[41]
As by the brightness of his beams
The moon lights up the firmament.

Now if the bodily perfume
Of virtuous bhikkhus can succeed
In pleasing even deities,
What of the perfume of his virtue ?

It is more perfect far than all
The other perfumes in the world,
Because the perfume virtue gives
Is borne unchecked in all directions.

The deeds done for a virtuous man,
Though they be few, will bear much fruit,
And so the virtuous man becomes
A vessel of honour and renown.

There are no cankers here and now
To plague the virtuous man at all;
The virtuous man digs out the root
Of suffering in lives to come.

Perfection among human kind
And even among deities,
If wished for, is not hard to gain
For him whose virtue is perfected;

41. An allusion to the Gosiṅga Suttas (M. Suttas 31 and 32).

But once his virtue is perfected,
His mind then seeks no other kind
Than the perfection of nibbana,
The state where utter peace prevails.

Such is the blessed fruit of virtue,
Showing full many a varied form,
So let a wise man know it well
This root of all perfection's branches.

160. The mind of one who understands thus, shudders at failure in virtue and reaches out towards the perfecting of virtue. So virtue should be cleansed with all care, seeing this danger of failure in virtue and this benefit of the perfection of virtue in the way stated.

161. And at this point in the Path of Purification, which is shown under the headings of Virtue, Concentration and Understanding by the stanza, 'When a wise man, established well in virtue' (§1), Virtue, firstly, has been fully illustrated.

The first chapter called 'The Description of Virtue' in the Path of Purification composed for the purpose of gladdening good people.

CHAPTER II

DESCRIPTION OF THE ASCETIC PRACTICES

(*Dhutaṅga-niddesa*)

1. [59] Now while a meditator is engaged in the pursuit of virtue, he should set about undertaking the ascetic practices in order to perfect those special qualities of fewness of wishes, contentment, etc., by which the virtue of the kind already described is cleansed. For when his virtue is thus washed clean of stains by the waters of such special qualities as fewness of wishes, contentment, effacement, seclusion, dispersal, energy, and modest needs, it will become quite purified; and his vows will succeed as well. And so, when his whole behaviour has been purified by the special quality of blameless virtue and vows and he has become established in the [first] three of the ancient Noble One's Heritages, he may become worthy to attain to the fourth called 'delight in development' (A. ii, 27). We shall therefore begin the explanation of the ascetic practices.

[The 13 Kinds of Ascetic Practices]

2. Thirteen kinds of ascetic practices have been allowed by the Blessed One to clansmen who have given up the things of the flesh and, regardless of body and life, are desirous of undertaking a practice in conformity [with their aim]. They are:

i. the refuse-rag-wearer's practice,
ii. the triple-robe-wearer's practice,
iii. the alms-food-eater's practice,
iv. the house-to-house-seeker's practice,
v. the one-sessioner's practice,
vi. the bowl-food-eater's practice,
vii. the later-food-refuser's practice,
viii. the forest-dweller's practice,
ix. the tree-root-dweller's practice,
x. the open-air-dweller's practice,
xi. the charnel-ground-dweller's practice,
xii. the any-bed-user's practice,
xiii. the sitter's practice,

3. Herein,

(1) As to meaning, (2) character. etcetera,
(3) The undertaking and directions,
And then the grade, and breach as well,
And benefits of each besides,
(4) As to the profitable triad,

(5) 'Ascetic' and so on distinguished,
(6) And as to groups, and also (7) singly,
The exposition should be known. [60]

4. 1. Herein, *as to meaning*, in the first place.

i. It is 'refuse (*paṃsukūla*)' since, owing to its being found on refuse in any such place as a street, a charnel ground, or a midden, it belongs, as it were, to the refuse in the sense of being dumped in any one of these places. Or alternatively: like refuse it gets to a vile state (*PAMSU viya KUcchita-bhāvaṃ ULAti*), thus it is 'refuse (*paṃsukūla*)'; it goes to a vile state, is what is meant. The wearing of a refuse-[rag], which has acquired its derivative name[1] in this way, is 'refuse-[rag-wearing] (*paṃsukūla*)'. That is his habit, thus he is a 'refuse-[rag-wear-]er (*paṃsukūlika*)'. The practice (*aṅga*) of the refuse-[rag-wear]-er is the 'refuse-[rag-wear-]er's practice (*paṃsukūlikaṅga*)'. It is the action that is called the 'practice'. Therefore it should be understood as a term for that by undertaking which one becomes a refuse-[rag-wear-]er.

ii. In the same way, he has the habit of [wearing] the triple robe (*ti-cīvara*)—in other words, the cloak of patches, the upper garment, and the inner clothing—, thus he is a 'triple-robe-[wear-]er (*tecīvarika*)'. His practice is called the 'triple-robe-wearer's practice'.

5. iii. The dropping (*pāta*) of the lumps (*piṇḍa*) of material-sustenance (*āmisa*) called alms (*bhikkhā*) is 'alms food (*piṇḍa-pāta*)'; the falling (*nipatana*) into the bowl of lumps (*piṇḍa*) given by others, is what is meant. He gleans that alms food (that falling of lumps), he seeks it by approaching such and such a family, thus he is called an 'alms-food-[eat-]er (*piṇḍa-pātika*)'. Or his vow is to gather (*patituṃ*)[2] the lump (*piṇḍa*), thus he is a 'lump-gatherer (*piṇḍapātin*)'. To 'gather' is to wander for. A 'lump-gatherer (*piṇḍapātin*)' is the same as an 'alms-food-eater (*piṇḍapātika*)'. The practice of the alms-food-eater is the 'alms-food-eater's practice'.

6. iv. It is a hiatus (*avakhaṇḍana*) that is called a 'gap (*dāna*)'.[3] It is removed (*apeta*) from a gap, thus it is called 'gapless (*apadāna*)'; the meaning is, it is without hiatus. It is together with (*saha*) what is gapless (*apadāna*), thus it is 'with the gapless, (*sapadāna*)'; devoid of hiatus—from house to house—is what is meant. His habit is to wander on what-is-with-the-gapless, thus he is a 'gapless wanderer (*sapadāna-cārin*)'. A gapless wanderer is the same as a 'house-to-house seeker (*sapadāna-cārika*)'. His practice is the 'house-to-house-seeker's practice'.

---

1. '*Nibbacana*—derivative name (or verbal derivative)'; gram. term not in P.T.S.; see MA, i, 61, 105; Vis. Ch. XVI, §16.
2. '*Patati*—to gather (or to wander)': not in P.T.S. Dict.
3. '*Avakhaṇḍana*—hiatus' and '*dāna*—gap': not in P.T.S. Dict.

7. v. Eating in one session is 'one-session'. He has that habit, thus he is a 'one-sessioner'. His practice is the 'one-sessioner's practice.'

vi. Alms (*piṇḍa*) in one bowl (*patta*) only, because of refusing a second vessel, is 'bowl-alms (*patta-piṇḍa*)'. Now, making 'bowl-alms (*patta-piṇḍa*)' the name for the taking of alms-food in the bowl: bowl-alms-food is his habit, thus he is a 'bowl-food-eater (*pattapiṇḍika*)'. His practice is the 'bowl-food-eater's practice'.

8. vii. 'No (*khalu*)' is a particle in the sense of refusing [61]. Food (*bhatta*) obtained later by one who has shown that he is satisfied is called 'later-food (*paccha-bhatta*)'. The eating of that later food is 'later-food-eating'. Making 'later-food (*pacchā-bhatta*)' the name for that later-food-eating: later-food is his habit, thus he is a 'later-food-[eat-]er (*pacchābhattika*)'. Not a later-food-eater is a 'no-later-food-[eat-]er (*khalu-pacchā-bhattika*)', [that is, a 'later-food-refuser'.] This is the name for one who as an undertaking refuses extra food. But it is said in the commentary[4] 'Khalu is a certain kind of bird. 'When it has taken a fruit into its beak and that drops, it 'does not eat any more. This [bhikkhu] is like that'. Thus he is 'a later-food-refuser (*khalu-paccha-bhattika*)'. His practice is the 'later-food-refuser's practice'.

9. viii. His habit is dwelling in the forest, thus he is a 'forest-dweller'. His practice is the 'forest-dweller's practice'.

ix. Dwelling at the root of a tree is 'tree-root-dwelling.' He has that habit, thus he is a 'tree-root-dweller'. The practice of the tree-root-dweller is the 'tree-root-dweller's practice'.

x., xi. Likewise with the open-air-dweller and the charnel-ground-dweller.

10. xii. Only what has been distributed (*yad eva santhata*) is 'as distributed *yathā-santhata*)'. This is a term for the resting place first allotted thus 'This one falls to you'. He has the habit of dwelling in that as distributed, thus he is an 'as-distributed user (*yathāsanthatika*)', [that is, an 'any-bed-user'.] His practice is the 'any-bed-user's pratice.'

xiii. He has the habit of keeping to the sitting, [posture when resting], refusing to lie down, thus he is a 'sitter'. His practice is the 'sitter's practice'.

11. All these, however. are the practices (*aṅga*) of a bhikkhu who is ascetic (*dhuta*) because he has shaken off (*dhuta*) defilement by undertaking one or other of them. Or the knowledge that has got the name 'ascetic (*dhuta*)' because it shakes off (*dhunana*) defilement is a practice (*aṅga*) belonging to these, thus they are 'ascetic practices (*dhut-aṅga*)'. Or

4. Such references to 'the Commentary' are to the old Sinhalese commentary, no longer extant, from which Bhadantācariya Buddhaghosa drew his material.

alternatively, they are ascetic (*dhuta*) because they shake off (*niddhunana*) opposition, and they are practices (*aṅga*) because they are a way (*paṭipatti*).

This, firstly, is how the exposition should be known here 'as to meaning'.

12. 2. All of them have as their characteristic the volition of undertaking. For this is said [in the commentary] 'He who 'does the undertaking is a person. That whereby he does the 'undertaking is states of consciousness and consciousness-'concomitants. The volition of the act of undertaking is 'the ascetic practice. What it rejects is the instance'. All have the function of eliminating cupidity, and they manifest themselves with the production of non-cupidity. For their proximate cause they have the noble states consisting of fewness of wishes, and so on. [62] This is how the exposition should be known *as to characteristic, etc.*, here.

13. 3. As regards the five beginning with *the undertaking and directions*: during the Blessed One's lifetime all ascetic practices should be undertaken in the Blessed One's presence. After his attainment of nibbana this should be done in the presence of a principal disciple. When he is not available it should be done in the presence of one whose cankers are destroyed, of a Non-returner, of a Once-returner, of a Stream-enterer, of one who knows the three Pitakas, of one who knows two of the Pitakas, of one who knows one of the Pitakas, of one who knows one Collection,[5] of a teacher of the Commentaries. When he is not available it should be done in the presence of an observer of an ascetic practice. When he is not available, then after one has swept out the shrine terrace they can be undertaken seated in a reverential posture as though pronouncing them in the Fully Enlightened One's presence. Also it is permitted to undertake them by oneself.

And here should be told the story of the senior of the two brothers who were Elders at Cetiyapabbata and their fewness of wishes with respect to the ascetic practices (see MA.ii, 140).[6]

This, firstly, is what applies to all [the practices].

14. Now we shall proceed to comment on the undertaking, directions, grade, breach, and benefits, of each one [separately].

---

5. ' "*Ekasaṅgītika*": one who knows one of the five Collections (*nikāya*) beginning with the Collection of Long Discourses (*Dīgha-nikāya*)' Pm. 76).

6. 'That Elder, it seems, was a sitter, but no one knew it. Then one night the other saw him by the light of a flash of lightning sitting up on his bed. He asked "Are you a sitter, venerable sir?". Out of fewness of wishes that his ascetic practice should get known, the Elder lay down. Afterwards he undertook the practice anew. So the story has come down' (Pm. 77).

i. First, the *refuse-rag-wearer's practice* is *undertaken* with one of these two statements: 'I refuse robes given by householders' or 'I undertake the refuse-rag-wearer's practice'. This, firstly, is the *undertaking*.

15. One who has done this should get a robe of one of the following kinds: one from a charnel ground, one from a shop, a cloth from a street, a cloth from a midden, one from a childbed, an ablution cloth, a cloth from a washing place, one worn going to and returning from [the charnel ground], one scorched by fire, one gnawed by cattle, one gnawed by ants, one gnawed by rats, one cut at the end, one cut at the edge, one carried as a flag, a robe from a shrine, an ascetic's robe, one from a consecration, one produced by supernormal power, one from a highway, one borne by the wind, one presented by deities, one from the sea. Taking one of these robe cloths, he should tear off and throw away the weak parts, and then wash the sound parts and make up a robe. He can use it after getting rid of his old robe given by householders.

16. Herein, '*one from a charnel ground*' is one dropped on a charnel ground.

'*One from a shop*' is one dropped at the door of a shop.

'*A cloth from a street*' is a cloth thrown into a street from inside a window by those who seek merit.

'*A cloth from a midden*' [63] is a cloth thrown onto a place for rubbish.

'*One from a childbed*' is a cloth thrown away after wiping up the stains of childbirth with it. The mother of Tissa the Minister, it seems, had the stains of childbirth wiped up with a cloth worth a hundred [pieces], and thinking 'The refuse-rag wearers will take it', she had it thrown onto the Tālaveli Road'.[7] Bhikkhus took it for the purpose of mending worn places.

17. '*An ablution cloth*' is one that people who are made by devil doctors to bathe themselves, including their heads, are accustomed to throw away as a 'cloth of ill luck.'

'*A cloth from a washing place*' is rags thrown away at a washing place where bathing is done.

'*One worn going to and returning from*' is one that people throw away after they have gone to a charnel ground and returned and bathed.

'*One scorched by fire*' is one partly scorched by fire; for people throw that away.

'*One gnawed by cattle,*' etc., are obvious; for people throw away such as these too.

'*One carried as a flag*': Those who board a ship do so after hoisting a flag. It is allowable to take this when they have gone out of sight. Also it is allowable, when the two armies

7. 'The name of a street in Mahāgāma (S.E. Ceylon). Also in Anurādhapura, they say' (Pm. 77).

have gone away, to take a flag that has been hoisted on a battlefield.

18. '*A robe from a shrine*' is an offering made by draping an ant-hill [in cloth].

'*An ascetic's robe*' is one belonging to a bhikkhu.

'*One from a consecration*' is one thrown away at the king's consecration place.

'*One produced by supernormal power*' is a 'come-bhikkhu' robe.[8]

'*One from a highway*' is one dropped in the middle of a road. But one dropped by the owner's negligence should be taken only after waiting a while.

'*One borne by the wind*' is one that falls a long way off, having been carried by the wind. It is allowable to take it if the owners are not in sight.

'*One presented by deities*' is one given by deities like that given to the Elder Anuruddha (See DhA. ii, 173–4).

'*One from the sea*' is one washed up on dry land by the sea waves.

19. One given thus 'We give it to the Order' or got by those who go out for alms-cloth is not a refuse-rag. And in the case of one presented by a bhikkhu, one given after it has been got [at a presentation of robes by householders] at the end of the Rains, or a 'resting-place robe', [that is, one automatically supplied by a householder to the occupant of a certain resting place,] is not a refuse-rag. It is a refuse-rag only when given after not having been so obtained. And herein, that placed by the donors at a bhikkhu's feet but given by that bhikkhu to the refuse-rag wearer by placing it in his hand is called pure in one way. That given to a bhikkhu by placing it in his hand but placed by him at the [refuse-rag wearer's] feet is also pure in one way. That which is both placed at a bhikkhu's feet and then given by him in the same way is pure in both ways. [64] One obtained by being placed in the hand and [given by being] placed in the hand too is not a strict man's robe. So a refuse-rag wearer should use the robe after getting to know about the kinds of refuse-rags.

These are the *directions* for it in this instance.

20. The *grades* are these. There are three kinds of refuse-rag wearers: the strict, the medium, and the mild. Herein, one who takes it only from a charnel ground is strict. One who takes one left [by someone, thinking] 'One gone forth will take it' is medium. One who takes one given by being placed at his feet [by a bhikkhu] is mild.

---

8. On certain occasions, when the Going Forth was given by the Buddha with only the words '*Ehi bhikkhu* (come, bhikkhu)', owing to the disciple's past merit robes appeared miraculously upon him (see *e.g.* Vin. Mahāvagga, Kh. 1).

The moment any one of these of his own choice or inclination agrees to [accept] a robe given by a householder, his ascetic practice is broken. This is the *breach* in this instance.

21. The *benefits* are these. He actually practises in conformity with the Dependence, because of the words 'The Going Forth by 'depending on the refuse-rag robe' (Vin. i, 58, 96) ; he is established in the first of the Noble One's Heritages (see A.ii, 27) ; there is no suffering due to protecting ; he exists independent of others ; there is no fear of robbers ; there is no craving connected with use [of robes] ; it is a requisite suitable for an ascetic ; it is a requisite recommended by the Blessed One thus 'valueless, easy to get, and blameless ' (A. ii, 26) ; it inspires confidence ; it produces the fruits of fewness of wishes, etc. ; the right way is cultivated ; a good example is set[9] to later generations.

22. While striving for Death's army's rout
The ascetic clad in rag-robe clout
Got from a rubbish heap, shines bright
As mail-clad warrior in the fight.

This robe the world's great teacher wore,
Leaving rare Kāsi cloth and more ;—
Who would not have a robe to keep
Of rags from off a rubbish heap ?

Minding the words he did profess
When he went into homelessness,
Let him to wear such rags delight
As one in seemly garb bedight.

This, firstly, is the commentary on the undertaking, directions, grades, breach, and benefits, in the case of the refuse-rag-wearer's practice.

23. ii. Next there is the *triple-robe-wearer's practice*. This is undertaken with one of the following statements : 'I refuse a fourth robe ' or ' I undertake the triple-robe-wearer's practice '. [65]

When a triple-robe wearer has got cloth for a robe, he can put it by for as long as, owing to ill-health, he is unable to make it up, or for as long as he does not find a helper, or lacks needle, etc., and there is no fault in his putting it by. But it is not allowed to put it by once it has been dyed. That is called cheating the ascetic practice. These are the *directions* for it.

24. This too has three *grades*. Herein, one who is strict should, at the time of dyeing, first dye either the inner cloth or the upper garment, and having dyed it, he should wear that round the waist and dye the other. Then he can put that on over

9. '*Apādana*—institution (or production) ': not in P.T.S. Dict.

the shoulder and dye the cloak of patches. But he is not allowed to wear the cloak of patches round the waist. This is the duty when in an abode inside a village. But it is allowable for him in the forest to wash and dye two together. However, he should sit in place near [to the robes] so that, if he sees anyone, he can pull a yellow cloth over himself. But for the medium one there is a yellow cloth in the dyeing room for use while dyeing, and it is allowable for him to wear that [as an inner cloth] or to put it on [as an upper garment] in order to do the work of dyeing. For the mild one it is allowable to wear, or put on, the robes of bhikkhus who are in communion (i.e. not suspended, etc.) in order to do the work of dyeing. A bedspread that remains where it is[10] is also allowable for him, but he must not take it about him. And it is allowed for him to use from time to time the robes of bhikkhus who are in communion. It is allowed to one who wears the triple robe as an ascetic practice to have a yellow shoulder-cloth too as fourth ; but it must be only a span wide and three hands long.

The moment anyone of these three agrees to [accept] a fourth robe, his ascetic practice is broken. This is the *breach* in this instance.

25. The *benefits* are these. The bhikkhu who is a triple-robe wearer is content with the robe as a protection for the body. Hence he goes taking it with him as bird does its wings (see M.i, 180) ; and such special qualities as having few undertakings, avoidance of storage of cloth, a frugal existence, the abandoning of greed for many robes, living in effacement by observing moderation even in what is permitted, production of the fruits of fewness of wishes, etc., are perfected. [66]

26. No risk of hoarding haunts the man of wit
Who wants no extra cloth for requisite ;
Using the triple robe where'er he goes,
The pleasant relish of content he knows.

So, would the adept wander undeterred
With naught else but his robes, as flies the bird
With its own wings, then let him too rejoice
That frugalness in garments be his choice.

This is the commentary on the undertaking, directions, grades, breach, and benefits, in the case of the triple-robe-wearer's practice.

27. iii. The *alms-food-eater's practice* is *undertaken* with one of the following statements : 'I refuse a supplementary [food] supply' or 'I undertake the alms-food-eater's practice'.

10. '*Tatra-ṭṭhaka-paccattharaṇa*—a bedspread that remains there': 'A name for what has been determined upon as a bedspread in one's own resting place or in someone else's. They say accordingly (it is said in a commentary) that there is no breach of the ascetic practice even when

Now this alms-food eater should not accept the following fourteen kinds of meal : a meal offered to the Order, a meal offered to specified bhikkhus, an invitation, a meal given by a ticket,one each half-moon day,one each Uposatha day, one each first of the half-moon, a meal given for visitors, a meal for travellers, a meal for the sick, a meal for sick-nurses, a meal supplied to a [particular] residence, a meal given in a principal house,[11] a meal given in turn.

If, instead of saying 'Take a meal given to the Order', [meals] are given saying 'The Order is taking alms in our house ; you may take alms too', it is allowable to consent. Tickets from the Order that are not for actual food,[12] and also a meal cooked in a monastery, are allowable as well.

These are the *directions* for it.

28. This too has three *grades*. Herein, one who is strict takes alms brought both from before and from behind, and he gives the bowl to those who take it while he stands outside a door. He also takes alms brought to the refectory and given there. But he does not take alms by sitting [and waiting for it to be brought later] that day. The medium one takes it as well by sitting [and waiting for it to be brought later] that day ; but he does not consent to [its being brought] next day. The mild one consents to alms [being brought] on the next day and on the day after. Both these last miss the joy of an independent life. There is, perhaps, a preaching on the Noble Ones' Heritages (A.ii,28) in some village. The strict one says to the others ' Let us go, friends, and listen to the Dhamma'. One of them says ' I have been made to sit [and wait] by a man, venerable sir', and the other 'I have consented to [receive] alms tomorrow, venerable sir'. So they are both losers. The other wanders for alms in the morning and then he goes and savours the taste of the Dhamma. [67]

The moment any one of these three agrees to the extra gain consisting of a meal given to the Order, etc., his ascetic practice is broken. This is the *breach* in this instance.

29. The *benefits* are these. He actually practices in conformity with the Dependence because of the words 'The Going Forth ' by depending on the eating of lumps of alms food ' (Vin. I, 58, 96) ; he is established in the second of the Noble Ones' Heritages ; his existence is independent of others ; it is a requisite recommended by the Blessed One thus 'Valueless, 'easy to get, blameless' (A. ii,26) ; idleness is eliminated; livelihood is purified; the practice of the minor Training Rules

these two, that is, the bedspread and the undyed cloth, are kept as extra robes ' (Pm. 78–9). For *tatratthaka* (fixture) see also §61.

11. 'A meal to be given by setting it out in a principal house only (Pm. 79). This meaning of *dhura-bhatta* not in P.T.S. Dict.

12. ' Tickets that are not for actual food, but deal with medicine, etc. ' (Pm. 79). *Paṭikkamana*—refectory ' (§28) = .*bojun hal* (eating hall) ' in Sinhalese translation.

[of the Pāṭimokkha] is fulfilled ; he is not maintained by another; he helps others; pride is abandoned; craving for tastes is checked ; the training precepts about eating as a group, substituting one meal [invitation for another] (See Vin. Pācittiya 33 and Comy.),and good behaviour,are not contravened;his life conforms to [the principles of] fewness of wishes; he cultivates the right way; he has compassion for later generations.

30. The monk content with alms for food
Has independent livelihood,
And greed in him no footing finds ;
He is as free as the four winds.

He never need be indolent,
His livelihood is innocent,
So let a wise man not disdain
Alms-gathering for his domain.

Since it is said :

'If a bhikkhu can support himself on alms
'And live without another's maintenance,
'And pay no heed as well to gain and fame,
'The very gods indeed might envy him' (Ud. 31).

This is the commentary on the undertaking, directions, grades, breach, and benefits, in the case of the alms-food-eater's practice.

31. iv. The *house-to-house-seeker's practice* is *undertaken* with one of the following statements : 'I refuse a greedy alms round' or 'I undertake the house-to-house-seeker's practice'.

Now the house-to-house seeker should stop at the village gate and make sure that there is no danger. If there is danger in any street or village, it is allowable to leave it out and wander for alms elsewhere. When there is a house door or a street or a village where he [regularly] gets nothing at all, he can go [past it] not counting it as the village. But wherever he gets anything at all it is not allowed [subsequently] to go [past] there and leave it out. This bhikkhu should enter the village early so that he will be able to leave out any inconvenient place and go elsewhere. [68] But if people who are giving a gift [of a meal] in a monastery or who are coming along the road take his bowl and give alms food, it is allowable. And as this [bhikkhu] is going along the road, he should, when it is the time, wander for alms in any village he comes to and not pass it by. If he gets nothing there or only a little, he should wander for alms in the next village in order. These are the *directions* for it.

32. This too has three *grades*. Herein, one who is strict does not take alms brought from before or brought from behind or brought to the refectory and given there. He hands over his bowl at a door, however ; for in this ascetic practice there is none equal to the Elder Mahā Kassapa, yet an instance in

which even he handed over his bowl is mentioned (see Ud. 29). The medium one takes what is brought from before and from behind and what is brought to the refectory, and he hands over his bowl at a door. But he does not sit waiting for alms. Thus he conforms to the rule of the strict alms-food eater. The mild one sits waiting [for alms to be brought] that day.

The ascetic practice of these three is broken as soon as the greedy alms round starts [by going only to the houses where good alms food is given]. This is the *breach* in this instance.

33. The *benefits* are these. He is always a stranger among families and is like the moon (see S. ii, 197); he abandons avarice about families; he is compassionate impartially; he avoids the dangers in being supported by a family; he does not delight in invitations; he does not hope for [meals] to be brought; his life conforms to [the principles of] fewness of wishes, and so on.

34. The monk who at each house his begging plies
Is moonlike, ever new to families,
Nor does he grudge to help all equally,
Free from the risks of house-dependency.

Who would the self-indulgent round forsake
And roam the world at will, the while to make
His downcast eyes range a yoke-length before,
Then let him wisely seek from door to door.

This is the commentary on the undertaking, directions, grades, breach, and benefits, in the case of the house-to-house-seeker's practice. [69]

35. v. The *one-sessioner's practice* is *undertaken* with one of the following statements: 'I refuse eating in several sessions' or 'I undertake the one-sessioner's practice'.

When the one-sessioner sits down in the sitting hall, instead of sitting on an elder's seat, he should notice which seat is likely to fall to him and sit down on that. If his teacher or preceptor arrives while the meal is still unfinished, it is allowable for him to get up and do the duties. But the Elder Tipiṭaka Cūḷa-Abhaya said 'He should either keep his seat [and finish his meal] or [if he gets up he should leave the rest of] his meal [in order not to break the ascetic practice]. And this is one whose meal is still unfinished; therefore let him do the duties, but in that case let him not eat the [rest of the] meal'. These are the *directions*.

36. This too has three *grades*. Herein, one who is strict may not take anything more than the food that he has laid his hand on, whether it is little or much. And if people bring him ghee, etc., thinking 'The Elder has eaten nothing', while these are allowable for the purpose of medicine, they are not so for the purpose of food. The medium one may take more as long as the meal in the bowl is not exhausted; for he is called 'One who stops when the food is finished.' The mild one may

eat as long as he does not get up from his seat. He is either 'One who stops with the water' because he eats until he takes [water for] washing the bowl, or 'One who stops with the session' because he eats until he gets up.

The ascetic practice of these three is broken at the moment when food has been eaten at more than one session. This is the breach in this instance.

37. The *benefits* are these. He has little affliction and little sickness ; he has lightness, strength, and a happy life ; there is no contravening [rules] about food that is not what is left over from a meal ; craving for tastes is eliminated ; his life conforms to the [principles of] fewness of wishes, and so on.

38. No illness due to eating shall he feel
Who gladly in one session takes his meal ;
No longing to indulge his sense of taste
Tempts him to leave his work to go to waste.

His own true happiness a monk may find
In eating in one session, pure in mind.
Purity and effacement wait on this ;
For it gives reason to abide in bliss.

This is the commentary on the undertaking, directions, grades, breach, and benefits, in the case of the non-sessioner's practice. [70]

39. vi. The *bowl-food-eater's practice* is *undertaken* with one of the following statements : 'I refuse a second vessel' or 'I undertake the bowl-food-eater's practice'.

When at the time of drinking rice gruel, the bowl-food eater gets curry that is put in a dish, he can first either eat the curry or drink the rice gruel. If he puts it in the rice gruel, the rice gruel becomes repulsive when a curry made with cured fish, etc., is put into it. So it is allowable [to do this] only in order to use it without making it repulsive. Consequently this is said with reference to such curry as that. But what is unrepulsive, such as honey, sugar,[13] etc., should be put into it. And in taking it he should take the right amount. It is allowable to take green vegetables with the hand and eat them. But unless he does that they should be put into the bowl. Because a second vessel has been refused it is not allowable [to use] anything else, not even the leaf of a tree. These are its *directions*.

40. This too has three *grades*. Herein, for one who is strict, except at the time of eating sugarcane, it is not allowed [while eating] to throw rubbish away, and it is not allowed while eating to break up rice-lumps, fish, meat and cakes. [The rubbish should be thrown away and the rice-lumps, etc., broken up before starting to eat.] The medium one is

13. '*Sakkarā*—sugar': spelt *sakkharā* in P.T.S. Dict.

allowed to break them up with one hand while eating ; and he is called a 'Hand Ascetic'. The mild one is called a 'Bowl Ascetic' ; anything that can be put into his bowl he is allowed, while eating, to break up, [that is, rice lumps, etc.,] with his hand or [such things as palm sugar, ginger, etc.,] with his teeth.

The moment any one of these three agrees to a second vessel his ascetic practice is broken. This is the *breach* in this instance.

41. The *benefits* are these. Craving for variety of tastes is eliminated ; excessiveness of wishes is abandoned ; he sees the purpose and the [right] amount in nutriment ; he is not bothered with carrying saucers, etc., about ; his life conforms to [the principles of] fewness of wishes and so on.

42. He baffles doubts that might arise
With extra dishes ; downcast eyes
The true devotedness imply[14]
Of one uprooting gluttony.

Wearing content as if 'twere part
Of his own nature, glad at heart ;
None but a Bowl-food Eater may
Consume his food in such a way.

This is the commentary on the undertaking, directions, grades, breach, and benefits, in the case of the bowl-food-eater's practice. [71]

43. vii. The *later-food-refuser's practice* is *undertaken* with one of the following statements : 'I refuse additional food' or 'I undertake the later-food-refuser's practice'.

Now when that later-food refuser has shown that he is satisfied, he should not again have the food made allowable [by having it put into his hands according to the rule for bhikkhus] and eat it. These are the *directions* for it.

44. This too has three *grades*. Herein, there is no showing that he has had enough with respect to the first lump, but there is when he refuses more while that is being swallowed. So when one who is strict has thus shown that he has had enough [with respect to the second lump], he does not eat the second lump after swallowing the first. The medium one eats also that food with respect to which he has shown that he has had enough. But the mild one who goes on eating until he gets up from his seat.

The moment any one of these three has eaten what has been made allowable [again] after he has shown that he has had enough, his ascetic practice is broken. This is the *breach* in this instance.

45. The *benefits* are these. One is far from committing an offence concerned with extra food; there is no overloading of the stomach ; there is no keeping food back ; there is no

14. '*Subbata*—truly devoted': fm. *su+vata* (having good vows). See also §59.

renewed search [for food] ; he lives in conformity with [the principles of] fewness of wishes, and so on.

46. When a wise man refuses later-food
He needs no extra search in weary mood,
Nor stores up food till later in the day,
Nor overloads his stomach in this way.

So, would the adept from such faults abstain,
Let him assume this practice for his gain,
Praised by the Blessed One, which will augment
The special qualities such as content.

This is the commentary on the undertaking, directions, grades, breach, and benefits, in the case of the later-food-refuser's practice.

47. viii. The *forest-dweller's practice* is *undertaken* with one of the following statements : ' I refuse an abode in a village ' or ' I undertake the forest-dweller's practice '.

48. Now that forest dweller must leave an abode in a village in order to meet the dawn in the forest. Herein, a village abode is the village itself with its precincts'. A 'village' may consist of one cottage or several cottages, it may be enclosed by a wall or not, have human inhabitants or not, and it can also be a caravan that is inhabited for more than four months. [72] The 'village precincts' cover the range of a stone thrown by a man of medium stature standing between the gate-posts of a walled village, if there are two gate-posts, as at Anurādhapura (Cf. Vin. iii, 46). The Vinaya experts say that this [stone's throw] is characterized as up to the place where a thrown stone falls, as, for instance, when young men exercise their arms and throw stones in order to show off their strength. But the Suttanta experts say that it is up to where one thrown to scare crows normally fails. In the case of an unwalled village, the house precinct is where the water falls when a woman standing in the door of the outermost house of all throws water from a basin. Within a stone's throw of the kind already described from that point is the village. Within a second stone's throw is the village precinct.

49. ' Forest ', according to the Vinaya method firstly, is described thus : ' Except the village and its precincts, all is forest' (Vin. iii, 46). According to the Abhidhamma method it is described thus : ' Having gone out beyond the boundary post, ' all that is forest ' (Vbh. 251 ; Ps. i, 176). But according to the Suttanta method its characteristic is this : ' A forest abode is ' five hundred bow-lengths distant ' (Vin. iv, 183). That should be defined by measuring it with a strung instructor's bow from the gate-post of a walled village, or from the range of the first stone's throw from an unwalled one, up to the monastery wall.

50. But if the monastery is not walled, it is said in the Vinaya commentaries, it should be measured by making the first dwelling of all the limit, or else the refectory or regular meeting place or Bodhi Tree or shrine, even if that is far from a dwelling [belonging to the monastery]. But in the Majjhima commentary it is said that, omitting the precincts of the monastery and the village, the distance to be measured is that between where the two stones fall. This is the measure here.

51. Even if the village is close by and the sounds of men are audible to people in the monastery, still if it is not possible to go straight to it because of rocks, rivers, etc., in between, the five hundred bow-lengths can be reckoned by that road even if one has to go by boat. But any one who blocks the path to the village here and there for the purpose of [lengthening it so as to be able to say that he is] taking up the practice is cheating the ascetic practice.

52. If a forest-dwelling bhikkhu's preceptor or teacher is ill and does not get what he needs in the forest, [73] he should take him to a village abode and attend him there. But he should leave in time to meet the dawn in a place proper for the practice. If the affliction increases towards the time of dawn, he must attend him and not bother about the purity of this ascetic practice.

These are the *directions*.

53. This too has three *grades*. Herein, one who is strict must always meet the dawn in the forest. The medium one is allowed to live in a village for the four months of the Rains. And the mild one, for the winter months too.

If in the period defined any one of these three goes from the forest and hears the Dhamma in a village abode, his ascetic practice is not broken if he meets the dawn there nor is it broken if he meets it as he is on his way back after hearing [the Dhamma]. But if, when the preacher has got up, he thinks 'We shall go after lying down awhile' and he meets the dawn while asleep or if of his own choice he meets the dawn while in a village abode, then his ascetic practice is broken. This is the *breach* in this instance.

54. The *benefits* are these. A forest-dwelling bhikkhu who has given attention to the perception of forest (see M. sutta 121) can obtain hitherto unobtained concentration, or preserve that already obtained. And the Master is pleased with him, according as it is said 'So, Nāgita, I am pleased with that bhikkhu's 'dwelling in the forest' (A. iii. 343). And when he lives in a remote abode his mind is not distracted by unsuitable visible objects, and so on. He is free from anxiety; he abandons attachment to life; he enjoys the taste of the bliss of seclusion, and the state of the refuse-rag wearer, etc., becomes him.

55. He lives secluded and apart,
Remote abodes delight his heart ;
The Saviour of the world, besides,
He gladdens that in groves abides.
The hermit that in woods can dwell
Alone, may gain the bliss as well
Whose savour is beyond the price
Of royal bliss in paradise.
Wearing the robe of rags he may
Go forth into the forest fray ;
Such is his mail, for weapons too
The other practices will do.
One so equipped can be assured
Of routing Māra and his horde.
So let the forest glades delight
A wise man for his dwelling's site.

This is the commentary on the undertaking, directions, grades, breach, and benefits, in the case of the forest-dweller's practice. [74]

56. ix. The *tree-root-dweller's practice* is *undertaken* with one of the following statements : 'I refuse a roof' or 'I undertake the tree-root-dweller's practice.

The tree-root dweller should avoid such trees as a tree near a frontier, a shrine tree, a gum tree, a fruit tree, a bats' tree, a hollow tree, or a tree standing in the middle of a monastery. He can choose a tree standing on the outskirts of a monastery. These are the *directions*.

57. This has three *grades* too. Herein, one who is strict is not allowed to have a tree that he has chosen tidied up. He can move the fallen leaves with his foot while dwelling there. The medium one is allowed to get it tidied up by those who happen to come along. The mild one can take up residence there after summoning monastery attendants and novices and getting them to clear it up, level it, strew sand and make a fence round with a gate fixed in it.

On a special day a tree-root dweller should sit in some concealed place elsewhere rather than there.

The moment any one of these three makes his abode under a roof, his ascetic practice is broken. The Reciters of the Anguttara say that it is broken as soon as he knowingly meets the dawn under a roof. This is the *breach* in this instance.

58. The *benefits* are these. He practices in conformity with the Dependence, because of the words. 'The Going Forth by 'depending on the root of a tree as an abode' (Vin. i. 58, 96) ; it is a requisite recommended by the Blessed One thus, 'Valueless, easy to get, and blameless' (A. ii, 26) ; perception of impermanence is aroused through seeing the continual alteration of young leaves ; avarice about abodes and love of

[building] work are absent ; he dwells in the company of dieties ; he lives in conformity with [the principles of] fewness of wishes, and so on.

59. The Blessed One praised roots of trees
As one of the Dependencies (Vin. i, 58) ;
Can he that loves secludedness
Find such another dwelling place ?
Secluded at the roots of trees
And guarded well by deities
He lives in true devotedness
Nor covets any dwelling place. [75]
And when the tender leaves are seen
Bright red at first, then turning green,
And then to yellow as they fall
He sheds belief once and for all
In permanence. Tree roots have been
Bequeathed by Him ; secluded scene
No wise man will disdain at all
For contemplating [Rice and Fall].

This is the commentary on the undertaking, directions, grades, breach, and benefits, in the case of the tree-root-dweller's practice.

60. x. The *open-air-dweller's practice* is *undertaken* with one of the following statements : ' I refuse a roof and a tree root ' or ' I undertake the open-air-dweller's practice '.

An open-air dweller is allowed to enter the Uposatha-house for the purpose of hearing the Dhamma or for the purpose of the Uposatha. If it rains while he is inside, he can go out when the rain is over instead of going out while it is still raining. He is allowed to enter the eating hall or the fire room in order to do the duties, or to go under a roof in order to ask elder bhikkhus in the eating hall about a meal, or when teaching and taking lessons, or to take beds, chairs, etc., inside that have been wrongly left outside. If he is going along a road with a requisite belonging to a senior and it rains, he is allowed to go into a wayside rest house. If he has nothing with him, he is not allowed to hurry in order to get to a rest house ; but he can go at his normal pace and enter it and stay there as long as it rains. These are the *directions* for it. And the same rule applies to the tree-root dweller too.

61. This has three *grades* too. Herein, one who is strict is not allowed to live near a tree or a rock or a house. He should make a robe-tent right out in the open and live in that. The medium one is allowed to live near a tree or a rock or a house so long as he is not covered by them. The mild one is allowed these : a [rock] overhang without a drip-ledge cut in it,[15] a

15. Reading *acchinna-mariyādam* with Pm., which says " *Without a dripledge cut* (*acchinnamariyādam*) " means without a drip-ledge (*mari-*

hut of branches, cloth stiffened with paste, and a tent treated as a fixture, that has been left by field watchers, and so on.

The moment any one of these three goes under a roof or to a tree root to dwell there, [76] his ascetic practice is broken. The Reciters of the Aṅguttara say that it is broken as soon as he knowingly meets the dawn there. This is the *breach* in this case.

62. The *benefits* are these : the impediment of dwellings is severed ; stiffness and torpor are expelled ; his conduct deserves the praise ' Like deer the bhikkhus live unattached and ' homeless ' (S. i, 199) he is detached ; he is [free to go in] any direction ; he lives in conformity with [the principles of] fewness of wishes, and so on.

63.
The open air provides a life
That aids the homeless bhikkhu's strife,
Easy to get, and leaves his mind
Alert as a deer, so he shall find

Stiffness and torpor brought to halt.
Under the star-bejewelled vault
The moon and sun furnish his light,
And concentration his delight.

The joy seclusion's savour gives
He shall discover soon who lives
In open air ; and that is why
The wise prefer the open aky.

This is the commentary on the undertaking, directions, grades, breach, and benefits, in the case of the open-air-dweller's practice.

64. xi. The *charnel-ground-dweller's practice* is *undertaken with* one of the following statements : ' I refuse what is not a charnel ground ' or ' I undertake the charnel-ground-dweller's practice '.

Now the charnel-ground dweller should not live in some place just because the people who built the village have called it ' the charnel ground ' for it is not a charnel ground unless a dead body has been burnt on it. But as soon as one has been burnt on it it becomes charnel ground. And even if it has been neglected for a dozen years, it is so still.

---

yāda) made above, which might come under the heading of a drip-ledge (*mariyādasaṅkhepena*) made to prevent rain water from coming in. But if the rain water comes under the overhang (*pabbhāra*) and is allowed to go in under it, then this comes under the heading of the open air (*abbhokāsikasankhepa*) ' (Pm. 84). This seems to refer to the widespread habit in ancient Ceylon of cutting a drip-ledge on overhanging rocks used for bhikkhu's dwellings so that the rain that falls on top of the rock drips down in front of the space under the overhang instead of trickling down under the rock and wetting the back and floor. *Pabbhāra* in this context is ' overhang ' rather than ' slope '.

65. One who dwells there, should not be the sort of person who gets walks, pavilions, etc., built, has beds and chairs set out and drinking and washing water kept ready, and preaches Dhamma; for this ascetic practice is a momentous thing. Whoever goes to live there should be diligent. And he should first inform the senior elder of the Order or the king's local representative in order to prevent trouble. When he walks up and down, he should do so looking at the pyre with half an eye. [77] On his way to the charnel ground he should avoid the main roads and take a by-path. He should define all the objects [there] while it is day, so that they will not assume frightening shapes for him at night. Even if non-human beings wander about screeching, he must not hit them with anything. It is not allowed to miss going to the charnel ground even for a single day. The Reciters of the Anguttara say that after spending the middle watch in the charnel ground he is allowed to leave in the last watch. He should not take such foods as sesamum flour, pease pudding, fish, meat, milk, oil, sugar, etc., which are liked by non-human beings. He should not enter the homes of families.[16] These are the *directions* for it.

66. This has three *grades* too. Herein, one who is strict should live where there are always burnings and corpses and mourning. The medium one is allowed to live where there is one of these three. The mild one is allowed to live in a place that possesses the bare characteristics of a charnel ground already stated.

When any one of these three makes his abode in some place not a charnel ground, his ascetic practice is broken. It is on the day on which he does not go to the charnel ground, the Aṅguttara Reciters say. This is the *breach* in this case.

67. The *benefits* are these. He acquires mindfulness of death; he lives diligently; the sign of foulness is available (see Ch. VI); greed for sense desires is removed; he constantly sees the body's true nature; he has a great sense of urgency; he abandons vanity of health, etc.; he vanquishes fear and dread (see M. Sutta 4); non-human beings respect and honour him; he lives in conformity with [the principles of] fewness of wishes, and so on.

68. Even in sleep the dweller in a charnel ground shows naught
Of negligence, for death is ever present to his thought;
He may be sure there is no lust after sense pleasure preys
Upon his mind, with many corpses present to his gaze.
Rightly he strives because he gains a sense of urgency,
While in his search for final peace he curbs all vanity.

---

16. 'He should not go into families' houses because he smells of the dead and is followed by *Pisāca* goblins' (Pm. 84).

Let him that feels a leaning to nibbana in his heart
Embrace this practice for it has rare virtues to impart.

This is the commentary on the undertaking, directions, grades, breach, and benefits, in the case of the charnel-ground dweller's practice. [78]

69. xii. The *any-bed-user's practice* is *undertaken* with one of the following statements : ' I refuse greed for resting places ' or ' I undertake the any-bed-user's practice '.

The any-bed user should be content with whatever resting place he gets thus : ' This falls to your lot '. He must not make anyone else shift [from his bed]. These are the *directions*.

70. This has three *grades* too. Herein, one who is strict is not allowed to ask about the resting place that has fallen to his lot ' Is it far ?' or ' Is it too near ?' or ' Is it infested by inhuman beings, snakes, and so on ?' or ' Is it hot ?' or ' Is it cold ?'. The medium one is allowed to ask, but not to go and inspect it. The mild one is allowed to inspect it and, if he does not like it, to choose another.

As soon as greed for resting places arises in any one of these three, his ascetic practice is broken. This is the *breach* in this instance.

71. The *benefits* are these. The advice ' He should be content ' with what he gets ' (Jā. i, 476 ; Vin. iv, 259) is carried out ; he regards the welfare of his fellows in the life of purity ; he gives up caring about inferiority and superiority ; approval and disapproval are abandoned ; the door is closed against excessive wishes ; he lives in conformity with [the principles] of fewness of wishes, and so on.

72. One vowed to any bed will be
Content with what he gets, and he
Can sleep in bliss without dismay
On nothing but a spread of hay.

He is not eager for the best,
No lowly couch does he detest,
He aids his young companions too
That to the monk's good life are new.

So for a wise man to delight
In any kind of bed is right ;
A Noble One this custom loves
As one the Sage's Lord approves.

This is the commentary on the undertaking, directions, grades, breach, and benefits, in the case of any-bed-user's practice.

73. xiii. The *sitter's practice* is *undertaken* with one of the following statements : ' I refuse lying down ' or ' I undertake the sitter's practice '.

The sitter can get up in any one of three watches of the night and walk up and down ; for lying down is the only posture not allowed. These are the *directions*. [79]

74. This has three *grades* too. Herein, one who is strict is not allowed a back-rest or cloth band or binding-strap [to prevent falling while asleep].[17] The medium one is allowed any one of these three. The mild one is allowed a back-rest, a cloth band, a binding-strap, a cushion, ' five-limb ' and a ' seven-limb '. A ' five-limb ' is [a chair] made with [four legs and] a support for the back. A ' seven-limb ' is one made with [four legs], a support for the back and an [arm] support on each side. They made that, it seems, for the Elder Pīṭhābhaya (Abhaya of the Chair). The Elder became a Non-returner, and then attained nibbana.

As soon as any one of these three lies down, his ascetic practice is broken. This is the *breach* in this instance.

75. The *benefits* are these. The mental shackle described thus, 'He ' dwells indulging in the pleasure of lying prone, the pleasure ' of lolling, the pleasure of torpor ' (M. i, 102), is severed ; his state is suitable for devotion to any meditation subject ; his deportment inspires confidence ; his state favours the application of energy ; he develops the right practice.

76. The adept that can place crosswise
His feet to rest upon his thighs
And sit with back erect shall make
Foul Māra's evil heart to quake.

No more in supine joys to plump
And wallow in lethargic dump ;
Who sits for rest and finds it good
Shines forth in the Ascetics' Wood.

The happiness and bliss it brings
Has naught to do with worldly things ;
So must the Sitter's Vow befit
The manners of a man of wit.

This is the commentary on the undertaking, directions, grades, breach, and benefits, in the case of the sitter's practice.

77. Now there is the commentary according to the stanza :

(4) As to the Profitable Triad,
(5) ' Ascetic ' and so on distinguished,
(6) As to groups, and also (7) singly,
The exposition should be known (see §3).

78. 4. Herein, *as to the Profitable Triad* (see Dhs. p. 1) : all the ascetic practices, that is to say, those of trainers, ordinary men, and men whose cankers have been destroyed, may be

17. ' *Āyogapaṭṭa*—a binding-strap ' : this is probably the meaning. But cf. Vin. ii, 135 and Vin. A. 891.

either profitable or [in the Arahant's case] indeterminate. [80] No ascetic practice is unprofitable. But if someone should say : There is also an unprofitable ascetic practice because of the words 'One of evil wishes, a prey to wishes, becomes a forest dweller' (A. iii, 219), etc., he should be told : We have not said that he does not live in the forest with unprofitable consciousness. Whoever has his dwelling in the forest is a forest dweller ; and he may be one of evil wishes or of few wishes. But, as it was said above (§ 11), they 'are the practices (*aṅga*) of a bhikkhu who is ascetic (*dhuta*) because he has shaken off (*dhuta*) defilement by undertaking one or other of them. Or the knowledge that has got the name "ascetic (*dhuta*)" because it shakes off (*dhunana*) defilement is a practice (*aṅga*) belonging to these, thus they are "ascetic practices (*dhutaṅga*)". Or alternatively, they are ascetic (*dhuta*) because they shake off (*niddhunana*) opposition, and they are practices (*aṅga*) because they are a way (*paṭipatti*)'. Now no one called 'ascetic' on account of what is unprofitable could have these as his practices ; nor does what is unprofitable shake off anything so that those things to which it belonged as a practice could be called 'ascetic practices'. And what is unprofitable does not both shake off cupidity for robes, etc., and become the practice of the way. Consequently it was rightly said that no ascetic practice is unprofitable.

79. And those who hold that an ascetic practice is outside the Profitable Triad[18] have no ascetic practice as regards meaning. Owing to the shaking off of what could what is non-existent be called an ascetic practice ? Also there are the words 'Proceeded to undertake the ascetic qualities' (Vin. iii, 15), and it follows[19] that those words are contradicted. So that should not be accepted.

This, in the first place, is the commentary on the Profitable Triad.

80. 5. *As to 'ascetic' and so on distinguished* ; the following things should be understood, that is to say, ascetic, a preacher of asceticism, ascetic states, ascetic practices, and for whom the cultivation of ascetic practices is suitable.

81. Herein, *ascetic* means either a person whose defilements are shaken off, or a state that entails shaking off defilements.

---

18. For the triads of the Abhidhamma Mātikā (Abhidhamma Schedule) see Ch. XIII, n. 20.

"'*Those who hold*" : a reference to the inhabitants of the Abhayagiri Monastery at Anurādhapura. For they say that ascetic practice is a concept consisting in a name (*nāma-paññatti*). That being so, they could have no meaning of shaking off defilements, or possibility of being undertaken, because in the ultimate sense they would be non-existent [concepts having no existence]' (Pm. 87). Cf. Ch. IV, §29.

19. *Āpajjati* (and its noun *āpatti*) is the normal word used for undesirable consequences that follow on some unsound logical proposition. See Ch. XVI, § 68f. This meaning not in P.T.S. Dict.

A preacher of asceticism : one is ascetic but not a preacher of asceticism, another is not ascetic but a preacher of asceticism, another is neither ascetic nor a preacher of asceticism, and another is both ascetic and a preacher of asceticism.

82. Herein, one who has shaken off his defilements with an ascetic practice but does not advise and instruct another in an ascetic practice, like the Elder Bakkula, is ' ascetic but not a preacher of asceticism ', according as it is said ' Now the vener- 'able Bakkula was ascetic but not a preacher of asceticism '. One who [81] has not shaken off his own defilements but only advises and instructs another in an ascetic practice, like the Elder Upananda is ' not ascetic but a preacher of asceticism', according as it is said 'Now the venerable Upananda ' son of the Sakyans was not ascetic but a preacher of ' asceticism '. One who has failed in both, like Lāludāyin, is ' neither ascetic nor a preacher of asceticism ', according as it is said ' Now the venerable Lāludāyin was neither ascetic nor ' a preacher of asceticism '. One who has succeeded in both, like the General of the Dhamma, is ' both ascetic and a preacher of asceticism ', according as it is said ' Now the venerable ' Sāriputta was ascetic and a preacher of asceticism '.

83. *Ascetic states :* the five states that go with the volition of an ascetic practice, that is to say, fewness of wishes, content- ment, effacement, seclusion, and that specific quality[20] are called ' ascetic states ' because of the words ' Depending ' on fewness of wishes ' (A. iii, 219), and so on.

84. Herein, *fewness of wishes* and *contentment* are non-agreed. *Effacement* and *seclusion* belong to the two states, non- green and non-delusion. *That specific quality* is knowledge. Herein, by means of non-greed a man shakes off greed for things that are forbidden. By means of non-delusion he shakes off the declusion that hides the dangers in those same things. And by means of non-greed he shakes off indulgence in pleasure due to sense desires that occurs under the heading of using what is allowed. And by means of non-delusion he shakes off indulgence in self mortification that occurs under the heading of excessive effacement in the ascetic practices. That is why these states should be understood as ' ascetic states '.

85. *Ascetic practices :* these should be understood as the thirteen that is to say, the refuse-rag-wearer's practice, ... the sitter's practice, which have already been described as to meaning and as to characteristic, and so on.

---

20. *Idamatthitā*—That specific quality ' : ' Owing to these profitable states it exists, (thus it is " specific by those " *imehi kusaladhammehi atthi= idam-atthi*). The knowledge by means of which one who has gone forth should be established in the refuse-rag-wearer's practice, etc., and by means of which, on being so instructed, one undertakes and persists in the ascetic qualities—that knowledge is *idamatthitā* ' (Pm. 88).

86. *For whom the cultivation of ascetic practices is suitable :* [they are suitable] for one of greedy temperament and for one of deluded temperament. Why ? Because the cultivation of ascetic practices is both a difficult progress[21] and an abiding in effacement ; and greed subsides with the difficult progress, while delusion is got rid of in those diligent by effacement. Or the cultivation of the forest-dweller's practice and the tree-root-dweller's practice here are suitable for one of hating temperament ; for hate too subsides in one who dwells there without coming into conflict.

This is the commentary ' as to " ascetic " and so on distinguished '. [82]

87. 6. and 7. *As to groups and also singly.* Now 6. *as to groups :* these ascetic practices are in fact only eight, that is to say, three principal and five individual practices. Herein, the three, namely, the house-to-house-seeker's practice, the one-sessioner's practice, and the open-air-dweller's practice, are principal practices. For one who keeps the house-to-house-seeker's practice will keep the alms-food-eater's practice ; and the bowl-food-eater's practice and the later-food-refuser's practice will be well kept by one who keeps the one-sessioner's practice. And what need has one who keeps the open-air-dweller's practice to keep the tree-root-dweller's practice or the any-bed-user's practice ? So there are these three principal practices that, together with the five individual practices, that is to say, the forest-dweller's practice, the refuse-rag-wearer's practice, the triple-robe-wearer's practice, the sitter's practice, and the charnel-ground-dweller's practice, come to eight only.

88. Again they come to four, that is to say, two connected with robes, five connected with alms food, five connected with the resting place, and one connected with energy. Herein, it is the sitter's practice that is connected with energy ; the rest are obvious.

Again they all amount to two only, since twelve are dependent on requisites and one on energy. Also they are two according to what is and what is not to be cultivated. For when one cultivating an ascetic practice finds that his meditation subject improves, he should cultivate it ; but when he is cultivating one and finds that his meditation subject deteriorates, he should not cultivate it. But when he finds that, whether he cultivates one or not, his meditation subject only improves and does not deteriorate, he should cultivate them out of compassion for later generation. And when he finds that, whether he cultivates them or not, his meditation subject does not improve, he should still cultivate them for the sake of acquiring the habit for the future. So

21. See Ch. XXI, §117.

they are of two kinds as what is and what is not to be cultivated.

89. And all are of one kind as volition. For there is only one ascetic practice, namely, that consisting in the volition of undertaking. Also it is said in the Commentary 'It is the volition that is the ascetic practice, they say'.

90. 7. *Singly :* with thirteen for bhikkhus, eight for bhikkhunis, twelve for novices, seven for female probationers and female novices, and two for male and female lay followers, there are thus forty-two.

91. If there is a charnel ground in the open that complies with the forest-dweller's practice, one bhikkhu is able to put all the ascetic practices into effect simultaneously. But the two, namely, the forest-dweller's practice and the later-food-refuser's practice are forbidden to bhikkhunis by training precept. [83] And it is hard for them to observe the three, namely, the open-air-dweller's practice, the tree-root-dweller's practice, and the charnel-ground-dweller's practice, because a bhikkhuni is not allowed to live without a companion, and it is hard to find a female companion with like desire for such a place, and even if available, she would not escape having to live in company. This being so, the purpose of cultivating the ascetic practice would scarcely be served. It is because they are reduced by five owing to this inability to make use of certain of them that they are to be understood as eight only for bhikkhunis.

92. Except for the triple-robe-wearer's practice all the other twelve as stated should be understood to be for novices, and all the other seven for female probationers and female novices.

The two, namely, the one-sessioner's practice and the bowl-food-eater's practice, are proper for male and female lay followers to employ. In this way there are two ascetic practices.

This is the commentary 'as to groups and also singly'.

93. And this is the end of the treatise on the ascetic practices to be undertaken for the purpose of perfecting those special qualities of fewness of wishes, contentment, etc., by means of which there comes about the cleansing of virtue as described in the Path of Purification, which is shown under the three headings of virtue, concentration and understanding, contained in the stanza,

'When a wise man, established well in virtue' (Ch. I, §1).

The second chapter called 'the Description of the Ascetic Practices' in the Path of Purification composed for the purpose of gladdening good people.

PART II. CONCENTRATION

CHAPTER III. DESCRIPTION OF CONCENTRATION—TAKING A MEDITATION SUBJECT

(*Kammaṭṭhāna-gahaṇa-niddesa*)

1. [84] Now concentration is described under the heading of 'consciousness' in the phrase 'develops consciousness and understanding' (Ch. I, §1). It should be developed by one who has taken his stand on virtue that has been purified by means of the special qualities of fewness of wishes, etc., and perfected by observance of the ascetic practices. But that concentration has been shown only very briefly and so it is not even easy to understand, much less to develop. There is therefore the following set of questions, the purpose of which is to show the method of its development in detail :

(i) What is concentration ?

(ii) In what sense is it concentration ?

(iii) What are its characteristic, function, manifestation, and proximate cause ?

(iv) How many kinds of concentration are there ?

(v) What is its defilement ?

(vi) What is its cleansing ?

(vii) How should it be developed ?

(viii) What are the benefits of the development of concentration ?[1]

2. Here are the answers :

(i) WHAT IS CONCENTRATION ? Concentration is of many sorts and has various aspects. An answer that attempted to cover it all would accomplish neither its intention nor its purpose and would, besides, lead to distraction ; so we shall confine ourselves to the kind intended here, calling concentration profitable unification of mind.[2]

---

1. The answer to question (vii) stretches from Ch. III, §27 to Ch. XI, §119. That to question (viii) from Ch. XI, §120 up to the end of Ch. XIII.

2. '*Cittass' ekaggatā*' is rendered here as 'unification of mind' in the sense of agreement or harmony (cf. *samagga*) of consciousness and its concomitants in focussing on a single object (see A. i, 70). It is sometimes rendered 'one-pointedness' in that sense, or in the sense of the focussing of a searchlight. It may be concluded that this term is simply a synonym for *samādhi* and nothing more firstly from its use in the suttas and secondly from the fact that it is given no separate definition in the description of the formations aggregate in Ch. XIV. Cf. gloss at MA. i, 124.

3. (ii) IN WHAT SENSE IS IT CONCENTRATION ? It is concentration (*samādhi*) in the sense of concentrating (*samādhāna*). What is this concentrating ? It is the centering (*ādhāna*) of consciousness and consciousness-concomitants evenly (*samaṃ*) and rightly (*sammā*) on a single object ; placing, is what is meant. [85] So it is the state, in virtue of which consciousness and its concomitants remain evenly and rightly on a single object undistracted and unscattered, that should be understood as concentrating.

4. (iii) WHAT ARE ITS CHARACTERISTIC, FUNCTION, MANIFESTATION, AND PROXIMATE CAUSE ? Concentration has non-distraction as its characteristic.[3] Its function is to eliminate distraction. It is manifested as non-wavering. Because of the words 'Being blissful, his 'mind becomes concentrated' (D. i, 73) its proximate cause is bliss.

5. (iv) HOW MANY KINDS OF CONCENTRATION ARE THERE ?

(1) First of all it is of one kind with the characteristic of non-distraction. (2) Then it is of two kinds as access and absorption ;[4] (3) likewise as mundane and supramundane,[5] (4) as with happiness and without happiness, and (5) as accompanied by bliss and accompanied by equanimity.[6] It is of three kinds (6) as inferior, medium and superior ;

---

3. 'The characteristic of non-distraction is the individual essence peculiar to concentration. Hence no analysis of it is possible, which is why he said "*It is of one kind with the characteristic of non-distraction*"' (Pm. 91).

4. 'Applied-thought that occurs as though absorbing (*appento*) associated states in the object is absorption (*appanā*). Accordingly it is described as "absorption, absorbing (*appanā vyappanā*)" (M. iii, 73). Now since that is the most important, the usage of the commentaries is to call all exalted and unsurpassed jhana states "absorption" [as well as the applied thought itself], and likewise to apply the term of common usage "access" to the limited [*i.e.* sense-sphere] jhana that heralds the arising of the former, just as the term "village access", etc. is applied to the neighbourhood of a village' (Pm. 91).

5. 'The round (*vaṭṭa*, see Ch. XVII, §298) [including fine-material and immaterial heavens] is called the world (*loka*) because of its crumbling *lujjana*) and disintegrating (*palujjana*). "*Mundane* (*loktya*)" means connected with the world because of being included in it or found there. "*Supramundane* (*lokuttara*)" means beyond the world, excepted from it, because of not being included in it [through being associated with nibbana]' (Pm. 91). See also 'Nine supramundane states', Ch. VII, §68, 74f.

6. In loose usage *pīti* (happiness) and *sukha* (pleasure or bliss) are almost synonyms. They become differentiated in the jhana formulas (see Ch, IV, §100), and then technically *pīti*, as the active thrill of rapture, is classed under the formations aggregate and *sukha* under the feeling aggregate. The valuable word 'happiness' was chosen for *pīti* rather than the possible alternatives of 'joy' (needed for *somanassa*),

likewise (7) as with applied thought and sustained thought, etc., (8) as accompanied by happiness, etc., and (9) as limited, exalted, and measureless. It is of four kinds (10) as of difficult progress and sluggish direct-knowledge, etc.; likewise (11) as limited with limited object, etc., (12) according to the factors of the four jhanas, (13) as partaking of diminution, etc., (14) as of the sense sphere; etc., and (15) as predominance, and so on. (16) It is of five kinds according to the factors of the five jhanas reckoned by the five-fold method.

6. 1. Herein, the section dealing with that of one kind is evident in meaning.

2. In the section dealing with that of two kinds, *access* concentration is the unification of mind obtained by the following, that is to say, the six Recollections, Mindfulness of death, the Recollection of Peace, the Perception of Repulsiveness in Nutriment, and the Defining of the Four Elements, and it is the unification that precedes absorption concentration. *Absorption* concentration is the unification that follows immediately upon the preliminary-work (Ch. IV, §74) because of the words 'The first-jhana preliminary-work is a condition, 'as proximity condition, for the first jhana' Ptn2. 350, Siamese ed.). So it is of two kinds as access and absorption.

7. 3. In the second dyad *mundane* concentration is profitable unification of mind in the three planes. *Supramundane* concentration is the unification associated with the noble paths. So it is of two kinds as mundane and supramundane.

8. 4. In the third dyad concentration *with happiness* is the unification of mind in two jhanas in the fourfold reckoning and in three jhanas in the fivefold reckoning. [86] Concentration *without happiness* is the unification in the remaining two jhanas. But access concentraion may be with happiness or without happiness. So it is of two kinds as with happiness and without happiness.

9. 5. In the fourth dyad concentration *accompanied by bliss* is the unification in three jhanas in the fourfold and four in the fivefold reckoning. That *accompanied by equanimity* is that in the remaining jhana. Access concentration may be accompanied by bliss or accompanied by equanimity. So it is

---

'interest' (which is too flat), 'rapture' (which is overcharged), or 'zest.' For *sukha*, while 'pleasure' seemed to fit admirably where ordinary pleasant feeling is intended, another, less crass, word seemed necessary for the refined pleasant feeling of jhana and the 'bliss' of nibbana (which is not feeling aggregate—see M. i, 400). 'Ease' is sometimes used.

'Neither-painful-nor-pleasant feeling is intended here by "equanimity (*upekkha* lit. onlooking)"; for it "looks on (*upekkhati*)" at the occurrence of [bodily] pleasure and pain by maintaining the neutral (central) mode' (Pm. 92).

of two kinds as accompanied by bliss and accompanied by equanimity.

10. 6. In the first of the triads what has only just been acquired is *inferior*. What is not very well developed is *medium*. What is well developed and has reached mastery is *superior*. So it is of three kinds as inferior, medium, and superior.

11. 7. In the second triad that *with applied thought and sustained thought* is the concentration of the first jhana together with access concentration. That *without applied thought*, with *sustained thought only* is the concentration of the second jhana in the fivefold reckoning. For when a man sees danger only in applied thought and not in sustained thought, he aspires only to abandon applied thought when he passes beyond the first jhana, and so he obtains concentration without applied thought and with sustained thought only. This is said with reference to him. Concentration *without applied thought and sustained thought* is the unification in the three jhanas beginning with the second in the fourfold reckoning and with the third in the fivefold reckoning (See D. iii, 219). So it is of three kinds as with applied thought and sustained thought, and so on.

12. 8. In the third triad concentration *accompanied by happiness* is the unification in the two first jhanas in the fourfold reckoning and in the three first jhanas in the fivefold reckoning. Concentration *accompanied by bliss* is the unification in those same jhanas and in the third and the fourth respectively in the two reckonings. That *Accompanied by equanimity* is that in the remaining jhana. Access concentration may be accompanied by bliss and happiness or accompanied by equanimity. So it is of three kinds as accompanied by happiness, and so on.

13. 9. In the fourth triad *limited* concentration is unification on the plane of access. *Exalted* concentration is unification in profitable [consciousness, etc.,] of the fine-material sphere and immaterial sphere. *Measureless* concentration is unification associated with the noble paths. So it is of three kinds as limited, exalted, and measureless.

14 10. In the first of the triads there is concentration of *difficult progress and sluggish direct-knowledge*. There is that of difficult progress and swift direct-knowledge. There is that of easy progress and sluggish direct-knowledge. And there is that of easy progress and swift direct-knowledge.

15. Herein, the development of concentration that occurs from the time of the first conscious reaction up to the arising of the access of a given jhana is called *progress*. And the understanding that occurs from the time of access until absorption is called *direct-knowledge*. That progress is difficult for some, being troublesome owing to the tenacious

resistance of the inimical states beginning with the hindrances. The meaning is that it is cultivated without ease. [87] It is easy for others because of the absence of those difficulties. Also the direct-knowledge is sluggish in some and occurs slowly, not quickly. In others it is swift and occurs rapidly, not slowly.

16. Herein, we shall comment below upon the suitable and unsuitable (Ch. IV, §35f.), the preparatory tasks consisting in the severing of impediments (Ch. IV, §20), etc., and skill in absorption (Ch. IV, §42). When a man cultivates what is unsuitable, his progress is difficult and his direct-knowledge sluggish. When he cultivates what is suitable, his progress is easy and his direct-knowledge swift. But if he cultivates the unsuitable in the earlier stage and the suitable in the later stage, or if he cultivates the suitable in the earlier stage and the unsuitable in the later stage, then it should be understood as mixed in his case. Likewise if he devotes himself to development without carrying out the preparatory tasks of severing impediments, etc., his progress is difficult. It is easy in the opposite case. And if he is not accomplished in skill in absorption, his direct-knowledge is sluggish. It is swift if he is so accomplished.

17. Besides, they should be understood as classed according to craving and ignorance, and according to whether one has had practice in serenity and insight.[7] For if a man is overwhelmed by craving, his progress is difficult. If not, it is easy. And if he is overwhelmed by ignorance, his direct-knowledge is sluggish. If not, it is swift. And if he has had no practice in serenity, his progress is difficult. If he has, it is easy. And if he has had no practice in insight, his direct-knowledge is sluggish. If he has, it is swift.

18. Also they should be understood as classed according to defilements and faculties. For if a man's defilements are sharp and his faculties dull, then his progress is difficult and his direct-knowledge sluggish ; but if his faculties are keen, his direct-knowledge is swift. And if his defilements are blunt and his faculties dull, then his progress is easy and his direct-knowledge sluggish ; but if his faculties are keen, his direct-knowledge is swift.

19. So as regards this progress and this direct-knowledge, when a person reaches concentration with difficult progress and sluggish direct-knowledge, his concentration is called *concentration of difficult progress and sluggish direct-knowledge.* Similarly in the cases of the remaining three.

---

7. '*Samatha*— serenity' is a synonym for absorption concentration, and 'insight (*vipassanā*)' a synonym for understanding. *Samatha* is sometimes rendered by 'tranquillity' (reserved here for *passaddhi*), or 'calm' or 'quiet'.

So it is of four kinds as of difficult progress and sluggish direct-knowledge, and so on.

20. 11. In the second tetrad there is limited concentration with a limited object, there is limited with a measureless object, there is measureless with a limited object, and there is measureless with a measureless object. Herein, concentration that is unfamiliar and incapable of being a condition for a higher jhana [88] is *limited.* When it occurs with an unextended object (Ch. IV, §126), it is *with a limited object.* When it is familiar, well developed and capable of being a condition for a higher jhana, it is *measureless.* And when it occurs with an extended object, it is *with a measureless object.* The mixed method can be understood as the mixture of the characteristics already stated. So it is of four kinds as limited with limited object, and so on.

21. 12. In the third tetrad the first jhana has five factors, that is to say, applied thought, sustained thought, happiness, bliss, and concentration, following suppresion of the hindrances. The second has the three factors remaining after the elimination of applied and sustained thought. The third has two factors with the fading away of happiness. The fourth, where bliss is abandoned, has two factors with concentration and the equanimous feeling that accompanies it. Thus there are four kinds of concentration according to the factors of these four jhanas. So it is of four kinds according to the factors of the four jhanas.

22. 13. In the fourth tetrad there is concentration partaking of diminution, there is concentration partaking of stagnation, there is concentration partaking of distinction, and there is concentration partaking of penetration. Herein, it should be understood that the state of *partaking of diminution* is accessibility to opposition, the state of *partaking of stagnation* (*ṭhiti*) is stationariness (*saṇṭhāna*) of the mindfulness that is in conformity with that [concentration], the state of *partaking of distinction* is the attaining of higher distinction, and the state of *partaking of penetration* is accessibility to perception and attention accompanied by dispassion, according as it is said 'When a man has attained the first jhana and he is 'accessible to perception and attention accompanied by sense 'desire, then his understanding partakes of diminution. 'When his mindfulness that is in conformity with that stag- 'nates, then his understanding partakes of stagnation. When 'he is accessible to perception and attention unaccompanied 'by applied thought, then his understanding partakes of 'distinction. When he is accessible to perception and attent- 'ion accompanied by dispassion and directed to fading away, 'then his understanding partakes of penetration' (Vbh. 330). The kinds of concentration associated with that [fourfold]

understanding are also four in number. So it is of four kinds as partaking of diminution, and so on.

23. 14. In the fifth tetrad there are the following four kinds of concentration, that is to say, sense-sphere concentration, fine-material-sphere concentration, immaterial-sphere concentration, and unincluded, [that is, path,] concentration. Herein, *sense sphere concentration* is all kinds of access unification. Likewise the other three are respectively profitable unification of mind associated with fine-material, [immaterial, and path, jhana.] So it is of four kinds as of the sense-sphere, and so on.

24. 15. In the sixth tetrad 'If a bhikkhu obtains concentration, obtains unification of mind, by making zeal (desire) 'predominant, [89] this is called concentration due to zeal. 'If . . . by making energy predominant, . . . If . . . by making '[natural purity of] consciousness predominant, . . . If . . . by 'making inquiry predominant, this is called concentration 'due to inquiry' (Vbh. 216-9). So it is of four kinds as predominance.

25. 16. In the pentad there are five jhanas by dividing in two what is called the second jhana in the fourfold reckoning (see §21), taking the second jhana to be due to the surmounting of only applied thought and the third jhana to be due to the surmounting of both applied and sustained thought. There are five kinds of concentration according to the factors of these five jhanas. So its fivefoldness should be understood according to the five sets of jhana factors.

26. (v) WHAT IS ITS DEFILEMENT, (vi) WHAT IS ITS CLEANSING? Here the answer is given in the Vibhanga: 'defilement is the state partaking of diminution, cleansing 'is the state partaking of distinction' (Vbh. 343). Herein, the state partaking of diminution should be understood in this way: 'When a man has attained the first 'jhana and he is accessible to perception and attention 'accompanied by sense desire, then his understanding 'partakes of diminution' (Vbh. 330). And the state partaking of distinction should be understood in this way: 'When he is accessible to perception and attention unaccom- 'panied by applied thought, then his understanding partakes 'of distinction' (Vbh. 330).

27. (vii) HOW SHOULD IT BE DEVELOPED?

[*A. Development in Brief*]

The method of developing the kind of concentration associated with the noble paths mentioned (§7) under that 'of two kinds as mundane and supramundane', etc., is included in the method of developing understanding (Ch. XXII) ; for in developing [path] understanding that is developed too. So we shall say nothing separately [here] about how that is to be developed.

28. But mundane concentration should be developed by one who has taken his stand on virtue that is quite purified in the way already stated. He should sever any of the ten impediments that he may have. He should then approach the Good friend, the giver of a meditation subject, and he should apprehend from among the forty meditation subjects one that suits his own temperament. After that he should avoid a monastery unfavourable to the development of concentration and go to live in one that is favourable. Then he should sever the lesser impediments and not overlook any of the directions for development. This is in brief.

[*B. Development in Detail*]

29. The detail is this :

[*The Ten Impediments*]

Firstly it was said above, *he should sever any of the ten impediments that he may have.* [90] Now the ' ten impediments ' are:

' A dwelling, family, and gain,
' A class, and building too as fifth,
' And travel, kin, affliction, books,
' And supernormal powers : ten.

Herein the dwelling itself is the ' impediment ' due to the dwelling '. So too with the family and so on.

30. 1. Herein, a single inner room or a single hut or a whole monastery for the Community is called a *dwelling*. This is not an impediment for everyone. It is an impediment only for anyone whose mind is exercised about the building, etc., that goes on there, or who has many belongings stored there, or whose mind is caught up by some business connected with it. For any other it is not an impediment.

31. Here is a relevant story. Two clansmen left Anurādhapura, it seems, and eventually went forth at the Thūpārāma.[8] One of them made himself familiar with the Two Codes,[9] and when he had acquired five years' seniority, he took part in the Pavarana[10] and then left for the place called Pācīna-

---

8. One of the principal monasteries in Anurādhapura.
9. *Dve Mātikā*—'the Two Codes ' : see Ch. I, n. II. But. Pm says here : ' " *Observers of the Codes* " are observers of the codes (summaries) of the Dhamma and Vinaya ' (Pm. 117).
10. ' *Pavāraṇā* : Ceremony held at the end of the Rains, during three months of which season bhikkhus have to undertake to live in one place in order to avoid travel while crops are growing. It consists in a meeting of the bhikkhus who have spent the Rains together, at which each member present invites (*pavāreti*) the Community to point out

khaṇḍarājī.[11] The other stayed on where he was. Now when the one who had gone to Pācīnakhaṇḍarājī had lived there a long time and had become an elder,[12] he thought 'This place is good for retreat; suppose I told my friend about it?'. So he set out, and in due course he entered the Thūpārāma. As he entered, the Elder of the same seniority saw him, went to meet him, took his bowl and robe and did the duties.

32. The visiting Elder went into his lodging. He thought 'Now my friend will be sending me ghee or molasses or a drink; for he has lived long in this city'. He got nothing that night, and in the morning he thought 'Now he will be sending me rice gruel and solid food sent by his supporters'. When he saw none, he thought 'There is no one to bring it. No doubt they will give it when we go into the town'. Early in the morning they went into the town together. When they had wandered through one street and had got only a ladleful of gruel, they sat down in a sitting hall to drink it.[13]

33. Then the visitor thought 'Perhaps there is no individual giving of gruel. But as soon as it is the time for the meal people will give special food'. But when it was time for the meal, they ate what they had got by wandering for alms. Then the visitor said 'Venerable sir, how is this? Do you live in this way all the time?'—'Yes, friend'.—'Venerable sir, Pācīnakhaṇḍarājī is comfortable; let us go there'. Now as the Elder came out from the city [91] by the southern gate he took the Kumbhakāragāma road [which leads to Pācīnakhaṇḍarāji]. The visitor asked 'But, venerable sir, why do you take this road?'—'Did you not recommend Pācīnakhaṇḍarājī, friend?'—But how is this, venerable sir, have you no extra belongings in the place you have lived in for so long?'—'That is so, friend. The bed and chair belong to the Community, and they are put away [as usual]. There is nothing else'.—'But, venerable sir, I have left my staff and my oil tube and my sandal bag there'.—'Have you already collected so much, friend, living there for just one day?'—'Yes, venerable sir'.

34. He was glad in his heart, and he paid homage to the Elder: 'For those like you, venerable sir, everywhere is a forest

---

his faults (breaches of Vinaya rules) committed during the preceding three months (Vin. i, 155).

11. '*Pācīnakhaṇḍarājī ti puratthimadisāya pabbatakhaṇḍānaṃ antare vanarājiṭṭhānaṃ*' (Pm. 97).

12. For the first five years after the admission (*upasampadā*) a bhikkhu is called a 'new (*nava*) bhikkhu'; from five to ten years' he is called a 'middle (*majjhima*) bhikkhu'; with ten or more years' seniority he is called an 'elder (*thera*) bhikkhu'.

13. The last sentence here might refer to a free mass distribution of gruel (*yāgu*), which appears to have been more or less constantly maintained at Anurādhapura.

dwelling. The Thūpārāma is a place where the relics of four Buddhas are deposited ; there is suitable hearing of the Dhamma in the Brazen Palace ; there is the Great Shrine to be seen ; and one can visit Elders. It is like the time of the Buddha. It is here that you should live '. On the following day he took his bowl and [outer] robe and went away by himself. It is no impediment for one like that.

35. 2. *Family* means a family consisting of relatives or of supporters. For even a family consisting of supporters is an impediment for someone who lives in close association with it in the way beginning ' He is pleased when they are pleased ' (S.iii,11), and who does not even go to a neighbouring monastery to hear the Dhamma without members of the family. But even mother and father are not an impediment for another,

36. as in the case of the young bhikkhu, the nephew of the Elder who lived at the Koraṇḍaka Monastery.

We went to Rohana for instruction, it seems. The Elder's sister who was a lay devotee was always asking the Elder how her son was getting on. One day the Elder set out for Rohaṇa to fetch him back.

37. The young bhikkhu too thought ' I have lived here for a long time. Now I might go and visit my Preceptor and find out how the lay devotee is ', and he left Rohaṇa. The two met on the banks of the [Mahaveli] River. He did the duties to the Elder at the foot of a tree. When asked ' Where are you going ?', he told his purpose. The Elder said ' You have done well. The lay devotee is always asking after you. That was why I came. You may go, but I shall stay here for the Rains ', and he dismissed him. [92] He arrived at the monastery on the actual day for taking up residence for the Rains. The lodging alloted to him happened to be the one for which his father had undertaken responsibility.

38. His father came on the following day and asked ' To whom was our lodging allotted, venerable sirs' ?'. When he heard that it had fallen to a young visitor, he went to him. After paying homage to him, he said Venerable sir, there is an obligation for him who has taken up residence for the Rains in our lodging '.—' What is it, lay follower ?'—' It is to take alms food only in our house for the three months, and to let us know the time of departure after the *Pavāraṇā* ceremony. He consented in silence. The lay devotee went home and told his wife ' There is a visiting lord who has taken up residence for the Rains in our lodging. He must be carefully looked after ', and she agreed. She prepared good food of various kinds for him.[14] Though the youth went to his relatives' home at the time of the meal, no one recognized him.

14. It is usual to render the set phrase '*paṇītaṃ khādanīyaṃ bhojanīyaṃ* ' by some such phrase as ' sumptuous food both hard and soft ', which is literal but unfamiliar-sounding.

39. When he had eaten alms food there during the three months and had completed the residence for the Rains, he announced his departure. Then his relatives said ' Let it be tomorrow, venerable sir ', and on the following day, when they had fed him in their house and filled his oil tube and given him a lump of sugar and a nine-cubit length of cloth, they said ' Now you are leaving venerable sir '. He gave his blessing and set out for Rohana.

40. His preceptor had completed the *Pavāraṇā* ceremony and was on his way back. They met at the same place as before. He did the duties to the Elder at the foot of a tree. The Elder asked him ' How was it, my dear, did you see the good woman lay devotee ?' He replied ' Yes, venerable sir ', and he told him all that had happened. He then anointed the Elder's feet with the oil, made him a drink with the sugar and presented him with the length of cloth. He then, after paying homage to the Elder, told him ' Venerable sir, only Rohana suits me ', and he departed. The Elder too arrived back at his monastery, and next day he went into the village of Koraṇḍaka.

41. The lay devotee, his sister, had always kept looking down the road, thinking ' My brother is now coming with my son '. When he saw him coming alone, she thought ' My son must be dead ; that is why the elder is coming alone ', and she fell at the Elder's feet, lamenting and weeping. Suspecting that it must have been out of fewness of wishes that the youth had gone away without announcing himself, [93] the Elder comforted her and told her all that had happened, and he took the length of cloth out of his bag and showed it to her.

42. She was appeased. She prostrated herself in the direction taken by her son, and she said ' Surely the Blessed One taught the way of the Rathavinīta, the way of the Nāḷaka, the way of the Tuvaṭaka and the way of the Great Noble Ones' Heritages[15] showing contentment with the four requisites and delight in development, making a bhikkhu such as my son a body-witness. So, although for three months he ate in the house of the mother who bore him, yet he never said " I am your son, you are my mother "! 'Oh admirable man ' !. Even mother and father are no impediment for one such as him, so how much less any other family that supports him.

43. 3. *Gain* is the four requisites. How are they an impediment ? Wherever a meritorious bhikkhu goes people give him a large supply of requisites. With giving blessings to them

15. ' The way of the Rathavinīta (*Rathavinīta-paṭipadā*) ': this is a reference to certain suttas that were adopted by bhikkhus as a ' way (*paṭipadā*) ' or guide to practice. The suttas mentioned here are Rathavinīta (M. i, 145), Nāḷaka (Sn., p. 131), Tuvaṭaka (Sn., p. 179), Noble One's Heritages (*ariyavamsa*—A. ii, 27). Other such suttas are mentioned at MA., i, 92 ; iii, 6 ; S.A. iii, 291. The Ariyavamsa Sutta (A. ii, 207

and teaching them the Dhamma he gets no chance to do the ascetic's duties. From sunrise till the first watch of the night he never breaks his association with people. Again even at dawn alms-food eaters fond of opulence come and say 'Venerable sir, such and such a man lay follower, woman lay follower, friend, friend's daughter, wants to see you', and being ready to go, he replies 'Take the bowl and robe, friend'. So he is always on the alert. Thus these requisites are an impediment for him. He should leave his group and wander by himself where he is not known. This is the way his impediment is severed.

44. 4. *Class* is a class (group) of students of Suttas or students of Abhidhamma. If with the group's instruction and questioning he gets no opportunity for the ascetic's duties, then that group is an impediment for him. He should sever that impediment in this way: if those bhikkhus have already acquired the main part and little still remains, he should finish that off and then go to the forest. If they have only acquired little and much still remains, [94] he should, without travelling more than a league, approach another instructor of a class within the radius of a league and say 'Help those venerable ones with instruction, etc.' If he does not find anyone in this way, he should take leave of the class, saying 'I have a task to see to, friends; go where it suits you', and he should do his own work.

45. 5. *Building* (*kamma*) is new building work (*nava-kamma*). Since one engaged in this must know about what [material] has and has not been got by carpenters, etc., and must see about what has and has not been done, it is always an impediment. It should be severed in this way. If little remains, it should be completed. If much remains, it should be handed over to the Community or to bhikkhus who are entrusted with the Community's affairs, if it is a new building for the Community; or if it is for himself, it should be handed over to those whom he entrusts with his own affairs, but if these are not available, he should relinquish it to the Community and depart.

46. 6. *Travel* is going on a journey. If someone is expected to give the Going Forth somewhere else, or if some requisite is obtainable there and he cannot rest content without getting it [that will be an impediment; for] even if he goes into the forest to do the ascetic's duties, he will find it hard to get rid of thoughts about the journey. So one in this position should apply himself to the ascetic's duties after he has done the journey and transacted the business.

itself has a long commentary on practice, and it is mentioned in the commentaries as a popular subject for preaching (see *e.g.* a story in the commentary to A. Tikanipāta 42).

47. 7. *Kin* in the case of the monastery means Teacher, Preceptor, co-resident, pupil, those with the same Preceptor, as oneself, and those with the same Teacher as oneself ; and in the case of the house it means mother, father, brother, and so on. When they are sick they are an impediment for him. Therefore that impediment should be severed by curing them with nursing.

48. Herein, when the preceptor is sick he must be cared for as long as life lasts if the sickness does not soon depart. Likewise the Teacher at the Going Forth, the Teacher at the Admission, the co-resident, the pupils to whom one has given the Admission and the Going Forth, and those who have the same Preceptor. But the teacher from whom one takes the Dependence, the teacher who gives one instruction, the pupil to whom one has given the Dependence, the pupil to whom one is giving instruction, and those who have that same teacher as oneself, should be looked after as long as the Dependence or the instruction has not been terminated. If one is able to do so, one should look after them even beyond that [period].

49. Mother and father should be treated like the Preceptor. If they live within the kingdom and look to their son for help, it should be given. [95] Also if they have no medicine, he should give them his own. If he has none, he should go in search of it as alms and give that. But in the case of brothers or sisters, one should only give them what is theirs. If they have none, then one should give one's own temporarily and later get it back, but one should not complain if one does not get it back. It is not allowed either to make medicine for or to give it to a sister's husband who is not related by blood ; but one can give it to one's sister, saying ' Give it to your husband '. The same applies to one's brother's wife. But it is allowed to make it for their children since they are blood relatives.

50. 8. *Affliction* is any kind of illness. It is an impediment when it is actually afflicting ; therefore it should be severed by treatment with medicine. But if it is not cured after taking medicine for a few days, then the ascetic's duties should be done after apostrophizing one's person in this way ' I am not your slave, or your hireling. I have come to suffering through maintaining you through the beginningless round of rebirths '.

51. 9. *Books* mean responsibility for the scriptures. That is an impediment only for one who is constantly busy with recitations, etc., but not for others. Here are relevant stories. The Elder Revata, it seems, the Majjhima reciter, went to the Elder Revata, the dweller in Malaya (the Hill Country), and asked him for a meditation subject. The Elder asked him ' How are you in the scriptures, friend ?'—' I am studying the Majjhima [Nikāya], venerable sir '.—' The Majjhima is a hard

responsibility, friend. When a man is still learning the First Fifty by heart, he is faced with the Middle Fifty; and when he is still learning that by heart, he is faced with the Last Fifty. How can you take up a meditation subject?' — 'Venerable sir, when I have taken a meditation subject from you, I shall not look at the scriptures again.' He took the meditation subject, and doing no recitation for nineteen years, he reached Arahantship in the twentieth year. He told bhikkhus who came for recitation 'I have not looked at the scriptures for twenty years, friends, [96] yet I am familiar with them. You may begin'. And from beginning to end he had no hesitation even over a single syllable.

52. The Elder Mahā-Nāga, too, who lived at Karuliyagiri (Karaliyagiri) put aside the scriptures for eighteen years, and then he recited the Dhātukathā to the bhikkhus. When they checked this with the town-dwelling elders [of Anurādhapura], not a single question was found out of its order.

53. In the Great Monastery too the Elder Tipitaka-Cūla-Abhaya had the golden drum struck, saying 'I shall expound the three Piṭakas in the circle of [experts in] the Five Collections of discourses', and this was before he had learnt the commentaries. The community of Bhikkhus said 'Which teachers' teaching is it? Unless you give only the teaching of our own teachers we shall not let you speak'. Also his Preceptor asked him when he went to wait on him 'Did you have the drum beaten, friend?'. — 'Yes, venerable sir.' — 'For what reason?' — 'I shall expound the scriptures, venerable sir.'— 'Friend Abhaya, how do the teachers explain this passage?'— 'They explain it in this way, venerable sir.' The Elder dissented, saying 'Hum'. Again three times, each time in a different way, he said 'They explain it in this way, venerable sir'. The elder always dissented, saying 'Hum'. Then he said 'Friend, your first explanation was the way of the teachers. But it is because you have not actually learnt it from the teachers' lips that you are unable to maintain that the teachers say such and such. Go and learn it from our own teachers'.— 'Where shall I go, venerable sir.' — 'There is an Elder named Mahā-Dhammarakkhita living in the Tulādhārapabbata Monastery in the Rohaṇa country beyond the [Mahaveli] River. He knows all the scriptures. Go to him.' Saying 'Good, venerable sir', he paid homage to the Elder. He went with five hundred bhikkhus to the Elder Mahā-Dhammarakkhita, and when he had paid homage to him, he sat down. The Elder asked 'Why have you come?'. —'To hear the Dhamma, venerable sir.' — 'Friend Abhaya, they ask me about the Dīgha and the Majjhima from time to time, but I have not looked at the others for thirty years. Still you may repeat them in my presence by night, and I shall explain them to

you by day.' He said 'Good, venerable sir', and he acted accordingly.

54\. The inhabitants of the village had a large pavilion built at the door of his dwelling, and they came daily to hear the Dhamma. Explaining by day what had been repeated by night, [97] the Elder [Dhammarakkhita] eventually completed the instruction. Then he sat down on a mat on the ground before the Elder Abhaya and said 'Friend, explain a meditation subject to me'. — 'What are you saying, venerable sir, have I not heard it all from you? What can I explain to you that you do not already know?' The senior Elder said 'This path is
55\. different for one who has actually travelled by it'. The Elder Abhaya was then, it seems, a Stream Enterer.

When the Elder Abhaya had given his teacher a meditation subject, he returned to Anurādhapura. Later, while he was expounding the Dhamma in the Brazen Palace, he heard that the Elder had attained nibbana. On hearing this, he said 'Bring me [my] robe, friends'. Then he put on the robe and said 'The Arahant path befits our teacher, friends. Our teacher was a true thoroughbred. He sat down on a mat before his own Dhamma pupil and said "Explain a meditation subject to me". The Arahant path befits our teacher, friends'.

For such as these books are no impediment.

56\. 10. *Supernormal powers* are the supernormal powers of the ordinary man. They are hard to maintain, like a prone infant or like a baby hare, and the slightest thing breaks them. But they are an impediment for insight, not for concentration, since they are obtainable through concentration. So the supernormal powers are an impediment that should be severed by one who seeks insight: the others are impediments to be severed by one who seeks concentration.

This in the first place is the detailed explanation of the impediments.

57\. *Approach the Good Friend, the giver of a meditation subject* (§28): meditation subjects are of two kinds, that is, generally useful meditation subjects and special meditation subjects.

Herein, lovingkindness towards the Community of Bhikkhus etc., and also mindfulness of death are what are called generally useful meditation subjects. Some say perception of foulness, too.

58\. When a bhikkhu takes up a meditation subject, he should first develop lovingkindness towards the Community of Bhikkhus within the boundary,[16] limiting it at first [to 'all bhikkhus in this monastery'], in this way: 'May they be happy

16\. '*Sīmā*—boundary': loosely used in this sense, it corresponds vaguely to what is meant by 'parish'. In the strict sense it is the actual area (usually a 'chapter house') agreed according to rule laid down in the Vinaya and marked by boundary stones, within which the Community *saṅgha*) carries out its formal acts.

and free from affliction'. Then he should develop it towards all deities within the boundary. Then towards all the principal people in the village that is his alms resort; then to [all human beings there and to] all living beings dependent on the human beings. With lovingkindness towards the Community of Bhikkhus he produces kindliness in his co-residents; then they are easy for him to live with. With lovingkindness towards the deities within the boundary he is protected by kindly deities with lawful protection. [98] With lovingkindness towards the principal people in the village that is his alms resort his requisites are protected by well-disposed principal people with lawful protection. With lovingkindness to all human beings there he goes about without incurring their dislike since they trust him. With lovingkindness to all living beings he can wander unhindered everywhere.

With mindfulness of death, thinking 'I have got to die', he gives up improper search (see S. ii, 194; MA. i, 115), and with a growing sense of urgency he comes to live without attachment.

When his mind is familiar with the perception of foulness, then even divine objects do not tempt his mind to greed.

59. So these are called generally useful and they are called meditation subjects since they are needed[17] generally and desirable owing to their great helpfulness and since they are subjects for the meditation work intended.

60. What is called a 'special meditation subject' is that one from among the forty meditation subjects that is suitable to a man's own temperament. It is 'special (*pārihāriya*)' because he must carry it (*pariharitabbattā*) constantly about with him, and because it is the proximate cause for each higher stage of development.

So it is the one who gives this twofold meditation subject that is called *the giver of meditation subject.*

61. *The Good Friend* is one who possesses such special qualities as these:

'He is revered and dearly loved,
'And one who speaks and suffers speech;
'The speech he utters is profound,
'He does not urge without a reason' (A.iv,32), and so on.

He is wholly solicitous of welfare and partial to progress.

62. Because of the words beginning 'Ānanda, it is owing to my being a good friend to them that living beings subject to birth are freed from birth' (S. i, 88) it is only the Fully Enlightened One who possesses all the aspects of the Good Friend. Since that is so, while he is available only a meditation subject taken in the Blessed One's presence is well taken.

17. '*Atthayitabba*—needed': not in P.T.S. Dict., not in T.C.P. Dict.

But after his final attainment of nibbana, it is proper to take it from any one of the eighty great disciples still living. When they are no more available, one who wants to take a particular meditation subject should take it from someone with cankers destroyed, who has, by means of that particular meditation subject, produced the fourfold and fivefold jhana, and has reached the destruction of cankers by augmenting insight that had that jhana as its proximate cause.

63. But how then, does someone with cankers destroyed declare himself thus: 'I am one whose cankers are destroyed'? Why not? He declares himself when he knows that his instructions will be carried out. Did not the Elder Assagutta [99] spread out his leather mat in the air and sitting cross-legged on it explain a meditation subject to a bhikkhu who was starting his meditation subject, hecause he knew that that bhikkhu was one who would carry out his instructions for the meditation subject?

64. So if someone with cankers destroyed is available, that is good. if not, then one should take it from a Non-returner, a Once-returner, a Stream Enterer, an ordinary man who has obtained jhana, one who knows three Pitakas, one who knows two Pitakas, one who knows one Pitaka, in descending order [according as available]. If not even one who knows one Pitaka is available, then it should be taken from one who is familiar with one Collection together with its commentary, and one who is himself conscientious. For a teacher such as this who knows the texts guards the heritage, and protects the tradition, will follow the teachers' opinion rather than his own. Hence the Ancient Elders said three times 'One who is conscientious will guard it'.

65. Now those beginning with one whose cankers are destroyed mentioned above will describe only the path they have themselves reached. But with a learned man, his instructions and his answers to questions are purified by his having approached such and such teachers, and so he will explain a meditation subject showing a broad track, like a big elephant going through a stretch of jungle, and he will select suttas and reasons from here and there, adding [explanations of] what is suitable and unsuitable. So a meditation subject should be taken by approaching the Good Friend such as this, the giver of a meditation subject, and by doing all the duties to him.

66. If he is available in the same monastery, it is good. If not, one should go to where he lives.

When [a bhikkhu] goes to him, he should not do so with feet washed and anointed, wearing sandals, with an umbrella, surrounded by pupils, and bringing oil tube, honey, molasses, etc.; he should do so fulfilling the duties of a bhikkhu setting out on a journey, carrying his bowl and robes himself, doing all the duties in each monastery on the way, with few belongings, and living in the greatest effacement. When entering that monastery, he should do so [expecting nothing, and even provided] with a tooth-stick that he has had made allowable on the way [according to the rules]. And he should not enter some other room, thinking 'I shall go to the teacher after resting awhile and after washing and annointing my feet, and so on'.

67. Why? If there are bhikkhus there who are hostile to the teacher, they might ask him the reason for his coming and speak dispraise of the teacher, saying 'You are done for if you go to him'; [100] they might make him regret his coming and turn him back. So he should ask for the teacher's dwelling and go straight there.

68. If the teacher is junior, he should not consent to the teacher's receiving his bowl and robe, and so on. If the teacher is senior, then he should go and pay homage to him and remain standing. When told 'Put down the bowl and robe, friend', he may put them down. When told 'Have some water to drink', he can drink if he wants to. When told 'You may wash your feet', he should not do so at once, for if the water has been brought by the teacher himself, it would be improper. But when told 'Wash, friend, it was not brought by me, it was brought by others', then he can wash his feet, sitting in a screened place out of sight of the teacher, or in the open to one side of the dwelling.

69. If the teacher brings an oil tube, he should get up and take it carefully with both hands. If he did not take it, it might make the teacher wonder 'Does this bhikkhu resent sharing so soon?'; but having taken it, he should not anoint his feet at once. For if it were oil for anointing the teacher's limbs, it would not be proper. So he should first anoint his head, then his shoulders, etc.; but when told 'This is meant for all the limbs, friend, anoint your feet', he should put a little on his head and then anoint his feet. Then he should give it back, saying when the teacher takes it 'May I return this oil tube, venerable sir?'.

70. He should not say 'Explain a meditation subject to me, venerable sir' on the very day he arrives. But starting from the next day, he can, if the teacher has a habitual attendant, ask his permission to do the duties. If he does not allow it when asked, they can be done when the opportunity offers. When he does them, three tooth-sticks should be brought, a small, a medium, and a big one, and two kinds of mouth-washing water and bathing water, that is, hot and cold, should be set out. Whichever of these the teacher uses for three days should then be brought regularly. If the teacher uses

either kind indiscriminately, he can bring whatever is available.

71. Why so many words? All should be done as prescribed by the Blessed One in the Khandhakas as the Right Duties in the passage beginning 'Bhikkhus, a pupil should perform the duties 'to the teacher [101] rightly. Herein, this is the right per-'formance of duties. He should rise early; removing his sandals 'and arranging his robe on one shoulder, he should give the 'tooth-sticks and the mouth-washing water, and he should 'prepare the seat. If there is rice gruel, he should wash the 'dish and bring the rice gruel' (Vin. i, 61).

72. To please the teacher by perfection in the duties he should pay homage in the evening, and he should leave when dismissed with the words 'You may go'. When the teacher asks him 'Why have you come?', he can explain the reason for his coming. If he does not ask but agrees to the duties being done, then after ten days or a fortnight have gone by he should make an opportunity by staying back one day at the time of his dismissal, and announcing the reason for his coming; or he should go at an unaccustomed time, and when asked 'What have you come for?', he can announce it. If the teacher
73. says 'Come in the morning', he should do so. But if his stomach burns with a bile affliction at that hour, or if his food does not get digested owing to sluggish digestive heat, or if some other ailment afflicts him, he should let it be known, and proposing a time that suits himself, he should come at that time. For if a meditation subject is expounded at an inconvenient time, one cannot give attention.

This is the detailed explanation of the words 'approach the Good Friend, the giver of a meditation subject'.

74. Now as to the words, *one that suits his temperament* (§28): there are six kinds of temperament, that is, greedy temperament, hating temperament, deluded temperament, faithful temperament, intelligent temperament, and speculative temperament. Some would have fourteen, taking these six single ones together with the four made up of the three double combinations and one triple combination with the greed triad and likewise with the faith triad. But if this classification is admitted, there are many more kinds of temperament possible by combining greed, etc., with faith etc.; therefore the kinds of temperament should be understood briefly as only six. As to meaning the temperaments are one, that is to say, personal nature, idiosyncrasy. According to [102] these there are only six types of persons, that is, one of greedy temperament, one of hating temperament, one of deluded temperament, one of faithful temperament, one of intelligent temperament, and one of speculative temperament.

75. Herein, one of faithful temperament is parallel to one of greedy temperament because faith is strong when profitable [kamma] occurs in one of greedy temperament, owing to its special qualities being near to those of greed. For, in an unprofitable way, greed is affectionate and not over-austere, and so, in a profitable way, is faith. Greed seeks out sense desires as object, while faith seeks out the special qualities of virtue and so on. And greed does not give up what is harmful, while faith does not give up what is beneficial.

76. One of intelligent temperament is parallel to one of hating temperament because understanding is strong when profitable [kamma] occurs in one of hating temperament, owing to its special qualities being near to those of hate. For, in an unprofitable way, hate is disaffected and does not hold to its object, and so, in a profitable way, is understanding. Hate seeks out only unreal faults, while understanding seeks out only real faults. And hate occurs in the mode of condemning living beings, while understanding occurs in the mode of condemning formations.

77. One of speculative temperament is parallel to one of deluded temperament because obstructive applied thoughts arise often in one of deluded temperament who is striving to arouse unarisen profitable states, owing to their special qualities being near to those of delusion. For just as delusion is restless owing to perplexity, so are applied thoughts that are due to thinking over various aspects. And just as delusion vacillates owing to superficiality, so do applied thoughts that are due to facile conjecturing.

78. Others say that there are three more kinds of temperament with craving, pride, and views. Herein craving is simply greed; and pride[18] is associated with that. So neither of them exceeds greed. And since views have their source in delusion, the temperament of views falls within the deluded temperament.

79. What is the source of these temperaments? And how is it to be known that such a person is of greedy temperament, that such a person is of one of those beginning with hating temperament? What suits one of what kind of temperament?

---

18. *Māna*, usually rendered by 'pride', is rendered here both by 'pride' and 'conceit'. Etymologically derived perhaps from *māneti* (to honour) or *mināti* (to measure). In sense, however, it tends to become associated with *maññati* to conceive (false notions, see M. i, 1), to imagine, to think (as *e.g.* at Nd1. 80, Vbh. 390 and comy.). As one of the 'defilements' (see M. i, 36) it is probably best rendered by 'pride'. In the expression *asmi-māna* (often rendered by 'the pride that says "I am"') it more nearly approaches *maññanā* (false imagining, misconception, see M. iii, 246) and is better rendered by 'the conceit "I am"', since the word 'conceit' straddles both the meanings of 'pride (haughtiness)' and 'conception'.

80. Herein, as some say,[19] the first three kinds of temperament to begin with have their source in previous habit; and they have their source in the elements and humours. Apparently one of greedy temperament has formerly had plenty of desirable tasks and gratifying work to do, or has reappeared here after dying in a heaven. And one of hating temperament has formerly had plenty of stabbing and torturing and brutal work to do or has reappeared here after dying in one of the hells or the Nāga (serpent) existences. And one [103] of deluded temperament has formerly drunk a lot of intoxicants and neglected learning and questioning, or has reappeared here after dying in the animal existence. It is in this way that they have their source in previous habit, they
81. say. Then a person is of deluded temperament because two elements are prominent, that is to say, the earth element and the fire element. He is of hating temperament because the other two elements are prominent. But he is of greedy temperament because all four are equal. And as regards the humours, one of greedy temperament has phlegm in excess and one of deluded temperament has wind in excess. Or one of deluded temperament has phlegm in excess and one of greedy temperament has wind in excess. So they have their source in the elements and the humours, they say.

82. [Now it can rightly be objected that] not all of those who have had plenty of desirable tasks and gratifying work to do, and who have reappeared here after dying in a heaven, are of greedy temperament, or the others respectively of hating and deluded temperament; and there is no such law of prominence of elements (See Ch. XIV, §43f.) as that asserted; and only the pair, greed and delusion, are given in the law of humours, and even that subsequently contradicts itself; and no source for even one among those beginning with one of faithful temperament is given. Consequently this definition is indecisive.

83. The following is the exposition according to the opinion of the teachers of the commentaries; for this is said in the Explanation of Prominence: 'The fact that these beings have prominence of greed, prominence of hate, prominence of delusion, prominence of non-greed, prominence of non-hate, prominence of non-delusion, is governed by previous root-cause.

'For when in one man at the moment of his accumulating [rebirth-producing] kamma greed is strong and non-greed is weak, non-hate and non-delusion are strong and hate and

19. '"*Some*" is said with reference to the Elder Upatissa. For it is put in his way by him in the Vimutti-magga. The word "*apparently*" indicates dissent from what follows' (Pm. 103). A similiar passage to that referred to appears in Ch. 6 of the Chinese version of the Vimutti-magga, the only one extant.

delusion are weak, then his weak non-greed is unable to prevail over his greed, but his non-hate and non-delusion being strong are able to prevail over his hate and delusion. That is why, on being reborn through rebirth-linking given by that kamma, he has greed, is good-natured and unangry, and possesses understanding with knowledge like a lightning flash.

84. 'When at the moment of another's accumulating kamma greed and hate are strong and non-greed and non-hate weak, and non-delusion is strong and delusion weak, then in the way already stated he has both greed and hate but possesses understanding with knowledge like a lightning flash; like the Elder Datta-Abhaya.

'When at the moment of his accumulating kamma greed, non-hate and delusion are strong and the others are weak, then in the way already stated he both has greed and is dull but is good-tempered[20] and unangry like the Elder Bahula.

'Likewise when at the moment of his accumulating kamma the three, namely, greed, hate and delusion are strong and non-greed, etc., are weak, then in the way already stated he has both greed and hate and is deluded. [104]

85. 'When at the moment of his accumulating kamma non-greed, hate and delusion are strong and the others are weak, then in the way already stated he has little defilement and is unshakable even on seeing a heavenly object but he has hate and is slow in understanding.

'When at the moment of his accumulating kamma non-greed, non-hate and delusion are strong and the rest weak, then in the way already stated he has no greed and no hate, and is good-tempered but slow in understanding.

'Likewise when at the moment of his accumulating kamma non-greed, hate and non-delusion are strong and the rest weak, then in the way already stated he both has no greed and possesses understanding but has hate and is irascible.

'Likewise when at the moment of his accumulating kamma the three, that is, non-hate, non-greed, and non-delusion, are strong and greed, etc., are weak, then in the way already stated he has no greed and no hate and possesses understanding like the Elder Mahā-Saṅgharakkhita'.

86. One who, as it is said here, 'has greed' is one of greedy temperament; one who 'has hate' and one who 'is dull' are respectively of hating temperament and deluded temperament. One who 'possesses understanding' is one of intelligent temperament. One who 'has no greed' and one who 'has no hate' are of faithful temperament because they are naturally trustful. Or just as one who is reborn through kamma accompanied by non-delusion is of intelligent temperament, so one

---

20. '*Sīlaka*—good-tempered'=*sukhasīla* (good-natured—see §83), which =*sakhila* (kindly—Pm. 104). Not in P. T. S. Dict.

who is reborn through kamma accompanied by strong faith is of faithful temperament, one who is reborn through kamma accompanied by thoughts of sense desire is of speculative temperament, and one who is reborn through kamma accompanied by mixed greed, etc., is of mixed temperament. So it is the kamma productive of rebirth-linking and accompanied by some one among the things beginning with greed that should be understood as the source of the temperaments.

87. But it was asked, *and how is it to be known that 'This person is of greedy temperament'* (§79), and so on. This is explained as follows:

'By the posture, by the action,
'By eating, seeing, and so on,
'By the kind of states occurring,
'May temperament be recognized.'

88. Herein, *by the posture*: when one of greedy temperament is walking in his usual manner, he walks carefully, puts his foot down slowly, puts it down evenly, lifts it up evenly, and his step is springy.[21]

One of hating temperament walks as though he were digging with the points of his feet, puts his foot down quickly, lifts it up quickly, and his step is dragged along.

One of deluded temperament walks with a perplexed gait, puts his foot down hesitantly, lifts it up hesitantly, [105] and his step is pressed down suddenly.

And this is said in the account of the origin of the Māgandiya Sutta:

'The step of one of greedy nature, will be springy;
'The step of one of hating nature, dragged along;
Deluded, he will suddenly press down his step;
'And one without defilement has a step like this'
(see SnA. 544)

89. The stance of one of greedy temperament is confident and graceful. That of one of hating temperament is rigid. That of one of deluded temperament is muddled. Likewise in sitting. And one of greedy temperament spreads his bed unhurriedly, lies down slowly, composing his limbs, and he sleeps in a confident manner. When woken instead of getting up quickly, he gives his answer slowly as though doubtful. One of hating temperament spreads his bed hastily anyhow; with his body flung down he sleeps with a scowl. When woken, he gets up quickly and answers as though annoyed. One of deluded temperament spreads his bed all awry and sleeps mostly face downwards with his body sprawling. When woken, he gets up slowly, saying 'Hum'.

21. '*Ukkuṭika*—springy' is glossed here by *asamphuṭṭhamajjham* (not touching in the middle—Pm. 106). This meaning is not in P. T. S. Dict.

90. Since those of faithful temperament, etc., are parallel to those of greedy temperament, etc., their postures are therefore like those described above.

This firstly is how the temperaments may be recognized by the posture.

91. *By the action*: also in the acts of sweeping, etc., one of greedy temperament grasps the broom well, and he sweeps cleanly and evenly without hurrying or scattering the sand, as if he were strewing *sinduvāra* flowers. One of hating temperament grasps the broom tightly, and he sweeps uncleanly and unevenly with a harsh noise, hurriedly throwing up the sand on each side. One of deluded temperament grasps the broom loosely, and he sweeps neither cleanly nor evenly, mixing the sand up and turning it over.

92. As with sweeping so too with any action such as washing and dyeing robes, and so on. One of greedy temperament acts skilfully, gently, evenly and carefully. One of hating temperament acts tensely, stiffly and unevenly. One of deluded temperament acts unskilfully as if muddled, unevenly, and indecisively. [106]

Also one of greedy temperament wears his robe neither too tightly nor too loosely, confidently and level all round. One of hating temperament wears it too tight and not level all round. One of deluded temperament wears it loosely and in a muddled way.

Those of faithful temperament, etc., should be understood in the same way as those just described, since they are parallel.

This is how the temperaments may be recognized by the actions.

93. *By eating*: one of greedy temperament likes eating rich sweet food. When eating, he makes a round lump not too big and eats unhurriedly, savouring the various tastes. He enjoys getting something good. One of hating temperament likes eating rough sour food. When eating he makes a lump that fills his mouth, and he eats hurriedly without savouring the taste. He is aggrieved when he gets something not good. One of deluded temperament has no settled choice. When eating, he makes a small unrounded lump, and as he eats he drops bits into his dish, smearing his face, with his mind astray, thinking of this and that.

Also those of faithful temperament, etc., should be understood in the same way as those just described since they are parallel.

This is how the temperament may be recognized by eating.

94. And by *seeing and so on*: when one of greedy temperament sees even a slightly pleasing visible object, he looks long as if surprised, he seizes on trivial virtues, discounts genuine

faults, and when departing, he does so with regret as if unwilling to leave. When one of hating temperament sees even a slightly unpleasing visible object, he avoids looking long as if he were tired, he picks out trivial faults, discounts genuine virtues, and when departing, he does so without regret as if anxious to leave. When one of deluded temperament sees any sort of visible object, he copies what others do: if he hears others criticizing, he criticizes; if he hears others praising, he praises; but actually he feels equanimity in himself—the equanimity of unknowing. So too with sounds, and so on.

And those of faithful temperament, etc., should be understood in the same way as those just described since they are parallel.

This is how the temperaments may be recognized by seeing and so on.

95. *By the kind of states occurring*: in one of greedy temperament there is frequent occurrence of such states as deceit, fraud, pride, evilness of wishes, greatness of wishes, discontent, foppery and personal vanity.[22] [107] In one of hating temperament there is frequent occurrence of such states as anger, enmity, disparaging, domineering, envy and avarice. In one of deluded temperament there is frequent occurrence of such states as stiffness, torpor, agitation, worry, uncertainty, and holding on tenaciously with refusal to relinquish.

In one of faithful temperament there is frequent occurrence of such states as free generosity, desire to see Noble Ones, desire to hear the Good Dhamma, great gladness, ingenuousness, honesty, and trust in things that inspire trust. In one of intelligent temperament there is frequent occurrence of such states as readiness to be spoken to, possession of good

---

22. '*Siṅga*—foppery' is not in P.T.S. Dict. in this sense. See Vbh. 351 and commentary.

'*Cāpalya* (*cāpalla*)—personal vanity': noun from adj. *capala*. The word '*capala*' comes in an often-repeated passage... '*sāṭhā māyāvino keṭubhino uddhatā unnalā capalā mukharā*...' (M. i, 32); cf. S. i, 203; A. iii. 199, etc.), and also at M. i, 470 '*uddhato hoti capalo*', with two lines lower '*uddhaccaṃ cāpalyaṃ*'. *Cāpalya* also occurs at Vbh. 351 (and M. ii, 167). At MA. i, 152 (commenting of M. i, 32) we find '*capalā ti pattacīvaramaṇḍanādinā cāpallena yuttā* (interested in personal vanity consisting in adorning bowl and robe and so on)', and at MA. iii, 185 (commenting on M. i, 470) '*Uddhato hoti capalo ti uddhaccapakatiko c'eva hoti cīvaramaṇḍanā pattamaṇḍanā senāsanamaṇḍanā imassa vā pūtikāyassa kelāyanamaṇḍanā ti evaṁ vuttena taruṇadārakacāpallena samannāgato* ("he is distracted—or puffed up—and personally vain": he is possessed of the callow youth's personal vanity described as adorning the robe, adorning the bowl, adorning the lodging, or prizing and adorning this filthy body)'. This meaning is confirmed in the commentary to Vbh. 251. P.T.S. Dict. does not give this meaning at all but only 'fickle', which is unsupported by the commentary. T.C.P. Dict. (*acapala*) also does not give this meaning.

As to the other things listed here in the Vis. Text, most will be found at M. i, 36. For 'holding on tenaciously', etc., see M. i, 43.

friends, knowledge of the right amount in eating, mindfulness and full awareness, devotion to wakefulness, a sense of urgency about things that should inspire a sense of urgency, and wisely directed endeavour. In one of speculative temperament there is frequent occurrence of such states as talkativeness, sociability, boredom with devotion to the profitable, failure to finish undertakings, smoking by night and flaming by day (see M.I,144—that is to say, hatching plans at night and putting them into effect by day), and mental running hither and thither (see Ud. 37).

This is how the temperaments may be recognized by the kind of states occurring.

96. However, these directions for recognizing the temperaments have not been handed down in their entirety in either the texts or the commentaries; they are only expressed according to the opinion of the teachers and cannot therefore be treated as authentic. For even those of hating temperament can exhibit postures, etc., ascribed to the greedy temperament when they try diligently. And postures, etc., never arise with distinct characteristics in a person of mixed temperament. Only such directions for recognizing temperament as are given in the commentaries should be treated as authentic; for this is said: 'A teacher who has acquired penetration of minds will know the temperament and will explain a meditation subject accordingly; one who has not should question the pupil'. So it is by penetration of minds or by questioning the person, that it can be known whether he is one of greedy temperament or one of those beginning with hating temperament.

97. What suits one of what kind of temperament? (§79). A suitable lodging for one of greedy temperament has an unwashed sill and stands level with the ground, and it can be either an overhanging [rock with an] unprepared [drip-ledge] (see Ch. II, note 15), a grass hut, or a leaf house, etc.; it ought to be spattered with dirt, full of bats,[23] dilapidated, too high or too low, in bleak surroundings, threatened [by lions, tigers, etc.,] with a muddy, uneven path, [108] where even the bed and chair are full of bugs. And it should be ugly and unsightly, exciting loathing as soon as looked at. Suitable inner and outer garments are those that have torn-off edges with threads hanging down all round like a 'net cake',[24] harsh to the touch like hemp, soiled, heavy and hard to wear. And the right kind of bowl for him is an ugly clay bowl disfigured by stoppings and joins, or a heavy and misshapen iron bowl

---

23. '*Jatukā*—a bat': not in P.T.S. Dict. Also at Ch. XI. §7.
24. '*Jalapūvasadisa*—like a net cake': 'A cake made like a net' (Pm. 108); possibly what is now known in Ceylon as a 'string hopper', or something like it.

as unappetising as a skull. The right kind of road for him on which to wander for alms is disagreeable, with no village near, and uneven. The right kind of village for him in which to wander for alms is where people wander about as if oblivious of him, where, as he is about to leave without getting alms even from a single family, people call him into the sitting hall, saying 'Come, venerable sir', and give him gruel and rice, but do so as casually as if they were putting a cow in a pen. Suitable people to serve him are slaves or workmen who are unsightly, ill-favoured, with dirty clothes, ill-smelling and disgusting, who serve him his gruel and rice as if they were throwing it rudely at him. The right kind of gruel and rice and hard food is poor, unsightly, made up of millet, *kudusaka*, broken rice, etc., stale buttermilk, sour gruel, curry of old vegetables, or anything at all that is merely for filling the stomach. The right kind of posture for him is either standing or walking. The object of his contemplation should be any of the colour kasinas, beginning with the blue, whose colour is not pure. This is what suits one of greedy temperament.

98. A suitable resting place for one of hating temperament is not too high or too low, provided with shade and water, with well-proportioned walls, posts and steps, with well-prepared frieze work and lattice work, brightened with various kinds of painting, with an even, smooth, soft floor, adorned with festoons of flowers and a canopy of many-coloured cloth like a Brahmā-god's divine palace, with bed and chair covered with well-spread clean pretty covers, smelling sweetly of flowers, and perfumes and scents set about for homely comfort, which makes one happy and glad at

99. the mere sight of it. The right kind of road to his lodging is free from any sort of danger, traverses clean, even ground, and has been properly prepared. [109] And here it is best that the lodging's furnishings are not too many in order to avoid hiding-places for insects, bugs, snakes and rats: even a single bed and chair only. The right kind of inner and outer garments for him are of any superior stuff such as China cloth, Somāra cloth, silk, fine cotton, fine linen, of either single or double thickness, quite light, and well dyed, quite pure in colour to befit an ascetic. The right kind of bowl is made of iron, as well shaped as a water bubble, as polished as a gem, spotless, and of quite pure colour to befit an ascetic. The right kind of road on which to wander for alms is free from dangers, level, agreeable, with the village neither too far nor too near. The right kind of village in which to wander for aims is where people, thinking 'Now our lord is coming', prepare a seat in a sprinkled, swept place, and going out to meet him, take his bowl, lead him to the house,

seat him on a prepared seat and serve him carefully with their
100. own hands. Suitable people to serve him are handsome, pleasing, well bathed, well anointed, scented[25] with the perfume of incense and the smell of flowers, adorned with apparel made of variously-dyed clean pretty cloth, who do their work carefully. The right kind of gruel, rice, and hard food has colour, smell and taste, possesses nutritive essence, and is inviting, superior in every way, and enough for his wants. The right kind of posture for him is lying down or sitting. The object of his contemplation should be any one of the colour kasinas, beginning with the blue, whose colour is quite pure. This is what suits one of hating temperament.

101. The right lodging for one of deluded temperament has a view and is not shut in, where the four quarters are visible to him as he sits there. As to the postures, walking is right. The right kind of object for his contemplation is not small, that is to say, the size of a winnowing basket or the size of a saucer; for his mind becomes more confused in a confined space; so the right kind is an amply large kasina. The rest is as stated for one of hating temperament. This is what suits one of deluded temperament.

102. For one of faithful temperament all the directions given for one of hating temperament are suitable. As to the object of his contemplation, one of the Recollections is right as well.

For one of intelligent temperament there is nothing unsuitable as far as concerns the lodging and so on.

For one of speculative temperament an open lodging with a view, [110] where gardens, groves and ponds, pleasant prospects, panoramas of villages, towns and countryside, and the blue gleam of mountains, are visible to him as he sits there, is not right; for that is a condition for the running hither and thither of applied thought. So he should live in a lodging such as a deep cavern screened by woods like the Overhanging Rock of the Elephant's Belly (*Hatthikucchipabbhāra*), or Mahinda's Cave. Also an ample-sized object of contemplation is not suitable for him; for one like that is a condition for the running hither and thither of applied thought. A small one is right. The rest is as stated for one of greedy temperament. This is what suits one of speculative temperament.

These are the details, with definition of the kind, source, recognition, and what is suitable, as regards the various temperaments handed down here with the words 'that suits his own temperament' (§28).

103. However, the meditation subject that is suitable to the temperament has not been cleared up in all its aspects yet.

25. '*Surabhi*—scented, perfume': not in P.T.S. Dict.; also at Ch. VI, §90; X, §60 and Pm. 445.

This will become clear automatically when those in the following list are treated in detail.

Now it was said above 'and he should apprehend from among the forty meditation subjects one that suits his own temperament' (§28). Here the exposition of the meditation subject should be first understood in these ten ways: (1) as to enumeration, (2) as to which bring only access and which absorption, (3) as to the kinds of jhana, (4) as to surmounting, (5) as to extension and non-extension, (6) as to object, (7) as to plane, (8) as to apprehending, (9) as to condition, (10) as to suitability to temperament.

104. 1. Herein, *as to enumeration*: it was said above 'from among the forty meditation subjects' (§28). Herein, the forty meditation subjects are these:

ten kasinas (totalities),
ten kinds of foulness,
ten recollections,
four divine abidings,
four immaterial states,
One perception,
One defining.

105. Herein, the ten kasinas are these: earth kasina, water kasina, fire kasina, air kasina, blue kasina, yellow kasina, red kasina, white kasina, light kasina, and limited-space kasina.[26]

The ten kinds of foulness are these: the bloated, the livid, the festering, the cut-up, the gnawed, the scattered, the hacked and scattered, the bleeding, the worm-infested, and a skeleton.[27]

The ten kinds of recollection are these: recollection of the Buddha (the Enlightened One), recollection of the Dhamma (the Law), recollection of the Saṅgha (the Community), recollection of virtue, recollection of generosity, recollection of deities, recollection (or mindfulness) of death, mindfulness occupied with the body, mindfulness of breathing, and recollection of peace. [111]

---

26. '"*Kasiṇa*" is in the sense of entirety (*sakalaṭṭhena*)' (MA. iii, 260), See Ch. IV, §119.

27. Here ten kinds of foulness are given. But in the suttas only either five or six of this set appear to be mentioned, that is, 'Perception of a skeleton, perception of the worm-infested, perception of the livid, perception of the cut-up, perception of the bloated' (see A. i, 42 and S. v, 131; A. ii, 17 adds 'perception of the festering'). No details are given. All ten appear at Dhs. 263-4 and Ps. i, 49. It will be noted that no order of progress of decay in the kinds of corpse appears here; also the instructions in Ch. VI are for contemplating actual corpses in these states. The primary purpose here is to cultivate 'repulsiveness'.

Another set of nine progressive stages in the decay of a corpse, mostly differing from these, is given at M. i, 58, 89, etc., beginning with a corpse one day old and ending with bones turned to dust. From the

The four divine abidings are these: lovingkindness, compassion, gladness, and equanimity.

The four immaterial states are these: the base consisting of boundless space, the base consisting of boundless consciousness, the base consisting of nothingness, and the base consisting of neither perception nor non-perception.

The one perception is the perception of repulsiveness in nutriment.

The one defining is the defining of the four elements.

This is how the exposition should be understood 'as to enumeration'.

106. 2. *As to which bring access only and which absorption*: the eight recollections – excepting mindfulness occupied with the body and mindfulness of breathing—, the perception of repulsiveness in nutriment, and the defining of the four elements, are ten meditation subjects that bring access only. The others bring absorption. This is 'as to which bring access only and which absorption'.

107. 3. *As to the kind of jhana*: among those that bring absorption, the ten kasinas together with mindfulness of breathing bring all four jhanas. The ten kinds of foulness together with mindfulness occupied with the body bring the first jhana. The first three divine abidings bring three jhanas. The fourth divine abiding and the four immaterial states bring the fourth jhana. This is 'as to the kind of jhana'.

108. 4. *As to surmounting*: there are two kinds of surmounting, that is to say, surmounting of factors and surmounting of object. Herein, there is surmounting of factors in the case of all meditation subjects that bring three and four jhanas because the second jhana, etc., have to be reached in those same objects by surmounting the jhana factors of applied thought and sustained thought, and so on. Likewise in the case of the fourth divine abiding; for that too has to be reached by surmounting joy in the same object as that of lovingkindness, and so on. But in the case of the four immaterial states there is surmounting of the object; for the base consisting of boundless space has to be reached by surmounting one or other of the first nine kasinas, and the base consisting

---

words 'suppose a bhikkhu saw a corpse thrown on a charnel ground... he compares this same body of his with it thus "This body too is of like nature, awaits a like fate, is not exempt from that" ' (M. i, 58) it can be assumed that these nine, which are given in progressive order of decay in order to demonstrate the body's impermanence, are not necessarily intended as contemplations of actual corpses so much as mental images to be created, the primary purpose being to cultivate impermanence. This may be why these nine are not used here (see Ch. VIII, §43).

The word *asubha* (foul, foulness) is used both of the contemplations of corpses as here and of the contemplation of the parts of the body (A. v, 109).

of boundless consciousness, etc., have respectively to be reached by surmounting space, and so on. With the rest there is no surmounting. This is 'as to surmounting'.

109. 5. *As to extension and non-extension*: only the ten kasinas among these forty meditation subjects need be extended. For it is within just so much space as one is intent upon with the kasina that one can hear sounds with the divine ear element, see visible objects with the divine eye, and know the minds of other beings with the mind.

110. Mindfulness occupied with the body and the ten kinds of foulness need not be extended. Why? Because they have a definite location and because there is no benefit in it. The definiteness of their location will become clear in explaining the method of development (Ch. VIII, §83-138 and Ch. VI, §40, 41, 79). If the latter are extended, it is only a quantity of corpses that is extended [112] and there is no benefit. And this is said in answer to the question of Sopāka 'Perception of visible forms is quite clear, Blessed One, perception of 'bones is not clear' ( ); for here the perception of visible forms is called 'quite clear' in the sense of extension of the sign, while the perception of bones is called 'not

111. quite clear' in the sense of its non-extension. But the words 'I was intent upon this whole earth with the perception of a 'skeleton' (Thag. 18) are said of the manner of appearance to one who has acquired that perception. For just as in [the Emperor] Dhammāsoka's time the *Karavīka* bird uttered a sweet song when it saw its own reflection in the looking-glass walls all round and perceived *Karavīkas* in every direction,[28] so the Elder [Siṅgāla Pitar] thought, when he saw the sign appearing in all directions through his acquisition of the perception of a skeleton, that the whole earth was covered with bones.

28. The full story, which occurs at MA. iii, 382-3 and elsewhere, is this: 'It seems that when the Karavīka bird has pecked a sweet-flavoured mango with its beak and savoured the dripping juice, and, flapping its wings, begins to sing, then quadrupeds caper as if mad. Quadrupeds grazing in their pastures drop the grass in their mouths and listen to the sound. Beasts of prey hunting small animals pause with one foot raised. Hunted animals lose their fear of death and halt in their tracks. Birds flying in the air stay with wings outstretched. Fishes in the water keep still, not moving their fins. All listen to the sound, so beautiful is the Karavīka's song. Dhammāsoka's queen Asandhamittā asked the Community "Venerable sirs, is there anything that sounds like the Buddha?"—"The Karavīka bird does."—"Where are those birds, venerable sirs?"—"In the Himalaya." She told the king "Sire, I wish to hear a Karavīka bird". The king despatched a gold cage with the order "Let a Karavīka bird come and sit in this cage." The cage travelled and halted in front of a Karavīka. Thinking "The cage has come at the king's command; it is imposible not to go", the bird got in. The cage returned and stopped before the king. They could not get the Karavīka to utter a sound. When the king asked "When do they utter a sound?", they replied "On seeing their kin".

112. If that is so, then is what is called the measurelessness of the object of jhana produced on foulness contradicted?[29] It is not contradicted. For one man apprehends the sign in a large bloated corpse or skeleton, another in a small one. In this way the jhana of the one has a limited object and that of the other a measureless object. Or alternatively 'With a measureless object' (Dhs. 182–4 in elision) is said of it referring to one who extends it, seeing no disadvantage in doing so. But it need not be extended because no benefit results.

113. The rest need not be extended likewise. Why? When a man extends the sign of in-breaths and out-breaths, only a quantity of wind is extended, and it has a definite location, [the nose-tip.] So it need not be extended because of the disadvantage and because of the definiteness of the location. And the divine abidings have living beings as their object. When a man extends the sign of these, only the quantity of living beings would be extended, and there is no purpose in that. So that also need not be extended.

114. When it is said 'Intent upon one quarter with his 'heart endued with lovingkindness' (D. i, 250), etc., that is said for the sake of comprehensive inclusion. For it is when a man develops it progressively by including living beings in one direction by one house, by two houses, etc., that he is said to be 'intent upon one direction', [113] not when he extends the sign. And there is no counterpart sign here that he might extend. Also the state of having a limited or measureless object can be understood here according to the way of inclusion, too.

115. As regards the immaterial states as object, space need not be extended since it is the mere removal of the kasina [materiality]; for that should be brought to mind only as the disappearance of the kasina [materiality]; if he extends it, nothing further happens. And consciousness need not be extended since it is a state consisting in an individual essence, and it is not possible to extend a state consisting in an individual essence. The disappearance of consciousness need not be extended since it is mere non-existence of consciousness. And the base consisting of neither perception

Then the king had it surrounded with looking-glasses. Seeing its own reflection and imagining that its relatives had come, it flapped its wings and cried out with an exquisite voice as if sounding a crystal trumpet. All the people in the city rushed about as if mad. Asandhamittā thought "If the sound of this creature is so fine, what indeed can the sound of the Blessed One have been like since he had reached the glory of omniscient knowledge?", and arousing a happiness that she never again relinquished, she became established in the fruition of Stream Entry'.

29. See Dhs., p. 55; but it comes under the '...*pe*...', which must be filled in from pp. 37-8, §182 and §184.

nor non-perception as object need not be extended since it too is a state consisting in an individual essence.[30]

116. The rest need not be extended because they have no sign. For it is the counterpart sign[31] that would be extendable, and the object of the recollection of the Buddha, etc., is not a counterpart sign. Consequently there is no need for extension there.

This is 'as to extension and non-extension'.

117. 6. *As to object*: of these forty meditation subjects, twenty-two have counterpart signs as object, that is to say, the ten kasinas, the ten kinds of foulness, mindfulness of breathing, and mindfulness occupied with the body; the rest do not have counterpart signs as object. Then twelve have states consisting in individual essences as object, that is to say, eight of the ten recollections—except mindfulness of breathing and mindfulness occupied with the body—, the perception of repulsiveness in nutriment, the defining of the four elements, the base consisting of boundless consciousness, and the base consisting of neither perception nor non-perception ; and twenty-two have [counterpart] signs as object, that is to say, the ten kasinas, the ten kinds of foulness, mindfulness of breathing, and mindfulness occupied with the body; while the remaining six have 'not-so-classifiable'[32] objects. Then eight have mobile objects in the early stage though the counterpart is stationary, that is to say, the festering, the bleeding, the worm-infested, mindfulness of breathing, the water kasina, the fire kasina, the air kasina, and in the case of the light kasina the object consisting of a circle of sunlight, etc.; the rest have immobile objects.[33] This is 'as to object'.

---

30. 'It is because only an abstract (*parikappaja*) object can be extended, not any other kind, that he said "*it is not possible to extend a state consisting in an individual essence*"' (Pm. 110).

31. The word '*nimitta*' in its technical sense is consistently rendered here by the word 'sign', which corresponds very nearly if not exactly to most uses of it. It is sometimes rendered by 'mark' (which over-emphasizes the concrete), and by 'image' (which is not always intended). The three kinds, that is, the 'preliminary-work sign, learning sign and counterpart sign' do not appear in the Pitakas. There the use rather suggests association of ideas as, for example, at M. i, 180, M. i, 119, A. i, 4, etc., than the more definitely visualized 'image' in some instances of the 'counterpart sign' described in the following chapters.

32. '*Na-vattaba*—not-so-classifiable' is an Abhidhamma shorthand term for something that, when considered under one of the triads or dyads of the Abhidhamma Mātikā (Dhs., p. 1f.), cannot be placed under any one of the three, or two, headings.

33. '"*The festering*" is a mobile object because of the oozing of the pus, "*the bleeding*" because of the trickling of the blood, "*the worm-infested*" because of the wriggling of the worms. The mobile aspect of the sunshine coming in through a window opening is evident, which explains why an object consisting of a circle of sunlight is called mobile' (Pm. 110).

118. 7. *As to plane*: here the twelve, namely, the ten kinds of foulness, mindfulness occupied with the body, and perception of repulsiveness in nutriment, do not occur among deities. These twelve and mindfulness of breathing do not occur in the Brahmā world. But none except the four immaterial states occur in the immaterial becoming. All occur among human beings. This is 'as to plane'. [114]

119. 8. *As to apprehending*: here the exposition should be understood according to sight, touch and hearsay. Herein, these nineteen, that is to say, nine kasinas omitting the air kasina and the ten kinds of foulness, must be apprehended by sight. The meaning is that in the early stage their sign must be apprehended by constantly looking with the eye. In the case of mindfulness occupied with the body the five parts ending with skin must be apprehended by sight and the rest by hearsay, so its object must be apprehended by sight and hearsay. Mindfulness of breathing must be apprehended by touch; the air kasina by sight and touch; the remaining eighteen by hearsay. The divine abiding of equanimity and the four immaterial states are not apprehendable by a beginner; but the remaining thirty-five are. This is 'as to apprehending'.

120. 9. *As to condition*: of these meditation subjects nine kasinas omitting the space kasina are conditions for the immaterial states. The ten kasinas are conditions for the kinds of direct-knowledge. Three divine abidings are conditions for the fourth divine abiding. Each lower immaterial state is a condition for each higher one. The base consisting of neither perception nor non-perception is a condition for the attainment of cessation. All are conditions for living in bliss, for insight, and for the fortunate kinds of becoming. This is 'as to condition'.

121. 10. *As to suitability to temperament*: here the exposition should be understood according to what is suitable to the temperaments. That is to say: firstly the ten kinds of foulness and mindfulness occupied with the body are eleven meditation subjects suitable for one of greedy temperament. The four divine abidings and four colour kasinas are eight suitable for one of hating temperament. Mindfulness of breathing is the one [recollection as a] meditation subject suitable for one of deluded temperament and for one of speculative temperament. The first six recollections are suitable for one of faithful temperament. Mindfulness of death, the recollection of peace, the defining of the four elements, and the perception of repulsiveness in nutriment, are four suitable for one of intelligent temperament. The remaining kasinas and the immaterial states are suitable for all kinds of temperament. And any one of the kasinas should be limited for one

of speculative temperament and measureless for one of deluded temperament. This is how the exposition should be understood here 'as to suitability to temperament'.

122. All this has been stated in the form of direct opposition and complete suitability. But there is actually no profitable development that does not suppress greed, etc., and help faith, and so on. And this is said in the Meghiya Sutta: '[One] should, in addition,[34] develop these four things: 'foulness should be developed for the purpose of abandoning greed (lust). Lovingkindness should be developed for the 'purpose of abandoning ill will. [115] Mindfulness of breathing should be developed for the purpose of cutting off 'applied thought. Perception of impermanence should be 'cultivated for the purpose of eliminating the conceit "I 'am" ' (A.iv, 358). Also in the Rāhula Sutta in the passage beginning 'Develop lovingkindness, Rāhula' (M. i, 424) seven meditation subjects are given for a single temperament. So instead of insisting on the mere letter, the intention should be sought in each instance.

This is the explanatory exposition of the meditation subject referred to by the words *and he should apprehend...one* [meditation subject] (§28).

123. Now the words *and he should apprehend* are illustrated as follows. After approaching the Good Friend of the kind described in the explanation of the words *then approach the Good Friend, the giver of a meditation subject* (§28 and §57–73), the meditator should dedicate himself to the Blessed One, the Enlightened One, or to a teacher, and he should ask for the meditation subject with a sincere inclination [of the heart] and sincere resolution.

124. Herein, he should dedicate himself to the Blessed One, the Enlightened One, in this way: 'Blessed One, I relinquish this my person to you'. For without having thus dedicated himself when living in a remote abode he might be unable to stand fast if a frightening object made its appearance, and he might return to a village abode, become associated with laymen, take up improper search and come to ruin. But when he has dedicated himself in this way no fear arises in him if a frightening object makes its appearance; in fact only joy arises in him as he reflects 'Have you not wisely already dedicated yourself to the Enlightened One?'

125. Suppose a man had a fine piece of Kāsi cloth. He would feel grief if it were eaten by rats or moths; but if he gave it to a bhikkhu needing robes, he would feel only joy if he saw the

34. 'In addition to the five things' (not quoted) dealt with earlier in the sutta, namely, perfection of virtue, good friendship, hearing suitable things, energy, and understanding.

bhikkhu tearing it up [to make his patched cloak]. And so it is with this.

126. When he dedicates himself to a teacher, he should say 'I relinquish this my person to you, venerable sir'. For one who has not dedicated his person thus becomes unresponsive to correction, hard to speak to, and unamenable to advice, or he goes where he likes without asking the teacher. Consequently the teacher does not help him with either material things or the Dhamma, and he does not train him in the cryptic books.[35] Failing to get these two kinds of help [116] he finds no footing in the Dispensation, and he soon comes down to misconducting himself or to the lay state. But if he has dedicated his person, he is not unresponsive to correction, does not go about as he likes, is easy to speak to, and lives only in dependence on the teacher. He gets the twofold help from the teacher and attains growth, increase and fulfilment in the Dispensation. Like the Elder Cūḷa-Piṇḍapātika-Tissa's pupils.

127. Three bhikkhus came to the Elder, it seems. One of them said 'Venerable sir, I am ready to fall from a cliff the height of one hundred men, if it is said to be to your advantage'. The second said 'Venerable sir, I am ready to grind away this body from the heels up without remainder on a flat stone, if it is said to be to your advantage'. The third said 'Venerable sir, I am ready to die by stopping breathing, if it said to be to your advantage'. Observing 'These bhikkhus are certainly capable of progress', the Elder expounded a meditation subject to them. Following his advice, the three attained Arahantship.

This is the benefit in self dedication. Hence it was said above 'dedicating himself to the Blessed One, the Enlightened One, or to a teacher'.

128. *With a sincere inclination [of the heart] and sincere resolution* (§123): the meditator's inclination should be sincere in the six modes beginning with non-greed. For it is one of such sincere inclination who arrives at one of the three kinds of enlightenment, according as it is said 'Six kinds 'of inclination lead to the maturing of the enlightenment of the Bodhisattas. With the inclination to non-greed 'Bodhisattas see the fault in greed. With the inclina- 'tion to non-hate Bodhisattas see the fault in hate. 'With the inclination to non-delusion Bodhisattas see 'the fault in delusion. With the inclination to renun- 'ciation Bodhisattas see the fault in house life. With the 'inclination to seclusion Bodhisattas see the fault in society.

35. '"*The cryptic books*": the meditation-subject books dealing with the truths, the dependent origination, etc., which are profound and associated with voidness' (Pm. III), Cf. MA. ii, 264; AA. commentary to A. Catukka-nipāta, 180.

'With the inclination to relinquishment Bodhisattas see the 'fault in all kinds of becoming and destiny' ( ). For Stream Enterers, Once-returners, Non-returners, those with Cankers Destroyed, Pacceka Buddhas, and Fully Enlightened Ones, whether past, future or present, all arrive at the distinction peculiar to each by means of these same six modes. That is why he should have sincerity of inclination in these six modes.

129. He should be whole-heartedly resolved on that. The meaning is [117] that he should be resolved upon concentration, respect concentration, incline to concentration, be resolved upon nibbana, respect nibbana, incline to nibbana.

130. When with sincerity of inclination and whole-hearted resolution in this way he asks for a meditation subject, then a teacher who has acquired the penetration of minds can know his temperament by snrveying his mental conduct; and a teacher who has not can know it by putting such questions to him as 'What is your temperament?' or 'What states are usually present in you?' or 'What do you like bringing to mind?' or 'What meditation subject does your mind favour?'. When he knows, he can expound a meditation subject suitable to that temperament. And in doing so, he can expound it in three ways: it can be given to one who has already learnt the meditation subject by having him recite it at one or two sessions; it can be expounded to one who lives in the same place each time he comes; and to one who wants to learn it and then go elsewhere it can be expounded in such a manner that it is neither too brief nor too long.

131. Herein, when firstly he is explaining the earth kasina, there are nine aspects that he should explain. They are the four faults of the kasina, the making of a kasina, the method of development for one who has made it, the two kinds of sign, the two kinds of concentration, the seven kinds of suitable and unsuitable, the ten kinds of skill in absorption, evenness of energy, and the directions for absorption.

In the case of the other meditation subjects, each should be expounded in the way appropriate to it. All this will be made clear in the directions for development. But when the meditation subject is being expounded in this way, the meditator must apprehend the sign as he listens.

132. *Apprehend the sign* means that he must connect each aspect thus, 'This is the preceding clause, this is the subsequent clause, this is its meaning, this is its intention, this is the simile'. When he listens attentively, apprehending the sign in this way, his meditation subject is well apprehended. Then, and because of that, he successfully attains distinction, but

not otherwise. This clarifies the meaning of the words 'and he must apprehend'.

133. At this point the clauses *approach the Good Friend, the giver of a meditation subject, and he should apprehend from among the forty meditation subjects one that suits his own temperament* (§28) have been expounded in detail in all their aspects.

The third chapter called 'The Description of taking a Meditation Subject' in the Treatise on the Development of Concentration in the Path of Purification composed for the purpose of gladdening good people.

CHAPTER IV

DESCRIPTION OF CONCENTRATION— THE EARTH KASINA

(*paṭhavī-kasiṇa-niddesa*)

1. [118] Now it was said earlier *After that he should avoid a monastery unfavourable to the development of concentration and go to live in one that is favourable* (Ch. III, §28). In the first place one who finds it convenient to live with the teacher in the same monastery can live there while he is making certain of the meditation subject. If it is inconvenient there, he can live in another monastery—a suitable one—a quarter or a half or even a whole league distant. In that case, when he finds he is in doubt about, or has forgotten, some passage in the meditation subject, then he should do the duties in the monastery in good time and set out afterwards, going for alms on the way and arriving at the teacher's dwelling place after his meal. He should make certain about the meditation subject that day in the teacher's presence. Next day, after paying homage to the teacher, he should go for alms on his way back and so he can return to his own dwelling place without fatigue. But one who finds no convenient place within even a league should clarify all difficulties about the meditation subject and make quite sure it has been properly attended to. Then he can even go far away and, avoiding a monastery unfavourable to development of concentration, live in one that is favourable.

[The 18 Faults of a Monastery]

2. Herein, one that is unfavourable has any one of eighteen faults. These are largeness, newness, dilapidatedness, a nearby road, a pond, [edible] leaves, flowers, fruits, famousness, a nearby city, nearby timber trees, nearby arable fields, presence of incompatible persons, a nearby port of entry, nearness to the border countries, nearness to the frontier of a kingdom, unsuitability, lack of good friends. [119] One with any of these faults is not favourable. He should not live there. Why?

3. 1. Firstly people with varying aims collect in a *large monastery*. They conflict with each other and so neglect the duties. The Enlightenment-tree terrace, etc., remain unswept, the water for drinking and washing is not set out. So if he thinks 'I shall go to the alms-resort village for alms' and takes his bowl and robe and sets out, perhaps he sees that the duties have not been done or that a drinking-water pot is empty, and so the duty has to be done by him

unexpectedly. Drinking water must be maintained. By not doing it he would commit a wrongdoing in the breach of a duty. But if he does it, he loses time. He arrives too late at the village and gets nothing because the almsgiving is finished. Also when he goes into retreat, he is distracted by the loud noises of novices and young bhikkhus, and by acts of the Community [being carried out]. However, he can live in a large monastery where all the duties are done and where there are none of the other disturbances.

4. 2. In a *new monastery* there is much new building activity. People criticize someone who takes no part in it. But he can live in such a monastery where the bhikkhus say 'Let the venerable one do the ascetic's duties as much as he likes. We shall see to the building work'.

5. 3. In a *dilapidated monastery* there is much that needs repair. People criticize someone who does not see about the repairing of at least his own lodging. When he sees to the repairs, his meditation subject suffers.

6. 4. In a monastery with *a nearby road*, by a main street, visitors keep arriving night and day. He has to give up his own lodging to those who come late, and he has to go and live at the root of a tree or on the top of a rock. And next day it is the same. So there is no opportunity [to practise] his meditation subject. But he can live in one where there is no such disturbance by visitors.

7. 5. A *pond* is a rock pool. Numbers of people come there for drinking water. Pupils of city-dwelling elders supported by the royal family come to do dyeing work. When they ask for vessels, wood, tubs, etc., [120] they must be shown where these things are. So he is kept all the time on the alert.

8. 6. If he goes with his meditation subject to sit by day where there are many sorts of edible *leaves*, then women vegetable-gatherers, singing as they pick leaves nearby, endanger his meditation subject by disturbing it with sounds of the opposite sex.

7. And where there are many sorts of *flowering* shrubs in bloom there is the same danger too.

9. Where there are many sorts of *fruits* such as mangoes, rose-apples and jack-fruits people who want fruits come and ask for them, and they get angry if he does not give them any, or they take them by force. When walking in the monastery in the evening he sees them and asks 'Why do you do so, lay followers?', they abuse him as they please and even try to evict him.

10. 9. When he lives in a monastery that is *famous* and renowned in the world, like Dakkhiṇagiri,[1] Hatthikucchi, Cetiyagiri

1. 'They say it is the Dakkhiṇagiri in the Magadha country' (Pm. 116). There is mention of a Dakkhiṇagiri-vihāra at MA. ii, 293 and elsewhere.

or Cittalapabbata, there are always people coming who want to pay homage to him, supposing that he is an Arahant, which inconveniences him. But if it suits him, he can live there at night and go elsewhere by day.

11. 10. In one with a *nearby city* objects of the opposite sex come into focus. Women water-pot carriers go by bumping into him with their jars and giving no room to pass. Also important people spread out carpets in the middle of the monastery and sit down.

12. 11. One with *nearby timber trees* where there are timber trees and osiers useful for making framework is inconvenient because of the wood-gatherers there, like the gatherers of branches and fruits already mentioned. If there are trees in a monastery, people come and cut them down to build houses with. When he has come out of his meditation room in the evening and is walking up and down in the monastery, if he sees them and asks 'Why do you do so, lay followers?', they abuse him as they please and even try to evict him.

13. 12. People make use of one with *nearby arable fields*, quite surrounded by fields. They make a threshing floor in the middle of the monastery itself. They thresh corn there, dry it in the forecourts,[2] and cause great inconvenience. And where there is extensive property belonging to the Community, the monastery attendants impound cattle belonging to families and deny the water supply [to their crops]. [121] Then people bring and ear of paddy and show it to the Community saying 'Look at your monastery attendants' work'. For one reason or another he has to go to the portals of the king or the king's ministers. This [matter of property belonging to the Community] is included by [a monastery that is] near arable fields.

14. 13. *Presence of incompatible persons*: where there are bhikkhus living who are incompatible and mutually hostile, when they clash and it is protested 'Venerable sirs, do not do so' they exclaim 'We no longer count now that this refuse-rag wearer has come'.

15. 14. One with a nearby water *port of entry* or land port of entry[3] is made inconvenient by people constantly arriving respectively by ship or by caravan and crowding round, asking for space or drinking water or salt.

16. 15. In the case of one *near the Border Countries*, people have no trust in the Buddha, etc., there.

16. In one *near the frontier of a kingdom* there is fear of kings. For perhaps one king attacks that place, thinking 'It does not submit to my rule', and the other does likewise.

2. Read *pamukhesu sosayanti*. *Pamukha* not thus in P.T.S. Dict.
3. 'A "*water port of entry*" is a port of entry on the sea or on an estuary. A "*land port of entry*" is one on the edge of a forest and acts as the gateway on the road of approach to great cities' (Pm. 116).

thinking 'It does not submit to my rule'. A bhikkhu lives there when it is conquered by one king and when it is conquered by the other. Then they suspect him of spying, and they bring about his undoing.

17. 17. *Unsuitability* is that due to the risk of encountering visible data, etc., of the opposite sex as objects or to haunting by non-human beings. Here is a story. An elder lived in a forest, it seems. Then an ogress stood in the door of his leaf hut and sang. The elder came out and stood in the door. She went to the end of the walk and sang. The elder went to the end of the walk. She stood in a chasm a hundred fathoms deep and sang. The elder recoiled. Then she suddenly grabbed him saying 'Venerable sir, it is not just one or two of the likes of you I have eaten'.

18. 18. *Lack of good friends*: where it is not possible to find a good friend as a teacher or the equivalent of a teacher or a preceptor or the equivalent of a preceptor, the lack of good friends there is a serious fault.

One that has any of these eighteen faults should be understood as unfavourable. And this is said in the commentaries:

'A large abode, a new abode,
'One tumbling down, one near a rode,
'One with a pond, or leaves, or flowers,
'Or fruits, or one that people seek; [122]
'In cities, among timber, fields,
'Where people quarrel, in a port,
'In Border Lands, on frontiers,
'Unsuitableness, and no good friend—
'These are the eighteen instances
'A wise man needs to recognize
'And give them full as wide a berth
'As any footpad-haunted road'.

[The 5 Factors of the Resting Place]

19. One that has the five factors beginning with 'not too far from and not too near to' the alms resort is called favourable. For this is said by the Blessed One 'And how has a lodging 'five factors, bhikkhus? Here, bhikkhus, (1) a lodging is 'not too far, not too near, and has a path for going and 'coming. (2) It is little frequented by day with little sound 'and few voices by night. (3) There is little contact with 'gadflies, flies, wind, burning [sun] and creeping things. '(4) One who lives in that lodging easily obtains robes, alms 'food, lodging, and the requisite of medicine as cure for the 'sick. (5) In that lodging there are elder bhikkhus living who 'are learned, versed in the scriptures, observers of the 'Dhamma, observers of the Vinaya, observers of the Codes,

'and when from time to time one asks them questions "How 'is this, venerable sir? what is the meaning of this?", then those 'venerable ones reveal the unrevealed, explain the unex-'plained, and remove doubt about the many things that 'raise doubts. This, bhikkhus, is how a lodging has five 'factors' (A. v, 15).

These are the details for the clause 'After that he should avoid a monastery unfavourable to the development of concentration and go to live in one that is favourable' (Ch. III, §28).

[THE LESSER IMPEDIMENTS]

20. *Then he should sever the lesser impediments* (Ch. III, §28): one living in such a favourable monastery should sever any minor impediments that he may still have, that is to say, long head hair, nails, and body hair, should be cut, mending and patching of old robes should be done or those that are soiled should be dyed. If there is a stain on the bowl, the bowl should be baked. The bed, chair, etc., should be cleaned up. These are the details for the clause 'Then he should sever the lesser impediments'.

* * *

[DETAILED INSTRUCTIONS FOR DEVELOPMENT]

21. Now with the clause *And not overlook any of the directions for development* (Ch.III,§28) the time has come for the detailed exposition of all meditation subjects, starting with the earth kasina.

[THE EARTH KASINA]

[123] When a bhikkhu has thus severed the lesser impediments, then, on his return from his alms round after his meal and after he has got rid of drowziness due to the meal, he should sit down comfortably in a secluded place and apprehend the sign in earth that is either made up or not made up.
22. For this is said[4] : 'One who is learning the earth kasina apprehends the sign in earth that is either made up or not made up, that is bounded not unbounded, limited not unlimited, with

4. 'Said in the Old Commentary. "*One who is learning the earth kasina*" one who is apprehending, grasping, an earth kasina as a "learning sign". The meaning is, one who is producing an earth kasina that has become the sign of learning; and here "arousing" should be regarded as the establishing of the sign in that way. "*In earth*" in an earth disk of the kind about to be described. "*Apprehends the sign*": he apprehends in that with knowledge connected with meditative development the sign of earth of the kind about to be described, as one does with the eye the sign of the face in a looking-glass. "*Made up*": prepared in the manner about to be described. "*Not made up*": in a disk of earth consisting of an ordinary threshing-floor disk, and so on. "*Bounded*":

a periphery not without a periphery, circumscribed not uncircumscribed, either the size of a bushel (*suppa*) or the size of a saucer (*sarāva*). He sees to it that that sign is well apprehended, well attended to, well defined. Having done that, and seeing its advantages and perceiving it as a treasure, building up respect for it, making it dear to him, he anchors his mind to that object, thinking "Surely in this way I shall be freed from ageing and death". Secluded from sense desires,...he enters upon and dwells in the first jhana...'

23. Herein, when in a previous becoming a man has gone forth into homelessness in the Dispensation or [outside it] with the Rishis' Going Forth and has already produced the jhana tetrad or pentad on the earth kasina, and so has such merit and the support [of past practice of jhana] as well, then the sign arises in him on earth that is not made up, that is to say, on a ploughed area or on a threshing floor, as in the Elder Mallaka's case.

It seems that while that venerable one was looking at a ploughed area the sign arose in him the size of that area. He extended it and attained the jhana pentad. Then by establishing insight with the jhana as the basis for it, he reached Arahantship.

[Making an Earth Kasina]

24. But when a man has had no such previous practice, he should make a kasina, guarding against the four faults of a kasina and not overlooking any of the directions for the meditation subject learnt from the teacher. Now the four faults of the earth kasina are due to the intrusion of blue, yellow, red or white. So instead of using clay of such colours he should make the kasina of clay like that in the stream of the Gangā,[5] which is the colour of the dawn. [124] And he

---

only in one that has bounds. As regards the words "*the size of a bushel*", etc., it would be desirable that a bushel and a saucer were of equal size, but some say that "*the size of a saucer*" is a span and four fingers, and that "*the size of a bushel*" is larger than that. "*He sees to it that that sign is well apprehended*": that meditator makes that disk of earth a well-apprehended sign. When after apprehending the sign in it by opening the eyes and looking and then closing them again it appears to him as he adverts to it just as it did at the moment of looking with open eyes, then he has made it well apprehended. Having thoroughly established his mindfulness there, observing it again and again with his mind not straying outside, he sees that it is "*well attended to*". When it is well attended to thus by adverting and attending again and again, by producing much repetition and development instigated by that, he sees that it is "*well defined*". "*To that object*" to that object called earth kasina, which has appeared rightly owing to its having been well apprehended. "*He anchors his mind*": by bringing his own mind to access jhana he anchors it, keeps it from other objects' (Pm. 119).

5. '*Gangā* (= 'river') is the name for the Ganges in India and for the

should make it not in the middle of the monastery in a place where novices, etc., are about but on the confines of the manastery in a screened place, either under an overhanging rock or in a leaf hut. He can make it either portable or as a fixture.

25. Of these, a portable one should be made by tying rags or leather or matting onto four sticks and smearing thereon a disk of the size already mentioned, using clay picked clean of grass, roots, gravel, and sand, and well kneaded. At the time of the preliminary work it should be laid on the ground and looked at.

A fixture should be made by knocking stakes into the ground in the form of a lotus calyx, lacing them over with creepers. If the clay is insufficient, then other clay should be put underneath and a disk a span and four fingers across made on top of that with the quite pure dawn-coloured clay. For it was with reference only to measurement that it was said above *either the size of a bushel or the size of a saucer* (§22). But *that is bounded not unbounded* was said to show its delimitedness.

26. So, having thus made it delimited and of the size prescribed, he should scrape it down with a stone trowel—a wooden trowel turns it a bad colour, so that should not be employed—and make it as even as the surface of a drum. Then he should sweep the place out and have a bath. On his return he should seat himself on a well-covered chair with legs a span and four fingers high, prepared in a place that is two and a half cubits, [that is, two and a half times elbow to finger-tip,] from the kasina disk. For the kasina does not appear plainly to him if he sits further off than that; and if the sits nearer than that, faults in the kasina appear. If he sits higher up, he has to look at it with his neck bent; and if he sits lower down, his knees ache.

[Starting Contemplation]

27. So after seating himself in the way stated, he should review the dangers in sense desires in the way beginning 'Sense 'desires give little enjoyment' (M. i, 91) and arouse longing for the escape from sense desires, for the renunciation that is the means to the surmounting of all suffering. He should next arouse joy of happiness by recollecting the special qualities of the Buddha, the Dhamma, and the Sangha; then awe by thinking 'Now this is the way of renunciation entered upon By all Buddhas, Pacceka Buddhas and Noble Disciples'; and then eagerness by thinking 'In this way I shall surely

Mahavaeli-gangā, Ceylon's principal river. However, In the Island of Ceylon there is a river, it seems, called the Rāvaṇagangā. The Clay in the places where the banks are cut away by its stream is the colour of dawn' (Pm. 119).

come to know the taste of the bliss of seclusion'. [125] After that he should open his eyes moderately, apprehend the sign[6] and so proceed to develop it.

28. If he opens his eyes too wide, they get fatigued and the disk becomes too obvious, which prevents the sign becoming apparent to him. If he opens them too little, the disk is not obvious enough, his mind becomes drowzy, which also prevents the sign becoming apparent to him. So he should develop it by apprehending the sign (*nimitta*), keeping his eyes open moderately, as if he were seeing the reflection of his face (*mukha-nimitta*) on the surface of a looking-glass.[7]

29. The colour should not be reviewed. The characteristic should not be given attention.[8] But rather, while not ignoring the colour, attention should be given by setting the mind on the [name] concept as the most outstanding mental datum, relegating the colour to the position of a property of its physical support. That [conceptual state] can be called by any one he likes among the names for earth (*paṭhavī*), such as 'earth (*paṭhavī*)', 'the Great One (*mahī*)', 'the Friendly One (*medinī*)', 'ground (*bhūmi*)', 'The Pro-

---

6. ' "*Apprehend the sign*": apprehend with the mind the sign apprehended by the eye in the earth kasina. "*And develop it*": the apprehending of the sign as it occurs should be continued intensively and constantly practised' (Pm. 120).

7. 'Just as one who sees his reflection (*mukha-nimitta*—lit. face-sign) on the surface of a looking-glass does not open his eyes too widely or too little [in order to get the effect], nor does he review the colour of the looking-glass or give attention to its characteristic, but rather looks with moderately opened eyes and sees only the sign of his face, so too this meditator looks with moderately opened eyes at the earth kasina and is occupied only with the sign' (Pm. 121).

8. 'The dawn colour that is there in the kasina should not be thought about, though it cannot be denied that it is apprehended by eye consciousness. That is why, instead of saying here "should not be looked at", he says that it should not be apprehended by reviewing. Also the earth element's characteristic of hardness, which is there, should not be given attention because the apprehension has to be done through the channel of seeing. And after saying "*while not ignoring the colour*" he said "*relegating the colour to the position of a property of the physical support*", showing that here the concern is not with the colour, which is the channel, but rather that this colour should be treated as an accessory of the physical support; the meaning is that the kasina [disk] should be given attention with awareness of both the accompanying earth-aspect and its ancillary colour-aspect, but taking the earth-aspect with its ancillary concomitant colour as both supported equally by that physical support [the disk]. "*On the concept as the mental datum since that is what is outstanding*": the term of ordinary usage "earth (*paṭhavī*)" as applied to earth with its accessories, since the prominence of its individual effect is due to outstandingness of the earth element: "*setting the mind*" on that mental datum consisting of a [name-] concept (*paññatti-dhamma*), the kasina should be given attention as "earth, earth".—If the mind is to be set on a mere concept through the means of a term of common usage, ought earth to be given attention by means of different names?—It can be. What is wrong? It is to show that that is done he said "*Mahī, medinī*", and so on' (Pm. 122).

vider of Wealth (*vasudhā*)', 'the Bearer of Wealth (*vasudharā*)', etc., whichever suits his manner of perception. Still 'earth' is also a name that is obvious, so it can be developed with the obvious one by saying 'Earth, earth'. It should be adverted to now with eyes open, now with eyes shut. And he should go on developing it in this way a hundred times, a thousand times, and even more than that, until the learning sign arises.

30. When, while he is developing it in this way, it comes into focus[9] as he adverts with his eyes shut exactly as it does with his eyes open, then the learning sign is said to have been produced. After its production he should no longer sit in that place;[10] he should return to his own quarters and go on developing it sitting there. But in order to avoid the delay of foot washing, a pair of single-soled sandals and a walking stick are desirable. Then if the new concentration vanishes through some unsuitable encounter, he can put his sandals on, take his walking stick and go back to the place to re-apprehend the sign there. When he returns he should seat himself comfortably and develop it by reiterated reaction to it and by striking at it with thought and applied thought.

[THE COUNTERPART SIGN]

31. As he does so, the hindrances eventually become suppressed, the defilements subside, the mind becomes concentrated with access concentration, and the counterpart sign arises.

The difference between the earlier learning sign and the counterpart sign is this. In the learning sign any fault in the kasina is apparent. But the counterpart sign [126] appears as if breaking out from the learning sign, and a hundred times, a thousand times, more purified, like a looking-glass disk drawn from its case, like a mother-of-pearl dish well washed, like the moon's disk coming out from behind a cloud, like cranes against a thunder cloud. But it has neither colour nor shape; for if it had, it would be cognizable by the eye, gross, susceptible of comprehension [by insight—(see Ch. XX, §2f.)] and stamped with the three characteristics.[11] But it is not like that. For it is born only of perception in one who has obtained concentration, being a mere mode of appearance.[12]

---

9. '"*Comes into focus*": becomes the resort of mind-door impulsion' (Pm. 122).

10. 'Why should he not? If, after the learning sign was produced, he went on developing it by looking at the disk of the earth, there would be no arising of the counterpart sign' (Pm. 122).

11. 'Stamped with the three characteristics of the formed beginning with rise (see A.i,152), or marked with the three characteristics beginning with impermanence' Pm. 122).

12. 'If "*it is not like that*"—is not possessed of colour, etc.—then how is it the object of jhana? It is in order to answer that question that the

But as soon as it arises the hindrances are quite suppressed, the defilements subside, and the mind becomes concentrated in access concentration.

[The Two Kinds of Concentration]

32. Now concentration is of two kinds, that is to say, access concentration and absorption concentration: the mind becomes concentrated in two ways, that is, on the plane of access and on the plane of obtainment. Herein, the mind becomes concentrated on the plane of access by the abandonment of the hindrances, and on the plane of obtainment by the manifestation of the jhana factors. The difference between
33. the two kinds of concentration is this. The factors are not strong in access. It is because they are not strong that when access has arisen, the mind now makes the sign its object and now re-enters the life-continuum,[13] just as when a young child is lifted up and stood on its feet, it repeatedly falls down on the ground. But the factors are strong in absorption. It is because they are strong that when absorption concentration has arisen, the mind, having once interrupted the flow of the life-continuum, carries on with a stream of profitable impulsion[13] for a whole night and for a whole day, just as a healthy man, after rising from his seat, could stand for a whole day.

---

sentence beginning "*For it is . . .*" is given. "*Born of the perception*". produced by the perception during development, simply born from the perception during development. Since there is no arising from anywhere of what has no individual essence, he therefore said "*Being the mere mode of appearance*" ' (Pm. 122). See Ch. VIII. n. 11.

13. *Bhavanga* (life-continuum lit. constituent of becoming) and *javana* (impulsion) are first mentioned in this work at Ch. I, §57 (see n. 16); this is the second mention. The 'cognitive series (*citta-vīthi*)' so extensively used here is unknown as such in the *Piṭakas*. Perhaps the seed from which it sprang may exist in, say, such passages as 'Due to eye and to visible data eye consciousness arises. The coincidence of the three is contact. With contact as condition there is feeling. What he feels he perceives. What he perceives he thinks about. What he thinks about he diversifies [by means of craving, pride and false view] . . . Due to mind and to mental data. . .' (M. i, 111), and 'Is the eye permanent or impermanent?. . . Are visible objects permanent or impermanent?. . . Is the mind permanent or impermanent? Are mental data . . . Is mind consciousness. . . Is mind contact. . . Is any feeling, any perception, any formation, any consciousness, that arises with mind contact as condition permanent or impermanent. . .' (M. iii. 279). and 'These five faculties [of eye, etc. .] each with its separate objective field and no one of them experiencing as its objective field the province of any other, have mind as their refuge, and mind experiences their provinces as its objective field' (M. i. 295). This treatment of consciousness implies, as it were, more than even a 'double thickness' of consciousness. An already-formed nucleus of the cognitive series, based on such Sutta-Pitaka material, appears in the Abhidhamma Pitaka. The following two quotations show how the commentary (bracketted italics) expands the Abhidhamma-Pitaka treatment.

(i) 'Herein, what is eye-consciousness element? Due to eye and to visible data (*as support condition, and to functional mind element* (=5-

[GUARDING THE SIGN]

34. The arousing of the counterpart sign, which arises together with access concentration, is very difficult. Therefore if he is able to arrive at absorption in that same session by extending the sign, it is good. If not, then he must guard the sign diligently as if it were the embryo of a Wheel-turning Monarch (Word-ruler).

So guard the sign, nor count the cost,
And what is gained will not be lost;
Who fails to have this guard maintained
Will lose each time what he has gained. [127]

35. Herein, the way of guarding it is this:

(1) Abode, (2) resort, (3) and speech, (4) and person,
(5) the food, (6) the climate, (7) and the posture—

---

door adverting), *as disappearance condition, and to the remaining three immaterial aggregates as conascence condition*) there arises consciousness . . .which is eye-consciousness element. [Similarly with the other four sense elements.] Herein, what is mind element? Eye consciousness having arisen and ceased, next to that there arises consciousness,. . . which is appropriate (*profitable or unprofitable*) mind element (*in the mode of receiving*). [Similarly with the other four sense elements.] Or else it is the first reaction to any mental datum (*to be taken as functional mind element in the mode of mind-door adverting*). Herein, what is mind-consciousness element? Eye consciousness having arisen and ceased, next to that there arises mind element. (*Resultant*) mind element having arisen and ceased, also (*next to that there arises resultant mind-consciousness element in the mode of investigating; and that having arisen and ceased, next to that there arises functional mind-consciousness element in the mode of determining; and that having arisen and ceased,*) next to that there arises consciousness, . . .which is appropriate mind-consciousness element (*in the mode of impulsion*). [Similarly with the other four sense elements.] Due to (*life continuum*) mind and to mental data there arises consciousness,. . .which is appropriate (*impulsion*) mind-consciousness element (*following on the above-mentioned mind-door adverting*)' (Vbh. 87-90 and VbhA. 81f.).

(2) Eye consciousness and its associated states are a condition as proximity condition, for (*resultant*) mind element and for its associated states. Mind element and its associated states are a condition, as proximity condition, for (*root-causeless resultant*) mind-consciousness element (*in the mode of investigating*) and for its associated states. (*Next to that, the mind consciousness elements severally in the modes of determining, impulsion, registration, and life-continuum should be mentioned, though they are not since the teaching is abbreviated*). [Similarly for the other four senses and mind-consciousness element.] Preceding profitable (*impulsion*) states are a condition, as proximity condition, for subsequent indeterminate (*registration, life-continuum*)-states. . . [etc.]' (Ptn 2, and (Comy.) 33-4).

The form that the two kinds (5-door and mind-door) of the cognitive series take is shown in Table V. The following are some Pitaka refs. for the individual modes: *bhavaṅga* (life-continuum) Ptn1. 159, 160, 169, 324. *Āvajjana* (adverting) Ptn1. 159, 160, 169, 324. *Sampaṭicchana* (receiving), *santīraṇa* (investigating), *voṭṭhapana* (determining), and *tadārammaṇa* (registration) appear only in the commentaries. *Javana* (impulsion) Ps. ii, 73, 76. The following references may also be noted here: *anuloma* (conformity) Ptn1. 325. *Cuti-citta* death consciousness) Ptn1. 324. *Paṭisandhi* (rebirth-linking) Ptn1. 320, etc.; Ps, ii, 72, etc.

Eschew these seven different kinds
Whenever found unsuitable.
But cultivate the suitable;
For one perchance so doing finds
He need not wait too long until
Absorption shall his wish fulfil.

36. 1. Herein, an *abode* is unsuitable if, while he lives in it, the unarisen sign does not arise in him or is lost when it arises, and where unestablished mindfulness fails to become established and the unconcentrated mind concentrated. That is suitable in which the sign arises and becomes confirmed, in which mindfulness becomes established and the mind concentrated, as in the Elder Padhāniya-Tissa, resident at Nāgapabbata. So if a monastery has many abodes he can try them one by one, living in each for three days, and stay on where his mind becomes unified. For it was due to suitability of abode that five hundred bhikkhus reached Arahantship while still dwelling in the Lesser Nāga Cave (*Cūla-nāga-leṇa*) in Tambapaṇṇi Island (Ceylon) after apprehending their meditation subject there. But there is no counting the Stream Enterers who have reached Arahantship there after reaching the noble plane elsewhere. So too in the monastery of Cittalapabbata, and others.

37. 2. An alms-*resort* village lying to the north or south of the lodging, not too far, within one *kosa* and a half, and where alms food is easily obtained, is suitable. The opposite kind is unsuitable.[14]

38. 3. *Speech*: that included in the thirty-two kinds of aimless talk is unsuitable; for it leads to the disappearance of the sign. But talk based on the ten examples of talk is suitable; though even that should be discussed with moderation.[15]

39. 4. *Person*: one not given to aimless talk, who has the special qualities of virtue, etc., by acquaintanceship with whom the unconcentrated mind becomes concentrated, or the concentrated mind more so, is suitable. One who is much concerned with his body[16], who is addicted to aimless talk, is unsuitable; for he only creates disturbances, like muddy water added to clear water. And it was owing to one such as this that the attainments of the young bhikkhu who lived at Koṭapabbata vanished, not to mention the sign. [128]

---

14. North or south to avoid facing the rising sun in coming or going'. *kosa* is not in P. T. S. Dict.;'$1\frac{1}{2}$ kosas—3,000 bows' (Pm. 123).

15. Twenty-six kinds of 'aimless' (lit. 'animal') talk are given in the suttas (*e. g.* M. ii, 1; iii, 113), which the commentary increases to thirty-two (MA. iii, 223). The ten instances of talk are those given in the suttas (*e. g.* M. i, 145; iii, 113). See Ch. I, Note 12.

16. 'One who is occupied with exercising and caring for the body' (Pm. 124).

40. 5. *Food*: Sweet food suits one, sour food another. 6. *Climate*: a cool climate suits one, a warm one another. So when he finds that by using certain food or by living in a certain climate he is comfortable, or his unconcentrated mind becomes concentrated, or his concentrated mind more so, then that food or that climate is suitable. Any other food or climate is unsuitable.

41. 7. *Postures*: walking suits one; standing or sitting or lying down another. So he should try them, like the abode, for three days each, and that posture is suitable in which his unconcentrated mind becomes concentrated or his concentrated mind more so. Any other should be understood as unsuitable.

So he should avoid the seven unsuitable kinds and cultivate the suitable. For when he practises in this way, assiduously cultivating the sign, then 'he need not wait too long until absorption shall his wish fulfil'.

[The Ten Kinds of Skill in Absorption]

42. However, if this does not happen while he is practising in this way, then he should have recourse to the ten kinds of skill in absorption. Here is the method. Skill in absorption needs [to be dealt with in] ten aspects: (1) making the basis clean, (2) maintaining balanced faculties, (3) skill in the sign, (4) he exerts the mind on an occasion when it should be exerted, (5) he restrains the mind on an occasion when it should be restrained, (6) he encourages the mind on an occasion when it should be encouraged, (7) he looks on at the mind with equanimity when it should be looked on at with equanimity, (8) avoidance of unconcentrated persons, (9) cultivation of concentrated persons, (10) resoluteness upon that (concentration).

43. 1. Herein, *making the basis clean* is cleansing the internal and the external basis. For when his head, hair, nails and body hair are long, or when the body is soaked with sweat, then the internal basis is unclean and unpurified. But when an old dirty smelly robe is worn or when the lodging is dirty, then the external basis is unclean and unpurified. [129] When the internal and external bases are unclean, then the knowledge in the consciousness and consciousness-concomitants that arise is unpurified, like the light of a lamp's flame that arises with an unpurified lamp-bowl, wick and oil as its support; formations do not become evident to one who tries to comprehend them with unpurified knowledge, and when he devotes himself to his meditation subject, it does
44. not come to growth, increase and fulfilment. But when the internal and external bases are clean, then the knowledge in the consciousness and consciousness-concomitants that

arise is clean and purified, like the light of a lamp's flame that arises with a purified lamp bowl, wick and oil as its support; formations become evident to one who tries to comprehend them with purified knowledge and, as he devotes himself to his meditation subject it comes to growth, increase and fulfilment.

45. 2. *Maintaining balanced faculties* is equalizing the [five] faculties of faith and the rest. For if his faith faculty is strong and the others weak, then the energy faculty cannot perfom its function of exerting, the mindfulness faculty its function of establishing, the concentration faculty its function of not distracting, and the understanding faculty its function of seeing. So in that case the faith faculty should be modified either by reviewing the individual essences of the states [concerned, that is, the objects of attention,] or by not giving [them] attention in the way in which the faith faculty became too strong. And this is illustrated by the story of the Elder Vakkali (S. iii, 119). Then if the energy faculty is too
46. strong, the faith faculty cannot perform its function of resolving, nor can the rest of the faculties perfom their several functions. So in that case the energy faculty should be modified by developing tranquillity, and so on. And this should be illustrated by the story of the Elder Soṇa (Vin. i, 179—85; A. iii, 374—6). So too with the rest; for it should be understood that when any one of them is too strong the others cannot perform their several functions.

47. However, what is particularly recommended is balancing faith with understanding, and concentration with energy. For one strong in faith and weak in understanding has confidence uncritically and groundlessly. One strong in understanding and weak in faith errs on the side of cunning and is as hard to cure as one sick of a disease caused by medicine. With the balancing of the two a man has confidence only when there are grounds for it.

Then idleness overpowers one strong in concentration and weak in energy since concentration favours idleness. [130] Agitation overpowers one strong in energy and weak in concentration since energy favours agitation. But concentration coupled with energy cannot lapse into idleness, and energy coupled with concentration cannot lapse into agitation. So these two should be balanced; for absorption comes with the balancing of the two.

48. Again, [concentration and faith should be balanced.] One working on concentration needs strong faith, since it is with such faith and confidence that he reaches absorption. Then there is [balancing of] concentration and understanding. One working on concentration needs strong unification, since that is how he reaches absorption; and one working on insight

needs strong understanding, since that is how he reaches penetration of characteristics; but with the balancing of the two he reaches absorption as well.

49. Strong mindfulness, however, is needed in all instances; for mindfulness protects the mind from lapsing into agitation through faith, energy and understanding, which favour agitation, and from lapsing into idleness through concentration, which favours idleness. So it is as desirable in all instances as a seasoning of salt in all sauces, as a prime minister in all the king's business. Hence it is said [in the commentaries(?)] 'And mindfulness has been called universal by the Blessed One. For what reason? Because the mind has mindfulness as its refuge, and mindfuluess is manifested as protection, and there is no exertion and restraint of the mind without mindfulness'.

50. 3. *Skill in the sign* is skill in producing the as yet unproduced sign of unification of mind through the earth kasina, etc.; and it is skill in developing [the sign] when produced, and skill in protecting [the sign] when obtained by development. The last is what is intended here.

51. 4. How does he *exert the mind on an occasion when it should be exerted*? when his mind is slack with over-laxness of energy, etc., then, instead of developing the three enlightenment factors beginning with tranquillity, he should develop those beginning with investigation-of-states. For this is said by the Blessed One: 'Bhikkhus, suppose a man wanted to make 'a small fire burn up, and he put wet grass on it, put wet 'cowdung on it, put wet sticks on it, sprinkled it with water, 'and scattered dust on it, would that man be able to make the 'small fire burn up? [131]—No, venerable sir.—So too, 'bhikkhus, when the mind is slack, that is not the time to 'develop the tranquillity enlightenment factor, the con-'centration enlightenment factor or the equanimity enlight-'enment factor. Why is that? Because a slack mind cannot 'well be roused by those states. When the mind is slack, that 'is the time to develop the investigation-of-states enlighten-'ment factor, the energy enlightenment factor and the happi-'ness enlightenment factor. Why is that? Because a slack 'mind can well be roused by those states.

'Bhikkhus, suppose a man wanted to make a small fire 'burn up, and he put dry grass on it, put dry cowdung on it, 'put dry sticks on it, blew it with his mouth, and did not 'scatter dust on it, would that man be able to make that small 'fire burn up?—Yes, venerable sir' (S. v, 112).

52. And here the development of the investigation-of-states enlightenment factor, etc., should be understood as the nutriment for each one respectively, for this is said: 'Bhikkhus, 'there are profitable and unprofitable states, reprehensible

'and blameless states, inferior and superior states, dark and 'bright states the counterpart of each other. Wise attention 'much practised therein is the nutriment for the arising 'of the unarisen investigation-of-states enlightenment factor, 'or leads to the growth, fulfilment, development and per- 'fection of the arisen investigation-of-states enlightenment 'factor'. Likewise: 'Bhikkhus there is the element of 'initiative, the element of launching, and the element of 'persistence. Wise attention much practised therein is the 'nutriment for the arising of the unarisen energy enlighten- 'ment factor, or leads to the growth, fulfilment, development 'and perfection of the arisen energy enlightenment factor'. Likewise: 'Bhikkhus, there are states productive of the 'happiness enlightenment factor. Wise attention much prac- 'tised therein is the nutriment for the arising of the unarisen 'happiness enlightenment factor, or leads to the growth, 'fulfilment, development and perfection of the arisen happiness 'enlightenment factor' (S. v, 104). [132]

53. Herein, *wise attention* given to the *profitable*, etc., is attention occurring in penetration of individual essences and of [the three] general characteristics. *Wise attention* given to the *element of initiative*, etc., is attention occurring in the arousing of the element of initiative, and so on. Herein, initial energy is called the *element of initiative*. The *element of launching* is stronger than that because it launches out from idleness. The *element of persistence* is still stronger than that because it goes on persisting in successive later stages. *States productive of the happiness enlightenment factor* is a name for happiness itself; and attention that arouses that is *wise attention*.

54. There are, besides, seven things that lead to the arising of the investigation-of-states enlightenment factor: (i) asking questions, (ii) making the basis clean, (iii) balancing the faculties, (iv) avoidance of persons without understanding, (v) cultivation of persons with understanding, (vi) reviewing the field for the exercise of profound knowledge, (vii) resoluteness upon that [investigation of states].

55. Eleven things lead to the arising of the energy enlightenment factor: (i) reviewing the fearfulness of the States of Loss, etc., (ii) seeing benefit in obtaining the mundane and supramundane distinctions dependent on energy, (iii) reviewing the course of the journey [to be travelled] thus 'The path taken by the Buddhas, Pacceka Buddhas, and the Great Disciples has to to be taken by me, and it cannot be taken by an idler', (iv) being a credit to the alms food by producing great fruit for the givers, (v) reviewing the greatness of the Master thus 'My Master praises the energetic, and this unsurpassable Dispensation that is so helpful to us is honoured in the practice, not otherwise,' (vi) reviewing the greatness

of the heritage thus 'It is the great heritage called the Good Dhamma that is to be acquired by me, and it cannot be acquired by an idler', (vii) removing stiffness and torpor by attention to perception of light, change of postures, frequenting the open air, etc., (viii) avoidance of idle persons, (ix) cultivation of energetic persons, (x) reviewing the Right Endeavours, (xi) resoluteness upon that [energy].

56. Eleven things lead to the arising of the happiness enlightenment factor: the recollections (i) of the Buddha, (ii) of the Dhamma (iii) of the Sangha, (iv) of virtue, (v) of generosity, and (iv) of deities, (vii) the Recollection of Peace, (viii) [133] avoidance of rough persons, (ix) cultivation of refined persons (x) reviewing encouraging discourses, (xi) resoluteness upon that [happiness].

So by arousing these things in these ways he develops the investigation-of-states enlightenment factor, and the others. This is how he exerts the mind on an occasion when it should be exerted.

57. How does he *restrain the mind on an occasion when it should be restrained?* When his mind is agitated through over-energeticness, etc., then, instead of developing the three enlightenment factors beginning with investigation-of-states, he should develop those beginning with tranquillity; for this is said by the Blessed One: 'Bhikkhus, suppose a man wanted 'to extinguish a great mass of fire, and he put dry grass on it, '...and did not scatter dust on it, would that man be able 'to extinguish that great mass of fire?—No, venerable sir.— 'So too, bhikkhus, when the mind is agitated, that is not the 'time to develop the investigation-of-states enlightenment 'factor, the energy enlightenment factor or the happiness 'enlightenment factor. Why is that? Because an agitated 'mind cannot well be quieted by those states. When the mind 'is agitated, that is the time to develop the tranquillity 'enlightenment factor, the concentration enlightenment 'factor and the equanimity enlightenment factor. Why is 'that? Because an agitated mind can well be quieted by those 'states.

'Bhikkhus, suppose a man wanted to extinguish a great 'mass of fire, and he put wet grass on it,...and scattered 'dust on it, would that man be able to extinguish that great 'mass of fire?—Yes, venerable sir' (S. v, 114).

58. And here the development of the tranquillity enlightenment factor, etc., should be understood as the nutriment for each one respectively, for this is said: 'Bhikkhus, there is 'bodily tranquillity and mental tranquillity. [134] Wise 'attention much practised therein is the nutriment for the 'arising of the unarisen tranquillity enlightenment factor, 'or leads to the growth, fulfilment, development and per-'fection of the arisen tranquillity enlightenment factor'.

Likewise: 'Bhikkhus, there is the sign of serenity, the sign of 'non-diversion. Wise attention much practised therein is the 'nutriment for arising of the unarisen concentration en- 'lightenment factor, or leads to the growth, fulfilment, 'development and perfection of the arisen concentration 'enlightenment factor'. Likewise: 'Bhikkhus, there are 'states productive of the equanimity enlightenment factor. 'Wise attention much practised therein is the nutriment for 'the arising of the unrisen equanimity enlightenment 'factor, or leads to the growth, fulfilment, development and 'perfection of the arisen equanimity enlightenment factor' (S.v, 104).

59. Herein *wise attention* given to the three instances is attent-ion occuring in arousing tranquillity, etc., by observing the way in which they arose in him earlier. The *sign of serenity* is a term for serenity itself, and *non-diversion* is a term for that too in the sense of non-distraction.

60. There are, besides, seven things that lead to the arising of the tranquillity enlightenment factor: (i) using superior food, (ii) living in a good climate, (iii) maintaining a pleasant posture, (iv) keeping to the middle, (v) avoidance of violent persons, (vi) cultivation of persons tranquil in body, (vii) resoluteness upon that [tranquillity].

61. Eleven things lead to the arising of the concentration enlightenment factor: (i) making the basis clean, (ii) skill in the sign, (iii) balancing the faculties, (iv) restraining the mind on occasion, (v) exerting the mind on occasion, (vi) encourag-ing the listless mind by means of faith and a sense of urgency, (vii) looking on with equanimity at what is occurring rightly, (viii) avoidance of unconcentrated persons, (ix) cultivation of concentrated persons, (x) reviewing of the jhanas and liberations, (xi) resoluteness upon that con-centration].

62. Five things lead to the arising of the equanimity enlighten-ment factor: (i) maintenance of neutrality towards living beings, (ii) maintenance of neutrality towards forma-tions (inanimate things), (iii) avoidance of persons who show favouritism towards beings and formations, (iv) culti-vation of persons who maintain neutrality towards beings and formations, (v) resoluteness upon that [equanimity]. [135]

So by arousing these things in these ways he develops the tranquillity enlightenment factor, as well as the others. This is how he restrains the mind on an occasion when it should be restrained.

63. 6. How does he *encourage the mind on an occasion when it should be encouraged*? When his mind is listless owing to sluggishness in the exercise of understanding or to failure to attain the bliss of peace, then he should stimulate it by

reviewing the eight grounds for a sense of urgency. These are the four, namely, birth, ageing, sickness, and death, with the suffering of the States of Loss as the fifth, and also the suffering in the past rooted in the round [of rebirths], the suffering in the future rooted in the round [of rebirths], and the suffering in the present rooted in the search for nutriment. And he creates confidence by recollecting the special qualities of the Buddha, the Dhamma, and the Sangha. This is how he encourages the mind on an occasion when it should be encouraged.

64. 7. How does he *look on at the mind with equanimity on an occasion when it should be looked on at with equanimity*? When he is practising in this way and his mind follows the road of serenity, occurs evenly on the object, and is unidle, unagitated and not listless, then he is not interested to exert or restrain or encourage it; he is like a charioteer when the horses are progressing evenly. This is how he looks on at the mind with equanimity on an occasion when it should be looked on at with equanimity.

65. 8. *Avoidance of unconcentrated persons* is keeping far away from persons who have never trodden the way of renunciation, who are busy with many affairs, and whose hearts are distracted.

9. *Cultivation of concentrated persons* is approaching periodically persons who have trodden the way of renunciation and obtained concentration.

10. *Resoluteness upon that* is the state of being resolute upon concentration; the meaning is, giving concentration importance, tending, leaning and inclining to concentration.

This is how the tenfold skill in concentration should be undertaken.

66. Any man who acquires this sign
This tenfold skill will need to heed
In order absorption to gain
Thus achieving his bolder gold.
But if in spite of his efforts
No result comes that might requite
His work, still a wise wight persists
Never this task relinquishing, [136]
Since a tiro, if he gives up,
Thinking not to continue in
The task, never gains distinction
Here no matter how small at all.
A man wise in temperament[17]
Notices how his mind inclined:
Energy and serenity
Always he couples each to each.

---

17. '*Buddha*—possessed of wit': not in P. T. S. Dict.; see MA. i, 39.

Now his mind, seeing that it holds back,
He prods, now the restraining rein
Tightening, seeing it pull too hard;
Guiding with even pace the race.
Well-controlled bees get the pollen;
Well-balanced efforts meet to treat
Leaves, thread, and ships, and oil-tubes too,
Gain thus, not otherwise, the prize.
Let him set aside then this lax
Also this agitated state,
Steering here his mind at the sign
As the bee and the rest suggest.

[The Four Similes]

67. Here is the explanation of the meaning.
When a too clever bee learns that a flower on a tree is blooming, it sets out hurriedly, overshoots the mark, turns back, and arrives when the pollen is finished; and another, not clever enough, bee who sets out with too slow a speed arrives when the pollen is finished too; but a clever bee sets out with balanced speed, arrives with ease at the cluster of flowers, takes as much pollen as it pleases and enjoys the honey-dew.

68. Again, when a surgeon's pupils are being trained in the use of the scalpel on a lotus leaf in a dish of water, one who is too clever applies the scalpel hurriedly and either cuts the lotus leaf in two or pushes it under the water, and another who is not clever enough does not even dare to touch it with the scalpel for fear of cutting it in two or pushing it under; but one who is clever shows the scalpel stroke on it by means of a balanced effort, and being good at his craft he is rewarded on such occasions.

69. Again when the King announces 'Anyone who can draw out a spider's thread four fathoms long shall receive four thousand', one man who is too clever breaks the spider's thread here and there by pulling it hurriedly, and another who is not clever enough does not dare to touch it with his hand for fear of breaking it, but a clever man pulls it out starting from the end with a balanced effort, winds it on a stick, and so wins the prize.

70. Again, a too clever [137] skipper hoists full sails in a high wind and sends his ship adrift, and another, not clever enough, skipper lowers his sails in a light wind and remains where he is, but a clever skipper hoists full sails in a light wind, takes in half his sails in a high wind and so arrives safely at his desired destination.

71. Again, when a teacher says 'Anyone who fills the oil-tube without spilling any oil will win a prize', one who is too clever fills it hurriedly out of greed for the prize, and he spills

the oil, and another who is not clever enough does not dare to pour the oil at all for fear of spilling it, but one who is clever fills it with a balanced effort and wins the prize.

72. Just as in these four similes, so too when the sign arises, one bhikkhu forces his energy, thinking 'I shall soon reach absorption'. Then his mind lapses into agitation because of his mind's over-exerted energy and he is prevented from reaching absorption. Another who sees the defect in over-exertion slacks off his energy, thinking 'What is absorption to me now?'. Then his mind lapses into idleness because of his mind's too lax energy and he too is prevented from reaching absorption. Yet another who frees his mind from idleness even when it is only slightly idle and from agitation when only slightly agitated, confronting the sign with balanced effort, reaches absorption. One should be like the last-named.

73. It was with reference to this meaning that it was said above:

> 'Well-controlled bees get the pollen;
> Well-balanced efforts meet to treat
> Leaves, thread, and ships, and oil-tubes too,
> Gain thus, not otherwise, the prize.
> Let him set aside then this lax
> Also this agitated state,
> Steering here his mind at the sign
> As the bee and the rest suggest'.

[Appearance of Absorption in the Cognitive Series]

74. So, while he is guiding his mind in this way, confronting the sign, [then knowing] 'now absorption will succeed', there arises in him mind-door adverting with that same earth kasina as its object, interrupting the [occurrence of consciousness as] life-continuum, and evoked by the constant repeating of 'earth, earth'. After that, either four or five impulsions impel on that same object. The last one of which is an impulsion of the fine-material sphere. The rest are of the sense sphere, but they have stronger applied thought, sustained thought, happiness, bliss, and unification of mind, than the normal ones. They are called 'preliminary work' [consciousnesses] because they are the preliminary work for absorption [138] and they are also called 'access' [consciousnesses] because of their nearness to absorption or because they happen in its neighbourhood, just as the words 'village access' and 'city access' are used for a place near to a village, etc., and they are also called 'conformity' [consciousnesses] because they conform to those that precede the 'preliminary-work' [consciousnesses] and to the absorption that follows. And the last of these is also called 'change-of-lineage' because it transcends the limited [sense-sphere] lineage and

brings into being the exalted [fine-material-sphere] lineage.[18]

75. But omitting repetitions,[19] then either the first is the 'preliminary-work', the second 'access', the third 'conformity', and the fourth 'change-of-lineage', or else the first is 'access', the second 'conformity', and the third 'change-of-lineage'. Then either the fourth [in the latter case] or the fifth [in the former case] is the absorption consciousness. For it is only either the fourth or the fifth that fixes in absorption. And that is according as there is swift or sluggish direct-knowledge (cf. Ch. XXI, § 177). Beyond that, impulsion lapses and the life-continuum[20] takes over.

76. But the Abhidhamma scholar, the Elder Godatta, quoted this text 'Preceding profitable states are a condition, as 'repetition condition, for succeeding profitable states' (Ptn 1.5), adding, 'It is owing to the repetition condition that each succeeding state is strong, so there is absorption also in the sixth and seventh'. That is rejected by the commentaries with the remark that it is merely that Elder's
77. opinion, adding that 'It is only either in the fourth or the fifth[21] that there is absorption. Beyond that, impulsion

18. It guards the line (*gaṃ tāyati*), thus it is lineage (*gotta*). When it occurs limitedly, it guards the naming (*abhidhāna*) and the recognition (*buddhi*) of the naming as restricted to a definite scope (*ekaṃsa-visayatā*). For just as recognition does not take place without a meaning (*attha*) for its objective support (*ārammaṇa*,) so naming (*abhidhāna*) does not take place without what is named (*abhidheyya*). So it (the *gotta*) is said to protect and keep these. But the limited should be regarded as the materiality peculiar to sense-sphere states, which are the resort of craving for sense desires, and destitute of the exalted (fine-material and immaterial) or the unsurpassed (supramundane). The exalted lineage is explainable in the same way' (Pm. 134).

19. See Ch. XVII, §189 and note.

20. 'The intention is that it is as if the sixth and seventh impulsions had lapsed since impulsion beyond the fifth is exhausted. The Elder's opinion was that just as the first impulsion, which lacks the quality of repetition, does not arouse change-of-lineage because of its weakness, while the second or the third, which have the quality of repetition, can do so because they are strong on that account, so too the sixth and seventh fix in absorption owing to their strength due to their quality of repetition. But it is unsupported by a sutta or by any teacher's statement in conformity with a sutta. And the text quoted is not a reason because strength due to the quality of repetition is not a principle without exceptions (*anekantikattā*); for the first volition, which is not a repetition has result experienceable here and now, while the second to the sixth, which are repetitions, have result experienceable in future becomings' (Pm. 135).

21. '"*Either in the fourth or the fifth*", etc., is said for the purpose of concluding [the discussion] with a paragraph showing the correctness of the meaning already stated.—Herein, if the sixth and seventh impulsions are said to have lapsed because impulsion is exhausted, how does seventh-impulsion volition come to have result experienceable in the next rebirth and to be of immediate effect on rebirth?—This is not owing to strength got through a repetition condition.—What then?—It is owing to the difference in the function's position (*kiriyāvatthā*). For the function [of impulsion] has three positions,

lapses. It is said to do so because of nearness of the life-continuum'. And that has been stated in this way after consideration, so it cannot be rejected. For just as a man who is running towards a precipice and wants to stop cannot do so when he has his foot on the edge but falls over it, so there can be no fixing in absorption in the sixth or the seventh because of the nearness to the life-continuum. That is why it should be understood that there is absorption only in the fourth or the fifth.

78. But that absorption is only of a single conscious moment. for there are seven instances in which the normal extent[22] [of the cognitive series] does not apply. They are in the cases of the first absorption, the mundane kinds of direct-knowledge, the four paths, fruition next after the path, life-continuum jhana in the fine-material and immaterial kinds of becoming, the base consisting of neither perception nor non-perception as condition for cessation [of perception and feeling], and the fruition attainment in one emerging from cessasion. Here the fruition next after the path does not exceed three [consciousnesses in number]; [139] the [consciousnesses] of the base consisting of neither perception nor non-perception as condition for cessation do not exceed two [in number]; there is no measure of the [number of consciousnesses in the] life-continuum in the fine-material and immaterial [kinds of becoming]. In the remaining instances [the number of consciousnesses is] one only. So absorption is of a single consciousness moment. After that it lapses into the life-continuum. Then the life-continuum is interrupted by adverting for the purpose of reviewing the jhana, next to which comes the reviewing of the jhana.

[The First Jhana]

79. At this point, 'Quite secluded from sense desires, secluded ' from unprofitable things he enters upon and dwells in the ' first jhana, which is accompanied by applied and sustained ' thought with happiness and bliss born of seclusion' (Vbh. 245), and so he has attained the first jhana, which abandons five factors, possesses five factors, is good in three ways, possesses ten characteristics, and is of the earth kasina.

---

that is, initial, medial and final. Herein, experience ability of result in the next rebirth and immediateness of effect on rebirth are due to the last volition's final position, not to its strength . . . So the fact that the sixth and seventh lapse because impulsion is used up cannot be objected to' (Pm. 135). See Table V.

22. ' "*The normal extent does not apply*" here "*in the seven instances*" because of the immeasurability of the conscious moment in some, and the extreme brevity of the moment in others; for "*extent*" is inapplicable here in the sense of complete congnitive series, which is why "in fruition next to the path", etc., is said' (Pm. 136).

80. Herein, *quite secluded from sense desires* means having secluded himself from, having become without, having gone away from, sense desires. Now this word *quite* (*eva*) should be understood to have the meaning of absoluteness. Precisely because it has the meaning of absoluteness it shows how on the actual occasion of entering upon and dwelling in the first jhana sense desires as well as being non-existent then are the first jhana's contrary opposite, and it also shows that the arrival takes place only (*eva*) through the letting go of sense desires. How?

81. When absoluteness is introduced thus 'quite secluded from sense desires', what is expressed is this: sense desires are certainly incompatible with this jhana; when they exist, it does not occur, just as when there is darkness, there is no lamplight; and it is only by letting go of them that it is reached just as the further bank is reached by letting go of the near bank. That is why absoluteness is introduced.

82. Here it might be asked: But why is this [word 'quite'] mentioned only in the first phrase and not in the second? How is this, might he enter upon and dwell in the first jhana even when not secluded from unprofitable things?—It should not be regarded in that way. It ts mentioned in the first phrase as the escape from them; for this jhana is the escape from sense desires since it surmounts the sense-desire element and since it is incompatible with greed for sense desires, according as it is said 'The escape from sense desires is this, 'that is to say, renunciation' (D. iii, 275). But in the second phrase [140] the word *eva* should be adduced and taken as said, as in the passage 'Bhikkhus, only (*eva*) here is there 'an ascetic, here a second ascetic' (M. i, 63). For it is impossible to enter upon and dwell in jhana unsecluded also from unprofitable things, in other words, the hindrances other than that [sense desire]. So this word must be read in both phrases thus: Quite secluded from sense desires, quite secluded from unprofitable things'. And although the word 'secluded' as a general term includes all kinds of seclusion, that is to say, seclusion by substitution of opposites, etc., and bodily seclusion, etc.,[23] still only the three, namely, bodily exclusion, mental seclusion and seclusion by suppression (suspension), should be regarded here.

83. But this term 'sense desires' should be regarded as including all kinds, that is to say, 'sense-desires' object given in the Niddesa in the passage beginning 'What are sense-desires

23. The *five* (see *e.g.* Ps. ii, 220; MA. i, 85) are suppression (by concentration), substitution of opposites (by insight), cutting off (by the path), tranquillization (by fruition), and escape (as nibbana); cf. five kinds of deliverance (*e.g.* MA. iv, 168). The *three* (see *e.g.* Ndi. 26; MA. ii, 143) are bodily seclusion (retreat), mental seclusion (jhana) and seclusion from the substance or circumstances of becoming (nibbana).

'as object? They are agreeable visible objects . . .' (Nd I.I) and the sense-desires as defilement given there too and in the Vibhaṅga thus 'Zeal as sense-desire (*kāma*), greed as sense-'desire, zeal and greed as sense-desire, thinking as sense-'desire, greed as sense-desire, thinking and greed as sense-'desire' (Nd 1.2; Vbh. 256).[24] That being so, the words 'quite secluded from sense desires' properly mean 'quite secluded from sense-desires as object', and express bodily seclusion, while the words 'secluded from unprofitable things' properly mean 'secluded from sense-desires as defilement or from all unprofitable things' and express mental seclusion. And in this case giving up of pleasure in sense-desires is indicated by the first since it only expresses seclusion from sense-desires as object, while acquisition of pleasure in renunciation is indicated by the second since it expresses seclusion from sense-desire as defilement.

84. And with sense-desires as object and sense-desires as defilement expressed in this way it should also be recognized that the abandoning of the objective basis for defilement is indicated by the first of these two phrases and the abandoning of the [subjective] defilement by the second; also that the giving up of the cause of cupidity is indicated by the first and [the giving up of the cause] of stupidity by the second; also that the purification of one's occupation is indicated by the first and the educating of one's inclination by the second.

This, firstly, is the method here when the words *from sense-desires* are treated as referring to sense-desires as object.

85. But if they are treated as referring to sense-desires as defilement, then it is simply just (*kāmacchanda*) in the various forms of 'zeal (*chanda*)', 'greed (*rāga*)', etc., that is intended as 'sense-desire (*kāma*)' (§83, 2nd quotation). [141] And although that [lust] is also included by [the word] 'unprofitable', it is nevertheless stated separately in the Vibhaṅga in the way beginning 'Herein, what are sense-desires? Zeal

24. Here '*sankappa* (thinking)' has the meaning of 'hankering'. *Chanda kāma* and *rāga*, and their combinations need sorting out. *Chanda* (zeal, desire) is much used, neutral in colour, good or bad according to context and glossed by 'desire to act'; technically also one of the four Roads to Power and four Predominances. *Kāma* (sense-desire, sensuality) loosely represents enjoyment of the five sense pleasures (*e.g.* sense-desire sphere). More narrowly it refers to sexual enjoyment (third of the Five Precepts). Distinguished as subjective desire (defilement) and objective things that arouse it (Nd I. I; cf. Ch. XIV, n. 36). The figure 'five cords of sense-desire' signifies simply these desires with the five-sense objects that attract them. *Rāga* (greed) is the general term for desire in its bad sense and identical with *lobha*, which latter, however appears technically as one of the three root-causes of unprofitable action. *Rāga* is renderable also by 'lust' in its general sense. *Kāmacchanda* (lust): a technical term for the first of the five Hindrances. *Chanda-rāga* (zeal and greed) and *kāma-rāga* (greed for sense-desires) have no technical use.

as sense-desire, . . .' (Vbh. 256) because of its incompatibility with jhana. Or alternatively it is mentioned in the first phrase because it is sense-desire as defilement and in the second phrase because it is included in the 'unprofitable'. And because this [lust] has various forms, therefore 'from sense desires' is said instead of 'from sense desire'.

86. And although there may be unprofitableness in other states as well, nevertheless only the hindrances are mentioned subsequently in the Vibhaṅga thus, 'Herein, what states are unprofitable? Lust . . . ' (Vbh. 256), etc., in order to show their opposition to, and incompatibility with, the jhana factors. For the hindrances are the contrary opposites of the jhana factors: what is meant is that the jhana factors are incompatible with them, eliminate them, abolish them. And it is said accordingly in the Peṭaka 'Concentration is incompatible with lust, happiness with ill will, applied thought with stiffness and torpor, bliss with agitation and worry, and sustained thought with uncertainty' (not in Peṭakopadesa).

87. So in this case it should be understood that seclusion-by-suppression (suspension) of lust is indicated by the phrase *quite secluded from sense desires*, and seclusion-by-suppression (suspension) of [all] five hindrances by the phrase *secluded from unprofitable things*. But omitting repetitions, that of lust is indicated by the first and that of the remaining hindrances by the second. Similarly with the three unprofitable roots, that of greed, which has the five cords of sense desire (M. i, 85) as its province, is indicated by the first, and that of hate and delusion, which have as their respective provinces the various grounds for annoyance (A. iv, 408; v, 150), etc., by the second. Or with the states consisting of the floods, etc., that of the flood of sense-desires, of the bond of sense-desires, of the canker of sense-desires, of sense-desire clinging, of the bodily tie of covetousness, and of the fetter of greed for sense-desires, is indicated by the first, and that of the remaining floods, bonds, cankers, clingings, ties, and fetters, is indicated by the second. Again that of craving and of what is associated with craving is indicated by the first, and that of ignorance and of what is associated with ignorance is indicated by the second. Furthermore, that of the eight thought-arisings associated with greed (Ch. XIV, §90) is indicated by the first, and that of the remaining kinds of unprofitable thought-arisings is indicated by the second.

This, in the first place, is the explanation of the meaning of the words 'quite secluded from sense desires, secluded from unprofitable things'.

88. So far the factors abandoned by the jhana have been shown. And now, in order to show the factors associated with it,

which is accompanied by applied and sustained thought is said. [142] Herein, applied thinking (*vitakkana*) is *applied thought* (*vitakka*); hitting upon, is what is meant.[25] It has the characteristic of directing the mind onto an object (mounting the mind on its object). Its function is to strike at and thresh—for the meditator is said, in virtue of it, to have the object struck at by applied thought, threshed by applied thought. It is manifested as the leading of the mind onto an object. Sustained thinking (*vicaraṇa*) is *sustained thought* (*vicāra*); continued sustainment (*anusañcaraṇa*), is what is meant. It has the characteristic of continued pressure on (occupation with) the object. Its function is to keep conascent [mental] states [occupied] with that. It is manifested as keeping consciousness anchored [on that object].

89. And though sometimes not separate, *applied thought* is the first compact of the mind in the sense that it is both gross and inceptive, like the striking of a bell. *Sustained thought* is the act of keeping the mind anchored, in the sense that it is subtle with the individual essence of continued pressure, like the ringing of the bell. *Applied thought* intervenes, being the interference of conciousness at the time of first arousing [thought], like a bird's spreading out its wings when about to soar into the air, and like a bee's diving towards a lotus when it is minded to follow up the scent of it. The behaviour of *sustained thought* is quiet, being the near non-interference of conciousness, like the birds planing with outspread wings after soaring into the air, and like the bee's buzzing above the lotus after it has dived towards it.

90. In the commentary to the Book of Twos [of the Anguttara Nikāya (?)] this is said: 'Applied thought occurs as a state of directing the mind onto an object, like the movement of a large bird taking off into the air by engaging the air with both wings and forcing them downwards. For it causes absorption by being unified.[26] Sustained thought occurs with the individual essence of continued pressure, like the bird's movement when it is using (activating) its wings for the purpose of keeping hold on the air. For it keeps pressing the object'.[26] That fits in with the latter's occurrence as anchoring. This difference of theirs becomes evident in the first and second jhanas [in the fivefold reckoning].

91 Furthermore, *applied thought* is like the hand that grips firmly and *sustained thought* is like the hand that rubs, when one grips a tarnished metal dish firmly with one hand and rubs it with powder and oil and a woollen pad with

25. '*Uhana*—hitting upon': possibly connected with *ūhanati* (to disturb—see M. i, 243; ii, 193). Obviously connected here with the meaning of *āhananapariyāhanana* (striking and threshing) in the next line. For the similes that follow here see Pe. 142.

26. These two sentences, '*So hi ekaggo hutvā appeti*' and '*So hi ārammaṇaṃ anumajjati*' are not in the Burmese and Harvard editions.

the other hand. Likewise, when a potter has spun his wheel with a stroke on the stick and is making a dish [143], his supporting hand is like *applied thought* and his hand that moves back and forth is like *sustained thought*. Likewise, when one is drawing a circle, the pin that stays fixed down in the centre is like *applied thought*, which directs onto the object, and the pin that revolves round it is like *sustained thought*, which continuously presses.

92. So this jhana occurs together with this applied thought and this sustained thought; and it is called 'accompanied by applied and sustained thought' as a tree is called 'accompanied by flowers and fruits'. But in the Vibhaṅga the teaching is given in terms of a person[27] in the way beginning ' He is possessed, fully possessed, of this applied thought and ' this sustained thought' (Vbh. 257). The meaning should be regarded in the same way there too.

93 *Born of seclusion*: here secludedness (*vivitti*) is seclusion (*viveka*); the meaning is, disappearance of hindrances. Or alternatively, it is secluded (*vivitta*), thus it is seclusion; the meaning is, the collection of states associated with the jhana is secluded from hindrances. 'Born of seclusion' is born of or in that kind of seclusion.

94. *Happiness and bliss*: It refreshes (*pīṇayati*), thus it is happiness (*pīti*). It has the characteristic of endearing (*sampiyāyana*). Its function is to refresh the body and the mind; or its function is to pervade (thrill with rapture). It is manifested as elation. But it is of five kinds as minor happiness, momentary happiness, showering happiness, uplifting happiness, and pervading (rapturous) happiness.

Herein, *minor happiness* is only able to raise the hairs on the body. *Momentary happiness* is like flashes of lightning at different moments. *Showering happiness* breaks over the body again and again like waves on the sea shore.

Uplifting happiness can be powerful enough to levitate the
95. body and make it spring up into the air. For this was what happened to the Elder Mahā-Tissa, resident at Puṇṇavallika. He went to the shrine terrace on the evening of the full-moon day. Seeing the moonlight, he faced in the direction of the Great Shrine [at Anurādhapura], thinking 'At this very hour the four assemblies[28] are worshipping at the Great Shrine!'. By means of objects formerly seen [there] he aroused uplifting

27. '*Puggalādhiṭṭhāna*—in terms of a person'; a technical commentarial term for one of the ways of presenting a subject. They are *dhamma-desanā* (discourse about principles), and *puggala-desanā* (discourse about persons), both of which may be treated either as *dhammādhiṭṭhāna* (in terms of principles) or *puggalādhiṭṭhāna* (in terms of persons). See MA. i, 24.

28. The four assemblies (*Parisā*) are the bhikkhus, bhikkhunis, laymen followers and laywomen followers.

happiness with the Enlightened One as object, and he rose into the air like a painted ball bounced off a plastered floor and alighted on the terrace of the Great Shrine.

96. And this was what happened to the daughter of a clan in the village of Vattakālaka near the Girikaṇḍaka Monastery when she sprang up into the air owing to strong uplifting happiness with the Enlightened One as object. As her parents were about to go to the monastery in the evening, it seems, in order to hear the Dhamma [144], they told her 'My dear, you are expecting a child; you cannot go out at an unsuitable time. We shall hear the Dhamma and gain merit for you'. So they went out. And though she wanted to go too, she could not well object to what they said. She stepped out of the house onto a balcony and stood looking at the Ākāsacetiya Shrine at Girikaṇḍaka lit by the moon. She saw the offering of lamps at the shrine, and the four communities as they circumambulated it to the right after making their offerings of flowers and perfumes; and she heard the sound of the massed recital by the Community of Bhikkhus. Then she thought 'How lucky they are to be able to go to the monastery and wander round such a shrine terrace and listen to such sweet preaching of Dhamma!' Seeing the shrine as a mound of pearls and arousing uplifting happiness, she sprang up into the air, and before her parents arrived she came down from the air into the shrine terrace, where she paid homage and

97. stood listening to the Dhamma. When her parents arrived, they asked her 'What road did you come by?'. She said 'I came through the air, not by the road' and when they told her 'My dear, those whose cankers are destroyed come through the air. But how did you come?', she replied 'As I was standing looking at the shrine in the moonlight a strong sense of happiness arose in me with the Enlightened One as its object. Then I knew no more whether I was standing or sitting, but only that I was springing up into the air with the sign that I had grasped, and I came to rest on this shrine terrace'.

So uplifting happiness can be powerful enough to levitate the body make it spring up into the air.

98. But when *pervading* (*rapturous*) *happiness* arises, the whole body is completely pervaded, like a filled bladder, like a rock cavern invaded by a huge inundation.

99. Now this fivefold happiness, when conceived and matured, perfects the twofold tranquillity, that is, bodily and mental tranquillity. When tranquillity is conceived and matured, it perfects the twofold bliss, that is, bodily and mental bliss. When bliss is conceived and matured, it perfects the threefold concentration, that is, momentary concentration, access concentration, and absorption concentration.

Of these, what is intended in this context by happiness is pervading happiness, which is the root of absorption and comes by growth into association with absorption. [145]

100. But as to the other word: pleasing (*sukhana*) is bliss (*sukha*). Or alternatively: it thoroughly (*Suṭṭhu*) devours (*KHĀdati*), consumes (*KHAṇati*),[29] bodily and mental affliction, thus it is bliss (*sukha*). It has gratifying as its characteristic. Its function is to intensify associated states. It is manifested as aid.

And wherever the two are associated, happiness is the contentedness at getting a desirable object, and bliss is the actual experiencing of it when got. Where there is happiness there is bliss (pleasure); but where there is bliss there is not necessarily happiness. Happiness is included in the formations aggregate; bliss is included in the feeling aggregate. If a man exhausted[30] in a desert saw or heard about a pond on the edge of a wood, he would have happiness; if he went into the wood's shade and used the water, he would have bliss. And it should be understood that this is said because they are obvious on such occassions.

101. Accordingly, (*a*) this happiness and this bliss are of this jhana, or in this jhana; so in this way this jhana is qualified by the words *with happiness and bliss*, [and also *born of seclusion*]. Or alternatively: (*b*) the words *happiness and bliss* (*pītisukhaṃ*) can be taken as 'the happiness and the bliss' independently, like 'the Law and the Discipline (*dhammavinaya*)', and so then it can be taken as seclusion-born happiness-and-bliss of this jhana, or in this jhana; so in this way it is the happiness and bliss [rather than the jhana] that are born of seclusion. For just as the words 'born of seclusion' can [as at (*a*)] be taken as qualifying the word jhana', so too they can be taken here [as at (*b*)] as qualifying the expression 'happiness and bliss', and then that [total expression] is predicated of this [jhana]. So it is also correct to call 'happiness-and-bliss born-of-seclusion' a single expression. In the Vibhaṅga it is stated in the way beginning 'This bliss accompanied by this happiness' (Vbh. 257). The meaning should be regarded in the same way there too.

102. *First jhana*: this will be explained below (§119).

Enters upon (*upasampajja*): arrives at; reaches, is what is meant; or else, taking it as 'makes enter (*upasampādayitvā*)', then producing, is what is meant. In the Vibhaṅga this is

---

29. For this word play see also Ch. XVII, §48. *Khaṇati* is only given its normal meaning of 'to dig' in P. T. S. Dict. There seems to be some confusion of meaning with *khayati* (to destroy) here, perhaps suggested by *khādati* (to eat). This suggests a rendering here and in Ch. XVII of 'to consume' which makes sense. Glossed by *avadāriyati*; to break or dig: not in P. T. S. Dict. see T. C. P. Dict. *avadārana*'.

30. *Kantāra-khinna*—exhausted in a desert'; *khinna* is not in P. T. S. Dict.

said: ' "Enters upon": the gaining, the regaining, the reaching ' the arrival at, the touching, the realizing of, the entering ' upon (*upasampadā*), the first jhana' (Vbh. 257), the meaning of which should be regarded in the same way.

103. *And dwells in* (*viharati*): by becoming possessed of jhana of the kind described above through dwelling in a posture favourable to that [jhana] he produces a posture, a procedure, a keeping, an enduring, a lasting, a behaviour, a dwelling, of the person. For this is said in the Vibhaṅga "Dwells 'in": poses, proceeds, keeps, endures, lasts, behaves, dwells; '[146] hence "dwells" is said' (Vbh. 252).

104. Now it was also said above *Which abandons five factors, possesses five factors* (§79cf. M. i, 294). Herein, the abandoning of the five factors should be understood as the abandoning of these five hindrances, namely, lust, ill will, stiffness and torpor, agitation and worry, and uncertainty; for no jhana arises until these have been abandoned, and so they are called the factors of abandoning. For although other unprofitable things too are abandoned at the moment of jhana, still only these are specifically obstructive to jhana.

105. The mind affected through lust by greed for varied objective fields does not become concentrated on an object consisting in unity, or being overwhelmed by lust, it does not enter on the way to abandoning the sense-desire element. When pestered by ill-will towards an object, it does not occur uninterruptedly. When overcome by stiffness and torpor, it is unwieldy. When seized by agitation and worry, it is unquiet and buzzes about. When stricken by uncertainty, it fails to mount the way to accomplish the attainment of jhana. So it is these only that are called factors of abandoning because they are specifically obstructive to jhana.

106. But applied thought directs the mind onto the object; sustained thought keeps it anchored there. Happiness produced by the success of the effort refreshes the mind whose effort has succeeded through not being distracted by those hindrances; and bliss intensifies it for the same reason. Then unification aided by this directing onto, this anchoring, this refreshing and this intensifying, evenly and rightly centers (Ch. III, §3) the mind with its remaining associated states on the object consisting in unity. Consequently possession of five factors should be understood as the arising of these five, namely, applied thought, sustained thought, happiness, bliss and unification of mind.

107. For it is when these are arisen that jhana is said to be arisen, which is why they are called the five factors of possesion. Therefore it should not be assumed that the jhana is something other which possesses them. But just as 'The army 'with the four factors' (Vin. iv, 104) and 'Music with the

'five factors' (MA. ii, 300) and 'The path with the eight 'factors (eightfold path)' are stated simply in terms of their factors, so this too [147] should be understood as stated simply in terms of its factors, when it is said to 'have five factors' or 'possess five factors'.

108. And while these five factors are present also at the moment of access and are stronger in access than in normal consciousness, they are still stonger here than in access and acquire the characteristic of the fine-material sphere. For applied thought arises here directing the mind on to the object in an extremely lucid manner, and sustained thought does so pressing the object very hard, and the happiness and bliss pervade the entire body. Hence it is said 'And there is ' nothing of his whole body not permeated by the happiness ' and bliss born of seclusion' (D. i, 73). And unification too arises in the complete contact with the object that the surface of a box's lid has with the surface of its base. This is how they differ from the others.

109. Although unification of mind is not actually listed among these factors in the [summary] version [beginning] 'which is ' accompanied by applied and sustained thought' (Vbh. 245), nevertheless it is mentioned [later] in the Vibhaṅga as follows, ' "jhana": it is applied thought, sustained thought, happiness, ' bliss, unification' (Vbh. 257), and so it is a factor too; for the intention with which the Blessed One gave the summary is the same as that with which he gave the exposition that follows it.

110. *Is good in three ways, possesses ten characteristics* (§79): the goodness in three ways is in the beginning, middle, and end. The possession of the ten characteristics should be understood as the characteristics of the beginning, middle, and end, too. Here is the text :

111. 'Of the first jhana purification of the way is the beginning, ' intensification of equanimity is the middle, and satisfaction ' is the end.

' "Of the first jhana purification of the way is the beginning": how many characteristics has the beginning? The ' beginning has three characteristics: the mind is purified of ' obstructions to that [jhana]; because it is purified the mind ' makes way for the central [state of equilibrium, which is the] ' sign of serenity; because it has made way the mind enters ' into that state. And it is since the mind becomes purified ' of obstructions and, through being purified, makes way for ' the central [state of equilibrium, which is the] sign of ' serenity and, having made way, enters into that state, that ' the purification of the way is the beginning of the first jhana. ' These are the three characteristics of the beginning. Hence 'it is said: The first jhana is good in the beginning which 'possesses three characteristics. [148]

112. '"Of the first jhana intensification of equanimity is the 'middle": how many characteristics has the middle? 'The middle has three characteristics. He [now] looks 'on with equanimity at the mind that is purified; he 'looks on with equanimity at it as having made way 'for serenity; he looks on with equanimity at the appear-'ance of unity.[31] And in that he [now] looks on with 'equanimity at the mind that is purified and looks on with 'equanimity at it as having made way for serenity and looks 'on with equanimity at the appearance of unity, that 'intensification of equanimity is the middle of the first jhana. 'These are the three characteristics of the middle. Hence it 'is said: The first jhana is good in the middle which 'possesses three characteristics.

113. '"Of the first jhana satisfaction is the end": how many 'characteristics has the end? The end has four charac-'teristics. The satisfaction in the sense that there was 'non-excess of any of the states arisen therein, and 'the satisfaction in the sense that the faculties had a 'single function, and the satisfaction in the sense that the 'appropriate energy was effective, and the satisfaction in the 'sense of repetition, are the satisfaction in the end of the 'first jhana. These are the four characteristics of the end. 'Hence it is said: The first jhana is good in the end which 'possesses four characteristics' (Ps. i, 167—8).

114. Herein, *purification of the way* is access together with its concomitants. *Intensification of equanimity* is absorption. *Satisfaction* is reviewing. So some comment.[32] But it is said in the text 'The mind arrived at unity enters into 'purification of the way, is intensified in equanimity, and 'is satisfied by knowledge' (Ps. i, 167), and therefore it is from the standpoint within actual absorption that *purification of the way* firstly should be understood as the approach, with *intensification of equanimity* as the function of equanimity consisting in specific neutrality, and *satisfaction* as the manifestation of clarifying knowledge's function in accomplishing non-excess of states. How?

---

31. Four unities (*ekatta*), are given in the preceding paragraph of the same Paṭisambhidā ref.: 'The unity consisting in the appearance of relinquishment in the act of giving, which is found in those resolved upon generosity (giving up); the unity consisting in the appearance of the sign of serenity, which is found in those who devote themselves to the higher consciousness; the unity consisting in the appearance of the characteristic of fall, which is found in those with insight; the unity consisting in the appearance of cessation, which is found in Noble Persons' (Ps. i, 167). The second is meant here.

32. 'The inmates of the Abhayagiri Monastery in Anurādhapura' (Pm. 144).

115. Firstly in a cycle [of consciousness] in which absorption arises the mind becomes purified from the group of defilements called hindrances that are an obstruction to jhana. Being devoid of obstruction because it has been purified, it makes way for the central [state of equilibrium, which is the] sign of serenity. Now it is the absorption concentration itself occurring evenly that is called *the sign of serenity.* But the consciousness immediately before that [149] reaches that state by way of change in a single continuity (cf. Ch. XXII, §1—6), and so it is said that it *makes way for the central [state of equilibrium, which is the] sign of serenity.* And it is said that it *enters into that state* by approaching it through having made way for it. That is why in the first place *purification of the way,* while referring to aspects existing in the preceding consciousness, should nevertheless be understood as the approach at the moment of the first jhana's actual arising.

116. Secondly, when he has no more interest in purifying, since there is no need to re-purify what has already been purified thus, it is said that *he looks on with equanimity at the mind that is purified.* And when he has no more interest in concentrating again what has already made way for serenity by arriving at the state of serenity, it is said that *he looks on with equanimity at it as having made way for serenity.* And when he has no more interest in again causing appearance of unity in what has already appeared as unity through abandonment of its association with defilement in making way for serenity, it is said that *he looks on with equanimity at the appearance of unity.* That is why *intensification of equanimity* should be understood as the function of equanimity that consists in specific neutrality.

117. And lastly, when equanimity was thus intensified, the states called concentration and understanding produced there occurred coupled together without either one exceeding the other. And also the [five] faculties beginning with faith occurred with the single function (taste) of deliverance owing to deliverance from the various defilements. And also the energy appropriate to that, which was favourable to their state of non-excess and single function, was effective. And also its repetition occurs at that moment.[33] Now all these [four] aspects are only produced because it is after seeing with knowledge the various dangers in defilement and advantages in cleansing that satisfiedness, purifiedness and clarifiedness ensue accordingly. That is the reason why it was said that *satisfaction* should be understood as the manifestation of

33. '"*Its*": of that jhana consciousness. "*At that moment*": at the moment of dissolution; for when the moment of arising is past, repetition occurs starting with the moment of presence' (Pm. 145). A curious argument, see § 182.

clarifying knowledge's function in accomplishing non-access, etc., of states (§114).

118. Herein, satisfaction as a function of knowledge is called 'the end' since the knowledge is evident as due to onlooking (equanimity), according as it is said: 'He looks on with ' complete equanimity at the mind thus exerted; then the ' understanding faculty it outstanding as understanding ' due to equanimity. Owing to equanimity the mind is ' liberated from the many sorts of defilements; then the ' understanding faculty is outstanding as understanding due ' to liberation. Because of being liberated these states come ' to have a single function; then [the understanding faculty ' is outstanding as understanding due to] development in the ' sense of the single function'[34] (Ps. ii. 25).

119. Now as to the words *and so he has attained the first jhana, . . . of the earth kasina* (§79). Here it is *first* because it starts a numerical series; [150] also it is first because it arises first. It is called *jhāna* because of lighting (*upanijjhāna*) the object and because of burning up (*jhāpana*) opposition (Ps. i, 49). The disk of earth is called *earth kasina* (*paṭhavī-kasiṇa*—lit. earth-universal) in the sense of entirety,[35] and the sign acquired with that as its support and also the jhana acquired in the earth-kasina sign are so called too. So that jhana should be understood as *of the earth kasina* in this sense, with reference to which it was said above 'and so he has attained to the first jhana, . . . of the earth kasina'.

120. When it has been attained in this way, the mode of its attainment must be discerned by the meditator as if he were a hair-splitter or a cook. For when a very skilful archer, who is working to split a hair, actually splits the hair on one occasion, he discerns the modes of the position of his feet, the bow, the bowstring, and the arrow thus: 'I spilt the hair as I stood thus, with the bow thus, the bowstring thus, the arrow thus'. From then on he recaptures those same modes and repeats the splitting of the hair without fail. So too the meditator must discern such modes as that of suitable food, etc., thus: 'I attained this after eating this food, attending on such a person, in such a lodging, in this posture at this time'. In this way, when that [absorption] is lost, he will be able to recapture those modes and renew the absorption, or while familiarizing himself with it he will be able to repeat that
121. absorption again and again. And just as when a skilled cook is serving his employer, he notices whatever he chooses to eat and from then on brings only that sort and so obtains a reward, so too this meditator discerns such modes as that of

34. The quotation is incomplete and the end should read '. . . *ekarasaṭṭhena bhāvanāvasena paññāvasena paññindriyaṁ adhimattaṁ hoti*'.

35. 'In the sense of the jhana's entire object. It is not made its partial object' (Pm. 147).

the food, etc., at the time of the attaining, and he recaptures them and re-obtains absorption each time it is lost. So he must discern the modes as a hair-splitter or a cook does.

122. And this has been said by the Blessed One: 'Bhikkhus, 'suppose a wise, clever, skilful cook set various kinds of 'sauces before a king or a king's minister, such as sour, 'bitter, sharp, [151] sweet, peppery and unpeppery, salty 'and unsalty sauces; then the wise, clever, skilful cook 'learned his masters sign thus "today this sauce pleased my 'master" or "he held out his hand for this one" or "he took 'a lot of this one" or "he praised this one" or "today the 'sour kind pleased my master" or "he held out his hand for 'the sour kind" or "he took a lot of the sour kind" or "he 'praised the sour kind" . . . or "he praised the unsalty kind"; 'then the wise, clever, skilful cook is rewarded with clothing 'and wages and presents. Why is that? Because that 'wise, clever, skilful cook learned his master's sign in this way. 'So too, bhikkhus, here a wise, clever, skilful bhikkhu dwells 'contemplating the body as a body,... He dwells contemplat-'ing feelings as feelings, . . . consciousness as consciousness, '. . . mental objects as mental objects, ardent, fully aware 'mindful, having put away covetousness and grief for the 'world. As he dwells contemplating mental objects as mental 'objects, his mind becomes concentrated, his defilements are 'abandoned. He learns the sign of that. Then that wise, 'clever, skilful bhikkhu is rewarded with a happy abiding 'here and now, he is rewarded with mindfulness and full 'awareness. Why is that? Because that wise, clever, 'skilful bhikkhu learned his consciousness's sign' (S.v, 151-2).

123. And when he recaptures those modes by apprehending the sign, he just succeeds in reaching absorption, but not in making it last. It lasts when it is absolutely purified from states that obstruct concentration.

124. When a bhikkhu enters upon a jhana without [first] completely suppressing lust by reviewing the dangers in sense desires, etc., and without [first] completely tranquillizing bodily irritability[36] by tranquillizing the body, and without [first] completely removing stiffness and torpor by bringing to mind the elements of initiative, etc. (§55), and without [first] completely abolishing agitation and worry by bringing to mind the sign of serenity, etc., [152] and without [first] completely purifying his mind of other states that obstruct concentration, then that bhikkhu soon comes out of

36. '*Kāya-duṭṭhulla*—bodily irritability': explained here as 'bodily disturbance (*daratha*), excitement of the body (*kāya-sāraddhatā*') by Pm. (p. 148); here it represents the hindrance of ill will; cf. M. iii, 151, 159, where commented on as *kāyālasiya*—bodily inertia' (MA. iv, 202, 208). P. T. S. Dict. only gives meaning of 'wicked, lewd' for *duṭṭhulla* for which meaning see *e.g.* A. i, 88; Vin A. 528, cf. Ch. IX, §69.

that jhana again, like a bee that has gone into an unpurified hive, like a king who has gone into an unclean park.

125. But when he enters upon a jhana after [first] completely purifying his mind of states that obstruct concentration, then he remains in the attainment even for a whole day, like a bee that has gone into a completely purified hive, like a king who has gone into a perfectly clean park. Hence the Ancients said:

'So let him dispel any sensual lust, and resentment,
'Agitation as well, and then torpor, and doubt as the fifth;
'There let him find joy with a heart that is glad in seclusion,
'Like a king in a garden where all and each corner is clean'.

126. So if he wants to remain long in the jhana, he must enter upon it after [first] purifying his mind from obstructive states.

[EXTENSION OF THE SIGN]

In order to perfect the development of consciousness he should besides extend the counterpart sign according as acquired. Now there are two planes for extension, namely, access and absorption; for it is possible to extend it on reaching access and on reaching absorption. But the extending should be done consistently in one [or the other], which is why it was said 'he should besides extend the counterpart sign according as acquired'.

127. The way to extend it is this. The meditator should not extend the sign as a clay bowl or a cake or boiled rice or a creeper or a piece of cloth is extended. He should first delimit with his mind successive sizes for the sign, according as acquired, that is to say, one finger, two fingers, three fingers, four fingers, and then extend it by the amount delimited, just as a ploughman delimits with the plough the area to be ploughed and then ploughs within the area delimited, or just as bhikkhus fixing a boundary first observe the marks and then fix it. He should not, in fact, extend it without having delimited [the amount it is to be extended by]. After that has been done, he can further extend it, doing so by delimiting successive boundaries of, say, a span, a *ratana* (=2 spans), the verandah, the surrounding space,[37] the monastery, and the boundaries of the village, the town, the district, the kingdom, and the ocean, [153] making the extreme limit the world-sphere or even beyond.

---

37. For '*pamukha*—verandah' see this Ch. n. 2. '*Pariveṇa*—surrounding space': this meaning, not given in P. T. S. Dict., is brought out clearly in Ch. XI, §7.

128. Just as young swans first starting to use their wings soar a little distance at a time, and by gradually increasing it eventually reach the presence of the moon and sun, so too when a bhikkhu extends the sign by successive delimitations in the way described, he can extend it up to the limit of the world-sphere or even beyond.

129. Then that sign [appears] to him like an ox hide stretched out with a hundred pegs[38] over the earth's ridges and hollows, river ravines, tracts of scrub and thorns, and rocky inequalities (see M. iii, 105) in any area to which it has been extended.

When a beginner has reached the first jhana in this sign he should enter upon it often without reviewing it much. For the first jhana factors occur crudely and weakly in one who reviews it much. Then because of that they do not become conditions for higher endeavour. While he is endeavouring for the unfamiliar [higher jhana] he falls away from the first jhana and fails to reach the second.

130. Hence the Blessed One said: 'Bhikkhus, suppose there 'were a foolish, stupid mountain cow, with no knowledge of 'fields and no skill in walking on craggy mountains, who 'thought "What if I walked in a direction I never walked in 'before, ate grass I never ate before, drank water I never 'drank before?", and without placing her fore foot properly 'she lifted up her hind foot; then she would not walk in the 'direction she never walked in before or eat the grass she never 'ate before or drink the water she never drank before, and 'also she would not get back safely to the place where she had 'thought "What if I walked in a direction I never walked in 'before,...drank water I never drank before?". Why is that? 'Because that mountain cow was foolish and stupid with no 'knowledge of fields and no skill in walking on craggy moun-'tains. So too, bhikkhus, here is a certain foolish, stupid 'bhikkhu with no knowledge of fields and no skill quite 'secluded from sense desires, secluded from unprofitable 'things, in entering upon and dwelling in the first jhana, 'which is accompanied by applied thought and sustained 'thought with happiness and bliss born of seclusion. He 'does not repeat, develop or cultivate that sign or properly 'establish it. He thinks "What if with the subsiding of 'applied and sustained thought I entered upon and dwelt in 'the second jhana, which is ... with happiness and bliss born 'of concentration?". [154] He is unable with the subsiding of

38. '*Samabbhāhata*—stretched flat': not in this sense in P. T. S. Dict. This word replaces the word *suvihata* used at M. iii, 105 where this clause is borrowed from. At Ch. XI, §92 the same word (apparently in another sense) is glossed by *pellana*=pushing (not in P. T. S. Dict.) at Pm. 362. MA. (iv, 153) glosses *suvihata* with '*pasāretvā suṭṭhu vihata*' which suggests 'stretched' rather than 'beaten'; *harati* rather than *hanati*.

'applied and substained thought to enter upon and dwell in 'the second jhana, which is . . . with happiness and bliss 'born of concentration. Then he thinks "What if quite 'secluded from sense desires, secluded from unprofitable 'things I entered upon and dwelt in the first jhana, which 'is . . . with happiness and bliss born of seclusion?". He is 'unable quite secluded from sense desires, secluded from 'unprofitable things to enter upon and dwell in the first jhana, 'which is . . . with happiness and bliss born of seclusion. 'This bhikkhu is called one who has slipped between the two, 'who has fallen between the two just like the foolish, 'stupid mountain cow, with no knowledge of fields and no 'skill in walking on craggy mountains. . .' (A. iv, 418-9).

131. Therefore he should acquire mastery in the five ways first of all with respect to the first jhana. Herein, these are the five kinds of mastery: mastery in adverting, mastery in attaining, mastery in resolving (steadying the duration), mastery in emerging, and mastery in reviewing. 'He 'adverts to the first jhana where, when, and for as 'long as, he wishes; he has no difficulty in adverting; 'thus it is mastery in adverting. He attains the first 'jhana where, . . . he has no difficulty in attaining; thus 'it is mastery in attaining' (Ps. i, 100), and all the rest should be quoted in detail (Ch. XXIII, §27).

132. The explanation of the meaning here is this. When he emerges from the first jhana and first of all adverts to the applied thought, then, next to the adverting that arose interrupting the life-continuum, either four or five impulsions impel with that applied thought as their object. Then there are two life-continuum [consciousness]. Then there is adverting with the sustained thought as its object and followed by impulsions in the way just stated. When he is able to prolong his conscious process uninterruptedly in this way with the five jhana factors, then his mastery of adverting is successful. But this mastery is found at its acme of perfection in the Blessed One's Twin Marvel (Ps. i, 125), or for others on the aforesaid occasions. There is no quicker mastery in adverting than that.

133. The venerable Mahā-Moggallāna's ability to enter upon jhana quickly, as in the taming of the Royal Nāga-Serpent Nandopananda (Ch. XII, §106f.), is called mastery in attaining.

134. Ability to remain in jhana for a moment consisting in exactly a finger-snap or exactly ten finger-snaps is called mastery in resolving (steadying the duration).

Ability to emerge quickly in the same way is called mastery in emerging.

135. The story of the Elder Buddharakkhita may be told in order to illustrate both these last. [155] Eight years after

his admission to the Community that Elder was sitting in the midst of thirty thousand bhikkhus possessed of supernormal powers who had gathered to attend upon the sickness of the Elder Mahā-Rohanogutta at Therambatthala. He saw a Royal Supaṇṇa (demon) swooping down from the sky intending to seize an attendant Royal Nāga-serpent as he was getting rice gruel accepted for the Elder. The Elder Budddharakkhita created a rock meanwhile, and seizing the Royal Nāga by the arm, he pushed him inside it. The Royal Supanna gave the rock a blow and made off. The Senior Elder remarked: 'Friends, if Rakkhita had not been there, we should all have been put to shame'.[39]

136. Mastery in reviewing is described in the same way as mastery in adverting; for the reviewing impulsions are in fact those next to the adverting mentioned there (§132).

137. When he has once acquired mastery in these five ways, then on emerging from the now familiar first jhana he can regard the flaws in it in this way: This attainment is threatened by the nearness of the hindrances, and its factors are weakened by the grossness of the applied and sustained thought. He can bring the second jhana to mind as quieter and so end his attachment to the first jhana and set about doing what is needed for attaining the second.

138. When he has emerged from the first jhana, applied and sustained thought appear gross to him as he reviews the jhana factors with mindfulness and full awareness, while happiness and bliss and unification of mind appear peaceful. Then, as he brings that same sign to mind as 'earth, earth' again and again with the purpose of abandoning the gross factors and obtaining the peaceful factors, [knowing] 'now the second jhana will arise' there arises in him mind-door adverting with that same earth kasina as its object, interrupting the life-continuum. After that, either four or five impulsions impel on that same object, the last one of which is an impulsion of the fine-material sphere belonging to the second jhana. The rest are of the sense sphere of the kinds already stated (§74).

[The Second Jhana]

139. And at this point, 'With the stilling of applied and sustained 'thought he enters upon and dwells in the second jhana, which 'has internal confidence and singleness of mind without 'applied thought, without sustained thought, with happiness

---

39. What the story is intended to illustrate is the rapidity with which the Elder entered the jhana, controlled its duration, and emerged, which is the necessary preliminary to the working of a marvel (the creation of a rock in this case; Ch. XII, §57). The last remark seems to indicate that all the others would have been too slow (see Pm. 150).

'and bliss born of concentration' (Vbh. 245), and so he has attained the second jhana, which abandons two factors, possesses three factors, is good in three ways, possesses ten characteristics and is of the earth kasina. [156]

140. Herein, *with the stilling of applied and sustained thought*: with the stilling, with the surmounting, of these two, namely, applied thought and sustained thought; with their non-manifestation at the moment of the second jhana, is what is meant. Herein, although none of the states belonging to the first jhana exist in the second jhana—for the contact, etc., (see M. iii, 25), in the first jhana are one and here they are another—it should be understood all the same that the phrase 'with the stilling of applied and sustained thought' is expressed in this way in order to indicate that the attaining of the other jhanas, beginning with that of the second from the first, is effected by the surmounting of the gross factor in each case.

141. *Internal*: here one's own internal[40] is intended; but that much is actually stated in the Vibhaṅga too with the words 'internally in oneself' (Vbh. 258). And since one's own internal is intended, the meaning here is this: born in oneself, generated in one's own continuity.

142. *Confidence*: it is faith that is called confidence. The jhana 'has confidence' because it is associated with confidence as a cloth 'has blue colour' because it is associated with blue colour. Or alternatively, that jhana is stated to 'have confidence' because it makes the mind confident with the confidence possessed by it and by stilling the disturbance created by applied and sustained thought. And with this conception of the meaning the word construction must be taken as 'confidence of mind'. But with the first-mentioned conception of the meaning the words 'of mind' must be construed with 'singleness'.[41]

143. Here is the construction of the meaning in that case. Unique (*eka*) it comes up (*udeti*), thus it is single (*ekodi*); the meaning is, it comes up as the superlative, the best, because it is not overtopped by applied and sustained thought, for the best is called 'unique' in the world. Or it is permissible to say that when deprived of applied and sustained thought it is unique, without companion. Or alternatively: it evokes (*udāyati*) associated states, thus it is an evoker (*udi*); the meaning is, it arouses. And that is unique (*eka*) in the sense of best, and it is an evoker (*udi*), thus it is a unique evoker (*ekodi*=single). This

40. See Ch. XIV, §198 and note.
41. In the Pali, *sampasādanam cetaso ekodibhāvam*', '*cetaso* (of mind)' comes between '*sampasādanaṁ* (confidence)' and '*ekodibhāvaṁ* (singleness)' and so can be construed with either.

is a term for concentration. Then, since the second jhana gives existing-ness to (*bhāveti*), augments, this single [thing], it 'gives single-ness (*ekodibhāva*)'. But as this single [thing] is a mind's, not a being's or a soul's so 'singleness of mind' is said.

144. It might be asked: But does not this faith exist in the first jhana too, and also this concentration with the name of the 'single [thing]'? Then why is only this second jhana said to have confidence and singleness of mind?—It may be replied as follows: It is because that first jhana [157] is not fully confident owing to the disturbance created by applied and sustained thought, like water ruffled by ripples and wavelets. That is why, although faith does exist in it, it is not called 'confidence'. And there too concentration is not fully evident because of the lack of full confidence. That is why it is not called 'singleness' there. But in this second jhana faith is strong, having got a footing in the absence of the impediments of applied and sustained thought; and concentration is also evident through having strong faith as its companion. That may be understood as the reason why only this jhana it
145. described in this way. But that much is actually stated in the Vibhaṅga too with the words '"Confidence" is faith, having 'faith, trust, full confidence. "Singleness of mind" is steadi- 'ness of consciousness,......right concentration' (Vbh. 258). And this commentary on the meaning should not be so understood as to conflict with the meaning stated in the way, but on the contrary so as to agree and concur with it.

146. *Without applied thought, without sustained thought*: since it has been abandoned by development, there is no applied thought in this, or of this, [jhana], thus it is without applied thought. The same explanation applies to sustained thought. Also it is said in the Vibhaṅga: 'So this applied thought 'and this sustained thought are quieted, quietened, stilled, 'set at rest, set quite at rest, done away with, quite done away 'with,[42] dried up, quite dried up, made an end of; hence it 'is said: without applied thought, without sustained 'thought' (Vbh. 258).

Here it may be asked: Has not this meaning already been established by the words 'with the stilling of applied and sustained thought'? So why is it said again 'without applied thought, without sustained thought'?—It may be replied: Yes, that meaning has already been established. But this does not indicate that meaning. Did we not say earlier: 'The phrase "with the stilling of applied and sustained thought" is expressed in this way in order to indicate

42. '*Appita*—done away with': '"*Appitā*" *ti vināsaṁ gamitā* (*Appita* means made to go to annihilation)' (Pm. 153). This meaning, though not in P.T.S. Dict., is given in T.C.P. Dict.

that the act of attaining the other jhanas, beginning with that of the second from the first, is effected by the
147. surmounting of the gross factor in each case'? (§140). Besides, this confidence comes about with the act of stilling, not the darkness of defilement, but the applied and sustained thought. And the singleness comes about, not as in access jhana with the abandoning of the hindrances, nor as in the first jhana with the manifestation of the factors, but with the act of stilling the applied and sustained thought. So that [first] clause indicates the cause of the confidence and singleness. In the same way this jhana is without applied thought and without sustained thought, not as in the third and fourth jhanas or as in eye consciousness, etc., with just absence, but with the actual act of stilling the applied and sustained thought. So that [first clause] also indicates the cause of the state without applied and sustained thought; it does not indicate the bare absence of applied and sustained thought. [158] The bare absence of applied and sustained thought is indicated by this [second] clause, namely, 'without applied thought, without sustained thought'. Consequently it needs to be stated notwithstanding that the first has already been stated.

148. *Born of concentration*: born of the first-jhana concentration, or born of associated concentration, is the meaning. Herein, although the first was born of associated concentration too, still it is only this concentration that is quite worthy to be called 'concentration' because of its complete confidence and extreme immobility due to absence of disturbance by applied and sustained thought. So only this [jhana] is called 'born of concentration', and that is in order to recommend it.

With happiness and bliss is as already explained. *Second*: second in numerical series. Also second because entered upon second.

149. Then it was also said above *which abandons two factors, possesses three factors* (§139). Herein, the abandoning of two factors should be understood as the abandoning of applied thought and sustained thought. But while the hindrances are abandoned at the moment of the access of the first jhana, in the case of this jhana the applied thought and sustained thought are not abandoned at the moment of its access. It is only at the moment of actual absorption that the jhana arises without them. Hence they are called its factors of abandoning.

150. Its possession of three factors should be understood as the arising of the three, that is, happiness, bliss, and unification of mind. So when it is said in the Vibhaṅga '"Jhana": confi'dence, happiness, bliss, unification of mind' (Vbh. 258), this is said figuratively in order to show that jhana with its equipment. But, excepting the confidence, this jhana has

literally three factors *quâ* factors that have attained to the characteristic of lighting (see §119), according as it is said: 'What is jhana of three factors on that occasion? It is 'happiness, bliss, unification of mind' (Vbh. 263).

The rest is as in the case of the first jhana.

151. Once this has been obtained in this way, and he has mastery in the five ways already described, then on emerging from the now familiar second jhana he can regard the flaws in it thus: This attainment is threatened by the nearness of applied and sustained thought; 'Whatever there is in it of happiness, 'of mental excitement, proclaims its grossness' (D. i, 37), and its factors are weakened by the grossness of the happiness so expressed. He can bring the third jhana to mind as quieter and so end his attachment to the second jhana and set about doing what is needed for attaining the third.

152. When he has emerged from the second jhana [159] happiness appears gross to him as he reviews the jhana factors with mindfulness and full awareness, while bliss and unification appear peaceful. Then as he brings that same sign to mind as 'earth, earth' again and again with the purpose of abandoning the gross factor and obtaining the peaceful factors, [knowing] 'now the third jhana will arise' there arises in him mind-door adverting with that same earth kasina as its object, interrupting the life-continuum. After that, either four or five impulsions impel on that same object, the last one of which is an impulsion of the fine-material sphere belonging to the third jhana. The rest are of the kinds already stated (§74).

[The Third Jhana]

153. And at this point, 'With the fading away of happiness as 'well he dwells in equanimity, and mindful and fully aware 'he feels bliss with his body, he enters upon and dwells in the 'third jhana, on account of which the Noble Ones announce: 'He dwells in bliss who has equanimity and is mindful' (Vbh. 245), and so he has attained the third jhana, which abandons one factor, possesses two factors, is good in three ways, possesses ten characteristics, and is of the earth kasina.

154. Herein, *with the fading away of happiness* as well (*pītiyā ca virāgā*): fading away is distaste for, or surmounting of, happiness of the kind already described. But the words 'as well (*ca*)' between the two [words *pītiyā* and *virāgā*] have the meaning of a conjunction;[43] they conjoin [to them] either the word 'stilling' or the expression 'the stilling of applied and sustained thought' [in the description of the second jhana]. Herein, when taken as conjoining 'stilling', the construction to be understood is 'with the fading away and,

---

43. '*Sampiṇḍana*—conjunction': gram. term for the word *ca* (and). This meaning not given in P.T.S. Dict. Cf. MA, i, 40.

what is more, with the stilling, of happiness', With this construction 'fading away' has the meaning of distaste; so the meaning can be regarded as 'with distaste for, and with the stilling of, happiness'. But when taken as conjoining the words 'stilling of applied and sustained thought', then the construction to be understood is 'with the fading of happiness and, what is more, with the stilling of applied and sustained thought'. With this construction 'fading away' has the meaning of surmounting; so this meaning can be regarded as 'with the surmounting of happiness and with the stilling of applied and sustained thought'.

155. Of course, applied and sustained thought have already been stilled in the second jhana, too. However, this is said in order to show the path to this third jhana and in order to recommend it. For when 'with the stilling of applied and sustained thought' is said, it is declared that the path to this jhana is necessarily by the stilling of applied and sustained thought. And just as, although mistaken view of individuality, etc., are not abandoned in the attaining of the third Noble Path [but in the first], yet when it is recommended by describing their abandonment thus 'With the abandoning of the 'five lower fetters' (A. i, 232), [160] then it awakens eagerness in those trying to attain that third Noble Path,—so too, when the stilling of applied and sustained thought is mentioned, though they are not actually stilled here [but in the second], this is a recommendation. Hence the meaning expressed is this: 'With the surmounting of happiness and with the stilling of applied and sustained thought.'

156. *He dwells in equanimity*: it watches [things] as they arise (*UPApattito IKKHATI*), thus it is equanimity (*upekkha*—or onlooking); it sees fairly, sees without partiality (*a-pakkha-patita*), is the meaning. A possessor of the third jhana is said to 'dwell in equanimity' since he possesses equanimity that is clear, abundant and sound.

Equanimity is of ten kinds: six-factored equanimity, equanimity as a divine abiding, equanimity as an enlightenment factor, equanimity of energy, equanimity about formations, equanimity as a feeling, equanimity about insight, equanimity as specific neutrality, equanimity of jhana, and equanimity of purification.

157. Herein, *six-factored equanimity* is a name for the equanimity in one whose cankers are destroyed. It is the mode of non-abandonment of the natural state of purity when desirable or undesirable objects of the six kinds come into focus in the six doors described thus: 'Here a bhikkhu whose can-'kers are destroyed is neither glad nor sad on seeing a visible 'object with the eye: he dwells in equanimity, mindful and 'fully aware' (A. iii, 279).

158. *Equanimity as a divine abiding* is a name for equanimity consisting in the mode of neutrality towards beings described thus: 'He dwells intent upon one quarter with his heart 'endued with equanimity' (D. i, 251).

159. *Equanimity as an enlightenment factor* is a name for equanimity consisting in the mode of neutrality in conascent states described thus: 'He develops the equanimity enlightenment 'factor depending on relinquishment' (M. i, II).

160. *Equanimity of energy* is a name for the equanimity otherwise known as neither over-strenuous nor over-lax energy described thus: 'From time to time he brings to mind the sign 'of equanimity' (A. i, 257).

161. *Equanimity about formations* is a name for equanimity consisting in neutrality about apprehending reflexion and composure regarding the hindrances, etc., described thus: 'How 'many kinds of equanimity about formations arise through 'concentration? How many kinds of equanimity about formations arise through insight? Eight kinds of equanimity 'about formations arise through concentration. Ten kinds 'of equanimity about formations arise through insight' '(Ps. i, 64).[44] [161].

162. *Equanimity as a feeling* is a name for the equanimity known as neither-pain-nor-pleasure described thus: 'On the occasion 'on which a sense-sphere profitable consciousness has arisen 'accompanied by equanimity' (Dhs. 156).

163. *Equanimity about insight* is a name for equanimity consisting in neutrality about investigation described thus: 'What 'exists, what has become, that he abandons, and he obtains 'equanimity' (   ).

164. *Equanimity as specific neutrality* is a name for equanimity consisting in the equal efficiency of conascent states: it is contained among the 'or-whatever states' beginning with zeal (Ch. XIV, §133; DhsA. 132).

165. *Equanimity of jhana* is a name for equanimity producing impartiality towards even the highest bliss described thus: 'He dwells in equanimity' (Vbh. 245).

166. *Purifying equanimity* is a name for equanimity purified of all opposition, and so consisting in uninterestedness in stilling opposition described thus: 'The fourth jhana, which... 'has mindfulness purified by equanimity' (Vbh. 245).

167. Herein, six-factored equanimity, equanimity as a divine abiding, equanimity as an enlightenment factor, equanimity as specific neutrality, equanimity of jhana and purifying equanimity are one in meaning, that is, equanimity as specific neutrality. Their difference, however, is one of position,[45]

44. The 'eight kinds' are those connected with the eight jhana attainments. The 'ten kinds' are those connected with the four paths, the four fruitions, the void liberation, and the singleness liberation.

45. '*Avatthā*—position, occasion': Not in P.T.S. Dict.; see T.C.P. Dict.

like the difference in a single being as a boy, a youth, an adult a general, a king, and so on. Therefore of these it should be understood that equanimity as an enlightenment factor, etc., are not found where there is six-factored equanimity; or that six-factored equanimity, etc., are not found where there is equanimity as enlightenment factor.

And just as these have one meaning, so also equanimity about formations and equanimity about insight have one meaning too; for they are simply understanding classed
168. in these two ways according to function. Just as, when a man has seen a snake go into his house in the evening and has hunted for it with a forked stick, and then when he has seen it lying in the grain store and has looked to discover whether it is actually a snake or not, and then by seeing three marks[46] has no more doubt, and so there is neutrality in him about further investigating whether or not it is a snake, [162] so too, when a man has begun insight, and he sees with insight-knowledge the three characteristics, then there is neutrality in him about further investigating the impermanence, etc., of formations,
169. and that neutrality is called *equanimity about insight.* But just as, when the man has caught hold of the snake securely with the forked stick and thinks 'How shall I get rid of the snake without hurting it or getting bitten by it?', then as he is seeking only the way to get rid of it, there is neutrality in him about the catching hold of it, so too, when a man, through seeking the three characteristics, sees the three kinds of becoming as if burning, then there is neutrality in him about catching hold of formations: and that neutrality is
170. called *equanimity about formations.* So when equanimity about insight is established, equanimity about formations is established too. But it is divided into two in this way according to function, in other words, according to neutrality about investigating and about catching hold.

Equanimity of energy and *equanimity as feeling* are different both from each other and from the rest.

171. So, of these kinds of equanimity, it is equanimity of jhana that is intended here. That has the characteristic of neutrality. Its function is to be unconcerned. It is manifested as uninterestedness. Its proximate cause is the fading away of happiness.

Here it may be said: Is this not simply equanimity as specific neutrality in the meaning? And that exists in the first and second jhanas as well; so this clause 'He dwells in equanimity' ought to be stated of those also. Why is it not?—[It may be replied:] Because its function is unevident there. For its function is unevident there

46. '*Sovatthika-ttaya*—three marks'; cf. Ch. XXI, §49.

since it is overshadowed by applied thought, and the rest. But it appears here with a quite evident function, with head erect, as it were, because it is not overshadowed by applied thought and sustained thought and happiness. That is why it is stated here.

The commentary on the meaning of the clause 'He dwells in equanimity' is thus completed in all its aspects.

172. Now as to *mindful and fully aware*: here, he remembers (*sarati*), thus he is mindful (*sata*); He has full-awareness (*sampajānāti*), thus he is fully aware (*sampajāna*). This is mindfulness and full-awareness stated as personal attributes. Herein, mindfulness has the characteristic of remembering. Its function is not to forget. It is manifested as guarding. Full-awareness has the characteristic of non-confusion. Its function is to investigate (judge). It is manifested as scrutiny.

173. Herein, although this mindfulness, and this full-awareness exist in the earlier jhanas as well—for one who is forgetful and not fully aware does not attain even access, let alone absorption—, yet, because of the [comparative] grossness of those jhanas the mind's going is easy [there], like that of a man on [level] ground, and so the functions of mindfulness and full awareness are not evident in them. [163] But it is only stated here because the subtlety of this jhana, which is due to the abandoning of the gross factors, requires that the mind's going always includes the functions of mindfulness and full-awareness, like that of a man on a razor's edge.

174. What is more, just as a calf that follows a cow returns to the cow when taken away from her if not prevented, so too, when this third jhana is led away from happiness, it would return to happiness if not prevented by mindfulness and full awareness, and would rejoin happiness. And besides, beings are greedy for bliss, and this kind of bliss is exceedingly sweet since there is none greater. But here there is non-greed for the bliss owing to the influence of the mindfulness and full-awareness, not for any other reason. And so it should also be understood that it is stated only here in order to emphasize this meaning too.

175. Now, as to the clause *he feels bliss with his body*: here although in one actually possessed of the third jhana there is no concern about feeling bliss, nevertheless he would feel the bliss associated with his mental body, and after emerging from the jhana he would also feel bliss since his material body would have been affected by the exceedingly superior matter originated by that bliss associated with the mental body.[47] It is in order to point to this meaning that the words 'he feels bliss with his body' are said.

---

47. For consciousness-originated materiality see Ch. XX, §30ff.

176. Now, as to the clause, *that...on account of which the Noble Ones announce: He dwells in bliss who has equanimity and is mindful:* here it is the jhana, *on account of which* as cause, on account of which as reason, *the Noble Ones*, that is to say, the Enlightened Ones, etc., '*announce*, teach, declare establish, reveal, expound, explain, clarify' (Vbh. 259) *that* person who possesses the third jhana—they praise, is what is intended. Why? Because '*he dwells in bliss who has equanimity and is mindful. He enters upon and dwells in that third jhana* (*taṁ ...tatiyaṁ jhānaṁ upasampajja viharati*) is how the construction should be understood here. But why do they praise

177. him thus? Because he is worthy of praise. For this man is worthy of praise since he has equanimity towards the third jhana though it possesses exceedingly sweet bliss and has reached the perfection of bliss, and he is not drawn towards it by a liking for the bliss, and he is mindful with the mindfulness established in order to prevent the arising of happiness, and he feels with his mental body the undefiled bliss beloved of Noble Ones, cultivated by Noble Ones. Because he is worthy of praise in this way, it should be understood, Noble Ones praise him with the words 'He dwells in bliss who has equanimity and is mindful', thus declaring the special qualities that are worthy of praise. [164]

Third: it is the third in the numerical series; and it is third because it is entered upon third.

178. Then it was said, *which abandons one factor, possesses two factors* (§153): here the abandoning of the one factor should be understood as the abandoning of happiness. But that is abandoned only at the moment of absorption, as applied thought and sustained thought are at that of the second jhana; hence it is called its factor of abandoning.

179. The possession of the two factors should be understood as the arising of the two, namely, bliss and unification. So when it is said in the Vibhaṅga, '"Jhana": equanimity, 'mindfulness, full-awareness, bliss, unification of mind' (Vbh. 260), this is said figuratively in order to show that jhana with its equipment. But, excepting the equanimity and mindfulness and full-awareness, this jhana has literally only two factors *quâ* factors that have attained to the characteristic of lighting (see §119), according as it is said 'What 'is the jhana of two factors on that occasion? It is bliss 'and unification of mind' (Vbh. 264).

The rest is as in the case of the first jhana.

180. Once this has been obtained in this way, and once he has mastery in the five ways already described, then on emerging from the now familiar third jhana, he can regard the flaws in it thus. This attainment is threatened by the nearness of happiness; 'Whatever there is in it of mental concern about

'bliss proclaims its grossness' (D. i, 37; see Ch. IX, n. 20), and its factors are weakened by the grossness of the bliss so expressed. He can bring the fourth jhana to mind as quieter and so end his attachment to the third jhana and set about doing what is needed for attaining the fourth.

181. When he has emerged from the third jhana, the bliss, in other words, the mental joy appears gross to him as he reviews the jhana factors with mindfulness and full awareness, while the equanimity as feeling and the unification of mind appear peaceful. Then as he brings that same sign to mind as 'earth, earth' again and again with the purpose of abandoning the gross factor and obtaining the peaceful factors [knowing] 'now the fourth jhana will arise' there arises in him mind-door adverting with that same earth kasina as its object, interrupting the life-continuum After that either four or five impulsions impel on that same object, [165] the last one of which is an impulsion of the fine-material sphere belonging to the fourth jhana. The rest are of the kinds already stated (§ 74).

182. But there is this difference: blissful (pleasant) feeling is not a condition, as repetition condition, for neither-painful-nor-pleasant feeling, and [the preliminary-work] must be aroused in the case of the fourth jhana with neither-painful-nor-pleasant feeling, consequently these [consciousnesses of the preliminary-work] are associated with neither-painful-nor-pleasant feeling, and here happiness vanishes simply owing to their association with equanimity.

[The Fourth Jhana]

183. And at this point, 'With the abandoning of pleasure and 'pain and with the previous disappearance of joy and grief the enters upon and dwells in the fourth jhana, which has 'neither-pain-nor-pleasure and has purity of mindfulness due 'to equanimity' (Vbh. 245), and so he has attained the fourth jhana, which abandons one factor, possesses two factors, is good in three ways, possesses ten characteristics, and is of the earth kasina.

184. Herein, *with the abandoning of pleasure and pain* is with the abandoning of bodily pleasure and bodily pain. *With the previous*: which took place before, not in the moment of the fourth jhana. *Disappearance of joy and grief*: with the previous disappearance of the two, that is, mental bliss (pleasure) and mental pain; with the abandoning, is what is meant.

185. But when does the abandoning of these take place? At the moment of access of the four jhanas. For [mental] joy is only abandoned at the moment of the fourth-jhana access, while [bodily] pain, [mental] grief, and [bodily] bliss

(pleasure) are abandoned respectively at the moments of access of the first, second, and third jhanas. So although the order in which they are abandoned is not actually mentioned, nevertheless the abandoning of the pleasure, pain, joy, and grief, is stated here according to the order in which the faculties are summarized in the Indriya Vibhaṅga (Vbh. 122).

186. But if these are only abandoned at the moments of access of the several jhanas, why is their cessation said to take place in the jhana itself in the following passage: 'And where does 'the arisen pain faculty cease without remainder? Here, 'bhikkhus, quite secluded from sense desires, secluded from 'unprofitable things, a bhikkhu enters upon and dwells in the 'first jhana, which is...born of seclusion. It is here that the 'arisen pain faculty ceases without remainder...Where does 'the arisen grief faculty [cease without remainder?...in the 'second jhana]... Where does the arisen pleasure faculty '[cease without remainder?...in the third jhana]... Where 'does the arisen joy faculty cease without remainder? [166] 'Here, bhikkhus, with the abandoning of pleasure and pain '[and with the previous disappearance of joy and grief] a 'bhikkhu enters upon and dwells in the fourth jhana, which '...has mindfulness purified by equanimity. It is here 'that the arisen joy faculty ceases without remainder' (S. v,213–5)?

It is said in that way there referring to reinforced cessation. For in the first jhana, etc., it is their reinforced cessation, not just their cessation, that takes place. At the moment of access it is just their cessation, not their reinforced cessation, that
187. takes place. For accordingly, during the first jhana access, which has multiple adverting, there could be rearising of the [bodily] pain faculty[48] due to contact with gadflies, flies, etc., or due to the discomfort of an uneven seat, though that pain faculty had already ceased, but not so during absorption. Or alternatively, though it has ceased during access, it has not absolutely ceased there since it is not quite beaten out by opposition. But during absorption the whole body is showered

48. 'They say that with the words "*There could be the arising of the pain faculty*" it is shown that since grief arises even in obtainers of jhana it is demonstrated thereby that hate can exist without being a hindrance just as greed can; for grief does not arise without hate. Nor, they say, is there any conflict with the Paṭṭhāna text to be fancied here, since what is shown there is only grief that occurs making lost jhana its object because the grief that occurs making its object a jhana that has not been lost is not relevant there. And they say that it cannot be maintained that grief does not arise at all in those who have obtained jhana since it did arise in Asita who had the eight attainments (Sn. 691), and he was not one who had lost jhana. So they say. That is wrong because there is no hate without the nature of a hindrance. If there were, it would arise in fine-material and immaterial beings, and it does not. Accordingly when in such passages as "In the immaterial state, due to the hindrance of lust there is the hindrance of stiffness and

with bliss owing to pervasion by happiness. And the pain faculty has absolutely ceased in one whose body is showered with bliss, since it is beaten out then by opposition. And
188. during the second-jhana access too, which has multiple adverting, there could be rearising of the [mental] grief faculty, although it had already ceased there, because it arises when there is bodily weariness and mental vexation, which have applied thought and sustained thought as their condition, but it does not arise when applied and sustained thought are absent. When it arises, it does so in the presence of applied and sustained thought, and they are not abandoned in the second-jhana access; but this is not so in the second jhana itself
189. because its conditions are abandoned there. Likewise in the third-jhana access there could be rearising of the abandoned [bodily] pleasure faculty in one whose body was pervaded by the superior materiality originated by the [consciousness associated with the] happiness.[48] But not so in the third jhana itself. For in the third jhana the happiness that is a condition for the [bodily] bliss (pleasure) has ceased entirely. Likewise in the fourth-jhana access there could be rearising of the abandoned [mental] joy faculty becaue of its nearness and because it has not been properly surmounted owing to the absence of equanimity brought to absorption strength. But not so in the fourth jhana itself. And that is why in each case (§ 186) the words 'without remainder' are included thus: ' It is here that the arisen pain faculty ceases without remainder'.

190. Here it may be asked: Then if these kinds of feelıng are abandoned in the access in this way, why are they brought in here?

It is done so that they can be readily grasped. For the neither-painful-nor-pleasant feeling described here by the words 'which has neither-pain-nor-pleasure' is subtle, hard to recognize and not readily grasped. So just as, when a cattle-herd[49] wants to catch a refractory ox that cannot be caught at all by approaching it, he collects all the cattle into one pen [167] and lets them out one by one, and then [he says] 'That is it; catch it', and so it gets caught as well, so too the Blessed One has collected all these [five kinds of feeling] together so that they can be grasped readily;

torpor....the hindrance of agitation, the hindrance of ignorance" (Ptn. 2. 291) ill will and worry are not mentioned as hindrances, that does not imply that they are not hindrances even by supposing that it was because lust, etc., were not actually hindrances and were called hindrances there figuratively because of resemblance to hindrances. And it is no reason to argue "it is because it arose in Asita", since there is falling away from jhana with the arising of grief. The way to regard that is that when the jhana is lost for some trivial reason such men reinstate it without difficulty' (Pm. 158—9).

49. '*Gopa*—cowherd (or guardian)': not in P.T.S. Dict.

for when they are shown collected together in this way, then what is not [bodily] pleasure (bliss) or [bodily] pain or [mental] joy or [mental] grief can still be grasped in this way:
191. This is neither-painful-nor-pleasant feeling. Besides, this may be understood as said in order to show the condition for the neither-painful-nor-pleasant mind-deliverance. For the abandoning of [bodily] pain, etc., are conditions for that, according as it is said: 'There are four conditions, friend, 'for the attainment of the neither-painful-nor-pleasant 'mind-deliverance. Here, friend, with the abandoning of 'pleasure and pain and with the previous disappearance of 'joy and grief a bhikkhu enters upon and dwells in the fourth 'jhana...equanimity. These are the four conditions for the 'attainment of the neither-painful-nor-pleasant mind-deliver-
192. 'ance' (M.i,296). Or alternatively, just as, although mistaken view of individuality, etc., have already been abandoned in the earlier paths, they are nevertheless mentioned as abandoned in the description of the third path for the purpose of recommending it (cf. §155), so too these kinds of feeling can be understood as mentioned here for the purpose of recommending this jhana. Or alternatively, they can be understood as mentioned for the purpose of showing that greed and hate are very far away owing to the removal of their conditions; for of these, pleasure (bliss) is a condition for joy, and joy for greed; pain is a condition for grief and grief for hate. So with the removal of pleasure (bliss), etc., greed and hate are very far away since they are removed along with their conditions.

193. *Which has neither-pain-nor-pleasure*: no pain owing to absence of pain; no pleasure owing to absence of pleasure (bliss). By this he indicates the third kind of feeling that is in opposition both to pain and to pleasure, not the mere absence of pain and pleasure. This third kind of feeling named 'neither-pain-nor-pleasure' is also called 'equanimity'. It has the characteristic of experiencing what is contrary to both the desirable and the undesirable. Its function is neutral. Its manifestation is unevident. Its proximate cause should be understood as the cessation of pleasure (bliss).

194. *And has purity of mindfulness due to equanimity*: has purity of mindfulness brought about by equanimity. For the mindfulness in this jhana is quite purified, and its purification is effected by equanimity, not by anything else. That is why it is said to have purity of mindfulness due to equanimity. Also it is said in the Vibhaṅga: 'This mindfulness is cleared, 'purified, clarified, by equanimity; hence it is said to have purity of mindfulness due to equanimity (Vbh. 261). [168] And the equanimity due to which there comes to be this purity of mindfulness should be understood as specific neutrality

in meaning. And not only mindfulness is purified by it here, but also all associated states. However, the teaching is given under the heading of mindfulness.

195. Herein, this equanimity exists in the three lower jhanas too; but just as, although a crescent moon exists by day but is not purified or clear since it is outshone by the sun's radiance in the daytime or since it is deprived of the night, which is its ally owing to gentleness and owing to helpfulness to it, so too, this crescent moon of equanimity consisting in specific neutrality exists in the first jhana, etc., but it is not purified since it is outshone by the glare of the opposing states consisting in applied thought, etc., and since it is deprived of the night of equanimity-as-feeling for its ally; and because it is not purified, the conascent mindfulness and other states are not purified either, like the unpurified crescent moon's radiance by day. That is why no one among these [first three jhanas] is said to have purity of mindfulness due to equanimity. But here this crescent moon consisting in specific neutrality is utterly pure because it is not outshone by the glare of the opposing states consisting in applied thought, etc., and because it has the night of equanimity-as-feeling for its ally. And since it is purified, the conascent mindfulness and other states are purified and clear also, like the purified crescent moon's radiance, That, it should be understood, is why only this jhana is said to have purity of mindfulness due to equanimity.

196. *Fourth*: it is fourth in numerical series; and it is fourth because it is entered upon fourth.

197. Then it was said, *which abandons one factor, possesses two factors* (§183); here the abandoning of the one factor should be understood as the abandoning of joy. But that joy is actually abandoned in the first impulsions of the same cognitive series (cf. §185). Hence it is called its factor of abandoning.

The possession of the two factors should be understood as the arising of the two, namely, equanimity as feeling and unification of mind.

The rest is as stated in the case of the first jhana.

This, in the first place, is according to the fourfold reckoning of jhana.

[The Fivefold Reckoning of Jhana]

198. When, however he is developing fivefold jhana, then, on emerging from the now familiar first jhana, he can regard the flaws in it in this way: This attainment is threatened by the nearness of the hindrances, and its factors are weakened by the grossness of applied thought. [169] He can bring the second jhana to mind as quieter and so end his attachment

to the first jhana and to what is needed for attaining the second.

199. Now he emerges from the first jhana mindful and fully aware; and only applied thought appears gross to him as he reviews the jhana factors, while the sustained thought, etc., appear peaceful. Then as he brings that same sign to mind as 'earth, earth' with the purpose of abandoning the gross factor and obtaining the peaceful factors the second jhana arises in him in the way already described.

Its factor of abandoning is applied thought only. The four beginning with sustained thought are the factors that it possesses. The rest is as already stated.

200. When this has been obtained in this way, and once he has mastery in the five ways already described, then on emerging from the now familiar second jhana he can regard the flaws in it in this way: This attainment is threatened by the nearness of applied thought, and its factors are weakened by the grossness of sustained thought. He can bring the third jhana to mind as quieter and so end his attachment to the second jhana and set about doing what is needed for attaining the third.

201. Now he emerges from the second jhana mindful and fully aware; only sustained thought appears gross to him as he reviews the jhana factors, while happiness, etc., appear peaceful. Then as he brings that same sign to mind as 'earth, earth' again and again with the purpose of abandoning the gross factor and obtaining the peaceful factors the third jhana arises in him in the way already described.

Its factor of abandoning is sustained thought only. The three beginning with happiness, as in the second jhana in the fourfold reckoning, are the factors that it possesses. The rest is as already stated.

202. So that which is the second in the fourfold reckoning becomes the second and third in the fivefold reckoning by being devided into two. And those which are the third and fourth in the former reckoning become the fourth and fifth in this reckoning. The first remains the first in each case.

The fourth chapter called 'The Description of the Earth Kasina' in the Treatise on the Development of Concentration in the Path of Purification composed for the purpose of gladdening good people.

CHAPTER V

DESCRIPTION OF CONCENTRATION —THE REMAINING KASINAS

(*Sesa-kasiṇa-niddesa*)

[The Water Kasina]

1. [170] Now the water kasina comes next after the earth kasina (Ch. III, §105). Here is the detailed explanation.

One who wants to develop the water kasina should, as in the case of the earth kasina, seat himself comfortably and apprehend the sign in water that 'is either made up or not made up', etc.; and so all the rest should be repeated in detail (Ch. IV, §22). And as in this case, so with all those that follow [in this chapter]. We shall in fact not repeat even this much and shall only point out what is different.

2. Here too, when someone has had practice in previous [lives], the sign arises for him in water that is not made up, such as a pool, a lake, a lagoon, or the ocean as in the case of the Elder Cūḷa-Sīva.

The venerable one, it seems, thought to abandon gain and honour and live a secluded life. He boarded a ship at Mahātittha (Mannar) and sailed to Jambudīpa (India). As he gazed at the ocean meanwhile the kasina sign, the counterpart of that ocean, arose in him.

3. Someone with no such previous practice should guard against the four faults of a kasina (Ch. IV, §24) and not apprehend the water as one of the colours, blue, yellow, red or white. He should fill a bowl or a four-footed water pot[1] to the brim with water uncontaminated by soil, taken in the open through a clean cloth [strainer], or with any other clear unturbid water. He should put it in a screened place on the outskirts of the monastery as already described and seat himself comfortably. He should neither review its colour nor bring its characteristic to mind. Apprehending the colour as belonging to its physical support he should set his mind on the [name] concept as the most outstanding mental datum, and using any among the [various] names for water (*āpo*) such as 'rain (*ambu*)', 'liquid (*udaka*)', 'dew (*vāri*),' 'fluid (*salila*)',[2] he should develop [the kasina] by using [preferably] the obvious 'Water, water'.

4. As he develops it in this way, the two signs eventually arise in him in the way already described. Here, however, the

1. '*Kuṇḍika*—a four-footed water pot': not in P.T.S. Dict.
2. English cannot really furnish five words for water.

learning sign has the appearance of moving. [171] If the water has bubbles of froth mixed with it, the learning sign has the same appearance, and it is evident as a fault in the kasina. But the counterpart sign appears inactive, like a crystal fan set in space, like the disk of a looking-glass made of crystal. With the appearance of that sign he reaches access jhana and the jhana tetrad and pentad in the way already described.

The water kasina

[The Fire Kasina]

5. Anyone who wants to develop the fire kasina should apprehend the sign in fire.

Herein, when someone with merit, having had previous practice, is apprehending the sign, it arises in him in any sort of fire, not made up, as he looks at the fiery combustion in a lamp's flame or in a furnace or in a place for baking bowls or in a forest conflagration, as in the Elder Cittagutta's case.

The sign arose in that Elder as he was looking at a lamp's flame while he was in the Uposatha house on the dav of preaching the Dhamma.

6. Anyone else should make one up. Here are the directions for making it. He should split up some damp heartwood, dry it, and break it up into short lengths. He should go to a suitable tree root or to a shed and there make a pile in the way done for baking bowls, and have it lit. He should make a hole a span and four fingers wide in a rush mat or a piece of leather or a cloth, and after hanging it in front of the fire, he should sit down in the way already described. Instead of giving attention to the grass and sticks below or the smoke above, he should apprehend the sign in the dense combustion in the middle.

7. He should not review the colour as blue or yellow, etc., or give attention to its characteristic as heat, etc., but taking the colour as belonging to its physical support, and setting his mind on the [name] concept as the most outstanding mental datum, and using any among the names for fire (*tejo*) such as 'the Bright One (*pāvaka*),' 'the Leaver of the Black Trail (*kaṇhavattani*)', 'the Knower of Creatures (*jāta-veda*)', 'the Altar of Sacrifice (*hutāsana*)', etc., he should develop [the kasina] by using [preferably] the obvious 'Fire, fire'.

8. As he develops it in this way the two signs eventually arise in him as already described. Herein, the learning sign appears like [the fire to keep] sinking down as the flame keeps detaching itself. [172] But when someone apprehends it in a kasina that is not made up, any fault in the kasina is evident [in

the learning sign], and any firebrand, or pile of embers or ashes, or smoke appears in it. The counterpart sign appears motionless like a piece of red cloth set in space, like a gold fan, like a gold column. With its appearance he reaches access jhana and the jhana tetrad and pentad in the way already described.

The fire kasina

[The Air Kasina]

9. Anyone who wants to develop the air kasina should apprehend the sign in air. And that is done either by sight or by touch. For this is said in the Commentaries: 'One who is learning the air kasina apprehends the sign in air. He notices the tops of [growing] sugarcane moving to and fro; or he notices the tops of bamboos, or the tops of trees, or the ends of the hair, moving to and fro; or he notices the touch of it on the body'.

10. So when he sees sugarcanes with dense foliage standing with tops level or bamboos or trees, or else hair four fingers long on a man's head, being struck by the wind, he should establish mindfulness in this way: 'This wind is striking on this place'. Or he can establish mindfulness where the wind strikes a part of his body after entering by a window opening or by a crack in a wall, and using any among names for wind (*vāta*) beginning with 'wind (*vāta*)', 'breeze (*māluta*)', 'blowing (*anila*)', he should develop [the kasina] by using [preferably] the obvious 'Air, air'.

11. Here the learning sign appears to move like the swirl of hot [steam] on rice gruel just withdrawn from an oven. The counterpart sign is quiet and motionless. The rest should be understood in the way already described.

The air kasina.

[The Blue Kasina]

12. Next it is said [in the commentaries] 'One who is learning the blue kasina apprehends the sign in blue, whether in a flower or in a cloth or in a colour element'.[3] Firstly, when someone has merit, having had previous practice, the sign arises in him when he sees a bush with blue flowers, or such flowers spread out on a place of offering, or any blue cloth or
13. gem. [173] But anyone else should take flowers such as blue lotuses, *girikaṇṇikā* (morning glory) flowers, etc., and spread them out to fill a tray or a flat basket completely so that no stamen or stalk shows, or with only their petals. Or he can fill it with blue cloth bunched up together; or he can fasten the cloth over the rim of the tray or basket

3. '*Vaṇṇa-dhātu*—colour element' should perhaps have been rendered simply by 'paint'. The one Pāli word '*nīla*' has to serve for the English blue, green, and sometimes black.

like the covering of a drum. Or he can make a kasina disk, either portable as described under the earth kasina or on a wall, with one of the colour elements such as bronze-green, leaf-green, anjana-ointment black, surrounding it with a different colour. After that, he should bring it to mind as 'Blue, blue' in the way already described under the earth kasina.

14. And here too any fault in the kasina is evident in the learning sign; the stamens and stalks and the gaps between the petals, etc., are apparent. The counterpart sign appears like a crystal fan in space, free from the kasina disk. The rest should be understood as already described.

The blue kasina

[The Yellow Kasina]

15. Likewise with the yellow kasina; for this is said: 'One who is learning the yellow kasina apprehends the sign in yellow, either in a flower or in a cloth or in a colour element'. Therefore here too, when someone has merit, having had previous practice, the sign arises in him when he sees a flowering bush or flowers spread out, or yellow cloth or colour element, as in the case of the Elder Cittagutta.

That venerable one, it seems, saw an offering being made on the flower altar, with *pattaṅga* flowers[4] at Cittalapabbata, and as soon as he saw it the sign arose in him the size of the flower altar.

16. Anyone else should make a kasina, in the way described for the blue kasina, with *kaṇikāra* flowers, etc., or with yellow cloth or with a colour element. He should bring it to mind as 'Yellow, yellow'. The rest is as before.

The yellow kasina

[The Red Kasina]

17. Likewise with the red kasina; for this is said: 'One who is learning the red kasina apprehends the sign in red, [174] either in a flower or in a cloth or in a colour element'. Therefore here too, when someone has merit, having had previous practice, the sign arises in him when he sees a *bandhujīvaka* (hibiscus) bush, etc., in flower, or such flowers spread out, or a red cloth or gem or colour element. But anyone else
18. should make a kasina, in the way already described for the blue kasina, with *jayasumana* flowers or *bandhujīvaka* or red *koraṇḍaka* flowers, etc., or with red cloth or with a colour element. He should bring it to mind as 'Red, red'. The rest is as before.

The red kasina

4. '*Pattaṅga*': not in P.T.S. Dict. '*Āsana*—altar': not in this sense in P.T.S. Dict.

[THE WHITE KASINA]

19. Of the white kasina it is said 'One who is learning the white kasina apprehends the sign in white, either in a flower or in a cloth or in a colour element'. So firstly, when someone has merit, having had previous practice, the sign arises in him when he sees a flowering bush of such a kind or *vassikasumana* (jasmine) flowers, etc.; spread out, or a heap of white lotuses or lilies, white cloth or colour element; and it also arises in a tin disk, a silver disk, and the moon's disk.
20. Anyone else should make a kasina, in the way already described for the blue kasina, with the white flowers already mentioned, or with cloth or colour element. He should bring it to mind as 'White, white'. The rest is as before.

The white kasina

[THE LIGHT KASINA]

21. Of the light kasina it is said 'One who is learning the light kasina apprehends the sign in light in a hole in a wall, or in a keyhole, or in a window opening'. So firstly, when someone has merit, having had previous practice, the sign arises in him when he sees the circle thrown on a wall or a floor by sunlight or moonlight entering through a hole in a wall, etc., or when he sees a circle thrown on the ground by sunlight or moonlight coming through a gap in the branches of a dense-leaved tree or through a gap in a hut made of closely packed branches. Anyone else should use that same kind of circle of
22. luminosity just described, developing it as 'Luminosity, luminosity' or 'Light, light'. If he cannot do so, he can light a lamp inside a pot, close the pot's mouth, make a hole in it and place it with the hole facing a wall. The lamplight coming out of the hole throws a circle on the wall. He should develop that [175] as 'Light, light'. This lasts longer than
23. the other kinds. Here the learning sign is like the circle thrown on the wall or the ground. The counterpart sign is like a compact bright cluster of lights. The rest is as before.

The light kasina

[THE LIMITED-SPACE KASINA]

24. Of the limited-space kasina it is said 'One who is learning the space kasina apprehends the sign in a hole in a wall, or in a keyhole, or in a window opening, and so firstly, when someone has merit, having had previous practice, the sign arises in him when he sees any [such gap as a] hole in a wall.
25. Anyone else should make a hole a span and four fingers broad in a well-thatched hut, or in a piece of leather, or in a rush mat, and so on. He should develop one of these, or a hole
26. such as a hole in a wall, as 'Space, space'. Here the learning sign resembles the hole together with the wall, etc., that

surrounds it. Attempts to extend it fail. The counterpart sign appears only as a circle of space. Attempts to extend it succeed. The rest should be understood as described under the earth kasina.[5]

The limited-space kasina

[GENERAL]

27. He with Ten Powers, who all things did see,
Tells ten kasinas, each of which can be
The cause of fourfold and of fivefold jhana,
The fine-material sphere's own master key.
Now knowing their descriptions and the way
To tackle each and how they are developed,
There are some further points that will repay
Study, each with its special part to play.

28. Of these, the earth kasina is the basis for such powers as the state described as 'Having been one, he becomes many' (D. i, 78), etc., and stepping or standing or sitting on space or on water by creating earth, and the acquisition of the bases of mastery (M. ii, 13) by the limited and measureless method.

29. The water kasina is the basis for such powers as diving in and out of the earth (D.i, 78), causing rain storms, creating rivers and seas, making the earth and rocks and palaces quake (M. i, 253).

30. The fire kasina is the basis for such powers as smoking, flaming, causing showers of sparks, countering fire with fire, ability to burn only what one wants to burn (S. iv, 290), [176] causing light for the purpose of seeing visible objects with the divine eye, burning up the body by means of the fire element at the time of attaining nibbana (MA.iv, 196).

5. In the suttas the first eight kasinas are the same as those given here, and they are the only ones mentioned in the Dhammasaṅgaṇī (§160-203) and Paṭisambhidā (Ps. i, 6). The suttas give space and consciousness as ninth and tenth respectively (M.ii, 14-5; D.iii, 268, Netti 89 etc.). But these last two appear to coincide with the first two immaterial states, that is, boundless space and boundless consciousness. The light kasina given here as ninth does not appear in the suttas. It is perhaps a development from the 'perception of light (*āloka-saññā*)' (A. ii, 45). The limited-space kasina given here as tenth has perhaps been made 'limited' in order to differentiate it from the first immaterial state. The Commentary on the consciousness kasina (MA. iii, 261) says nothing on this aspect. As to space, Pm. (p. 373) says 'The attainment of the immaterial states is not produced by means of the space kasina, and with the words "ending with the white kasina" (Ch. XXI, §2) the light kasina is included in the white kasina'. For description of space (*ākāsa*) see DhsA. 325, Netti 29. Also Pm. (p. 393) defines space thus 'Wherever there is no obstruction, that is called space'. Again the Majjhima-nikāya Ṭīkā (commenting on M. sutta 106) remarks '[Sense desires] are not called empty (*ritta*) in the sense that space, which is entirely devoid of individual essence, is called empty'.

31. The air kasina is the basis for such powers as going with the speed of the wind, causing wind storms.

32. The blue kasina is the basis for such powers as creating black forms, causing darkness, acquisition of the bases of mastery by the method of fairness and ugliness, and attainment of the liberation by the beautiful (see M. ii, 12),

33. The yellow kasina is the basis for such powers as creating yellow forms, resolving that something shall be gold (S. i, 116), acquisition of the bases of mastery in the way stated, and attainment of the liberation by the beautiful.

34. The red kasina is the basis for such powers as creating red forms, acquisition of the bases of mastery in the way stated and attainment of the liberation by the beautiful.

35. The white kasina is the basis for such powers as creating white forms, banishing stiffness and torpor, dispelling darkness, causing light for the purpose of seeing visible objects with the divine eye.

36. The light kasina is the basis for such powers as creating luminous forms, banishing stiffness and torpor, dispelling darkness, causing light for the purpose of seeing visible objects with the divine eye.

37. The space kasina is the basis for such powers as revealing the hidden, maintaining postures inside the earth and rocks by creating space inside them, travelling unobstructed through walls, and so on.

38. The classification 'above, below, around, exclusive, measureless' applies to all kasinas; for this is said: 'He perceives 'the earth kasina above, below, around, exclusive measure-'less' (M. ii, 14), and so on.

39. Herein, *above* is upwards towards the sky's level. *Below* is downwards towards the earth's level. *Around* is marked off all round like the perimeter of a field. For one extends a kasina upwards only, another downwards, another all round; or for some reason another projects it thus as one who wants to see visible objects with the divine eye projects light. [177] Hence 'above, below, around' is said. The word *exclusive*, however, shows that any one such state has nothing to do with any other. Just as there is water and nothing else in all directions for one who is actually in water, so too, the earth kasina is the earth kasina only; it has nothing in common with any other kasina. Similarly in each instance. *Measureless* means measureless intentness. He is intent upon the entirety with his mind, taking no measurements in this way 'This is its beginning, this is its middle'.

40. No kasina can be developed by any living being described as follows: 'Beings hindered by kamma, by defilement or by 'kamma-result, who lack faith, zeal and understanding, will

'be incapable of entering into the certainty of rightness 'in profitable states' (Vbh. 341).

41. Herein, the words *hindered by kamma* refer to those who possesses bad kamma entailing immediate effect [on rebirth].[6] *By defilement*: who have fixed wrong view[7] or are hermaphrodites or eunuchs. *By kamma-result*: who have had a rebirth-linking with no [profitable] root-cause or with only two [profitable] root-causes. *Lack faith*: are destitute of faith in the Buddha, Dhamma and Sangha. *Zeal*: are destitute of zeal for the Unopposed Way. *Understanding*: are destitute of mundane and supramundane right view. *Will be incapable of entering into the certainty of rightness in profitable states* means that they are incapable of entering into the Noble Path called 'certainty' and rightness in profitable states'.

42. And this does not apply only to kasinas; for none of them will succeed in developing any meditation subject at all. So the task of devotion to a meditation subject must be undertaken by a clansman who has no hindrance by kamma-result, who shuns hindrance by kamma and by defilement, and who fosters faith, zeal and understanding by listening to the Dhamma, frequenting good men, and so on.

The fifth chapter called 'The Description of the Remaining Kasinas' in the Treatise on the Development of Concentration in the Path of Purification composed for the purpose of gladdening good people.

---

6. The five kinds of bad kamma with immediate effect on rebirth are, in that order of priority, matricide, parricide, arahanticide, intentional shedding of a Buddha's blood, and causing a schism in the Community, all of which cause rebirth in hell and remaining there for the remainder of the aeon (*kappa*), whatever other kinds of kamma may have been performed (MA. iv, 109f.).

7. The no-cause view, moral-inefficacy-of-action view, the nihilistic view that there is no such thing as giving, and so on (see D. Sutta 2).

CHAPTER VI

DESCRIPTION OF CONCENTRATION —FOULNESS AS A MEDITATION SUBJECT

(*Asubha-kammaṭṭhāna-niddesa*)

[General Definitions]

1. [178] Now ten kinds of foulness, [as corpses] without consciousness, were listed next after the kasinas thus: the bloated, the livid, the festering, the cut up, the gnawed, the scattered, the hacked and scattered, the bleeding, the worm-infested, a skeleton (Ch. III, §105).

The bloated: it is bloated (*uddhumāta*) because bloated by gradual dilation and swelling after (*uddhaṁ*) the close of life, as a bellows is with wind. What is bloated (*uddhumāta*) is the same as 'the bloated (*uddhumātaka*)'. Or alternatively what is bloated (*uddhumāta*) is vile (*kucchita*) because of repulsiveness, thus it is 'the bloated (*uddhumātaka*)'. This is a term for a corpse in that particular state.

2. *The livid*: what has patchy discolouration is called livid (*vinīla*). What is livid is the same as 'the livid (*vinīlaka*)'. Or alternatively, what is livid (*vinīla*) is vile (*kucchita*) because of repulsiveness, thus it is 'the livid *vinīlaka*'.[1] This is a term for a corpse that is reddish-coloured in places where flesh is prominent, whitish-coloured in places where pus has collected, but mostly blue-black (*nīla*), as if draped with blue-black cloth in the blue-black places.

3. *The festering*: what is trickling with pus in broken places is festering (*vipubba*). What is festering is the same as 'the festering (*vipubbaka*)'. Or alternatively, what is festering (*vipubba*) is vile (*kucchita*) because of repulsiveness, thus it is 'the festering (*vipubbaka*)'. This is a term for a corpse in that particular state.

4. *The cut up*: what has been opened up[2] by cutttng it in two is called cut up (*vicchidda*). What is cut up is the same as 'the cut up (*vicchiddaka*)'. Or alternatively what is cut up (*vicchidda*) is vile (*kucchita*) because of repulsiveness, thus it is 'the cut up (*vicchiddaka*)'. This is a term for a corpse cut in the middle. [179]

5. *The gnawed*: what has been chewed here and there in various ways by dogs, jackals, etc., is what is gnawed (*vikkhāyita*). What is gnawed is the same as 'the gnawed (*vikkhāyitaka*)'.

---

1. It is not possible to render such associative and alliterative derivations of meaning into English. They have nothing to do with the historical development of words, and their purpose is purely mnemonic.
2. '*Apavārita*—opened up': not in P. T. S. Dict.

Or alternatively, what is gnawed (*vikkhāyita*) is vile (*kucchita*) because of repulsiveness, thus it is 'the gnawed (*vikkhāyitaka*)'. this is a term for a corpse in that particular state.

6. *The scattered*: what is strewed about (*vividhaṃ khittaṃ*) is scattered (*vikkhittaṁ*). What is scattered is the same as 'the scattered (*vikkhittaka*)'. Or alternatively, what is scattered (*vikkhitta*) is vile (*kucchita*) because of repulsiveness, thus it is 'the scattered *vikkhittaka*)'. This is a term for a corpse that is strewed here and there in this way: 'Here a hand, there a foot, there the head' (cf. M. i, 58).

7. *The hacked and scattered*: it is hacked, and it is scattered in the way just described, thus it is 'hacked and scattered *hatavikkhitaka*)'. This is a term for a corpse scattered in the way just described after it has been hacked with a knife in a crow's-foot pattern on every limb.

8. *The bleeding*: it sprinkles (*kirati*), scatters, blood (*lohita*), and it trickles here and there, thus it is 'the bleeding (*lohitaka*)'. This is a term for a corpse smeared with trickling blood.

9. *The worm-infested*: it is maggots that are called worms (*puḷuva*); it sprinkles worms (*puḷuve kirati*) thus it is worm-infested (*puḷuvaka*). This is a term for a corpse full of maggots.

10. *A skeleton*: bone (*aṭṭhi*) is the same as skeleton (*aṭṭhika*). Or alternatively, bone (*aṭṭhi*) is vile (*kucchita*) because of repulsiveness, thus it is a skeleton (*aṭṭhika*). This is a term both for a single bone and for a framework of bones.

11. These names are also used both for the signs that arise with the bloated, etc., as their support, and for the jhanas obtained in the signs.

[The Bloated]

12. Herein, when a meditator wants to develop the jhana called 'of the bloated' by arousing the sign of the bloated on a bloated body, he should in the way already described approach a teacher of the kind mentioned under the earth kasina and learn the meditation subject from him. In explaining the meditation subject to him, the teacher should explain it all, that is, the directions for going with the aim of acquiring the sign of foulness, the characterizing of the surrounding signs, the eleven ways of apprehending the sign, the reviewing of the path gone by and come by, concluding with the directions for absorption. And when the meditator has learnt it all well, he should go to an abode of the kind already described and live there while seeking the sign of the bloated.

13. Meanwhile, when he hears people saying that at some village gate or on some road or at some forest's edge or at the base of some rock or at the root of some tree [180] or on some charnel ground a bloated corpse is lying, he should not go there at once, like one who plunges into a river where there

14. is no ford. Why not? Because this foulness is beset by wild beasts and non-human beings, and he might risk his life there. Or perhaps the way to it goes by a village gate or a bathing place or an irrigated field, and there a visible object of the opposite sex might come into focus. Or perhaps the body is of the opposite sex; for a female body is unsuitable for a man, and a male body for a woman. If only recently dead, it may even look beautiful; hence there might be danger to the life of purity. But if he judges himself thus 'This is not difficult for one like me', then he can go there.

15. And when he goes, he should do so only after he has spoken to the senior elder of the Community or to some well-known
16. bhikkhu. Why? Because if all his limbs are seized with shuddering at the charnel ground, or if his gorge rises when he is confronted with disagreeable objects such as the visible forms and sounds of non-human beings, lions, tigers, etc., or something else afflicts him, then he whom he told will have his bowl and robe well looked after in the monastery, or he will care for him by sending young bhikkhus or novices to him.

17. Besides, robbers may meet there thinking a charnel ground a safe place for them whether or not they have done anything wrong. And when men chase them, they drop their goods near the bhikkhu and run away. Perhaps the men seize the bhikkhu, saying 'We have found the thief with the goods', and bully him. Then he whom he told will explain to the men 'Do not bully him; he went to do this special work after telling me', and he will rescue him. This is the advantage of going only after informing someone.

18. Therefore he should inform a bhikkhu of the kind described and then set out eager to see the sign, and as happy and joyful as a warrior-noble (*khattiya*) on his way to the scene of anointing, as one going to offer libations at the hall of sacrifice, or as a pauper on his way to unearth a hidden treasure. And he should go there in the way advised by the Com-
19. mentaries. For this is said: One who is learning the bloated sign of foulness goes alone with no companion, with unremitting mindfulness established, with his sense faculties turned inwards, with his mind not turned outwards, reviewing the path gone by and come by. In the place where the bloated sign of foulness [181] has been left he notes any stone or ant-hill or tree or bush or creeper there each with its particular sign and in relation to the object. When he has done this, he characterizes the bloated sign of foulness by the fact of its having attained that particular individual essence (see §84). Then he sees that the sign is properly apprehended, that it is properly remembered, that it is properly defined, by its colour, by its mark, by its shape, by its direction, by its location, by its delimitation, by its joints, by its openings, by

20. its concavities, by its convexities, and all round. When he has properly apprehended the sign, properly remembered it, properly defined it, he goes alone with no companion, with unremitting mindfulness established, with his sense faculties turned inwards, with his mind not turned outwards, reviewing the path gone by and come by. When he walks, he resolves that his walk is oriented towards it; when he sits, he prepares
21. a seat that is oriented towards it. What is the purpose, what is the advantage of characterizing the surrounding signs? Characterizing the surrounding signs has non-delusion for its purpose, it has non-delusion for its advantage. What is the purpose, what is the advantage of apprehending the sign in the [other] eleven ways? Apprehending the sign in the [other] eleven ways has anchoring [the mind] for its purpose, it has anchoring [the mind] for its advantage. What is the purpose, what is the advantage of reviewing the path gone by and come by? Reviewing the path gone by and come by has keeping [the mind] on the track for its purpose, it has keeping [the mind]
22. on the track for its advantage. When he has established reverence for it by seeing its advantages and by perceiving it as a treasure and so come to love it, he anchors his mind upon that object: "Surely in this way I shall be liberated from ageing and death". Quite secluded from sense desires, secluded from unprofitable things he enters upon and dwells in the first jhana ... [seclusion.] He has arrived at the first jhana of the fine-material sphere. His is a heavenly abiding and an instance of the meritorious action consisting in [meditative] development'.

23. So if he goes to the charnel ground to test his control of mind, let him do so after striking the gong or summoning a chapter. If he goes there mainly for [developing that] meditation subject, let him go alone with no companion, without renouncing his basic meditation subject and keeping it always in mind, taking a walking stick or a staff to keep off attacks by dogs, etc., [182] ensuring unremitting mindfulness by establishing it well, with his mind not turned outwards because he has ensured that his faculties, of which his mind is the sixth, are turned inwards.

24. As he goes out of the monastery he should note the gate: 'I have gone out in such a direction by such a gate'. After that he should define the path by which he goes: 'This path goes in an easterly direction...westerly...northerly... southerly direction' or 'It goes in an intermediate direction'; and 'In this place it goes to the left, in this place to the right'; and 'In this place there is a stone, in this an ant-hill, in this a tree, in this a bush, in this a creeper'. He should go to the place where the sign is, defining in this way the path by which

25. he goes. And he should not approach it up wind; for if he did so and the smell of corpses assailed his nose, his brain[3] might get upset, or he might throw up his food, or he might repent his coming, thinking 'What a place of corpses I have come to!'. So instead of approaching it up wind, he should go down wind. If he cannot go by a down-wind path—if there is a mountain or a ravine or a rock or a fence or a patch of thorns or water or a bog in the way—, then he should go stopping his nose with the corner of his robe. These are the duties in going.

26. When he has gone there in this way, he should not at once look at the sign of foulness; he should make sure of the direction. For perhaps if he stands in a certain direction, the object does not appear clearly to him and his mind is not wieldy. So rather than there he should stand where the object appears clearly and his mind is wieldy. And he should avoid standing to leeward or to windward of it. For if he stands to leeward he is bothered by the corpse smell and his mind strays; and if he stands to windward and non-human beings are dwelling there, they may get annoyed and do him a mischief. So he should move round a little and not stand too much to windward. [183]

27. Then he should stand not too far off or too near, or too much towards the feet or the head. For if he stands too far off, the object is not clear to him, and if he stands too near, he may get frightened. If he stands too much towards the feet or the head, not all the foulness becomes manifest to him equally. So he should stand not too far off or too near, opposite the middle of the body, in a place convenient for him to look at it.

28. Then he should characterize the surrounding signs in the way stated thus: 'In the place where the bloated sign of foulness has been left he notes any stone ... or creeper there with its sign' (§19).

29. These are the directions for characterizing them. If there is a rock in the eye's focus near the sign, he should define it in this way: 'This rock is high or low, small or large, brown or black or white, long or round', after which he should observe [the relative positions] thus: 'In this place, this is a rock, this is the sign of foulness; this is the sign of foulness, this is a rock'.

30. If there is an ant-hill, he should define it in this way: 'This is high or low, small or large, brown or black or white, long or round,' after which he should observe [the relative positions] thus: 'In this place, this is an ant-hill, this is the sign of foulness'.

3. This does not imply what we, now, might suppose. See the description of 'brain' in Ch. VIII, §126 and especially §136. What is meant is perhaps that he might get a cold or catarrh.

31. If there is a tree, he should define it in this way: 'This is a pippul tree or a banyan tree or a *kacchaka* tree or a wood-apple tree; it is tall or short, small or large, black or white', after which he should observe [the relative positions] thus: 'In this place, this is a tree, this is the sign of foulness'.

32. If there is a bush, he should define it in this way: 'This is a *sindi* bush or a *karamanda* bush or a *kaṇavīra* bush or a *koraṇḍaka* bush; it is tall or short, small or large', after which he should observe [the relative positions] thus: 'In this place, this is a bush, this is the sign of foulness'.

33. If there is a creeper, he should define it in this way: 'This is a pumpkin creeper or a gourd creeper or a brown creeper or a black creeper or a stinking creeper', after which he should observe [the relative positions] thus: 'In this place, this is a creeper, this is the sign of foulness; this is the sign of foulness, this is a creeper'.

34. Also *with its particular sign and in relation to the object* was said (§ 19); but that is included by what has just been said; for he 'characterizes it with its particular sign' when he defines it again and again, and he 'characterizes it in relation to the object' when he defines it by combining it each time in pairs thus: 'This is a rock, this is the sign of foulness; this is the sign of foulness, this is a rock'.

35. Having done this, again he should bring to mind the fact that it has an individual essence, its own state of being bloated, which is not common to anything else, since it was said that he defines[4] it *by the fact of its having attained that particular individual essence.* The meaning is that it should be defined according to its individual essence, according to its own nature, as 'the inflated,[5] the bloated'.

Having defined it in this way, he should apprehend the sign in the following six ways, that is to say, (1) by its colour, (2) by its mark (3) by its shape [184] (4) by its direction, (5 by its location, (6) by its delimitation. How?

36. (1) The meditator should define it *by its colour* thus: 'This is the body of one who is black or white or yellow-skinned'.

37. (2) Instead of defining it by the female mark or the male mark, he should define it *by its mark* thus: 'This is the body of one who was in the first phase of life, in the middle phase, in the last phase'.

38. (3) *By its shape*: he should define it only by the shape of the bloated thus: 'This is the shape of its head, this is the shape of its neck, this is the shape of its hand, this is the shape of its chest, this is the shape of its belly, this is the shape of its navel, this is the shape of its hips, this is the shape of

4. Reference back to §19 requires *sabhāvato upalakkhati* rather than *s. vavatthāpeti*, but so the readings have it.

5. '*Vaṇita*—inflated': glossed by Pm. with *sūna* (swollen). Not in P. T.S. Dict. in this sense.

its thigh, this is the shape of its calf, this is the shape of its foot'.

39. (4) He should define it *by its direction* thus: 'There are two directions in this body, that is, down from the navel as the lower direction, and up from it as the upper direction'. Or alternatively he can define it thus: 'I am standing in this direction; the sign of foulness is in that direction'.

40. (5) He should define it *by its location* thus: 'The hand is in this location, the foot in this, the head in this, the middle of the body in this'. Or alternatively, he can define it thus: I am in this location; the sign of foulness is in that'.

41. (6) He should define it *by its delimitation* thus: 'This body is delimited below by the soles of the feet, above by the tips of the hair, all round by the skin; the space so delimited is filled up with thirty-two pieces of corpse'. Or alternatively, he can define it thus: 'This is the delimitation of its hand, this is the delimitation of its foot, this is the delimitation of its head, this is the delimitation of the middle part of its body'. Or alternatively, he can delimit as much of it as he has apprehended thus: 'Just this much of the bloated is like this'.

42. However, a female body is not appropriate for a man or a male one for a woman; for the object, [namely, the repulsive aspect], does not make its appearance in a body of the opposite sex, which merely becomes a condition for the wrong kind of excitement.[6] To quote the Majjima Commentary: 'Even when decaying[7] a woman invades a man's mind and stays there'. That is why the sign should be apprehended in the six ways only in a body of the same sex.

43. But when a clansman has cultivated the meditation subject under former Enlightened Ones, kept the ascetic practices, threshed out the great primary elements, discerned formations, defined mentality-materiality, eliminated the perception of a being, done the ascetic's [185] duties, lived the moral life, and developed the development, when he contains the seed [of Turning Away from formations], and has mature knowledge and little defilement, then the counterpart sign appears to

6. '*Vipphandana*—wrong kind cf excitement': Pm. says here '*Kilesa-paripphandanass'eva nimittaṃ hotī ti attho* (the meaning is, it becomes the sign for the interference by (activity of) defilement)' Pm. 170). *Phandati* and *vipphandati* are both given only such meanings as 'to throb, stir, twitch and *paripphandati* is not in P.T.S. Dict. For the sense of wrong (*vi-*) excitement (*phandana*) cf. Ch. IV, §89, and Ch XIV, §132 and note. There seems to be an association of meaning between *vipphāra*, *vyāpāra*, *vipphandana*, *īhaka*, and *paripphandana* (perhaps also *abhoga*) in the general senses of interestedness, activity, concern, interference, intervention, etc.

7. The Harvard text has *uggkāṭita*, but Pm. (p. 170) reads '*ugghāṇitā* (not in P.T.S. Dict.) *pī ti uddhumātakabhāvappattā pi sabbaso kuthita-sarīrā pī ti attho*'.

him in the place while he keeps looking. If it does not appear in that way, then it appears to him as he is apprehending the sign in the six ways.

44. But if it does not appear to him even then, he should apprehend the sign again in five more ways: (7) by its joints, (8) by its openings, (9) by its concavities, (10) by its convexities, and (11) all round.

45. Herein, (7) *by its joints* is [properly] by its hundred and eighty joints. But how can he define the hundred and eighty joints in the bloated? Consequently he can define it by its fourteen major joints thus: Three joints in the right arm, three in the left arm, three in the right leg, three in the left leg, one neck joint, one waist joint.

46. (8) *By its openings* an 'opening' is the hollow between the arm [and the side], the hollow between the legs, the hollow of the stomach, the hollow of the ear. He should define it by its openings in this way. Or alternatively, the opened or closed state of the eyes and the opened or closed state of the mouth can be defined.

47. (9) *By its concavities*: he should define any concave place on the body such as the eye sockets or the inside of the mouth or the base of the neck. Or he can define it thus: 'I am standing in a concave place, the body is in a convex place'.

48. (10) *By its convexities* he should define any raised place on the body such as the knee or the chest or the forehead. Or he can define it thus: 'I am standing in a convex place, the body is in a concave place'.

49. (11) *All round*: the whole body should be defined all round. After working over the whole body with knowledge, he should establish his mind thus, 'The bloated, the bloated', upon any part that appears clearly to him. If it has not appeared even yet, and if there is special intensity of the bloatedness in the belly,[8] he should establish his mind thus, 'The bloated, the bloated', on that.

50. Now as to the words, *he sees that the sign is properly apprehended*, etc., the explanation is this. The meditator should apprehend the sign thoroughly in that body in the way of apprehending the sign already described. He should advert to it with well-established mindfulness. He should see that it is properly remembered, properly defined, by doing that again and again. Standing in a place not too far from and not too near to the body, he should open his eyes, look and apprehend the sign. [186] He should open his eyes and look a hundred times, a thousand times, [thinking], 'Repulsiveness of the bloated, repulsiveness of the bloated', and he should close his eyes and advert to it.

8. '*Udara-pariyosānaṃ uparisarīraṃ*' (Pm. 172). *Pariyosāna* here means 'intensity' though normally it means 'end'; but see P.T.S. Dict. *pariyosita*.

51. As he does so again and again, the learning sign becomes properly apprehended by him. When is it properly apprehended? When it comes into focus alike whether he opens his eyes and looks or closes his eyes and adverts, then it is called properly apprehended.

52. When he has thus properly apprehended the sign, properly remembered it, and properly defined it, then if he is unable to conclude his development on the spot, he can go to his own lodging, alone, in the same way as described of his coming, with no companion, keeping that same meditation subject in mind, with mindfulness well established, and with his mind not turned outwards owing to his faculties being turned inwards.

53. As he leaves the charnel ground he should define the path he comes back by thus: 'The path by which I have left goes in an easterly direction, westerly . . . northerly . . . southerly direction,' or 'It goes in an intermediate direction'; or 'In this place it goes to the left, in this place to the right'; and 'In this place there is a stone, in this an ant-hill, in this a tree, in this a bush, in this a creeper'.

54. When he has defined the path he has come back by and when, once back, he is walking up and down, he should see that his walk is oriented towards it too; the meaning is that he should walk up and down on a piece of ground that faces in the direction of the sign of foulness. And when he sits, he should prepare a seat oriented towards it too.

55. But if there is a bog or a ravine or a tree or a fence or a swamp in that direction, if he cannot walk up and down on a piece of ground facing in that direction, if he cannot prepare his seat thus because there is no room for it, then he can both walk up and down and sit in a place where there is room, even though it does not face that way; but he should turn his mind in that direction.

56. Now as to the questions beginning with *what is the purpose . . . characterizing the surrounding signs*? the intention of the answer that begins with the words, *has non-delusion for its purpose*, is this: If someone goes at the wrong time to the place where the sign of the bloated is, and opens his eyes for the purpose of apprehending the sign by characterizing the surrounding signs, then as soon as he looks the dead body appears [187] as if were standing up and threatening[9] and pursuing him, and when he sees the hideous and fearful object, his mind reels, he is like one demented, gripped by panic fear and terror, and his hair stands on end. For among the thirty-eight meditation subjects expounded in the texts there is no object so frightening as this one. There are some who

9. There is no sense of *ajjhottharatti* given in P.T.S. Dict. that fits here. See Ch. I, §56.

lose jhana in this meditation subject. Why? Because it is so frightening.

57. So the meditator must stand firm. Establishing his mindfulness well, he should remove his fears in this way: 'No dead body gets up and pursues one. If that stone or that creeper close to it were to come, the body might come too; but since that stone or that creeper does not come, the body will not come either. Its appearance to you in this way is born of your perception, created by your perception. Today your meditation has appeared to you. Do not be afraid, bhikkhu'. He should laugh it off and direct his mind to the sign. In that way he will arrive at distinction. The words 'Characterizing the surrounding signs has non-delusion for its purpose' are said on this account.

58. To succeed in apprehending the sign in the eleven ways is to anchor the meditation subject. For the opening of his eyes and looking conditions the arising of the learning sign; and as he exercises his mind on that the counterpart sign arises; and as he exercises his mind on that he reaches absorption. When he is sure of absorption, he works up insight and realizes Arahantship. Hence it was said: *apprehending the sign in the [other] eleven ways has anchoring [the mind] for its purpose*.

59. *The reviewing of the path gone by and come by has keeping [the mind] on the track for its purpose*: the meaning is that the reviewing of the path gone by and of the path come back by mentioned is for the purpose of keeping properly to the track of the meditation subject.

60. For if this bhikkhu is going along with his meditation subject and people on the way ask him about the day, 'What is today, venerable sir'?, or they ask him some question [about Dhamma], or they welcome him, he ought not to go on in silence, thinking 'I have a meditation subject'. The day must be told, the question must be answered, even by saying 'I do not know' if he does not know, a legitimate welcome must be responded to. [188] As he does so, the newly acquired sign vanishes. But even if it does vanish, he should still tell the day when asked; if he does not know the answer to the question, he should still say 'I do not know', and if he does know it, he should explain it surely;[10] and he must respond to a welcome. Also reception of visitors must be attended to on seeing a visiting bhikkhu, and all the remaining duties in the Khandhakas must be carried out too, that is, the duties of the shrine terrace, the duties of the Bodhi-tree terrace, the duties of the Uposatha house, the duties of the refectory and the bath house, and those to the teacher, the preceptor, visitors, departing bhikkhus, and the rest.

10. Reading *ekaṁsena* (surely) with Harvard text rather than *ekadesena* (partly).

61. And the newly acquired sign vanishes while he is carrying out these too. When he wants to go again, thinking 'I shall go and take up the sign', he finds he cannot go to the charnel ground because it has been invaded by non-human beings or by wild beasts, or the sign has disappeared. For a bloated corpse only lasts one or two days and then turns into a livid corpse. Of all the meditation subjects there is none so hard to come as by this.

62. So when the sign has vanished in this way, the bhikkhu should sit down in his night quarters or in his day quarters and first of all review the path gone by and come by up to the place where he is actually sitting cross-legged, doing it in this way: 'I went out of the monastery by this gate, I took a path leading in such and such a direction, I turned left at such and such a place, I turned right at such and such a place, in one part of it there was a stone, in another an ant-hill or a tree or a bush or a creeper; having gone by that path, I saw the Foulness in such and such a place, I stood there facing in such and such a direction and observed such and such surrounding signs, I apprehended the sign of foulness in this way; I left the charnel ground in such and such a direction, I came back by such and such a path doing this and this, and I am now sitting here'.

63. As he reviews it in this way, the sign becomes evident and appears as if placed in front of him; the meditation subject rides in its track as it did before. Hence it was said: *the reviewing of the path gone by and come by has keeping [the mind] on the track for its purpose.*

64. Now as to the words, *when he has established reverence for it by seeing its advantages and by perceiving it as a treasure and so come to love it, he anchors the mind on that object*: here, having gained jhana by exercising his mind on the repulsiveness in the bloated, he should increase insight with the jhana as its proximate cause, and then he should see the advantages in this way: [189] 'Surely in this way I shall be liberated from ageing and death'.

65. Just as a pauper who acquired a treasure of gems would guard and love it with great affection, feeling reverence for it as one who appreciates the value of it, 'I have got what is hard indeed to get!', so too [this bhikkhu] should guard the sign, loving it and feeling reverence for it as one who appreciates the value of it, 'I have got this meditation subject, which is indeed as hard to get as a very valuable treasure is for a pauper to get. For one whose meditation subject is the four elements discerns the four primary elements in himself, one whose meditation subject is breathing discerns the wind in his own nostrils, and one whose meditation subject is a kasina makes a kasina and develops it at his ease, so these

other meditation subjects are easily got. But this one lasts only one or two days, after which it turns into a livid corpse. There is none harder to get than this one'. In his night quarters and in his day quarters he should keep his mind anchored there thus 'Repulsiveness of the bloated, repulsiveness of the bloated'. And he should advert to the sign, bring it to mind and strike at it with thought and applied thought over and over again.

66. As he does so, the counterpart sign arises. Here is the difference between the two signs. The learning sign appears as a hideous, dreadful and frightening sight; but the counterpart sign appears like a man with big limbs lying down after eating his fill.

67. Simultaneously with his acquiring the counterpart sign his lust is abandoned by suppression owing to his giving no attention externally to sense desires [as object]. And owing to his abandoning of approval, ill will is abandoned too, as pus is with the abandoning of blood. Likewise stiffness-and-torpor is abandoned through exertion of energy, agitation-and-worry is abandoned through devotion to peaceful things that cause no remorse; and uncertainty about the Master who teaches the way, about the way, and about the fruit of the way, is abandoned through the actual experience of the distinction attained. So the five hindrances are abandoned. And there are present applied thought with the characteristic of directing the mind on to that same sign, and sustained thought accomplishing the function of pressing on the sign, and happiness due to the acquisition of distinction, and tranquillity due to the production of tranquillity in one whose mind is happy, and bliss with that tranquillity as its sign, [190] and unification that has bliss as its sign due to the production of concentration in one whose mind is blissful. So the jhana factors become manifest.

68. Thus access, which is the obverse of the first jhana, is produced in him too at that same moment. All after that up to absorption in the first jhana and mastery in it should be understood as described under the earth kasina.

69. As regards the livid and the rest: the characterizing already described, starting with the going in the way beginning 'One who is learning the bloated sign of foulness goes alone with no companion, with unremitting mindfulness established' (§19), should all be understood with its exposition and intention, substituting for the word 'bloated' the appropriate word in each case thus: One who is learning the livid sign of foulness . . .', 'One who is learning the festering
70. sign of foulness. . . '. But the differences are as follows.

[THE LIVID]

The livid should be brought to mind as 'Repulsiveness of the livid, repulsiveness of the livid'. Here the learning sign appears blotchy-coloured; but the counterpart sign's appearance has the colour which is most prevalent.

[THE FESTERING]

71. *The festering* should be brought to mind as 'Repulsiveness of the festering, repulsiveness of the festering'. Here the learning sign appears as though trickling; but the counterpart sign appears motionless and quiet.

[THE CUT UP]

72. *The cut up* is found on a battle field or in a robbers' forest or on a charnel ground where kings have robbers cut up or in the jungle in a place where men are torn up by lions and tigers. So, if when he goes there, it comes into focus at one adverting although lying in different places, that is good. If not, then he should not touch it with his own hand; for by doing so he would become familiar with it.[11] He should get a monastery attendant or one studying to become an ascetic or someone else to put it together in one place. If he cannot find anyone to do it, he should put it together with a walking stick or a staff in such a way that there is only a finger's breadth separating [the parts]. Having put it together thus, he should bring it to mind as 'Repulsiveness of the cut up, repulsiveness of the cut up'. Herein, the learning sign appears as though cut in the middle; but the counterpart sign appears whole. [191]

[THE GNAWED]

73. *The gnawed* should be brought to mind as 'Repulsiveness of the gnawed, repulsiveness of the gnawed'. Here the learning sign appears as though gnawed here and there; but the counterpart sign appears whole.

[THE SCATTERED]

74. After getting *the scattered* put together or putting it together in the way described under the Cut-up so that there is only a finger's breadth separating [the pieces], it should be brought to mind as 'Repulsiveness of the scattered, repulsiveness of the scattered'. Here the learning sign appears with the gaps evident; but the counterpart sign appears whole.

[THE HACKED AND SCATTERED]

75. *The hacked and scattered* is found in the same places as those described under the Cut-up. Therefore after going there and

11. 'He would come to handle it without disgust as a corpse-burner would' (Pm. 176.).

getting it put together or putting it together in the way described under the Cut-up so that there is only a finger's breadth separating [the pieces], it should be brought to mind as 'Repulsiveness of the hacked and scattered, repulsiveness of the hacked and scattered'. Here when the learning sign becomes evident, it does so with the fissures of the wounds; but the counterpart sign appears whole.

[THE BLEEDING]

76. *The bleeding* is found at the time when [blood] is trickling from the openings of wounds received on battle fields, etc., or from the openings of burst boils and abscesses when the hands and feet have been cut off. So on seeing that, it should be brought to mind as 'Repulsiveness of the bleeding, repulsiveness of the bleeding'. Here the learning sign appears to have the aspect of moving like a red banner struck by wind; but the counterpart sign appears quiet.

[THE WORM-INFESTED]

77. There is a *worm-infested* corpse when at the end of two or three days a mass of maggots oozes out from the corpse's nine orifices, and the mass lies there like a heap of paddy or boiled rice as big as the body, whether the body is that of a dog, a jackal, a human being,[12] an ox, a buffalo, an elephant, a horse, a python, or what you will. It can be brought to, mind with respect to any one of these as 'Repulsiveness of the worm-infested, repulsiveness of the worm-infested'. For the sign arose for the Elder Cūḷa-Piṇḍapātika-Tissa in the corpse of an elephant's carcase in the Kāḷadīghavāpi reservoir. Here the learning sign appears as though moving; but the counterpart sign appears quiet, like a ball of boiled rice.

[A SKELETON]

78. *A skeleton* is described in various aspects in the way beginning 'As though he were looking at a corpse thrown onto 'a charnel ground, a skeleton with flesh and blood, held 'together by sinews' (D. ii, 296). [192] So he should go in the way already described to where it has been put, and noticing any stones, etc., with their surrounding signs and in relation to the object, he should characterize it *by the fact of its having attained that particular individual essence* thus 'This is a skeleton' and apprehend the sign in the eleven ways by colour and the rest. But if he looks at it, [apprehending it only] *by its colour as* white, it does not appear to him [with its individual essence as repulsive], but only as a variant of the white kasina.

12. Reading *manussa* with Sinhalese ed.

Consequently he should only look at it as 'a skeleton' in
79. the repulsive aspect. 'Mark' is a term for the hand, etc., here, so he should define it *by its mark* according to hand, foot, head, chest, arm, waist, thigh, and shin. He should define it *by its shape*, however, according as it is long, short, square, round, small or large. *By its direction* and *by its location* are as already described (§39–40). Having defined it *by its delimitation* according to the periphery of each bone, he should reach absorption by apprehending whichever appears most evident to him. But it can also be defined *by its concavities* and *by its convexities* according to the concave and convex places in each bone. And it can also be defined by position thus: 'I am standing in a concave place, the skeleton is in a convex place; or I am standing in a convex place, the skeleton is in a concave place'. It should be defined *by its joints* according as any two bones are joined together. It should be defined *by its openings* according to the gaps separating the bones. It should be defined *all round* by directing knowledge to it comprehensively thus: 'In this place there is this skeleton'. If the sign does not arise even in this way, then the mind should be established on the frontal bone. And in this case, just as in the case of those that precede it beginning with the worm-infested, the apprehending of the sign should be observed in this elevenfold manner as appropriate.

80. This meditation subject is successful with a whole skeleton frame and even with a single bone as well. So having learnt the sign in any one of these in the eleven ways, he should bring it to mind as 'Repulsiveness of a skeleton, repulsiveness of a skeleton'. Here the learning sign and the counterpart sign are alike, so it is said. That is correct for a single bone. But when the learning sign becomes manifest in a skeleton frame, what is correct [to say] is that there are gaps in the learning sign while the counterpart sign appears whole. [193] And the learning sign even in a single bone should be dreadful and terrifying; but the counterpart sign produces happiness and joy because it brings access.

81. What is said in the Commentaries in this context allows that deduction. For there, after saying this, 'There is no counterpart sign in the four divine abidings and in the ten kinds of foulness; for in the case of the divine abidings the sign is the breaking down of boundaries itself, and in the case of the ten kinds of foulness the sign comes into being as soon as the repulsiveness is seen, without any thinking about it', it is again said immediately next 'Here the sign is twofold: the learning sign and the connterpart sign. The learning sign appears hideous, dreadful and terrifying', and so on. So what we said was well considered. And it is only this that is correct here. Besides, the appearance of a woman's

whole body as a collection of bones to the Elder Mahā-Tissa through his merely looking at her teeth demonstrates this here (see Ch. I, §55).

[GENERAL]

82. The Divine Ruler with ten hundred eyes
Did him with the Ten Powers eulogize,
Who, fair in fame, made known as cause of jhana
This Foulness of ten species in suchwise.
Now knowing their description and the way
To tackle each and how they are developed,
There are some further points that will repay
Study, each with its special part to play.

83. One who has reached jhana in any one of these goes free from cupidity; he resembles [an Arahant] without greed because his greed has been well suppressed. At the same time, however, this classification of foulness should be understood as stated in accordance with the particular individual essences successively reached by the [dead] body and also in accordance with the particular subdivisions of the greedy temperament.

84. When a corpse has entered upon the repulsive state, it may have reached the individual essence of the bloated or any one of the individual essences beginning with that of the livid. So the sign should be apprehended as 'Repulsiveness of the bloated', 'Repulsiveness of the livid', according to whichever he has been able to find. This, it should be understood, is how the classification of foulness comes to be tenfold with the body's arrival at each particular individual essence.

85. And individually *the bloated* suits one who is greedy about shape since it makes evident the disfigurement of the body's shape. *The livid* suits one who is greedy about the body's colour since it makes evident the disfigurement of the skin's colour. *The festering* [194] suits one who is greedy about the smell of the body aroused by scents, perfumes, etc., since it makes evident the evil smells connected with this sore, the body. *The cut up* suits one who is greedy about compactness in the body since it makes evident the hollowness inside it. *The gnawed* suits one who is greedy about accumulation of flesh in such parts of the body as the breasts since it makes it evident how a fine accumulation of flesh comes to nothing. *The scattered* suits one who is greedy about the grace of the limbs since it makes it evident how limbs can be scattered. *The hacked and scattered* suits one who is greedy about a fine body as a whole since it makes evident the disintegration and alteration of the body as a whole. *The bleeding* suits one who is greedy about elegance produced by ornaments since it makes evident its repulsiveness when smeared with blood. The

worm-infested suits one who is greedy about ownership of the body since it makes it evident how the body is shared with many families of worms. *A skeleton* suits one who is greedy about fine teeth since it makes evident the repulsiveness of the bones in the body. This, it should be understood, is how the classification of foulness comes to be tenfold according to the subdivisions of the greedy temperament.

86. But as regards the tenfold foulness, just as it is only by virtue of its rudder that a boat keeps steady in a river with turbulent[13] waters and a rapid current, and it cannot be steadied without a rudder, so too [here], owing to the weak hold on the object, consciousness when unified only keeps steady by virtue of applied thought, and it cannot be steadied without applied thought, which is why there is only the first jhana here, not the second and the rest.

87. And repulsive as this object is, still it arouses joy and happiness in him by his seeing its advantages thus '*Surely in this way I shall be liberated from ageing and death*', and by his abandoning the hindrances' oppression; just as a garbage heap does in a flower-scavenger by his seeing the advantages thus 'Now I shall get a high wage', and as the workings of purges and emetics do in a man suffering the pains of sickness.

88. This Foulness, while of ten kinds, has only one characteristic. For though it is of ten kinds, nevertheless its characteristic is only its impure, stinking, disgusting and repulsive state (essence). And foulness appears with this characteristic not only in a dead body but also in a living one, as it did to the Elder Mahā-Tissa who lived at Cetiyapabbata (Ch. I, §55), and to the novice attendant on the Elder Saṅgharakkhita while he was watching the king riding an elephant. For a living body is just as foul as a dead one, [195] only the characteristic of foulness is not evident in a living body, being hidden by adventitious embellishments.

89. This is the body's nature: it is a collection of over three hundred bones, jointed by one hundred and eighty joints, bound together by nine hundred sinews, plastered over with nine hundred pieces of flesh, enveloped in the moist inner skin, enclosed in the outer cuticle, with orifices here and there, constantly dribbling and trickling like a grease pot, inhabited by a community of worms, the home of disease, the basis of painful states, perpetually oozing from the nine orifices like a chronic open carbuncle, from both of whose eyes eye-filth trickles, from whose ears ear-filth, from whose nostrils snot, from whose mouth food and bile and phlegm and blood, from whose lower outlets excrement and urine, and from whose ninety-nine thousand pores the broth of

13. "*Aparisaṇṭhita*—turbulent" *parisaṇṭhāti* (to quiet) is not in P.T.S. Dict. *aparisaṇṭhita* is not in T.C.P. Dict.

stale sweat seeps, with bluebottles and their like buzzing round it, which when untended with tooth sticks and mouth-washing and head-anointing and bathing and underclothing and dressing would, judged by the universal repulsiveness of the body, make even a king, if he wandered from village to village with his hair in its natural wild disorder, no different from a flower-scavenger or an outcaste or what you will. So there is no distinction between a king's body and an outcaste's in so far as its impure stinking nauseating repulsiveness is concerned.

90. But by rubbing out the stains on its teeth with tooth sticks and mouth-washing and all that, by concealing its private parts under several cloths, by daubing it with various scents and salves, by pranking it with nosegays and such things, it is worked up into a state that permits of its being taken as 'I' and 'mine'. So men delight in women and women in men without perceiving the true nature of its characteristic foulness, now masked by this adventitious adornment. But in the ultimate sense there is no place here even the size of an atom fit to lust after.

91. And then, when any such bits of it as head hairs, body hairs, nails, teeth, spittle, snot, excrement or urine have dropped off the body, beings will not touch them; they are ashamed, humiliated and disgusted. But as long as any one of these things remains, in it, though it is just as repulsive, they take it as agreeable, desirable, permanent, [196] pleasant, self, because they are wrapped in the murk of ignorance and dyed with affection and greed for self. Taking it as they do, they resemble the old jackal who saw a flower not yet fallen from a *kiṁsuka* tree in a forest and yearned after it, thinking, 'This is a piece of meat, it is a piece of meat'.

92. There was a jackal chanced to see
A flowering *kiṁsuka* in a wood;
In haste he went to where it stood:
'I have found a meat-bearing tree!'

He chewed the blooms that fell, but could,
Of course, find nothing fit to eat;
He took it thus: 'Unlike the meat
There on the tree, *this* is no good'.

A wise man will not think to treat
As foul only the part that fell,
But treats as foul the part as well
That in the body has its seat.

Fools cannot in their folly tell;
They take the body to be fair,
And soon get caught in Evil's snare
Nor can escape its painful spell.

But since the wise have thus laid bare
This filthy body's nature, so,
Be it alive or dead, they know
There is no beauty lurking there.

93. For this is said:

'This filthy body stinks outright
Like ordure, like a privy's site;
This body men that have insight
Condemn, is object of a fool's delight.

A tumour where nine holes abide
Wrapped in a coat of clammy hide
And trickling filth on every side,
Polluting the air with stenches far and wide.

If it perchance should come about
That what is inside it came out,
Surely a man would need a knout
With which to put the crows and dogs to rout'.

94. So a capable bhikkhu should apprehend the sign wherever the aspect of foulness is manifest, whether in a living body or in a dead one, and he should make the meditation subject reach absorption.

The sixth chapter called 'The Description of Foulness as a Meditation Subject' in the Treatise on the Development of Concentration in the Path of Purification composed for the purpose of gladdening good people.

CHAPTER VII

DESCRIPTION OF CONCENTRATION —SIX RECOLLECTIONS

(Cha-anussati-niddesa)

1. [197] Now ten recollections were listed next after the kinds of foulness (Ch. III, §105). As to these:

Mindfulness (*sati*) itself is recollection (*anussati*) because it arises again and again; or alternatively, the mindfulness (*sati*) that is proper (*anurūpa*) for a clansman gone forth out of faith since it occurs only in those instances where it should occur is 'recollection (*anussati*)'.

The recollection arisen inspired by the Enlightened One is the *recollection of the Buddha.* This is a term for mindfulness with the Enlightened One's special qualities as its object.

The recollection arisen inspired by the Law is the *recollection of the Dhamma.*[1] This is a term for mindfulness with the special qualities of the Law's being well proclaimed, etc., as its object.

---

1. The word '*dhamma*'—perhaps the most important and frequently used of Pali words—has no single equivalent in English because no English word has both a generalization so wide and loose as the word '*dhamma*' in its widest sense (which includes 'everything' that can be known or thought of in any way) and at the same time an ability to be, as it were, focussed in a set of well-defined specific uses. Roughly *dhamma*=what-can-be-remembered or what-can-be-borne-in-mind (*dhāretabba*) as *kamma*=what-can-be-done (*kātabba*). The following two principal (and overlapping) senses are involved here. (i) the Law as taught, and (ii) objects of consciousness. (i) In the first case the word has either been left untranslated as 'Dhamma' or 'dhamma' or it has been rendered as 'Law' or 'law'. This ranges from the loose sense of the 'Good Law', 'cosmic law' and 'teaching' to such specific technical senses as the 'discrimination of law', 'causality', 'being subject to or having the nature of'. (ii) In the second case the word in its looser sense of 'something known or thought of' has either been left untranslated as 'dhamma' or rendered by 'state' (more rarely by 'thing' or 'phenomenon'), while in its technical sense as one of the twelve bases or eighteen elements 'mental object' and 'mental datum' have been used. The sometimes indiscriminate use of 'dhamma', 'state' and 'law' in both the looser senses is deliberate. The English words have been reserved as far as possible for rendering 'dhamma' (except that 'state' has sometimes been used to render '*bhāva*', etc., in the sense of '-ness'). Other subsidiary meanings of a non-technical nature have occasionally been otherwise rendered according to context.

In order to avoid muddle it is necessary to distinguish renderings of the word *dhamma* and renderings of the words used to define it. The word itself is a gerundive of the verb *dharati* (caus. *dhāreti*—to bear) and so is the literal equivalent of '(quality) that is to be borne'. But since the grammatical meanings of the two words *dharati* (to bear) and *dahati* (to put or sort out, whence *dhātu* element) sometimes

The recollection arisen inspired by the Community is the *recollection of the Saṅgha.* This is a term for mindfulness with the Community's special qualities of being entered on the good way, etc., as its object.

The recollection arisen inspired by virtue is the *recollection of virtue.* This is a term for mindfulness with the special qualities of virtue's untornness, etc., as its object.

The recollection arisen inspired by generosity is the *recollection of generosity.* This is a term for mindfulness with generosity's special qualities of free generosity, etc., as its object.

The recollection arisen inspired by deities is the *recollection of deities.* This is a term for mindfulness with the special qualities of one's own faith, etc., as its object with deities standing as witnesses.

The recollection arisen inspired by death is the *recollection of death.* This is a term for mindfulness with the termination of the life faculty as its object.

[*Mindfulness occupied with the body* (*kāya-gatā sati*—lit. body-gone mindfulness):] it is gone (*gata*) to the material body (*kāya*) that is analysed into head-hairs, etc., or it is gone into the body, thus it is 'body-gone (*kāya-gatā*)'. It is body-gone (*kāya-gatā*) and it is mindfulness (*sati*), thus it is 'body-gone-mindfulness (*kāyagatasati*—single compound)'; but instead of shortening [the vowel] thus in the usual way, 'body-gone mindfulness (*kāyagatā sati*—compound adj. +noun)' is said. This is a term for mindfulness that has as its object the sign of the bodily parts consisting of head-hairs and the rest.

The mindfulness arisen inspired by breathing (*ānāpāna*) is *mindfulness of breathing.* This is a term for mindfulness that has as its object the sign of in-breaths and out-breaths.

---

coalesce it often comes very close to *dhātu* (but see Ch. VIII, n. 68 and Ch. XI, §104). If it is asked, what bears the qualities to be borne? a correct answer here would probably be that it is the event (*samaya*) as stated in the Dhammasaṅgaṇī (§1 onwards) in which the various dhammas listed there arise and are present, variously related to each other. The word *dhammin* (thing qualified or 'bearer of what is to be borne') is a late introduction as a logical term (perhaps first used in Pali by Pm., see p. 534).

As to the definitions of the word, there are several. At DA. i, 99 four meanings are given: moral (meritorious) special quality (*guṇa*), preaching of the Law (*desanā*), scripture (*pariyatti*), and 'no-living-being-ness' (*nissattatā*). Four meanings are also given at Dhs A. 38: scripture (*pariyatti*), cause (of effect) as law (*hetu*), moral (meritorious) special quality (*guṇa*), and 'no-living-being-ness and soullessness' (*nissatta-nijjīvatā*). A wider definition is given at MA, i, 17, where the following meanings are distinguished: scripture or mastery (*pariyatti*—A. iii, 86), truth (*sacca*—Vin. i, 12), concentration (*samādhi*—D. ii, 54), understanding (*paññā*—Jā. i, 280), nature (*pakati*—M. i, 162), individual essence (*sabhāva*—Dhs. 1), voidness (*suññatā*—Dhs. 25), merit (*puñña*—Sn. 182), offence (*āpatti*—Vin. iii, 187), what is knowable (*ñeyya*—Ps. ii, 194), '*and so on*' (see also Ch. VIII n. 68).

The recollection arisen inspired by peace is the *recollection of peace*. This is a term for mindfulness that has as its object stilling of all suffering.

*

[(1) RECOLLECTION OF THE ENLIGHTENED ONE]

2. [198] Now a meditator with absolute confidence[2] who wants to develop firstly the recollection of the Enlightened One among these ten should go into solitary retreat in a favourable abode and recollect the special qualities of the Enlightened One, the Blessed One, as follows:

'That Blessed One is such since he is accomplished, fully 'enlightened, endowed with [clear] vision and [virtuous] 'conduct, sublime, the knower of worlds, the incomparable 'leader of men to be tamed, the teacher of gods and men, 'enlightened and blessed' (M.i,37; A.iii,285).

3. Here is the way he recollects: 'That Blessed One is such since he is accomplished, he is such since he is fully enlightened, . . . he is such since he is blessed'—he is so for these several reasons, is what is meant.

[*Accomplished*]

4. Herein, what he recollects firstly is that the Blessed One is *accomplished* (*arahanta*) for the following reasons: (i) because of remoteness (*āraka*), and (ii) because of his enemies (*ari*) and (iii) the spokes (*ara*) having been destroyed (*hata*), and (iv) because of his worthiness (*araha*) of requisites, etc., and (v) because of absence of secret (*rahābhāva*) evil-doing.[3]

5. (i) He stands utterly remote and far away from all defilements because he has expunged all trace of defilement by means of the path—because of such remoteness (*āraka*) he is accomplished (*arahanta*).

A man remote (*āraka*) indeed we call
From something he has not at all;
The Saviour too that has no stain
May well the name 'accomplished (*arahanta*)' gain.

6. (ii) And these enemies (*ari*), these defilements, are destroyed (*hata*) by the path—because the enemies are thus destroyed he is accomplished (*arahanta*) also.

The enemies (*ari*) that were deployed,
Greed and the rest, have been destroyed (*hata*)
By His, the Helper's, Wisdom's sword,
So he is 'accomplished (*arahanta*)', all accord.

2. '"*Absolute confidence*" is the confidence afforded by the noble path. Development of the recollection comes to success in him who has that, not in any other' (Pm. 181). 'Absolute confidence' is a constituent of the first three 'factors of Stream Entry' (see S. v, 196).

3. Cf. derivation of the word '*ariya* (noble)' at MA. i, 21.

7. (iii) Now this wheel of the round of rebirths with its hub made of ignorance and of craving for becoming, with its spokes consisting of formations of merit and the rest, with its rim of ageing and death, which is joined to the chariot of the triple becoming by piercing it with the axle made of the origin of cankers (see M.i,55), has been revolving throughout time that has no beginning. All this wheel's spokes (*ara*) were destroyed (*hata*) by him at the Place of Enlightenment, as he stood firm with the feet of energy on the ground of virtue, wielding with the hand of faith the axe of knowledge that destroys kamma—because the spokes are thus destroyed he is *accomplished* (*arahanta*) also.

8. Or alternatively, it is the beginningless round of rebirths that is called the 'Wheel of the round of rebirths'. Ignorance is its hub because it is its root. Ageing-and-death is its rim because it terminates it. The remaining ten states [of the dependent origination] are its spokes because ignorance is their root and ageing-and-death their termination.

9. Herein, ignorance is unknowing about suffering and the rest. And ignorance in sensual becoming [199] is a condition for formations in sensual becoming; ignorance in fine-material becoming is a condition for formations in fine-material becoming. Ignorance in immaterial becoming is a condition for formations in immaterial becoming.

10. Formations in sensual becoming are a condition for rebirth-linking consciousness in sensual becoming. And similarly with the rest.

11. Rebirth-linking consciousness in sensual becoming is a condition for mentality-materiality in sensual becoming. Similarly in fine-material becoming. In immaterial becoming it is a condition for mentality only.

12. Mentality-materiality in sensual becoming is a condition for the sixfold base in sensual becoming. Mentality-materiality in fine-material becoming is a condition for three bases in fine-material becoming. Mentality in immaterial becoming is a condition for one base in immaterial becoming.

13. The sixfold base in sensual becoming is a condition for six kinds of contact in sensual becoming. Three bases in fine-material becoming are conditions for three kinds of contact in fine-material becoming. The mind base alone in immaterial becoming is a condition for one kind of contact in immaterial becoming.

14. The six kinds of contact in sensual becoming are conditions for six kinds of feeling in sensual becoming. Three kinds of contact in fine-material becoming are conditions for three kinds of feeling there too. One kind of contact in immaterial becoming is a condition for one kind of feeling there too.

15. The six kinds of feeling in sensual becoming are conditions for the six groups of craving in sensual becoming. Three in the fine-material becoming are for three there too. One kind of feeling in the immaterial becoming is a condition for one group of craving in the immaterial becoming.

The craving in the several kinds of becoming is a condition for the clinging there.

16. Clinging, etc., are the respective conditions for becoming and the rest. In what way? Here someone thinks 'I shall enjoy sense desires', and with sense-desire clinging as condition he misconducts himself in body, speech, and mind. Owing to the fulfilment of his misconduct he reappears in a state of loss (deprivation). The kamma that is the cause of his reappearance there is kamma-process becoming, the aggregates generated by the kamma are rebirth-process becoming, the generating of the aggregates is birth, their maturing is ageing, their dissolution is death.

17. Another thinks 'I shall enjoy the delights of heaven', and in the parallel manner he conducts himself well. Owing to the fulfilment of his good conduct he reappears in a [sensual-sphere] heaven. The kamma that is the cause of his reappearance there is kamma-process becoming, and the rest as before.

18. Another thinks 'I shall enjoy the delights of the Brahmā World', and with sense-desire clinging as condition he develops lovingkindness, compassion, gladness, and equanimity.[4] [200] Owing to the fulfilment of the meditative development he is reborn in the Brahmā World. The kamma that is the cause of his rebirth there is kamma-process becoming, and the rest is as before.

19. Yet another thinks 'I shall enjoy the delights of immaterial becoming' and with the same condition he develops the attainments beginning with the base consisting of boundless space. Owing to the fulfilment of the development he is reborn in one of these states. The kamma that is the cause of his rebirth there is kamma-process becoming, the aggregates generated by the kamma are rebirth-process becoming, the generating of the aggregates is birth, their maturing is ageing, their dissolution is death (see M.ii; 263).

The remaining kinds of clinging are construable in the same way.

20. So, 'Understanding of discernment of conditions thus '"Ignorance is a cause, formations are causally arisen, and 'both these states are causally arisen" is knowledge of the

4. 'Because of the words "Also all dhammas of the three planes are sense desires (*kāma*) in the sense of being desirable (*kamanīya*)" ( ), greed for becoming is sense-desire clinging' (Pm. 184). See Ch. XXII, §72. For the 'Way to the Brahmā World' see M. ii, 194-6; 207f.).

'causal relationship of states. Understanding of discernment 'of conditions thus "In the past and in the future ignorance 'is a cause, formations are causally arisen, and both these 'states are causally arisen" is knowledge of the causal 'relationship of states' (Ps. i, 50), and all the clauses should be given in detail in this way.

21. Herein, ignorance and formations are one summarization; consciousness, mentality-materiality, the sixfold base, contact, and feeling, are another; craving, clinging, and becoming, are another; and birth and ageing-and-death are another. Here the first summarization is past, the two middle ones are present, and birth and ageing-and-death are future. When ignorance and formations are mentioned, then also craving, clinging and becoming are included too, so these five states are the round of kamma in the past. The five beginning with consciousness are the round of kamma-result in the present. When craving, clinging and becoming are mentioned, then also ignorance and formations are included too, so these five states are the round of kamma in the present. And because [the five] beginning with consciousness, are described under the heading of birth and ageing-and-death these five states are the round of kamma-result in the future. These make twenty aspects in this way. And here there is one link between formations and consciousness, one between feeling and craving, and one between becoming and birth (see Ch. XVII, §288f.).

22. Now the Blessed One knew, saw, understood and penetrated in all aspects this dependent origination with its four summarizations its three times, its twenty aspects, and its three links. 'Knowledge is in the sense of 'that being known[5] and understanding is in the sense 'of the act of understanding that. Hence it was said: '"Understanding of discernment of conditions is knowledge 'of the causal relationship of states"' (Ps. i, 52). Thus when the Blessed One, by correctly knowing these states with knowledge of relations of states, became dispassionate towards them, when his greed faded away, when he was liberated, then he destroyed, quite destroyed, abolished, the spokes of this Wheel of the round of rebirths of the kind just described.

Because the spokes are thus destroyed he is accomplished (*arahanta*) also. [201]

> The spokes (*ara*) of Rebirth's Wheel have been
> Destroyed (*hata*) with wisdom's weapon keen
> By Him, the Helper of the world,
> And so 'accomplished (*arahanta*)' he is called.

5. Reading '*taṁ ñātaṭṭhena ñāṇaṁ*' with Pm.

23. (iv) And he is worthy (*arahati*) of the requisites of robes, etc., and of the distinction of being accorded homage because it is he who is most worthy of offerings. For when a Perfect One has arisen, important deities and human beings pay homage to none else; for Brahmā Sahampati paid homage to the Perfect One with a jewelled garland as big as Sineru, and other deities did so according to their means, as well as such human beings as king Bimbisāra [of Magadha] and the king of Kosala. And after the Blessed One had finally attained nibbana king Asoka renounced wealth to the amount of ninety-six millions for his sake and founded eighty-four thousand monasteries throughout all Jambudīpa (India). And so, with all these, what need to speak of others ?—Because of worthiness of requisites he is accomplished (*arahanta*) also.

So he is worthy, the Helper of the world,
Of homage paid with requisites; the word
'Accomplished (*arahanta*)' has this meaning in the world,
Hence the Victor is worthy of that word.

24. (v) And he does not act like those fools in the world who vaunt their cleverness and yet do evil, but in secret for fear of getting a bad name.—Because of absence of secret (*rahā-bhāva*) evil-doing he is accomplished (*arahanta*) also.

No secret evil deed may claim
An author so august; the name
'Accomplished (*arahanta*)' is his deservedly
By absence of such secrecy (*rahābhāva*)

25. So in all ways,

The Sage of remoteness unalloyed,
Vanquished defiling foes deployed,
The spokes of rebirth's wheel destroyed,
Worthy of requisites employed,
Secret evil he does avoid :
For these five reasons he may claim
This word 'accomplished' for his name.

[*Fully Enlightened*]

26. He is fully enlightened (*sammāsambuddha*) because he has discovered (*buddha*) all things rightly (*sammā*) and by himself (*sāmam*).

In fact all things were discovered by him rightly by himself in that he discovered of the things to be directly-known that they must be directly known, [that is, learning about the Four Truths,] of the things to be fully understood that they must be fully understood, [that is, penetration of suffering,] of the things to be abandoned that they must be abandoned, [that is, penetration of the origin of suffering,] of the things to be realized that they must be realized, [that is, penetration of the cessation of suffering,] and of the things to be developed that they must be developed, [that is, penetration of the path.] Hence it is said:

'What must be directly-known is directly-known,
'What has to be developed has been developed,
'What has to be abandoned has been abandoned ;
'And that, brahman, is why I am enlightened' (Sn.558).

27. [202] Besides, he has discovered all things rightly by himself step by step thus: The eye is the Truth of Suffering; the prior craving that originates it by being its root-cause is the Truth of Origin; the non-occurrence of both is the Truth of Cessation; the way that is the act of understanding cessation is the Truth of the Path. And so too in the case of the ear, the nose, the tongue, the body, and the mind.

28. And the following things should be construed in the same way:

The six bases beginning with visible objects,
The six groups of consciousness beginning with eye consciousness,
The six kinds of contact beginning with eye contact,
The six kinds of feeling beginning with the eye-contact-born,
The six kinds of perception beginning with perception of visible objects,
The six kinds of volition beginning with volition about visible objects,
The six groups of craving beginning with craving for visible objects,
The six kinds of applied thought beginning with applied thought about visible objects,
The six kinds of sustained thought beginning with sustained thought about visible objects,
The five aggregates beginning with the aggregate of matter,
The ten kasinas,
The ten recollections,
The ten perceptions beginning with perception of the bloated,
The thirty-two aspects [of the body] beginning with head hairs,
The twelve bases,
The eighteen elements,
The nine kinds of becoming beginning with sensual becoming[6]
The four jhanas beginning with the first,

6. See Ch. XVII, §253–4. The word *bhava* is rendered here both by 'existence' and by 'becoming'. The former, while less awkward to the ear, is inaccurate if it is allowed a flavour of staticness. 'Becoming' will be more frequently used as this work proceeds. Loosely the two

The four measureless states beginning with the development of lovingkindness,

The four immaterial attainments,

The factors of the dependent origination in reverse order beginning with ageing-and-death and in forward order beginning with ignorance (cf. Ch. XX, §9).

29. Herein, this is the construction of a single clause [of the dependent origination]: Ageing-and-death is the Truth of Suffering, birth is the Truth of Origin, the escape from both is the Truth of Cessation, the way that is the act of understanding cessation is the Truth of the Path.

In this way he has discovered, progressively discovered, completely discovered, all states rightly and by himself step by step. Hence it was said above: 'He is fully enlightened because he has discovered all things rightly and by himself' (§26).[7]

---

senses tend to merge. But technically, 'existence' should perhaps be used only for *atthitā*, which signifies the momentary existence of a *dhamma* 'possessed of the three instants of arising, presence and dissolution'. 'Becoming' then signifies the continuous flow or flux of such tripple-instant moments; and it occurs in three main modes: sensual, fine-material, and immaterial. For remarks on the words 'being' and 'essence' see Ch. VIII, note 68.

7. 'Is not Unobstructed Knowledge (*anāvaraṇa-ñāṇa*) different from Omniscient Knowledge (*sabbaññuta-ñāṇa*)? Otherwise the words "Six kinds of knowledge unshared [by disciples]" (Ps. i, 3) would be contradicted? [Note: the six kinds are: knowledge of what faculties prevail in beings, knowledge of the inclinations and tendencies of beings, knowledge of the Twin Marvel, knowledge of the attainment of the Great Compassion, Omniscient Knowledge, and Unobstructed Knowledges (see Ps. i, 133)]—There is no contradiction, because two ways in which a single kind of knowledge's objective field occurs are described for the purpose of showing by means of this difference how it is not shared by others. It is only one kind of knowledge; but it is called omniscient knowledge because its objective field consists of formed, unformed and conventional (*sammuti*) [*i.e.* conceptual] dhammas without remainder, and it is called unobstructed knowledge because of its unrestricted access to the objective field, because of absence of obstruction. And it is said accordingly in the Paṭisambhidā "It knows all the formed and the unformed without remainder, thus it is omniscient knowledge. It has no obstruction therein, thus it is unobstructed knowledge" (Ps. i, 131) and so on. So they are not different kinds of knowledge. And there must be no reservation, otherwise it would follow that omniscient and unobstructed knowledge had obstructions and did not make all dhammas its object. There is not in fact a minimal obstruction to the Blessed One's knowledge; and if his unobstructed knowledge did not have all dhammas as its object, there would be presence of obstruction where it did not occur, and so it would not be unobstructed.

'Or alternatively, even if we suppose that they are different, still it is omniscient knowledge itself that is intended as "unhindered" since it is that which occurs unhindered universally. And it is by his attainment of that that the Blessed One is known as Omniscient, All-seer, Fully Enlightened, not because of awareness (*avabodha*) of every dhamma at once, simultaneously (see M. ii, 127). And it is said accordingly in the Paṭisambhidā "This is a name derived from the final liberation of the

[*Endowed with Clear Vision and Virtuous Conduct*]

30. He is *endowed with* [*clear*] *vision and* [*virtuous*] *conduct*: *vijjācaraṇasampanno=vijjāhi caraṇena ca sampanno* (resolution of compound).

Herein, as to [*clear*] *vision*: there are three kinds of clear vision and eight kinds of clear vision. The three kinds should be understood as stated in the Bhayabherava Sutta (M. 1,

---

Enlightened Ones, the Blessed Ones, together with the acquisition of omniscient knowledge at the root of the Enlightenment Tree; this name 'Buddha' is a designation based on realization" (Ps. i, 174). For the ability in the Blessed One's continuity to penetrate all dhammas without exception was due to his having completely attained to knowledge capable of becoming aware of all dhammas.

'Here it may be asked: But how then? When this knowledge occurs, does it do so with respect to every field simultaneously, or successively? For firstly, if it occurs simultaneously with respect to every objective field, then with the simultaneous appearance of formed dhammas classed as past, future and present, internal and external, etc., and of unformed and conventional (conceptual) dhammas, there would be no awareness of contrast (*paṭibhāga*), as happens in one who looks at a painted canvas from a distance. That being so, it follows that all dhammas become the objective field of the Blessed One's knowledge in an undifferentiated form (*anirūpita-rūpana*), as they do through the aspect of not-self to those who are exercising insight thus "All dhammas are not-self" (Dh. 279; Thag. 678; M. i, 230; ii. 64; S. iii, 132; A. i, 286; iv, 14; Ps. ii, 48, 62; Vin. v, 86. Cf. also A. iii, 444; iv, 88, 338; Sn. 1076). And those do not escape this difficulty who say that the Enlightened One's knowledge occurs with the characteristic of presence of all knowable dhammas as its objective field, devoid of discriminative thinking (*vikappa-rahita*), and universal in time (*sabba-kāla*) and that is why they are called "All-seeing" and why it is said "The Nāga is concentrated walking and he is concentrated standing" ( ). They do not escape the difficulty since the Blessed One's knowledge would then have only a partial objective field, because, by having the characteristic of presence as its object, past, future and conventional dhammas, which lack that characteristic, would be absent. So it is wrong to say that it occurs simultaneously with respect to every objective field. Then secondly, if we say that it occurs successively with respect to every objective field, that is wrong too. For when the knowable, classed in the many different ways according to birth, place, individual essence, etc., and direction, place, time, etc., is apprehended successively, then penetration without remainder is not effected since the knowable is infinite. And those are wrong too who say that the Blessed One is All-seeing owing to his doing his defining by taking one part of the knowable as that actually experienced (*paccakkha*) and deciding that the rest is the same because of the unequivocalness of its meaning, and that such knowledge is not inferential (*anumānika*) since it is free from doubt, because it is what is doubtfully discovered that is meant by inferential knowledge in the world. And they are wrong because there is no such defining by taking one part of the knowable as that actually experienced and deciding that the rest is the same because of the unequivocalness of its meaning, without making all of it actually experienced. For then that "rest" is not actually experienced; and if it were actually experienced, it would no longer be "the rest".

'All that is no argument—Why not?—Because this is not a field for ratiocination; for the Blessed One has said this: "The objective field of Enlightened Ones is unthinkable, it cannot be thought out; anyone who tried to think it out would reap madness and frustration" (A. ii, 80).

22f.), and the eight kinds as stated in the Ambaṭṭha Sutta (D.i,100). For there eight kinds of clear vision are stated, made up of the six kinds of direct-knowledge together with insight and the supernormal power of the mind-made [body].

31. [*Virtuous*] *conduct* should be understood as fifteen things, that is to say: restraint by virtue, guarding the doors of the sense faculties, knowledge of the right amount in eating, devotion to wakefulness, the seven good states,[8] and the four jhanas of the fine-material sphere. For it is precisely by means of these fifteen things that a noble disciple conducts himself, that he goes, towards the deathless. That is why it is called '[*virtuous*] *conduct*', according as it is said 'Here, 'Mahānāma, a noble disciple has virtue' (M.i,355), etc., the whole of which should be understood as it is given in the Middle Fifty [of the Majjhima Nikāya].

[203] Now the Blessed One is endowed with these kinds of clear vision and with this conduct as well; hence he is called 'endowed with [clear] vision and [virtuous] conduct'.

32. Herein, the Blessed One's possession of clear vision consists in the fulfilment of Omniscience (Ps.1,131), while his possession of conduct consists in the fulfilment of the Great Compassion

---

The agreed explanation here is this: Whatever the Blessed One wants to know—either entirely or partially—there his knowledge occurs as actual experience because it does so without hindrance. And it has constant concentration because of the absence of distraction. And it cannot occur in association with wishing of a kind that is due to absence from the objective field of something that he wants to know. There can be no exception to this because of the words "All dhammas are available to the adverting of the Enlightened One, the Blessed One, are available at his wish, are available to his attention, are available to his thought" (Ps. ii, 195). And the Blessed One's knowledge that has the past and future as its objective field is entirely actual experience since it is devoid of assumption based on inference, tradition or conjecture.

'And yet, even in that case, suppose he wanted to know the whole in its entirety, then would his knowledge not occur without differentiation in the whole objective field simultaneously? and so there would still be no getting out of that dfficulty?

'That is not so, because of its purifiedness. Because the Enlightened One's objective field is purified and it is unthinkable. Otherwise there would be no unthinkableness in the knowledge of the Enlightened One, the Blessed One, if it occurred in the same way as that of ordinary people. So, although it occurs with all dhammas as its object, it nevertheless does so making those dhammas quite clearly defined, as though it had a single dhamma as its object. This is what is unthinkable here. "There is as much knowledge as there is knowable, there is as much knowable as there is knowledge; the knowledge is limited by the knowable, the knowable is limited by the knowledge" (Ps. ii, 195). So he is Fully Enlightened because he has rightly and by himself discovered all dhammas together and separately, simultaneously and successively, according to his wish' (Pm. 190–1).

8. A possessor of 'the seven' has faith, conscience, shame, learning, energy, mindfulness, and understanding (see D. iii, 252). P.T.S. Dict. traces *saddhamma* (as 'the true dhamma', etc.) to *sant+dhamma*; but it is as likely traceable to *srad+dhamma*=(good ground) for the placing of faith (*saddhā*).

(Ps. 1, 126). He knows through omniscience what is good and harmful for all beings, and through compassion he warns them of harm and exhorts them to do good. That is how he is possessed of clear vision and conduct, which is why his disciples have entered upon the good way instead of entering upon the bad way as the self-mortifying disciples of those who are not possessed of clear vision and conduct have done.[9]

[*Sublime*]

33. He is called *Sublime* (*sugata*)[10] (i) because of a manner of going that is good (*sobhaṇa-gamana*), (ii) because of being gone to an excellent place (*Sundaraṁ ṭhānaṁ gatattā*), (iii) because of having gone rightly (*sammāgatattā*), and (iv) because of enunciating rightly (*sammāgadattā*).

(i) A manner of going (*gamana*) is called 'gone (*gata*)', and that in the Blessed One is good (*sobhaṇa*), purified, blameless. But what is that? It is the Noble Path; for by

---

9. 'Here the Master's possession of vision shows the greatness of understanding, and his possession of conduct the greatness of his compassion. It was through understanding that the Blessed One reached the kingdom of the Law, and through compassion that he became the bestower of the Law. It was through understanding that he felt revulsion for the round of rebirths, and through compassion that he bore it. It was through understanding that he fully understood others' suffering, and through compassion that he undertook to counteract it. It was through understanding that he was brought face to face with nibbana, and through compassion that he attained it. It was through understanding that he himself crossed over, and through compassion that he brought others across. It was through understanding that he perfected the Enlightened One's state, and through compassion that he perfected the Enlightened One's task.

'Or it was through compassion that he faced the round of rebirths as a Bodhisatta, and through understanding that he took no delight in it. Likewise it was through compassion that he practised non-cruelty to others, and through understanding that he was himself fearless of others. It was through compassion that he protected others to protect himself, and through understanding that he protected himself to protect others. Likewise it was through compassion that he did not torment others, and through understanding that he did not torment himself; so of the four types of persons beginning with the one who practises his own welfare (A. ii, 96) he perfected the fourth and best type. Likewise it was through compassion that he became the world's Helper, and through understanding that he became his own helper. It was through compassion that he had humility [as a Bodhisatta], and through understanding that he had dignity [as a Buddha]. Likewise it was through compassion that he helped all beings as a father while owing to the understanding associated with it his mind remained detached from them all, and it was through understanding that his mind remained detached from all dhammas while owing to the compassion associated with it he was helpful to all beings. For just as the Blessed One's compassion was devoid of sentimental affection or sorrow, so his understanding was free from the thoughts of "I" and "mine"' (Pm. 192–3).

10. The following renderings have been adopted for the most widely-used epithets for the Buddha. *Tathāgata* (Perfect One—for definitions see MA.i,45f.), *Bhagavant* (Blessed One), *Sugata* (Sublime One). These

means of that manner of going he has 'gone' without attachment in the direction of safety—Thus he is sublime (*sugata*) because of a manner of going that is good.

(ii) And it is to the excellent (*sundara*) place that he has gone (*gata*), to the deathless nibbana—Thus he is sublime (*sugata*) also because of having gone to an excellent place.

34. (iii) And he has rightly (*sammā*) gone (*gata*), without going back again to the defilements abandoned by each path. For this is said: 'He does not again turn, return, go back, to the 'defilements abandoned by the Stream-entry path, thus he is 'sublime . . . he does not again turn, return, go back, to the 'defilements abandoned by the Arahant path, thus he is 'sublime' (old commentary?). Or alternatively, he has rightly gone from the time of [making his resolution] at the feet of Dīpaṅkara up till the Enlightenment Session, by working for the welfare and happiness of the whole world through the fulfilment of the thirty perfections and through following the right way without deviating towards either of the two extremes, that is to say, towards eternalism or annihilationism, towards indulgence in sense pleasures or self-mortification—Thus he is sublime also because of having gone rightly.

35. (iv) And he enunciates[11] (*gadati*) rightly (*sammā*); he speaks only fitting speech in the fitting place—Thus he is sublime also because of enunciating rightly.

Here is a sutta that confirms this: 'Such speech as the 'Perfect One knows to be untrue and incorrect, conducive to 'harm, and displeasing and unwelcome to others, that he does 'not speak. And such speech as the Perfect One knows to be 'true and correct, but conducive to harm, and displeasing and 'unwelcome to others, that he does not speak. [204] And 'such speech as the Perfect One knows to be true and correct, 'conducive to good, but displeasing and unwelcome to others, 'that speech the Perfect One knows the time to expound. 'Such speech as the Perfect One knows to be untrue and in-'correct, and conducive to harm but pleasing and welcome to 'others, that he does not speak. And such speech as the 'Perfect One knows to be true and correct, but conducive to 'harm, though pleasing and welcome to others, that he does 'not speak. And such speech as the Perfect One knows to be 'true and correct, conducive to good, and pleasing and 'welcome to others, that speech the Perfect One knows the 'time to expound' (M.i,395)—Thus he is sublime also because of enunciating rightly.

---

renderings do not pretend to literalness. Attempts to be literal here are apt to produce a bizarre or quaint effect, and for that very reason fail to render what is in the Pali.

11. '*Gadati*—to enunciate': only noun *gada*. in P.T.S. Dict.

[*Knower of Worlds*]

36. He is the *knower of worlds* because he has known the world in all ways. For the Blessed One has experienced, known and penetrated the world in all ways as to its individual essence, its arising, its cessation, and the means to its cessation, according as it is said: 'Friend, that there is a world's end where 'one neither is born nor ages nor dies nor passes away nor re- 'appears, which is to be known or seen or reached by travel— 'that I do not say. Yet I do not say that there is ending 'of suffering without reaching the world's end. Rather it is 'in the fathom-long carcase with its perceptions and its 'consciousness that I make known the world, the arising of the 'world, the cessation of the world, and the way leading to the 'cessation of the world.

> ' 'Tis utterly impossible
> 'To reach by travel the world's end;
> 'But there is no escape from pain
> 'Until the world's end has been reached.
> 'It is a sage, a knower of the worlds,
> 'Who gets to the world's end, and it is he
> 'Whose Life Divine is lived out to its term;
> 'He is at peace who the world's end has known
> 'And hopes for neither this world nor the next' (S.i,62

37. Moreover, there are three worlds: the world of formations, the world of beings and the world of location. Herein in the passage 'One world: all beings subsist by nutriment' (Ps. i, 122) [205] the world of formations is to be understood. In the passage ' " The world is eternal " or " The world is not ' " eternal " ' (M.i,426) it is the world of beings. In the passage

> 'As far as moon and sun do circulate
> 'Shining[12] and lighting up the [four] directions,
> 'Over a thousand times as great a world
> 'Your power holds unquestionable sway' (M.i,328).

it is the world of location. The Blessed One has known that in all ways too.

38. Likewise, because of the words 'One world: all beings 'subsist by nutriment. Two worlds: mentality and mate- 'riality. Three worlds : Three kinds of feeling. Four 'worlds : four kinds of nutriment. Five worlds: five 'aggregates as objects of clinging. Six worlds : six internal 'bases. Seven worlds : seven stations of consciousness. 'Eight worlds : eight worldly states. Nine worlds : nine 'abodes of beings. Ten worlds: ten bases. Twelve worlds: 'twelve bases. Eighteen worlds : eighteen elements'

---

12. '*Bhanti*—they shine' : this form is not given in P. T. S. Dict. under *bhāti*.

(Ps.i,122),[13] this world of formations was known to him in all ways.

39. But he knows all beings' habits, knows their inherent tendencies, knows their temperaments, knows their bents; knows them as with little dust on their eyes and with much dust on their eyes, with keen faculties and with dull faculties, with good behaviour and with bad behaviour, easy to teach and hard to teach, capable and incapable [of achievement] (cf.Ps.i,121), therefore this world of beings was known to him in all ways.

40. And as the world of beings so also the world of location. For accordingly this [world measures as follows]:

One world-sphere[14] is twelve hundred thousand leagues and thirty-four hundred and fifty leagues (1,203,450) in breadth and width. In circumference, however,

[The measure of it] all around
Is six and thirty hundred thousand
And then ten thousand in addition,
Four hundred too less half a hundred (3,610,350).

---

13. To take what is not self-evident in this paragraph, *three kinds of feeling* are pleasant, painful and neither-painful-nor-pleasant (see M. Sutta 59). *Four kinds of nutriment* are physical nutriment, contact, mental volition, and consciousness (see M. i, 48, and MA. i, 207f.). *The seven stations of consciousness* are: (1) sense sphere, (2) Brahmā's Retinue, (3) Ābhassara (Brahmā-world) Deities, (4) Subhakiṇṇa (Brahmā-world) Deities, (5) base consisting of boundless space, (6) base consisting of boundless consciousness, (7) base consisting of nothingness (see D. iii, 253). *The eight wordly states* are gain, fame, blame, pleasure, and their opposites (see D. iii, 260). *The nine abodes of beings*: (1)–(4) as in stations of consciousness, (5) unconscious beings, (6)–(9) the four immaterial states (see D. iii, 263). *The ten bases* are eye, ear, nose, tongue, body, visible object, sound, odour, flavour, tangible object.

14. *Cakkavāḷa* (world-sphere or universe) is a term for the concept of a single complete universe as one of an infinite number of such universes. This concept of the cosmos, in its general form, is not peculiar to Buddhism, but appears to have been the already generally accepted one. The term *loka-dhātu* (world-element) in its most restricted sense, is one world-sphere, but it can be extended to mean any number, for example, the set of world-spheres dominated by a particular Brahmā (see M. Sutta 120).

As thus conceived, a circle of 'world-sphere mountains' 'like the rim of a wheel' (*cakka*—Pm. 198) encloses the ocean. In the centre of the ocean stands Mount Sineru (or Meru), surrounded by seven concentric rings of mountains separated by rings of sea. In the ocean between the outermost of these seven rings and the enclosing 'world-sphere mountain' ring are the 'four continents'. 'Over forty-two thousand leagues away' (DhsA. 313) the moon and the sun circulate above them inside the world-sphere-mountain ring, and night is the effect of the sun's going behind Sineru. The orbits of the moon and sun are in the sense-sphere heaven of the Four Kings (Catumahārājā), the lowest heaven, which is a layer extending from the world-sphere mountains to the slopes of Sineru. The stars are on both sides of them (DhsA. 318). Above that come the successive layers of the other five sense-sphere heavens—the four highest not touching the earth—and above them the fine-material Brahmā worlds, the higher of which extend over

41. Herein,

Two times a hundred thousand leagues
And then four *nahutas* as well (240,000):
This Earth, this 'Bearer of All Wealth',
Has that much thickness, as they tell.

And its support:

Four times a hundred thousand leagues
And then eight *nahutas* as well (480,000):
The water resting on the air
Has that much thickness, as they tell.

And the support of that: [206]

Nine times a hundred thousand goes
The air out in the firmament
And sixty thousand more besides (960,000)
So this much is the world's extent.

42. Such is its extent. And these features are to be found in it:

Sineru, tallest of all mountains plunges down into the sea
Full four and eighty thousand leagues, and towers up in like degree.
Seven concentric mountain rings surround Sineru in suchwise
That each of them in depth and height is half its predecessor's size:

---

more than one world-sphere (see A. v, 59). The world-sphere rests on water, which rests on air, which rests on space. World-spheres 'lie adjacent to each other in contact like bowls, leaving a triangular unlighted space between each three' (Pm. 199) which is called a 'world-interspace' (see also MA. iv, 178), and their numbers extend thus in all four directions to infinity on the supporting water's surface.

The southern continent of Jambudīpa is the known inhabited world (but see *e.g.* D. Sutta 26). Various hells (see *e.g.* M. Sutta 130; A. v. 173; Vin. iii, 107) are below the earth's surface. The lowest sensual-sphere heaven, is that of the Deities of the Four Kings ((*Cātumahārājika*). The four are Dhaṭarattha Gandhabba-rāja (King of the East), Virūḷha Kumbhaṇḍa-rāja (King of the South), Virūpaka Nāga-rāja (King of the West), and Kuvera or Vessavaṇa Yakkha-rāja (King of the North—see D. Sutta 32). Here the moon and sun circulate. The deities of this heaven are often at war with the Asura demons (see *e.g.* D. ii, 285) for possession of the lower slopes of Sineru. The next higher is Tāvatimsa (the Heaven of the Thirty-three), governed by Sakka, Ruler of Gods (*sakka-devinda*). Above this is the heaven of the Yāma Deities (Deities who have Gone to Bliss) ruled by King Suyāma (not to be confused with Yama King of the Underworld—see M. iii, 179). Higher still come the Deities of the Tusita (Contented) Heaven with King Santusita. The fifth of these heavens is that of the Nimmānarati Deities (Deities who Delight in Creating) ruled by King Sunimmita. The last and highest of the sensual-sphere heavens is the Paranimmitavasavatti Heaven (Deities who Wield Power over Others' Creations). Their King is Vasavatti (see A. i, 227; for details see VbhA. 519f.). Māra (Death) lives in a remote part of this heaven with his hosts, like a rebel with a band of brigands (MA. i, 33f.). For destruction and renewal of all this at the end of the aeon see Ch. XIII.

Vast ranges called Yugandhara, Isadhara, Karavīka,
Sudassana, Nemindhara, Vinataka, Assakaṇṇa.
Heavenly [breezes fan] their cliffs agleam with gems, and here reside
The Four Kings of the Cardinal Points, and other gods and sprites beside.[15]
Himālaya's lofty mountain mass rises in height five hundred leagues,
And in its width and in its breadth it covers quite three thousand leagues,
And then it is bedecked besides with four and eighty thousand peaks.[16]
The Jambu Tree called Naga lends the name, by its magnificence,
To Jambudīpa's land; its trunk, thrice five leagues in circumference,
Soars fifty leagues, and bears all round branches of equal amplitude,
So that a hundred leagues define diameter and altitude.

43. The World-sphere Mountains' line of summits plunges down into the sea
Just two and eighty thousand leagues, and towers up in like degree,
Enringing one world-element all round in its entirety.

And the size of the *Jambu* (Rose-apple) Tree is the same as that of the *Citrapāṭaliya* Tree of the *Asura* demons, the

15. 'Sineru is not only 84,000 leagues in height but measures the same in width and breadth. For this is said: "Bhikkhus, Sineru King of Mountains is eighty-four thousand leagues in width and it is eighty-four thousand leagues in breadth" (A. iv, 100). Each of the seven surrounding mountains is half as high as that last mentioned, that is, Yugandhara is half as high as Sineru, and so on. The great ocean gradually slopes from the foot of the world-sphere mountains down as far as the foot of Sineru, where it measures in depth as much as Sineru's height. And Yugandhara, which is half that height, rests on the earth as Isadhara and the rest do; for it is said "Bhikkhus, the Great Ocean gradually slopes, gradually tends, gradually inclines" (Ud. 53). Between Sineru and Yugandhara, and so on, the oceans are called "bottomless (*sīdanta*)". Their widths correspond respectively to the heights of Sineru and the rest. The mountains stand all round Sineru, enclosing it, as it were. Yugandhara surrounds Sineru, then Isadhara surrounds Yugandhara, and likewise with the others' (Pm. 199).

'The moon's disk is below and the sun's disk above. It is because it is nearer that the moon's disk appears deficient [when new] owing to its own shadow. They are a league apart and circulate in space at the height of Yugandhara's summit. The Asura Realm is beneath Sineru. Avīci is beneath Jambudīpa. Jambudīpa is the shape of a cart. Aparagoyāna is the shape of an adāsa [bird]. Pubbavideha is the shape of a half-moon. Uttarakurū is the shape of a chair. And they say that the faces of the people who inhabit each of these and who inhabit the small islands belonging to each have respectively those shapes' (Pm. 200).

16. For the commentarial description of *Himavant* (Himalaya) with its five peaks and seven great lakes see MA. iii, 54.

Simbali Tree of the *Garuḷa* demons, the *Kadamba* Tree in [the western continent of] Aparagoyāna, the *Kappa* Tree [in the northern continent] of the Uttarakurūs, the *Sirīsa* Tree in [the eastern continent of] Pubbavideha, and the *Pāricchattaka* Tree [in the heaven] of the Deities of the Thirty-three (Tāvatiṁsa).[17] Hence the Ancients said:

'The Pātali, Simbali, and Jambu, the deities'
'Pāricchattaka,
'The Kadamba, the Kappa Tree and the Sirīsa as the seventh'.

44. [207] Herein, the moon's disk is forty-nine leagues [across] and the sun's disk is fifty leagues. The realm of Tāvatiṁsa (the Thirty-three Gods) is ten thousand leagues. Likewise the realm of the Asura demons, the great Avīci (unremitting) Hell, and Jambudīpa (India). Aparagoyāna is seven thousand leagues. Likewise Pubbavideha. Uttarakurū is eight thousand leagues. And herein, each great continent is surrounded by five hundred small islands. And the whole of that constitutes a single world-sphere, a single world-element. Between [this and the adjacent world-spheres] are the Lokantariya (world-inter-space) hells.[18] So the world-spheres are infinite in number, the world-elements are infinite, and the Blessed One has experienced, known and penetrated them with the infinite knowledge of the Enlightened Ones.

45. Therefore this world of location was known to him in all ways too. So he is 'Knower of worlds' because he has seen the world in all ways.

[*Incomparable leader of men to be tamed*]

46. In the absence of anyone more distinguished for special qualities than himself there is no one to compare with him, thus he is *incomparable*. For in this way he surpasses the whole world in the special quality of virtue, and also in the special qualities of concentration, understanding, deliverance, and knowledge and vision of deliverance. In the special quality of virtue he is without equal, he is the equal only of those [other Enlightened Ones] without equal, he is without like, without double, without counterpart; . . . in the special quality of knowledge and vision of deliverance he is . . . without counterpart, according as it is said; 'I do not see in the 'world with its deities, its Māras and its Brahmās, in this 'generation with its ascetics and brahmans, with its princes 'and men,[19] anyone more perfect in virtue than myself'

---

17. AA. commenting on A. i, 35 ascribes the *Simbali* Tree to the *Supaṇṇas* or winged demons. The commentary to Udāna V. 5, incidentally, gives a further acccount of all these things, only a small proportion of which are discoverable in the Suttas.
18. See note 14.
19. The rendering of *sadevamanussānaṁ* by 'with its princes and men' is supported by the commentary. See MA. ii, 20 and also MA. i, 33 where

(S. i, 139), with the rest in detail, and likewise in the Aggappasāda Sutta (A. ii, 34; Iti. 87), and so on, and in the stanzas beginning 'I have no teacher and my like does not exist in all 'the world' (M. i, 171), all of which should be taken in detail.

47. He guides (*sāreti*) men to be tamed (*purisa-damme*) thus he is *leader of men to be tamed* (*purisadammasārathi*); he tames, he disciplines, is what is meant. Herein, animal males (*purisā*) and human males and non-human males that are not tamed but fit to be tamed (*dametum yuttā*) are 'men to be tamed (*purisadammā*)'. For the animal males, namely, the Royal Nāga (Serpent) Apalāla, Cūḷodara, Mahodara, Aggisikha, Dhūmasikha the Royal Nāga Āravāḷa, the elephant Dhanapālaka, and so on, were tamed by the Blessed One, freed from the poison [of defilement] and established in the refuges and the precepts of virtue, and also the human males, namely, Saccaka the Nigaṇṭhas' (Jains') son, the brahman student Ambaṭṭha, [208] Pokkharasāti, Soṇadaṇḍa, Kūṭadanta, and so on, and also the non-human males. namely, the spirits Āḷavaka, Sūciloma and Kharaloma, Sakka Ruler of Gods, etc.,[20] were tamed and disciplined by various disciplinary means. And the following sutta should be given in full here: 'I discipline men to be tamed 'sometimes gently, Kesi, and I discipline them sometimes 'roughly, and I discipline them sometimes gently and 'roughly' (A.ii,112).

48. Then the Blessed One moreover further tames those already tamed, doing so by announcing the first jhana, etc., respectively to those whose virtue is purified, etc., and also the way to the higher path to Stream-enterers, and so on.

Or alternatively the words *incomparable leader of men to be tamed* can be taken together as one clause. For the Blessed One so guides men to be tamed that in a single session they may go in the eight directions [by the eight liberations] without hesitation. Thus he is called *the incomparable leader of men to be tamed*. And the following Sutta passage should be given in full here: 'Guided by the elephant-tamer, bhikkhus, the elephant to be tamed goes in one direction ...' M.iii,222).

---

the use of '*sammuti-deva*' for a royal personage, not an actual god, is explained. *Deva* is the normal mode of addressing a king. Besides, the first half of the sentence deals with deities and it would be out of place to refer to them again in the clause relating to mankind.

20- The references are these; Apalāla (Mahāvamsa p. 242. 'Dwelling in the Himalayas'—Pm. 202), Cūḷodara and Mahodara (Mahāvamsa, p. 7–8; Dīpavamsa, p. 21–3), Aggisikha and Dhūmasikha ('Inhabitant of Ceylon' —Pm. 202), Āravāḷa and Dhanapālaka (Vin. ii, 194–6; Jā. v, 333–7). Saccaka (M. Suttas 35 and 36), Ambaṭṭha (D. Sutta 3), Pokkharasāti (D. i, 109), Soṇadaṇḍa (D. Sutta 4), Kūṭadanta (D. Sutta 5), Āḷavaka (Sn., p. 31), Sūciloma and Kharaloma (Sn., p. 47f.), Sakka (D. i, 263f.).

[*Teacher of Gods and men*]

49. He teaches (*anusāsati*) by means of the here and now, of the life to come, and of the ultimate goal, according as befits the case, thus he is the *Teacher* (*satthar*).

And furthermore this meaning should be understood according to the Niddesa thus: '"Teacher (*satthar*)": the 'Blessed One is a caravan leader (*satthar*) since he brings home 'caravans (*sattha*). Just as one who brings a caravan home 'gets caravans across a wilderness, gets them accross a robber-'infested wilderness, gets them across a wild-beast-infested 'wilderness, gets them across a foodless wilderness, gets them 'across a waterless wilderness, gets them right across, gets 'them quite across, gets them properly across, gets them to 'reach a land of safety, so too the Blessed One is a caravan 'leader, one who brings home the caravans, he gets them 'across a wilderness, gets them across the wilderness of 'birth' (Nd1.446).

50. *Of gods and men*: *devamanussānaṁ*=*devānañ ca manussānañ ca* (resolution of compound). This is said in order to denote those who are the best and also to denote those persons capable of progress. For the Blessed One as a teacher bestowed his teaching upon animals as well. For even animals can, through listening to the Blessed One's Law, acquire the benefit of a [suitable rebirth as] support [for progress], and with the benefit of that same support they come, in their second or their third rebirth, to partake of the path and its fruition.

51. Maṇḍūka the deity's son and others illustrate this. While the Blessed one was teaching the Dhamma to the inhabitants of the City of Campā on the banks of the Gaggarā Lake, it seems, a frog (*maṇḍūka*) apprehended a sign in the Blessed One's voice. [209] A cowherd who was standing leaning on a stick put his stick on the frog's head and crushed it. He died and was straight away reborn in a gilded divine palace twelve leagues broad in the realm of the Thirty-three (*Tāvatiṁsa*). He found himself there, as if waking up from sleep, amidst a host of celestial nymphs, and he exclaimed 'So I have actually been reborn here. What deed did I do?'. When he sought for the reason, he found it was none other than his apprehension of the sign in the Blessed One's voice. He went with his divine palace at once to the Blessed One and paid homage at his feet. Though the Blessed One knew about it, he asked him:

'Who now pays homage at my feet,
'Shining with glory of success,
'Illuminating all around
'With beauty so outstanding?

'In my last life I was a frog,

'The waters of a pond my home;
'A cowherd's crook ended my life
'While listening to your Dhamma' (Vv. 49).

The Blessed One taught him the Dhamma. Eighty-four thousand creatures gained penetration to the Dhamma. As soon as the deity's son became established in the fruition of Stream Entry he smiled and then vanished.

[*Enlightened*]

52. He is *enlightened* (*buddha*) with the knowledge that belongs to the fruit of liberation, since everything that can be known has been discovered (*buddha*) by him.

Or alternatively, he discovered (*bujjhi*) the four truths by himself and awakened (*bodhesi*) others to them, thus and for other such reasons he is enlightened (*buddha*). And in order to explain this meaning the whole passage in the Niddesa beginning thus 'He is the discoverer (*bujjhitar*) of the truths, 'thus he is enlightened (*buddha*). He is the awakener (*bodhe-* '*tar* of the generation, thus he is enlightened (*buddha*)' (Nd1.457), or the same passage from the Patisambhidā (Ps.i,174), should be quoted in detail.

[*Blessed*]

53. *Blessed* (*bhagavant*) is a term signifying the respect and veneration accorded to him as the highest of all beings and distinguished by his special qualities.[21] Hence the Ancients said:

'"Blessed" is the best of words,
'"Blessed" is the finest word;
'Deserving awe and veneration,
'Blessed is the name therefore'.

54. Or alternatively, names are of four kinds: denoting a period of life, describing a particular mark, signifying a particular acquirement, and fortuitously arisen,[22] which last in the current usage of the world is called 'capricious'. Herein, [210] *names denoting a period of life* are those such as 'yearling calf (*vaccha*)', 'steer to be trained (*damma*)', 'yoke ox (*balivaddha*)', and the like. *Names describing a particular mark* are those such as 'staff-bearer (*daṇḍin*)', umbrella-bearer (*chattin*)', 'topknot-wearer (*sikhin*)', 'hand possessor (*karin*—elephant)', and the like. *Names signifying a particular acquirement* are those such as 'possessor of the three clear vision (*tevijja*)', possessor of the six direct-knowledges (*chaḷabhiñña*)', and the

21. For the breaking up of this compound cf. parallel passage at MA. 1,10.
22. '*Āvatthika*—denoting a period in life' (from *avatthā* see Ch. IV, §167); not in P.T.S. Dict., the meaning given in P.T.S. Dict for '*lingika*—describing a particular mark' is hardly adequate for this ref.; '*nemittika*—signifying a particular acquirement' is not in this sense in P.T.S. Dict. For more on names see Dhs A.S90.

like. Such names as 'Sirivaḍḍhaka (Augmenter of Lustre)', 'Dhanavaḍḍhaka (Augmenter of Wealth)', etc., are *fortuitously arisen names*; they have no reference to the word-meanings.

55. This name, *Blessed*, is one signifying a particular acquirement; it is not made by Mahā-Māyā, or by king Suddhodhana, or by the eighty thousand kinsmen, or by distinguished deities like Sakka, Santusita, and others. And this is said by the General of the Law:[23] ' " Blessed ": this is not a name ' made by a mother, . . . This [name] "Buddha", which signifies final liberation, is a realistic description of Buddhas (Enlightened Ones), the Blessed Ones, together with their obtainment of ommiscient knowledge at the root of an Enlightenment [Tree]' (Ps. i, 174; NdI. 143).

56. Now in order to explain also the special qualities signified by this name they cite the following stanza .

' *Bhagī bhajī bhāgī vibhattavā iti*
' *Akāsi bhaggan ti garū ti bhāgyavā.*
' *Bahūhi ñāyehi subhāvitattano*
' *Bhavantago so bhagavā ti vuccati*'.

' The reverend one (*garu*) has blessings) (*bhagī*), is a frequenter (*bhajī*), a partaker (*bhāgī*), a possessor of what has been analysed (*vibhattavā*),
' He has caused abolishing (*bhagga*), he is fortunate (*bhāgyavā*),
' He has fully developed himself (*subhāvitattano*) in many ways ;
' He has gone to the end of becoming (*bhavantago*); thus he is called " Blessed (*bhagavā*)" '.

The meaning of these words should be understood according to the method of explanation given to the Niddesa (NdI. 142).[24]

---

23. The commentarial name for the Elder Sāriputta to whom the authorship of the Paṭisambhidā is traditionally attributed. The Ps. text has ' Buddha ' not ' Bhagavā '.

24. ' The Niddesa method is this : " The word Blessed (*bhagavā*) is a term of respect. Moreover, he has abolished (*bhagga*) greed, thus he is blessed (*bhagavā*); he has abolished hate,......delusion,...... views,...... craving,......defilement, thus he is blessed.

' " He divided (*bhaji*), analysed (*vibhaji*), and classified (*paṭivibhaji*) the Dhamma treasure, thus he is blessed (*bhagavā*). He makes an end of the kinds of becoming (*bhavānaṃ antakaroti*), thus he is blessed (*bhagavā*). He has developed (*bhāvita*) the body and virtue and the mind and understanding, thus he is blessed (*bhagavā*).

' " Or the Blessed One is a frequenter (*bhajī*) of remote jungle-thicket resting places with little noise, with few voices, with a lonely atmosphere, where one can lie hidden from people, favourable to retreat, thus he is blessed (*bhagavā*).

' " Or the Blessed One is a partaker (*bhāgī*) of robes, alms food, resting place, and the requisite of medicine as cure for the sick, thus he is blessed (*bhagavā*). Or he is a partaker of the taste of meaning, the taste

57. But there is this other way:

‘ *Bhāgyavā bhaggavā yutto bhagehi ca vibhattavā.*
‘ *Bhattavā vanta-gamano bhavesu*: *bhagavā tato.*
‘ He is fortunate (*bhāgyavā*)., possessed of abolishment (*bhaggavā*), associated with blessings (*yutto bhagehi*), and a possessor of what has been analysed (*vibhattavā*),
‘ He has frequented (*bhattavā*), and he has rejected going in the kinds of becoming (*VAnta-GAmano BHAvesu*), thus he is Blessed (*BHAGAVĀ*)’.

58. Herein, by using the Characteristic of Language beginning with ‘Vowel augmentation of syllable, elision of syllable’ (see Kasikā vi, 3, 109), or by using the Characteristic of Insertion beginning with [the example of] *Pisodara*, etc. (see Pāṇini, Gaṇapatha 6, 3, 109) it may be known that he [can also] be called ‘Blessed (*Bhagavā*)’ when he can be called ‘fortunate (*bhāgyavā*) ’ owing to the fortunateness (*bhāgya*) to have reached the further shore [of the ocean of perfection] of giving, virtue, etc., which produce mundane and supramundane bliss. (See Khp A. 108).

59. [Similarly] he [can also] be called ‘blessed (*bhagavā*)’ when he can be called ‘possessed of abolishment (*bhaggavā*)’ owing to the following menaces having been abolished; for he has abolished (*abhañji*) all the hundred thousand kinds of trouble, anxiety and defilement classed as greed, as hate, as delusion, and as misdirected attention; as consciencelessness and shamelessness, as anger and enmity, as contempt and domineering, as envy and avarice, as deceit and fraud, as obduracy and presumption, as pride and haughtiness, as vanity and negligence, as craving and ignorance; as the three roots of the unprofitable, kinds of misconduct, defilement, stains, [211] fictitious perceptions, applied thoughts, and diversifications; as the four perversenesses, cankers, ties, floods, bonds, bad ways, cravings, and clingings; as the five wildernesses in the

of the law, the taste of deliverance, the higher virtue, the higher consciousness, the higher understanding, thus he is blessed (*bhagavā*). Or he is a partaker of the four jhanas, the four measureless states, the four immaterial states, thus he is blessed. Or he is a partaker of the eight liberations, the eight bases of mastery, the nine successive attainments, thus he is blessed. Or he is a partaker of the ten developments of perception, the ten kasina attainments, concentration due to mindfulness of breathing, the attainment due to foulness, thus he is blessed. Or he is a partaker of the four foundations of mindfulness, the four right endeavours, the four roads to power, the five spiritual faculties, the five powers, the seven enlightenment factors, the noble eightfold path, thus he is blessed. Or he is a partaker of the ten powers of Perfect Ones (see M. Sutta 12), of the four kinds of perfect confidence (same ref.), of the four discriminations, of the six kinds of direct-knowledge, of the six Enlightened Ones’ states [not shared by disciples (see note 7)] thus he is blessed. Blessed One (*bhagavā*): this is not a name made by a mother,....this name, Blessed One, is a designation based on realization" ’ (Pm. 207).

heart, shackles in the heart, hindrances, and kinds of delight; as the six roots of discord, and groups of craving; as the seven inherent tendencies; as the eight wrongnesses; as the nine things rooted in craving; as the ten courses of unprofitable action; as the sixty-two kinds of [false] view; as the hundred and eight ways of behaviour of craving[25]—or in brief, the five Māras, that is to say, the Māras of defilement, of the aggregates, and of kamma-formations, Māra as deity, and Māra as death.

And in this context it is said:

'He has abolished (*bhagga*) greed and hate,
'Delusion too, he is canker-free;
'Abolished every evil state,
'"Blessed" his name may rightly be',

60. And by his fortunateness (*bhāgyavatā*) is indicated the excellence of his material body which bears a hundred characteristics of merit; and by his having abolished defects (*bhaggadosatā*)] is indicated the excellence of his Dhamma body. Likewise, [by his fortunateness is indicated] the esteem of worldly [people: and by his having abolished defects, the esteem of] those who resemble him. [And by his fortunateness it is indicated] that he is fit to be relied on[26] by laymen; and [by his having abolished defects that he is fit to be relied on by] those gone forth into homelessness; and when both have relied on him, they acquire relief from bodily and mental pain as well as help with both material and dhamma gifts, and they are rendered capable of finding both mundane and supramundane bliss.

61. He is also called 'blessed (*bhagavā*)' since he is '*associated with blessings* (*bhagehi yuttattā*)' such as those of the following kind, in the sense that he 'has those blessings *bhagā assa*

---

25. Here are explanations of those things in this list that cannot be discovered by reference to the index: The pairs, 'anger and enmity' to 'conceit and negligence' (M. i, 16). The 'three roots' are greed, hate and delusion (D. iii, 214). The 'three kinds of misconduct' are that of body, speech and mind (S. v, 75). The 'three defilements' are misconduct, craving, views (Ch. I. §9, 13). The 'three erroneous perceptions (*visama-saññā*)' are those connected with greed, hate and delusion (Vibh. 368). The three 'applied thoughts' are thoughts of sense-desire, ill will and cruelty (M. i, 114). The 'three diversifications (*papañca*)' are those due to craving, conceit and [false] views (see Ch. XVI, n. 17). 'Four perversenesses': seeing permanence, pleasure, self, and beauty, where there is none (Vbh. 376). 'Four cankers', etc. (Ch. XXII, §47ff.). 'Five wildernesses' and 'shackles' (M. i, 101). 'Five kinds of delight': delight in the five aggregates (Ch. XVI, §93). 'Six roots of discord': anger, contempt, envy, fraud, evilness of wishes and adherence to one's own view (D. iii, 246). 'Nine things rooted in craving' (D. iii, 288–9). 'Ten courses of unprofitable action': killing, stealing, sexual misconduct; lying, slander, harsh speech, gossip, covetousness, ill will, wrong view (M. i, 47, 286f.). 'Sixty-two kinds of view': (D. i, 12ff.; M. Sutta 102). 'The hundred and eight ways of behaviour of craving' (Vbh. 400).

26. '*Abhigamanīya*—fit to be relied on': *abhigacchati* not in P. T. S. Dict.

santi)'. Now in the world the word 'blessing' is used for six things, namely, lordship, dhamma, fame, glory, wish, and endeavour. He has supreme *lordship* over his own mind either of the kind reckoned as mundane and consisting in 'minuteness, lightness', etc.,[27] or that complete in all aspects, and likewise the supramundane *Dhamma*. And he has the exceedingly pure *fame*, spread through the three worlds, acquired through the special quality of veracity. And he has *glory* of all limbs, perfect in every aspect, which is capable of comforting the eyes of people eager to see his material body. And he has his *wish*, in other words, the production of what is wanted, since whatever is wanted and needed by him as beneficial to himself or others is then and there produced for him. And he has the *endeavour*, in other words, the right effort, which is the reason why the whole world venerates him.

62. [He can also] be called 'blessed (*bhagavā*)' when he can be called '*a possessor of what has been analysed* (*vibhattavā*)' owing to his having analysed [and clarified] all states into the [three]classes beginning with the profitable; or profitable, etc., states into such classes as aggregates, bases, elements, truths, faculties, dependent origination, etc.; [212] or the Noble Truth of suffering into the senses of oppressing, being formed, burning, and changing; and that of Origin into the senses of accumulating, source, bond, and impediment; and that of Cessation into the senses of escape, seclusion, being unformed, and deathless; and that of the Path into the senses of outlet, cause, seeing, and predominance. Having analysed, having revealed, having shown, them, is what is meant.

63. He [can also] be called 'blessed (*bhagavā*)' when he can be called one who '*has frequented* (*bhattavā*)' owing to his having frequented (*bhaji*), cultivated, repeatedly practised, such mundane and supramundane higher-than-human states as the heavenly, the divine, and the noble, abidings,[28] as bodily, mental, and existential seclusion, as the void, the desireless, and the signless, liberations, and others as well.

---

27. Pm. says 'the word "*etc.*" includes the following six: *mahimā, patti, pākammaṃ, īsitā, vasitā,* and *yatthakāmāvasāyitā*. 'Herein, *aṇimā* means making the body minute (the size of an atom—*aṇu*). *Laghimā* means lightness of body; walking on air, and so on. *Mahimā* means enlargement producing hugeness of the body. *Patti* means arriving where one wants to go. *Pākamma* means producing what one wants by resolving, and so on. *Isitā* means self-mastery, lordship. *Vasitā* means mastery of miraculous powers. *Yatthakāmāvasāyitā* means attainment of perfection in all ways in one who goes through the air or does anything else of the sort' (Pm . 210). Yogabhāsya 3. 45.

28. The three 'abidings' are these: heavenly abiding=kasina jhana, divine abiding=lovingkindness jhana, etc., noble abiding=fruition attainment.

For the three kinds of seclusion, see Ch. IV, note 23.

64. He [can also] be called 'blessed (*bhagavā*)' when he can be called one who '*has rejected going in the kinds of becoming* (*vantagamano bhavesu*)' because in the three kinds of becoming (*bhava*), the going (*gamana*), in other words, craving, has been rejected (*vanta*) by him. And the syllables *bha* from the word *bhava*, and *ga* from the word *gamana*, and *va* from the word *vanta* with the letter *a* lengthened, make the word '*bhagavā*', just as is done in the world with the word '*mekhalā*' since '*MEhanassa KHAssa māLĀ*' can be said.[29]

65. As long as [the meditator] recollects the special qualities of the Buddha in this way 'For this and this reason the Blessed One is accomplished,......for this and this reason he is blessed', then 'On that occasion his mind is not obsessed ' by greed, or obsessed by hate, or obsessed by delusion; ' his mind has rectitude on that occasion, being inspired by ' the Perfect One (A.iii,285).[30]

66. So when he has thus suppressed the hindrances by preventing obsession by greed, etc., and his mind faces the meditation subject with rectitude, then his applied thought and sustained thought occur with a tendency towards the Enlightened One's special qualities. As he continues to exercise applied thought and sustained thought upon the Enlightened One's special qualities, happiness arises in him. With his mind happy, with happiness as proximate cause, his bodily and mental disturbance are tranquillized by tranquillity. When the disturbance has been tranquillized, bodily and mental bliss arise in him. When he is blissful, his mind, with the Enlightened One's special qualities for its object, becomes concentrated, and so the jhana factors eventually arise in a

29. *Mehana* is not in P.T.S. Dict.

30. Pm. adds seven more plays on the word *bhagavā*, which in brief are these: he is *bhāgavā* (a possessor of parts) because he has the Dhamma aggregates of virtue, etc. (*bhagā*=part, =*vant*=possessor of). He is *bhatavā* (possessor of what is borne) because he has borne (*bhata*) the Perfections to their full development. He has cultivated the parts (*bhāge vani*), that is, he has developed the various classes of attainments. He has cultivated the blessings (*bhage vani*), that is, the mundane and supramundane blessings. He is *bhattavā* (possessor of devotees) because devoted (*bhatta*) people show devotion (*bhatti*) to him on account of his attainments. He has rejected blessings (*bhage vami*) such as glory, lordship, fame and so on. He has rejected the parts (*bhāge vami*) such as the five aggregates of experience, and so on (Pm. 241-6).

As to the word '*bhattavā*': at Vis. Ch. VII, §63 it is explained as ' one who has frequented (*bhaji*) ' attainments. In this sense the attainments have been ' frequented (*bhatta*)' by him. Pm. (p. 214-5) uses the same word in another sense as ' possessor of devotees ', expanding it as ' *bhattā dalhabhattikā assa bahu atthi* (he has many devoted firm devotees—Skr. *bhakta*). In P.T.S. Dict. under *bhattavant* (citing also Vis. 212) only the second meaning is given. *Bhatta* is from the same root *bhaj*) in both cases.

For a short exposition of this recollection see commentary to A., Ekanipāta, XVI, 1.

single moment. But owing to the profundity of the Enlightened One's special qualities, or else owing to his being occupied in recollecting special qualities of many sorts, the jhana is only access and does not reach absorption. And that access jhana itself is known as 'recollection of Buddha' too, because it arises with the recollection of the Enlightened One's special qualities as the means.

67. When a bhikkhu is devoted to this recollection of the Buddha, he is respectful and deferential towards the Master. He attains fullness of faith, mindfulness, understanding and merit. He has much happiness and gladness. He conquers fear and dread. [213] He is able to endure pain. He comes to feel as if he were living in the Master's presence. And his body, when the recollection of the Buddha's special qualities dwells in it, becomes as worthy of veneration as a shrine room. His mind tends towards the plane of the Buddhas. When he encounters an opportunity for transgression, he has awareness of conscience and shame as vivid as though he were face to face with the Master. And if he penetrates no higher, he is at least headed for a happy destiny.

Now when a man is truly wise,
His constant task will surely be
This recollection of the *Buddha*
Blessed with such mighty potency.

This, firstly, is the section dealing with the Recollection of the Enlightened One in the detailed explanation.

•

[(2) Recollection of the Dhamma]

68. One who wants to develop the Recollection of the Dhamma (Law) should go into solitary retreat and recollect the special qualities of both the Dhamma (Law) of the scriptures and the ninefold supramundane Dhamma (state) as follows:

'The Dhamma is well proclaimed by the Blessed One, 'visible here and now, not delayed (timeless), inviting of 'inspection, onward-leading, and directly experienceable by 'the wise' (M. i, 37; A. iii, 285).

69. *Well proclaimed*: in this clause the Dhamma of the scriptures is included as well as the other; in the rest of the clauses only the supramundane Dhamma is included.

Herein, the Dhamma of the scriptures is well proclaimed because it is good in the beginning, the middle, and the end and because it announces the life of purity that is utterly perfect and pure with meaning and with detail (see M.i, 179).

Even a single stanza of the Blessed One's teaching is good in the beginning with the first word, good in the middle with the second, third, etc., and good in the end with the last word, because the Dhamma is altogether admirable. A sutta with a single sequence of meaning[31] is good in the beginning with the introduction, good in the end with the conclusion, and good in the middle with what is in between. A sutta with several sequences of meaning is good in the beginning with the first sequence of meaning, good in the end with the last sequence of meaning, and good in the middle with the sequences of meaning in between. Furthermore, it is good in the beginning with the introduction [giving the place of] and the origin [giving the reason for] its utterance, it is good in the middle because it suits those susceptible of being taught since it is unequivocal in meaning and reasoned with cause and example. It is good in the end with its conclusion that inspires faith in the hearers.

70. Also the entire Dhamma of the Dispensation is good in the beginning with virtue as one's own well-being. It is good in the middle with serenity and insight and with path and fruition. It is good in the end with nibbana. Or alternatively, it is good in the beginning with virtue and concentration. [214] It is good in the middle with insight and the path. It is good in the end with fruition and nibbana. Or alternatively, it is good in the beginning because it is the good discovery made by the Buddha. It is good in the middle because it is the well-regulatedness of the Dhamma. It is good in the end because it is the good way entered upon by the Saṅgha. Or alternatively, it is good in the beginning as the discovery of what can be attained by one who enters upon the way of practice in conformity after hearing about it. It is good in the middle as the unproclaimed enlightenment [of Pacceka Buddhas]. It is good in the end as the enlightenment of disciples.

71. And when listened to, it does good through hearing it because it suppresses the hindrances, thus it is good in the beginning. And when made the way of practice it does good through the way being entered upon because it brings the bliss of serenity and insight, thus it is good in the middle. And when it has thus been made the way of practice and the fruit of the way is ready, it does good through the fruit of the way because it brings [unshakable] equipoise, thus it is good in the end.

So it is 'well proclaimed' because of being good in the beginning, the middle and the end.

---

31. '*Anusandhi*—sequence of meaning': a technical commentarial term signifying both a particular subject treated in a discourse, and also the way of linking one subject with another in the same discourse. At MA.i,175 three kinds are distinguished: sequence of meaning in answer to a question (*pucchānusandhi*—e.g. M.i, 36), that to suit a personal idiosyncrasy (*ajjhāsayānusandhi*—e.g. M.i, 23), and that due to the natural course of the teaching (*yathānusandhi*—e.g. the whole development of M. Sutta 6).

Now the life of purity, that is to say, the life of purity of the dispensation and the life of purity of the path, which the Blessed One announces, which he shows in various ways when he teaches the Dhamma, is 'with meaning' because of perfection of meaning, and it is 'with detail' because of perfection of detail, as it is proper that it should be. It is 'with meaning' because it conforms to the words declaring its meaning by pronouncing, clarifying, revealing, expounding, and explaining it. It is 'with detail' because it has perfection of syllables, words, details, style, language, and descriptions. It is 'with meaning' owing to profundity of meaning and profundity of penetration. It is 'with detail' owing to profundity of Law and profundity of teaching. It is 'with meaning' because it is the province of the Discriminations of meaning and of perspicuity. It is 'with detail' because it is the province of the Discriminations of law and of language (see Ch. XIV, §21). It is 'with meaning' since it inspires confidence in persons of discretion, being experienceable by the wise. It is 'with detail' since it inspires confidence in worldly persons, being a fit object of faith. It is 'with meaning' because its intention is profound. It is 'with detail' because its words are clear. It is 'utterly perfect' with the complete perfection due to absence of anything that can be added. It is 'pure' with the immaculateness due to absence of anything to be subtracted.

Furthermore, it is 'with meaning' because it provides the particular distinction[32] of achievement through practice of the way, and it is 'with detail' because it provides the particular distinction of learning through mastery of scripture. It is 'utterly perfect' because it is connected with the five Aggregates of Dhamma beginning with Virtue.[33] It is 'pure' because it has no imperfection, because it exists for the purpose of crossing over [the round of rebirths' flood (see M.i, 134)], and because it is not concerned with worldly things.

So it is 'well proclaimed' because it 'announces the life of purity that is utterly perfect and pure with meaning and with detail'.

Or alternatively, it is *well proclaimed* since it has been properly proclaimed with no perversion of meaning. For the meaning of other sectarians' law suffers perversion since there is actually no obstruction in the [215] things described there as obstructive and actually no outlet in the things described there as outlets, which is why their law is ill-proclaimed; but not so the Blessed One's Law, whose meaning suffers

32. '*Vyatti* (*byatti*)—Particular distinction' (n. fm. *vi*+*añj*) not so spelt in. P.T.S. Dict. but see *viyatti*. Glossed by Pm. with *veyyatti*.

33. These 'five aggregates' are those of virtue, concentration, understanding, deliverance, and knowledge and vision of deliverance.

no perversion since the things described there as obstructions and the things described there as outlets are so in actual fact.

So, in the first place, the Dhamma of the scriptures is 'well proclaimed'.

74. The Supramundane Dhamma is *well proclaimed* since both the way that accords with nibbana and the nibbana that accords with the way have been proclaimed, according as it is said: 'The way leading to nibbana has been properly 'declared to the disciples by the Blessed One, and nibbana 'and the way meet. Just as the water of the Ganges meets 'and joins with the water of the Yamunā, so too the way 'leading to nibbana has been properly declared to the dis'ciples by the Blessed One, and nibbana and the way meet' (D.ii,223).

75. And here the Noble Path, which is the middle way since it does not approach either extreme, is *well proclaimed* in being proclaimed to be the middle way.

The fruits of asceticism, where defilements are tranquillized, are *well proclaimed* too in being proclaimed to have tranquillized defilement.

Nibbana, whose individual essence is eternal, deathless, the refuge, the shelter, etc., is *well proclaimed* too in being proclaimed to have an individual essence that is eternal, and so on.

So the supramundane Dhamma is also 'well proclaimed'.

76. *Visible here and now*: firstly the noble path is 'visible here and now' since it can be seen by a noble person himself when he has done away with greed, etc., in his own continuity according as it is said: 'When a man is dyed with greed, 'brahman, and is overwhelmed and his mind is obsessed 'by greed, then he thinks for his own affliction, he thinks 'for others' affliction, he thinks for the affliction of both, 'and he experiences mental suffering and grief. When greed 'has been abandoned, he neither thinks for his own affliction, 'nor thinks for others' affliction, nor thinks for the affliction 'of both, and he does not experience mental suffering and 'grief. This, brahman, is how the Dhamma is visible here and 'now' (A.1,156). [216]

77. Furthermore, the ninefold supramundane Dhamma is also *visible here and now*, since when any one has attained it, it is visible to him through reviewing knowledge without his having to rely on faith in another.

78. Or alternatively, the view (*diṭṭhi*) that is recommended (*pasattha*—pp. of root *saṃs*) is 'proper view (*sandiṭṭhi*)'. It conquers by means of proper view, thus it 'has proper view (*sandiṭṭhika*—visible here and now)'. For in this way the noble path conquers defilements by means of the proper view

associated with it, and the noble fruition does so by means of the proper view that is its cause, and nibbana does so by means of the proper view that has nibbana as its objective field. So the ninefold supramundane Dhamma 'has the proper view (*sandiṭṭhika*—is visible here and now)' since it conquers by means of proper view, just as a charioteer (*rathika*) is so called because he conquers by means of a chariot (*ratha*).

79. Or alternatively, it is seeing (*dassana*) that is called 'the seen (*diṭṭha*)'; then *diṭṭha* and *sandiṭṭha* are identical in meaning as 'seeing'. It is worthy of being seen (*diṭṭha*), thus it is 'visible here and now *sandiṭṭhika*'. For the supramundane Dhamma (law) arrests the fearful round (of kamma, etc.,] as soon as it is seen by means of penetration consisting in development [of the path] and by means of penetration consisting in realization [of nibbana]. So it is 'visible here and now (*sandiṭṭhika*)' since it is worthy of being seen (*diṭṭha*), just as one who is clothable (*vatthika*)[34] is so called because he is worthy of clothes (*vattha*).

80. [*Not delayed*]: it has no delay (lit. takes no time—*kāla*) in the matter of giving its own fruit, thus it is 'without delay (*akāla*)'. 'Without delay' is the same as 'not delayed (*akālika*'. What is meant is that instead of giving its fruit after creating a delay (using up time), say, five days, seven days, it gives its fruit immediately next to its own occurrence (see Sn. 226).

81. Or alternatively, what is delayed (*kālika*—lit. what takes time) is what needs some distant[35] time to be reached before it can give its fruit. What is that? It is the mundane law of profitable [kamma]. This, however, is undelayed (*na kālika*) because its fruit comes immediately next to it, so it is 'not delayed (*akālika*)'.

This is said with reference to the path.

82. [*Inviting of inspection*:] it is worthy of an invitation to inspect (*ehipassa-vidhi*) given thus 'come and see this Dhamma' (*ehi passa imaṃ dhammaṃ*)', thus it is 'inviting of inspection (*ehipassika*)'. But why is it worthy of this invitation? Because it is found and because of its purity. For if a man has said that there is money or gold in an empty fist, he cannot say 'Come and see it'. Why not? Because it is not found. And on the other hand, while dung or urine may well be found, a man cannot, for the purpose of cheering the mind by exhibiting beauty, say 'Come and see this'; on the contrary they have to be covered up with grass and leaves. Why? Because of their impurity. But this ninefold supramundane Dhamma is actually found as such in its individual essence, and it is as pure as the full moon's

34. '*Vatthika*—clothable': not in P.T.S. Dict.
35. '*Pakaṭṭha*—distant': not in P.T.S. Dict. (=*dura*—Pm. 297).

disk in a cloudless sky, as a gem of pure water on bleached cloth. [217] Consequently, it is worthy of the invitation to inspect since it is found and pure, thus it is 'inviting of inspection'.

83. The word '*opanayika* (onward-leading)' is [equivalent to the gerund] *upanetabba* (ought to—can—be induced). Here is an exposition. An inducing (*upanayana* is an inducement (*upanaya*). [As the four paths and four fruitions] this [Dhamma] is worth inducing (*upanayanam arahati*) [, in other words, arousing,] *in* one's own mind [subjectively] by means of development, without any question of whether or not one's clothing or one's head is on fire (see A. iv, 320), thus it is 'onward-leading (*opanayika*'. This applies to the [above-mentioned eight] formed supramundane states (dhammas). But the unformed [dhamma] is worth inducing *by* one's own mind [to become the mind's object], thus it is 'onward-leading', too; the meaning is that it is worth treating as one's shelter by realizing it. Or alternatively, what

84. induces (*upaneti*) [the noble person] onwards to nibbana is the noble path, which is thus inducive (*upaneyya*). Again, what can (ought to) be induced (*upanetabba*) to realizability is the Dhamma consisting in fruition and nibbana, which is thus inducive (*upaneyya*), too. The word *upaneyya* is the same as the word *opanayika*.[36]

85. *Is directly experienceable by the wise*: it can be experienced by all the kinds of wise men beginning with the 'acutely 'wise' (see A. ii, 135) each in himself thus: 'The path has been developed, fruition attained, and cessation realized, by me'. For it does not happen that when a preceptor has developed the Path his co-resident abandons his defilements, nor does a co-resident dwell in comfort owing to the preceptor's attainment of fruition, nor does he realize the nibbana realized by the preceptor. So this is not visible in the way that an ornament on another's head is, but rather it is visible only in one's own mind. What is meant is that it can be undergone by wise men, but it is not the province of fools.

---

36. This passage is only loosely renderable because the exegesis here is based almost entirely on the substitution of one Pali grammatical form for another (*pada—siddhi*). The reading *opaneyyiko* (for *opanayiko*) does not appear in any Sinhalese text (generally the most reliable); consequently the sentence '*opanayiko*' *va opaneyyiko*' (see Harvard text) is absent in them, being superfluous. Pm.'s explanations are incorporated. This paragraph depends on the double sense of *upaneti* (*upa*+*neti* to lead on or induce) and its derivatives as (1) an attractive inducement and (2) a reliable guide and so the word *induce* is stretched a bit and *inducive* coined on the analogy of conducive. *Upanaya* (inducement) is not in P.T.S. Dict., nor is *upanayana* (inducing) in this sense (see also Ch. XIV §68). *Upanayana* means in logic 'application', subsumption'; and also *upanetabba* means 'to be added', see end of §72. For *allīyana* (treating as one's shelter) see refs. in Glossary.

86. Now in addition, this Dhamma is well proclaimed. Why? Because it is visible here and now. It is visible here and now because it is not delayed. It is not delayed because it invites inspection. And what invites inspection is onward-leading.

87. As long as [the meditator] recollects the special qualities of the Dhamma in this way, then 'on that occasion his mind 'is not obsessed by greed, or obsessed by hate, or obsessed 'by delusion; his mind has rectitude on that occasion, being 'inspired by the Law' (A. iii, 285).

So when he has suppressed the hindrances in the way already described (§66), the jhana factors arise in a single conscious moment. But owing to the profundity of the Law's special qualities, or else owing to his being occupied in recollecting special qualities of many sorts, the jhana is only access and does not reach absorption. And that access jhana itself is known as 'recollection of the Dhamma' too because it arises with the recollection of the Law's special qualities as the means. [218]

88. When a bhikkhu is devoted to this recollection of the Dhamma, he thinks 'I never in the past met a master who taught a law that led onward thus, who possessed this talent, nor do I now see any such a master other than the Blessed One'. Seeing the Dhamma's special qualities in this way, he is respectful and deferential towards the Master. He entertains great reverence for the Dhamma and attains fullness of faith, and so on. He has much happiness and gladness. He conquers fear and dread. He is able to endure pain. He comes to feel as if he were living in the Law's presence. And his body, when the recollection of the Dhamma's special qualities dwells in it, becomes as worthy of veneration as a shrine room. His mind tends towards the realization of the peerless Dhamma. When he encounters an opportunity for transgression, he has vivid awareness of conscience and shame on recollecting the well-regulatedness of the Dhamma. And if he penetrates no higher, he is at least headed for a happy destiny.

Now when a man is truly wise,
His constant task will surely be
This recollection of the *Dhamma*
Blessed with such mighty potency.

This is the section dealing with the Recollection of the Law in the detailed explanation.

*

[(3) RECOLLECTION OF THE SANGHA]

89. One who wants to develop the recollection of the Community should go into solitary retreat and recollect the special

qualities of the Community of Noble Ones as follows:

'The community of the Blessed One's disciples has entered 'on the good way, the community of the Blessed One's dis-'ciples has entered on the straight way, the community of the 'Blessed One's disciples has entered on the true way, the 'community of the Blessed One's disciples has entered on the 'proper way, that is to say, the Four Pairs of Men, the Eight 'Persons; this community of the Blessed One's disciples is 'fit for gifts, fit for hospitality, fit for offerings, fit for reveren-'tial salutation, as an incomparable field of merit for the 'world' (A.iii,286).

90. Herein, *entered on the good way* (*supaṭipanna*) is thoroughly entered on the way (*suṭṭhu paṭipanna*). What is meant is that it has entered on a way (*paṭipanna*) that is the right way (*sammā-paṭipadā*), the way that is irreversible, the way that is in conformity [with truth], the way that has no opposition, the way that is regulated by the Dhamma. They hear (*suṇanti*) attentively the Blessed One's instruction, thus they are his disciples, (*sāvaka*—lit. hearers). *The community of the disciples* is the community of those disciples. The meaning is that the total of disciples forms a communality because it possesses in common both virtue and [right] view. [219] That right way, being *straight*, unbent, uncrooked, unwarped, is called noble and *true* and is known as *proper* owing to its becomingness, therefore the noble community that has entered on that is also said to have *entered on the straight way, entered on the true way,* and *entered on the proper way.*

91. Those who stand on the path can be understood to have *entered on the good way* since they possess the right way. And those who stand in fruition can be understood to have *entered on the good way* with respect to the way that is now past since by means of the right way they have realized what should be realized.

92. Furthermore, the Community *has entered on the good way* because it has entered on the way according as instructed in the well-proclaimed Law and Discipline (*dhamma-vinaya*), and because it has entered on the immaculate way. It *has entered on the straight way* because it has entered on the way avoiding the two extremes and taking the middle course, and because it has entered on the way of the abandonment of the faults of bodily and verbal crookedness, tortuousness and warpedness. It *has entered on the true way* because nibbana is what is called 'true' and it has entered on the way with that as the aim. It *has entered on the proper way* because it has entered on the way of those who are worthy of proper acts [of veneration].

93. The word '*yadidaṃ* (that is to say)'=*yāni imāni*. *The four pairs of men*: taking them pairwise, the one who stands on the

first path and the one who stands in the first fruition as one pair, in this way there are four pairs. *The eight persons*: taking them by persons, the one who stands on the first path as one and one who stands in the first fruition as one, in this way there are eight persons. And there in the compound *purisa-puggala* (persons) the words *purisa* and *puggala* have the same meaning, but it is expressed in this way to suit differing susceptibility to teaching.

This community of the Blessed One's disciples: this community of the Blessed One's disciples taken by pairs as the four pairs of men (*purisa*) and individually as the eight persons (*purisa-puggala*).

94. As to *fit for gifts*, etc.: what should be brought (*ānetvā*) and given (*hunitabba*) is a gift (*āhuna*—lit. sacrifice); the meaning is, what is to be brought even from far away and donated to the virtuous. It is a term for the four requisites. The Community is fit to receive that gift (sacrifice) because it makes it bear great fruit, thus it is 'fit for gifts (*āhuneyya*)'.

95. Or alternatively, all kinds of property, even when the bringer comes (*āgantvā*) from far away, can be given (*hunitabba*) here, thus the Community 'can be given to (*āhavanīya*)'; or it is fit to be given to by Sakka and others, thus it 'can be given to'. And the brahmans' fire is called 'to be given (sacrificed) to (*āhavanīya*)', for they believe that what is sacrificed to it brings great fruit. [220] But if something is to be sacrificed to for the sake of the great fruit brought by what is sacrificed to it, then surely the Community should be sacrificed to; for what is sacrificed (given) to the Community has great fruit, according as it is said:

'Were anyone to serve the fire
'Out in the woods a hundred years,
'And pay one moment's homage too
'To men of self development,
'His homage would by far excel
'His hundred years of sacrifice' (Dh. 107).

And the word '*āhavanīya* (to be sacrificed to)', which is used in the schools,[37] is the same in meaning as this word '*āhuneyya* (fit for gifts)' used here. There is only the mere trifling difference of syllables. So it is 'fit for gifts'.

96. *Fit for hospitality* (*pāhuneyya*): 'hospitality (*pāhuna*)' is what a donation to visitors is called, prepared with all honours for the sake of dear and beloved relatives and friends who have come from all quarters. But even more than to such objects of hospitality, it is fitting that it should be given also to the Community; for there is no object of hospitality so fit to receive hospitality as the Community since it is encountered after an interval between Buddhas and possesses wholly

37. 'In the Sarvastivādin school and so on' (Pm. 230).

endearing and lovable qualities. So it is 'fit for hospitality' since the hospitality is fit to be given to it and it is fit to receive it.

But those who take the text to be '*pāhavanīya* (fit to be given hospitality to)' have it that the Community is worthy to be placed first and so what is to be given should first of all be brought here and given (*sabba-Paṭhamaṃ Ānetvā ettha HUNItabbaṃ*), and for that reason it is 'fit to be given hospitality to (*pāhavanīya*)' or since it is worthy to be given to in all aspects (*sabba-Pakārena ĀHAVANAṃ arahati*), it is thus 'fit to be given hospitality to (*pāhavanīya*)'. And here this is called *pāhuneyya* in the same sense.

97. 'Offering (*dakkhiṇa*)' is what a gift is called that is to be given out of faith in the world to come. The Community is worthy of that offering, or it is helpful to that offering because it purifies it by making it of great fruit, thus it is *fit for offerings* (*dakkhiṇeyya*).

It is worthy of being accorded by the whole world the reverential salutation (*añjali-kamma*) consisting in placing both hands [palms together] above the head, thus it is *fit for reverential salutation* (*añjalikaraṇīya*).

98. *As an incomparable field of merit for the world*: as a place without equal in the world for growing merit; just as the place for growing the king's or a minister's rice or corn is the king's rice-field or the king's corn-field, so the Community is the place for growing the whole world's merit. For the world's various kinds of merit leading to welfare and happiness grow with the Community as their support. Therefore the Community is 'an incomparable field of merit for the world.'

99. As long as he recollects the special qualities of the Sangha in this way, classed as 'having entered on the good way, etc., [221] then 'On that occasion his mind is not obsessed by 'greed, or obsessed by hate, or obsessed by delusion; his 'mind has rectitude on that occasion, being inspired by the 'Saṅgha' (A.iii,286).

So when he has suppressed the hindrances in the way already described (§66), the jhana factors arise in a single conscious moment. But owing to the profundity of the Community's special qualities, or else owing to his being occupied in recollecting special qualities of many sorts, the jhana is only access and does not reach absorption. And that access jhana itself is known as 'recollection of the Saṅgha' too because it arises with the recollection of the Community's special qualities as the means.

100. When a bhikkhu is devoted to this recollection of the Community, he is respectful and deferential towards the Community. He attains fullness of faith, and so on. He has much happiness and bliss. He conquers fear and dread.

He is able to endure pain. He comes to feel as if he were living in the Community's presence. And his body, when the recollection of the Saṅgha's special qualities dwells in it, becomes as worthy of veneration as an Uposatha house where the Community has met. His mind tends towards the attainment of the Community's special qualities. When he encounters an opportunity for transgression, he has awareness of conscience and shame as vividly as if he were face to face with the Community. And if he penetrates no higher, he is at least headed for a happy destiny.

Now when a man is truly wise,
His constant task will surely be
This recollection of the *Saṅgha*
Blessed with such mighty potency.

This is the section dealing with the Recollection of the Community in the detailed explanation.

*

[(4) Recollection of Virtue]

101. One who wants to develop the recollection of virtue should go into solitary retreat and recollect his own different kinds of virtue in their special qualities of being untorn, etc., as follows:

Indeed my various kinds of virtue are 'untorn, unrent, 'unblotched, unmottled, liberating, praised by the wise, 'not adhered to, and conducive to concentration' (A.iii,286). And a layman should recollect them in the form of laymen's virtue while one gone forth into homelessness should recollect them in the form of the virtue of those gone forth.

102. Whether they are the virtues of laymen or of those gone forth, when no one of them is broken in the beginning or in the end, not being torn like a cloth ragged at the ends, then they are *untorn*. [222] When no one of them is broken in the middle, not being rent like a cloth that is punctured in the middle, then they are *unrent*. When they are not broken twice or thrice in succession, not being blotched like a cow whose body is some such colour as black or red with a discrepant-coloured oblong or round patch appearing on her back or belly, then they are *unblotched*. When they are not broken all over at intervals, not being mottled like a cow speckled with discrepant-coloured spots, then they are *unmottled*.

103. Or in general they are *untorn*, *unrent*, *unblotched*, *unmottled* when they are undamaged by the seven bonds of sexuality (Ch.I,§144) and by anger and enmity and the other evil things (see §59).

104. Those same virtues are *liberating* since they liberate by freeing from the slavery of craving. They are *praised by the*

wise because they are praised by such wise men as Enlightened Ones. They are *not adhered to* (*aparāmaṭṭha*) since they are not adhered to (*aparāmaṭṭhattā*) with craving and [false] view, or because of the impossibility of misapprehending (*parāmaṭṭhum*) that 'There is this flaw in your virtues'. They are *conducive to concentration* since they conduce to access concentration and absorption concentration, or to path concentration and fruition concentration.

105. As long as he recollects his own virtues in their special qualities of being untorn, etc., in this way, then 'On that 'occasion his mind is not obsessed by greed, or obsessed by 'hate, or obsessed by delusion, his mind has rectitude on that 'occasion, being inspired by virtue' (A.iii,286).

So when he has suppressed the hindrances in the way already described (§66), the jhana factors arise in a single conscious moment. But owing to the profundity of the virtues' special qualities, or owing to his being occupied in recollecting special qualities of many sorts, the jhana is only access and does not reach absorption. And that access jhana itself is known as 'recollection of virtue' too because it arises with the virtues' special qualities as the means.

106. And when a bhikkhu is devoted to this recollection of virtue, he has respect for the training. He lives in communion [with his fellows in the life of purity]. He is sedulous in welcoming. He is devoid of the fear of self-reproach and so on. He sees fear in the slightest fault. He attains fullness of faith, and so on. He has much happiness and gladness. And if he penetrates no higher, he is at least headed for a happy destiny.

Now when a man is truly wise,
His constant task will surely be
This recollection of his virtue
Blessed with such mighty potency.

This is the section dealing with the Recollection of Virtue in the detailed explanation. [223]

*

[(5) Recollection of Generosity]

107. One who wants to develop the recollection of generosity should be naturally devoted to generosity and the constant practice of giving and sharing. Or alternatively, if he is one who is starting the development of it, he should make the resolution 'From now on, when there is anyone present to receive, I shall not eat even a single mouthful without having given a gift'. And that very day he should give a gift by sharing according to his means and his ability with those who have distinguished qualities. When he has apprehended the sign in that, he should go into solitary retreat and recollect

his own generosity in its special qualities of being free from the stain of avarice, etc., as follows:

'It is gain for me, it is great gain for me, that in a genera-'tion obsessed by the stain of avarice I abide with my heart 'free from stain by avarice, and am freely generous and open-'handed, that I delight in relinquishing, expect to be asked, 'and rejoice in giving and sharing' (A.iii,287).

108. Herein, *it is gain for me*: it is my gain, advantage. The intention is: I surely partake of those kinds of gain for a giver that have been commended by the Blessed One as follows: 'A man who gives life [by giving food] shall have life either 'divine or human' (A.iii,42), and 'A giver is loved and fre-'quented by many' (A.iii,40), and 'One who gives is ever 'loved, according to the wise man's law' (A. iii, 41), and so on.

109. *It is great gain for me*: it is great gain for me that this Dispensation, or the human state, has been gained by me. Why? Because of the fact that 'I abide *with my mind free from stain by avarice . . . and rejoice in giving and sharing.*'

110. Herein, *obsessed by the stain of avarice* is overwhelmed by the stain of avarice. *Generation*: beings; so called owing to the fact of their being generated. So the meaning here is this: among beings who are overwhelmed by the stain of avarice, which is one of the dark states that corrupt the [natural] transparency of consciousness (see A. i, 10) and which has the characteristic of inability to bear sharing one's own good fortune with others.

111. *Free from stain by avarice* because of being free both from avarice and from the other stains, greed, hate, and the rest. *I abide with my heart*: I abide with my consciousness of the kind already stated, is the meaning. [224] But in the Sutta 'I live the home life with my heart free' (A. iii, 287; v,331), etc., is said because it was taught there as a [mental] abiding to depend on [constantly] to Mahānāma the Sakyan, who was a Stream-enterer asking about an abiding to depend on. There the meaning is 'I live overcoming . . .'

112. *Freely generous*: liberally generous. *Open-handed*: with hands that are purified. What is meant is: with hands that are always washed in order to give gifts carefully with one's own hands. *That I delight in relinquishing*: the act of relinquishing (*vos-sajjana*) is relinquishing (*vossagga*); the meaning is, giving up. To delight in relinquishing is to delight in constant devotion to that relinquishing. *Expect to be asked* (*yācayoga*): accus-tomed to being asked (*yācana-yogga*) because of giving what-ever others ask for, is the meaning. *Yājayoga* is a reading, in which case the meaning is: devoted (*yutta*) to sacrifice (*yāja*), in other words, to sacrificing (*yajana*). *And rejoice in sharing*: the meaning is, he recollects thus: 'I give gifts and I share out what is to be used by myself, and I rejoice in both.

113. As long as he recollects his own generosity in its special qualities of freedom from stain by avarice, etc., in this way, then 'On that occasion his mind is not obsessed by greed, 'or obsessed by hate, or obsessed by delusion; his mind has 'rectitude on that occasion, being inspired by generosity (A. iii, 287).

So when he has suppressed the hindrances in the way already described (§66), the jhana factors arise in a single conscious moment. But owing to the profundity of the generosity's special qualities, or owing to his being occupied in recollecting the generosity's special qualities of many sorts, the jhana is only access and does not reach absorption. And that access jhana itself is known as 'recollection of generosity' too because it arises with the generosity's special qualities as the means.

114. And when a bhikkhu is devoted to this recollection of generosity, he becomes ever more intent on generosity, his preference is for non-greed, he acts in conformity with loving-kindness, he is fearlesss. He has much happiness and gladness. And if he penetrates no higher, he is at least headed for a happy destiny.

Now when a man is truly wise,
His constant task will surely be
This recollection of his giving
Blessed with such mighty potency.

This is the section dealing with the Recollection of Generosity in the detailed explanation. [225]

*

[(6) Recollection of Deities]

115. One who wants to develop the recollection of deities should possess the special qualities of faith, etc., evoked by means of the noble path, and he should go into solitary retreat and recollect his own special qualities of faith, etc., with deities standing as witnesses, as follows:

'There are Deities of the Realm of the Four Kings (*devā* '*cātumahārājikā*), there are Deities of the Realm of the Thirty 'three (*devā tāvatiṃsā*), there are the Deities who are Gone 'to Divine Bliss (*yāmā*,) ... are Contented (*tusitā*), ... 'Delight in Creating (*nimmānarati*), ... Wield Power Over 'Others' Creations (*paranimmitavasavatti*), there are Deities 'of Brahmā's Retinue (*brahmakāyikā*), there are Deities 'higher than that. And those Deities were possessed of faith 'such that on dying here they were reborn there, and such 'faith is present in me too. And those Deities were possessed 'of virtue ... of learning ... of generosity ... of under'standing such that when they died here they were reborn 'there, and such understanding is present in me too' (A.iii,287).

116. In the Sutta, however, it is said: On the occasion, Mahā-'nāma, on which a noble disciple recollects the faith, the virtue, 'the learning, the generosity, and the understanding, that are 'both his own and those deities', on that occasion his mind is 'not obsessed by greed, . . .' (A,iii,287). Although this is said, it should nevertheless be understood as said for the purpose of showing that the special qualities of faith, etc., in oneself are those in the deities, making the deities stand as witnesses. For it is said definitely in the Commentary 'He recollects his own special qualities, making the deities stand as witnesses'.

117. As long as in the prior stage he recollects the deities' special qualities of faith, etc., and in the later stage he recollects the special qualities of faith, etc., existing in himself, then 'On that occasion his mind is not obsessed by greed, 'or obsessed by hate, or obsessed by delusion, his mind 'has rectitude on that occasion, being inspired by deities' (A.iii,288).

So when he has suppressed the hindrances in the way already stated (§66), the jhana factors arise in a single conscious moment. But owing to the profundity of the special qualities of faith, etc., or owing to his being occupied in recollecting special qualities of many sorts, the jhana is only access and does not reach absorption. And that access jhana itself is known as 'recollection of deities' too because it arises with the deities' special qualities as the means. [226]

118. And when a bhikkhu is devoted to this recollection of deities, he becomes dearly loved by deities. He obtains even greater fullness of faith. He has much happiness and gladness. And if he penetrates no higher, he is at least headed for a happy destiny.

Now when a man is truly wise,
His constant task will surely be
This recollection of deities
Blessed with such mighty potency

This is the section dealing with the Recollection of Deities in the detailed explanation.

*

[General]

119. Now in setting forth the detail of these recollections, after the words 'His mind has rectitude on that occasion, being 'inspired by the Perfect One', it is added 'When a noble 'disciple's mind has rectitude, Mahānāma, the meaning 'inspires him, the law inspires him, and the application

'of the law makes him glad. When he is glad, happi-'ness is born in him' (A.iii,285–8). Herein, *the meaning inspires* him should be understood as said of contentment inspired by the meaning beginning 'This blessed One is such since he is . . .' (§2). *The law inspires him* is said of contentment inspired by the text. The *application* of the *law makes him glad* is said of both (cf.MA.i, 173).

120. And when in the case of the recollection of Deities *inspired by deities* is said, this should be understood as said either of the consciousness that occurs in the prior stage inspired by deities or of the consciousness [that occurs in the later stage] inspired by the special qualities that are similar to those of the deities and are productive of the deities' state (cf. §117).

121. These six recollections succeed only in noble disciples. For the special qualities of the Enlightened One, the Law, and the Community, are evident to them; and they possess the virtue with the special qualities of untornness, etc., the generosity that is free from stain by avarice, and the special qualities of faith, etc., similar to those of deities.

122. And in the Mahānāma Sutta (A.iii,285f.) they are expounded in detail by the Blessed One in order to show to a Stream-enterer an abiding to depend upon when he asked for one.

123. Also in the Gedha Sutta they are expounded in order that a noble disciple should purify his consciousness by means of the recollections and so attain further purification in the ultimate sense thus: 'Here, bhikkhus, a noble disciple 'recollects the Perfect One in this way: That Blessed One 'is such since he is accomplished, . . . His mind has rectitude 'on that occasion. He has renounced, [227] got free from, 'emerged from cupidity. Cupidity, bhikkhus, is a term for 'the five cords of sense desire. Some beings gain purity 'here by making this [recollection] their prop' (A.iii,312).

124. And in the Sambādhokāsa Sutta taught by the venerable Mahā-Kaccāna they are expounded as the realization of the wide open through the susceptibility of purification that exists in the ultimate sense only in a noble disciple thus: 'It is 'wonderful, friends, it is marvellous how the realization of the 'wide-open in the crowded [house life] has been discovered 'by the Blessed One who knows and sees, accomplished and 'fully enlightened, for the purification of beings, [for] the 'surmounting of sorrow and lamentation, for the ending of 'pain and grief, for the attainment of the true way,] for the 'realization of nibbana, that is to say, the six stations of re-'collection. What six? Here, friends, a noble disciple recollects 'the Perfect One, . . . Some beings are susceptible of puri-'fication here in this way' (A. iii, 314–5).

125. Also in the Uposatha Sutta they are expounded, in order to show the greatness of the fruit of the Uposatha, as a mind-purifying meditation subject for a noble disciple who is observing the Uposatha; 'And what is the Noble Ones' 'Uposatha, Visākhā? It is the gradual cleansing of the mind 'still sullied by imperfections. And what is the gradual 'cleansing of the mind still sullied by imperfections? Here, 'Visākhā, a noble disciple recollects the Perfect One...' (A. i, 206–11).

126. And in the Book of Elevens, when a noble disciple has asked 'Venerable sir, in what way should we abide who abide 'various ways?' (A. v. 328), they are expounded to him in order to show the way of abiding in this way: 'One who has 'faith is successful, Mahānāma, not one who has no faith. 'One who is energetic ... One whose mindfulness is estab-'lished ... One who is concentrated ... One who has under-'standing is successful, Mahānāma, not one who has no under-'standing. Having established yourself in these five things, 'Mahānāma, you should develop six things. Here, Mahānāma, you should recollect the Perfect One; That Blessed 'One is such since ...' (A. v. 329—32).

127. Still, though this is so, they can be brought to mind by an ordinary man too, if he possesses the special qualities of purified virtue, and the rest. [228] For when he is recollecting the special qualities of the Buddha, etc., even only according to hearsay, his consciousness settles down, in virtue of which the hindrances are suppressed. In his supreme gladness he initiates insight, and he even attains to Arahantship, like the Elder Phussadeva who dwelt at Kaṭakandhakāra.

128. That venerable one, it seems, saw a figure of the Enlightened One created by Māra. He thought 'How good this appears despite its having greed, hate and delusion! What can the Blessed One's goodness have been like? for he was quite without greed, hate and delusion!' he acquired happiness with the Blessed One as object, and by augmenting his insight he reached Arahantship.

The seventh chapter called 'The Description of Six Recollections' in the Treatise on the Development of Concentration in the Path of Purification composed for the purpose of gladdening good people.

CHAPTER VIII

DESCRIPTION OF CONCENTRATION —OTHER RECOLLECTIONS AS MEDITATION SUBJECTS

(*Anussati-kammaṭṭhāna-niddesa*)

[(7) MINDFULNESS OF DEATH]

1. [229] Now comes the description of the development of Mindfulness of Death, which was listed next (Ch. III, § 105).

[*Definitions*]

Herein, *death* (*maraṇa*) is the interruption of the life faculty included within [the limits of] a single becoming (existence). But death as termination (cutting off), in other words, the Arahant's termination of the suffering of the round, is not intended here, nor is momentary death, in other words, the momentary dissolution of formations, nor the 'death' of conventional (metaphorical) usage in such expressions as 'dead tree', 'dead metal', and so on.

2. As intended here it is of two kinds, that is to say, timely death and untimely death. Herein, *timely death* comes about with the exhaustion of merit or with the exhaustion of a life span or with both. *Untimely death* comes about through kamma that interrupts [other, life-producing,] kamma.

3. Herein, death through *exhaustion of merit* is a term for the kind of death that comes about only owing to the result of [former] rebirth-producing kamma's having finished ripening although favourable conditions for prolonging the continuity of a life span may be still present. Death through *exhaustion of a life span* is a term for the kind of death that comes about owing to the exhaustion of the normal life span of men of today, which measures only a century owing to want of such excellence in destiny [as deities have] or in time [as there is at the beginning of an aeon] or in nutriment [as the Uttarakurūs and so on have]. [1] *Untimely death* is a term for the death of those whose continuity is interrupted by kamma capable of causing them to fall (*cāvana*) from their place at that very moment, as in the case of Dūsi-Māra (see M. i, 337), Kalāburājā (see Jā. iii, 39), etc.,[2] or for the death of those whose [life's] continuity is interrupted by assaults with

---

1. Amplifications are from Pm., p. 236.
2. 'The word "etc." includes Nanda-yakkha, Nanda-māṇava, and others' (Pm. 236). See AA. Commentary to A. Dukanipāta I, 3. and MA. iv, 8.

weapons, etc., due to previous kamma. [230] All these are included under the interruption of the life faculty of the kinds already stated. So Mindfulness of Death is the remembering of death, in other words, of the interruption of the life faculty.

[*Development*]

4. One who wants to develop this should go into solitary retreat and exercise attention wisely in this way: 'Death will take place; the life faculty will be interrupted', or 'Death, death'.

5. If he exercises his attention unwisely in recollecting the [possible] death of an agreeable person, sorrow arises, as in a mother on recollecting the death of her beloved child she bore; and gladness arises in recollecting the death of a disagreeable person, as in enemies on recollecting the death of their enemies; and no sense of urgency arises on recollecting the death of neutral people, as happens in a corpse-burner on seeing a dead body; and anxiety arises on recollecting one's own death, as happens in a timid person on seeing a murderer with a poised dagger.

6. In all that there is neither mindfulness nor sense of urgency nor knowledge. So he should look here and there at beings that have been killed or have died, and advert to the death of beings already dead but formerly seen enjoying good things, doing so with mindfulness, with a sense of urgency and with knowledge, after which he can exercise his attention in the way beginning 'Death will take place'. By so doing he exercises it wisely. He exercises it as a [right] means, is the meaning.[3]

7. When some exercise it merely in this way, their hindrances get suppressed, their mindfulness becomes established with death as its object, and the meditation subject reaches access.

[*Eight Ways of Recollecting Death*]

8. But one who finds that it does not get so far should do his recollecting of death in eight ways, that is to say: (1) as having the appearance of a murderer, (2) as the ruin of success, (3) by comparison, (4) as to sharing the body with many, (5) as to the frailty of life, (6) as signless, (7) as to the limitedness of the extent, (8) as to the shortness of the moment.

9. 1. Herein, *as having the appearance of a murderer*: he should do his recollecting thus, 'Just as a murderer appears with a sword, thinking "I shall cut this man's head off", and applies it to his neck, so death appears'. Why? Because it comes with birth and it takes away life.

10. As budding toadstools always come up lifting dust on their tops, so beings are born along with ageing and death. For

3. For the expression '*upāya-manasikāra*—attention as a [right] means' see MA. i, 64.

accordingly their rebirth-linking consciousness reaches ageing immediately next to its arising and then breaks up together with its associated aggregates, like a stone that falls from the summit of a rock. [231] So to begin with, momentary death comes along with birth. But death is inevitable for what is born ; consequently the kind of death intended here

11. also comes along with birth. Therefore, just as the risen sun moves on towards its setting and never turns back even for a little while from wherever it has got to, or just as a mountain torrent sweeps by with a rapid current, ever flowing and rushing on and never turning back even for a little while, so too this living being travels on towards death from the time when he is born, and he never turns back even for a little while. Hence it is said :

> 'Right from the very day a man has been conceived inside a womb
> 'He cannot but go on and on, nor going can he once turn back'
>
> (Jā. iv, 494).

12. And whilst he goes on thus death is as near to him as drying up is to rivulets in the summer heat, as falling is to the fruits of trees when the sap reaches their attachments in the morning, as breaking is to clay pots tapped by a mallet, as vanishing is to dew-drops touched by the sun's rays. Hence it is said:

> 'The nights and days go slipping by
> 'As life keeps dwindling steadily
> 'Till mortals' span, like water pools
> 'In failing rills, is all used up' (S. i, 109).
> 'As there is fear, when fruits are ripe,
> 'That in the morning they will fall,
> 'So mortals are in constant fear,
> 'When they are born, that they will die.
> 'And as the fate of pots of clay
> 'Once fashioned by the potter's hand,
> 'Or small or big or baked or raw,[4]
> 'Condemns them to be broken up,
> 'So mortals' life leads but to death' (Sn.576-7).
> 'The dew-drop on the blade of grass
> 'Vanishes when the sun comes up ;
> 'Such is a human span of life ;
> 'So, mother, do not hinder me' (Jā. iv, 122).

13. So this death, which comes along with birth, is like a murderer with poised sword. And, like the murderer who applies the sword to the neck, it carries off life and never returns to bring it back. [232] That is why, since death appears like a

---

4. This line is not in the Sutta-nipāta, but see D. ii, 120, note.

murderer with poised sword owing to its coming along with birth and carrying off life, it should be recollected as 'having the appearance of a murderer'.

14. 2. *As the ruin of success*: here success shines as long as failure does not overcome it. And the success does not exist that might endure out of reach of failure. Accordingly,

'He gave with joy a hundred millions
'After conquering all the earth,
'Till in the end his realm came down
'To less than half a gall-nut's worth.
'Yet when his merit was used up,
'His body breathing its last breath,
'The Sorrowless Asoka too[5]
'Felt sorrow face to face with death',

15. Furthermore, all health ends in sickness, all youth ends in ageing, all life ends in death; all worldly existence is procured by birth, haunted by ageing, surprised by sickness, and struck down by death. Hence it is said:

'As though huge mountains made of rock
'So vast they reached up to the sky
'Were to advance from every side,
'Grinding beneath them all that lives,
'So age and death roll over all,
'Warriors, priests, merchants, and craftsmen,
'The outcastes and the scavengers,
'Crushing all beings, sparing none.
'And here no troops of elephants,
'No charioteers, no infantry,
'No strategy in form of spells,
'No riches, serve to beat them off' (S. i, 102).

This is how death should be recollected as the 'ruin of success' by defining it as death's final ruining of life's success.

16. 3. *By comparison*: by comparing oneself to others. Herein, death should be recollected by comparison in seven ways, that is to say: with those of great fame, with those of great merit, with those of great strength, with those of great supernormal power, with those of great understanding, with Pacceka Buddhas, with fully enlightened Buddhas. How? [233]

17. Although Mahāsammata, Mandhātu, Mahāsudassana, Daḷhanemi, Nimi,[6] etc.,[7] were greatly famous and had a great

5. The Emperor Asoka is referred to. His name Asoka means 'Sorrowless'. This story is in the Asokāvadāna and Divya p. 429–434.

6. The references for the names here and in the following paragraphs are: Mahāsammata (Jā. iii, 454; ii, 311). Mandhātu (Jā. ii, 311), Mahāsudassana (D. ii, 169f.), Daḷhanemi (D. iii, 59f.), Nimi (Jā. vi, 96f.), Jotika (Ch. XII, §41), Jaṭila (Ch. XII, §41), Ugga (AA. i, 394), Meṇḍaka (Ch. XII, §41–2), Puṇṇaka (Ch. XII, §42), Vāsudeva (Jā. iv, 81f.), Baladeva (Jā. iv, 81f.), Bhīmasena (Jā. v, 426), Yuddhiṭṭhila (Jā. v, 426), Cāṇura (Jā. iv, 81).

7. '-ppabhuti—etc.': this meaning is not in P.T.S. Dict.; see §121.

following, and though they had amassed enormous wealth, yet death inevitably caught up with them at length, so how shall it not at length overtake me ?

Great kings like Mahāsammata,
Whose fame did spread so mightily,
All fell into death's power too;
What can be said of those like me ?

It should be recollected in this way, firstly, by comparison *with those of great fame*.

18. How by comparison *with those of great merit*?

Jotika, Jaṭila, Ugga,
And Meṇḍaka, and Puṇṇaka,
These, the world said, and others too
Did live most meritoriously;
Yet they came one and all to death;
What can be said of those like me?

It should be recollected in this way by comparison with those of great merit.

19. How by comparison *with those of great strength*?

Vāsudeva, Baladeva,
Bhīmasena, Yuddhiṭṭhila,
And Cāṇura the wrestler,
Were in the Exterminator's power.
Throughout the world they were renowned
As blessed with strength so mightily ;
They too went to the realm of death ;
What can be said of those like me?

It should be recollected in this way by comparison with those of great strength.

20. How by comparison *with those of great supernormal power*?

The second of the Chief Disciples,
The foremost in miraculous powers,
Who with the point of his great toe
Did rock Vejayanta's Palace towers,
Like a deer in a lion's jaw, he too,
Despite miraculous potency,
Fell in the dreadful jaws of death;
What can be said of those like me?

It should be recollected in this way by comparison with those of great supernormal power.

21. How by comparison *with those of great understanding*? [234]

The first of the two chief disciples
Did so excel in wisdom's art
That, save the Helper of the World,
No being is worth his sixteenth part.
But though so great was Sāriputta's

Understanding faculty,
He fell into death's power too;
What can be said of those like me?

It should be recollected in this way by comparison with those of great understanding.

22. How by comparison *with Pacceka Buddhas*? Even those who by the strength of their own knowledge and energy crushed all the enemy defilements and reached enlightenment for themselves, who [stood alone] like the horn of the rhinoceros (see Sn. 35f.), who were self-perfected, were still not free from death. So how should I be free from it?

To help them in their search for truth
The Sages various signs employed,
Their knowledge brought them self-perfection,
Their cankers were at length destroyed.

Like the rhinoceros's horn
They lived alone in constancy,
But death they could no wise evade;
What can be said of those like me?

It should be recollected in this way by comparison *with Pacceka Buddhas*.

23. How by comparison *with fully enlightened Buddhas*? Even the Blessed One, whose material body was embellished with the eighty lesser details and adorned with the thirty-two marks of a great man (see M. Sutta 91, D. Sutta 30), whose Dhamma body brought to perfection the treasured qualities of the aggregates of virtue, etc.,[8] made pure in every aspect, who overpassed greatness of fame, greatness of merit, greatness of strength, greatness of supernormal power and greatness of understanding, who had no equal, who was the equal of those without equal, without double, accomplished and fully enlightened,—even he was suddenly quenched by the downpour of death's rain, as a great mass of fire is quenched by the downpour of a rain of water.

And so the Greatest Sage possessed
Such mighty power in every way,
And it was not through fear or guilt
That over him Death held his sway.
No being, not even one without
Guilt or pusillanimity
But will be smitten down; so how
Will he not conquer those like me?

It should be recollected in this way by comparison with fully enlightened Buddhas.

---

8. Virtue, concentration, understanding, deliverance, knowledge and vision of deliverance.

24. When he does his recollecting in this way by comparing himself with others possessed of such great fame, etc., in the light of the universality of death, thinking 'Death will come to me even as it did to those distinguished beings', then his meditation subject reaches access.

This is how death should be recollected by comparison. [235]

25. 4. *As to the sharing of the body with many*: this body is shared by many. Firstly, it is shared by the eighty families of worms. There too, creatures live in dependence on the outer skin, feeding on the outer skin; creatures live in dependence on the inner skin, feeding on the inner skin; creatures live in dependence on the flesh, feeding on the flesh; creatures live in dependence on the sinews, feeding on the sinews; creatures live in dependence on the bones, feeding on the bones; and creatures live in dependence on the marrow, feeding on the marrow. And there they are born, grow old and die, evacuate, and make water; and the body is their maternity home, their hospital, their charnel ground, their privy and their urinal. The body can also be brought to death with the upsetting of these worms. And just as it is shared with the eighty families of worms, so too it is shared by the several hundred internal diseases, as well as by such external causes of death as snakes, scorpions, and what not.

26. And just as when a target is set up at a cross-roads and then arrows, spears, pikes, stones, etc., come from all directions and fall upon it, so too all kinds of accidents befall the body, and it also comes to death through these accidents befalling it. Hence the Blessed One said: 'Here, bhikkhus, when day is 'departing and night drawing on[9] a bhikkhu considers thus: 'In many ways I can risk death. A snake may bite me, 'or a scorpion may sting me, or a centipede may sting 'me. I might die of that, and that would set me back. Or 'I might stumble and fall, or the food I have eaten might 'disagree with me, or my bile might get upset, or my phlegm 'might get upset, or the forces (winds) [in my limbs] might 'get upset [and sever my joints as it were] like knives. I 'might die of that, and that would set me back' (A. iii, 306).

That is how death should be recollected as to sharing the body with many.

27. 5. *As to the frailty of life*: this life is impotent and frail. For the life of beings is bound up with breathing, it is bound up with the postures, it is bound up with cold and heat, it is bound up with the primary elements, and it is bound up with nutriment.

---

9. '*Paṭihitāya* drawing on': not in P. T. S. Dict.; Pm. (P.240) reads *paṇitāya* and explains by *paccāgatāya* (come back).

28. Life occurs only when the in-breaths and out-breaths occur evenly. But when the wind in the nostrils that has gone outside does not go in again, or when that which has gone inside does not come out again, then a man is reckoned to be dead.

And it occurs only when the four postures are found occurring evenly. [236] But with the prevailing of any one of them the life process is interrupted.

And it occurs only when cold and heat are found occurring evenly. But it fails when a man is overcome by excessive cold or heat.

And it occurs only when the four primary elements are found occurring evenly. But with the disturbance of the earth element even a strong man's life can be terminated if his body becomes rigid, or with the disturbance of one of the elements beginning with water if his body becomes flaccid and putrifies with a flux of the bowels, etc., or if he is consumed by a bad fever, or if he suffers a severing of his limb-joint ligatures (cf.Ch.XI,§102).

And life occurs only in one who gets physical nutriment at the proper time; but if he gets none, he uses his life up.

This is how death should be recollected as to the frailty of life.

29. 6. *As signless*: as indefinable. The meaning is that it is unpredictable. For in the case of all beings,

> The span, the sickness, and the time, and where
> The body will be laid, the destiny:
> The living world can never know[10] these things;
> There is no sign foretells when they will be.

30. Herein, firstly *the span* has no sign because there is no definition such as: just so much must be lived, no more than that. For beings [die in the various stages of the embryo, namely], at the time of the *kalala*, of the *abbuda*, of the *pesi*, of the *ghana*, at one month gone, two months gone, three months gone, four months gone, five months gone . . . ten months gone, and on the occasion of coming out of the womb. And after that they die this side or the other of the century.

31. And *the sickness* has no sign because there is no definition such as: Beings die only of this sickness, not of any other. For beings die of eye disease or of any one among those beginning with ear disease (see A. v, 110).

32. And *the time* has no sign because there is no definition such as: One has to die only at this time, not at any other. For beings die in the morning and at any of the other times such as noon.

10. '*Ñāyare*—can know': form not in P. T. S. Dict.; Pm. explains by *ñāyanti*.

33. And *where the body will be laid down* has no sign because there is no definition such as: When people die, they must drop their bodies only here, not anywhere else. For the person of those born inside a village is dropped outside the village, and that of those born outside the village is dropped inside it. Likewise that of those born on water is dropped on land, and that of those born on land on water. And this can be multiplied in many ways. [237]

34. And *the destiny* has no sign because there is no definition such as: One who dies there must be reborn here. For there are some who die in a divine world and are reborn in the human world, and there are some who die in the human world and are reborn in a divine world, and so on. And in this way the world goes round and round the five kinds of destinies like an ox harnessed to a machine.

This is how death should be recollected as signless.

35. 7. *As to the limitedness of the extent*: the extent of human life is short now. One who lives long lives a hundred years, more or less. Hence the Blessed One said: 'Bhikkhus, 'this human life span is short. There is a new life to be gone 'to, there are profitable [deeds] to be done, there is the life 'of purity to be led. There is no not dying for the born. 'He who lives long lives a hundred years, more or less . . .

'The life of human kind is short;
'A wise man holds it in contempt
'And acts as one whose head is burning;
'Death will never fail to come' (S. i, 108).

And he said further: 'Bhikkhus, there was once a teacher called Araka '. . .' (A. iv, 136), all of which sutta should be given in full, adorned as it is with seven similes.

36. And he said further: 'Bhikkhus, when a bhikkhu develops 'mindfulness of death thus, "Oh let me live a night and day 'that I may attend to the Blessed One's teaching, surely 'much could be done by me", and when a bhikkhu develops 'mindfulness of death thus, "Oh let me live a day that I may 'attend to the Blessed One's teaching, surely much could be 'done by me", and when a bhikkhu develops mindfulness of 'death thus, "Oh let me live as long as it takes to eat a meal 'that I may attend to the Blessed One's teaching, surely much 'could be done by me", and when a bhikkhu develops mind-'fulness of death thus, "Oh let me live as long as it takes to 'chew and swallow four or five mouthfuls that I may attend 'to the Blessed One's teaching, surely much could be done 'by me",—these are called bhikkhus who dwell in negligence 'and slackly develop mindfulness of death for the destruction 'of cankers. [238]

37. 'And, bhikkhus, when a bhikkhu develops mindfulness of 'death thus, "Oh let me live for as long as it takes to chew and

'swallow a single mouthful that I may attend to the Blessed 'One's teaching, surely much could be done by me", and when 'a bhikkhu develops mindfulness of death thus, "Oh let me 'live as long as it takes to breathe in and breathe out, or as 'long as it takes to breathe out and breathe in that I 'may attend to the Blessed One's teaching, surely much 'could be done by me",—these are called bhikkhus who dwell 'in diligence and keenly develop mindfulness of death for the 'destruction of cankers' (A.iii,305-6).

38. So short in fact is the extent of life that it is not certain even for as long as it takes to chew and swallow four or five mouthfuls.

This is how death should be recollected as to the limitedness of the extent.

39. 8. *As to the shortness of the moment*: in the ultimate sense the life-moment of living beings is extremely short, being only as much as the occurrence of a single conscious moment. Just as a chariot wheel, when it is rolling, rolls, [that is, touches the ground,] only on one point of [the circumference of] its tyre, and, when it is at rest, rests only on one point, so too, the life of living beings lasts only for a single conscious moment. When that consciousness has ceased, the being is said to have ceased, according as it is said: 'In a past conscious moment he did 'live, not he does live, not he will live. In a future conscious 'moment not he did live, not he does live, he will live. In 'the present conscious moment not he did live, he does live, 'not he will live.

' "Life, person, pleasure, pain—just these alone
' "Join in one conscious moment that flicks by.
' "Ceased aggregates of those dead or alive
' "Are all alike, gone never to return
' "No [world is] born if [consciousness is] not
' "Produced; when that is present, then it lives;
' "When consciousness dissolves, the world is dead:
' "The highest sense this concept will allow" '(NdI.42).[11]

11. ' "Person (*atta-bhāva*)" is the states other than the already-mentioned life, feeling and consciousness. The words "*just these alone*" mean that it is unmixed with self (*attā*) or permanence' (Pm. 242). *Atta-bhāva* as used in the Suttas and in this work is more or less a synonym for *sakkāya* in the sense of person (body and mind) or personality, or individual form. See Pitaka refs. in P. T. S. Dict. and *e.g.* this chapter §35 and Ch. IX, §54. ' "*When consciousness dissolves, the world is dead*": just as in the case of the death-consciousness, this world is also called "dead" in the highest (ultimate) sense with the arrival of any consciousness whatever at its dissolution, since its cessation has no rebirth-linking (is "cessation never to return"). Nevertheless though this is so, "*the highest sense this concept will allow* (*paññatti paramatthiyā*)" —the ultimate sense will allow this concept of continuity, which is what the expression of common usage "Tissa lives, Phussa lives" refers to, and which is based on consciousnesses [momentarily] existing along with a physical support; this belongs to the ulti-

This is how death should be recollected as to the shortness of the moment.

[*Conclusion*]

40. So while he does his recollecting by means of one or other of these eight ways, his consciousness acquires [the support of] repetition owing to the reiterated attention, mindfulness settles down with death as its object, the hindrances are

---

mate sense here, since, as they say, "It is not the name and surname that lives'" (Pm. 242 and 801).

Something may be said about the word *paññatti* here. Twenty-four kinds are dealt with in the Commentary to the Puggalapaññatti. The Puggalapaññatti Schedule gives the following six *paññatti* (here a making known a setting out): of aggregates, bases, elements, truths, faculties, and persons (Pug. 1). The Commentary explains the word in this sense as *paññāpana* (making known) and *thapana* (placing,) quoting 'He announces, teaches, declares (*paññāpeti*), establishes' (cf. M. iii, 248) and also 'a well-appointed (*supaññatta*) bed and chair' ( ). It continues: 'The making known of a name (*nāma-paññatti*) shows such and such dhammas and places them in such and such compartments, while the making known of the aggregates (*khandha-paññatti*) and the rest shows in brief the individual form of those makings-known (*paññatti*)'. It then gives six kinds of *paññatti* 'according to the commentarial method but not in the texts': (1) *Concept of the existent* (*vijjamāna-pannññatti*), which is the conceptualizing of (making known, a dhamma that is existent, actual, become, in the true and ultimate sense (e.g. aggregates, etc.). (2) *Concept of the non-existent*, which is, for example, the conceptualizing of 'female', 'male', 'persons', etc., which are non-existent by that standard and are only established by means of current speech in the world; similarly 'such impossibilities as concepts of a fifth Truth or the other sectarians' Atom, Primordial Essence, World Soul, and the like'. (3) *Concept of the non-existent based on the existent*, e. g., the expression 'One with the three clear-visions', where the 'person' ('one') is non-existent and the 'clear-visions', are existent. (4) *Concept of the existent based on the non-existent*, e. g., the 'female form', 'visible form'. (=visible datum base) being existent and 'female' non-existent. (5) *Concept of the existant based on the existent*, e. g., 'eye contact', both 'eye' and 'contact' being existent. (6) *Concept of the non-existent based on the non-existent*, e. g., 'banker's son', both being non-existent. Again two more sets of six are given as 'according to the Teachers, but not in the Commentaries'. The first is: (1) *Derivative concept* (*upādā-paññatti*); this for instance, is a 'being', which is a convention derived from the aggregates of materiality, feeling, etc., though it has no individual essence of its own apprehendable in the true ultimate sense, as materiality, say, has in its self-identity and its otherness from feeling, etc.; or 'a house' or a 'fist' or an 'oven' as apart from its component parts, or a 'pitcher' or a 'garment', which are all derived from those same aggregates; or 'time' or 'direction,' which are derived from the revolutions of the moon and sun; or the 'learning sign' or 'counterpart sign' founded on some aspect or other, which are a convention derived from some real sign as a benefit of meditative development: these are derived concepts, and this kind is a 'concept (*paññatti*)' in the sense of 'ability to be set up (*paññapetabba*=ability to be conceptualized)', but not in the sense of 'making known (*paññāpana*)'. Under the latter heading this would be a 'concept of the non-existent'. (2) *Appositional Concept* (*upanidhā-p.*): many varieties are listed, namely, Apposition of Reference ('second' as against 'first', 'third' as against 'second', 'long' as against 'short'), Apposition of What is in the Hand ('umbrella-in-hand', 'knife-in-hand'),

suppressed, and the jhana factors make their appearance. But since the object is states with individual essences,[12] and since it awakes a sense of urgency, the jhana does not reach absorption and is only access. [239] Now with special development the supramundane jhana and the second and the fourth immaterial jhanas reach absorption even with respect to states with individual essences. For the supramundane reaches absorption by means of progressive development of the Purifications and the immaterial jhanas do so by means of development consisting in the surmounting of the object (see Ch. X) since there [in those two immaterial jhanas] there is merely the surmounting of the object of jhana that had already reached absorption. But here [in mundane mindfulness of death] there is neither, so the jhana only reaches access. And that access is known as 'mindfulness of death' too since it arises through its means.

41. A bhikkhu devoted to mindfulness of death is constantly diligent. He acquires perception of disenchantment with all kinds of becoming (existence). He conquers attachment to life. He condemns evil. He avoids much storing. He has no

---

Apposition of Association ('earring-wearer', 'topknot-wearer', 'crest-wearer'), Apposition of Contents ('Corn-waggon', 'ghee-pot'), Apposition of Proximity ('Indasālā Cave', 'Piyangu Cave'), Apposition of Comparison ('golden coloured', 'with a bull's gait'), Apposition of Majority ('Padumassara-Brahman Village'), Apposition of Distinction ('diamond ring'); and so on. (3) *Collective Concept* (*samodhāna-p*·), e. g., 'eight-footed', 'pile of riches', (4) *Additive Concept* (*upanikkhitta-p.*), e. g., 'one', 'two', 'three'. (5) *Verisimilar Concept* (*tajjāp.*): refers to the individual essence of a given dhamma, e. g., 'earth', 'fire': 'hardness', 'heat'. (6) *Continuity Concept* (*santati-p.*): refers to the length of continuity of life, e. g., 'octagenarian,' 'nonagenarian'. In the second set there are: (i) *Concept According to Function* (*kicca-p.*), e. g., 'preacher' 'expounder of dhamma'. (ii) *Concept According to Shape* (*saṇṭhāna-p*), e. g., 'thin', 'stout'. 'round', 'square'. (iii) *Concept According to gender* (*liṅga-p.*), e. g., 'female', 'male', (iv) *Concept According to Location* (*bhūmi-p.*), e. g., 'of the sense sphere', 'Kosalan'. (v) *Concept as Proper Name* (*paccatta-p.*), e. g., 'Tissa', 'Nāga', 'Sumana', which are makings-known (appellations) by mere name-making. (vi) *Concept of the Unformed* (*asaṅkhata-paññatti*), e. g., 'cessation', 'nibbana', etc., which make the unformed dhamma known—an existent concept (From Commentary to Puggalapaññatti, condensed—see also DhsA. 390f.). All this shows that the word *paññatti* carries the meanings of *either* appellation *or* concept *or* both together, and that no English word quite corresponds.

12. ' "*But since the object is state with individual essences*": the break up of states with individual essences, their destruction, their fall,—[all] that has to do only with states with individual essences. Hence the Blessed One said "Bhikkhus, ageing-and-death is impermanent, formed, dependently arisen" (S. ii, 26) . . .If it cannot reach obsorption because of [its object being] states with individual essences, then what about the supramundane jhanas and certain of the immaterial jhanas? It was to answer this that he said "now with special development the supramundane jhana" and so on' (Pm. 243). Kasina jhana, for example, has a concept (*paññatti*) as its object (Ch. IV. §29) and a concept is a dhamma without individual essence (*asabhāva-dhamma*).

stain of avarice about requisites. Perception of impermanence grows in him, following upon which there appear the perceptions of pain and not-self. But while beings who have not developed [mindfulness of] death fall victims to fear, horror and confusion at the time of death as though suddenly seized by wild beasts, spirits, snakes, robbers, or murderers, he dies undeluded and fearless without falling into any such state. And if he does not attain the deathless here and now, he is at least headed for a happy destiny on the break up of the body.

Now when a man is truly wise,
His constant task will surely be
This recollection about death
Blessed with such mighty potency.

This is the section dealing with the recollection of death in the detailed explanation.

*

[(8) MINDFULNESS OCCUPIED WITH THE BODY]

42. Now comes the description of the development of Mindfulness Occupied with the Body as a meditation subject, which is never promulgated except after an Enlightened One's arising, and is outside the province of any sectarians. It has been commended by the Blessed One in various ways in different suttas thus, 'Bhikkhus, when one thing is developed and repeatedly practised, it leads to a supreme sense of urgency, to supreme benefit, to supreme surcease of bondage, to supreme mindfulness and full-awareness, to acquisition of knowledge and vision, to a happy life here and now, to realization of the fruit of clear vision and deliverance. What is that one thing? It is mindfulness occupied with the body' (A.i,43) and thus, 'Bhikkhus, they savour the deathless who savour mindfulness occupied with the body; they do not savour the deathless who do not savour mindfulness occupied with the body.[13] [240] They have savoured the deathless who have savoured mindfulness occupied with the body; they have not savoured ...They have neglected... they have not neglected...They have missed...they have found the deathless who have found mindfulness occupied with the body' (A.i.45). And it has been described in fourteen sections in the passage beginning 'And how developed, bhikkhu, how repeatedly practised is mindfulness occupied with the body of great fruit, of great benefit? Here, bhikkhus, bhikkhu, gone to the forest...' (M.iii, 89), that is to say, the sections on breathing, on postures, on the four kinds of full-awareness, on attention directed

13. In the A. text the negative and positive clauses are in the opposite order.

to repulsiveness, on attention directed to elements, and on the nine charnel-ground contemplations.

43. Herein, the three, that is to say, the sections on postures, on the four kinds of full-awareness (see MA, i,253f.), and on attention directed to elements, as they are stated [in that sutta], deal with insight. Then the nine sections on the charnel-ground contemplations, as stated there, deal with that particular phase of insight knowledge called Contemplation of Danger. And any development of concentration in the bloated, etc., that might be implied there has already been explained in the Description of Foulness (Ch. VI). So there are only the two that is, the sections on breathing and on directing attention to repulsiveness, that, as stated there, deal with concentration. Of these two, the section on breathing is a separate meditation subject, namely Mindfulness of Breathing.

[*Text*]

44. What is intended here as Mindfulness Occupied with the Body is the thirty-two aspects. This meditation subject is taught as the direction of attention to repulsiveness thus: 'Again, bhikkhus, a bhikkhu reviews this body, up from the 'soles of the feet and down from the top of the hair and con- 'tained in the skin as full of many kinds of filth thus: In this 'body there are head hairs, body hairs, nails, teeth, skin, 'flesh, sinews, bones, bone-marrow, kidney, heart, liver, 'midriff, spleen, lights, bowels, entrails, gorge, dung, bile, 'phlegm, pus, blood, sweet, fat, tears, grease, spittle, snot, oil 'of the joints, and urine' (M.iii,90), the brain being included in the bone marrow in this version [with a total of only thirty-one aspects].

45. Here is the description of the development introduced by a commentary on the text.

[*Word Commentary*]

This body: this filthy body constructed out of the four primary elements. *Up from the soles of the feet*: from the soles of the feet upwards. *Down from the top of the hair*: from the highest part of the hair downwards. *Contained in the skin:* terminated all round by the skin. *Reviews. . .as full of many kinds of filth*: [241] he sees that this body is packed with the filth of various kinds beginning with head hairs. How? 'In this body there are head hairs. . . .urine'.

46. Herein, *there are* means, there are found. *In this*: in this, which is expressed thus 'Up from the soles of the feet and down from the top of the hair and contained in the skin, as full of many kinds of filth'. *Body*: the carcase; for it is the carcase that is called 'body (*kāya*)' because it is a conglomeration of filth, because such vile (*kucchita*) things as the

head hairs, etc., and the hundred deseases beginning with eye disease, have it as their origin (*āya*).

Head hairs, body hairs: these things beginning with head hairs are the thirty-two aspects. The construction here should be understood in this way: In this body there are head hairs, in this body there are body hairs.

47. No one who searches throughout the whole of this fathom-long carcase, starting upwards from the soles of the feet, starting downwards from the top of the head, and starting from the skin all round, ever finds even the minutest atom at all beautiful in it, such as a pearl, or a gem, or beryl, or aloes,[14] or saffron, or camphor, or talcum powder; on the contrary he finds nothing but the various very malodorous, offensive, drab-looking sort of filth consisting of the head hairs, body hairs, and the rest. Hence it is said: 'In this body there are head hairs, body hairs. . .urine'.

This is the commentary on the word-construction here.

[*Development*]

48. Now a clansman who, as a beginner, wants to develop this meditation subject should go to a good friend of the kind already described (Ch.III,§61-73) and learn it. And the teacher who expounds it to him should tell him the sevenfold skill in learning and the tenfold skill in giving attention.

[*The Sevenfold Skill in Learning*]

Herein, the sevenfold skill in learning should be told thus: (1) as verbal recitation, (2) as mental recitation, (3) as to colour, (4) as to shape, (5) as to direction, (6) as to location, (7) as to delimitation.

49. 1. This meditation subject consists in giving attention to repulsiveness. Even if one is master of the Tipitaka, the *verbal recitation* should still be done at the time of first giving it attention. For the meditation subject only becomes evident to some through recitation, as it did to the two elders who learned the meditation subject from the Elder Mahā-Deva of the Hill Country (Malaya). On being asked for the meditation subject, it seems, the Elder, [242] gave the text of the thirty-two aspects, saying 'Do only this recitation for four months'. Although they were familiar respectively with two and three Pitakas, it was only at the end of four months recitation of the meditation subject that they became Stream Enterers, with right apprehension [of the text]. So the teacher who expounds the meditation subject should tell the pupil to do the recitation verbally first.

50. Now when he does the recitation, he should divide it up into the 'skin pentad', etc., and do it forwards and backwards.

14. '*Agaru*—aloes': not so spelt in P. T. S. Dict.; but see *agalu*.

After saying 'Head hairs body hairs, nails, teeth, skin', he should repeat it backwards 'Skin, teeth, nails, body hairs, head hairs'.

51. Next to that, with the 'kidney pentad' after saying 'Flesh, sinews, bones, bone marrow, kidney', he should repeat it backwards 'Kidney, bone marrow, bones, sinews, flesh; skin, teeth, nails, body hairs, head hairs'.

52. Next, with the 'lights pentad', after saying 'Heart, liver, midriff, spleen, lights', he should repeat it backwards 'Lights, spleen, midriff, liver, heart; kidney, bone marrow, bones, sinews, flesh; skin, teeth, nails, body hairs, head hairs'.

53. Next, with the 'brain pentad', after saying 'Bowels, entrails gorge, dung, brain', he should repeat it backwards 'Brain, dung, gorge, entrails, bowels; lights, spleen, midriff, liver, heart; kidney, bone marrow, bones, sinews, flesh; skin, teeth, nails, body hairs, head hairs'.

54. Next, with the 'fat sestad', after saying 'Bile, phlegm, pus, blood, sweat, fat', he should repeat it backwards 'Fat, sweat, blood, pus, phlegm, bile; brain, dung, gorge, entrails, bowels; lights, spleen, midriff, liver, heart; kidney, bone marrow, bones, sinews, flesh; skin, teeth, nails, body hairs, head hairs'.

55. Next, with the 'urine sestad', after saying 'Tears, grease, spittle, snot, oil of the joints, urine', he should repeat it backwards 'Urine, oil of the joints, snot, spittle, grease, tears; fat, sweat, blood, pus, phlegm, bile; brain, dung, gorge, entrails, bowels; lights, spleen, midriff, liver, heart; kidney, bone marrow, bones, sinews, flesh; skin, teeth, nails, body hairs, head hairs'. [243]

56. The recitation should be done verbally in this way a hundred times, a thousand times, even a hundred thousand times. For it is through verbal recitation that the meditation subject becomes familiar, and the mind being thus prevented from running here and there, the parts become evident and seem like [the fingers of] a pair of clasped hands,[15] like a row of fence posts.

57. 2. The *mental recitation* should be done just as it is done verbally. For the verbal recitation is a condition for the mental recitation, and the mental recitation is a condition for the penetration of the characteristic [of foulness].[16]

58. 3. *As to colour*: the colour of the head hairs, etc., should be defined.

4. *As to shape*: their shape should be defined too.

---

15. '*Hatthasaṅkhalikā*—the fingers of a pair of clasped hands'—'a row of fingers (*aṅgulīpanti*)'—(Pm. 246).

16. 'For the penetration of the characteristic of foulness, for the observation of repulsiveness as the individual essence' (Pm. 246).

5. *As to direction*: in this body, upwards from the navel is the upward direction, and downwards from it is the downward direction. So the direction should be defined thus: This part is in this direction.

6. *As to location*: the location of this or that part should be defined this: Thus part is established in this location.

59. 7. *As to delimitation*: there are two kinds of delimitation, that is, delimitation of the similar and delimitation of the dissimilar. Herein, delimitation of the similar should be understood in this way: This part is delimited above and below and around by this. Delimitation of the dissimilar should be understood as non-intermixed-ness in this way: Head hairs are not body hairs, and body hairs are not head hairs.

60. When the teacher tells the skill in learning in seven ways thus, he should do so knowing that in certain suttas this meditation subject is expounded from the point of view of repulsiveness and in certain suttas from the point of view of elements. For in the Mahā-Satipaṭṭhāna Sutta (D. Sutta 22) it is expounded only as repulsiveness. In the Mahā-Hatthipadopama Sutta (M. Sutta 28), in the Mahā-Rāhulovāda Sutta (M. Sutta 62), and the Dhātuvibhaṅga (M. Sutta 140, also Vbh. 82) it is expounded as elements. In the Kāyagatāsati Sutta (M. Sutta 119), however, *four* jhanas are expounded with reference to one to whom it has appeared as a colour [kasina] (see Ch. III, 107). Herein, it is an insight meditation subject that is expounded as elements and a serenity meditation subject that is expounded as repulsiveness. Consequently it is only the serenity meditation subject [that is relevant] here.

[*The Tenfold Skill in Giving Attention*]

61. Having thus told the sevenfold skill in learning, he should tell the tenfold skill in giving attention as follows: (1) as to following the order, (2) not too quickly, (3) not too slowly (4) as to warding off distraction, (5) as to surmounting the concept, (6) as to successive leaving, (7) as to absorption, (8)-(10) as to the three suttantas.

62. 1. Herein, *as to following the order*: from the time of beginning the recitation [244] attention should be given following the serial order without skipping. For just as when someone who has no skill climbs a thirty-two-rung ladder using every other step, his body gets exhausted and he falls without completing the climb, so too, one who gives it attention skipping [parts] becomes exhausted in his mind and does not complete the development since he fails to get the satisfaction that ought to be got with successful development.

63. 2. Also when he gives attention to it following the serial order, he should do so *not too quickly*. For just as when a

man sets out on a three-league journey, even if he has already done the journey out and back a hundred times rapidly without taking note of [turnings] to be taken and avoided, though he may finish his journey, he still has to ask how to get there, so too, when the meditator gives his attention to the meditation subject too quickly, though he may reach the end of the meditation subject, it still does not become clear or bring about any distinction. So he should not give his attention to it too quickly.

64. 3. And as 'not too quickly', so also *not too slowly*. For just as when a man wants to do a three-league journey in one day, if he loiters on the way among trees, rocks, pools, etc., he does not finish the journey in a day and needs two or three to complete it, so too, if the meditator gives his attention to the meditation subject too slowly, he does not get to the end and it does not become a condition for distinction.

65. 4. *As to warding off distraction*: he must ward off [temptation] to drop the meditation subject and to let his mind get distracted among the variety of external objects. For if not, just as when a man has entered on a one-foot-wide cliff path, if he looks about here and there without watching his step, he may miss his footing and fall down the cliff, which is perhaps as high as a hundred men, so too, when there is outward distraction, the meditation subject gets neglected and deteriorates. So he should give his attention to it warding off distraction.

66. 5. *As to surmounting the concept*: this [name-] concept beginning with 'head hairs, body hairs' must be surmounted and consciousness established on [the aspect] 'repulsive'. For just as when men find a water hole in a forest in a time of drought, they hang up some kind of signal there such as a palm leaf, and people come to bathe and drink guided by the signal [245] but when the way has become plain with their continual traffic, there is no further need of the signal and they go to bathe and drink there whenever they want, so too, when repulsiveness becomes evident to him as he is giving his attention to the meditation subject through the means of the [name-] concept 'head hairs, body hairs', he must surmount the concept 'head hairs, body hairs', and establish consciousness on only the actual repulsiveness.

67. 6. *As to successive leaving*: in giving his attention he should eventually leave out any [parts] that do not appear to him. For when a beginner gives his attention to head hairs, his attention then carries on till it arrives at the last part, that is, urine and stops there; and when he gives his attention to urine, his attention then carries on till it arrives back at the first part, that is, head hairs, and stops there. As he persists in giving his attention thus, some parts appear to him

and others do not. Then he should work on those that have appeared till one out of any two appears the clearer. He should arouse absorption by again and again giving attention to the one that has appeared thus.

68. Here is a simile. Suppose a hunter wanted to catch a monkey that lived in a grove of thirty-two palms, and he shot an arrow through a leaf of the palm that stood at the beginning and gave a shout; then the monkey went leaping successively from palm to palm till it reached the last palm; and when the hunter went there too and did as before, it came back in like manner to the first palm; and being followed thus again and again, after leaping from each place where a shout was given, it eventually jumped on to one palm and firmly seizing the palm shoot's leaf spike in the middle, would not leap any more even when shot—so it is with this.

69. The application of the simile is this. The thirty-two parts of the body are like the thirty-two palms in the grove. The monkey is like the mind. The meditator is like the hunter. The range of meditator's mind in the body with its thirty-two parts as object is like the monkey's inhabiting the palm grove of thirty-two palms. The settling down of the meditator's mind in the last part after going successively [from part to part] when he began by giving his attention to head hairs is like the monkey's leaping from palm to palm and going to the last palm, [246] when the hunter shot an arrow through the leaf of the palm where it was and gave a shout. Likewise in the return to the beginning. His doing the preliminary work on those parts that have appeared, leaving behind those that did not appear while, as he gave his attention to them again and again, some appeared to him and some did not, is like the monkey's being followed and leaping up from each place where a shout is given. The meditator's repeated attention given to the part that in the end appears the more clearly of any two that have appeared to him and his finally reaching absorption, is like the monkey's eventually stopping in one palm, firmly seizing the palm shoot's leaf spike in the middle and not leaping up even when shot.

70. There is another simile too. Suppose an alms-food-eater bhikkhu went to live near a village of thirty-two families and when he got two lots of alms at the first house he left out one [house] beyond it, and next day, when he got three lots of [alms at the first house] he left out two [houses] beyond it, and on the third day he got his bowl full at the first [house], and went to the sitting hall and ate—so it is with this.

71. The thirty-two aspects are like the village with the thirty-two families. The meditator is like the alms-food eater. The meditator's preliminary work is like the alms-food eater's

going to live near the village. The meditator's continuing to give attention after leaving out those parts that do not appear and doing his preliminary work on the pair of parts that do appear is like the alms-food eater's getting two lots of alms at the first house and leaving out one [house] beyond it, and like his next day getting three [lots of alms at the first house] and leaving out two [houses] beyond it. The arousing of absorption by giving attention again and again to that which has appeared the more clearly of two is like the alms-food eater's getting his bowl full at the first [house] on the third day and then going to the sitting hall and eating.

72. 7. *As to absorption*: as to absorption part by part. The intention here is this: it should be understood that absorption is brought about in each one of the parts.

73. 8-10. *As to the three Suttantas*: the intention here is this: it should be understood that the three Suttantas, namely, those on Higher Consciousness,[17] on Coolness, and on Skill in the Enlightenment Factors, have as their purpose the linking of energy with concentration.

74. 8. Herein, this Sutta should be understood to deal with Higher Consciousness: 'Bhikkhus, there are three signs that 'should be given attention from time to time by a bhikkhu 'intent on higher consciousness. The sign of concentration 'should be given attention from time to time, the sign of 'exertion should be given attention from time to time, the 'sign of equanimity should be given attention from time to 'time. [247] If a bhikkhu intent on higher consciousness 'gives attention only to the sign of concentration, then his 'consciousness may conduce to idleness. If a bhikkhu intent 'on higher consciousness gives attention only to the sign of 'exertion, then his consciousness may conduce to agitation. 'If a bhikkhu intent on higher consciousness gives attention 'only to the sign of equanimity, then his consciousness may 'not become rightly concentrated for the destruction of 'cankers. But, bhikkhus, when a bhikkhu intent on higher 'consciousness gives attention from time to time to the sign 'of concentration, . . . to the sign of exertion,. . .to the sign 'of equanimity, then his consciousness becomes malleable, 'wieldy and bright, it is not brittle and becomes rightly 'concentrated for the destruction of cankers.

75. 'Bhikkhus, just as a skilled goldsmith or goldsmith's 'apprentice prepares his furnace and heats it up and puts 'crude gold into it with tongs; and he blows on it from time 'to time, sprinkles water on it from time to time, and looks 'on at it from time to time; and if the goldsmith or gold-'smith's apprentice only blew on the crude gold, it would burn

17. 'The Higher Consciousness' is a term for jhana.

'and if he only sprinkled water on it, it would cool down, and 'if he only looked on at it, it would not get rightly refined; 'but when the goldsmith or goldsmith's apprentice blows on 'the crude gold from time to time, sprinkles water on it 'from time to time, and looks on at it from time to time, then 'it becomes malleable, wieldy and bright, it is not brittle, 'and it submits rightly to being wrought; whatever kind of 'ornament he wants to work it into, whether a chain or a ring
76. 'or a necklace or a gold fillet, it serves his purpose; so too, 'bhikkhus, there are three signs that should be given attention from time to time by a bhikkhu intent on higher consciousness . . . becomes rightly concentrated for the destruction of cankers. [248] He attains the ability to be a witness, 'through realization by direct-knowledge, of any state realizable by direct-knowledge to which he inclines his mind, 'whenever there is occasion' (A.i,256-8).[18]

77. 9. This Sutta deals with Coolness: 'Bhikkhus, when a 'bhikkhu possesses six things, he is able to realize the supreme 'coolness: What six? Here, bhikkhus, when consciousness 'should be restrained, he restrains it; when consciousness 'should be exerted, he exerts it; when consciousness should 'be encouraged, he encourages it; when consciousness should 'be looked on at with equanimity, he looks on at it with 'equanimity. He is resolute on the superior [state to be 'attained], he delights in nibbana. Possessing these six things 'a bhikkhu is able to realize the supreme 'coolness' (A.iii, 435).

78. 10. Skill in the Enlightenment Factors has already been dealt with in the explanation of skill in absorption (Ch. IV, §51,57) in the passage beginning 'Bhikkhus, when the mind 'is slack, that is not the time for developing the tranquillity 'enlightenment factor, . . .' (S.v,113).

79. So the meditator should make sure that he has apprehended this sevenfold skill in learning well and has properly defined this tenfold skill in giving attention, thus learning the meditation subject properly with both kinds of skill.

[*Starting the Practice*]

80. If it is convenient for him to live in the same monastery as the teacher, then he need not get it explained in detail thus [to begin with], but as he applies himself to the meditation subject after he has made quite sure about it he can have each successive stage explained as he reaches each distinction.

---

18. Pm. explains '*sati sati āyatane*' (rendered here by 'whenever there is occasion') with '*tasmiṃ tasmiṃ pubbahetu-ādi-kāraṇe sati* (when there is this or that reason consisting in a previous cause, etc.)'; MA. iv, 146 says '*Sati sati kāraṇe. Kim pan'ettha kāraṇan? ti. Abhiññā'va kāraṇaṃ* (whenever there is a reason. But what is the reason here? The direct-knowledge itself is the reason)'.

One who wants to live elsewhere, however, must get it explained to him in detail in the way already given, and he must turn it over and over, getting all the difficulties solved. He should leave an abode of an unsuitable kind as described in the Description of the Earth Kasina, and go to live in a suitable one. Then he should sever the minor impediments (Ch. IV, §20) and set about the preliminary work for giving attention to repulsiveness.

[*The 32 Aspects in Detail*]

81. When he sets about it, he should first apprehend the [learning] sign in head hairs. How? The *colour* should be defined first by plucking out one or two head hairs and placing them on the palm of the hand. [249] He can also look at them in the hair-cutting place, or in a bowl of water or rice gruel. If the ones he sees are black when he sees them, they should be brought to mind as 'black'; if white, as 'white'; if mixed, they should be brought to mind in accordance with those most prevalent. And as in the case of head hairs, so too the sign should be apprehended visually with the whole of the 'skin pentad'.

82. Having apprehended the sign thus and (*a*) defined all the other *parts of the body* by colour, shape, direction, location, and delimitation (§58), he should then (*b*) define *repulsiveness* in five ways, that is, by colour, shape, odour, habitat, and location.

83. Here is the explanation of all the parts given in successive order

[Head Hairs]

(*a*) Firstly head hairs are black in their normal *colour*, the colour of fresh *ariṭṭhaka* seeds.[19] As to *shape*, they are the shape of long round measuring rods.[20] As to *direction*, they lie in the upper direction. As to *location*, their location is the wet inner skin that envelops the skull; it is bounded on both sides by the roots of the ears, in front by the forehead, and behind by the nape of the neck.[21] As to *delimitation*, they are bounded below by the surface of their own roots, which are fixed by entering to the amount of the tip of a rice grain into the inner skin that envelops the head. They are bounded above by space, and all round by each other. There are no two hairs together. This is their delimitation by the similar. Head hairs are not body hairs, and body hairs are not head

19. '*Ariṭṭhaka*' as a plant is not in P. T. S. Dict; see T.C.P. Dict.—Sinh. *penela aṭa*.
20. There are various readings.
21. '*Galavāṭaka*,' here rendered by, 'nape of the neck', which the context demands. But elsewhere (e. g. Ch. VI. §47, Ch. VIII, §110) 'base of the neck' seems indicated, that is, where the neck fits on to the body, or 'gullet'.

hairs; being likewise not intermixed with the remaining thirty-one parts the head hairs are a separate part. This is their delimitation by the dissimilar. Such is the definition of head hairs as to colour and so on.

84. (*b*) Their definition *as to repulsiveness* in the five ways, that is, by colour, etc., is as follows.

Head hairs are repulsive in colour as well as in shape, odour,
85. habitat, and location. For on seeing the colour of a head hair in a bowl of inviting rice gruel or cooked rice people are disgusted and say 'This has got hairs in it. Take it away'. So they are repulsive in *colour*. Also when people are eating at night, they are likewise disgusted by the mere sensation of a hair-shaped *akka*-bark or *makaci*-bark fibre. So they are
86. repulsive in *shape*. And the *odour* of head hairs, unless dressed with a smearing of oil, scented with flowers, etc., is most offensive. And it is still worse when they are put in the fire. [250] Even if head hairs are not directly repulsive in colour and shape, still their odour is directly repulsive. Just as a baby's excrement, as to its colour, is the colour of turmeric and, as to its shape, is the shape of a piece of turmeric root, and just as the bloated carcase of a black dog thrown on a rubbish heap, as to its colour, is the colour of a ripe palmyra fruit and, as to its shape, is the shape of a [mandoline-shaped] drum left face down, and its fangs are like jasmine buds, and so even if both these are not directly repulsive in colour and shape, still their odour is directly repulsive, so too, even if head hairs are not directly repulsive
87. in colour and shape, still their odour is directly repulsive. But just as pot herbs that grow on village sewage in a filthy place are disgusting to civilized people and unusable, so also head hairs are disgusting since they grow on the sewage of pus, blood, urine, dung, bile, phlegm, and the like. This is the
88. repulsive aspect of the *habitat*. And these head hairs grow on the heap of the [other] thirty-one parts as fungus do on a dung hill. And owing to the filthy place they grow in they are quite as unappetizing as vegetables growing on a charnel ground, on a midden etc., as lotuses or water lilies growing in drains and so on. This is the repulsive aspect of their *location*.

89. And as in the case of head hairs, so also the repulsiveness of all the parts should be defined (*b*) in the same five ways by colour, shape, odour, habitat, and location.

All, however, must be defined individually (*a*) by colour, shape, direction, location, and delimitation, as follows.

[Body Hairs]

90. Herein, firstly, as to natural *colour*, body hairs are not pure black like head hairs but blackish brown. As to *shape*, they

are the shape of palm roots with the tips bent down. As to *direction*, they lie in the two directions. As to *location*, except for the locations where the head hairs are established, and for the palms of the hands and soles of the feet, they grow in most of the rest of the inner skin that envelops the body. As to *delimitation*, they are bounded below by the surface of their own roots, which are fixed by entering to the extent of a *likhā*[22] into the inner skin that envelops the body, above by space, and all round by each other. There are no two body hairs together. This is the delimitation by the similar. But their delimitation by the dissimilar is like that for the head hairs. [Note: These two last sentences are repeated verbatim at the end of the description of each part. They are not translated in the remaining thirty parts].

[Nails]

91. 'Nails' is the name for the twenty nail plates. They are all white as to *colour*. As to *shape*, they are the shape of fish scales. As to *direction*; the toe-nails are in the lower direction; the finger-nails are in the upper direction. [251] So they grow in the two directions. As to *location*, they are fixed on the tips of the backs of the fingers and toes. As to *delimitation*, they are bounded in the two directions by the flesh of the ends of the fingers and toes, and inside by the flesh of the backs of the fingers and toes, and externally and at the end by space, and all round by each other. There are no two nails together. . .

[Teeth]

92. There are thirty-two tooth bones in one whose teeth are complete. They too are white in *colour*. As to shape, they are of various shapes; for firstly in the lower row, the four middle teeth are the shape of pumpkin seeds set in a row in a lump of clay; that on each side of them has one root and one point and is the shape of a jasmine bud; each one after that has two roots and two points and is the shape of a waggon prop; then two each side with three roots and three points, then two each side four-rooted and four-pointed. Likewise in the upper row. As to *direction*, they lie in the upper direction. As to *location*, they are fixed in the jaw bones. As to *delimitation*, they are bounded by the surface of their own roots which are fixed in the jaw bones; they are bounded above by space, and all round by each other. There are no two teeth together. . .

[Skin (taca)]

93. The inner skin envelops the whole body. Outside it is what is called the outer cuticle, which is black, brown or yellow

22. A measure of length, as much as a 'louse's head'.

in colour, and when that from the whole of the body is compressed together, it amounts to only as much as a jujube-fruit kernel. But as to *colour*, the skin itself is white; and its whiteness becomes evident when the outer cuticle is destroyed by contact with the flame of a fire or the impact of a blow and so
94. on. As to *shape*, it is the shape of the body in brief. But in detail, the skin of the toes is the shape of silk-worms' cocoons; the skin of the back of the foot is the shape of shoes with uppers; the skin of the calf is the shape of a palm leaf wrapping cooked rice; the skin of the thighs is the shape of a long sack full of paddy; the skin of the buttock is the shape of a cloth strainer full of water; the skin of the back is the shape of hide stretched over a plank; the skin of the belly is the shape of the hide stretched over the body of a lute; the skin of the chest is more or less square; the skin of both arms is the shape of the hide stretched over a quiver; the skin of the backs of the hands is the shape of a razor box, or the shape of a comb case; the skin of the fingers is the shape of a key box; the skin of the neck is the shape of a collar for the throat; the skin of the face [252] is the shape of an insects' nest full of holes; the skin
95. of the head is the shape of a bowl bag. The meditator who is discerning the skin should first define the inner skin that covers the face, working his knowledge over the face beginning with the upper lip. Next, the inner skin of the frontal bone. Next, he should define the inner skin of the head, separating, as it were, the inner skin's connexion with the bone by inserting his knowledge in between the cranium bone and the inner skin of the head, as he might his hand in between the bag and the bowl put in the bag. Next, the inner skin of the shoulders. Next, the inner skin of the right arm forwards and backwards; and then in the same way the inner skin of the left arm. Next after defining the inner skin of the back, he should define the inner skin of the right leg forwards and backwards; then the inner skin of the left leg in the same way. Next the inner skin of the groin, the paunch, the bosom and the neck, should be successively defined. Then after defining the inner skin of the lower jaw next after that of the neck, he should finish on arriving at the lower lip. When he discerns it in the gross in this way, it becomes evident to him
96. more subtly too. As to *direction*, it lies in both directions. As to *location*, it covers the whole body. As to *delimitation*, it is bounded below by its fixed surface, and above by space. . .

[FLESH]

97. There are nine hundred pieces of flesh. As to *colour*, it is all red, like *kimsuka* flowers. As to *shape*, the flesh of the calves is the shape of cooked rice in a palm-leaf bag. The

flesh of the thighs is the shape of a rolling pin.[23] The flesh of the buttock is the shape of the end of an oven. The flesh of the back is the shape of a slab of palm sugar. The flesh between each two ribs is the shape of clay mortar squeezed thin in a flattened opening. The flesh of the breast is the shape of a lump of clay made into a ball and flung down. The flesh of the two upper arms is the shape of a large skinned rat and twice the size. When he discerns it grossly in this way it
98. becomes evident to him subtly too. As to *direction*, it lies in both directions. As to *location*, it is plastered over the three hundred and odd bones. [253] As to *delimitation*, it is bounded below by its surface, which is fixed on to the collection of bones, and above by the skin, and all round each by each other piece...

[SINEWS]

99. There are nine hundred sinews. As to *colour*, all the sinews are white. As to *shape*, they have various shapes. For five of the great sinews that bind the body together start out from the upper part of the neck and descend by the front, and five by the back, and then five by the right and five by the left. And of those that bind the right hand, five descend by the front of the hand and five by the back; likewise those that bind the left hand. And of those that bind the right foot, five descend by the front and five by the back; likewise those that bind the left foot. So there are sixty great sinews called 'body supporters' which descend [from the neck] and bind the body together; and they are also called 'tendons'. They are all the shape of yam shoots. But there are others scattered over various parts of the body, which are finer than the last-named. They are the shape of strings and cords. There are others still finer, the shape of creepers. Others still finer are the shape of large lute strings. Yet others are the shape of coarse thread. The sinews in the backs of the hands and feet are the shape of a bird's claw. The sinews in the head are the shape of children's head nets. The sinews in the back are the shape of a wet net spread out in the sun. The rest of the sinews, following the various limbs, are the shape
100. of a net jacket fitted to the body, As to *direction*, they lie in the two directions. As to *location*, they are to be found binding the bones of the whole body together. As to *delimitation*, they are bounded below by their surface, which is fixed on to the three hundred bones, and above by the portions

23. '*Nisadapota*—rolling pin': (—*silā-puttaka*—Pm. 250) what is meant is probably the stone roller, thicker in the middle than at the ends, with which curry spices, etc., are normally rolled by hand on a small stone slab in Ceylon today.

that are in contact with the flesh and the inner skin, and all round by each other...

[BONES]

101. Excepting the 32 teeth bones, these consist of the remaining 64 hand bones, 64 foot bones, 64 soft bones dependent on the flesh, 2 heel bones; then in each leg 2 ankle bones, 2 shin bones, 1 knee bone and 1 thigh bone; then 2 hip bones, 18 spine bones, [254] 24 rib bones, 14 breast bones, 1 heart bone (sternum), 2 collar bones, 2 shoulder blade bones,[24] 2 upper-arm bones, 2 pairs of forearm bones, 7 neck bones, 2 jaw bones, 1 nose bone, 2 eye bones, 2 ear bones, 1 frontal bone, 1 occiput bone, 9 sinciput bones. So there are exactly three hundred bones. As to *colour*, they are all white. As to *shape*, they
102. are of various shapes. Herein, the end bones of the toes are the shape of *kataka* seeds. Those next to them in the middle sections are the shape of jack-fruit seeds. The bones of the base sections are the shape of small drums. The bones of the back of the foot are the shape of a bunch of bruised yams. The heel bone is the shape of the seed of a single-
103. stone palmyra fruit. The ankle bones are the shape of [two] play balls bound together. The shin bones, in the place where they rest on the ankle bones, are the shape of a *sindi* shoot without the skin removed. The small shin bone is the shape of a [toy] bow stick. The large one is the shape of a shrivelled snake's back. The knee bone is the shape of a lump of froth melted on one side. Herein, the place where the shin bone rests on it is the shape of a blunt cow's horn. The thigh bone is the shape of a badly-pared[25] handle for an axe or hatchet. The place where it fits into the hip bone is the shape of a play ball. The place in the hip bone where it is set is the shape
104. of a big *punnāga* fruit with the end cut off. The two hip bones, when fastened together, are the shape of a potter's oven. Seperately they are the shape of the ring-fastening of a smith's hammer. The buttock bone on the end [of them] is the shape of an inverted snake's bood. It is perforated in seven or eight places. The spine bones are internally the shape of lead-sheet pipes put one on top of the other; externally they are the shape of a string of beads. They have two or three rows of projections next to each other like the
105. teeth of a saw. Of the twenty-four rib bones the incomplete ones are the shape of incomplete sabres, [255] and the

24. '*Kotthatthīni*—shoulder-blade bones': for *kottha* (—flat) cf. *kotthalika* §97; the meaning is demanded by the context, otherwise no mention would be made of these two bones, and the description fits. P. T. S. Dict. this ref. has, 'stomach bone' (?). Should one read *a-tikhiṇa* (blunt) *or ati-khiṇa* (very sharp)?

25. '*Duttacchita*—badly pared': *tacchita* pp. of *tacchati* to pare (e.g. with an adze); not in P.T.S. Dict.; see M.i. 31, 124; iii 166.

complete ones are the shape of complete sabres; all together they are like the outspread wings of a white cock. The fourteen breast bones are the shape of an old chariot frame.[26] The heart bone (sternum) is the shape of the bowl of a spoon. The collar bones are the shape of small metal knife handles. The shoulder-blade bones are the shape of a Sinhalese hoe
106. worn down on one side. The upper-arm bones are the shape of looking glass handles. The forearm bones are the shape of a twin palm's trunks. The wrist bones are the shape of lead-sheet pipes stuck together. The bones of the back of the hand are the shape of a bundle of bruised yams. As to the fingers, the bones of the base sections are the shape of small drums; those of the middle sections are the shape of immature jack-fruit seeds; those of the end sections are the
107. shape of *kataka* seeds. The seven neck bones are the shape of rings of bamboo stem threaded one after other on a stick. The lower jaw bone is the shape of a smith's iron hammer ring-fastening. The upper one is the shape of a knife for scraping [rind off sugarcane]. The bones of the eye sockets and nostril sockets are the shape of young palmyra seeds with the kernels removed. The frontal bone is the shape of an inverted bowl made of a shell. The bones of the ear-holes are the shape of barbers' razor boxes. The bone in the place where a cloth is tied [round the head] above the frontal bone and the ear holes is the shape of a piece of curled-up toffee flake.[27] The occiput bone is the shape of a lop-sided coconut with a hole cut in the end. The sinciput bones are the shape of a
108. dish made of an old gourd held together with stitches. As to *direction*, they lie in both directions. As to *location*, they are to be found indiscriminately throughout the whole body. But in particular here, the head bones rest on the neck bones, the neck bones on the spine bones, the spine bones on the hip bones, the hip bones on the thigh bones, the thigh bones on the knee bones, the knee bones on the shin bones, the shin bones on the ankle bones, the ankle bones on the bones of the back of the foot. As to *delimitation*, they are bounded inside by the bone marrow, above by the flesh, at the ends and at the roots by each other...

[BONE MARROW]

109. This is the marrow inside the various bones. As to *colour*, it is white. As to *shape*, [256] that inside each large bone is the shape of a large cane shoot moistened and inserted into

---

26. '*Pañjara*—frame': not quite in this sense in P. T. S. Dict.
27. '*Saṅkuṭitaghaṭapuṇṇapaṭalakhaṇḍa*—a piece of curled-up toffee flake' the Sinhalese translation suggests the following readings and resolution; *saṅkuthita* (thickened or boiled down (?), rather than *saṅkuṭita*...curled up) *Ghata-puṇṇa* [toffee?] 'full of ghee') *paṭala* (flake or slab) *khaṇḍa* (piece).

a bamboo tube. That inside each small bone is the shape of a slender cane shoot moistened and inserted in a section of bamboo twig. As to *direction*, it lies in both directions. As to *location*, it is set inside the bones. As to *delimitation*, it is delimited by the inner surface of the bones...

[KIDNEY]

110. This is two pieces of flesh with a single ligature. As to *colour*, it is dull red, the colour of *pālibhaddhaka* seeds. As to *shape*, it is the shape of a pair of child's play balls; or it is the shape of a pair of mango fruits attached to a single stalk. As to *direction*, it lies in the upper direction. As to *location*, it is to be found on either side of the heart flesh, being fastened by a stout sinew that starts out with one root from the base of the neck and divides into two after going a short way. As to *delimitation*, the kidney is bounded by what appertains to kidney...

[HEART]

111. This is the heart flesh. As to *colour*, it is the colour of the back of a red-lotus petal. As to *shape*, it is the shape of a lotus bud with the outer petals removed and turned upside down; it is smooth outside, and inside it is like the interior of a *kosātakī* (loofah gourd). In those who possess understanding it is a little expanded; in those without understanding it is still only a bud. Inside it there is a hollow the size of a *punnāga* seed's bed where half a *pasata* measure of blood is kept, with which as their support the mind element and mind-
112. consciousness element occur. That in one of greedy temperament is red; that in one of hating temperament is black; that in one of deluded temperament is like water that meat has been washed in; that in one of speculative temperament is like lentil soup in colour; that in one of faithful temperament is the colour of [yellow] *kanikāra* flowers, that in one of understanding temperament is limpid, clear, unturbid, bright, pure, like a washed gem of pure water, and it seems to shine.
113. As to *direction*, it lies in the upper direction. As to *location*, it is to be found in the middle between the two breasts, inside the body. As to *delimitation*, it is bounded by what appertains to heart... [257]

[LIVER]

114. This is a twin slab of flesh. As to *colour*, it is a brownish shade of red, the colour of the not-too-red backs of white water-lily petals. As to *shape*, with its single root and twin ends, it is the shape of a *kovilāra* leaf. In sluggish people it is single and large; in those possessed of understanding there are two or three small ones. As to *direction*, it lies in the

upper direction. As to *location*, it is to be found on the right side, inside from the two breasts. As to *delimitation*, it is bounded by what appertains to liver. . .

[MIDRIFF][28]

115. This is the covering of the flesh, which is of two kinds, namely, the concealed and the unconcealed. As to *colour*, both kinds are white, the colour of *dukūla* (muslim) rags. As to *shape*, it is the shape of its location. As to *direction*, the concealed midriff lies in the upper direction, the other in both directions. As to *location* the concealed midriff is to be found concealing the heart and kidney; the unconcealed is to be found covering the flesh under the inner skin throughout the whole body. As to *delimitation*, it is bounded below by the flesh, above by the inner skin, and all round by what appertains to midriff. . .

[SPLEEN]

116. This is the flesh of the belly's 'tongue'. As to *colour*, it is blue, the colour of *niggundi* flowers. As to *shape*, it is seven fingers in size, without attachments, and the shape of a black calf's tongue. As to *direction*, it lies in the upper direction. As to *location*, it is to be found near the upper side of the belly to the left of the heart. When it comes out through a wound a being's life is terminated. As to *delimitation*. It is bounded by what appertains to spleen. . .

[LIGHTS]

117. The flesh of the lights is divided up into two or three pieces of flesh. As to *colour*, it is red, the colour of not very ripe *udumbara* fig fruits. As to *shape*, it is the shape of an unevenly cut thick slice of cake. Inside, it is insipid and lacks nutritive essence, like a lump of chewed straw, because it is affected by the heat of the kamma-born fire [element] that springs up when there is need of something to eat and drink. As to *direction*, it lies in the upper direction. As to *location*, it is to be found inside the body between the two breasts, hanging above the heart [258] and liver and concealing them. As to *delimitation*, it is bounded by what appertains to lights. . .

[BOWEL]

118. This is the bowel tube; it is looped[29] in twenty-one places, and in a man it is thirty-two hands long, and in a woman, twenty-eight hands. As to *colour*, it is white, the colour of

28. '*Kilomaka*—midriff': the rendering is obviously quite inadequate for what is described here, but there is no appropriate English word.

29. '*Obhagga*—looped': not in this sense in P. T. S. Dict.; see ***obhañjati*** (Ch. XI, §64 and P. T. S. Dict.).

lime [mixed] with sand. As to *shape*, it is the shape of a beheaded snake coiled up and put in a trough of blood. As to *direction*, it lies in the two directions. As to *location*, it is fastened above at the gullet and below to the excrement passage (rectum), so it is to be found inside the body between the limits of the gullet and the excrement passage. As to *delimitation*, it is bounded by what pertains to bowel...

[ENTRAIL (MESENTERY)]

119. This is the fastening in the places where the bowel is coiled. As to *colour*, it is white, the colour of *dakasītalika*[30] (white edible water lily) roots. As to *shape*, it is the shape of those roots too. As to *direction* it lies in the two directions. As to *location*, it is to be found inside the twenty-one coils of the bowel, like the strings to be found inside rope-rings for wiping the feet on, sewing them together, and it fastens the bowels coils together so that they do not slip down in those working with hoes, axes, etc., as the marionette-strings do the marionette's wooden [limbs] at the time of the marionette's being pulled along. As to *delimitation*, it is bounded by what appertains to entrails...

[GORGE]

120. This is what has been eaten, drunk, chewed and tasted, and is present in the stomach. As to *colour*, it is the colour of swallowed food. As to *shape*, it is the shape of rice loosely tied in a cloth strainer. As to *direction*, it is in the upper
121. direction. As to *location*, it is in the stomach. What is called the 'stomach' is [a part of] the bowel-membrane, which is like the swelling [of air] produced in the middle of a length of wet cloth when it is being [twisted and] wrung out from the two ends. It is smooth outside. Inside, it is like a baloon of cloth[31] soiled by wrapping up meat refuse; or it can be said to be like the inside of the skin of a rotten jack fruit. It is the place where worms dwell seething in tangles: the thirty-two families of worms, such as round worms, boil-producing worms, 'palm-splinter' worms, needle-mouthed

---

30. '*Dakasītalika*'; not in P.T.S. Dict.; rendered in Sinhalese translation by '*helmaeli* (white edible water lily)'.

31. '*Maṁsakasambupalivethanakiliṭṭhapāvārapupphakasadisa*'.: this is rendered into Sinhalese by "*kuṇu mas kasaḷa velu porōnā kaḍek pup* (an inflated piece (or bag) of cloth, which has wrapped rotten meat refuse)'. In P.T.S. Dict. *pāvāra* is given as 'clock, mantle' and (this ref.) as 'the mango tree'; but there seems to be no authority for the rendering 'mango tree'; which has nothing to do with this contex. *Pupphaka* (balloon) is not in P.T.S. Dict. (cf. common Burmese spelling of *bubbuḷa* (bubble) as *pupphuḷa*).

worms, tape-worms, thread worms, and the rest.[32] When there is no food and drink, [259] etc., present, they leap up shrieking and pounce upon the heart's flesh; and when food and drink, etc., are swallowed, they wait with uplifted mouths and scramble to snatch the first two or three lumps swallowed. It is these worms' maternity home, privy, hospital and charnel ground. Just as when it has rained heavily in a time of drought and what has been carried by the water into the cesspit at the gate of an outcaste village—the various kinds of ordure[33] such as urine, excrement, bits of hide and bones and sinews, as well as spittle, snot, blood, etc.—gets mixed up with the mud and water already collected there; and after two or three days the families of worms appear, and it ferments, warmed by the energy of the sun's heat, frothing and bubbling on the top, quite black in colour, and so utterly stinking and loathsome that one can scarcely go near it or look at it, much less smell or taste it, so too, [the stomach is where] the assortment of food, drink, etc., falls after being pounded up by the pestle of the teeth, turned over by the hand of the tongue and stuck together with spittle and saliva, losing at that moment its virtues of colour, smell, taste, etc., and taking on the appearance of weavers' paste and dogs' vomit, then to get soused in the bile and phlegm and wind that have collected there, where it ferments with the energy of the stomach-fire's heat, seethes with the families of worms, frothing and bubbling on the top, till it turns into utterly stinking nauseating muck, even to hear about which takes away any appetite for food, drink, etc., let alone to see it with the eye of understanding. And when the food, drink, etc., fall into it, they get divided into five parts: the worms eat one part, the stomach-fire burns up another part, another part becomes urine, another part becomes excrement, and one part is turned into nourishment and sustains the blood,
122. flesh and so on. As to *delimitation*, it is bounded by the stomach-lining and by what appertains to gorge...

[DUNG]

123. This is excrement. As to *colour*, it is mostly the colour of eaten food. As to *shape*, it is the shape of its location. As to *direction*, it is in the lower direction. As to *location*, it is

---

32. It would be a mistake to take the renderings of these worm's names too literally. *Gaṇḍuppada* (boil-producing worm?) appears only as 'earth worm' in P.T.S. Dict., which will not do here. The more generally accepted reading seems to take *paḷatantuka* and *suttaka* (tape-worm and thread-worm) as two kinds rather than *paṭatantusuttaka;* neither is in P.T.S. Dict.

33. '*Kuṇapa*—ordure'; P.T.S. Dict. only gives the meaning 'cropse', which does not fit the meaning either here or, e.g., Ch. XI, §21, where he sense of a *dead* body is inappropriate.

124. to be found in the receptacle for digested food (rectum). The receptacle fcr digested food is the lowest part at the end of the bowel, between the navel and the root of the spine. [260] It measures eight fingerbreadths in height and resembles a bamboo tube. Just as when rain water falls on a higher level it runs down to fill a lower level and stays there, so too, the receptacle for digested food is where any food, drink etc., that have fallen into the receptacle for undigested food, have been continuously cooked and simmered by the stomach-fire, and have got as soft as though ground up on a stone, run down to through the cavities of the bowels; and it is pressed down there till it becomes impacted like brown clay pushed
125. into a bamboo joint, and there it stays. As to *delimitation*, it is bounded by the receptacle for digested food and by what appertains to dung. . .

[Brain]

126. This is the lumps of marrow to be found inside the skull. As to *colour*, it is white, the colour of the flesh of a toadstool; it can also be said that it is the colour of turned milk that has not yet become curd. As to *shape*, it is the shape of its location. As to *direction*, it belongs to the upper direction. As to *location*, it is to be found inside the skull, like four lumps of dough put together to correspond with the [skull's] four sutured sections. As to *delimitation*, it is bounded by the skull's inner surface and by what appertains to brain. . .

[Bile]

127. There are two kinds of bile: local bile and free bile Herein as to *colour*, the local bile is the colour of thick *madhuka* oil; the free bile is the colour of faded *ākulī* flowers. As to *shape*, both are the shape of their location. As to *direction*, the local bile belongs to the upper direction; the other belongs to both directions. As to *location*, the free bile spreads, like a drop of oil on water, all over the body except for the fleshless parts of the head hairs, body hairs, teeth, nails, and the hard dry skin. When it is disturbed, the eyes become yellow and twitch, and there is shivering and itching[34] of the body. The local bile is situated near the flesh of the liver between the heart and the lights. It is to be found in the bile container (gall bladder), which is like a large *kosātakī* (loofah) gourd pip. When it is disturbed, beings go crazy and demented, they throw off conscience and shame and do the undoable, speak the unspeakable, and think the unthinkable. As to *delimitation*, it is bounded by what appertains to bile . . .[261]

34. '*Kaṇḍūyati*—to itch': the verb is not in P. T. S. Dict.; see *kaṇḍu*.

[PHLEGM]

128. The phlegm is inside the body and it measures a bowlful. As to *colour*, it is white, the colour of the juice of *nāgabalā* leaves. As to *shape*, it is the shape of its location. As to *direction*, it belongs to the upper direction. As to *location*, it is to be found on the stomach's surface. Just as duckweed and green scum on the surface of water divide when a stick or a potsherd is dropped into the water and then spread together again, so too, at the time of eating and drinking, etc., when the food, drink, etc., fall into the stomach, the phlegm divides and then spreads together again. And if it gets weak the stomach becomes utterly disgusting with a smell of ordure, like a ripe boil or a rotten hen's egg, and then the eructations and the mouth reek with a stench like rotting ordure rising from the stomach, so that the man has to be told 'Go away, your breath smells'. But when it grows plentiful it holds the stench of ordure beneath the surface of the stomach, acting like the wooden lid of a privy. As to *delimitation*, it is bounded by what appertains to phlegm...

[PUS]

129. Pus is produced by decaying blood. As to *colour*, it is the colour of bleached leaves; but in a dead body it is the colour of stale thickened gruel. As to *shape*, it is the shape of its location. As to *direction*, it belongs to both directions. As to *location*, however, there is no fixed location for pus where it could be found stored up. Wherever blood stagnates and goes bad in some part of the body damaged by wounds with stumps and thorns, by burns with fire, etc., or where boils, carbuncles, etc., appear, it can be found there. As to *delimitation*, it is bounded by what appertains to pus...

[BLOOD]

130. There are two kinds of blood: stored blood and mobile blood. Herein, as to *colour*, stored blood is the colour of cooked and thickened lac solution; mobile blood is the colour of clear lac solution. As to *shape*, both are the shape of their locations. As to *direction*, the stored blood belongs to the upper direction; the other belongs to both directions. As to *location*, except for the fleshless parts of the head hairs, body hairs, teeth, nails, and the hard dry skin, the mobile blood permeates the whole of the clung-to (kammically-acquired)[35] body by following the net work of veins. The stored blood fills the lower part of the liver's site [262] to the extent of a bowlful, and by its splashing little by little over

35. '*Upādiṇṇa*—clung-to': See Ch. XIV, note 23.

the heart, kidney and lights, it keeps the kidney, heart liver and lights moist. For it is when it fails to moisten the kidney, heart, etc., that beings become thirsty. As to *delimitation*, it is bounded by what appertains to blood...

[SWEAT]

131. This is the water element that trickles from the pores of the body hairs, and so on. As to *colour*, it is the colour of clear sesamum oil. As to *shape*, it is the shape of its location. As to *direction*, it belongs to both directions. As to *location*, there is no fixed location for sweat where it could always be found like blood. But if the body is heated by the heat of a fire, by the sun's heat, by a change of temperature, etc., then it trickles from all the pore openings of the head hairs and body hairs, as water does from a bunch of unevenly cut lily-bud stems and lotus stalks pulled up from the water. So its shape should also be understood to correspond to the pore-openings of the head hairs and body hairs. And the meditator who discerns sweat should only give his attention to it as it is to be found filling the pore-openings of the head hairs and body hairs. As to *delimitation*, it is bounded by what appertains to sweat . . .

[FAT]

132. This is a thick unguent. As to *colour*, it is the colour of sliced turmeric. As to *shape*, firstly in the body of a stout man it is the shape of turmeric-coloured *dukūla* (muslin) rags placed between the inner skin and the flesh. In the body of a lean man it is the shape of turmeric-coloured *dukūla* (muslin) rags placed in two or three thicknesses on the shank flesh, thigh flesh, back flesh near the spine, and belly-covering flesh. As to *direction*, it belongs to both directions. As to *location*, it permeates the whole of a stout man's body; it is to be found on a lean man's shank flesh, and so on. And though it was described as 'unguent' above, still it is neither used as oil on the head nor as oil for the nose, etc., because of its utter disgustingness. As to *delimitation*, it is bounded below by the flesh, above by the inner skin, and all round by what appertains to fat...

[TEARS]

133. These are the water element that trickles from the eye. As to *colour*, they are the colour of clear sesamum oil. As to *shape*, they are the shape of their location. [263] As to *direction*, they belong to the upper direction. As to *location*, they are to be found in the eye sockets. But they are not stored in the eye sockets all the while as the bile is in the bile container. But when beings feel joy and laugh uproariously

or feel grief and weep and lament, or eat particular kinds of wrong food, or when their eyes are affected by smoke, dust, dirt, etc., then being originated by the joy, grief, wrong food, or temperature, they fill up the eye sockets or trickle out. And the meditator who discerns tears should discern them only as they are to be found filling the eye sockets. As to *delimitation*, they are bounded by what appertains to tears...

[GREASE]

134. This is a melted unguent. As to *colour*, it is the colour of coconut oil. Also it can be said to be the colour of oil sprinkled on gruel. As to *shape*, it is a film the shape of a drop of unguent spread out over still water at the time of bathing. As to *direction*, it belongs to both directions. As to *location*, it is to be found mostly on the palms of the hands, backs of the hands, soles of the feet, backs of the feet, tip of the nose, forehead, and points of the shoulders. And it is not always to be found in the melted state in these locations, but when these parts get hot with the heat of a fire, the sun's heat, upset of temperature or upset of elements then it spreads here and there in those places like the film from the drop of unguent on the still water at the time of bathing. As to *delimitation*, it is bounded by what appertains to grease...

[SPITTLE]

135. This is water element mixed with froth inside the mouth As to *colour*, it is white, the colour of the froth. As to *shape*, it is the shape of its location, or it can be called 'the shape of froth'. As to *direction*, it belongs to the upper direction. As to *location*, it is to be found on the tongue after it has descended from the cheeks on both sides. And it is not always to be found stored there; but when beings see particular kinds of food, or remember it, or put something hot or bitter or sharp or salt or sour into their mouths, or when their hearts are faint, or nausea arises on some account, then spittle appears and runs down from the cheeks on both sides to settle on the tongue. It is thin at the tip of the tongue, and thick at the root of the tongue. It is capable, without getting used up, of wetting unhusked rice or husked rice or anything else chewable that is put into the mouth, like the water in a pit scooped out in a river sand bank. [264] As to *delimitation* it is bounded by what appertains to spittle...

[SNOT]

136. This is impurity that trickles out from the brain. As to *colour*, it is the colour of a young palmyra kernel. As to *shape*, it is the shape of its location. As to *direction*, it belongs

to the upper direction. As to *location,* it is to be found filling the nostril cavities. And it is not always to be found stored there; but rather, just as though a man tied up curd in a lotus leaf, which he then pricked with a thorn underneath, and whey oozed out and dripped, so too, when beings weep or suffer a disturbance of elements produced by wrong food or temperature, then the brain inside the head turns into stale phlegm, and it oozes out and comes down by an opening in the palate, and it fills the nostrils and stays there or trickles out. And the meditator who discerns snot should discern it only as it is to be found filling the nostril cavities. As to *delimitation,* it is bounded by what appertains to snot...

[OIL OF THE JOINTS]

137. This is the slimy ordure inside the joints in the body. As to *colour,* it is the colour of *kaṇikāra* gum. As to *shape,* it is the shape of its location. As to *direction,* it belongs to both directions. As to *location,* it is to be found inside the hundred and eighty joints, serving the function of lubricating the bones' joints. If it is weak, when a man gets up or sits down, moves forward or backward, bends or stretches, then his bones creak, and he goes about making a noise like the snapping of fingers, and when he has walked only one or two leagues' distance, his air element gets upset and his limbs pain him. But if a man has plenty of it, his bones do not creak when he gets up, sits down, etc., and even when he has walked a long distance, his air element does not get upset and his limbs do not pain him. As to *delimitation,* it is bounded by what appertains to oil of the joints...

[URINE]

138. This is the urine solution. As to *colour,* it is the colour of bean brine. As to *shape,* it is the shape of water inside a water pot placed upside down. As to *direction,* it belongs to the lower direction. As to *location,* it is to be found inside the bladder. For the bladder sack is called the bladder. Just as when a porous pot with no mouth is put into a cesspool, [265] then the solution from the cesspool gets into the porous pot with no mouth even though no way of entry is evident, so too, while the urinary secretion from the body enters the bladder its way of entry is not evident. Its way of exit, however, is evident. And when the bladder is full of urine, beings feel the need to make water. As to *delimitation,* it is delimited by the inside of the bladder and by what is similar to urine. This is the delimitation by the similar. But its delimitation by the dissimilar is like that for the head hairs (see note at end of §90).

The Arising of Absorption

139. When the meditator has defined the parts beginning with the head hairs in this way by colour, shape, direction, location and delimitation (§58), and he gives his attention in the ways beginning with 'following the order, not too quickly' (§61) to their repulsiveness in the five aspects of colour, shape, smell, habitat, and location (§84f.), then, at last he surmounts the concept (§66). Then just as when a man with good sight is observing a garland of flowers of thirty-two colours knotted on a single string and all the flowers become evident to him simultaneously, so too, when the meditator observes this body thus 'There are in this body head hairs', then all these things become evident to him, as it were, simultaneously. Hence it was said above in the explanation of skill in giving attention: 'For when a beginner gives his attention to head hairs, his attention carries on till it arrives at the last part, that is, urine, and stops there' (§67).

140. If he applies his attention externally as well when all the parts have become evident in this way, then human beings, animals, etc., as they go about are divested of their aspect of beings and appear as just assemblages of parts. And when drink, food, etc., is being swallowed by them, it appears as though it were being put in among the assemblage of parts.

141. Then, as he gives his attention to them again and again as 'Repulsive, repulsive', employing the process of 'successive leaving', etc. (§67), eventually absorption arises in him. Herein, the appearance of the head hairs, etc., as to colour, shape, direction, location, and delimitation, is the learning sign; their appearance as repulsive in all aspects is the counterpart sign.

As he cultivates and develops that counterpart sign, absorption arises in him, but only of the first jhana, in the same way as described under Foulness as a meditation subject (Ch.IV,§74f.). And it arises singly in one to whom only one part has become evident, or who has reached absorption in
142. one part and makes no further effort about another. But several first jhanas, according to the number of parts, are produced in one to whom several parts have become evident, or who has reached jhana in one and also makes further effort about another. As in the case of Elder Mallaka. [266]

That Elder, it seems, took the Elder Abhaya, the Dīgha Reciter, by the hand,[36] and after saying 'Friend Abhaya, first learn this matter', he went on 'The Elder Mallaka is an obtainer of thirty-two jhanas in the thirty-two parts. If he

36. Reference is sometimes made to the 'hand-grasping question (*hattha-gahaka-pañhā*)'. It may be to this; but there is another mentioned at the end of the commentary to the Dhātu-Vibhaṅga.

enters upon one by night and one by day, he goes on entering upon them for over a fortnight; but if he enters upon one each day, he goes on entering upon them for over a month'.

143. And although this meditation is successful in this way with the first jhana, it is nevertheless called 'mindfulnes occupied with the body' because it is successful through the influence of the mindfulness of the colour, shape, and so on.

144. And the bhikkhu who is devoted to this mindfulness occupied with the body 'is a conqueror of boredom and delight, ' and boredom does not conquer him; he dwells transcending ' boredom as it arises. He is a conqueror of fear and dread, ' and fear and dread do not conquer him; he dwells transcend- ' ing fear and dread as they arise. He is one who bears cold ' and heat. . .who endures. . .arisen bodily feelings that are... ' menacing to life' (M.iii, 97); he becomes an obtainer of the four jhanas based on the colour aspect of the head hairs,[37] etc.; and he comes to penetrate the six kinds of direct knowledge (see M. sutta 6).

So let a man, if he is wise,
Untiringly devote his days
To mindfulness of body which
Rewards him in so many ways.

This is the section dealing with mindfulness occupied with the body in the detailed treatise.

*

[(9) Mindfulness of breathing]

145. Now comes the description of the development of mindfulness of Breathing as a meditation subject. It has been recommended by the Blessed One thus: 'And, bhikkhus, this ' concentration through mindfulness of breathing, when deve- ' loped and practised much, is both peaceful and sublime, it is ' an unadulterated blissfull abiding, and it banishes at once ' and stills evil unprofitable thoughts as soon as they arise' (S. v, 321; Vin. iii, 70).

[*Text*]

It has been described by the Blessed One as having sixteen bases thus: 'And how developed, bhikkhus, how practised ' much is concentration through mindfulness of breathing ' both peaceful and sublime, an unadulterated blissful ' abiding, banishing at once and stilling evil unprofitable ' thought as soon as they arise?

'Here, bhikkhus, a bhikkhu, gone to the forest or to the ' root of a tree or to an empty place, sits down; having

37. The allusion seems to be to the Bases of Mastery (*abhibhāyatana* —or better, Bases for Transcendence), see M. ii. 13 and MA. iii, 257f.; but see §60.

'folded his legs crosswise, set his body erect, established 'mindfulness in front of him, [367] ever mindful he breathes 'in, mindful he breathes out.

'(i) Breathing in long, he knows "I breathe in long"; or 'breathing out long, he knows "I breathe out long". (ii) 'Breathing in short, he knows "I breathe in short"; or 'breathing out short, he knows "I breathe out short". '(iii) He trains thus "I shall breathe in experiencing the whole 'body"; he trains thus "I shall breathe out experiencing the 'whole body". (iv) He trains thus "I shall breathe in tran-'quillizing the bodily formation"; he trains thus "I shall 'breathe out tranquillizing the bodily formation".

'(v) He trains thus "I shall breathe in experiencing happi-'ness"; he trains thus "I shall breathe out experiencing 'happiness". (vi) He trains thus "I shall breathe in ex-'periencing bliss"; he trains thus "I shall breathe out 'experiencing bliss". (vii) He trains thus "I shall breathe in 'experiencing the mental formation"; he trains thus "I shall 'breathe out experiencing the mental formation". (viii) He 'trains thus "I shall breathe in tranquillizing the mental 'formation"; he trains thus "I shall breathe out tranquilliz-'ing the mental formation".

'(ix) He trains thus "I shall breathe in experiencing the '[manner of] consciousness"; he trains thus "I shall breathe 'out experiencing the [manner of] consciousness". (x) He 'trains thus "I shall breathe in gladdening the [manner of] 'consciousness"; he trains thus "I shall breathe out gladden-'ing the [manner of] consciousness." (xi) He trains thus "I 'shall breathe in concentrating the [manner of] conscious-'ness"; he trains thus "I shall breathe out concentrating the '[manner of] consciousness". (xii) He trains thus "I shall 'breathe in liberating the [manner of] consciousness"; he 'trains thus "I shall breathe out liberating the [manner of] 'consciousness".

'(xiii) He trains thus "I shall breathe in contemplating 'impermanence"; he trains thus "I shall breathe out con-'templating impermanence". (xiv) He trains thus "I shall 'breathe in contemplating fading away"; he trains thus "I 'shall breathe out contemplating fading away". (xv) He 'trains thus "I shall breathe in contemplating cessation"; 'he trains thus "I shall breathe out contemplating cessation". '(xvi) He trains thus "I shall breathe in contemplating 'relinquishment"; he trains thus "I shall breathe out contem-'plating relinquishment"' (S. v, 321-2).

146. The description [of development] is complete in all respects, however, only if it is given in due course after a commentary on the text. So it is given here (§186) introduced by a commentary on the [first part of the] text.

[*Word Commentary*]

And how developed, bhikkhus, how practised much, is concentration through mindfulness of breathing: here in the first place *how* is a question showing desire to explain in detail the development of concentration through mindfulness of breathing in its various forms. *Developed, bhikkhus,...is concentration through mindfulness of breathing*: this shows the thing that is being asked about out of desire to explain it in its various forms. *How practised much...as soon as they arise*? here too the same explanation applies.

147. Herein, *developed* means aroused, or increased, *Concentration through mindfulness of breathing* (lit. 'breathing-mindful ness concentration') is either concentration associated with mindfulness that discerns breathing, or it is concentration on mindfulness of breathing. *Practised much*: practised again and again.

148. *Both peaceful and sublime* (*santo c'eva paṇīto ca*): it is peaceful in both ways and sublime in both ways; the two words should each be understood as governed by the word 'both' (*eva*). What is meant? Unlike Foulness, which as a meditation subject is peaceful and sublime only by penetration, but is neither (*n'eva*) peaceful no sublime in its object since its object [in the learning stage] is gross, and [after that] its object is repulsiveness—unlike that, this is not unpeaceful or unsublime in any way but on the contrary it is peaceful, stilled and quiet both on account of the peacefulness of its object and on account of the peacefulness of that one of its factors called penetration. And it is sublime, something one cannot have enough of, both on account of the sublimeness of its object and on [268] account the sublimeness of the aforesaid factor. Hence it is called 'both peaceful and sublime.'

149. *It is an unadulterated blissful abiding*: it has no adulteration, thus it is unadulterated; It is unalloyed, unmixed, particular, special. Here it is not a question of peacefulness to be reached through preliminary work [as with the kasinas] or through access [as with Foulness, for instance]. It is peaceful and sublime in its own individual essence too starting with the very first attention given to it. But some[38] say that it is 'unadulterated' because it is unalloyed, possessed of nutritive value and sweet in its individual essence too. So it should be understood to be 'unadulterated' and a 'blissful abiding' since it leads to the obtaining of bodily and mental bliss with every moment of absorption.

---

38. ' "*Some*" is said with reference to the inmates of the Uttara (Northern) monastery [in Anurādhapura]' (Pm. 256).

150. *As soon as they arise*: whenever they are not suppressed. *Evil*: bad. *Unprofitable* (*akusala*) *thoughts*: thoughts produced by unskilfulness (*akosalla*). *It banishes at once*: it banishes, suppresses, at that very moment. *Stills* (*vūpasameti*): it thoroughly calms (*suṭṭhu upasameti*); or else, when eventually brought to fulfilment by the noble path, it cuts off, because of partaking of penetration; it tranquillizes, is what is meant.

151. In brief, however, the meaning here is this: Bhikkhus, in what way, in what manner, by what system, is concentration through mindfulness of breathing developed, in what way is it practised much, that it is both peaceful. . .as soon as they arise?

152. He now said 'Here, bhikkhus', etc., giving the meaning of that in detail.

Herein, *here bhikkhus, a bhikhu* means, bhikkhus, in this dispensation a bhikkhu. For this word *here* signifies the [Buddha's] dispensation as the prerequisite for a person to produce concentration through mindfulness of breathing in all its modes,[39] and it denies that such a state exists in any other dispensation. For this is said: 'Bhikkhus, only here is ' there an ascetic, here a second ascetic, here a third ascetic, ' here a fourth ascetic; other dispensations are devoid of ' ascetics' (M. i, 63; A. ii, 238).[40] That is why it was said above 'in this dispensation a bhikkhu'.

153. *Gone to the forest. . .or to an empty place*: this signifies that he has found an abode favourable to the development of concentration through mindfulness of breathing. For this bhikku's mind has long been dissipated among visible data, etc., as its object, and it does not want to mount the object of concentration-through-mindfulness-of-breathing; it runs off the track like a chariot harnessed to a wild ox.[41] Now suppose a cowherd [269] wanted to tame a wild calf that had been reared on a wild cow's milk, he would take it away from the cow and tie it up apart with a rope to a stout post dug into the ground; then the calf might dash to and fro, but being unable to get away, it would eventually sit down or lie down by the post, so too, when a bhikkhu wants to tame his own mind which has long been spoilt by being reared on visible data, etc., as object for its food and drink, he should take it away from visible

---

39. 'The words "*in all its aspects*" refer to the sixteen bases; for these are only found in total in this dispensation. When outsiders know mindfulness of breathing, they only know the first four modes' (Pm. 257).

40. ' "*The ascetic*" is a Stream Enterer, the "*second ascetic*" is a Once-returner, the "*third ascetic*" is a Non-returner, the "*fourth ascetic*" is an Arahant' (MA. ii, 4).

41. '*Kūṭa*—wild: P. T. S. Dict. this ref. gives 'useless', which misses the point. Cf. MA. ii, 82; iv, 198.

data, etc., as object and bring it into the forest or to the root of a tree or to an empty place and tie it up there to the post of in-breaths and out-breaths with the rope of mindfulness. And so his mind may then dash to and fro when it no longer gets the objects it was formerly used to, but being unable to break the rope of mindfulness and get away, it sits down, lies down, by that object under the influence of access and absorption. Hence the Ancients said:

154. 'Just as a man who tames a calf would tie it to a post, so here

'Should his own mind by mindfulness be firmly to the object tied.'

This is how an abode is favourable to his development. Hence it was said above: 'This signifies that he has found an abode favourable to the development of concentration through mindfulness of breathing'.

155. Or alternatively, this mindfulness of breathing as a meditation subject—which is foremost among the various meditation subjects of all Buddhas, [some] Pacceka Buddhas and [some] Buddhas' disciples as a basis for attaining distinction and abiding in bliss here and now—is not easy to develop without leaving the neighbourhood of villages, which resound with the noises of women, men, elephants, horses, etc., noise being a thorn to jhana (seeA.v,135), whereas in the forest away from a village a meditator can at his ease set about discerning this meditation subject and achieve the fourth jhana in mindfulness of breathing; and then, by making that same jhana the basis for comprehension of formations [with insight] (Ch. XX, §2f.), he can reach Arahantship, the highest fruit. That is why the Blessed One said 'gone to the forest', etc., in pointing out a favourable abode for him.

156. For the Blessed one is like a master of the art of building sites (see D.i.9,12;ii,87). [270] As the master of the art of building sites surveys the proposed site for a town, thoroughly examines it, and then gives his directions 'Build the town here', and when the town is safely finished, he receives great honour from the royal family, so the Blessed One examines an abode as to its suitability for the meditator, and he directs 'Devote yourself to the meditation subject here', and later on, when the meditator has devoted himself to the meditation subject and has reached Arahantship and says 'The Blessed One is indeed fully enlightened', the Blessed One receives great honour.

157. And this bhikkhu is compared to a leopard. For just as a great leopard king lurks in a grass wilderness or a jungle wilderness or a rock wilderness in the forest and seizes wild beasts—the wild buffalo, wild ox, boar, etc.—, so too, the bhikkhu who devotes himself to his meditation subject in the

forest, etc., should be understood to seize successively the paths of Stream Entry, Once-return, Non-return, and Arahantship; and the noble fruitions as well. Hence the Ancients said:

> 'For as the leopard by his lurking [in the forest] seizes beasts
> 'So also will this Buddhas' son, with insight gifted, strenuous,
> 'By his retreating to the forest seize the highest fruit of all' (Miln. 369).

So the Blessed One said 'gone to the forest', etc., to point out a forest abode as a place likely to hasten his advancement.

158. Herein, *gone to the forest* is gone to any kind of forest possessing the bliss of seclusion among the kinds of forests characterized thus. 'Having gone out beyond the boundary post, all that is forest' (Ps.i,176;Vbh.251), and 'A forest abode is five hundred bow lengths distant' (Vin.iv,183). *To the root of a tree*: gone to the vicinity of a tree. *To an empty place*: gone to an empty, secluded space. And here he can be said to have gone to an 'empty place' if he has gone to any of the remaining seven kinds of abode (resting place).[42] [271]

159. Having thus indicated an abode that is suitable to the three seasons, suitable to humour and temperament,[43] and favourable to the development of mindfulness of breathing, he then said *sits down*, etc., indicating a posture that is peaceful and tends neither to idleness nor to agitation. Then he said *having folded his legs crosswise*, etc., to show firmness in the sitting position, easy occurence of the in-breaths and out-breaths, and the means for discerning the object.

160. Herein, *crosswise* is the sitting position with the thighs fully locked. *Folded*: having locked. *Set his body erect*: having placed the upper part of the body erect with the eighteen backbones resting end to end. For when he is seated like this, his skin, flesh and sinews are not twisted, and so the feelings that would arise moment by moment if they were twisted do not arise. That being so, his mind becomes unified, and the meditation subject, instead of collapsing, attains to growth and increase.

---

42. The nine kinds of abode (resting place) are the forest and the root of a tree already mentioned, and a rock, a hill cleft, a mountain cave, a charnel ground, a jungle thicket, an open space, a heap of straw (M.i, 181).

43. 'In the hot season the forest is favourable, in the cold season the root of a tree, in the rainy season an empty place. For one of phlegmatic humour, phlegmatic by nature, the forest is favourable, for one of bilious humour the root of a tree, for one of windy humour an empty place. For one of deluded temperament the forest, for one of hating temperament the root of a tree, for one of greedy temperament an empty place' (Pm. 258).

161. *Established mindfulness in front of him* (*parimukhaṃ satiṃ upaṭṭhapetvā*)=having placed (*ṭhapayitvā*) mindfulness (*satiṃ*) facing the meditation subject (*kammaṭṭhānābhimukhaṃ*). Or alternatively, the meaning can be treated here too according to the method of explanation given in the Paṭisambhidā, which is this: *Pari* has the sense of control (*pariggaha*), *mukhaṃ* (lit. mouth) has the sense of outlet (*niyyāna*), *sati* has the sense of establishment (*upaṭṭhāna*); that is why *parimukhaṃ satiṃ* (mindfulness as a controlled outlet)" is said' (Ps.i.176). The meaning of it in brief is: Having made mindfulness the outlet [from opposition, forgetfulness being thereby] controlled.[44]

162. *Ever mindful he breathes in, mindful he breathes out*: having seated himself thus, having established mindfulness thus, the bhikkhu does not abandon that mindfulness, ever mindful he breathes in, mindful he breathes out; he is a mindful worker, is what is meant.

[*Word Commentary Continued—First Tetrad*]

163. (1) Now *breathing in long*, etc., is said in order to show the different ways in which he is a mindful worker. For in the Paṭisambhidā, in the exposition of the clause 'Ever mindful he breathes in, mindful he breathes out', this is said: 'He is a 'mindful worker in thirty-two says: (1) when he knows 'unification of mind and non-distraction by means of long 'in-breath, mindfulness is established in him; owing to that 'mindfulness and that knowledge he is a mindful worker. '(2) When he knows unification of mind and non-distraction by 'means of long out-breath...(31)...by means of breathing in 'contemplating relinquishment...(32) When he knows unification of mind and non-distraction by means of breathing out 'contemplating relinquishment, mindfulness is established in 'him; owing to that mindfulness and that knowledge he is a 'mindful worker' (Ps.i,176).

164. Herein, *breathing in long* (*assasanto*) is producing a long in-breath. [272] '*Assāsa* is the wind issuing out; *passāsa* is the wind entering in' is said in the Vinaya Commentary. But in the Suttanta Commentaries it is given in the opposite sense. Herein, when any infant comes out from the mother's womb, first the wind from within goes out and subsequently the wind from without enters in with fine dust, strikes the palate and is extinguished [with the infant's sneezing]. This, firstly, is how *assāsa* and *passāsa* should be understood.

165. But their length and shortness should be understood by extent (*addhāna*). For just as water or sand that occupies an extent of space is called a 'long water', a 'long sand', a 'short water', a 'short sand', so in the case of elephants' and snakes'

44. The amplification is from Pm. 258.

bodies the in-breaths and out-breaths regarded as particles[45] slowly fill the long extent, in other words, their persons, and slowly go out again. That is why they are called 'long'. They rapidly fill a short extent, in other words, the person of a dog, a hare, etc., and rapidly go out again. That is why they are
166. called 'short'. And in the case of human beings some breathe in and breathe out long, by extent of time, as elephants, snakes, etc., do while others breathe in and breathe out short in that way as dogs, hares, etc., do. Of these, therefore, the breaths that travel over a long extent in entering in and going out are to be understood as long in time; and the breaths that travel over a little extent in entering in and going out, as short in time.

167. Now this bhikkhu knows 'I breathe in, I breathe out, long' while breathing in and breathing out long in nine ways. And the development of the Foundation of Mindfulness consisting in Contemplation of the Body should be understood to be perfected in one aspect in him who knows thus, according as it is said in the Paṭisambhidā:

168. 'How, breathing in long, does he know: "I breathe in long" ' breathing out long, does he know: "I breathe out long"? (1) ' He breathes in a long in-breath reckoned as an extent. (2) ' He breathes out a long out-breath reckoned as an extent. ' (3) He breathes in and breathes out long in-breaths and ' out-breaths reckoned as an extent. As he breathes in and ' breathes out long in-breaths and out-breaths reckoned as ' an extent, zeal arises.[46] (4) Through zeal he breathes in a

45. ' "*Regarded as particles*": as a number of groups (*kalapa*)' (Pm. 259). This conception of the occurrence of breaths is based on the theory of motion as 'successive arisings in adjacent locations (*desantaruppatti*)', see note 54 below. For 'groups' see Ch, XX, §2f.

46. ' "*Zeal arises*": additional zeal, which is profitable and has the characteristic of desire to act, arises due to the satisfaction obtained when the meditation has brought progressive improvement. "*More subtle than before*": more subtle than before the already-described zeal arose; for the breaths occur more subtly owing to the meditation's influence in tranquillizing the body's distress and disturbance, *Gladness arises*": fresh happiness arises of the kinds classed as 'minor', etc., which is the gladness that accompanies the consciousness occupied with the meditation and is due to the fact that the peacefulness of the object increases with the growing subtlety of the breaths and to the fact that the meditation subject keeps to its course. "*The mind turns away*": the mind turns away from the breaths, which have reached the point at which their manifestation needs investigating (see §177) owing to their gradually increasing subtlety. But some say (see Ps A. Sinhalese Ed., p. 351) "It is when the in-breaths and out-breaths have reached a subtler state owing to the influence of the meditation and the counterpart sign; for when that has arisen, the mind turns away from the normal breaths". "*Equanimity is established*": when concentration, classed as access and absorption, has arisen in that counterpart sign, then, since there is no need for further interest to achieve jhana, onlooking (equanimity) ensues, which is specific neutrality' (Pm. 260).

'long in-breath more subtle than before reckoned as an 'extent. (5) Through zeal he breathes out a long out-breath 'more subtle than before reckoned as an extent. (6) Through 'zeal he breathes in and breathes out long in-breaths and out- 'breaths more subtle than before reckoned as an extent. 'As, through zeal, he breathes in and breathes out long in- 'breaths and out-breaths more subtle than before reckoned as 'an extent, gladness arises. [273] (7) Through gladness he 'breathes in a long in-breath more subtle than before reckoned 'as an extent. (8) Through gladness he breathes out a long 'out-breath more subtle than before reckoned as an extent. '(9) Through gladness he breathes in and breathes out long 'in-breaths and out-breaths more subtle than before reckoned 'as an extent. As, through gladness, he breathes in and 'breathes out long in-breaths and out-breaths more subtle 'than before reckoned as an extent his mind turns away from 'the long in-breaths and out-breaths and equanimity is 'established.

'Long in-breaths and out-breaths in these nine ways are a 'body. The establishment (foundation)[47] is mindfulness. 'The contemplation is knowledge. The body is the establish- 'ment (foundation), but it is not the mindfulness. Mindful- 'ness is both the establishment (foundation) and the mindful- 'ness. By means of that mindfulness and that knowledge 'he contemplates that body. That is why "Development 'of the foundation (establishment) of mindfulness consisting

47. '"*In these nine ways*" that occur in the nine ways just described. "*Long in-breaths and out-breaths...are a body*": the in-breaths and out-breaths, which exist as particles though they have the aspect of length, constitute a "body" in the sense of a mass. And here the sign that arises with the breaths as its support is also called "in-breath and out-breath" (cf. e.g. §40 end). "*The establishment (foundation) is mindfulness*": mindfulness is called "establishment (foundation)—*upaṭṭhāna*)" since it approaches (*upagantvā*) the object and remains (*tiṭṭhati*) there. "*The contemplation is knowledge*": contemplation of the sign by means of serenity, and contemplation of mentality-materiality by defining with insight the in-breaths and out-breaths and the body, which is their support, as materiality, and the consciousness and the states associated with it as the immaterial (mentality), are knowledge, in other words, awareness of what is actually there (has actually become). "*The body is the establishment (foundation)*": there is that body, and mindfulness approaches it by making it its object and remains there, thus it is called "establishment". And the words "the body is the establishment" include the other (the mental) kind of body too since the above-mentioned comprehension by insight is needed here too. "*But it is not the mindfulness*": that body is not called "mindfulness" [though it in called "the establishment"]. "*Mindfulness is both the establishment (foundation) and the mindfulness*", being so both in the sense of remembering (*saraṇa*) and in the sense of establishing (*upatiṭṭhana*). "*By means of that mindfulness*": by means of that mindfulness already mentioned. "*And that knowledge*": and the knowledge already mentioned. "*That body*": that in-breath-and-out-breath body and that material body which is its support. "*He*

'in contemplation of the body as a body" (see D. ii, 290) is 'said' (Ps. i, 177).

169. (ii) The same method of explanation applies also in the case of *short* breaths. But there is this difference. While in the former case 'a long in-breath reckoned as an extent' is said, here 'A short in-breath reckoned as a little' (Ps. i, 182) is given. So it must be construed as 'short' as far as the phrase 'That is why "Development of the foundation '(establishment) of mindfulness consisting in contemplation 'of the body as a body" is said' (Ps.i,183).

170. So it should be understood that it is when this bhikkhu knows in-breaths and out-breaths in these nine ways as 'a [long] extent' and as 'a little [duration]' that, 'breathing in long, he knows "I breathe in long";...breathing out short, he knows "I breathe out short"' is said of him. And when he knows thus,

'The long kind and the short as well,
'The in-breath and the out-breath too,
'Such then are the four kinds that happen
'At the bhikkhu's nose tip here'.

171. (iii) *He trains thus 'I shall breathe in...I shall breathe out experiencing the whole body'*: he trains thus, I shall breathe in making known, making plain, the beginning, middle and end[48] of the entire in-breath body. I shall breathe out

---

contemplates (*anupassati*)": he keeps re-seeing (*anu anu passati*) with jhana knowledge and with insight knowledge. "*That is why 'Development of the foundation* (*establishment*) *of mindfulness consisting in contemplation of the body as a body' is said*": in virtue of that contemplation this is said to be development of the foundation (establishment) of mindfulness consisting in contemplation of the body as a body of the kind already stated. What is meant is this: the contemplation of the body as an in-breath-and-out-breath body as stated and of the physical body that is its [material] support, which is not contemplation of permanence, etc., in a body whose individual essence is impermanent, etc.—like the contemplation of a waterless mirage as water—, but which is rather contemplation of its essence as impermanent, painful, not self, and foul, according as is appropriate, or alternatively, which is contemplation of it is a mere body only, by not contemplating it as containing anything that can be apprehended as "I" or "mine" or "woman". or "man" all this is "contemplation of the body". The mindfulness associated with that contemplation of the body, which mindfulness is itself the establishment, is the "establishment". The development, the increase, of that is the "development of the foundation (establishment) of mindfulness consisting in contemplation of the body"' (Pm. 261).

The compound '*Satipaṭṭhāna*' is derived by the Paṭisambhidā from *sati* (mindfulness) and *upaṭṭhāna* (establishment—Ps. i, 182), but in the commentaries the resolution into *sati* and *paṭṭhāna* (foundation) is preferred (MA. i, 237-8). In the 118th Sutta of the Majjhimanikāya the first tetrad is called development of the first foundation of mindfulness, or contemplation of the body (M. Sutta 10; D. Sutta, 22). The object of the Paṭisambhidā passage quoted is to demonstrate this.

48. The beginning, middle and end are described in §197, and the way

making known, making plain, the beginning, middle and end of the entire out-breath body, thus he trains. Making them known, making them plain, in this way he both breathes in and breathes out with consciousness associated with knowledge. That is why it is said 'He trains thus "I shall breathe in...shall breathe out..." '

172. To one bhikkhu the beginning of the in-breath body or the out-breath body, distributed in particles, [that is to say, regarded as successive arisings (see note 45)] is plain, but not the middle or the end; he is only able to discern the beginning and has difficulty with the middle and the end. To another the middle is plain, not the beginning or the end; he is only able to discern the middle and has difficulty with the beginning and the end. To another the end is plain, not the beginning or the middle; he is only able to discern the end [274] and has difficulty with the beginning and the middle. To yet another all stages are plain; he is able to discern them all and has no difficulty with any of them. Pointing out that one should be like the last-mentioned bhikkhu, he said 'He trains thus "I shall breath in...shall breathe out experiencing the whole body" '.

173. Herein, *he trains*: he strives, he endeavours in this way. Or else the restraint here in one such as this is training in the higher virtue, his consciousness is training in the higher consciousness, and his understanding is training in the higher understanding (see Ps.i,184). So he trains in, repeats, develops, repeatedly practises, these three kinds of training, on that object, by means of that mindfulness, by means of that attention. This is how the meaning should be regarded here.

174. Herein, in the first part of the system (nos. (i) and (ii)[49] he should only breathe in and breathe out and not do anything else at all, and it is only afterwards that he should apply himself to the arousing of knowledge, and so on. Consequently the present tense is used here in the text 'He knows "I breathe in" ...he knows " I breathe out" '. But the future tense in the

---

they should be treated is given in § 199-201. What is meant is that the meditator should know what they are and be aware of them without his mindfulness leaving the tip of the nose to follow after the breaths inside the body or outside it, speculating on what becomes of them.

49. ' "*In the first part of the system*" : in the first part of the system of development; in the first two bases, is what is intended. Of course, arousing of knowledge must be admitted to take place here too because of the presence of awareness of the length and shortness of the breaths as they actually are (as they actually become) ; and it is not hard to do that; for it is merely the taking count of them as they occur. That is why it is put in the present tense here. But what follows is as hard as for a man to walk on a razor's edge; which is why the future tense is used for the subsequent stages in order to indicate the need for exceptional prior effort' (Pm. 263).

passage beginning '"I shall breathe in experiencing the whole body"' should be understood as used in order to show that the aspect of arousing knowledge, etc., has to be undertaken from then on.

175. (iv) He trains thus '*I shall breathe in...shall breathe out tranquillizing the bodily formation*'; he trains thus, I shall breathe in, shall breathe out tranquillizing, completely tranquillizing, stopping, stilling, the gross bodily formation.[50]

176. And here both the gross and subtle state and also [progressive] tranquillizing should be understood. For previously, at the time when the bhikkhu has still not discerned [the meditation subject], his body and his mind are disturbed and so they are gross. And while the grossness of the body and the mind has still not subsided the in-breaths and out-breaths are gross. They get stronger; his nostrils become inadequate, and he keeps breathing in and out through his mouth. But they become quiet and still when his body and mind have been discerned. When they are still then the in-breaths and out-breaths occur so subtly that he has to investigate whether they exist or not.

177. Suppose a man stands still after running, or descending from a hill, or putting down a big load from his head, then his in-breaths and out-breaths are gross, his nostrils become inadequate, and he keeps on breathing in and out through his mouth. But when he has rid himself of his fatigue and has bathed and drunk [275] and put a wet cloth on his heart, and is lying in the cool shade, then his in-breaths and out-breaths eventually occur so subtly that he has to investigate whether they exist or not; so too, previously, at the time when the bhikkhu has still not discerned,...he has to investigate whether they exist or not.

178. Why is that? Because previously, at the time when he has still not discerned there is no concern in him, no reaction, no attention, no reviewing, to the effect that 'I am [progressively] tranquillizing each grosser bodily formation'. But when he has discerned, there is. So his bodily formation at the time when he has discerned is subtle in comparison with that at the time when he has not. Hence the Ancients said:

> 'The mind and body are disturbed, and then in excess it occurs;
> But when the body is undisturbed, then it with subtlety occurs'.

179. In discerning [the meditation subject the formation] is gross, and it is subtle [by comparison] in the first-jhana

50. "*Bodily formation*": the in-breath and out-breath (see M. i, 301). For although it is consciousness-originated, it is nevertheless called "Bodily formation" since its existence is bound up with the kamma-born body and it is formed with that as the means' (Pm. 263).

access; also it is gross in that, and subtle [by comparison] in the first jhana; in the first jhana and second-jhana access it is gross, and in the second jhana subtle; in the second jhana and third-jhana access it is gross, and in the third jhana subtle; in the third jhana and fourth-jhana access it is gross, and in the fourth jhana it is so exceedingly subtle that it even reaches cessation. This is the opinion of the Dīgha and Saṃyutta Reciters. But the Majjhima reciters have it that it is subtler in each access than in the jhana below too in this way: In the first jhana it is gross, and in the second-jhana access it is subtle [by comparison, and so on]. It is however the opinion of all that the bodily formation occurring before the time of discerning becomes tranquillized at the time of discerning, and the bodily formation at the time of discerning becomes tranquillized in the first-jhana access...and the bodily formation occurring in the fourth-jhana access becomes tranquillized in the fourth jhana. This is the method of explanation in the case of serenity.

180. But in the case of insight, the bodily formation occurring at the time of not discerning is gross, and in discerning the primary elements it is [by comparison] subtle; that also is gross, and in discerning derived materiality it is subtle; that also is gross, and in discerning all materiality it is subtle; that also is gross, and in discerning the immaterial it is subtle; that also is gross, and in discerning the material and immaterial it is subtle; that also is gross, and in discerning conditions it is subtle; that also is gross, and in seeing mentality-materiality with its conditions it is subtle; that also is gross and in insight that has the characteristics [of impermanence, etc.,] as its object it is subtle; that also is gross in weak insight while in strong insight it is subtle.

Herein, the tranquillizing should be understood as [the relative tranquillity] of the subsequent compared with the previous. Thus should the gross and subtle state, and the [progressive] tranquillizing, be understood here. [276]

181. But the meaning of this is given in the Paṭisambhidā together with the objection and clarification thus:

'How is it that trains thus "I shall breathe in...shall 'breathe out tranquillizing the bodily formation? What are the 'bodily formations? Long in-breaths...out-breaths [experi'encing the whole body] belong to the body; these things being 'bound up with the body, are bodily formations; he trains in 'tranquillizing, stopping, stilling, those bodily formations.

'When there are such bodily formations whereby there is 'bending backwards, sideways in all directions, and forwards, 'and perturbation, vacillation, moving, and shaking of 'the body, he trains thus "I shall breathe in tranquillizing 'the bodily formation", he trains thus "I shall breathe 'out tranquillizing the bodily formation". When there are 'such bodily formations whereby there is no bending back- 'wards, sideways, in all directions, and forwards, and no 'perturbation, vacillation, moving and shaking of the body, 'quietly, subtly, he trains thus "I shall breathe in tranquilliz- 'ing the bodily formation", he trains thus "I shall breathe 'out tranquillizing the bodily formation".

182. '[Objection:] so then he trains thus "I shall breathe in 'tranquillizing the bodily formation", he trains thus "I shall 'breathe out tranquillizing the bodily formation": that being 'so there is no production of awareness of wind, and there is 'no production of in-breaths and out-breaths, and there is 'no production of mindfulness of breathing, and there is 'no production of concentration through mindfulness of 'breathing, and consequently the wise neither enter into 'nor emerge from that attainment.

183. '[Clarification:] So then, he trains thus "I shall breathe in 'tranquillizing the bodily formation", he trains thus "I shall 'breathe out tranquillizing the bodily formation": that being 'so, there is production of awareness of wind and there is 'production of in-breaths and out-breaths, and there is 'production of mindfulness of breathing, and there is pro- 'duction of concentration through mindfulness of breathing, 'and consequently the wise enter into and emerge from that 'attainment.

184. 'Like what? Just as when a gong is struck. At first gross 'sounds occur and consciousness [occurs] because the sign 'of the gross sounds is well apprehended, well attended to, 'well observed; and when the gross sounds have ceased, then 'afterwards faint sounds occur and [consciousness occurs] 'because the sign of the faint sounds is well apprehended, well 'attended to, well observed; and when the faint sounds have 'ceased, then [277] afterwards consciousness occurs because 'it has the sign of the faint sounds as its object,[51]—so too, 'at first gross in-breaths and out-breaths occur and [conscious- 'ness does not become distracted] because the sign of the 'gross in-breaths and out-breaths is well apprehended, well 'attended to, well observed; and when the gross in-breaths 'and out-breaths have ceased, then afterwards faint in-breaths 'and out-breaths occur and [consciousness does not become 'distracted] because the sign of the faint in-breaths and out-

51. 'The faint sound itself as a sign is the "*sign of the faint sounds*"; it has that as its object, What is meant? Of course, the faint sounds have ceased too then; but the sign of the sounds has been well apprehended and so consciousness occurs with the sign of fainter sounds as its object. For from the outset he ascertains with undistracted consciousness the sign of each sound as it ceases, eventually his consciousness occurs in the end with the sign of ultra subtle sounds too as its object' (Pm. 266).

'breaths is well apprehended, well attended to, well observed; 'and when the faint in-breaths and out-breaths have ceased, 'then afterwards consciousness does not become distracted 'because it has the sign of the faint in-breaths and out-breaths 'as its object.

'That being so, there is production of awareness of wind, 'and there is production of in-breaths and out-breaths, and 'there is production of mindfulness of breathing, and there 'is production of concentration through mindfulness of 'breathing, and consequently the wise enter into and em-'erge from that attainment.

185. 'In-breaths and out-breaths tranquillizing the bodily 'formation are a body. The establishment (foundation) is 'mindfulness. The contemplation is knowledge. The body 'is the establishment(foundation), but it is not the mindful-'ness. Mindfulness is both the establishment (foundation) 'and the mindfulness. By means of that mindfulness and 'that knowledge he contemplates that body. That is why '"Development of the foundation (establishment) of mind-'fulness consisting in contemplation of the body as a body" 'is said' (Ps. i, 184-6).

This, in the first place is the consecutive word commentary here on the first tetrad, which deals with contemplation of the body.

[*Method of development*]

186. The first tetrad is set forth as a meditation subject for a beginner;[52] but the other three tetrads are [respectively] set forth, as the contemplations of feeling, of [the manner of] consciousness, and of mental objects, for one who has already attained jhana in this tetrad. So if a clansman who is beginner wants to develop this meditation subject, and, through insight based on the fourth jhana produced in breathing, to reach Arahantship together with the discriminations, he should first do all the work connected with the purification of virtue, etc., in the way already described, after which he should learn the meditation subject in five stages from a teacher of the kind already described.

187. Here are the five stages: learning, questioning, establishing, absorption, characteristic.

Herein, *learning* is learning, the meditation subject. *Questioning* is questioning about the meditation subject. *Establishing* is establishing the meditation subject. *Absorption* [278] is the absorption of the meditation subject. *Characteristic* is the characteristic of the meditation subject; what

52. '"*As a meditation subject for a beginner*" is said with reference to the serenity (i.e. jhana) meditation subject; but the insight meditation subject applies to the other tetrads too' (Pm. 266).

is meant is that it is the ascertaining of the meditation subject's individual essense thus 'This meditation subject has
188. such a characteristic'. Learning the meditation subject in the five stages in this way, he neither tires himself nor worries the teacher.

So in giving this meditation subject consisting in mindfulness of breathing attention he can live either with the teacher or elsewhere in an abode of the kind already described, learning the meditation subject in the five stages thus, getting a little expounded at a time and taking a long time over reciting it. He should sever the minor impediments. After finishing the work connected with the meal and getting rid of any dizziness due to the meal he should seat himself comfortably. Then, making sure he is not confused about even a single word of what he has learned from the teacher, he should cheer his mind by recollecting the special qualities of the Three Jewels.

189. Here are the stages in giving attention to it: (1) counting, (2) connexion, (3) touching, (4) fixing, (5) observing, (6) turning away, (7) purification, and (8) looking back on these.

Herein, *counting* is just counting, *connexion* is carrying on, *touching* is the place touched [by the breaths], *fixing* is absorption, *observing* is insight, *turning away* is the path, *purification* is fruition, *looking back on these* is reviewing.

190. 1. Herein, this clansman who is a beginner should first give attention to this meditation subject by counting. And when counting, he should not stop short of five or go beyond ten or make any break in the series. By stopping short of five his thoughts get excited in the cramped space, like a herd of cattle shut in a cramped pen. By going beyond ten his thoughts take the number [rather than the breaths] for their support. By making a break in the series he wonders if the meditation subject has reached completion or not. So he should do his counting without those faults.

191. When counting, he should at first do it slowly, [that is, late,] as a grain measurer does. For a grain measurer having filled his measure, says 'One', and empties it, and then refilling it, he goes on saying 'One, one' while removing any rubbish he may have noticed. And the same with 'Two, two', and so on. So, taking the in-breath or the out-breath, whichever appears [most plainly], he should begin with 'One, one' [279] and count up to 'Ten, ten', noting each as it occurs.

192. As he does his counting in this way the in-breaths and out-breaths become evident to him as they enter in and issue out. Then he can leave off counting slowly (late), like a grain measurer, and he can count quickly, [that is, early,] as a cowherd does. For a skilled cowherd takes pebbles in his pocket and goes to the cow pen in the morning, whip in hand; sitting on the bar of the gate, prodding the cows in the

back, he counts each one as it reaches the gate, saying 'One, two', dropping a pebble for each. And the cows of the herd, which have been spending the three watches of the night uncomfortably in the cramped space, come out quickly in parties, jostling, each other as they escape. So he counts quickly (early) 'Three, four, five' and so up to ten. In this way the in-breaths, and out-breaths, which had already become evident to him while he counted them in the former way, now keep moving along quickly.

193. Then knowing that they keep moving along quickly, not apprehending them either inside or outside [the body], but apprehending them just as they reach the [nostril] door, he can do his counting quickly (early): 'One, two, three, four, five; one, two, three, four, five, six;...seven;...eight;... nine;...ten'. For as long as the meditation subject is connected with counting it is with the help of that very counting that the mind becomes unified, just as a boat in a swift current is steadied with the help of a rudder.

194. When he counts quickly, the meditation subject becomes apparent to him as an uninterrupted process. Then, knowing that it is proceeding uninterruptedly, he can count quickly (early in the way just described, not discerning the wind either inside or outside [the body]. For by bringing his consciousness inside along with the incoming breath it seems as if it were buffetted by the wind inside or filled with fat.[53] By taking his consciousness outside along with the outgoing breath it gets distracted by the multiplicity of objects outside. However, his development is successful when he fixes his mindfulness on the place touched [by the breaths]. That is why it was said above 'He can count quickly (early) in the way just described, not discerning the wind either inside or outside'.

195. But how long is he to go on counting? Until, without counting [280] mindfulness remains settled on the in-breaths and out-breaths as its object. For counting is simply a device for settling mindfulness on the in-breaths and out-breaths as object by cutting off the external dissipation of applied thoughts.

196. 2. Having given attention to it in this way by counting, he should now do so by *connexion*.

Connexion is the uninterrupted following of the in-breaths and out-breaths with mindfulness after counting has been given up. And that is not by following after the beginning, middle and end.[54]

---

53. '" *Buffetted by wind*": if he gives much attention to the wind that has gone inside, that place seems to him as if it were buffetted by the wind, as if filled with fat' (Pm. 268). No further explanation is given.

54. '"*Following* (*anugamana*)" is occurring along with (*anu anu pavattana*) going after (*anugacchana*), by means of mindfulness through making

197. The navel is the beginning of the wind issuing out, the heart is its middle and the nose-tip is its end. The nose-tip is the beginning of the wind entering in, the heart is its middle and the navel its end. And if he follows after that, his mind is distracted by disquiet and perturbation, according as it is said: 'When he goes in with mindfulness after the beginning, middle and end of the in-breath, his mind being distracted internally, both his body and his mind are disquieted and perturbed and shaky. When he goes out with mindfulness after the beginning, middle and end of the out-breath, his mind being distracted externally, both his body and his mind are disquieted and perturbed and shaky' (Ps.i,165).

3-4. So when he gives his attention to it by connexion, he should do so not by the beginning, middle and end, but rather by *touching* and by *fixing*.

198. There is no attention to be given to it by touching separate from fixing as there is by counting separate from connexion. But when he is counting the breaths in the place touched by each, he is giving attention to them by counting and touching. When he has given up counting and is connecting them by means of mindfulness in that same place and fixing consciousness by means of absorption, then he is said to be giving his attention to them by connexion, touching and fixing. And the meaning of this may be understood through the similes of the Man Who Cannot Walk and the Gate-keeper given in the commentaries, and through the simile of the Saw given in the Paṭisambhidā.

199. Here is the simile of the man who cannot walk: just as a man unable to walk, who is rocking a swing for the amusement of his children and their mother, sits at the foot of the swing post and sees both ends and the middle of the swing plank successively coming and going [281] yet does not move from his place in order to see both ends and the middle, so too, when a bhikkhu places himself with mindfulness, as it were, at the foot of the post for anchoring [mindfulness] and rocks

---

the breaths the object as they occur. Hence he said "*And that is not by following after the beginning, middle and end*". "*The navel is the beginning*" because of their first arising there. For the notion of a beginning (*ādi cintā*) is here in the sense of first arising not in the sense of just arising [once only]. For they actually go on arising throughout [the whole length] from the navel to the nose tip; and wherever they arise, there in that same place they dissolve, because there is no going (movement) of dhammas. The ordinary term "motion" (*gati-samaññā*) refers to successive arisings in adjacent locations (*desantarup-patti*) according to conditions. "*The heart is the middle*": near the heart, just above it is the middle. "*The nose tip is the end*": the place where the nostrils are is the end: that is the limit of the application of the ordinary term "in-breaths and out-breaths", for it is accordingly that they are called "consciousness-originated" there being no production externally of what is consciousness-originated' (Pm. 268).

the swing of the in-breaths and out-breaths; he sits down with mindfulness on the sign at that same place, and follows with mindfulness the beginning, middle and end of the in-breaths and out-breaths at the place touched by them as they come and go; keeping his mind fixed there, he then sees them without moving from his place in order to see them. This is the simile of the man who cannot walk.

200. This is the simile of the gate-keeper: just as a gate-keeper does not examine people inside and outside the town, asking 'Who are you? Where have you come from? Where are you going? What have you got in your hand?'—for those people are not his concern—, but does examine each man as he arrives at the gate, so too, the incoming breaths that have gone inside and the outgoing breaths that have gone outside are not this bhikkhu's concern, but they are his concern each time they arrive at the [nostril] gate itself.

201. Then the simile of the saw should he understood from its beginning. For this is said:

' Sign, in-breath, out-breath, are not object
' Of a single consciousness;
' By one who knows not these three things
' Development is not obtained.
' Sign, in-breath, out-breath, are not object
' Of a single consciousness;
' By one who does know these three things
' Development can be obtained.

202. 'How is it that these three things are not the object of a ' single consciousness, that they are nevertheless not unknown, ' that the mind does not become distracted, that he manifests ' effort, carries out a task, and achieves an effect?

'Suppose there were a tree trunk placed on a level piece of ' ground, and a man cut it with a saw. The man's mindfulness ' is established by the saw's teeth where they touch the tree ' trunk, without his giving attention to the saw's teeth as ' they approach and recede, though they are not unknown to ' him as they do so; and he manifests effort, carries out a task ' and achieves an effect. As the tree trunk placed on the level ' piece of ground, so the sign for the anchoring of mindfulness. ' As the saw's teeth, so the in-breaths and out-breaths. As ' the man's mindfulness, established by the saw's teeth where ' they touch the tree trunk, without his giving attention to the ' saws' teeth as they approach and recede, though they are ' not unknown to him as they do so, and so he manifests effort, ' carries out a task and achieves an effect, [282] so too the ' bhikkhu sits, having established mindfulness at the nose tip ' or on the upper lip, without giving attention to the in-' breaths and out-breaths as they approach and recede, 'though they are not unknown to him as they do so, and he 'manifests effort, carries out a task and achieves an effect.

203. '"Effort": what is the effort? The body and the mind of 'one who is energetic become wieldy—this is the effort. 'What is the task? Imperfections come to be abandoned in 'one who is energetic, and his applied thoughts are stilled—'this is the task. What is the effect? Fetters come to be 'abandoned in one who is energetic, and his inherent tendencies 'come to be done away with—this is the effect.

'So these three things are not the object of a single cons-'ciousness, and they are nevertheless not unknown, and the 'mind does not become distracted, and he manifests effort, 'carries out a task, and achieves an effect.

'Whose mindfulness of breathing in
'And out is perfect, well developed,
'And gradually brought to growth
'According as the Buddha taught,
' 'Tis he illuminates the world
'Just like the full moon free from cloud' (Ps.i,170-2; last line Dh. 172; whole verse Thag.548).

This is the simile of the saw. But here it is precisely his not giving attention [to the breaths] as [yet to] come and [already] gone[55] that should be understood as the purpose.

204. When someone gives his attention to this meditation subject, sometimes it is not long before the sign arises in him, and then the *fixing*, in other words, absorption adorned with the rest of the jhana factors, is achieved.

205. After someone has given his attention to counting, then just as when a body that is disturbed sits down on a bed or chair, the bed or chair sags down and creaks and the cover gets rumpled, but when a body that is not disturbed sits down, the bed or chair neither sags down nor creaks, the cover does not get rumpled, and it is as though filled with cotton-wool, why? because a body that is not disturbed is light, so too, after he has given his attention to counting, when the bodily disturbance has been stilled by the gradual cessation of gross in-breaths and out-breaths, then both the body and the mind become light: the physical body is as though it were ready to leap up into the air. [283]

206. When his gross in-breaths and out-breaths have ceased, his consciousness occurs with the sign of the subtle in-breaths and out-breaths as its object. And when that has ceased, it goes on occurring with the successively subtler signs as its object. How?

207. Suppose a man struck a bronze bell with a big iron bar and at once a loud sound arose, his consciousness would occur with

55. Reading '*āgata-gata-vasena*' with Pm. (p. 271).

the gross sound as its object; then, when the gross sound had ceased, it would occur afterwards with the sign of the subtle sound as its object; and when that had ceased, it would go on occurring with the sign of the successively subtler sound as its object. This is how it should be understood. And this is given in detail in the passage beginning 'Just as when a metal gong is struck' (§84).

208. For while other meditation subjects become clearer at each higher stage, this one does not: in fact, as he goes on developing it, it becomes more subtle for him at each higher stage, and it even comes to the point at which it is no longer manifest.

However, when it becomes unmanifest in this way, the bhikkhu should not get up from his seat, shake out his leather mat, and go away. What should be done? He should not get up with the idea 'Shall I ask the teacher?' or 'Is my meditation subject lost?'; for by going away, and so disturbing his posture, the meditation subject has to be started anew. So he should go on sitting as he was and [temporarily] substitute the place [normally touched for the actual breaths as the object of contemplation].[56]

209. These are the means for doing it. The bhikkhu should recognize the unmanifest state of the meditation subject and consider thus: 'Where do these in-breaths and out-breaths exist? Where do they not? In whom do they exist? In whom not?'. Then, as he considers thus, he finds that they do not exist in one inside the mother's womb, or in those drowned in water, or likewise in unconscious beings,[57] or in the dead, or in those attained to the fourth jhana, or in those born into a fine-material or immaterial existence, or in those attained to cessation [of perception and feeling]. So he should apostrophize himself thus: 'You with all your wisdom are certainly not inside a mother's womb or drowned in water or in the unconscious existence or dead or attained to the fourth jhana or born into the fine-material or immaterial existence or attained to cessation. Those in-breaths and out-breaths are actually existent in you, only you are not able to discern them because your understanding is dull'. Then, fixing his mind on the place normally touched [by the breaths], he should proceed to give his attention to that.

210. These in-breaths and out-breaths occur striking the tip of the nose in a long-nosed man [284] and the upper lip in a short-

56. The point made here is that if the breaths themselves get temporarily too faint to be observed, he should carry on by observing the tip of the nose where they normally touch till they become apparent again. He brings the meditation back to mind for the moment, 'as the place (*desato*)' where they were last noticed, instead of 'as breaths', which have temporarily vanished.

57. Those born in the world of unconscious beings in the fine-material Brahmā-world (D. i, 28).

nosed man. So he should fix the sign thus: 'This is the place where they strike'. This was why the Blessed One said; 'Bhikkhus, I do not say of one who is forgetful, who is not 'fully aware, [that he practises] development of mindfulness 'of breathing' (M.iii,84).

211. Although any meditation subject, no matter what, is successful only in one who is mindful and fully aware, yet any meditation subject other than this one gets more evident as he goes on giving it his attention. But this mindfulness of breathing is difficult, difficult to develop, a field in which only the minds of Buddhas, Pacceka Buddhas, and Buddhas' sons are at home. It is no trivial matter, nor can it be cultivated by trivial persons. In proportion as continued attention is given to it it becomes more peaceful and more subtle. So strong mindfulness and understanding are necessary here.

212. Just as when doing needlework on a piece of fine cloth a fine needle is needed, and a still finer instrument for boring the needle's eye, so too, when developing this meditation subject, which resembles fine cloth, both the mindfulness, which is the counterpart of the needle, and the understanding associated with it, which is the counterpart of the instrument for boring the needle's eye, need to be strong. A bhikkhu must have the necessary mindfulness and understanding and must look for the in-breaths and out-breaths nowhere else than the place normally touched by them.

213. Suppose a ploughman, after doing some ploughing, sent his oxen free to graze and sat down to rest in the shade, then his oxen would soon go into the forest. Now a skilled ploughman who wants to catch them and yoke them again does not wander through the forest following their tracks, but rather he takes his rope and goad and goes straight to the drinking place where they meet, and he sits or lies there. Then after the oxen have wandered about for a part of the day, they come to the drinking place where they meet, and they bathe and drink and when he sees that they have come out and are standing about, he secures them with the rope, and prodding them with the goad, he brings them back, yokes them, and goes on with his ploughing. So too, the bhikkhu should not look for the in-breaths and out-breaths anywhere else than the place normally touched by them. And he should take the rope of mindfulness and the goad of understanding, and fixing his mind on the place normally touched by them he should go on giving his attention to that. [285] For as he gives his attention in this way they reappear after no long time, as the oxen did at the drinking place where they met. So he can secure them with the rope of mindfulness, and yoking them in that same place

and prodding them with the goad of understanding, he can keep on applying himself to the meditation subject.

214. When he does so in this way, the sign[58] soon appears to him. But it is not the same for all; on the contrary, some say that when it appears it does so to certain people producing a
215. light touch like cotton or silk-cotton or a draught. But this is the exposition given in the commentaries: it appears to some like a star or a cluster of gems or a cluster of pearls, to others with a rough touch like that of silk-cotton seeds or a peg made of heartwood, to others like a long braid string or a wreath of flowers or a puff of smoke, to others like a stretched-out cobweb or a film of cloud or a lotus flower or a chariot wheel or the moon's disk or the sun's disk.

216. In fact this resembles an occasion when a number of bhikkhus are sitting together reciting a suttanta. When a bhikkhu asks 'What does this sutta appear like to you?', one says 'It appears to me like a great mountain torrent', another 'To me it is like a line of forest trees', another 'To me it is like a spreading fruit tree giving cool shade'. For the one sutta appears to them differently because of the difference in their perception. Similarly this single meditation subject appears differently because of difference in perception.[59] It is born of perception, its source is perception, it is produced by perception. Therefore it should be understood that when it appears differently it is because of difference in perception.

217. And here, the consciousness that has in-breath as its object is one, the consciousness that has out-breath as its object is another, and the consciousness that has the sign as its object is another. For the meditation subject reaches neither absorption nor even access in one who has not got these three things [clear]. But it reaches access and also absorption in one who has got these three things [clear]. For this is said:

'Sign, in-breath, out-breath, are not object
'Of a single consciousness;
'By one who knows not these three things
'Development is not obtained.
'Sign, in-breath, out-breath, are not object
'Of a single consciousness;
'By one who does know these three things
'Development can be obtained' (Ps.i.170). [286]

218. And when the sign has appeared in this way, the bhikkhu should go to the teacher and tell him 'Venerable sir, such and

58. '"*The sign*" is the learning sign and the counterpart sign, for both are stated here together. Herein, the three similes beginning with cotton are properly the learning sign, the rest are both. "*Some*" are certain teachers. The similes beginning with the "*cluster of gems*" are properly the counterpart sign' (Pm. 273).

59. "*Because of difference in perception*": because of the difference in the manner of perceiving that occurred before the arising of the sign, (Pm. 273).

such has appeared to me'. But [say the Dīgha Reciters] the teacher should say neither 'This is the sign' nor 'This is not the sign'; after saying 'It happens like this, friend', he should tell him 'Go on giving it attention again and again'; for if he were told 'It is the sign', he might [become complacent and] stop short at that (see M.i.193f.), and if he were told 'It is not the sign', he might get discouraged and give up; so he should encourage him to keep giving it his attention without saying either. So the Dīgha Reciters say, firstly. But the Majjhima Reciters say that he should be told 'This is the sign, friend. Well done. Keep giving attention to it again and again'.

219. Then he should fix his mind on that same sign; and so from now on, his development proceeds by way of fixing. For this is said by the Ancients:

'Fixing his mind upon the sign
'And putting away[60] extraneous aspects,
'The clever man anchors his mind
'Upon the breathings in and out'.

220. So as soon as the sign appears, his hindrances are suppressed, his defilements subside, his mindfulness is established, and his consciousness is concentrated in access concentration.

221. Then he should not give attention to the sign as to its colour, or review it as to its [specific] characteristic. He should guard it as carefully as a king's chief queen guards the child in her womb due to become a Wheel-turning Monarch,[61] or as a farmer guards the ripening crops; and he should avoid the seven unsuitable things beginning with the unsuitable abode and cultivate the seven suitable things. Then, guarding it thus, he should make it grow and improve with repeated attention, and he should practise the tenfold skill in absorption (Ch.IV,§42) and bring about evenness of energy (Ch.IV,§66).

222. As he strives thus, fourfold and fivefold jhana is achieved by him on that same sign in the same way as described under the earth kasina.

5-8. (See §189) However, when a bhikkhu has achieved the fourfold and fivefold jhana and wants to reach purity by developing the meditation subject through *observing* and through *turning away*, he should make that jhana familiar by attaining mastery in it in the five ways (Ch.IV,§131), and then embark upon insight by defining mentality-materiality. How?

223. On emerging from the attainment, [287] he sees that the in-breaths and out-breaths have the physical body and the mind as their origin; and that just as, when a blacksmith's bellows are being blown, the wind moves owing to the bag and

60. '*Vibhāvayaṃ*' can mean 'to do away with' or 'to explain'. Either is applicable here according to Pm. (p. 274).

61. For the 'Wheel-turning Monarch (*cakkavattin*)' see D. Sutta 26 and M. Sutta 129.

to the man's appropriate effort, so too, in-breaths and out-breaths are due to the body and the mind.

Next, he defines the in-breaths and out-breaths and the body as 'materiality', and the consciousness and the states associated with the consciousness as 'the immaterial [mind]'. This is in brief (cf.MA.i,249); but the detail will be explained later in the Defining of Mentality-materiality (Ch.XVIII,§3f.).

224. Having defined mentality-materialily in this way, he seeks its condition. With search he finds it, and so overcomes his doubts about the way of mentality-materiality's occurrence in the three divisions of time (Ch.XIX).

His doubts being overcome, he attributes the three characteristics [beginning with that of suffering to mentality and materiality], comprehending [them] by groups (Ch.XX, §2f.); he abandons the ten imperfections of insight beginning with illumination, which arise in the first stages of the Contemplation of Rise and Fall (Ch.XX,§105f.), and he defines as 'the path' the knowledge of the way that is free from these imperfections (Ch.XX,§126f.).

He reaches Contemplation of Dissolution by abandoning [attention to] arising. When all formations have appeared as terror owing to the contemplation of their incessant dissolution, he becomes dispassionate towards them (Ch. XXI), his greed for them fades away, and he is liberated from them (Ch.XXII).

After he has [thus] reached the four noble paths in due succession and has become established in the fruition of Arahantship, he at last attains to the nineteen kinds of Reviewing Knowledge (Ch.XXII,§18f.), and he becomes fit to receive the highest gifts from the world with its deities.

225. At this point his development of concentration through mindfulness of breathing, beginning with *counting* and ending with *looking back* (§189) is completed. This is the commentary on the first tetrad in all aspects.

[*Word Commentary Continued—Second Tetrad*]

226. Now since there is no separate method for developing the meditation subject in the case of the other tetrads, their meaning therefore needs only to be understood according to the word commentary.

(v) *He trains thus 'I shall breathe in......shall breathe out experiencing happiness'*, that is, making happiness known, making it plain. Herein, the happiness is experienced in two ways: (a) with the object, and (b) with non-confusion.[62]

62. '"*With the object*": under the heading of the object. The happiness included in the jhana that has that object is experienced "*because of the experiencing of the object*". What is meant? Just as, when a man who is looking for a snake discovers (experiences) its abode, the snake is, as it were, already discovered (experienced) and caught, owing to the

227. How is the happiness experienced with the object? He attains the two jhanas in which happiness is present. At the time when he has actually entered upon them the happiness is experienced with the object owing to the obtaining of the jhana, because of the experiencing of the object. How with non-confusion? When, after entering upon and emerging from one of the two jhanas accompanied by happiness, [288] he comprehends with insight that happiness associated with the jhana as liable to destruction and to fall, then at the actual time of the insight the happiness is experienced with non-confusion owing to the penetration of its characteristics [of impermanence, and so on].

228. For this is said in the Paṭisambhidā: 'When he knows 'unification of mind and non-distraction through long in-'breaths, mindfulness is established in him. By means of that 'mindfulness and that knowledge that happiness is experienc-'ed. When he knows unification of mind and non-distraction 'through long out-breaths...through short in-breaths,... 'through short out-breaths,...through in-breaths...out-'breaths experiencing the whole body,...through in-breaths '... out-breaths tranquillizing the bodily formation, mind-'fulness is established in him. By means of that mindfulness 'and that knowledge that happiness is experienced.

'(b) It is experienced by him when he adverts, when he 'knows, sees, reviews, steadies his mind, resolves with faith, 'exerts energy, establishes mindfulness, concentrates his mind, 'understands with understanding, directlyknows what is to be 'directly-known, fully-understands what is to be fully-under-'stood, abandons what is to be abandoned, develops what is to 'be developed, realizes what is to be realized. It is in this 'way that that happiness is experienced (Ps.i,187).

229. (vi)-(viii) The remaining [three] clauses should be understood in the same way as to meaning; but there is this difference here. The *experiencing* of *bliss* must be understood to be through three jhanas, and that of the *mental formation* through four. The mental formation consists of the two aggregates of feeling and perception. And in the case of the clause, *experiencing bliss*, it is said in the Paṭisambhidā in order to show the plane of insight here [as well]: '"Bliss" there are two

ease with which he will then be able to catch it with charms and spells, so too, when the object, which is the abode of the happiness, is experienced (discovered), then the happiness itself is experienced (discovered) too, owing to the ease with which it will be apprehended in its specific and general characteristics. "*By his penetration of its characteristics*": by penetration of the specific and general characteristics of happiness. For when the specific and general characteristics of anything are experienced then that thing is experienced according to reality' (Pm. 276).

'kinds of bliss, bodily bliss and mental bliss' (Ps.i,188). *Tranquillizing the mental formation*: tranquillizing the gross mental formation; stopping it, is the meaning. And this should be understood in detail in the same way as given under the bodily formation (see §176-85).

230. Here, moreover, in the 'happiness' clause feeling [which is actually being contemplated in this tetrad] is stated under the heading of 'happiness' [which is a formation] but in the 'bliss' clause feeling is stated in its own form. In the two 'mental-formation' clauses the feeling is that [necessarily] associated with perception because of the words 'Perception 'and feeling belong to the mind, these things being bound up 'with the mind are mental formations' (Ps.i.188). [289] So this tetrad should be understood to deal with contemplation of feeling.

[*Word Commentary Continued—Third Tetrad*]

231. (ix) In the third tetrad the *experiencing* of *the* [*manner of*] *consciousness* must be understood to be through four jhanas.

(x) *Gladdening the* [*manner of*] *consciousness*: he trains thus, making the mind glad, instilling gladness into it, cheering it, rejoicing it, I shall breathe in, shall breathe out. Herein, there is gladdening in two ways, through concentration and through insight.

How through concentration? He attains the two jhanas in which happiness is present. At the time when he has actually entered upon them he inspires the mind with gladness, instils gladness into it, by means of the happiness associated with the jhana. How through insight? After entering upon and emerging from one of the two jhanas accompanied by happiness he comprehends with insight that happiness associated with the jhana as liable to destruction and to fall, thus at the actual time of insight he inspires the mind with gladness, instils gladness into it by making the happiness associated with the jhana the object.

It is of one progressing in this way that the words 'He trains thus "I shall breathe in.. shall breathe out gladdening the [manner of] consciousness" ', are said.

232. (xi) *Concentrating* (*samādahaṁ*) *the* [*manner of*] *consciousness*: evenly (*samaṁ*) placing (*ādahanto*) the mind, evenly putting it on its object by means of the first jhana and so on. Or alternatively when, having entered upon those jhanas and emerged from them, he comprehends with insight the consciousness associated with the jhana as liable to destruction and to fall, then at the actual time of insight momentary unification of the mind[63]

63. '"*Momentary unification of the mind*": concentration lasting only for a moment. For that too, when it occurs uninterruptedly on its

arises through the penetration of the characteristics [of impermanence, and so on]. Thus the words 'He trains thus "I shall breathe in...shall breathe out concentrating the [manner of] consciousness"', are said also of one who evenly places the mind, evenly puts it on its object by means of the momentary unification of the mind arisen thus.

233. (xii) *Liberating the [manner of] consciousness,* he both breathes in and breathes out delivering, liberating, the mind from the hindrances by means of the first jhana, from applied and sustained thought by means of the second, from happiness by means of the third, from pleasure and pain by means of the fourth. Or alternatively, when, having entered upon those jhanas and emerged from them, he comprehends with insight the consciousness, associated with the jhana as liable to destruction and to fall, then at the actual time of insight he delivers, liberates, the mind from the perception of permanence by means of the contemplation of impermanence, from the perception of pleasure by means of the contemplation of pain, from the perception of self by means of the contemplation of not self, from delight by means of the contemplation of dispassion, from greed by means of the contemplation of fading away, from arousing by means of the contemplation of cessation, from grasping by means of the contemplation of relinquishment. Hence it is said [290] 'He trains thus "I shall breathe in....shall breathe out liberating the [manner of] consciousness"'.[64]

So this tetrad should be understood to deal with contemplation of mind.

---

object in a single mode and is not overcome by opposition, fixes the mind immovably, as if in absorption' (Pm. 278).

64. '"*Delivering*": secluding, separating, by means of deliverance consisting in suppression; abandoning the hindrances, is the meaning. "*At the actual time of insight*": at the time of contemplation of dissolution. For dissolution is the furthest extreme of impermanence. So the meditator who is contemplating dissolution by its means sees under the heading of *consciousness* the whole field of formations as impermanent, not as permanent; and because of the suffering inherent in what is impermanent, and because of the absence of self in what is painful he sees that same whole field of formations as painful, not as pleasant, and as not-self, not as self. But since what is impermanent, painful, and not self is not something to delight in, and what is not something to delight in is not something to be greedy for, consequently he becomes dispassionate towards that whole field of formations when it is seen in the light of dissolution as impermanent, painful, not self, he does not delight in it, and his greed for it fades away, does not dye him. Now, as he thus becomes dispassionate and his greed fades away, it is firstly by means of mundane knowledge only that he causes greed to cease and does not arouse it. The meaning is that he does not bring about its arising. Or alternatively his greed having thus faded away, he causes by means of his own knowledge the cessation of the unseen field of formations just as that of the seen, he does not arouse it; the meaning is that he brings about only its cessation, he does not bring about its arising. Having entered on this way, he relinquishes, he does not grasp. What

[*Word Commentary Continued—Fourth Tetrad*]

234. (xiii) But in the fourth tetrad, as to *contemplating impermanence*, here firstly, the impermanent should be understood, and impermanence, and the contemplation of impermanence, and one contemplating impermanence.

Herein, the five aggregates are *the impermanent*. Why? because their essence is rise and fall and change. *Impermanence* is the rise and fall and change in those same aggregates, or it is their non-existence after having been; the meaning is, it is the break-up of produced aggregates through their momentary dissolution since they do not remain in the same mode. *Contemplation of impermanence* is contemplation of materiality, etc., as 'impermanent' in virtue of that impermanence. *One contemplating impermanence* possesses that contemplation. So it is when one such as this is breathing in and breathing out that it can be understood of him 'He trains thus "I shall breathe in...shall breathe out contemplating impermanence" '.[65]

---

is meant? It is that this contemplation of impermanence, etc., is called relinquishment as giving up and relinquishment as entering into because it gives up defilements along with aggregate-producing kamma-formations and because, by seeing the flaws in what is formed and by inclining towards the opposite of what is formed, namely nibbana, it enters into that nibbana. Consequently the meditator who has that contemplation gives up defilements and enters into nibbana in the way stated. Herein, the contemplation of what is impermanent as only impermanent is "*contemplation of impermanence*"; this is a name for insight that occurs by taking formations of the three [mundane] planes [and leaving aside the supramundane] as impermanent. "*From the perception of permanence*": from the wrong perception that occurs perceiving formed things as permanent, eternal; also the various views should be regarded as included under the heading of perception. Likewise with the perception of pleasure and so on. "*By means of the contemplation of dispassion*": by means of the contemplation that occurs in the mode of dispassion for formations. "*From delight*": from craving accompanied by happiness. "*By means of the contemplation of fading away*": by means of the contemplation that occurs similarly in the mode of fading away; hence "*delivering from greed*" is said. "*By means of the contemplation of cessation*": by means of the successive seeing of formations' cessation. Or contemplating cessation is contemplation such that formations cease only and do not arise with future renewal. For this is Knowledge of Desire for Deliverance grown strong. Hence he said "*delivering from arousing*". Contemplation that occurs in the mode of relinquishing is "*contemplation of relinquishment*". "*From grasping*" from taking as permanent etc.; or the meaning can also here be regarded as "from grasping rebirth-linking"' (Pm. 279). See Chs. XX and XXI.

65. 'What is called "permanent" is what is lasting, eternal, like nibbana. What is called "impermanent" is what is not permanent, and is possessed of rise and fall. He said "*The five aggregates are 'the impermanent'*", signifying that they are formed dhammas as to meaning. Why? "*Because their essence is rise and fall and change;* the meaning is that their individual essences have rise and fall and change. Herein, formed dhammas' arising owing to cause and condition, their coming

235. (xiv) *Contemplating fading away*: there are two kinds of fading away, that is, fading away as destruction, and absolute fading away.[66] Herein, 'fading away as destruction' is the momentary dissolution of formations. 'Absolute fading away' is nibbana. Contemplation of fading away is insight and it is the path, which occur as the seeing of these two. It is when he possesses this twofold contemplation that it can be understood of him 'He trains thus "I shall breathe in... shall breathe out contemplating fading away"'.

(xv) The same method of explanation applies to the clause, *contemplating cessation*.

236. (xvi) *Contemplating relinquishment*: relinquishment is of two kinds too, that is to say, relinquishment as giving up, and relinquishment as entering into. Relinquishment itself as [a way of] contemplation is 'contemplation of relinquishment'. For insight is called both 'relinquishment as giving up' and 'relinquishment as entering into' since [firstly] through substitution of opposite qualities it gives up defilements with their aggregate-producing kamma formations, and [secondly], through seeing the wretchedness of what is formed, it also enters into nibbana by inclining towards nibbana, which is the opposite of the formed (ch. Ch. XXI, 18). Also the path is called both relinquishment as giving up' and 'relinquishment as entering into' since it gives up defilements with their aggregate-producing kamma-formations by cutting them off, and it enters into nibbana by making it its object. Also both [insight and path knowledge] are called contemplation (*anupassanā*) because of their re-seeing successively (*anu anu passanā*) each preceding kind of knowledge.[67] [291] It is when he possesses this twofold contemplation

---

to be after non-existence, their acquisition of an individual self (*atta-lābha*), is "rise". Their momentary cessation when arisen is "fall". Their changedness due to ageing is "change". For just as when the occasion of arising dissolves and the occasion of dissolution [succeeds it] there is no break in the object (*vatthu*), so also there is no break in the object on the occasion facing dissolution, in other words, presence, which is what the term of common usage "ageing" refers to. So it is proper that the ageing of a single dhamma is meant, which is called "momentary ageing". And without any reservation there must be no break in the object between the occasions of arising and dissolution, otherwise it follows that one thing arises and another dissolves' (Pm. 280).

66. '"*Destruction*" is the vanishing of formations, it is the act of those formations' fading away, their disintegration, that is "*fading away*". Destruction itself as fading away is "*fading away as destruction*", this is momentary cessation. Formations fade away absolutely here when this has been reached, thus it is "*absolute fading away*"; this is nibbana' (Pm. 280).

67. 'The act of relinquishing as the act of giving up by means of substituting for what should be abandoned its opposite quality or by cutting it off, is "*relinquishment as giving up*". Likewise the act of relinquishing of self that takes place in non-formation of kamma, which is the

that it can be understood of him 'He trains thus "I shall breathe in...shall breathe out contemplating relinquishment"'.

237. This tetrad deals only with pure insight while the previous three deal with serenity and insight.

This is how the development of mindfulness of breathing with its sixteen bases in four tetrads should be understood.

[*Conclusion*]

This mindfulness of breathing with its sixteen bases thus is of great fruit, of great benefit.

238. Its great beneficialness should be understood here as peacefulness both because of the words 'And, bhikkhus, this 'concentration through mindfulnes of breathing, when 'developed and much practised, is both peaceful and sublime' (S.v.321), etc., and because of its ability to cut off applied thoughts; for it is because it is peaceful, sublime, and an unadulterated blissful abiding that it cuts off the mind's running hither and thither with applied thoughts obstructive to concentration, and keeps the mind only on the breaths as object. Hence it is said 'Mindfulness of breathing should be 'developed in order to cut off applied thoughts' (A.iv.353).

239. Also its great beneficialness should be understood as the root condition for the perfecting of clear vision and deliverance for this has been said by the Blessed One: 'Bhikkhus, mind-'fulness of breathing, when developed and much practised, 'perfects the four foundations of mindfulness. The four 'foundations of mindfulness, when developed and much 'practised, perfect the seven enlightenment factors. The 'seven enlightenment factors, when developed and much 'practised, perfect clear vision and deliverance' (M.iii,82).

---

relinquishing of all substrata (circumstances) of becoming being the entering into that [nibbana] either by inclination towards it [in insight] or by having it as object [in the path] is "*relinquishment as entering into*". "*Through substitution of opposite qualities*": here contemplation of impermanence, firstly, gives up perception of permanence by abandoning through substitution of the opposite [e.g. substituting perception of impermanence for that of permanence in the case of all formed things]. And the giving up in this way is in the form of inducing non-occurrence. For all kamma-formations that are rooted in defilements due to apprehending [formations] as permanent, and the kamma-resultant aggregates rooted in both which might arise in the future, are abandoned by causing their non-occurrence. Likewise in the case of perception of pain, and so on. "*Through seeing the wretchedness of what is formed*": through seeing the fault of impermanence, etc., in the formed three-plane field of formations. It is "*the opposite of the formed*" owing to its permanence, and so on, When defilements are given up by the path, then kamma-formations are called "given up" through producing (*āpādana*) in them the nature of not causing result, and aggregates rooted in them are called "given up" through their being rendered fit for non-arising. So the path gives up all these, is what is meant' (Pm. 281). The word *pakkhandana* (rendered by 'entering into') is used to define the act of faith, and can also be rendered by 'launching out into' or by 'leap'.

240. Again its great beneficialness should be understood to reside in the fact that it causes the final in-breaths and out-breaths to be known; for this is said by the Blessed One: 'Rāhula, when mindfulness of breathing is thus developed, 'thus practised much, the final in-breaths and out-breaths, 'too, are known as they cease, not unknown' (M.i,425-6).

241. Herein, there are three kinds of [breaths that are] final because of cessation, that is to say, final in becoming, final in jhana, and final in death. For, among the various kinds of becoming (existence), in-breaths and out-breaths occur in the sensual-sphere becoming, not in the fine-material and immaterial kinds of becoming. That is why there are final ones in becoming. In the jhanas they occur in the first three but not in the fourth. That is why there are final ones in jhana. Those that arise along with the sixteenth consciousness preceeding the death consciousness [292] cease together with the death consciousness. They are called 'final in death'. It is these last that are meant here by 'final'.

242. When a bhikkhu has devoted himself to this meditation subject, it seems, if he adverts, at the moment of arising of the sixteenth consciousness before the death consciousness, to their arising, then their arising is evident to him, if he adverts to their presence, then their presence is evident to him; if he adverts to their dissolution, then their dissolution is evident to him; and it is so because he has thoroughly discerned in-breaths and out-breaths as object.

243. When a bhikkhu has attained Arahantship by developing some other meditation subject than this one, he may be able to define his life term or not. But when he has reached Arahantship by developing this mindfulness of breathing with its sixteen bases, he can always define his life term. He knows 'My vital formations will continue now for so long and no more'. Automatically he performs all the functions of attending to the body, dressing and robing, etc., after which he closes his eyes, like the Elder Tissa who lived at Koṭapabbata Monastery, like the Elder Mahā-Tissa who lived at the Mahā-Karañjiya Monastery, like the Elder Tissa the alms-food eater in the kingdom of Devaputta, like the Elders who were brothers and lived at the Cittalapabbata Monastery.

244. Here is one story as an illustration. After reciting the *Paṭimokkha*, it seems, on the Uposatha day of the full moon one of the two Elders who were brothers went to his own dwelling place surrounded by the Community of Bhikkhus. As he stood on the walk looking at the moonlight he calculated his own vital formations, and he said to the Community of Bhikkhus 'In what way have you seen bhikkhus attaining nibbana up till now?'. Some answered 'Till now

we have seen them attain nibbana sitting in their seats'. Others answered 'We have seen them sitting cross-legged in the air'. The Elder said 'I shall now show you one attaining nibbana while walking'. He then drew a line on the walk, saying 'I shall go from this end of the walk to the other end and return; when I reach this line I shall attain nibbana'. So saying, he stepped on to the walk and went to the far end. On his return he attained nibbana in the same moment in which he stepped on the line. [293]

So let a man, if he is wise,
Untiringly devote his days
To mindfulness of breathing, which
Rewards him always in these ways.

This is the section dealing with mindfulness of breathing in the detailed explanation.

*

[(10) Recollection of Peace]

245. One who wants to develop the recollection of peace mentioned next to mindfulnes of breathing (Ch.III,§105) should go into solitary retreat and recollect the special qualities of nibbana, in other words, the stilling of all suffering, as follows:

'Bhikkhus, in so far as there are dhammas, whether formed 'or unformed, fading away is pronounced the best of them, 'that is to say, the disillusionment of vanity, the elimination 'of thirst, the abolition of reliance, the termination of the 'round, the destruction of craving, fading away, cessation, 'nibbana' (A.ii,34).

246. Herein *in so far as* means as many as. *Dhammas* [means] individual essences.[68] *Whether formed or unformed*: whether

---

68. 'In such passages as "Dhammas that are concepts" (Dhs., p. 1; §1308) even a non-entity (*abhāva*) is thus called a "dhamma" since it is borne (*dhārīyati*) and affirmed (*avadhārīyati*) by knowledge. That kind of dhamma is excluded by his saying "*Dhammas* [*means*] *individual essences*". The act of becoming (*bhavana*), which constitutes existingness (*vijjamānatā*) in the ultimate sense, is essence (*bhāva*); it is with essence (*saha bhāvena*), thus it is an individual essence (*sabhāva*); the meaning is that it is possible (*labbhamānarūpa*) in the true sense, in the ultimate sense. For these are called "dhammas (bearers)" because they bear (*dhāraṇa*) their own individual essences (*sabhāva*), and they are called "individual essences" in the sense already explained' (Pm. 282; cf Ch. VII, n. 1).

In the Pitakas the word *sabhāva* seems to appear only once (Ps.ii,178). It next appears in the Netti (p.79), the Milindapañhā (pp.90,164,212, 360). It is extensively used for exegetical purposes in the Visuddhimagga and main commentaries and likewise in the sub-commentaries. As has just been shown, it is narrower than dhamma (see also Ch. XXIII,n.18). It often roughly corresponds to *dhātu* (element—see e.g.DhsA.263) and to

made by conditions going together, coming together, or

---

lakkhaṇa (characteristic—see below), but less nearly to the vaguer and (in Pali) untechnical *pakati* (nature), or to *rasa* (function—see Ch.I,§21). The Atthasālinī observers: 'It is the individual essence, or the generality, of such and such dhammas that is called their characteristic' (DhsA.63); on which the Mūla Ṭīkā comments: 'The *individual essence* consisting in, say, hardness as that of earth, or touching as that of contact, is not common to all dhammas. The *generality* is the individual essence common to all consisting in impermanence, etc.; also in this context (i.e.Dhs.§1) the characteristic of being profitable may be regarded as general because it is the individual essence common to all that is profitable; or alternatively it is their individual essence because it is not common to the unprofitable and indeterminate [kinds of consciousness]' (DhsAA.63). The individual essence of any formed dhamma is manifested in the three instants of its existence (*atthitā, vijjamānatā*), namely, arising, presence (=ageing) and dissolution. It comes from nowhere and goes nowhere (Ch.XV,§15) and is borne by the mind. Dhammas without individual essence (*asabhāva-dhamma*) include the Attainment of Cessation (see Ch.XXIII,n.18) and some concepts. Space and time belong to the last-mentioned. Of space (*ākāsa*) the Ṭīkā to the Majjima Nikāya says: 'Space, which is quite devoid of individual essence, is called empty' (commenting on M. Sutta 106), while of time (*kāla*) the Mūla Ṭīkā says: 'Though time is determined by the kind of consciousness [e.g. as specified in the first paragraph of the Dhammasanganī] and is non-existent (*avijjamāna*) as to individual essence, yet as the non-entity (*abhāva*) before and after the moment in which those [conascent and co-present] dhammas occur, it is called the "container *adhīkarana*"; it is perceived (symbolized) only as the state of a receptacle (*ādhāra-bhāva*)' (DhsAA.62). Of nibbana (for which see Ch. XVI,§64ff.), which has its own individual essence, the Mūla Ṭīkā says: Nibbana is not like other dhammas; because of its extreme profundity it cannot be made an object of consciousness (*ālambituṁ*) by one who has not realized it. That is why it has to be realized by Change-of-lineage. It has profundity surpassing any individual essence belonging to the three periods of time' (Vbh.AA.38).

'*Sabhāva*' has not the extreme vagueness of its parent '*bhāva*', which can mean anything between 'essence' (see e.g. DhsA. 61) and '-ness' (e.g. *natthi-bhāva*=non-existingness—Ch.X,§35). This may be remembered when *sabhāva* is defined as above thus 'It is with essence (*saha bhāvena*)' thus it is individual essence (*sabhāva*)' (Pm.282), and when it is defined again thus 'A dhamma's own essence or its existing essence (*sako vā bhāvo samāno vā bhāvo*) is its individual essence (*sabhāva*)' (Pm.433). *Sabhāva* can also be the basis of a wrong view, if regarded as the sole efficient cause or condition of any formed thing (Ch.XVI,n.23). The Sanskrit equivalent, *svabhāva*, had a great vogue and chequered history in philosophical discussions on the Indian mainland.

This (unlike the word, *dhamma*, which has many 'referents') is an instance in which it is of first importance to stick to one rendering. The word is a purely exegetical one; consequently vagueness is undesirable, 'Individual essence' has been chosen principally on etymological grounds, and the word 'essence' (an admittedly slippery customer) must be understood from the contexts in which it is used and not prejudged. Strictly it refers here to the triple moment of arising etc., of formed dhammas that can have such 'existence' in their own right and be experienced as such; and it refers to the realizability of nibbana. We are here in the somewhat magical territory of Ontology, a subject which is at present undergoing one of its periodical upheavals in Europe, this time in the hands of the Existentialists. Consequently it is important to approach the subject with an open mind.

not so made.[69] *Fading away is pronounced the best of them*: of these formed and unformed dhammas fading away is pronounced the best, is called the foremost, the highest.

247. Herein *fading away* is not mere absence of greed, but rather it is that unformed dhamma which, while given the names 'disillusionment of vanity', etc., in the clause 'that is to say, the disillusionment of vanity,...nibbana', is treated basically as *fading away*.[70] It is called *disillusionment of vanity* because on coming to it all kinds of vanity (intoxication), such as the vanity of conceit, and vanity of manhood, are disillusioned, undone, done away with.[71] And it is called *elimination of thirst* because on coming to it all thirst for sense desires is eliminated and quenched. But it is called *abolition of reliance* because on coming to it reliance on the five cords of sense desire is abolished. It is called *termination of the round* because on coming to it the round of the three planes [of existence] is terminated. It is called *destruction of craving* because on coming to it craving is entirely destroyed, fades away and ceases. It is called *nibbāna* (*extinction*) because it has gone away from (*nikkhanta*), has escaped from (*nissata*), is dissociated from, craving, which has acquired in common usage the name 'fastening (*vāna*)' because, by ensuring successive becoming, craving serves as a joining together, a binding together, a lacing together, of the four kinds of generation, five destinies, seven stations of consciousness and nine abodes of beings.[72] [294]

248. This is how peace, in other words, nibbana, should be recollected according to its special qualities beginning with disillusionment of vanity. But it should also be recollected according

---

69. '"*Made*" is generated. "*Not so made*" is not made by any conditions at all' (Pm. 281).

70. 'That dhamma possessing individual essence and having the characteristic of being not formed is to be treated basically as "*fading away*", since it is there that the dhamma of defilement fades away' (Pm. 282).

71. 'When they are being abandoned by the noble path, which occurs by making nibbana its object, it is said that they are abandoned by reaching that [nibbana], which is why he said "*Because on coming to it*", and so on. Herein, "*vanity of conceit* (*māna-mada*)" is conceit (*māna*) that occurs as conceiving (*maññanā*) "I am superior" (Vbh. 353). "*Vanity of manhood*" is vanity about being of the male sex. The words "*such as*" refer to vanity of birth, and so (Vbh. 345)' (Pm. 282).

72. Modern etymology derives the word '*nibbāna* (Skr. *nirvāna*)' from the negative prefix *nir* plus the root *vā* (to blow). The original literal meaning was probably 'extinction' of a fire by ceasing to blow on it with bellows (a smith's fire for example). It seems to have been extended to extinction of fire by any means, for example, the going out of a lamp's flame (*nibbāyati*—M. iii, 245). By analogy it was extended to the extinction of greed, etc., in the Arahant, with the resultant extinction of the five-aggregate process on the Arahant's death (see Iti. 38). *Nibbāna* is not the 'extinction of a self or of a living lasting being', such a mistaken opinion being the Annihilation View (see e.g. M.i, 140; S. iii, 109).

to the other special qualities of peace stated by the Blessed One in the suttas beginning with 'Bhikkhus, I shall teach you 'the unformed...the truth...the other shore...the hard-to-'see...the undecaying...the lasting...the undiversified... 'the deathless...the auspicious...the safe...the marvellous... 'the intact...the unafflicted...the purity...the island... 'the shelter...' (S.iv,360-72).[73]

249. As he recollects peace in its special qualities of disillusionment of vanity, etc., in this way, then 'On that occasion his 'mind is not obsessed by greed or obsessed by hate or 'obsessed by delusion; his mind has rectitude on that 'occasion, being inspired by peace' (see Ch.VII,§65,etc.).

So when he has suppressed the hindrances in the way already described under the Recollection of the Enlightened One, etc., the jhana factors arise in a single moment. But owing to the profundity of the special qualities of peace, or owing to his being occupied in recollecting special qualities of various kinds, the jhana is only access and does not reach absorption. And that jhana itself is known as 'recollection of peace' too because it arises by means of the special qualities of peace.

250. And as in the case of the six Recollections, this also comes to success only in a noble disciple. Still, though this is so, it can nevertheless also be brought to mind by an ordinary person who values peace. For even by hearsay the mind has confidence in peace.

251. A bhikkhu who is devoted to this recollection of peace sleeps in bliss and wakes in bliss, his faculties are peaceful, his mind is peaceful, he has conscience and shame, he is confident, he is resolved [to attain] the superior [state], he is respected and honoured by his fellows in the life of purity. And even if he penetrates no higher, he is at least headed for a happy destiny.

So that is why a man of wit
Untiringly devotes his days
To mind the Noble Peace, which can
Reward him in so many ways.

This is the section dealing with the recollection of peace in the detailed explanation.

The eighth chapter called 'Description of Recollections as Meditation Subjects' in the Treatise on the Development of Concentration in the Path of Purification composed for the purpose of gladdening people.

---

73. Some texts add *leṇa* (another word for shelter). Still others are given in the Samyutta text.

CHAPTER IX.

DESCRIPTION OF CONCENTRATION— THE DIVINE ABIDINGS

(Brahmavihāra-niddesa)

[(1) LOVINGKINDNESS]

1. [295] The four Divine Abidings were mentioned next to the Recollections as Meditation Subjects (Ch. III, §,105). They are lovingkindness, compassion, gladness and equanimity. A meditator who wants to develop firstly lovingkindness among these, if he is a beginner, should sever the impediments and learn the meditation subject. Then, when he has done the work connected with the meal and got rid of any dizziness due to it, he should seat himself comfortably on a well-prepared seat in a secluded place. To start with he should review the danger in hate and the advantage in
2. patience. Why? Because hate has to be abandoned and patience attained in the development of this meditation subject and he cannot abandon unseen dangers and attain unknown advantages.

Now the danger in hate should be seen in accordance with such suttas as this: 'Friends, when a man hates, is a prey to ' hate and his mind is obsessed by hate, he kills living things, ' and...' (A.i,216). And the advantage in patience should be understood according to such suttas as these:

' No higher rule, the Buddhas say, than patience,
' and no nibbana higher than forbearance' (D.ii,49; Dh.184),
' Patience in force, in strong array:
' 'Tis him I call a brahman' (Dh.399),
' No greater thing exists than patience' (S.i, 222).

3. Thereupon he should embark upon the development of lovingkindness for the purpose of secluding the mind from hate seen as a danger and introducing it to patience known as an advantage.

But when he begins, he must know that some persons are of the wrong sort at the very beginning and that lovingkindness should be developed towards certain kinds of persons
4. and not towards certain other kinds at first. [296] For lovingkindness should not be developed at first towards the following four kinds of persons: an antipathetic person, a very dearly loved friend, a neutral person, and a hostile person. Also it should not be developed specifically (see §49) towards the opposite sex, or towards a dead person.

5. What is the reason why it should not be developed at first towards an antipathetic person and the others? To put an antipathetic person in a dear one's place is fatiguing. To put a very dearly loved friend in a neutral person's place is fatiguing; and if the slightest mischance befalls the friend, he feels like weeping. To put a neutral person in a respected one's or a dear one's place is fatiguing. Anger springs up in him if he recollects a hostile person. That is why it should not be developed at first towards an antipathetic person and the rest.

6. Then if he develops it specifically towards the opposite sex, lust inspired by that person springs up in him. An Elder supported by a family was asked, it seems, by a friend's son 'Venerable sir, towards whom should lovingkindness be developed?' The Elder told him, 'Towards a person one loves'. He loved his own wife. Through developing lovingkindness towards her he was fighting against the wall all the night.[1] That is why it should not be developed specifically towards the opposite sex.

7. But if he develops it towards a dead person, he reaches neither absorption nor access. A young bhikkhu, it seems, had started developing lovingkindness inspired by his teacher. His lovingkindness made no headway at all. He went to a Senior Elder and told him 'Venerable sir, I am quite familiar with attaining jhana through lovingkindness, and yet I cannot attain it. What is the matter?'. The Elder said 'Seek the sign, friend, [the object of your meditation]'. He did so. Finding that his teacher had died, he proceeded with developing lovingkindness inspired by another and attained absorption. That is why it should not be developed towards one who is dead.

8. First of all it should be developed only towards oneself, doing it repeatedly thus: 'May I be happy and free from suffering' or 'May I keep myself free from enmity, affliction and anxiety and live happily'.

9. If that is so, does it not conflict with what is said in the texts? For there is no mention of any development of it towards oneself in what is said in the Vibhaṅga, 'And how 'does a bhikkhu dwell pervading one direction with his heart 'filled with lovingkindness? Just as he would feel loving- 'kindness on seeing a dearly loved person, so he pervades all 'beings with lovingkindness' (Vbh.272), and in what is said in the Paṭisambhidā, 'In what five ways is the mind-deliverance

1. '"*Fighting against the wall*": having undertaken the precepts of virtue and sat down on a seat in his room with the door locked, he was developing lovingkindness. Blinded by lust arisen under cover of the lovingkindness, he wanted to go to his wife, and without noticing the door he beat on the wall in his desire to get out even by breaking the wall down' (Pm. 286).

'angry person is a prey to anger, ruled by anger; he miscon-'ducts himself in body, speech and mind. Misconducting 'himself thus in body, speech and mind, on the break up of 'the body, after death, he reappears in a state of loss in an 'unhappy destiny in perdition, in hell, being a prey to anger' (A.iv,94)? and this, 'As a log from a pyre, burnt at both ends 'and fouled in the middle, serves neither for timber in the 'village nor for timber in the forest, so is such a person as 'this I say' (A. ii,95; Iti. 90)? If you are angry now, you will be one who does not carry out the Blessed One's teaching; by repaying an angry man in kind you will be worse than the angry man and not win the battle hard to win; you will yourself do to yourself the things that help your enemy; and you will be like a pyre log.

16. If his resentment subsides when he strives and makes effort in this way, it is good. If not, then he should remove irritation by remembering some controlled and purified state in that person, which inspires confidence when remembered.

17. For one person may be controlled in his bodily behaviour with his control in doing an extensive course of duty known to all, though his verbal and mental behaviour are not controlled. Then the latter should be ignored and the control in his bodily behaviour remembered.

18. Another may be controlled in his verbal behaviour, and his control known to all—he may naturally be clever at welcoming kindly, easy to talk with, congenial, open-countenanced, deferential in speech and he may expound the Dhamma with a sweet voice and give explanations of Dhamma with well-rounded phrases and details—, though his bodily and mental behaviour are not controlled. Then the latter should be ignored and the control in his verbal behaviour remembered.

19. Another may be controlled in his mental behaviour, and his control in worshipping at shrines, etc., evident to all. For when one who is uncontrolled in mind pays homage at a shrine or at an Enlightenment Tree or to Elders, he does not do it carefully, [300] and he sits in the Dhamma-preaching pavilion with mind astray or nodding, while one whose mind is controlled pays homage carefully and deliberately, listens to the Dhamma attentively, remembering it, and evincing the confidence in his mind through his body or his speech. So another may be only controlled in his mental behaviour, though his bodily and verbal behaviour are not controlled. Then the latter should be ignored and the control in his mental behaviour remembered.

20. But there may be another in whom not even one of these three things is controlled. Then compassion for that person should be aroused thus: Though he is going about in the human world now, nevertheless after a certain number of

days he will find himself in [one of] the eight great hells or the sixteen prominent hells.[4] For irritation subsides too through compassion.

In yet another all three may be controlled. Then he can remember any of the three in that person, whichever he likes; for the development of lovingkindness towards such a person is easy.

21. And in order to make the meaning of this clear the following sutta from the Book of Fives should be cited in full: 'Bhikkhus 'there are five ways of dispelling annoyance whereby annoy- 'ance arisen in a bhikkhu can be entirely dispelled' (A.iii, 186-90).

22. But if irritation still arises in him in spite of his efforts, then he should admonish himself thus:

'Suppose an enemy has hurt
'You now in what is his domain,
'Why try yourself as well to hurt
'Your mind?—That is not his domain.

'In tears you left your family.
'They had been kind and helpful too.
'So why not leave your enemy,
'The anger that brings harm to you?
'This anger that you entertain
'Is gnawing at the very roots
'Of all the virtues that you guard—
'Who is there such a fool as you?

'Another does ignoble deeds,
'So you are angry—How is this?
'Do you then want to copy too
'The sort of acts that he commits?

'Suppose another, to annoy,
'Provokes you with some odious act,
'Why suffer anger to spring up,
'And do as he would have you do?

'If you get angry, then may be
'You make *him* suffer, may be not;
'Though with the hurt that anger brings
'*You* certainly are punished now.

'If anger-blinded enemies
'Set out to tread the path of woe,
'Do you by getting angry too
'Intend to follow heel to toe?

4. 'The eight great hells beginning with that of Sañjīva (see Jā.). At each of the four doors of the Great Unmitigated (Avīci) Hell there are the four beginning with the Ember (Kukuḷa) Hell (M. iii, 185), which make up the sixteen prominent hells' (Pm. 291).

'If hurt is done you by a foe
'Because of anger on your part,
'Then put your anger down, for why
'Should you be harassed groundlessly? [301]

'Since states last but a moment's time
'Those aggregates, by which was done
'The odious act, have ceased, so now
'What is it you are angry with?

'Whom shall he hurt, who seeks to hurt
'Another, in the other's absence?
'*Your* presence is the cause of hurt;
'Why are you angry, then, with *him*?'

23. But if resentment does not subside when he admonishes himself thus, then he should review the fact that he himself and the other are owners of their deeds (*kamma*).

Herein, he should first review this in himself thus: Now what is the point of your getting angry with him? Will not this kamma of yours that has anger as its source lead to your own harm? For you are the owner of your deeds, heir of your deeds, having deeds as your parent, deeds as your kin, deeds as your refuge; you will become the heir of whatever deeds you do (see A.iii, 186). And this is not the kind of deed to bring you to full enlightenment, to undeclared enlightenment or to the disciple's grade, or to any such position as the status of Brahmā or Sakka, or the throne of a Wheel-turning Monarch or a regional king, etc., but rather this is the kind of deed to lead to your fall from the Dispensation, even to the status of the eaters of scraps, etc., and to the manifold suffering in the hells, and so on. By doing this you are like a man who wants to hit another and picks up a burning ember or excrement in his hand and so first burns himself or makes himself stink.

24. Having reviewed ownership of deeds in himself in this way, he should review it in the other also: And what is the point of his getting angry with you? Will it not lead to his own harm? For that venerable one is owner of his deeds, heir of his deeds, . . .he will become the heir of whatever deeds he does. And this is not the kind of deed to bring him to full enlightenment, to undeclared enlightenment or to the disciple's grade or to any such position as the status of Brahmā or Sakka, or to the throne of a Wheel-turning Monarch or a regional king, etc.; but rather this is the kind of deed to lead to his fall from the Dispensation even to the status of the eaters of scraps, etc., and to the manifold suffering in the hells and so on. By doing this he is like a man who wants to throw dust at another against the wind and only covers himself with it.

For this is said by the Blessed One:

'When a fool hates a man that has no hate,
'Is purified and free from every blemish, [302]
'Such evil he will find comes back on him,
'As does fine dust thrown up against the wind' (Dh.125).

25. But if it still does not subside in him when he reviews ownership of deeds in this way, then he should review the special qualities of the Master's former conduct.

26. Here is the way of reviewing it: Now you who have gone forth, is it not the fact that when your Master was a Bodhisatta before discovering full enlightenment, while he was still engaged in fulfilling the Perfections during the four incalculable ages and a hundred thousand aeons, he did not allow hate to corrupt his mind even when his enemies tried to murder
27. him on various occasions? For example, in the Sīlavant Birth Story (Jā. i, 261) when his friends rose to prevent his kingdom of three hundred leagues being seized by an enemy king who had been incited by a wicked minister in whose mind his own queen had sown hate for him, he did not allow them to lift a weapon. Again when he was buried, along with a thousand companions, up to the neck in a hole dug in the earth in a charnel ground, he had no thought of hate. And when, after saving his life by a heroic effort helped by jackals scrapping away soil when they had come to devour the corpses, he went with the aid of a spirit to his own bedroom and saw his enemy lying on his own bed, he was not angry but treated him as a friend, undertaking a mutual pledge, and he then exclaimed:

'The brave aspire, the wise will not lose heart;
'I see myself as I had wished to be' (Jā.i,267).

28. And in the Khantivādin Birth Story he was asked by the stupid king of Kāsi (Benares) 'What do you preach, monk?', and he replied 'I am a preacher of patience'; and when the king had him flogged with scourges of thorns and had his hands and feet cut off, he felt not the slightest anger (see Jā. iii, 39).

29. It is perhaps not so wonderful that an adult who had actually gone forth into homelessness should have acted in that way; but also as an infant he did so. For in the Cūḷa-Dhammapāla Birth Story his hands and feet were ordered to be lopped off like four bamboo shoots by his father, king Mahāpatāpa, and his mother lamented over him thus:

'Oh Dhammapāla's arms are severed
'That had been bathed in sandalwood;
'He was the heir to all the earth:
'O king, my breath is choking me!' (Jā.iii,181). [303]

Then his father, still not satisfied, commanded that his head be cut off as well. But even then he had not the least trace of hate, since he had firmly resolved thus: 'Now is the time to restrain your mind; now, good Dhammapāla, be impartial towards these four persons, that is to say, towards your father who is having your head cut off, the man who is beheading you, your lamenting mother, and yourself'.

30. And it is perhaps not so wonderful that one who had become a human being should have acted in that way; but also as an animal he did so. For while the Bodhisatta was the elephant called Chaddanta he was pierced in the navel by a poisoned shaft. But even then he allowed no hate towards the hunter who had wounded him to corrupt his mind, according as it is said:

' The elephant, when struck by the stout shaft,
' Addressed the hunter with no hate in mind:
' "What is your aim? What is the reason why
' "You kill me thus? What can your purpose be?" '
(Jā.v,51).

And when the elephant had spoken thus and was told 'Sir, I have been sent by the king of Kāsi's queen to get your tusks', in order to fulfil her wish he cut off his own tusks whose gorgeous radiance glittered with the flashes of the six-coloured rays and gave them to him.

31. And when he was the Great Monkey, the man whom he had pulled out of a rocky chasm thought,

' Now this is food for human kind
' Like other forest animals,
' So why then should a hungry man
' Not kill the ape to eat? [I ask.]
' I'll travel independently
' Taking his meat as a provision;
' Thus I shall cross the waste, and that
' Will furnish my viaticum' (Jā.v.71).

Then he took up a stone and dashed it on his head. But the Monkey looked at him with eyes full of tears and said,

' Oh act not so, good sir, or else
' The fate you reap will long deter
' All others from such deeds as this
' That you would do to me today (Jā.v,71),

and with no hate in his mind and regardless of his own pain he saw to it that the man reached his journey's end in safety.

32. And while he was the Royal Nāga (serpent) Būridatta[304] when he had undertaken the Uposatha precepts and was lying on the top of an ant-hill, though he was [caught and] sprinkled with medicinal charms resembling the fire that ushers in the end of an aeon, and was put into a box and treated as a plaything throughout the whole of Jambudīpa, yet he had no trace of hate for that brahman, according as it is said,

'While being put into the coffer
'And being crushed down with his hand,
'I had no hate for Ālambāna
'Lest I should break my precept vow' (Cp. 85).

33. And when he was the Royal Nāga Campeyya he let no hate spring up in his mind while he was being cruelly treated by a snake charmer, according as it is said,

'While I was living in the Law
'Observing the Uposatha
'A snake charmer took me away
'To play with at the royal gate.
'Whatever hue he might conceive,
'Blue and yellow, and red as well,
'So in accordance with his thought
'I would become what he had wished;
'I would turn dry land into water,
'And water into land likewise.
'Now had I given way to wrath
'I could have seared him into ash,
'Had I relaxed mind-mastery
'I should have let my virtue lapse;
'And one who lets his virtue lapse;
'Cannot attain the highest goal' (Cp. 85).

34. And when he was the Royal Nāga Saṅkhapāla, while he was being carried along on a carrying pole by the sixteen village boys after they had wounded him in eight places with sharp spears and inserted thorn creepers into the wounds' orifices, and while, after threading a strong rope through his nose, they were causing him great agony by dragging him along bumping his body on the surface of the ground, though he was capable of turning those village boys to cinders with a mere glance, yet he did not even show the least trace of hate on opening his eyes, according as it is said:

'On the Fourteenth and the Fifteenth too, Āḷāra,
'I regularly kept the Holy Day,
'Until there came those sixteen village boys
'Bearing a rope and a stout spear as well.
'The hunters cleft my nose, and through the slit
'They passed a rope and dragged me off like that.
'But though I felt such poignant agony,
'I let no hate disturb my Holy Day' (Jā.v,172). [305]

35. And he performed not only these wonders but also many others too such as those told in the Mātuposaka Birth Story (Jā,iv,90). Now it is in the highest degree improper and unbecoming to you to arouse thoughts of resentment, since you are emulating as your Master that Blessed One who reached omniscience and who has in the special quality of patience no equal in the world with its deities.

36. But if, as he reviews the special qualities of the Master's former conduct, the resentment still does not subside in him, since he has long been used to the slavery of defilement, then he should review the suttas that deal with the beginninglessness [of the round of rebirths]. Here is what is said: 'Bhikkhus, it is not easy to find a being who has not formerly been your mother. . .your father. . .your brother. . .your sister. . . your son. . .your daughter' (S.ii,189-90). Consequently he should think about that person thus: This person, it seems, as my mother in the past carried me in her womb for ten months and removed from me without disgust as if it were yellow sandalwood my urine, excrement, spittle, snot, etc., and played with me in her lap, and nourished me, carrying me about at her hip. And this person as my father went by goat paths and paths set on piles,[5] etc., to pursue the trade of merchant, and he risked his life for me by going into battle in double array, by sailing on the great ocean in ships and doing other difficult things and he nourished me by bringing back wealth by one means or another thinking to feed his children. And as my brother, sister, son, daughter, this person gave me such and such help. So it is unbecoming for me to harbour hate for him in my mind.

37. But if he is still unable to quench that thought in this way, then he should review the advantages of lovingkindness thus: Now you who have gone forth into homelessness, has it not been said by the Blessed One as follows: 'Bhikkhus, when the mind-deliverance of lovingkindness is cultivated, developed, much practised, made the vehicle, made the foundation, established, consolidated, and properly undertaken, eleven blessings can be expected. What are the eleven? A man sleeps in comfort, wakes in comfort, and dreams no evil dreams, he is dear to human beings, he is dear to non-human beings, deities guard him, fire and poison and weapons do not affect him, his mind is easily concentrated, the expression of his face is serene, he dies unconfused, if he penetrates no higher he will be reborn in the Brahmā World' (A. v, 342). [306]. If you do not stop this thought, you will be denied these advantages.

38. But if he is still unable to stop it in this way, he should try resolution into elements. How? Now you who have gone forth into homelessness, when you are angry with him, what is it you are angry with? Is it head hairs you are angry with? or body hairs? or nails?. . .or is it urine you are angry with? Or alternatively, is it the earth element in the head hairs etc,, you are angry with? or the water element? or the fire element?

5. '*Saṅku-patha*—paths set on piles': Pm. (p. 294) says '*Saṅku laggāpetvā te ālambhitvā gamanamaggo saṅkupatho*'. This disagrees with P. T. S. Dict. this ref.

or is it the air element you are angry with? Or among the five aggregates or the twelve bases or the eighteen elements with respect to which this venerable one is called by such and such a name, which then, is it the materiality aggregate you are angry with? or the feeling aggregate, the perception aggregate, the formations aggregate, the consciousness aggregate you are angry with? Or is it the eye base you are angry with? or the visible-object base you are angry with?...or the mind base you are angry with? or the mental-object base you are angry with? Or is it the eye element you are angry with? or the visible-object element? or the eye-consciousness element?... or the mind element? or the mental-object element? or the mind-consciousness element you are angry with? For when he tries the resolution into elements, his anger finds no foothold, like a mustard seed on the point of an awl or a painting on the air.

39. But if he cannot effect the resolution into elements, he should try the giving of a gift. It can either be given by himself to the other or accepted by himself from the other. But if the other's livelihood is not purified and his requisites are not proper to be used, it should be given by oneself. And in the one who does this the annoyance with that person entirely subsides. And in the other even anger that has been dogging him from a past birth subsides at the moment, as happened to the senior elder who received a bowl given to him at the Cittalapabbata Monastery by an almsfood-eater elder who had been three times made to move from his lodging by him, and who presented it with these words 'Venerable sir, this bowl worth eight ducats was given me by my mother who is a lay devotee, and it is rightly obtained; let the good lay devotee acquire merit'. So efficacious is this act of giving. And this is said:

'A gift for taming the untamed,
'A gift for every kind of good;
'Through giving gifts they do unbend
'and condescend to kindly speech'. [307]

[*The Breaking Down of the Barriers—The Sign*]

40. When his resentment towards that hostile person has been thus allayed, then he can turn his mind with lovingkindness towards that person too, just as towards the one who is dear, the very dear friend, and the neutral person. Then he should break down the barriers by practising lovingkindness over and over again, accomplishing mental impartiality towards the four persons, that is to say, himself, the dear person, the neutral person and the hostile person.

41. The characteristic of it is this. Suppose this person is sitting in a place with a dear, a neutral, and a hostile person,

himself being the fourth; then bandits come to him and say 'Venerable sir, give us a bhikkhu', and on being asked why, they answer 'So that we may kill him and use the blood of his throat as an offering', then if that bhikkhu thinks 'Let them take this one, or this one', he has not broken down the barriers. And also if he thinks 'Let them take me but not these three', he has not broken down the barriers either. Why? Because he seeks the harm of him whom he wishes to be taken and seeks the welfare of the others only. But it is when he does not see a single one among the four people to be given to the bandits and he directs his mind impartially towards himself and towards those three people that he has broken down the

42. barriers. Hence the Ancients said:

'When he discriminates between
'The four, that is himself, the dear,
'The neutral, and the hostile one,
'Then "Skilled" is not the name he gets,
'Nor "Having Amity At Will",
'But only "Kindly Towards Beings",
'Now when a bhikkhu's barriers
'Have all the four been broken down,
'He treats with equal amity
'The whole world with its deities;
'Far more distinguished than the first
'Is He Who Knows No Barriers'.

43. Thus the sign and access are obtained by this bhikkhu simultaneously with the breaking down of the barriers. But when breaking down of the barriers has been effected, he reaches absorption in the way described under the earth kasina without trouble by cultivating, developing, and repeatedly practising that same sign.

At this point he has attained the first jhana, which abandons five factors, possesses five factors, is good in three ways, is endowed with ten characteristics, and is accompanied by lovingkindness. And when that has been obtained, then by cultivating, developing, and repeatedly pratising that same sign, he successively reaches the second and third jhanas in the fourfold system, and the second, third and fourth in the fivefold system. [308]

[*Texts and Commentary*]

44. Now it is by means of one of these jhanas beginning with the first that he 'Dwells pervading (intent upon) one direction with
' his heart endued with lovingkindness, likewise the second di-
' rection, likewise the third direction, likewise the fourh direc-
' tion and so above, below, and around; everywhere and equally
' he dwells pervading the entire world with his heart endued
' with lovingkindness, abundant, exalted, measureless, free

from enmity, and free from affliction' (Vbh.272; D.i,250). For this versatility comes about only in one whose consciousness has reached absorption in the first jhana and the rest.

45. And here *endued with lovingkindness* means possessing lovingkindness. *With his heart* (*cetasā*): with his mind (*cittena*). *One direction*: this refers to any one direction in which a being is first discerned and means pervasion of the beings included in that one direction. *Pervading*: touching, making his object. *He dwells* (*viharati*): he causes the occurrence of an abiding (*vihāra*—dwelling or continuation) in postures that is devoted to the divine abidings (see Ch. VI, § 103). *Likewise the second*: just as he dwells pervading any one direction among those beginning with the eastern one, so he does with the next one, and the third

46. and the fourth is the meaning. *So above*: in that same way in the upper direction is what is meant. *Below, around*: so too the lower direction and the direction all round. Herein, *below* is underneath, and *around* is in the intermediate directions. So he sends his heart full of lovingkindness back and forth in all directions like a horse in a circus ground. Up to this point specified pervasion with lovingkindness is shown in the discernment of each direction separately.

47. *Everywhere*, etc., is said for the purpose of showing unspecified pervasion. Herein, *everywhere* means in all places. *Equally* (*sabbattatāya*): to all classed as inferior, medium, superior, friendly, hostile, neutral, etc., just as to oneself (*attatā*); equality with oneself (*atta-samatā*) without making the distinction 'This is another being', is what is meant. Or alternatively *equally* (*sabbattatāya*) is with the whole state of the mind; not reserving even a little, is what is meant. [309]*Entire* (*sabbāvant*): possessing all beings (*sabbasattavant*); associated with all beings, is the meaning. *World* is the world of beings.

48. *Endued with lovingkindness* is said again here in order to introduce the synonyms beginning with *abundant*; Or alternatively *endued with lovingkindness* is repeated because the word *likewise* or the word *so* is not repeated here as it was in the case of the [preceding] specified pervasion. Or alternatively, it is said as a way of concluding. And *abundant* should be regarded here as abundance in pervading. But it is *exalted* in plane [from the sensual-sphere plane to the fine-material-sphere plane], *measureless* through familiarity and through having measureless beings as its object, *free from enmity* through abandonment of ill will and hostility, and *free from affliction* through abandonment of grief; without suffering, is what is meant. This is the meaning of the versatility described in the way beginning 'With his heart endued with lovingkindness'.

49. And just as this versatility is successful only in one whose mind has reached absorption, so too that described in the Paṭisambhidā should be understood to be successful only in one whose mind has reached absorption, that is to say: 'The mind-deliverance of lovingkindness is [practised] with 'unspecified pervasion in five ways. The mind-deliverance 'of lovingkindness is [practised] with specified pervasion in 'seven ways. The mind-deliverance of lovingkindness is '[practised] with directional pervasion in ten ways' (Ps. ii, 130).

50. And herein, the mind-deliverance of lovingkindness is [practised] with unspecified pervasion in these five ways: 'May all beings be free from enmity, affliction and anxiety, 'and live happily. May all breathing things. . .all creatures '. . . all persons . . .all those who have a personality be 'free from enmity, affliction and anxiety, and live happily, (Ps. ii, 130).

51. The mind-deliverance of lovingkindness is [practised] with specified pervasion in these seven ways: 'May all women be 'free from enmity, affliction and anxiety and live happily. 'May all men. . . all Noble Ones . . . all not Noble Ones . . . 'all deities . . . all human beings . . . all in states of loss be 'free from enmity, affliction and anxiety, and live happily' (Ps. ii, 131).

52. The mind-deliverance of lovingkindness is [practised] with directional pervasion in these ten ways: 'May all 'beings in the eastern direction be free from enmity, affliction 'and anxiety, and live happily. May all beings in the wes- 'tern direction . . . northern direction . . . southern direction '[310] . . . eastern intermediate direction . . . western inter- 'mediate direction . . . northern intermediate direction . . . 'southern intermediate direction . . . downward direction '. . . upward direction be free from enmity, affliction and 'anxiety, and live happily. May all breathing things in 'the eastern direction. . .May all creatures in the eastern 'direction . . . May all persons in the eastern direction . . . 'May all who have a personality in the eastern direction . . . '[etc.] . . . in the upward direction be free from enmity, 'affliction and anxiety, and live happily. May all women in 'the eastern direction . . . May all men in the eastern direc- 'tion. . .May all Noble Ones in the eastern direction...May all 'not Noble Ones in the eastern direction... May all deities in 'the eastern direction. . .May all human beings in the eastern 'direction. . .May all those in states of loss in the eastern 'direction . . . [etc.] . . . be free from enmity, affliction and 'anxiety, and live happily' (Ps.ii,131).

53. Herein, *all* signifies inclusion without exception. *Beings* (*satta*): they are held (*satta*), gripped (*visatta*) by desire and

greed for the aggregates beginning with materiality, thus they are beings (*satta*). For this is said by the Blessed One, 'Any 'desire for matter, Rādha, any greed for it, any delight in it, 'any craving for it, has held (*satta*) it, has gripped (*visatta*) 'it, that is why "a being (*satta*)" is said' (S.iii,190). But in ordinary speech this term of common usage is applied also to those who are without greed, just as the term of common usage 'palm fan (*tālavanta*)' is used for different sorts of fans [in general] even if made of split bamboo. However, [in the world] etymologists (*akkhara-cintaka*) who do not consider meaning have it that it is a mere name, while those who do consider meaning have it that a 'being (*satta*)' is so called with reference to the 'Bright Principle (*satta*').[6]

54. *Breathing things* (*pāṇa*): so called because of their state of breathing (*pāṇanatā*); the meaning is, because their existence depends on in-breaths and out-breaths. *Creatures* (*bhūta*): so called because of being (*bhūtatta*=becomeness); the meaning is, because of their being fully become (*sambhūtatta*), because of their being generated (*abhinibbattatta*). *Persons* (*puggala* : '*pum*' is what hell is called; they fall (*galanti*) into that, is the meaning. *Personality* (*attabhāva*) is what the physical body is called; or it is just the pentad of aggregates, since it is actually only a concept derived from that pentad of aggregates.[7] [What is referred to is] included (*pariyāpanna*) in that personality, thus it 'has a personality (*attabhāva-pariyāpanna*)'. 'Included in' is delimited by; 'gone into' is the meaning.

55. And all the remaining [terms] should be understood as synonyms for 'all beings' used in accordance with ordinary speech as in the case of the term 'beings'. Of course, [311] there are other synonyms too for all 'beings' such as all 'folks', all 'souls', etc.; still it is for clarity's sake that 'The mind-deliverance of lovingkindness is [practised] with unspecified pervasion in five ways' is said and that only these five are mentioned.

56. Those who would have it that there is not only a mere verbal difference between 'beings', 'breathing things', etc., but also an actual difference in meaning are contradicted by the mention of unspecified pervasion. So instead of taking

6. '*Satta*—the bright principle': Skr. *sattva*; one of the three principles in the Samkhya system, the other two being *rajas* (Pali *rajo*) or turbulence and *tamas* (Pali *tamo*) or darkness. Not in P. T. S. Dict.

7. 'Here when the aggregates are not fully understood, there is naming (*abhidāna*) of them and of the consciousness of them as self (*attā*), that is to say, the physical body or alternatively the five aggregates. "*Derived from*"; apprehending, gripping, making a support. "*Since it is actually a mere concept*": because of presence (*sabbhāvato*) as a mere concept in what is called a being, though in the highest sense the "being" is non-existent' (Pm. 298). See also Ch. VIII, n. 11

the meaning in that way the unspecified pervasion with lovingkindness is done in any one of these five ways.

And here, *may all beings be free from enmity* is one absorption; *free from affliction* is one absorption — free from affliction (*abyābajjha*) is free from afflictedness (*byābādha-rahita*);[8]—*free from anxiety* is one absorption—free from anxiety is free from suffering—; *may they live happily* is one absorption. Consequently he should do his pervading with lovingkindness according to whichever of these phrases is clear to him. So with the four kinds of absorption in each of the five ways there are twenty kinds of absorption in unspecified pervasion.

57. In specified pervasion, with the four kinds of absorption in each of the seven ways, there are twenty-eight kinds of absorption. And here 'woman' and 'man' are stated according to sex; 'Noble Ones' and 'not Noble Ones' according to Noble Ones and ordinary people; 'deities' and 'human beings' and 'those in states of loss' according to the kind of rebirth.

58. In directional pervasion, with twenty kinds of absorption in each of the directions beginning with 'all beings in the eastern direction', there are two hundred kinds of absorption; and with twenty-eight kinds in each of the directions beginning with 'all woman in the eastern direction' there are two hundred and eighty kinds; so these make four hundred and eighty kinds of absorption. Consequently all the kinds of absorption mentioned in the Paṭisambhidā amount to five hundred and twenty-eight.

59. So when this meditator develops the mind-deliverance of lovingkindness through any one of these kinds of absorption he obtains the eleven advantages described in the way beginning 'A man sleeps in comfort' (§37).

60. Herein, *sleeps in comfort* means that instead of sleeping uncomfortably, turning over and snoring as other people do, he sleeps comfortably, he falls asleep as though entering upon an attainment.

61. He *wakes in comfort*: instead of waking uncomfortably, groaning and yawning and turning over as others do, he wakes comfortably without contortions, like a lotus opening. [312]

62. He *dreams no evil dreams*: when he sees dreams, he sees only auspicious ones, as though he were worshipping a shrine, as though he were making an offering, as though he were hearing the Dhamma. But he does not see evil dreams as others do, as though being surrounded by bandits, as though being threatened by wild beasts, as though falling into chasms (see Ch. XIV, n. 45).

8. Harvard text reads '*byāpādarahita*', which would be renderable as 'free from ill will'. Pm. (p. 299) supports a reading *byābādha*, which seems better.

63. *He is dear to human beings:* he is as dear to and beloved by human beings as a necklace worn to hang on the chest, as a wreath adorning the head.

64. *He is dear to non-human beings:* he is just as dear to non-human beings as he is to human beings, as in the Elder Visākha's case. He was a landowner, it seems, at Pāṭaliputta (Patna). While he was living there he heard this: 'The Island of Tambapaṇṇi (Ceylon), apparently, is adorned with a diadem of shrines and gleams with the yellow cloth, and there a man can sit or lie wherever he likes; there the climate is favourable, the abodes are favourable, the people are favourable, the Dhamma to be heard is favourable, and all these favourable things are easily obtained there'.

65. He made over his fortune to his wife and children and left his home with only a single ducat (*kahāpana*) sewn into the hem of his garment. He stopped for one month on the sea coast in expectation of a ship, and meanwhile by his skill in trading he made a thousand during the month by buying goods here and selling them there in lawful enterprise.

66. Eventually he came to the Great Monastery [(Mahāvihāra) at Anurādhapura], and there he asked for the Going Forth into homelessness. When he was being conducted to the Chapter House (*sīmā*) for the Going-forth ceremony, the purse containing the thousand pieces dropped out from under his belt. When asked 'What is that?', he replied 'It is a thousand ducats, venerable sirs'. They told him 'Lay follower, it is not possible to distribute them after the Going Forth. Distribute them now'. Then he said 'Let none who have come to the scene of Visākha's Going Forth depart empty handed', and opening [the purse] he strewed them over the Chapter House yard, after which he received the Going Forth and the Full Admission.

67. When he had acquired five years' seniority and had become familiar with the two Codes (see Ch. III, §31), he celebrated the *Pavāraṇā* at the end of the Rains, took a meditation subject that suited him and set out to wander, living for four months in each monastery and doing the duties on a basis of equality with the residents. While he was wandering in this way,

The Elder halted in a wood
To scan the tenor of his way;
He thundered forth this roundelay
Proclaiming that he found it good:
So from your Full-admission day
Till in this place you paused and stood
No stumbling mars your bhikkhuhood;
Be thankful for such grace, I say. [313]

68. On his way to Cittalapabbata he came to a road fork and stood wondering which turn to take. Then a deity living in a

rock held out a hand pointing out the road to him.

69. He came to the Cittalapabbata Monastery. After he had stayed there for four months he lay down thinking 'In the morning I depart'. Then a deity living in a *maṇila* tree at the end of the walk sat down on a step of the stair and burst into tears. The Elder asked 'Who is that?'—'It is I, Maṇiliyā, venerable sir.'—'What are you weeping for?'—'Because you are going away.'—'What good does my living here do you?'—'Venerable sir, as long as you live here non-human beings treat each other kindly. Now when you are gone, they will start quarrels and loose talk.'[9] The Elder said 'If my living here makes you live at peace, that is good', and so he stayed there another four months. Then he again thought of leaving, but the deity wept as before. And so the Elder lived on there, and it was there that he attained nibbana.

This is how a bhikkhu who abides in lovingkindness is dear to non-human beings.

70. *Deities guard him*: deities guard him as a mother and father guard their child.

71. *Fire, poison and weapons do not affect him*: they do not affect, do not enter into, the body of one who abides in lovingkindness, like the fire in the case of the lay woman devotee Uttarā (see Ch. XII, §34 and DhA. iii,310), like the poison in the case of the Samyutta Reciter the Elder Cūḷa-Sīva, like the knife in the case of the novice Saṅkicca (see DhA. ii, 249); they do not disturb the body, is what is meant.

72. And they tell the story of the cow here too. A cow was giving milk to her calf, it seems. A hunter thinking 'I shall shoot her', flourished a long-handled spear in his hand and flung it. It struck her body and bounced off like a palm leaf—and that was owing neither to access nor to absorption, but simply to the strength of her consciousness of love for her calf. So mightily powerful is lovingkindness.

73. *His mind is easily concentrated*: the mind of one who abides in lovingkindness is quickly concentrated, there is no sluggishness about it. [314]

74. *The expression of his face is serene*: his face has a serene expression, like a palmyra fruit loosed from its stem.

75. *He dies unconfused*: there is no dying deluded for one who abides in lovingkindness. He passes away undeluded as if falling asleep.

76. *If he penetrates no higher*: if unable to reach higher than the attainment of lovingkindness and attain Arahantship, then when he falls from this life, he reappears in the Brahmā World as one who wakes up from sleep.

9. For '*duṭṭhulla*' see Ch. IV. note 36. Here the meaning is more likely to be 'bad' or 'lewd' than 'inert'.

This is the detailed explanation of the development of lovingkindness.

[(2) COMPASSION]

77. One who wants to develop compassion should begin his task by reviewing the danger in lack of compassion and the advantage in compassion.

And when he begins it, he should not direct it at first towards the dear, etc., persons; for one who is dear simply retains the position of one who is dear, a very dear companion retains the position of a very dear companion, one who is neutral retains the position of one who is neutral, one who is antipathetic retains the position of one who is antipathetic, and one who is hostile retains the position of one who is hostile. One of the opposite sex and one who is dead are also not the field for it.

78. In the Vibhaṅga it is said 'And how does a bhikkhu dwell 'pervading one direction with his heart endued with compas'sion? Just as he would feel compassion on seeing an unlucky, 'unfortunate person, so he pervades all beings with compas'sion' (Vbh. 273). Therefore first of all, on seeing a wretched man, unlucky, unfortunate, in every way a fit object for compassion, unsightly, reduced to utter misery, with hands and feet cut off, sitting in the shelter for the helpless with a pot placed before him, with a mass of maggots oozing from his arms and legs, and moaning, compassion should be felt for him in this way: This being has indeed been reduced to misery; if only he could be freed from this suffering!

But if he does not encounter such a person, then he can arouse compassion for an evil-doing person, even though he is happy, by comparing him to one about to be executed. How?

79. Suppose a robber has been caught with stolen goods, and in accordance with the king's command to execute him, the king's men bind him and lead him off to the place of execution, giving him a hundred blows in sets of four. Then people give him things to chew and eat and also garlands and perfumes, unguents and betel leaves. Although [315] he goes along eating and enjoying these things as though he were happy and well off, still no one fancies that he is really happy and well off. On the contrary people feel compassion for him, thinking 'This poor wretch is now about to die; every step he takes brings him nearer to the presence of death'. So too a bhikkhu whose meditation subject is compassion should arouse compassion for an [evil-doing] person even if he is happy: 'Though this poor wretch is now happy, cheerful, enjoying his wealth, still for want of even one good deed done now in any one of the three doors [of body, speech and mind] he can come to experience untold suffering in the states of loss'.

80. Having aroused compassion for that person in that way, he should next arouse compassion for a dear person, next for a neutral person, and next for a hostile person, successively in the same way.

81. But if resentment towards the hostile person arises in the way already described, he should make it subside in the way described under lovingkindness (§14-39).

And here too when someone has done profitable deeds and the meditator sees or hears that he has been overtaken by one of the kinds of ruin beginning with ruin of health, relatives, property, etc., he deserves the meditator's compassion; and so he does too in any case, even with no such ruin, thus 'In reality he is unhappy', because he is not exempt from the suffering of the round [of becoming]. And in the way already described the meditator should break down the barriers between the four kinds of people, that is to say, himself, the dear person, the neutral person and the hostile person. Then cultivating that sign, developing it and repeatedly practising it, he should increase the absorption by the triple and quadruple jhana in the way already stated under lovingkindness.

82. But the order given in the Aṅguttara Commentary is that a hostile person should first be made the object of compassion, and when the mind has been made malleable with respect to him, next the unlucky person, next the dear person, and next oneself. That does not agree with the text, 'an unlucky, unfortunate person' (§78). Therefore he should begin the development, break down the barriers, and increase absorption only in the way stated here.

83. After that, the versatility consisting in the unspecified pervasion in five ways, the specified pervasion in seven ways, and the directional pervasion in ten ways, and the advantages described as 'He sleeps in comfort ', etc., should be understood in the same way as given under lovingkindness.

This is the detailed explanation of the development of compassion. [316]

[(3) GLADNESS]

84. One who begins the development of gladness[10] should not start with the dear person and the rest; for a dear person is not the proximate cause of gladness merely in virture of dearness, how much less the neutral and the hostile person. One of the opposite sex and one who is dead are also not the field for it.

85. However, the very dear companion can be the proximate cause for it—one who in the commentaries is called a 'boon

10. '*Muditā*—gladness' as one of the divine abidings is always in the sense of gladness at others' success. Sometimes rendered 'altruistic joy' and 'sympathetic gladness'.

companion'; for he is constantly glad: he laughs first and speaks afterwards. So he should be the first to be pervaded with gladness. Or on seeing or hearing about a dear person being happy, cheerful and glad, gladness can be aroused thus: 'This being is indeed glad. How good, how excellent!' For this is what is referred to in the Vibhaṅga: 'And how does 'a bhikkhu dwell pervading one direction with his heart 'endued with gladness? Just as he would be glad on seeing a 'dear and beloved person, so he pervades all beings with 'gladness' (Vbh. 274).

86. But if his boon companion or the dear person was happy in the past but is now unlucky and unfortunate, then gladness can still be aroused by remembering his past happiness and apprehending the glad aspect in this way: 'In the past he had great wealth, a great following and he was always glad'. Or gladness can be aroused by apprehending the future glad aspect in him in this way: 'In the future he will again enjoy similar success and will go about in gold palanquins, on the backs of elephants or on horseback, and so on'.

Having thus aroused gladness with respect to a dear person, he can then direct it successively towards a neutral one, and after that towards a hostile one.

87. But if resentment towards the hostile one arises in him the way already described, he should make it subside in the same way as described under lovingkindness (§14-39).

He should break down the barriers by means of mental impartiality towards the four, that is, towards these three and himself. And by cultivating that sign, developing and repeatedly practising it, he should increase the absorption to triple and quadruple jhana in the way already stated under lovingkindness.

Next, the versatility consisting in unspecified pervasion in five ways, specified pervasion in seven ways, and directional pervasion in ten ways, and also the advantages described as 'He sleeps in comfort', etc., should be understood in the same way as stated under lovingkindness.

This is the detailed explanation of the development of gladness. [317]

*

[(4) Equanimity]

88. One who wants to develop equanimity must have already obtained the triple or quadruple jhana in lovingkindness, and so on. He should emerge from the third jhana [in the fourfold reckoning], after he has made it familiar, and he should see danger in the former [three divine abidings] because they are linked with attention given to beings' enjoyment in the way beginning 'May they be happy', because

resentment and approval are near, and because their association with joy is gross. And he should also see the advantage in equanimity because it is peaceful. Then he should arouse equanimity (*upekkhā*) by looking on with equanimity (*ajjhupekkhitvā*) at a person who is normally neutral; after that at a dear person, and the rest. For this is said: 'And how 'does a bhikkhu dwell pervading one direction with his heart 'endued with equanimity? Just as he would feel equanimity 'on seeing a person who was neither beloved nor unloved, so 'he pervades all beings with equanimity' (Vbh. 275).

89. Therefore he should arouse equanimity towards the neutral person in the way already stated. Then through the neutral one he should break down the barriers in each case between the three people, that is, the dear person, then the boon companion, and then the hostile one, and lastly himself. And he should cultivate that sign, develop and repeatedly practise it.

90. As he does so the fourth jhana arises in him in the way described under the earth kasina.

But how then? Does this arise in one in whom the third jhana has already arisen on the basis of the earth kasina, etc.? It does not. Why not? Because of the dissimilarity of the object. It arises only in one in whom the third jhana has arisen on the basis of lovingkindness, etc., because the object is similar.

But after that, the versatility, and the obtaining of advantages should be understood in the same way as described under lovingkindness.

This is the detailed explanation of the development of equanimity.

*

[General]

91. Now having thus known these divine abidings
Told by the Divine (*brahma*) One supremely [wise],
There is this General Explanation too
Concerning them that he should recognize.

[*Meanings*]

92. Now as to the meaning firstly of lovingkindness, compassion, gladness and equanimity: it fattens (*mejjati*), thus it is lovingkindness (*mettā*); it is solvent (*siniyhati*) is the meaning. Also: it comes about with respect to a friend (*mitta*), [318] or it is behaviour towards a friend, thus it is lovingkindness (*mettā*).

When there is suffering in others it causes (*karoti*) good people's hearts to be moved (*kampana*), thus it is compassion (*karuṇā*). Or alternatively, it combats (*kiṇāti*)[11] others'

11. '*Kiṇāti*—it combats': Skr. *kṛṇāti* to injure or kill. P. T. S. Dict. gives this ref. under ordinary meaning 'to buy', which is wrong.

suffering, attacks and demolishes it, thus it is compassion. Or alternatively, it is scattered (*kiriyati*) upon those who suffer, it is extended to them by pervasion, thus it is compassion (*karuṇā*).

Those endowed with it are glad (*modanti*), or itself is glad (*modati*), or it is the mere act of being glad (*modana*), thus it is gladness (*muditā*).

It looks on at (*upekkhati*), abandoning such interestedness as thinking 'May they be free from enmity' and having recourse to neutrality, thus it is equanimity (*upekkhā*).

[*Characteristic, Etc.*]

93. As to the characteristic, etc., *lovingkindness* is characterized here as promoting the aspect of welfare. Its function is to prefer welfare. It is manifested as the removal of annoyance. Its proximate cause is seeing lovableness in beings. It succeeds when it makes ill will subside, and it fails when it produces (selfish) affection.

94. *Compassion* is characterized as promoting the aspect of allaying suffering. Its function resides in not bearing others' suffering. It is manifested as non-cruelty. Its proximate cause is to see helplessness in those overwhelmed by suffering. It succeeds when it makes cruelty subside and it fails when it produces sorrow.

95. *Gladness* is characterized as gladdening (produced by others' success).[12] Its function resides in being unenvious. It is manifested as the elimination of aversion (boredom), Its proximate cause is seeing beings' success. It succeeds when it makes aversion (boredom) subside, and it fails in when it produces merriment.

96. *Equanimity* is characterized as promoting the aspect of neutrality towards beings. Its function is to see equality in beings. It is manifested as the quieting of resentment and approval. Its proximate cause is seeing ownership of deeds (kamma) thus: 'Beings are owners of their deeds. Whose[13] [if not theirs] is the choice by which they will become happy, or will get free from suffering, or will not fall away from the success they have reached?' It succeeds when it makes resentment and approval subside, and it fails when it produces the equanimity of unknowing, which is that [worldly-minded indifference of ignorance] based on the house life.

[*Purpose*]

97. The general purpose of these four divine abidings is the bliss of insight and an excellent (form of future) existence.

12. So Pm., p. 309.
13. All texts read *kassa* (whose), which is confirmed in the quotation translated in note 20. It is tempting, in view of the context to read *kammassa* (kamma's), but there is no authority for it. The statement would then be an assertion instead of a question.

That peculiar to each is respectively the warding off of ill will, and so on. For here lovingkindness has the purpose of warding off ill will, while the others have the respective purposes of warding off cruelty, aversion (boredom), and greed or resentment. And this is said too: 'For this is the escape from ill will, friends, that is to say, the mind-'deliverance of lovingkindness. . .For this is the escape 'from cruelty, friends, that is to say, the mind-deliverance 'of compassion. . .For this is the escape from aversion '(boredom), friends, that is to say, the mind-deliverance 'of gladness. . .For this is the escape from greed, friends, 'that is to say the mind-deliverance of equanimity (D.iii,248),

[*The Near and Far Enemies*]

98. And here each one has two enemies, one near and one far. The divine abiding of *lovingkindness* [319] has greed as its near enemy[14] since both share in seeing virtues. Greed behaves like a foe who keeps close by a man, and it easily finds an opportunity. So lovingkindness should be well protected from it. And ill will, which is dissimilar to the similar greed, is its far enemy like a foe ensconced in a rock wilderness. So lovingkindness must be practised free from fear of that; For it is not possible to practise lovingkindness and feel anger simultaneously (see D.iii,247-8).

99. *Compassion* has grief based on the home life as its near enemy, since both share in seeing failure. Such grief has been described in the way beginning, 'When a man either regards 'as a privation failure to obtain visible objects cognizable by 'the eye that are sought after, desired, agreeable, gratifying 'and associated with worldliness, or when he recalls those 'formerly obtained that are past, ceased and changed, then 'grief arises in him. Such grief as this is called grief based on 'the home life' (M.iii, 218). And cruelty, which is dissimilar to the similar grief, is its far enemy. So compassion must be practised free from fear of that; for it is not possible to practise compassion and be cruel to breathing things simultaneously.

100. *Gladness* has joy based on the home life as its near enemy since both share in seeing success. Such joy has been described in the way beginning. 'When a man either regards as gain 'the obtaining of visible objects cognizable by the eye that 'are sought,. . .and associated with worldliness, or recalls 'those formerly obtained that are past, ceased, and changed, 'then joy arises in him. Such joy as this is called joy based 'on the home life' (M. iii, 217). And aversion (boredom),

14. 'Greed is the near enemy of Lovingkindness since it is able to corrupt owing to its similarity, like an enemy masquerading as a friend' (Pm. 309).

which is dissimilar to the similar joy, is its far enemy. So gladness should be practised free from fear of that; for it is not possible to practise gladness and be discontented with remote abodes and things connected with the higher profitableness simultaneously.

101. *Equanimity* has the equanimity of unknowing based on the home life as its near enemy since both share in ignoring faults and virtues. Such unknowing has been described in the way beginning, 'On seeing a visible object with the eye 'equanimity arises in the foolish infatuated ordinary man, in 'the untaught ordinary man who has not conquered his 'limitations, who has not conquered future [kamma] result, 'who is unperceiving of danger. Such equanimity as this 'does not surmount the visible object. Such equanimity as 'this is called equanimity based on the home life' (M.iii,219). And greed and resentment, which are dissimilar to the similar unknowing, are its far enemies. Therefore equanimity must be practised free from fear of that; [320] for it is not possible to look on with equanimity and be inflamed with greed or be resentful[15] simultaneously.

[*The Beginning, Middle and End, Etc.*]

102. Now zeal consisting in desire to act is the beginning of all these things. Suppression of the hindrances, etc., is the middle. Absorption is the end. Their object is a single living being or many living beings, as a mental object consisting in a concept.

[*The Order in Extension*]

103. The extension of the object takes place either in access or in absorption. Here is the order of it. Just as a skilled ploughman first delimits an area and then does his ploughing, so first a single dwelling should be delimited and lovingkindness developed towards all beings there in the way beginning 'In this dwelling may all beings be free from enmity'. When his mind has become malleable and wieldy with respect to that, he can then delimit two dwellings. Next he can successively delimit three, four, five, six, seven, eight, nine, ten, one street, half the village, the whole village, the district, the kingdom, one direction, and so on up to one world-sphere, or even beyond that, and develop lovingkindness towards the beings in such areas. Likewise with compassion and so on. This is the order in extending here.

[*The Outcome*]

104. Just as the immaterial states are the outcome of the kasinas, and the base consisting of neither perception nor non-percep-

15. '*Paṭihaññati*—to be resentful': not in P. T. S. Dict.; the verb has been needed to correspond to 'resentment (*paṭigha*)' as the verb 'to be inflamed with greed (*rajjati*)' corresponds with 'greed (*rāga*)'.

tion is the outcome of concentration and fruition attainment is the outcome of insight, and the attainment of cessation is the outcome of serenity coupled with insight, so the divine abiding of equanimity is the outcome of the first three divine abidings. For just as the gable rafters cannot be placed in the air without having first set up the scaffolding and built the framework of beams, so it is not possible to develop the fourth jhana in these without having already developed the third jhana in them.

[*Four Questions*]

105. And here it may be asked: But why are lovingkindness, compassion, gladness, and equanimity, called divine abidings? And why are they only four? And what is their order? And why are they called Measureless States in the Abhidhamma?

106. It may be replied: The divineness of the abiding (*brahmavihāratā*) should be understood here in the sense of best and in the sense of immaculate. For these abidings are the best in being the right attitude towards beings. And just as *Brahmā* Gods abide with immaculate minds, so the meditators who associate themselves with these abidings abide on an equal footing with *Brahmā* Gods. So they are called divine abidings in the sense of best and in the sense of immaculate. [321]

107. Here are the answers to the questions beginning with 'Why are they only four?':

Their number four is due to paths to purity
And other sets of four; their order to their aim
As welfare and the rest. Their scope is found to be
Immeasurable, so 'Measureless States' their name.

108. For among these, lovingkindness is the way to purity for one who has much ill will, compassion is that for one who has much cruelty, gladness is that for one who has much aversion (boredom), and equanimity is that for one who has much greed. Also attention given to beings is only fourfold, that is to say, as bringing welfare, as removing suffering, as being glad at their success, and as unconcern, [that is to say, impartial neutrality.] And one abiding in the Measureless States should practise lovingkindness and the rest like a mother with four sons, namely, a child, an invalid, one in the flush of youth, and one busy with his own affairs; for she wants the child to grow up, wants the invalid to get well, wants the one in the flush of youth to enjoy for long the benefits of youth, and is not at all bothered about the one who is busy with his own affairs. That is why the Measureless States are only four as 'due to paths to purity and other sets of four'.

109. One who wants to develop these four should practise them towards beings first as the promotion of the aspect of welfare—and lovingkindness has the promotion of the aspect of welfare

as its characteristic—; and next, on seeing or hearing or judging[16] that beings whose welfare has been thus wished for are at the mercy of suffering, they should be practised as the promotion of the aspect of the removal of suffering—and compassion has the promotion of the aspect of the removal of suffering as its characteristic—; and then, on seeing the success of those whose welfare has been wished for and the removal of whose suffering has been wished for, they should be practised as being glad—and gladness has the act of gladdening as its characteristic—; but after that there is nothing to be done and so they should be practised as the neutral aspect, in other words, the state of an onlooker—and equanimity has the promotion of the aspect of neutrality as its characteristic—; therefore since their respective aims are the aspect of welfare, etc., their order should be understood to correspond, with lovingkindness stated first, then compassion, gladness and equanimity.

110. All of them, however, occur with a measureless scope, for their scope is measureless beings; and instead of assuming a measure such as 'Lovingkindness, etc., should be developed only towards a single being, or in an area of such an extent', they occur with universal pervasion. That is why it was said: [322]

' Their number four is due to paths to purity
' And other sets of four; their order to their aim
' As welfare and the rest. Their scope is found to be
' Immeasurable, so "Measureless States" their name'.

[*As Producing Three Jhanas and Four Jhanas*]

111. Though they have a single characteristic in having a measureless scope, yet the first three are only of triple and quadruple jhana [respectively in the fourfold and fivefold reckonings]. Why? Because they are not dissociated from joy. But why are their aims not dissociated from joy? Because they are the escape from ill will, etc., which are originated by grief. But the last one belongs only to the remaining single jhana. Why? Because it is associated with equanimous feeling. For the divine abiding of equanimity that occurs in the aspect of neutrality towards beings does not exist apart from equanimous [that is to say, neither-painful-nor-pleasant,] feeling.

112. However, someone might say this: It has been said by the Blessed One in the Book of Eights, speaking of the measureless states in general: 'Next, bhikkhu, you should develop the 'concentration with applied thought and sustained thought, ' and you should develop it without applied thought and with

16. '*Sambhāvetvā*—judging': not in this sense in P. T. S. Dict.; Pm. (p. 313) explains by *parikappetvā* (conjecturing).

'sustained thought only, and you should develop it without 'applied thought and without sustained thought, and you 'should develop it with happiness, and you should develop 'it without happiness, and you should develop it accompanied 'by gratification and you should develop it accompanied by 'equanimity' (A.iv,300). Consequently all four measureless states have quadruple and quintuple jhana.

113. He should be told: Do not put it like that. For if that were so, then contemplation of the body, etc., would also have quadruple and quintuple jhana. But there is not even the first jhana in the contemplation of feeling or in the other two.[17] So do not misrepresent the Blessed One by adherence to the letter. The Enlightened One's word is profound and should be taken as it is intended, giving due weight to the teachers.

114. And the intention here is this: The Blessed One, it seems, was asked to teach the Dhamma thus, Venerable Sir, it would be 'good if the Blessed One would teach me the Dhamma in 'brief, so that, having heard the Blessed One's Dhamma, I may 'dwell alone, withdrawn, diligent, ardent and self-exerted' (A.iv,299). But the Blessed One had no confidence yet in that bhikkhu, since although he had already heard the Dhamma he had nevertheless gone on living there instead of going to do the ascetic's duties, [and the Blessed One expressed his lack of confidence] thus, 'So too, some misguided men merely question me, and when the Dhamma is expounded [to them], they still fancy that they need not follow me' (A.iv,299). However, the bhikkhu possessed the potentiality for the attainment of Arahantship, and so he advised him once again, [323] saying 'Therefore, bhikkhu you should train thus: My 'mind shall be steadied, quite steadied, internally and arisen 'evil unprofitable things shall not obsess my mind and remain. 'You should train thus' (A. iv ,299). But what is stated in that advice is basic concentration consisting in mere unification of mind internally in the sense of in oneself (See Ch.
115. XIV,n.75). After that he told him about its development by means of lovingkindness in order to show that he should

17. For which kinds of Body Contemplation give which kinds of concentration see Ch. VIII, §43 and MA. i, 247.

'"*Mere unification of the mind*": the kind of concentrating (*Samādhāna*) that is undeveloped and just obtained by one in pursuit of development. That is called "*basic concentration*", however, since, it is the basic reason for the kinds of more distinguished concentration to be mentioned later in this connexion. This "mere unification of the mind" is intended as momentary concentration as in the passage beginning "I internally settled, steadied, unified and concentrated my mind" (M. i, 116). For the first unification of the mind is recognized as momentary concentration here as it is in the first of the two successive descriptions: "Tireless energy was aroused in me...my mind concentrated and unified" followed by "Quite secluded from sense desires ...." (M.i, 21)' (Pm. 314).

not rest content with just that much but should intensify his basic concentration in this way, 'As soon as your mind has 'become steadied, quite steadied internally, bhikkhu, and 'arisen evil unprofitable things do not obsess your mind and 'remain, then you should train thus: The mind-deliverance 'of lovingkindness will be developed by me, frequently 'practised, made the vehicle, made the foundation, establish- 'ed, consolidated, and properly undertaken. You should train 'thus, bhikkhu' (A.iv,299-300), after which he said further, 'As soon as this concentration has been thus developed by 'you, bhikkhu,[18] and frequently practised, then you should 'develop this concentration with applied thought and sus- 'tained thought, . .and you should develop it accompanied
116. 'by equanimity' (A.iv,300). The meaning is this: Bhikkhu, when this basic concentration has been developed by you by means of lovingkindness, then, instead of resting content with just that much, you should make this basic concentration reach quadruple and quintuple jhana in other objects by [further] developing it in the way beginning 'With applied
117. thought'. And having spoken thus, he further said, 'As 'soon as this concentration has been thus developed by you, 'bhikkhu, and frequently practised, then you should train 'thus: The mind-deliverance of compassion will be developed 'by me. . .' (A.iv,300), etc., pointing out that 'you should effect its [further] development by means of quadruple and quintuple jhana in other objects, this [further] development being preceded by the remaining divine abidings of compassion
118. and the rest.' Having thus shown how its [further] development by means of quadruple and quintuple jhana is preceded by lovingkindness, etc., and having told him, 'As soon as this 'concentration has been developed by you, bhikkhu, and 'frequently practised, then you should train thus: I shall 'dwell contemplating the body as a body', etc., he concluded the discourse with Arahantship as its culmination thus, 'As soon as this concentration has been developed by you, 'bhikkhu, completely developed, then wherever you go you 'will go in comfort, wherever you stand you will stand in 'comfort, wherever [324] you sit you will sit in comfort, 'wherever you make your couch you will do so in comfort' (A.iv,301). From that it must be understood that the [three] beginning with lovingkindness have only triple-quadruple jhana, and that equanimity has only the single

18. '"*Thus developed*": just as a fire started with wood and banked up with cowdung, dust etc., although it arrives at the state of a "cowdung fire", etc. (cf. M. i, 259), is nevertheless called after the original fire that was started with the wood, so too it is the basic concentration that is spoken of here, taking it as banked up with lovingkindness, and so on. "*In other objects*" means in such objects as the earth kasina' (Pm. 315).

remaining jhana. And they are expounded in the same way in the Abhidhamma as well.

[*The Highest Limit of Each*]

119. And while they are twofold by way of the triple-quadruple jhana and the single remaining jhana, still they should be understood to be distinguishable in each case by a different efficacy consisting in having 'beauty as the highest', etc., for they are so described in the *Haliddavasana* Sutta, according as it is said: 'Bhikkhus, the mind-deliverance of lovingkind-'ness has beauty as the highest, I say...The mind-deliverance 'of compassion has the base consisting of boundless space as 'the highest, I say,. . .The mind-deliverance of gladness has 'the base consisting of boundless consciousness as the highest 'I say, ... The mind-deliverance of equanimity has the base, 'consisting of nothingness as the highest, I say' (S.v,119-21).[19]

120. But why are they described in this way? Because each is the respective basic support for each. For beings are unrepulsive to one who abides in lovingkindness. Being familiar with the unrepulsive aspect, when he applies his mind to unrepulsive pure colours such as blue-black, his mind enters into them without difficulty. So lovingkindness is the basic support for the Liberation by the Beautiful (see M.ii,12; MA.iii,256), but not for what is beyond that. That is why it is called 'Having beauty as highest'.

121. One who abides in compassion has come to know thoroughly the danger in materiality sincc compassion is aroused in him when he sees the suffering of beings that has as its material sign (cause) beating with sticks, and so on. So, well knowing the danger in materiality, when he removes whichever kasina [concept he was contemplating], whether that of the earth kasina or another and applies his mind to the space [that remains (see Ch.X, §6)], which is the escape from materiality, then his mind enters into that [space] without difficulty. So compassion is the basic support for the sphere of boundless space, but not for what is beyond that. That is why it is called 'Having the base consisting of boundless space as the highest'.

122. When he abides in gladness, his mind becomes familiar with apprehending consciousness since gladness is aroused in him when he sees beings' consciousness arisen in the form of rejoicing over some reason for joy. Then when he surmounts the sphere of boundless space that he had already attained in due course and applies his mind to the consciousness that had as its object the sign of space, (325) his mind enters into it without difficulty. So gladness is the basic support for the

19. 'The beautiful (*subha*)' is the third of the eight Liberations (*vimokkha*—see M. ii, 12; MA. iii, 255).

base consisting of boundless consciousness, but not for what is beyond that. That is why it is called 'Having the sphere of boundless consciousness as the highest'.

123. When he abides in equanimity, his mind becomes skilled[20] in apprehending what is (in the ultimate sense) non-existent, because his mind has been diverted from apprehension of (what is existent in) the ultimate sense, namely, pleasure, (release from) pain, etc., owing to having no further concern such as 'May beings be happy' or 'May they be released from pain' or 'May they not lose the success they have obtained'. Now his mind has become used to being diverted from apprehension of (what is existent in) the ultimate sense, and his mind has become skilled in apprehending what is non-existent in the ultimate sense, (that is to say, living beings, which are a concept,) and so when he surmounts the base consisting of boundless consciousness attained in due course and applies his mind to the absence, which is non-existent as to individual essence, of consciousness, which is a reality (is become—see M.i,260) in the ultimate sense, then his mind enters into that (nothingness, that non-existence,) without difficulty (see Ch. X,§32). So equanimity is the basic support for the base consisting of nothingness, but not for what is beyond that. That is why it is called 'Having the base consisting of nothingness as the highest,

124. When he has understood thus that the special efficacy of each resides respectively in 'Having beauty as the highest', etc., he should besides understand how they bring to perfection all the good states beginning with giving. For the Great Beings' minds retain their balance by giving preference to beings' welfare, by dislike of beings' suffering, by desire for the various successes achieved by beings to last, and by impart-

20. Reading in both cases '*avijjamāna-gahaṇa-dakkhaṁ cittaṁ*, not *-dukkhaṁ*.' "*Because it has no more concern* (*ābhoga*)": because it has no further act of being concerned (*ābhujana*) by hoping (*āsimsana*) for their pleasure, etc., thus "May they be happy". The development of lovingkindness, etc., occurring as it does in the form of hope for beings' pleasure, etc., makes them its object by directing [the mind] to apprehension of [what is existent in] the ultimate sense [i.e. pleasure etc.] But development of equanimity, instead of occurring like that, makes beings its object by simply looking on.—But does not the divine abiding of equanimity itself too make beings its object by directing the mind to apprehension of [what is existent in] the ultimate sense, because of the words "Beings are owners of their deeds. Whose [if not theirs] is the choice by which they will become happy . . ."? (§96)—Certainly that is so. But that is in the prior stage of development of equanimity. When it has reached its culmination, it makes beings its object by simply looking on. So its occurrence is specially occupied with what is non-existent in the ultimate sense [i. e. beings, which are a concept]. And so skill in apprehending the non-existent should be understood as avoidance of bewilderment due to misrepresentation in apprehension of beings, which avoidance of bewilderment has reached absorption' (Pm.).

iality towards all beings. And to all beings they give *gifts*, which are a source of pleasure, without discriminating thus : 'It must be given to this one ; it must not be given to this one'. And in order to avoid doing harm to beings they undertake the precepts of *virtue*. They practise *renunciation* for the purpose of perfecting their virtue. They cleanse their *understanding* for the purpose of non-confusion about what is good and bad for beings. They constantly arouse *energy*, having beings' welfare and happiness at heart. When they have acquired heroic fortitude through supreme energy, they become *patient* with beings' many kinds of faults. They *do not deceive* when promising ' We shall give you this; We shall do this for you'. They are unshakably *resolute* upon beings' welfare and happiness. Through unshakable *lovingkindness* they place them first [before themselves]. Through *equanimity* they expect no reward. Having thus fulfilled the [Ten] Perfections, these [divine abidings] then perfect all the good states classed as the Ten powers, the Four kinds of fearlessness, the Six Kinds of Knowledge Not Shared [by Disciples] and the Eighteen States of the Enlightened One.[21] This is how they bring to perfection all the good states beginning with giving.

The Ninth Chapter called the 'Description of the Divine Abidings' in the Treatise on the Development of Concentration in the Path of Purification composed for the purpose of gladdening good people.

21. For the ' Ten Powers' and ' Four Kinds of Fearlessness ' see M. Sutta 12. For the ' Six Kinds of Knowledge Not Shared by Disciples' see Ps. i, 121f. For the ' Eighteen States of the Enlightened One' see Cp. Commentary.

CHAPTER X.

DESCRIPTION OF CONCENTRATION— THE IMMATERIAL STATES

(*Āruppa-niddesa*)

[(1) The Base Consisting of Boundless Space]

1. [326] Now as to the four Immaterial States mentioned next to the Divine Abidings (Ch. III, §105), one who wants firstly to develop the base consisting of boundless space sees in gross physical matter danger through the wielding of sticks, etc., because of the words ' "It is in virtue of matter ' that wielding of sticks, wielding of knives, quarrels, brawls ' and disputes take place; but that does not exist at all in the ' immaterial state", and in this expectation he enters upon the ' way to dispassion for only material things, for the fading and ' cessation of only those' (M.i,410), and he sees danger in it too through the thousand afflictions beginning with eye disease. So in order to surmount that he enters upon the fourth jhana in any one of the nine kasinas beginning with the earth kasina and omitting the limited-space kasina.

2. Now although he has already surmounted gross physical matter by means of the fourth jhana of the fine-material sphere, nevertheless he still wants also to surmount the kasina materiality since it is the counterpart of the former. How does he do this?

3. Suppose a timid man is pursued by a snake in a forest and flees from it as fast as he can, then if he sees in the place he has fled to a palm leaf with a streak painted on it or a creeper or a rope or a crack in the ground, he is fearful, anxious and will not even look at it. Suppose again a man is living in the same village as a hostile man who ill-uses him, and on being threatened by him with a flogging and the burning down of his house, he goes away to live in another village, then if he meets another man there of similar appearance, voice and manner, he is fearful, anxious and will not even look at him.

4. Here is the application of the similes. The time when the bhikkhu has the gross physical matter as his object is like the time when the men were respectively threatened by the snake and by the enemy. [327] The time when the bhikkhu surmounts the gross physical matter by means of the fourth jhana of the fine-material sphere is like the first man's fleeing as fast as he can and the other man's going away to another village. The bhikkhu's observing that even the matter of the

kasina is the counterpart of that gross physical matter and his wanting to surmount that also is like the first man's seeing in the place he had fled to the palm leaf with a streak painted on it, etc., and the other man's seeing the man who resembled the enemy in the village he had left, and their unwillingness to look owing to fear and anxiety.

And here the similes of the dog attacked by a boar, and that of the *pisāca* goblin and the timid man[1] should be understood too.

5. So when he has thus become disgusted with (dispassionate towards) the kasina materiality, the object of the fourth jhana, and wants to get away from it, he achieves mastery in the five ways. Then on emerging from the now familiar fourth jhana of the fine-material sphere, he sees the danger in that jhana in this way 'This makes its object the materiality with which I have become disgusted', and 'It has joy as its near enemy', and 'It is grosser than the Peaceful Liberations'. There is, however, no [comparative] grossness of factors here [as in the case of the four fine-material jhanas]; for the immaterial states have the same two factors as this fine-material [jhana].

6. When he has seen the danger in that [fine-material fourth jhana] in this way and has ended his attachment to it, he gives his attention to the Base Consisting of Boundless Space as peaceful. Then, when he has spread out the kasina to the limit of the world-sphere, or as far as he likes, he removes the kasina [materiality] by giving his attention to the space touched by it, [regarding that] as 'space' or 'boundless-space'.

7. When he is removing it, he neither folds it up like a mat nor withdraws it like a cake from a tin. It is simply that he does not advert to it or give attention to it or review it; it is when he neither adverts to it nor gives attention to it nor reviews it but gives his attention exclusively to the space touched by it [regarding that] as 'Space, space', that he is said to 'remove the kasina'.

8. And when the kasina is being removed, it does not roll up or roll away. It is simply that it is called 'removed' on account of his non-attention to it, his attention being given to 'space, space,'. This is conceptualized as the mere space left by the removal of the kasina [materiality]. Whether it is called 'space left by the removal of the kasina' or 'space touched by the kasina' or 'space secluded from the kasina', it is all the same.

---

1. 'A dog, it seems, was attacked in the forest by a boar and fled. When it was dusk he saw in the distance a cauldron for boiling rice, and perceiving it as a boar, he fled in fear and terror. Again, a man who was afraid of *pisāca* goblins saw a decapitated palm stump at night in a place that was unfamiliar to him, and perceiving it as a *pisāca* goblin, he fell down in his fear, horror and confusion' (Pm. 320).

9. He adverts again and again to the sign of the space left by the removal of the kasina [328] as 'Space, space', and he strikes at it with thought and applied thought. As he adverts to it again and again and strikes at it with thought and applied thought the hindrances are suppressed, mindfulness is established and his mind becomes concentrated in access. He cultivates that sign again and again, develops and repeatedly practises it.

10. As he again and again adverts to it and gives attention to it in this way consciousness belonging to the Base Consisting of Boundless Space arises in absorption with the space [as its object], as the consciousness belonging to the fine-material sphere did in the case of the earth kasina, and so on. And here too in the prior stage there are either three or four sensual-sphere impulsions associated with equanimous feeling, while the fourth or the fifth is of the immaterial sphere. The rest is the same as in the case of the earth kasina (Ch. IV, §74).

11. There is however, this difference. When the immaterial-sphere consciousness has arisen in this way, the bhikkhu, who has been formerly looking at the kasina disk with the jhana eye, finds himself looking at only space after that sign has been abruptly removed by the attention given in the preliminary work thus 'Space, space'. He is like a man who has plugged an opening in a [covered] vehicle, a sack or a pot[2] with a piece of blue rag or with a piece of rag of some such colour as yellow, red or white and is looking at that, and then when the rag is removed by the force of the wind or by some other agency, he finds himself looking at space.

[*Text and Commentary*]

12. And at this point it is said: With the complete surmounting '(*samatikkamā*) of perceptions of matter, with the disappearance 'of perceptions of resistance, with non-attention to per-'ceptions of variety, [aware of] "Unbounded space", he 'enters upon and dwells in the base consisting of boundless 'space' (Vbh.245).

13. Herein, *complete* is in all aspects or of all [perceptions]; without exception, is the meaning. *Of perceptions of matter*: both (a) of the fine-material jhanas mentioned [here] under the heading of 'perception' and (b) of those things that are their object. For (a) the jhana of the fine-material sphere

2. P. T. S. Dict., this ref. reads *yānapuṭosā* for *yānapattoli*, taking it as one compound (see under *yāna* and *mutoḷī*), but this does not fit the context happily. Pm. (p. 321) has '"*Yānappatoḷikumbhimukhādīnan*" *ti oguṇṭhana-sivikādi-yānaṁ mukhaṁ=yāna-mukhaṁ*; *patoḷiyā kuddakadvārassa mukhaṁ=patoli-mukhaṁ*; *kumbhi-mukhan ti paccekaṁ mukha-saddo sambandhitabbo*'. This necessitates taking *yāna* separately.

is called 'matter' in such passages as 'Possessed of visible 'matter he sees instances of matter' (D.ii,70;M.ii,12), and (b) it is its object too [that is called 'matter'] in such passages as 'He sees instances of visible matter externally, . . . fair and ugly' (D.ii,110;M.ii,13).[3] Consequently here the words 'perceptions of matter (*rūpa-saññā*—lit. matter-perceptions)', in the sense of 'perceptions about matter', are used (a) for fine-material jhana stated thus under the heading of 'perceptions'. [Also] (b) it has the label (*saññā*) 'matter (*rūpa*)', thus it (the jhana's object) is 'labelled matter (*rūpa-saññaṁ*)'; what is meant is that 'matter' is its name. So it should be understood that this is also a term for (b) what is classed as the earth kasina, etc., which is the object of that [jhana].[4] [329]

14. *With the surmounting*: with the fading away and with the cessation. What is meant? With the fading away and with the cessation, both because of the fading away and because of the cessation, either in all aspects or without exception, of these perceptions of matter, reckoned as jhana, which number fifteen with the [five each of the] profitable, resultant and functional,[5] and also of these things labelled matter, reckoned as objects [of those perceptions], which number nine with the earth kasina, etc. (§1), he enters upon and dwells in the base consisting of boundless space. For he cannot enter upon and dwell in that without completely surmounting perceptions of matter.

15. Herein, there is no surmounting of these perceptions in one whose greed for the object [of those perceptions] has not faded away; and when the perceptions have been surmounted, their objects have been surmounted as well. That is why in the Vibhaṅga only the surmounting of the perceptions and not that of the objects is mentioned as follows: 'Herein, what are 'perceptions of matter? They are the perception, perceiving, perceivedness, in one who has attained a fine-material-sphere attainment or in one who has been reborn there or in one who is abiding in bliss there in this present life. These are what are called perceptions of matter. These perceptions of matter are passed, surpassed, surmounted. Hence, "With the complete surmounting of perceptions of matter" is said' (Vbh. 261). But this commentary should be understood to

3. These two quotations refer respectively to the first of the Eight Liberations and the first of the Eight Bases of Mastery (See MA. iii, 255ff.)

4. This explanation depends on a play on the word *saññā* as the (subjective) perception and as the (objective) sign, signal or label perceived.

5. See Ch. XIV, §129, description of perception aggregate, which is classified in the same way as the consciousness aggregate. Those referred to here are the fifteen fine-material kinds, corresponding to nos. (9)-(13), (57)-(61) and (81)-(85) in Table II.

deal also with the surmounting of the object because these attainments have to be reached by surmounting the object; they are not reached by retaining the same object as in the first and subsequent jhanas.

16. *With the disappearance of perceptions of resistance*: perceptions of resistance are perceptions arisen through the impact of the physical base consisting of the eye, etc., and the respective objects consisting of visible objects, etc.; and this is a term for perceptions of visible objects (*rūpa*) and so on, according as it is said: 'Here, what are perceptions of resistance? Perceptions of visible objects, perceptions of sounds, perceptions of odours, perceptions of flavours, perceptions of tangible objects—these are called "perceptions of resistance"' (Vbh. 261); with the complete disappearance the abandoning, the non-arising, of these ten kinds of perceptions of resistance, that is to say, of the five profitable-resultant and five unprofitable-resultant;[6] causing their non-occurrence, is what is meant.

17. Of course, these are not to be found in one who has entered upon the first jhana, etc., either; for consciousness at that time does not occur by way of the five doers. Still [330] the mention of them here should be understood as a recommendation of this jhana for the purpose of arousing interest in it, just as in the case of the fourth jhana there is mention of the pleasure and pain already abandoned elsewhere, and in the case of the third path there is mention of the [false] view of personality, etc., already abandoned earlier.

18. Or alternatively, though these are also not to be found in one who has attained the fine-material sphere, still their not being there is not due to their having been abandoned; for development of the fine-material sphere does not lead to fading of greed for materiality, and the occurrence of those [fine-material jhanas] is actually dependent on materiality. But this development [of the immaterial] does lead to the fading of greed for materiality. Therefore it is allowable to say that they are actually abandoned here; and not only to say it, but to maintain it absolutely.

19. In fact it is because they have not been abandoned already before this that it was said by the Blessed One that sound is a thorn to one who has the first jhana (A. v, 135). And it is precisely because they are abandoned here that the imperturbability (see Vbh.135) of the immaterial attainments and their state of peaceful liberation are mentioned (M.i,33), and that Āḷāra Kālāma neither saw the five hundred carts that passed close by him nor heard the sound of them while he was in an immaterial attainment (D.ii,130).

---

6. See Ch. XIV, §96f. nos. (34)–(38) and (50)–(54) in Table II.

20. *With non-attention to perceptions of variety*: either to perceptions occurring with variety as their domain, or to perceptions themselves various. For 'Perceptions of variety' are so called [for two reasons:] firstly, because the kinds of perception included along with the mind element and mind-consciousness element in one who has not attained—which kinds are intended here as described in the Vibhaṅga thus: 'Herein, what are perceptions of variety? The perception, 'perceiving, perceivedness, in one who has not attained and 'possesses either mind element or mind-consciousness element: 'these are called "perceptions of variety"' (Vbh.261)—occur with respect to a domain that is varied in individual essence with the variety classed as visible-object, sound, etc.; and secondly, because the forty-four kinds of perception—that is to say, eight kinds of sense-sphere profitable perception, twelve kinds of unprofitable perception, eleven kinds of sense-sphere profitable resultant perception, two kinds of unprofitable-resultant perception, and eleven kinds of sense-sphere functional perception—themselves have variety, have various individual essences, and are dissimiliar from each other. With the complete non-attention to, non-adverting to, non-reaction to, non-reviewing of, these perceptions of variety; what is meant is that because he does not advert to them, give them attention or review them, therefore. . .

21. And [two things] should be understood: firstly, that their absence is stated here in the two ways as 'surmounting' and 'disappearance' because the earlier perceptions of matter and perceptions of resistance do not exist even in the kind of existence produced by this jhana on rebirth, let alone when this jhana is entered upon and dwelt in that existence; [331] and secondly, in the case of perceptions of variety, 'non-attention' to them is said because twenty-seven kinds of perception—that is to say, eight kinds of sense-sphere profitable perception, nine kinds of functional perception, and ten kinds of unprofitable perception—still exist in the kind of existence produced by this jhana; For when he enters upon and dwells in this jhana there too, he does so by non-attention to them also, but he is not attained when he does give attention to them.

22. And here briefly it should be understood that the abandoning of all fine-material-sphere states is signified by the words *with the surmounting of perceptions of matter*, and the abandoning of and non-attention to all sense-sphere consciousness and its concomitants is signified by the words *with the disappearance of perceptions of resistance with non-attention to perceptions of variety*.

23. *Unbounded space*: here it is called 'unbounded (*ananta*—lit. endless)' because neither its end as its arising nor its end

as its fall are made known.[7] It is the space left by the removal of the kasina that is called 'space' And here unboundedness (endlessness) should be understood as [referring to] the attention also, which is why it is said in the Vibhanga: 'He places, 'settles, his consciousness in that space, he pervades un-'boundedly (*anantaṁ*), hence "Unbounded (*ananto*) space" 'is said' (Vbh. 262).

24. *He enters upon and dwells in the base consisting of boundless space*: it has no bound (*anta*), thus it is unbounded (*ananta*). What is spacially unbounded (*ākāsaṁ anantaṁ*) is unbounded space (*ākāsānantaṁ*). Unbounded space is the same as boundless space (*ākāsānañcaṁ*—lit. space-boundlessness). That 'boundless space' is a 'base (*āyatana*)' in the sense of habitat for the jhana whose nature it is to be associated with it, as the 'deities' base' is for deities, thus it is the 'base consisting of boundless space (*ākāsānañcāyatana*)'. *He enters upon and dwells in*: having reached that base consisting of boundless space, having caused it to be produced, he dwells (*viharati*) with an abiding (*vihāra*) consisting in postures that are in conformity with it.

This is the detailed explanation of the base consisting of boundless space as a meditation subject.

*

[(2) The Base Consisting of Boundless Consciousness]

25. When he wants to develop the base consisting of boundless consciousness, he must first achieve mastery in the five ways in the attainment of the base consisting of boundless space. Then he should see the danger in the base consisting of boundless space in this way: 'This attainment has fine-material jhana as its near enemy, and it is not as peaceful as the base consisting of boundless consciousness'. So having ended his attachment to that, he should give his attention to the base consisting of boundless consciousness as peaceful, adverting again and again as 'Consciousness, consciousness' to the consciousness that occurred pervading that space [as its object]; He should give it attention, review it, and strike at it with applied and sustained thought; [332] but he should not give attention [simply] in this way 'Boundless, boundless'.[8]

---

7. 'A [formed] dhamma with an individual essence is delimited by rise and fall because it is produced after having not been, and because after having been it vanishes. But space is called boundless since it has neither rise nor fall because it is a dhamma without individual essence' (Pm. 323).

8. 'He should not give attention to it only as "Boundless, boundless"; instead of developing it thus, he should give attention to it as "Boundless consciousness, boundless consciousness" or as "Consciousness, consciousness" ' (Pm. 324).

26. As he directs his mind again and again on to that sign in this way, the hindrances are suppressed, mindfulness is established, and his mind becomes concentrated in access. He cultivates that sign again and again, develops and repeatedly practises it. As he does so, consciousness belonging to the base consisting of boundless consciousness arises in absorption with the [past] consciousness that pervaded the space [as its object], just as that belonging to the base consisting of boundless space did with the space [as its object]. But the method of explaining the process of absorption here should be understood in the way already described.

[*Text and Commentary*]

27. And at this point it is said: 'By completely surmounting '(*samatikamma*) the base consisting of boundless space, [aware 'of] "unbounded consciousness", he enters upon and dwells 'in the base consisting of boundless consciousness' (Vbh.245).

28. Herein, ***completely*** is as already explained. ***By . . . surmounting the base consisting of boundless space***: the jhana is called the 'base consisting of boundless space' in the way already stated (§24), and its object is so called too. For the object, too, is 'boundless space (*ākāsānañcaṁ*)' in the way already stated (§24), and then, because it is the object of the first immaterial jhana, it is its 'base' in the sense of habitat, as the 'deities' base' is for deities, thus it is the 'base consisting of boundless space'. Likewise: it is 'boundless space', and then, because it is the cause of the jhana's being of that species, it is its 'base' in the sense of locality of the species, as Kambojā is the 'base' of horses, thus it is the 'base consisting of boundless space' in this way also. So it should be understood that the words 'By. . . surmounting the base consisting of boundless space' include both [the jhana and its object] together, since this base consisting of boundless consciousness is to be entered upon and dwelt in precisely by surmounting, by causing the non-occurrence of, and by not giving attention to, both the jhana and its object.

29. *Unbounded consciousness*: What is meant is that he gives his attention thus 'Unbounded consciousness' to that same consciousness that occurred in pervading [as its object the space] as Unbounded space'. Or 'unbounded' refers to the attention. For when he gives attention without reserve to the consciousness that had the space as its object, then the attention he gives to it is 'unbounded'.

30. For it is said in the Vibhanga: '"Unbounded consciousness": 'he gives attention to that same space pervaded by conscious'ness, he pervades boundlessly, hence "Unbounded conscious'ness" is said' (Vbh. 262). But in that passage (*taṁ yeva*

ākāsaṁ viññāṇena phuṭaṁ) the instrumental case 'by consciousness' must be understood in the sense of accusative; for the teachers of the Commentary explain its meaning in that way. What is meant by 'He prevades boundlessly' is that 'he gives attention to that same consciousness which had pervaded that space (*taṁ yeva ākāsaṁ phutaṁ viññāṇaṁ*)'.

31. *He enters upon and dwells in the base consisting of boundless consciousness*: [333] it has no bound (*anta* lit. end), thus it is unbounded (*ananta*). What is unbounded is boundless (*ānañca* lit. unboundedness), and unbounded consciousness is called 'boundless consciousness' that is, '*viññāṇañcaṁ*' [in the contracted form] instead of '*viññāṇānañcam*' [which is the full number of syllables]. This is an idiomatic form. That boundless consciousness (*viññāṇañca*) is the base (*āyatana*) in the sense of foundation for the jhana whose nature it is to be associated with it, as the 'deities' base' is for deities, thus it is the 'base consisting of boundless consciousness (*viññāṇañcāyatana*)'. The rest is the same as before.

This is the detailed explanation of the base consisting of boundless consciousness as a meditation subject.

*

[(3) THE BASE CONSISTING OF NOTHINGNESS]

32. When he wants to develop the base consisting of nothingness, he must first achieve mastery in the five ways in the attainment of the base consisting of boundless consciousness. Then he should see the danger in the base consisting of boundless consciousness in this way: 'This attainment has the base consisting of boundless space as its near enemy, and it is not as peaceful as the base consisting of nothingness'. So having ended his attachment to that, he should give his attention to the base consisting of nothingness as peaceful. He should give attention to the [present] non-existence, voidness, secluded aspect, of that same [past] consciousness belonging to the base consisting of boundless space which became the object of [the consciousness belonging to] the base consisting of boundless consciousness. How does he do this ?

33. Without giving [further] attention to that consciousness, he should [now] advert again and again in this way 'There is not, there is not' or 'Void, void' or 'Secluded, secluded', and give his attention to it, review it, and strike at it with thought and applied thought.

34. As he directs his mind on to that sign thus, the hindrances are suppressed, mindfulness is established, and his mind becomes concentrated in access. He cultivates that sign again and again, develops and repeatedly practises it. As he does so, consciousness belonging to the base consisting of

nothingness arises in absorption, making its object the void, secluded, non-existent state of that same [past] exalted consciousness that occurred in pervading the space, just as the [consciousness belonging to the] base consisting of boundless consciousness did the [then past] exalted consciousness that had pervaded the space. And here too the method of explaining the absorption should be understood in the way already described.

35. But there is this difference. Suppose a man sees a community of bhikkhus gathered together in a meeting hall or some such place and then goes elsewhere; then after the bhikkhus have risen at the conclusion of the business for which they had met and have departed, the man comes back, and as he stands in the doorway looking at that place again, he sees it only as void, he sees it only as secluded, he does not think 'So many bhikkhus have died, so many have left the district', but rather [334] he sees only the non-existence thus, 'This is void, secluded'—so too, having formerly dwelt seeing with the jhana eye belonging to the base consisting of boundless consciousness the [earlier] consciousness that had occurred making the space its object, [now] when that consciousness has disappeared owing to his giving attention to the preliminary work in the way beginning 'There is not, there is not', he dwells seeing only its non-existence, in other words its departedness when this consciousness has arisen in absorption.

[*Text and Commentary*]

36. And at this point it is said: 'By completely surmounting the 'base consisting of boundless consciousness, [aware that] ' "There is nothing", he enters upon and dwells in the base 'consisting of nothingness' (Vbh.245).

37. Herein, *completely* is as already explained. *By... surmounting the base consisting of boundless consciousness*: here too the jhana is called the 'base consisting of boundless consciousness' in the way already stated, and its object is so-called too. For the object too is 'boundless consciousness (*viññāṇañcaṁ*)' in the way already stated, and then, because it is the object of the second immaterial jhana, it is its 'base' in the sense of habitat, as the 'deities' base' is for deities, thus it is the 'base consisting of boundless consciousness'. Likewise it is 'boundless consciousness', and then because it is the cause of the jhana's being of that species, it is its 'base' in the sense of locality of the species, as Kambojā is the 'base' of horses, thus it is the 'base consisting of boundless consciousness' in this way also. So it should be understood that the words 'By .. surmounting the base consisting of boundless consciousness' include both [the jhana and its object] together, since this base consisting of nothingness is to be entered upon

and dwelt in precisely by surmounting, by causing the non-occurrence of, not by giving attention to, both jhana and its object.

38. *There is nothing* (*natthi kiñci*): what is meant is that he gives his attention thus 'There is not, there is not' or 'void, void' or 'secluded, secluded'. It is said in the Vibhaṅga '"There is 'nothing": he makes that same consciousness non-existent, 'makes it absent, makes it disappear, sees that "there is 'nothing", hence "There is nothing" is said' (Vbh.262), which is expressed in a way that resembles comprehension [by insight] of liability to destruction, nevertheless the meaning should be understood in the way described above. For the words 'He makes that same consciousness non-existent, makes it absent, makes it disappear' are said of one who does not advert to it or give attention to it or review it, and only gives attention to its non-existence, its voidness, its secludedness; they are not meant in the other way (cf.Ch.XXI.§17).

39. *He enters upon and dwells in the base consisting of nothingness*: it has no owning (*kiñcana*)[9] thus it is non-owning (*akiñcana*); what is meant is that it has not even the mere act of its dissolution remaining. The state (essence) of non-owning is nothingness (*ākiñcañña*). This is a term for the disappearance of the consciousness belonging to the base consisting of boundless space. [335] That nothingness is the 'base' in the sense of foundation for that jhana, as the 'deities' base' is for deities, thus it is the 'base consisting of nothingness'. The rest is as before.

This is the detailed explanation of the base consisting of nothingness as a meditation subject.

*

[(4) THE BASE CONSISTING OF NEITHER PERCEPTION NOR NON-PERCEPTION]

40. When, however, he wants to develop the base consisting of neither perception nor non-perception, he must first achieve mastery in the five ways in the attainment of the base consisting of nothingness. Then he should see the danger in the base consisting of nothingness and the advantage in what is superior to it in this way, 'This attainment has the base consisting of boundless consciousness as its near enemy, and it is

9. There is a play on the words '*natthi kiñci* (there is nothing) and '*akiñcana* (non-owning)'. At M. i, 298 there occurs the expression '*Rāgo kho āvuso kiñcano* (greed, friend is an owning)', which is used in connexion with this attainment. The commentary (MA. ii, 354) says '*Rāgo uppajjitvā puggalaṁ kiñcati, maddati, palibujjhati, tasmā kiñcano ti vutto* (greed having arisen owns, presses, impedes, a person, that is why it is called an owning)' (Cf. MA. i, 27; also Ch. XXI, §53 and note 19.). Pm. (p. 327) here says '*Kiñcanan ti kiñci pi*'. The word *kiñcati* is not in P. T. S. Dict.

not as peaceful as the base consisting of neither perception nor non-perception' or in this way 'Perception is a disease, 'perception is a boil, perception is a dart, . . . this is peaceful, 'this is sublime, that is to say, neither perception nor non-'perception' (M.ii,231); So having ended his attachment to the base consisting of nothingness, he should give attention to the base consisting of neither perception nor non-perception as peaceful. He should advert again and again to that attainment of the base consisting of nothingness that has occurred making non-existence its object, adverting to it as 'Peaceful, peaceful', and he should give his attention to it, review it and strike at it with thought and applied thought.

41. As he directs his mind again and again on to that sign in this way the hindrances are suppressed, mindfulness is established, and his mind becomes concentrated in access. He cultivates that sign again and again, develops and repeatedly practises it. As he does so, consciousness belonging to the base consisting of neither perception nor non-perception arises in absorption, making its object the four [mental] aggregates that constitute the attainment of the base consisting of nothingness, just as the [consciousness belonging to the] base consisting of nothingness did the disappearance of the [previous] consciousness. And here too the method of explaining the absorption should be understood in the way already described.

[*Text and Commentary*]

42. And at this point it is said: 'By completely surmounting 'the base consisting of nothingness he enters upon and dwells 'in the base consisting of neither perception nor non-'perception' (Vbh. 245).

43. Herein, *completely* is as already explained. *By . . . surmounting the base consisting of nothingness*: here too the jhana is called the 'base consisting of nothingness' in the way already stated, and its object is so called too. For the object too is nothingness (*ākiñcaññaṁ*)' in the way already stated, and then, because it is the object of the third immaterial jhana, it is its 'base' in the sense of habitat, as the 'deities' base' is for deities, thus it is the 'base consisting of nothingness'. Likewise: it is 'nothingness', and then, because it is the cause of the jhana's being of that species, it is its 'base' in the sense of locality of the species, as Kambojā is the 'base' of horses, thus it is the base consisting of nothingness' in this way also. [336] So it should be understood that the words 'By . . . surmounting the base consisting of nothingness' include both [the jhana and its object] together, since the base consisting of neither perception nor non-perception is to be entered upon

and dwelt in precisely by surmounting, by causing the non-occurrence of, by not giving attention to, both the jhana and its object.

44. *Base consisting of neither perception nor non-perception*: then there is he who so practises that there is in him the perception on account of the presence of which this [attainment] is called the 'Base Consisting of Neither Perception Nor Non-perception', and in the Vibhaṅga, in order to point out that [person] firstly one specified as 'Neither-percipient-nor-non-percipient', it is said, 'gives attention to that same base 'consisting of nothingness as peaceful, he develops the 'attainment with residual formations, hence "neither-percipi-'ent nor non-percipient" is said' (Vbh.263).

45. Herein, *he gives attention. . . as peaceful*, means that he gives attention to it as 'peaceful' because of the peacefulness of the object thus: How peaceful this attainment is; for it can make even non-existence its object and still subsist!

If he brings it to mind as 'peaceful' then how does there come to be surmounting? Because there is no actual desire to attain it. For although he gives his attention to it as 'peaceful', yet there is no concern in him or reaction or attention such as 'I shall advert to this' or 'I shall attain this' or 'I shall resolve upon [the duration of] this' or 'I shall emerge from this' or 'I shall review this '. Why not? Because the base consisting of neither perception nor non-perception is more peaceful and better than the base consisting of nothingness.

46. Suppose a king is proceeding along a city street with the great pomp of royalty,[10] splendidly mounted on the back of an elephant, and he sees craftsmen wearing one cloth tightly as a loin-cloth and another tied round their heads, working at the various crafts such as ivory carving, etc., their limbs covered with ivory dust, etc.; now while he is pleased with their skill, thinking 'How skilled these craft-masters are, and what crafts they practise!', he does not, however, think 'Oh that I might abandon royalty and become a craftsman like that!'; why not? because of the great benefits in the majesty of kings; he leaves the craftsmen behind and proceeds on his way—so too, though this [meditator] gives attention to that attainment as 'peaceful', yet there is no concern in him or reaction or attention such as 'I shall advert to this attainment' or 'I shall attain this' or 'I shall resolve upon [the duration of] it' or 'I shall emerge from it' or 'I shall review it'.

47. As he gives attention to it as 'peaceful' in the way already described, [337] he reaches the ultra-subtle absorbed perception in virtue of which he is called 'neither percipient nor

10. *Mahacca* (see D. i. 49 and DA. i, 148); the form is not given in P.T.S. Dict.; probably a form of *mahatiya.*

non-percipient' and it is said of him that 'He develops the attainment with residual formations'.

The attainment with residual formations is the fourth immaterial attainment whose formations have reached a state of extreme subtlety.

48. Now in order to show the meaning of the kind of perception that has been reached, on account of which [this jhana] is called the 'base consisting of neither perception nor non-perception', it is said: ' "base consisting of neither perception 'nor non-perception": states of consciousness or its concomi-'tants in one who has attained the base consisting of 'neither perception nor non-perception or in one who has 'been reborn there or in one who is abiding in bliss there in 'this present life' (Vbh.263). Of these, what is intended here is the states of consciousness and its concomitants in one who has attained.

49. The word meaning here is this: that jhana with its associated states neither has perception nor has no perception because of the absence of gross perception and presence of subtle perception, thus it is 'neither-perception-nor-non-perception (*n'eva-saññā-nāsaññaṁ*)'. It is 'neither-perception-nor-non-perception' and it is a base (*āyatana*) because it is included in the mind base (*manāyatana*) and the mental-object base (*dhammāyatana*), thus it is the 'base consisting of neither perception nor non-perception (*nevasaññānāsaññāya-*
50. *tana*)'. Or alternatively: the perception here is neither perception, since it is incapable of performing the decisive function of perception, nor yet non-perception, since it is present in a subtle state as a residual formation, thus it is 'neither-perception-nor-non-perception'. It is 'neither-perception-nor-non-perception' and it is a 'base' in the sense of a foundation for the other states, thus it is the 'base consisting of neither perception nor non-perception'.

And here it is not only perception that is like this, but feeling as well is neither-feeling-nor-non-feeling, consciousness is neither-consciousness-nor-non-consciousness, and contact is neither-contact-nor-non-contact, and the same description applies to the rest of the associated states; but it should be understood that this presentation is given in terms of perception.

51. And the meaning should be illustrated by the similes beginning with the smearing of oil on the bowl. A novice smeared a bowl with oil, it seems, and laid it aside. When it was time to drink gruel, an Elder told him to bring the bowl. He said 'Venerable sir, there is oil in the bowl'. But then when he was told 'Bring the oil, novice, I shall fill the oil tube', he replied 'There is no oil, venerable sir'. Herein, just as 'There is oil' is in the sense of incompatibility with the gruel

because it has been poured into [the bowl] and just as 'There is no oil' is in the sense of filling the oil tube, etc., so too this perception is 'Neither perception' since it is incapable of performing the decisive function of perception and it is 'Nor non-perception' because it is present in a subtle form as a residual formation. [338]

52. But in this context what is perception's function? It is the perceiving of the object, and it is the production of dispassion if [that attainment and its object are] made the objective-field of insight. But it is not able to make the function of perceiving decisive, as the heat element in tepid[11] water is not able to make the function of burning decisive; and it is not able to produce dispassion by treatment of its objective field with insight in the way that perception is in the case of the other attainments.

53. There is in fact no bhikkhu capable of reaching dispassion by comprehension of aggregates connected with the base consisting of neither perception nor non-perception unless he has already done his interpreting with other aggregates (see Ch. XX, §2f. and XXI, §23). And furthermore, when the venerable Sāriputta, or someone very wise and naturally gifted with insight as he was, is able to do so, even he has to do it by means of comprehension by groups (Ch.XX, §2) in this way, 'So it seems, these states, not having been, come to be; having come to be, they vanish' (M. iii, 28) and not by means of [actual direct] insight into states one by one as they arise, such is the subtlety that this attainment reaches.

54. And this meaning should be illustrated by the simile of the water on the road, as it was by the simile of the oil-smearing on the bowl. A novice was walking in front of an elder, it seems, who had set out on a journey. He saw a little water and said 'There is water, venerable sir, remove your sandals'. Then the elder said 'If there is water, bring me the bathing cloth and let us bathe', but the novice said 'There is none, venerable sir'. Herein, just as 'There is water' is in the sense of mere wetting of the sandals, and 'There is none' is in the sense of bathing. So too, this perception is 'neither perception' since it is incapable of performing the decisive function of perception, and it is 'nor non-perception' because it is present
55. in a subtle form as a residual formation. And this meaning should be illustrated not only by these similes but by other appropriate ones as well.

Enters upon and dwells in is as already explained.

This is the detailed explanation of the base consisting of neither perception nor non-perception as a meditation subject.

---

11. '*Sukhodaka—tepid water*': see Monier Williams Skr. Dict,; this meaning of *sukha* not given in P. T. S. Dict.

[GENERAL]

56. Thus has the Peerless Helper told
The fourfold Immaterial State;
To know these general matters too
Will not be inappropriate.

57. For these immaterial states,
While reckoned by surmounting of
The object they are four, the wise
Do not admit surmounting of
Factors that one can recognize.

58. Of these [four], the first is due to surmounting signs of materiality, the second is due to surmounting space, the third is due to surmounting the consciousness that occurred with that space as its object, and the fourth is due to surmounting the disappearance of the consciousness that occurred with that space as its object. So they should be understood as four in number with the surmounting of the object in each case. [339] But the wise do not admit any surmounting of [jhana] factors; for there is no surmounting of factors in them as there is in the case of the fine-material-sphere attainments. Each one has just the two factors, namely, equanimity and unification of mind.

59. That being so,
They progress in refinement; each
Is finer than the one before.
Two figures help to make them known :
The cloth lengths, and each palace floor.

60. Suppose there were a four-storied palace: on its first floor the five objects of sense pleasure were provided in a very fine form as divine dancing, singing and music, and perfumes, scents, garlands, food, couches, clothing, etc., and on the second they were finer than that, and on the third finer still, and on the fourth they were finest of all; yet they are still only palace floors, and there is no difference between them in the matter of their state (essence) as palace floors; it is with the progressive refinement of the five objects of sense pleasure that each one is finer than the one below;—again suppose there were lengths of cloth of quadruple, treble, double and single thickness, and [made] of thick, thin, thinner, and very thin, thread spun by one woman, all of the same measure in width and breadth; now although these lengths of cloth are four in number, yet they measure the same in width and breadth, there is no difference in their measurement; but in softness to the touch, fineness, and costliness each is finer than the one before;—so too, although there are only the two factors in all four [immaterial states], that is to say, equanimity and unification of mind, still each one should be understood as

finer than the one before with the progressive refinement of the factors due to successful development.

61. And for the fact that each of them is finer than the last [there is this figure:]

One hangs upon a tent that stands
On filth; on him another leans.
Outside a third not leaning stands,
Against the last another leans
Between the four men and these states
The correspondence then is shown,
And so how each to each relates
Can by a man of wit be known.

62. This is how the meaning should be construed. There was a tent in a dirty place, it seems. Then a man arrived, and being disgusted with the dirt, he rested himself on the tent with his hands and remained as if hung or hanging on to it. Then another man came and leant upon the man hanging on to the tent. Then another man came and thought 'The one who is hanging on to the tent and the one who is leaning upon him are both badly off, and if the tent falls they will certainly fall. I think I shall stand outside'. [340] So instead of leaning upon the one leaning upon the first, he remained outside. Then another arrived, and taking account of the insecurity of the one hanging on to the tent and the one leaning upon him, and fancying that the one standing outside was well placed, he stood leaning upon him.

63. Herein, this is how it should be regarded. The space from which the kasina kas been removed is like the tent in the dirty place. The [consciousness of the] base consisting of boundless space, which makes space its object owing to disgust with the sign of the fine-material, is like the man who hangs on to the tent owing to disgust with the dirt. The [consciousness of the] base consisting of boundless consciousness, the occurrence of which is contingent upon [the consciousness of] the base consisting of boundless space whose object is space, is like the man who leans upon the man who hangs on to the tent. The [consciousness of the] base consisting of nothingness, which instead of making the [consciousness of the] base consisting of boundless space its object has the non-existence of that as its object, is like the man who, after considering the insecurity of those two, does not lean upon the one hanging on to the tent, but stands outside. The [consciousness of the] base consisting of neither perception nor non-perception, the occurrence of which is contingent upon [the consciousness of] the base consisting of nothingness, which stands in a place outside, in other words, in the non-existence of [the past] consciousness, is like the man who stands leaning upon the last-named, having considered the insecurity of the one

hanging on to the tent and the one leaning upon him, and fancying that the one standing outside is well placed.

64. And while occurring in this way,

It takes this for its object since
There is no other one as good,
As men depend upon a king,
Whose fault they see, for livelihood.

65. For although this [consciousness of the] base consisting of neither perception nor non-perception has seen the flaw in the base consisting of nothingness in this way 'This attainment has the base consisting of boundless consciousness as its near enemy', notwithstanding that fact it takes it as its object in the absence of any other. Like what? As men for the sake of livelihood depend on kings whose faults they see. For just as, for the sake of livelihood and because they cannot get a livelihood elsewhere, people put up with some king, ruler of all quarters, who is unrestrained, and harsh in bodily, verbal and mental behaviour, though they see his faults thus 'He is harshly behaved', so too the [consciousness of the] base consisting of neither perception nor non-perception takes that base consisting of nothingness as its object in spite of seeing its faults in this way, and it does so since it cannot find another [better] object.

66. As one who mounts a lofty stair
Leans on its railing for a prop,
As one who climbs an airy peak
Leans on the mountain's very top,
As one who stands on a crag's edge
Leans for support on his own knees—
Each jhana rests on that below;
For so it is with each of these.

The Tenth Chapter called 'The Description of the Immaterial States' in the Treatise on the Development of Concentration in the Path of Purification composed for the purpose of gladdening good people.

CHAPTER XI.

DESCRIPTION OF CONCENTRATION—CONCLUSION

(*Samādhi-niddesa*)

[PERCEPTION OF REPULSIVENESS IN NUTRIMENT]

1. [341] Now comes the description of the development of the perception of repulsiveness in nutriment, which was listed as the 'One Perception'[1] next to the Immaterial States (Ch. III,§105).

Herein: it nourishes (*āharati* lit. brings on), thus it is nutriment (*āhāra* lit. bringing on). That is of four kinds as physical nutriment, nutriment consisting of contact, nutriment consisting of mental volition, and nutriment consisting of consciousness.[2]

2. But what is it here that nourishes (brings on), what? Physical nutriment (*kabalinkārāhāra*) nourishes (brings on) the materiality of the octad that has nutritive essence as eighth.[3] Contact as nutriment nourishes (brings on) the three kinds of feeling. Mental volition as nutriment nourishes (brings on)

---

1. 'The word "perception (*saññā*)" is used for the dhamma with the characteristic of perceiving (*sañjānana*), as in the case of "perception of visible objects", "perception of sound", etc., and it is used for insight, as in the case of "perception of impermanence", "perception of suffering", etc., and it is used for serenity, as in the passage "Perception of the bloated and perception of visible objects, have these one meaning or different meanings Sopāka?" ( ), and so on. Here, however, it should be understood as the preliminary work for serenity; for it is the apprehending of the repulsive aspect in nutriment, or the access jhana produced by means of that, that is intended here by "perception of repulsiveness in nutriment"' (Pm. 334–5).

2. A more detailed exposition of nutriment is given at MA. i, 107ff. '"*It nourishes* (*āharati*)": the meaning is that it leads up, fetches, produces, its own fruit through its state as a condition for the fruit's arising or presence, which state is called "nutriment condition". It is made into a mouthful (*kabalaṁ karīyati*), thus it is physical (*kabaliṅkāra*). In this way it gets its designation from the concrete object; but as to characteristic, it should be understood to have the characteristic of nutritive-essence (*ojā*). It is physical and it is nutriment in the sense stated, thus it is physical nutriment. So with the rest. It touches (*phusati*), thus it is contact (*phassa*); for although this is an immaterial state, it occurs also as the aspect of touching on an object (*ārammaṇa*—lit. What is to be leaned on), which is why it is said to have the characteristic of touching. It wills (*cetayati*), thus it is volition (*cetanā*); the meaning is that it arranges (collects) itself together with associated states upon the object. Mental volition is volition occupied with the mind. It cognizes (*vijānāti*) by conjecturing about rebirth (see Ch. XVII, §303), thus it is consciousness (*viññāṇa*=cognition)' (Pm. 335).

3. For the 'octad with nutritive-essence as eighth (*ojaṭṭhamaka*)' see Ch. XVIII, §5ff. and XX, §27ff.

rebirth-linking in the three kinds of becoming. Consciousness as nutriment nourishes (brings on) mentality-materiality at the moment of rebirth-linking.

3. Now when there is physical nutriment there is attachment, which brings peril; when there is nutriment as contact there is approaching, which brings peril; when there is nutriment as mental volition there is reappearance, which brings peril; when there is nutriment as consciousness there is rebirth-linking, which brings peril.[4] And to show how they bring fear thus, physical nutriment should be illustrated by the simile of the child's flesh (S.ii,98), contact as nutriment by the simile of the hideless cow (S.ii,99), mental volition as nutriment by the simile of the pit of live coals (S.ii,99), and consciousness as nutriment by the simile of the hundred spears (S.ii,100).

4. But of these four kinds of nutriment it is only physical nutriment, classed as what is eaten, drunk, chewed, and tasted that is intended here as 'nutriment' in this sense. The perception arisen as the apprehension of the repulsive aspect in that nutriment is 'perception of repulsiveness in nutriment'.

5. One who wants to develop that perception of repulsiveness in nutriment should learn the meditation subject and see that he has no uncertainty about even a single word of what he

---

4. Im. (p. 355) explains *attachment* here as craving which is 'perilous because it brings harm' (see e.g. D. ii, 58–9), or in other words 'greed for the five aggregates (lust after five-aggregate experience)'. It cites the following: 'Bhikkhus, when there is physical nutriment, there is greed (lust), there is delighting, there is craving; consciousness being planted therein, grows. Wherever consciousness being planted grows, there is the combination of mind-and-matter. Wherever there is the combination of mind-and-matter, there is ramification of formations. Wherever there is ramification of formations, there is production of further becoming in the future. Wherever there is production of further becoming in the future, there is future birth, ageing and death. Wherever there is future birth, ageing and death, bhikkhus, the end is sorrow, I say, with woe and despair' (S. ii, 101; cf. S. ii, 66). *Approaching* is explained as 'meeting, coinciding, with unabandoned perversions [of perception] due to an object [being, perceived as permanent, etc., when it is not]'. That is 'perilous since it is not free from the three kinds of suffering'. The quotation given is: Bhikkhus due to contact of the kind to be felt as pleasant pleasant feeling arises. With that feeling as condition there is craving , . . . thus there is the arising of this whole mass of suffering' (cf. S. iv, 215). *Reappearance* is 'rebirth in some kind of becoming or other. Being flung into a new becoming is perilous because there is no immunity from the risks rooted in reappearance'. The following is quoted: 'Not knowing, bhikkhus, a man forms the formation of merit, and his [rebirth] consciousness accords with the merit [he performed] he forms the formation of demerit, . . . he forms the formation of the imperturbable, . . . ' (S. ii, 82). *Rebirth-linking* is the actual linking with the next becoming, which 'is perilous since it is not immune from the suffering due to the signs of [the impending] rebirth-linking'. The quotation given is: 'Bhikkhus, when there is consciousness as nutriment there is greed (lust), there is delighting, . . . ' (S. ii, 102—complete as above).

has learnt. Then he should go into solitary retreat and [342] review repulsiveness in ten aspects in the physical nutriment classified as what is eaten, drunk, chewed, and tasted, that is to say, as to going, seeking, using, secretion, receptacle, what is uncooked (undigested), what is cooked (digested), fruit, outflow, and smearing.

6. 1. Herein, *as to going*: even when a man has gone forth in so mighty a dispensation, still after he has perhaps spent all night reciting the Enlightened One's word or doing the ascetic's work, after he has risen early to do the duties connected with the shrine terrace and the Enlightenment-Tree terrace, to set out the water for drinking and washing, to sweep the grounds and to see to the needs of the body, after he has sat down on his seat and given attention to his meditation subject twenty or thirty times[5] and got up again, then he must take his bowl and [outer] robe, he must leave behind the ascetics' woods that are not crowded with people, offer the bliss of seclusion possess shade and water, and are clean, cool, delightful places, he must disregard the Noble Ones' delight in seclusion, and he must set out for the village in order to get nutriment, as a jackal for the charnel ground.

7. And as he goes thus, from the time when he steps down from his bed or chair he has to tread on a carpet[6] covered with the dust of his feet, geckos' droppings, and so on. Next he has to see the doorstep,[7] which is more repulsive than the inside of the room since it is often fouled with the droppings of rats, bats,[8] and so on. Next the lower terrace, which is more repulsive than the terrace above since it is all smeared with the droppings of owls, pigeons,[9] and so on. Next the grounds,[10] which are more repulsive than the lower floor since they are defiled by old grass and leaves blown about

5. '"*Twenty or thirty times*": here some say that the definition of the number of times is according to what is present-by-continuity (see Ch. XIV, §188). But others say that it is by way of "warming up the seat" (see MA. i, 255); for development that has not reached suppression of hindrances does not remove the bodily discomfort in the act of sitting, because of the lack of pervading happiness. So there is inconstancy of posture too. Then "twenty or thirty" is taken as the number already observed by the time of setting out on the alms round. Or alternatively from "going to" up to "smearing" is one turn; then it is after giving attention to the meditation subject by twenty or thirty turns in this way' (Pm. 339).

6. '*Paccattharaṇa*—carpet': the word normally means a coverlet, but here, according to Pm. (p. 339), it is 'a spread *attharana*) consisting of a rug (*cilimika*) to be spread on the ground for protecting the skin'.

7. For '*pamukha*—doorstep', perhaps an open upper floor gallery here, see Ch. XIII, §6.

8. '*Jatukā*—bat' = *khuddaka-vaggulī* (Pm. 339): not in P. T. S. Dict.; see Ch. III, §97.

9. '*Pārāvata*—pigeon': only spelling *pārāpata* given in P. T. S. Dict.

10. For this meaning of *pariveṇa* see Ch. IV, note 37.

by the wind, by sick novices' urine, excrement, spittle and snot, and in the rainy season by water, mud, and so on. And he has to see the road to the monastery, which is more repulsive than the grounds.

8. In due course, after standing in the debating lodge[11] when he has finished paying homage at the Enlightenment Tree and the shrine, he sets out thinking 'Instead of looking at the shrine that is like a cluster of pearls, and the Enlightenment Tree that is as lovely as a bouquet of peacock's tail feathers, and the abode that is as fair as a god's palace, I must now turn my back on such a charming place and go abroad for the sake of food'; and on the way to the village, the view of a road of stumps and thorns and an uneven road broken up by the force of water awaits him.

9. Next, after he has put on his waist cloth as one who hides an abscess, and tied his waist band as one who ties a bandage on a wound, and robed himself in his upper robes as one who hides a skeleton, and taken out his bowl as one who takes out a pan for medicine, [343] when he reaches the vicinity of the village gate, perhaps the sight of an elephant's carcase, a horse's carcase, a buffalo's carcase, a human carcase, a snake's carcase, or a dog's carcase, awaits him, and not only that but he has to suffer his nose to be assailed by the smell of them.

Next, as he stands in the village gateway, he must scan the village streets in order to avoid danger from savage elephants, horses, and so on.

10. So this repulsive [experience] beginning with the carpet that has to be trodden on and ending with the various kinds of carcases that have to be seen and smelt, [has to be undergone] for the sake of nutriment: 'Oh nutriment is indeed a repulsive thing!'

This is how repulsiveness should be reviewed as to going.

11. 2. How *as to seeking?* When he has endured the repulsiveness of going in this way, and has gone into the village, and is clothed in his cloak of patches, he has to wander in the village streets from house to house like a beggar with a dish in his hand. And in the rainy season wherever he treads his feet sink into water and mire up to the flesh of the calves.[12] He has to hold the bowl in one hand and his robe up with the otner. In the hot season he has to go about with his body covered with the dirt, grass and dust blown about by the wind. On reaching such and such a house door he has to see

---

11. '*Vitakka-māḷaka*—debating lodge': Pm. (p. 339) says '"*Kattha nu kho ajja bhikkhāya caritabban*" *ti ādinā vitakkamāḷake*' (in a lodge for thinking in the way beginning 'Where must I go for alms today').

12. '*Piṇḍika-maṁsa* — flesh of the calves = *jaṅghapiṇḍikamaṁsapadesa* (Pm. 340). Cf. Ch. VIII, §97; also AA. 417. Not in this sense in P. T. S. Dict.

and even to tread in gutters and cesspools covered with bluebottles and seething with all the species of worms, all mixed up with fish washings, meat washings, rice washings, spittle, snot, dogs' and pigs' excrement, and what not, from which flies come up and settle on his outer cloak of patches and on his bowl and on his head.

12. And when he enters a house, some give and some do not. And when they give, some give yesterday's cooked rice and stale cakes and rancid jelly, sauce and so on.[13] Some, not giving, say 'Please pass on, venerable sir', others keep silent as if they did not see him. Some avert their faces. Others treat him with harsh words such as 'Go away, you bald-head'. When he has wandered for alms in the village in this way like a beggar, he has to depart from it.

13. So this [experience] beginning with the entry into the village and ending with the departure from it, which is repulsive owing to the water, mud, etc., that has to be trodden in and seen and endured, [has to be undergone] for the sake of nutriment: 'Oh nutriment is indeed a repulsive thing!'

This is how repulsiveness should be reviewed as to seeking, [344]

14. 3. How *as to using*? After he has sought the nutriment in this way and is sitting at ease in a comfortable place outside the village, then so long as he has not dipped his hand into it he would be able to invite a respected bhikkhu or a decent, person, if he saw one, [to share it;] but as soon as he has dipped his hand into it out of desire to eat he would be ashamed to say 'Take some'. And when he has dipped his hand in and is squeezing it up, the sweat trickling down his five fingers wets any dry crisp food there may be and makes it sodden.

15. And when its good appearance has been spoilt by his squeezing it up, and it has been made into a ball and put into his mouth, then the lower teeth function as a mortar, the upper teeth as a pestle, and the tongue as a hand. It gets pounded there with the pestle of the teeth like a dog's dinner in a dog's trough, while he turns it over and over with his tongue; then the thin spittle at the tip of the tongue smears it, and the thick spittle behind the middle of the tongue smears it, and the filth from the teeth in the parts where a tooth-stick cannot reach smears it.

16. When thus mashed up and besmeared this peculiar compound now destitute of the [original] colour and smell is reduced to a condition as utterly nauseating as a dog's vomit in a dog's trough. Yet, notwithstanding that it is like this it can still be swallowed because it is no longer in range of the eye's focus.

---

13. '*Kummāsa*—jelly': usually rendered 'junket', but the Vinaya commentaries give it as made of corn (*yava*).

This is how repulsiveness should be reviewed as to using.

17. 4. How *as to secretion*? Buddhas and Pacceka Buddhas and Wheel-turning Monarchs have only one of the four secretions consisting of bile, phlegm, pus and blood, but those with weak merit have all four. So when [the food] has arrived at the stage of being eaten and it enters inside, then in one whose secretion of bile is in excess it becomes as utterly nauseating as if smeared with thick *madhuka* oil; in one whose secretion of phlegm is in excess it is as if smeared with the juice of *nāgabalā*[14] leaves; in one whose secretion of pus is in excess it is as if smeared with rancid buttermilk; and in one whose secretion of blood is in excess it is as utterly nauseating as if smeared with the dye. This is how repulsiveness should be reviewed as to secretion.

18. 5. How *as to receptacle*? When it has gone inside the belly and is smeared with one of these secretions, then the receptacle it goes into is no gold dish or crystal or silver dish and so on. On the contrary, if it is swallowed by one ten years old, it finds itself in a place like a cesspit unwashed for ten years. [345] If it is swallowed by one twenty years old, thirty, forty, fifty, sixty, seventy, eighty, ninety years old, if it is swallowed by one a hundred years old, it finds itself in a place like a cesspit unwashed for a hundred years. This is how repulsiveness should be reviewed as to receptacle.

19. 6. How *as to what is uncooked* (*undigested*)? After this nutriment has arrived at such a place for its receptacle, then for as long as it remains uncooked it stays in that same place just described, which is shrouded in absolute darkness, pervaded by draughts,[15] tainted by various smells of ordure and utterly fetid and loathsome. And just as when a cloud out of season has rained during a drought and bits of grass and leaves and rushes and the carcases of snakes, dogs and human beings that have collected in a pit at the gate of an outcaste village remain there warmed by the sun's heat until the pit becomes covered with froth and bubbles, so too, what has been swallowed that day and yesterday and the day before remains there together, and being smothered by the layer of phlegm and covered with froth and bubbles produced by digestion through being fermented by the heat of the bodily fires, it becomes quite loathsome. This is how repulsiveness should be reviewed as to what is uncooked.

20. How as to *what is cooked*? When it has been completely cooked there by the bodily fires, it does not turn into gold, silver etc., as the ores[16] of gold, silver, etc., do [through

14. '*Nāgabalā*'—a kind of plant; not in P. T. S. Dict.
15. '*Pavana*—draught': not in this sense in P. T. S. Dict.; see Ch. XVI, §37.
16. '*Dhātu*—ore': not in this sense in P. T. S. Dict. See also Ch. XV, §20.

smelting]. Instead, giving off froth and bubbles, it turns into excrement and fills the receptacle for digested food, like brown clay squeezed with a smoothing trowel and packed into a tube, and it turns into urine and fills the bladder. This is how repulsiveness should be reviewed as to what is cooked.

21. 8. How *as to fruit*? When it has been rightly cooked, it produces the various kinds of ordure consisting of head hairs, body hairs, nails, teeth, and the rest. When wrongly cooked it produces the hundred diseases beginning with itch, ringworm, smallpox, leprosy, plague, consumption, coughs, flux, and so on. Such is its fruit. This is how repulsiveness should be reviewed as to fruit.

22. 9. How *as to outflow*? On being swallowed, it enters by one door, after which it flows out by several doors in the way beginning 'Eye-dirt from the eye, ear-dirt from the ear' (Sn. 197). And on being swallowed it is swallowed even in the company of large gathering. But on flowing out, now converted into excrement, urine, etc., it is excreted only in solitude. [346] On the first day one is delighted to eat it, elated and full of happiness and joy. On the second day one stops one's nose to void it, with a wry face, disgusted and dismayed. And on the first day one swallows it lustfully, greedily, gluttonously, infatuatedly. But on the second day, after a single night has passed, one excretes it with distaste, ashamed, humiliated and disgusted. Hence the Ancients said:

23. 'The food and drink so greatly prized—
'The crisp to chew, the soft to suck—
'Go in all by a single door,
'But by nine doors come oozing out.

'The food and drink so greatly prized—
'The crisp to chew the soft to suck—
'Men like to eat in company,
'But to excrete in secrecy.

'The food and drink so greatly prized—
'The crisp to chew, the soft to suck—
'These a man eats with high delight,
'And then excretes with dumb disgust.

'The food and drink so greatly prized—
'The crisp to chew, the soft to suck—
'A single night will be enough
'To bring them to putridity'.

This is how repulsiveness should be reviewed as to outflow.

24. 10. How *as to smearing*? At the time of using it he smears his hands, lips, tongue and palate, and they become repulsive by being smeared with it. And even when washed, they have to be washed again and again in order to remove the smell.

And, just as, when rice is being boiled, the husks, the red powder covering the grain, etc., rise up and smear the mouth, rim and lid of the cauldron so too, when eaten it rises up during its cooking and simmering by the bodily fire that pervades the whole body, it turns into tartar, which smears the teeth, and it turns into spittle, phlegm etc., which respectively smear the tongue, palate, etc.; and it turns into eye-dirt, ear-dirt snot, urine, excrement, ete., which respectively smear the eyes, ears, nose and nether passages. And when these doors are smeared by it, they never become either clean or pleasing even though washed every day. And after one has washed a certain one of these, the hand has to be washed again.[17] And after one has washed a certain one of these, the repulsiveness does not depart from it even after two or three washings with cowdung and clay and scented powder. This is how repulsiveness should be reviewed as to smearing.

25. As he reviews repulsiveness in this way in ten aspects and strikes at it with thought and applied thought, physical nutriment [347] becomes evident to him in its repulsive aspect. He cultivates that sign[18] again and again, develops and repeatedly practises it. As he does so, the hindrances are suppressed, and his mind is concentrated in access concentration, but without reaching absorption because of the profundity of physical nutriment as a state with an individual essence. But perception is evident here in the apprehension of the repulsive aspect, which is why this meditation subject goes by the name of 'perception of repulsiveness in nutriment'.

26. When a bikkhu devotes himself to this perception of repulsiveness in nutriment, his mind retreats, retracts and recoils from craving for flavours. He nourishes himself with nutriment without vanity and only for the purpose of crossing over suffering, as one who seeks to cross over the desert his own dead child's flesh (S. ii, 98). Then his greed for the five cords of sense desire comes to be fully-understood without dificulty through the means of the fully-understanding of the physical nutriment. He fully-understands the materiality

17. '"*A certain one*" is said with reference to the anal orifice. But those who are scrupulously clean by nature wash their hands again after washing the mouth, and so on' (Pm. 342).

18. '"*That sign*"; that object as the sign for development, which sign is called physical nutriment and has appeared in the repulsive aspect to one who gives his attention to it repeatedly in the ways already described. And there, while development occurs through the repulsive aspect, it is only the dhammas on account of which there comes to be the concept of physical nutriment that are repulsive, not the concept. But it is because the occurrence of development is contingent only upon dhammas with an individual essence, and because the profundity is due to that actual individual essence of dhammas that have individual essences, that the jhana cànnot reach absorption in it through apprehension of the repulsive aspect. For it is owing to profundity that the first pair of truths is hard to see' (Pm. 342-3).

aggregate through the means of the full-understanding of five cords of sense desire. Development of mindfulness occupied with the body comes to perfection in him through the repulsiveness of 'what is uncooked' and the rest. He has entered upon a way that is in conformity with the Perception of Foulness. And by keeping to this way, even if he does not experience the deathless goal in this life, he is at least bound for a happy destiny.

This is the detailed explanation of the development of the perception of repulsiveness in nutriment.

*

[DEFINING OF THE ELEMENTS: WORD DEFINITIONS]

27. Now comes the description of the development of the Definition of the Four Elements, which was listed as the 'One Defining' next to the Perception or Repulsiveness in Nutriment (Ch. III, §105).

Herein, 'defining (*vavaṭṭhāna*)' is determining by characterizing individual essences[19] [the compound] '*Catudhātuvavaṭṭhāna* (four-element defining)' is [resolvable into] '*catunnaṁ dhātūnaṁ vavaṭṭhānaṁ* (defining of the four elements)'. 'Attention Given to Elements', 'The Meditation Subject Consisting of Elements' and 'Defining of the Four Elements' all mean the same thing.

This is given in two ways: in brief and in detail. It is given in brief in the Mahāsatipaṭṭhāna Sutta (D.ii,294), and in detail in the Mahāhatthipadūpamā Sutta (M.i.185), the Rāhulovāda Sutta (M.i,421) and the Dhātuvibhaṅga Sutta (M.iii,240).

[TEXTS AND COMMENTARY IN BRIEF]

28. It is given in brief in the Mahāsatipaṭṭhāna Sutta, for one of quick understanding whose meditation subject is elements, as follows: 'Bhikkhus, just as though a skilled butcher or ' butcher's apprentice had killed a cow and were seated at the ' cross-roads [348] with it cut up into pieces, so too, bhikkhus, ' a bhikkhu reviews this body however placed, however ' disposed, as consisting of elements: In this body there are

19. ' "*By characterizing individual essences*": by making certain (*upadhāraṇa*) of the specific characteristics of hardness, and so on. For this meditation subject does not consist in the observing of a mere concept, as in the case of the earth kasina as a meditation subject, neither does it consist in the observing of the colour blue, etc., as in the case of the blue kasina as a meditation subject, nor as the observing of the general characteristics of impermanence, etc., in formations, as in the case of insight as a meditation subject; but rather it consists in the observing of the individual essences of earth, and so on. That is why "by characterizing individual essences" is said, which means "by making certain of the specific characteristics of hardness, and so on"' (Pm. 344).

'the earth element, the water element, the fire element, and 'the air element' (D.ii,294).[20]

29. The meaning is this: *just as though* a clever *butcher*, or his *apprentice* who worked for his keep, *had killed a cow* and divided it up *and were seated at the cross-roads*, reckoned as the intersection of the main roads going in the four directions, having laid it out part by part, *so too a bhikkhu reviews* the *body, however placed* because it is in some one of the four postures and *however disposed* because it is so placed, thus: *In this body there are the earth element, the water element, the fire element, the air element.*

30. What is meant? Just as the butcher, while feeding the cow, bringing it to the shambles, keeping it tied up after bringing it there, slaughtering it, and seeing it slaughtered and dead, does not lose the perception 'cow' so long as he has not carved it up and divided it into parts; but when he has divided it up and is sitting there, he loses the perception 'cow' and the perception 'meat' occurs; he does not think 'I am selling cow' or 'They are carrying cow away', but rather he thinks 'I am selling meat' or 'They are carrying meat away'; so too this bhikkhu, while still a foolish ordinary person—both formerly as a layman and as one gone forth into homelessness—, does not lose the perception 'living being' or 'man' or 'person' so long as he does not, by resolution of the compact into elements, review this body, however placed, however disposed, as consisting of elements. But when he does review it as consisting of elements, he loses the perception 'living being' and his mind establishes itself upon elements. That is why the Blessed One said: 'Bhikkhus, just as though a skilled butcher . . . were seated at the cross-roads. So too, bhikkhus a bhikkhu . . . air element'.

[IN DETAIL]

31. In the Mahāhatthipadūpamā Sutta it is given in detail for one of not over-quick understanding whose meditation subject

20. 'Herein, as regards "*earth element*", etc., the meaning of element is the meaning of individual essence, the meaning of individual essence is the meaning of voidness, the meaning of voidness is the meaning of not-a-living-being. So it is just earth in the sense of individual essence, voidness, and not-a-living-being that is the element; hence it is earth element. So too in the case of the water element, and the rest. The earth element is the element that is the foothold for the conascent material states. Likewise the water element is the element of their cohesion; the fire element is the element of their ripening; and the air element is the element of their conveyance and distension' (Pm. 345).

To avoid confusion, it might be mentioned here that in 'physical' earth, fire, water, and air, it would be held that all four elements are present in each equally, but that in 'physical' earth the earth element is dominant in efficacy as the mode of hardness; and correspondingly with water and the rest. See e.g. Ch. XIV, §45.

is elements—and as here so also in the Rāhulovāda and Dhātuvibhaṅga Suttas—as follows:

'And what is the internal earth element, friends? Whatever there is internally in oneself that is hard, harsh,[21] and clung to (acquired through kamma), that is to say, head hairs, body hairs, teeth, nails, skin, flesh, sinews, bones, bone-marrow, kidney, heart, liver, midriff, spleen, lights, bowels, entrails, gorge, dung, or whatever else there is internally in oneself that is hard, harsh, and clung to—this is called the earth element' (M.i.185), [349]

and 'What is the internal water element, friends? Whatever there is internally in oneself that is water, watery, and clung to, that is to say, bile, phlegm, pus, blood, sweat, fat, tears, grease, spittle, snot, oil of the joints, and urine, or whatever else there is internally in oneself that is water, watery, and clung to—this is called the internal water element' (M.i,187),

and 'What is the internal fire element, friends? Whatever there is internally in oneself that is fire, fiery, clung to, that is to say, that whereby one is warmed, ages, and burns up, and whereby what is eaten, drunk, chewed and tasted gets completely digested, or whatever else there is internally in oneself that is fire, fiery, and clung to—this is called the internal fire element' (M.i,188),

and 'What is the internal air element friends? Whatever there is internally in oneself that is air airy, and clung to, that is to say, up-going winds, down-going winds, winds in the belly, winds in the bowels, winds that course through all the limbs, in-breath and out-breath, or whatever else there is internally in one self that is air, airy, and clung to—this is called the internal air element' (M.i,188),

32. Here is the commentary on the words that are not clear. *Internally in oneself* (*ajjhattaṁ paccattaṁ*): both these words are terms for what is one's own (*niyaka*), since what is one's own is what is produced in one's own self (*attani jātaṁ*); the meaning is, included in one's continuity (*sasantati-pariyā-panna*). 'This is called 'internal (*ajjhattaṁ*=*adhi*+*attā* lit. belonging-to-self)' because it occurs in self (*attani*—locative case, just as in the world speech among women (*itthīsu*—loc. case) is called [speech] belonging-to-women (*adhitthi*)'. And it is called 'in oneself (*paccattaṁ*)' because it occurs owing to self (*attānaṁ paṭicca*).[22]

33. *Hard*: rigid. *Harsh*: rough. Herein, the first is a word for the characteristic, while the second is a word for the mode; for the

21. '*Kharigata*—harsh': not in P. T. S. Dict., but see *khara*.

22. 'What occurs in attendance (*adhikicca*) upon self (*attā*) by its pertaining to the state that may be taken as 'self' because it is included in one's own continuity as internal (*ajjhatta*)' Pm. 347).

earth element is characterized as hard, but its mode is rough, which is why it is called 'harsh'. *Clung to*: taken firmly [by kamma]; the meaning is, firmly taken, seized, adhered to, as 'I', 'mine' (see §89f.).

34. *That is to say*: the word *seyyathidaṁ* (that is to say) is a particle; its meaning is 'What is that?'. Next, showing what that is, 'Head hairs, body hairs', etc., is said. And here the *brain* must be added since it has to be understood that the earth element needs to be described in twenty modes. *Or whatever else*: the earth element included in the remaining three portions.

35. [350] It flows (*appoti*), flows on (*pappoti*), to such and such a place as a state of streaming, thus it is water (*āpo*). The *watery* (*āpo-gata*) is what is gone (*gata*) among such various kinds of water (*āpo*) as the kamma-originated, and so on. What is that? It is what has the water element's characteristic of cohesion.

36. *Fire* (*tejo*) [is definable] as heating (*tejana*). The *fiery* (*tejo-gata*) is what is gone (*gata*), in the way already described, among the kinds of fire (*tejo*). What is that? It is what has the characteristic of heat. *Whereby*: by means of which fire element, when excited, this body *is warmed*, becomes heated by the state of one-day fever,[23] and so on. *Ages*: whereby this body grows old, reaches the decline of the faculties, loss of strength, wrinkles, greyness, and so on. *Burns up*: whereby, when excited, it causes this body to burn, and the person cries out 'I am burning, I am burning!' and longs for ghee a hundred times washed and for *gosīsa* sandalwood ointment, etc., and for the breeze of a fan. *And whereby what is eaten, drunk, chewed and tasted gets completely digested*: whereby the boiled rice, etc., that is eaten, or the beverage, etc., that is drunk, or the hard food consisting of flour biscuits, etc., that is chewed, the mango fruit, honey, molasses, etc., that is tasted, gets completely cooked; gets its juice, etc., extracted, is the meaning. And here the first three kinds of fire element, [that is to say, 'is warmed', 'ages', and 'burns up',] are of fourfold origination (Ch.XX,§27ff.), while the last is only kamma-originated.

37. *Air* (*vāyo*) [is definable] as blowing (*vāyana*). The *airy* (*vāyo-gata*) is what is gone (*gata*), in the way already described, among the kinds of air. What is that? It is what has the characteristic of destination.[24] *Up-going winds*: winds (forces) mounting upwards that cause the occurrence of vomiting,

---

23. '*Jara*—fever': not in P. T. S. Dict.; see A. v, 100; Nd1. 17.
24. '*Vitthambhana*—distension': the word most usually employed to describe the air element. It is often rendered by 'supporting', a word earmarked here for *nissaya*. The twofold function of the air element is (a) to uphold (*sandhāraṇa*) by distending (*vitthambhana*) and preven-

belching, and so on. *Down-going-winds*: winds (forces) descending downwards that expel excrement and urine. *Winds in the belly*: winds (forces) outside the bowels. *Winds in the bowels*: winds (forces) inside the bowels. *Winds that course through all the limbs*: winds (forces) that produce flexing, extending, etc., and are distributed over the limbs and the whole body by means of the network of veins (nerves). *In-breath*: wind in the nostrils entering in. *Out-breath*: wind in the nostrils issuing out. And here the first five are of fourfold origination. In-breath and out-breath are consciousness-originated. [351]

In each instance the phrase *or whatever else* comprises respectively the water element, the fire element, or the air element, included in the other three portions.

38. So the four elements have been detailed in forty-two aspects, that is to say, the earth element in twenty aspects, the water element in twelve, the fire element in four, and the air element in six.

This, firstly, is the commentary on the texts here.

[Method of Development in Brief]

39. As regards the method of development here, however, to discern the elements in detail in this way 'The head hairs are the earth element, the body hairs are the earth element' appears redundant to a bhikkhu of quick understanding, though the meditation subject becomes clear to him if he gives his attention to it in this way 'What has the characteristic of stiffenedness is the earth element, what has the characteristic of cohesion is the water element, what has the characteristic of ripening (maturing) is the fire element, what has the characteristic distending (supporting) is the air element'. But when one of not over-quick understanding gives his attention to it in this way, it appears obscure and unevident, and it only becomes plain to him if he gives his attention to it in the first-mentioned way. Why?

40. Suppose two bhikkhus are reciting a text with many elided repetitions, then the bhikkhu with the quicker understanding fills out the elided repetitions once or twice, after which he goes on doing the recital with only the two end parts of the elisions. Here the one of less quick understanding says 'What is he reciting? Why, he does not even give one time to

---

ting collapse (§92) and (b) to move (*samudīrana*) or more strictly, cause the appearance of motion (*calana* see n. 37). In Ch. XIV, §61 it is said to cause *thambhana*, rendered by 'stiffening'; but there is the description of the earth element as *thaddha* (e.g., §39; pp. of *thambhati*, from which the n. *thambhana* comes), rendered by 'stiffenedness'. It may also be noted that the word *sandhāraṇa* (upholding) is used to describe both the earth element (Ch. XIV, §47) and the air element (Ch. XIV, §61).

move one's lips! If the recitation is done like this, when shall we ever get familiar with the text!', and so he does his recitation filling out each elision as it comes. Then the other says 'What is he reciting? Why, he never lets one get to the end of it! If the recitation is done like this, when shall we ever get to the end of it!'. So too, the detailed discerning of the elements by head hairs, etc., appears redundant to one of quick understanding, though the meditation subject becomes clear to him if he gives his attention to it in brief in this way 'What has the characteristic of stiffenedness is the earth element', and so on. But when the other gives his attention to it in this way, it appears obscure and unevident, and it only becomes plain to him if he gives his attention in detail by head hairs and so on.

41. So firstly, one of quick understanding who wants to develop this meditation subject should go into solitary retreat. Then he should advert to his own entire material body and discern the elements in brief in this way 'In this body what is stiffenedness or harshness is the earth element, what is cohesion or fluidity[25] [352] is the water element, what is maturing (ripening) or heat is the fire element, what is distension or movement is the air element', and he should advert and give attention to it and review it again and again as 'earth element, water element', that is to say, as mere elements, not a being, and soulless.

42. As he makes effort in this way it is not long before concentration arises in him, which is reinforced by understanding that illuminates the classification of the elements, and which is only access and does not reach absorption because it has states with individual essences as its object.

43. Or alternatively, there are these four [bodily] parts mentioned by the General of the Law [the Elder Sāriputta] for the purpose of showing the absence of any living being in the four great primary elements thus: 'When a space is enclosed with ' bones and sinews and flesh and skin, there comes to be the ' term "material form (*rūpa*)" ' (M.i,190). And he should resolve each of these [as a separate entity], separating them out by the hand of knowledge, and then discern them in the way already stated thus 'In these what is stiffenedness or harshness is the earth element'. And he should again and again advert to them, give attention to them and review them as 'mere elements', 'not a living being', 'not a soul'.

44. As he makes effort in this way it is not long before concentration arises in him, which is reinforced by understanding that illuminates the classification of the elements, and which is only access and does not reach absorption because it has states with individual essences as its object.

25. '*Drava-bhāva*—fluidity': not in P. T. S. Dict.

1024-N

This is the method of development when the definition of the elements is given in brief.

[Method of Development in Detail]

45. The method given in detail should be understood in this way. A meditator of not over-quick understanding who wants to develop this meditation subject should learn the elements in detail in the forty-two aspects from a teacher, and he should live in an abode of the kind already described. Then when he has done all the duties, he should go into solitary retreat and develop the meditation subject in four ways thus: (1) with constituents in brief, (2) with constituents by analysis, (3) with characteristics in brief, and (4) with characteristics by analysis.

[(1) With Constituents in Brief]

46. Herein, how does he develop it *with constituents in brief*? Here a bhikkhu does his defining in this way. 'In twenty of the parts what has the stiffened mode is the earth element', and he does his defining thus 'In twelve parts the liquid called water with the mode of cohesion is the water element', [353] and he does his defining thus 'In four parts what matures (what has the mode of ripening) is the fire element', and he does his defining thus 'In six parts what has the mode of distending is the air element', As he defines them in this way they become evident to him. As he again and again adverts to them and gives his attention to them, concentration arises as access only.

[(2) With Constituents by Analysis]

47. However, if his meditation subject is not successful while he develops it in this way, then he should develop it *with constituents by analysis*. How? Firstly the bhikkhu should carry out all the directions given for the thirty-two-fold aspect in the Description of Mindfulness Occupied with the Body as a meditation subject (Ch.VIII,§48-78), namely, the sevenfold skill in learning and the tenfold skill in giving attention, and he should start with the verbal recitation, in direct and reverse order, of the skin pentad and so on, without omitting any of it. The only difference is this: there, after giving attention to the head hairs, etc., as to colour, shape, direction, location, and delimitation, the mind had to be fixed by means of repulsiveness (Ch.VIII,§83), but here it is done by means of elements. Therefore at the end of each part after giving attention to head hairs, etc., each in the five ways beginning with colour, (Ch.VIII,§83) attention should be given as follows.

48. These things called *head hairs* grow on the inner skin that envelops the skull. Herein, just as when *kuṇṭha* grasses

grow on the top of an ant-hill, the top of the ant-hill does not know '*Kuṇṭha* grasses are growing on me', nor do the *kuṇṭha* grasses know 'We are growing on the top of an ant-hill', so too, the inner skin that covers the skull does not know 'Head hairs grow on me', nor do the head hairs know 'We grow on inner skin that envelops a skull'. These things are devoid of mutual concern and reviewing. So what are called head hairs are a particular component of this body, without thought, [morally] indeterminate, void, not a living being, rigid (stiffened) earth element.

49. *Body hairs* grow on the inner skin that envelops the body, Herein, just as, when *dabba* grasses grow on the square in an empty village, the square in the empty village does not know '*Dabba* grasses grow on me', nor do the *dabba* grasses know 'We grow on the square in an empty village', so too, the inner skin that envelops the body does not know 'Body hairs grow on me' nor do the body hairs know 'We grow on inner skin that envelops a body'. These things are devoid of mutual concern and reviewing. So what are called body hairs are a particular component of this body, without thought, indeterminate, void, not a living being, rigid earth element.

50. *Nails* grow on the tips of the fingers and toes. Herein, just as, when children play a game by piercing *madhuka*-fruit kernels with sticks, the sticks [354] do not know '*Madhuka*-fruit kernels are put on us', nor do the *madhuka*-fruit kernels know 'We are put on sticks', so too, the fingers and toes do not know 'Nails grow on our tips', nor do the nails know 'We grow on the tips of fingers and toes'. These things are devoid of mutual concern and reviewing. So what are called nails are a particular component of this body, without thought, indeterminate, void, not a living being, rigid earth element.

51. *Teeth* grow in the jaw bones. Herein, just as, when posts are placed by builders in stone sockets and fastened with some kind of cement,[26] the sockets do not know 'Posts are placed in us', nor do the posts know 'We are placed in sockets', so too, the jaw bones do not know 'Teeth grow in us', nor do the teeth know 'We grow in jaw bones'. These things are devoid of mutual concern and reviewing. So what are called teeth are a particular component of this body, without thought, indeterminate, void, not a living being, rigid earth element.

52. *Skin* is to be found covering the whole body. Herein, just as, when a big lute is covered with damp ox hide, the lute does not know 'I am covered with damp ox-hide', nor does the damp ox-hide know 'A lute is covered by me', so too, the body does not know 'I am covered by skin', nor does the skin know 'A body is covered by me'. These things are devoid of

26. '*Silesa*—cement': not in this meaning in P. T. S. Dict.; MA. i, 37 *saṁ*—.

mutual concern and reviewing. So what is called skin is a particular component of this body, without thought, indeterminate, void, not a living being, rigid earth element.

53. *Flesh* is to be found plastered over the framework of bones. Herein, just as, when a wall is plastered with thick clay, the wall does not know 'I am plastered with thick clay', nor does the thick clay know 'A wall is plastered with me', so too, the framework of bones does not know 'I am plastered with flesh consisting of nine hundred pieces of flesh', nor does the flesh know 'A framework of bones is plastered with me'. These things are devoid of mutual concern and reviewing. So what is called flesh is a particular component of this body, without thought, indeterminate, void, not a living being, rigid earth element.

54. *Sinews* are to be found in the interior of the body binding the bones together. Herein, just as, when withies and sticks are bound together with creepers, the withies and sticks do not know [355] 'We are bound together with creepers', nor do the creepers know 'Withies and sticks are bound together by us', so too, the bones do not know 'We are bound together by sinews', nor do the sinews know 'Bones are bound together by us'. These things are devoid of mutual concern and reviewing. So what are called sinews are a particular component of this body, without thought, indeterminate, void, not a living being, rigid earth element.

55. As to the *bones*, the heel bone is to be found holding up the ankle bone, the ankle bone holding up the shin bone, the shin bone the thigh bone, the thigh bone the hip bone, the hip bone the backbone, the backbone the neck bone, and the neck bone is to be found holding up the cranium bone. The cranium bone rests on the neck bone, the neck bone on the backbone, the backbone on the hip bone, the hip bone on the thigh bone, the thigh bone on the shin bone, the shin bone on the
56. ankle bone, the ankle bone on the heel bone. Herein, just as, when bricks, timber or [blocks of dried] cow-dung are built up, those below do not know 'We each stand holding up those above us', nor do those above know 'We each rest on those below us', so too, the heel bone does not know 'I stand holding up the ankle bone', nor does the ankle bone know 'I stand holding up the shin bone', nor does the shin bone know 'I stand holding up the thigh bone', nor does the thigh bone know 'I stand holding up the hip bone', nor does the hip bone know 'I stand holding up the backbone', nor does the backbone know 'I stand holding up the neck bone', nor does the neck bone know 'I stand holding up the cranium bone', nor does the cranium bone know 'I rest on the neck bone', nor does the neck bone know 'I rest on the backbone', nor does the backbone know 'I rest on

the hip bone' nor does the hip bone know 'I rest on the thigh bone', nor does the thigh bone know 'I rest on the shin bone', nor does the shin bone know 'I rest on the ankle bone', nor does the ankle bone know 'I rest on the heel bone'. These things are devoid of mutual concern and reviewing. So what are called bones [356] are a particular component of this body, without thought, indeterminate, void, not a living being, rigid earth element.

57. *Bone marrow* is to be found inside the various bones. Herein, just as, when boiled bamboo sprouts, etc., are put inside bamboo joints, etc., the bamboo joints, etc., do not know 'Bamboo sprouts, etc., are put in us', nor do the bamboo sprouts, etc., know 'We are inside bamboo joints, etc.', so too, the bones do not know 'Marrow is inside us', nor does the bone marrow know 'I am inside bones.' These things are devoid of mutual concern or reviewing. So what is called bone marrow is a particular component of this body, without thought, indeterminate, void, not a living being, rigid earth element.

58. *Kidney* is to be found on each side of the heart flesh, being fastened by the stout sinew that starts out with a single root from the base of the neck and divides into two after going a short way. Herein just as, when a pair of mango fruits are bound together by their stalk, the stalk does not know 'A pair of mango fruits is bound together by me', nor do the pair of mango fruits know 'We are bound together by a stalk', so too, the stout sinew does not know 'Kidneys are bound together by me', nor does the kidney know 'I am bound together by a stout sinew'. These things are devoid of mutual concern and reviewing. So what is called kidney is a particular component of this body, without thought, indeterminate, void, not a living being, rigid earth element.

59. *Heart* is to be found in the inside of the body near the middle of the frame of the ribs. Herein, just as, when a piece of meat is placed near the framework of an old cart, the inside of the framework of the old cart does not know 'A piece of meat is placed near the middle of me', nor does the piece of meat know 'I am near the middle of the inside of the framework of an old cart', so too, the inside of the framework of the ribs does not know 'A heart is near the middle of me,' nor does the heart know 'I am near the middle of the inside of a framework of ribs'. These things are devoid of mutual concern and reviewing. So what is called heart is a particular component of this body, without thought, indeterminate, void, not a living being, rigid earth element.

60. *Liver* is to be found inside the body, near the right side between the two breasts. Herein, just as, when a twin lump of meat is stuck on the side of a cooking pot, the side of the

cooking pot does not know 'A twin lump of meat is stuck on me', nor does the twin lump of meat know [357] 'I am stuck on the side of a cooking pot', so too, the right side between the breasts does not know 'Liver is near me', nor does the liver know 'I am near a right side between two breasts'. These things are devoid of mutual concern and reviewing. So what is called liver is a particular component of this body, without thought, indeterminate, void, not a living being, rigid earth element.

61. As to the *midriff*, the concealed midriff is to be found surrounding the heart and kidney, while the unconcealed midriff is to be found covering the flesh under the skin in the whole body. Herein, just as, when meat is wrapped in a rag, the meat does not know 'I am wrapped in a rag', nor does the rag know 'Meat is wrapped in me', so too, the heart and kidney, and the flesh in the whole body, do not know 'I am concealed by midriff', nor does the midriff know 'Heart and kidney, and flesh in a whole body, are concealed by me'. These things are devoid of mutual concern and reviewing. So what is called midriff is a particular component of this body, without thought, indeterminate, void, not a living being, rigid earth element.

62. *Spleen* is to be found near the upper side of the belly lining on the left side of the heart. Herein, just as, when a lump of cowdung is near the upper side of a barn, the upper side of the barn does not know 'A lump of cowdung is near me', nor does the lump of cowdung know 'I am near the upper side of a barn,' so too, the upper side of the belly lining does not know 'Spleen is near me', nor does the spleen know 'I am near the upper side of a belly lining'. These things are devoid of mutual concern and reviewing. So what is called spleen is a particular component of this body, without thought, indeterminate, void, not a living being, rigid earth element.

63. *Lights* are to be found inside the body between the two breasts, hanging over the heart and liver and concealing them. Herein, just as when a bird's nest is hanging inside an old barn, the inside of the old barn does not know 'A bird's nest is hanging in me', nor does the bird's nest know 'I am hanging inside an old barn', so too, [358] the inside of the body does not know 'Lights are hanging in me', nor do the lights know 'We are hanging inside such a body'. These things are devoid of mutual concern and reviewing. So what is called lights is a particular component of this body, without thought, indeterminate, void, not a living being, rigid earth element.

64. *Bowel* is to be found inside the body extending from the base of the neck to the excrement passage. Herein, just as,

when the carcase of a large beheaded rat-snake[27] is coiled up and put into a trough of blood, the red trough does not know 'A rat snake's carcase has been put in me', nor does the rat snake's carcase know 'I am in a red trough', so too, the inside of the body does not know 'A bowel is in me', nor does the bowel know 'I am in a body'. These things are devoid of mutual concern and reviewing. So what is called the bowel is a particular component of this body, without thought, indeterminate, void, not a living being, rigid earth element.

65. *Entrails* are to be found in the interspaces between the twenty-one coils of the bowel, binding them together. Herein, just as, when ropes are found sewing together a rope ring for wiping the feet, the rope ring for wiping the feet does not know 'Ropes are to be found sewing me together', nor do the ropes know 'We are to be found sewing together a rope ring', so too, the bowel does not know 'Entrails are to be found binding me together', nor do the entrails know 'We are to be found binding a bowel together'. These things are devoid of mutual concern and reviewing. So what is called entrails is a particular component of this body, without thought, indeterminate, void, not a living being, rigid earth element.

66. *Gorge* is what is eaten, drunk, chewed and tasted that lies in the stomach. Herein, just as, when a dog's vomit lies in a dog's bowl, the dog's bowl does not know 'Dog's vomit is lying in me', nor does the dog's vomit know 'I am living in a dog's bowl', so too, the stomach does not know 'Gorge is lying in me', nor does the gorge know 'I am lying in a stomach'. These things are devoid of mutual concern and reviewing. So what is called gorge is a particular component of this body, without thought, indeterminate, void, not a living being, rigid earth element.

67. *Dung* is to be found at the end of the bowel, which resembles a bamboo joint eight fingerbreadths long and is called the 'receptacle for digested food'. [359] Herein, just as, when soft brown clay is impacted in a bamboo joint, the bamboo joint does not know 'Brown clay is in me', nor does brown clay know 'I am in a bamboo joint', so too, the receptacle for digested food does not know 'Dung is in me,' nor does the dung know 'I am in a receptacle for digested food'. These things are devoid of mutual concern and reviewing. So what is called dung is a particular component of this body, without thought, indeterminate, void, not a living being, rigid earth element.

68. *Brain* is to be found in the interior of the skull. Herein, just as, when a lump of dough is put inside an old gourd rind, the gourd rind does not know 'A lump of dough is in me', nore

27. '*Dhammani*—rat snake': not in this sense in P. T. S. Dict.; see AA. 459.

does the lump of dough know 'I am inside a gourd rind', so too, the inside of the skull does not know 'Brain is in me', nor does the brain know 'I am inside a skull'. These things are devoid of mutual concern and reviewing. So what is called brain is a particular component of this body, without thought, indeterminate, void, not a living being, rigid earth element.

69. As to *bile*, the free bile, which is bound up with the life faculty, is to be found soaking the whole body, while the local bile is to be found in the bile container (gall-bladder). Herein, just as, when oil has soaked a cake, the cake does not know 'Oil soaks me', nor does the oil know 'I soak a cake', so too, the body does not know 'Free bile soaks me', nor does the free bile know 'I soak a body'. And just as, when a *kosātakī* (loofah) creeper bladder is filled with rain water, the *kosātakī* creeper bladder does not know 'Rain water is in me', nor does the rain water know 'I am in a *kosātakī* creeper bladder', so too, the bile bladder does not know 'Local bile is in me', nor does the local bile know 'I am in a bile bladder'. These things are devoid of mutual concern and reviewing. So what is called bile is a particular component of this body, without thought, indeterminate, void, not a living being, liquid water element in the mode of cohesion.

70. *Phlegm* is to be found on the surface of the stomach and measures a bowlful. Herein, just as, when a cesspool has a surface of froth, the cesspool does not know 'A surface of froth is on me', nor does the surface of froth [360] know 'I am on a cesspool', so too, the surface of the stomach does not know 'Phlegm is on me', nor does the phlegm know 'I am on the surface of a stomach'. These things are devoid of mutual concern and reviewing, eg. So what is called phlegm is a particular component of this body, without thought, indeterminate, void, not a living being, liquid water element in the mode of cohesion.

71. *Pus* has no fixed location. It is to be found wherever the blood stagnates and goes bad in a part of the body damaged by wounds caused by splinters and thorns, and by burns due to fire, or where boils, carbuncles, etc., appear. Herein, just as, when a tree oozes gum through being hit by, say, an axe, the parts of the tree that have been hit do not know 'Gum is in us', nor does the gum know 'I am in a part of a tree that has been hit', so too, the parts of the body wounded by splinters, thorns, etc., do not know 'Pus is in us', nor does the pus know 'I am in such places'. These things are devoid of mutual concern and reviewing. So what is called pus is a particular component of this body, without thought, indeterminate, void, not a living being, liquid water element in the mode of cohesion.

72. As to *blood* the mobile blood is to be found, like the bile, soaking the whole body. The stored blood is to be found

filling the lower part of the liver's site to the extent of a bowlful, wetting the kidney, heart, liver and lights. Herein, the definition of the mobile blood is similar to that of the free bile. But as to the other, just as, when rain water seeps through an old pot and wets clods and stumps below, the clods and stumps do not know 'We are being wetted with water', nor does the water know 'I am wetting clods and stumps', so too, the lower part of the liver's site, or the kidney, etc., respectively do not know 'Blood is in me', or 'We are being wetted', nor does the blood know 'I fill the lower part of a liver's site, am wetting a kidney, and so on'. These things are devoid of mutual concern and reviewing. So what is called blood is a particular component of this body, without thought, indeterminate, void, not a living being, liquid water element in the mode of cohesion.

73. *Sweat* is to be found filling the openings of the pores of the head hairs and body hairs when there is heat due to fires, etc., and it trickles out of them. Herein, just as, when [361] bunches of lily bud stems and lotus stalks are pulled up out of water, the openings in the bunches of lilies, etc., do not know 'Water trickles from us', nor does the water trickling from the openings in the bunches of lilies, etc., know 'I am trickling from openings in bunches of lilies, etc.,' so too, the openings of the pores of the head hairs and body hairs do not know 'Sweat trickles from us', nor does the sweat know 'I trickle from openings of pores of head hairs and body hairs'. These things are devoid of mutual concern and reviewing. So what is called sweat is a particular component of this body, without thought, indeterminate, void, not a living being, liquid water element in the mode of cohesion.

74. *Fat* is the thick unguent to be found pervading the whole body of one who is stout, and on the shank flesh, etc., of one who is lean. Herein, just as, when a heap of meat is covered by a yellow rag, the heap of meat does not know 'A yellow rag is next to me', nor does the yellow rag know 'I am next to a heap of meat', so too, the flesh to be found on the whole body, or on the shanks, etc., does not know 'Fat is next to me', nor does the fat know 'I am next to flesh on a whole body, or on the shanks, and so on'. These things are devoid of mutual concern and reviewing. So what is called fat is a particular component of this body, without thought, indeterminate, void, not a living being, thick-liquid water element in the mode of cohesion.

75. *Tears* when produced, are to be found filling the eye sockets or trickling out of them. Herein, just as, when the sockets of young palm kernels are filled with water, the sockets of the young palm kernels do not know 'Water is in us', nor does the water in the sockets of the young palm kernels know 'I am in sockets of young palm kernels', so too, the eye sockets do not

know 'tears are in us', nor do the tears know 'We are in eye sockets'. These things are devoid of mutual concern and reviewing. So what is called tears is a particular component of this body, without thought, indeterminate, void, not a living being, liquid water element in the mode of cohesion.

76. *Grease* is the melted unguent to be found on the palms and backs of the hands, on the soles and backs of the feet, on the nose and forehead and on the points of the shoulders, when heated by fire, and so on. Herein, just as, when rice gruel has oil put on it, the rice gruel does not know 'Oil is spread over me', nor does the oil know 'I am spread over rice gruel', so too, the place consisting of the palm of the hand, etc., [362] does not know 'Grease is spread over me', nor does the grease know 'I am spread over places consisting of the palm of the hand, and so on'. These things are devoid of mutual concern and reviewing. So what is called grease is a particular component of this body, without thought, indeterminate, void, not a living being, liquid water element in the mode of cohesion.

77. *Spittle* is to be found on the surface of the tongue after it has descended from the cheeks on both sides, when there is a condition for the arising of spittle. Herein, just as, when a hollow in a river bank is constantly oozing with water, the surface of the hollow does not know 'Water lies on me,' nor does the water know 'I lie on the surface of a hollow', so too, the surface of the tongue does not know 'Spittle that has descended from cheeks on both sides is on me', nor does the spittle know 'I have descended from cheeks on both sides and am on the surface of a tongue'. These things are devoid of mutual concern and reviewing. So what is called spittle is a particular component of this body, without thought, indeterminate, void, not a living being, liquid water element in the mode of cohesion.

78. *Snot* when produced, is to be found filling the nostrils or trickling out of them. Herein, just as, when a bag[28] is loaded with rotting curd, the bag does not know 'Rotting curd is in me', nor does the rotting curd know 'I am in a bag', so too, the nostrils do not know 'Snot is in us', nor does the snot know 'I am in nostrils'. These things are devoid of mutual concern and reviewing. So what is called snot is a particular component of this body, without thought, indeterminate, void, not a living being, liquid water element in the mode of cohesion.

79. *Oil of the joints* is to be found in the hundred and eighty joints serving the function of lubricating the joints of the bones. Herein, just as, when an axle is lubricated with oil, the axle does not know 'Oil lubricates me', nor does the oil know 'I lubricate an axle', so too, the hundred and eighty

28. '*Sippikā*—bag (?)': not in this sense in P. T. S. Dict.

joints do not know 'Oil of the joints lubricates us', nor does the oils of the joints know 'I lubricate a hundred and eighty joints'. These things are devoid of mutual concern and reviewing. So what is called oil of the joints is a particular component of this body, without thought, indeterminate, void, not a living being, liquid water element in the mode of cohesion.

80. *Urine* is to be found inside the bladder. Herein, just as, when a porous pot is put upside down in a cesspool, the porous pot does not know 'Cesspool filtrate is in me,' nor does the cesspool filtrate know 'I am in a porous pot', so too, the bladder does not know [363] 'Urine is in me', nor does the urine know 'I am in a bladder'. These things are devoid of mutual concern and reviewing. So what is called urine is a particular component of this body, without thought, indeterminate, void, not a living being, liquid water element in the mode of cohesion.

81. When he has given his attention in this way to the body hairs, etc., he should then give his attention to the [four] fire components thus: *That whereby one is warmed*—this is a particular component of this body, without thought, indeterminate, void, not a living being; it is fire element in the mode of maturing (ripening).

That whereby one ages. . .

That where one burns up. . .

That whereby what is eaten, drunk, chewed and tasted becomes completely digested—this is a particular component of this body, without thought, indeterminate, void, not a living being; it is fire element in the mode of maturing (ripening).

82. After that, having discovered the *up-going winds* (*forces*) as up-going, the *down-going winds* (*forces*) as down-going, the *winds* (*forces*) *in the belly* as in the belly, the *winds* (*forces*) *in the bowels* as in the bowels, the *winds* (*forces*) *that course through all the limbs* as coursing through all the limbs, and *in-breath and out-breath* as in-breath and out-breath, he should give his attention to these [six] air components in this way: What is called *up-going winds* (*forces*) is a particular component of this body, without thought, indeterminate, void, not a living being; it is air element in the mode of distending.

What is called *down-going winds* (*forces*). . .

What is called *winds* (*forces*) *in the belly*. . .

What is called *winds* (*forces*) *in the bowels*. . .

What is called *winds* (*forces*) *that course through all the limbs*...

What is called *in-breath and out-breath* is a particular component of this body, without thought, indeterminate, void, not a living being; it is air element in the mode of distending.

83. As he gives his attention in this way the elements become evident to him. As he adverts and gives attention to them

again and again access concentration arises in him in the way already described.

[(3) WITH CHARACTERISTICS IN BRIEF]

84. But if his meditation subject is still not successful when he gives his attention to it in this way, then he should develop it *with characteristics in brief*. How? In the *twenty components* the characteristic of stiffenedness should be defined as the earth element, and the characteristic of cohesion, which is there too, is the water element, and the characteristic of maturing (ripening), which is there too, is the fire element, and the characteristic of distension, which is there too, is the air element. In the *twelve components* the characteristic of cohesion should be defined as the water element, the characteristic of maturing (ripening), which is there too, as the fire element, the characteristic of distension, which is there too, as the air element, the characteristic of stiffenedness, which is there too, as the earth element. In the *four components* the characteristic of maturing (ripening) should be defined as the fire element, the characteristic of distension unresolvable (inseparable) from it is the air element, [364] the characteristic of stiffenedness is the earth element, and the characteristic of cohesion is the water element. In the *six components* the characteristic of distension should be defined as the air element, the characteristic of stiffenedness there too is the earth element, the characteristic of cohesion is the water element, and the characteristic of maturing (ripening) is the fire element.

As he defines them in this way the elements become evident to him. As he adverts to them and gives attention to them again and again access concentration arises in him in the way already stated.

[(4) WITH CHARACTERISTICS BY ANALYSIS]

85. However, if he still does not succeed with his meditation subject when he gives his attention to it in this way, then he should develop it *with characteristics by analysis*. How? After discerning head hairs, etc., in the way already described the characteristic of stiffenedness in head hairs should be defined as the earth element, the characteristic of cohesion there too is the water element, the characteristic of maturing (ripening) is the fire element, and the characteristic of distension is the air element. The four elements should be defined in this way in the case of each component.

As he defines them in this way the elements become evident to him. As he adverts and gives attention to them again and again access concentration arises in him in the way already described.

[ADDITIONAL WAYS OF GIVING ATTENTION]

86. In addition, attention should be given to the elements in the following ways: (1) as to word meaning, (2) by groups, (3) by particles, (4) by characteristic, etc., (5) as to how originated, (6) as to variety and unity, (7) as to resolution (separability) and non-resolution (inseparability), (8) as to the similar and the dissimilar, (9) as to distinction between internal and external, (10) as to inclusion, (11) as to condition, (12) as to lack of conscious reaction, (13) as to analysis of conditions.

87. 1. Herein, one who gives his attention to them *as to word meaning* should do so separately and generally thus: [separately] it is earth (*paṭhavi*) because it is spread out (*patthaṭa*); it flows (*appoti*) or it glides (*āpiyati*) or it satisfies (*appāyati*), thus it is water (*āpo*); it heats (*tejati*), thus it is fire (*tejo*); it blows (*vāyati*,) thus it is air (*vāyo*). But without differentiation they are elements (*dhātu*) because of bearing (*dhāraṇa*) their own characteristics, because of grasping (*ādāna*) suffering, and because of sorting out (*ādhāna*) suffering (see Ch.XV,§19).[29] This is how they should be given attention as to word meaning.

88. 2. *By groups*: there is the earth element described under the twenty aspects (modes) beginning with head hairs, body hairs, and also the water element described under the twelve (modes) aspects beginning with bile, phlegm. Now as to these,

Colour, odour, taste, and nutritive
Essence, and the four elements—
From combination of these eight
There comes the common usage head hairs;
And separately from these eight[30]
There is no common usage head hairs.

Consequently head hairs are only a mere group of eight states. Likewise body hairs, [365] and the rest. A component here

29. ' "*Because of bearing their own characteristics*": these are not like the Primordial Essence (*pakati*—Skr. *prakṛti*) and the Self (*attā*) imagined by the theorists, which are non-existent as to individual essence. On the contrary these do bear their own characteristics, which is why they are elements' (Pm. 359). Capitals have been used here and elsewhere though Indian alphabets do not justify it. 'Appāyati—to satisfy' is not in P. T. S. Dict.; see VbhA. 9.

30. ' "*From resolution of these eight*": the eight dhammas beginning with colour, when resolved by means of understanding, are apprehendable (*upalabbhanti*) in the ultimate sense through mutual negation (*aññam-añña-vyatirekena*); but head hairs are not apprehendable in the ultimate sense through negation of colour and so on. Consequently the term of common usage "head hairs" is applied to these dhammas in their co-arisen state; but if they are each taken separately "*There is no common-usage head hair*". The meaning is that it is a mere conventional term. "*Only a mere group of eight states*" is said, taking the colour, etc., which are real (*bhūta*—lit. become), as a unity by means of the concept (*paññatti*) "a head hair", not only because they are merely the eight states' (Pm. 360).

that is kamma-originated is a group of ten states, [that is to say, the former eight] together with the life faculty and sex. But it is on account of respective prominence [of stiffenedness or cohesion] that it comes to be styled 'earth element' or 'water element'. This is how they should be given attention 'by groups'.

89. 3. *By particles*: in this body the earth element taken as reduced to fine dust and powdered to the size of the smallest atom[31] might amount to an average *doṇa* measure full; and that is held together[32] by the water element measuring half as much. Being maintained[33] by the fire element, and distended by the air element, it does not get scattered or dissipated. Instead of getting scattered or dissipated, it arrives at the alternative states of the female and male sex, etc., and manifests smallness, bigness, length, shortness, toughness, rigidity, and so on.

90. The liquid water element that is the mode of cohesion, being founded on earth, maintained by fire, and distended by air, does not trickle or run away.[34] Instead of trickling or running away it provides continued refreshments.[35]

91. And here the fire element that cooks what is eaten, drunk, etc., and is the mode of warming and has the characteristic of heat, being established on earth, held together by water, and distended by air, maintains this body and ensures its proper appearance. And this body, being maintained by it, shows no putrefaction.

92. The air element that courses through all the limbs and has the characteristic of moving and distending, being founded upon earth, held together by water, and maintained by fire, distends this body. And this body, being distended by the latter kind of air, does not collapse, but stands erect, and being propelled[36] by the other [motile] air, it shows intimation and it flexes and extends and it wriggles the hands and feet, doing so in the postures comprising walking, standing, sitting

31. '*Param-aṇu*—the smallest atom'; see VbhA. 343, According to VbhA. the size of a *paramaṇu* works out at 1/581,147,136th part of an *aṅgula* (fingerbreadth or inch). Pm. remarks (p. 361) 'Therefore... a *paramaṇu* as a particle of space is not the province of the physical eye, it is the province of the divine eye'.

32. '*Saṅgahita*—held together': not quite in this sense in P. T. S. Dict.; 'Held (*gahita*) by conjoining through cohesion and prevented from being scattered' (Pm. 361).

33. 'Kept guarded (*anurakkhita*) so that it may not lapse into a wet and slippery state through the water element, which has trickling as its essence' (Pm. 361).

34. '*Parissavati*—to run away': not in P. T. S. Dict;—*vissarati* (Pm. 361).

35. 'This is said with reference to the water element as a juice that helps growth' (Pm. 361).

36. '*Samabbhāhata*—propelled': see Ch. IV, note 38.

and lying down. So this mechanism of elements carries on like a magic trick, deceiving foolish people with the male and female sex and so on.

This is how they should be given attention by particles.

93. 4. *As to characteristic etc.*: he should advert to the four elements in this way. 'The earth element—what are its characteristic, function, manifestation?', [defining them in this way:]The earth element has the characteristic of hardness. Its function is to act as foundation. It is manifested as receiving. The water element has the characteristic of trickling. Its function is to intensify. It is manifested as holding together. The fire element has the characteristic of heat. Its function is to mature (maintain). It is manifested as a continued supply of softness. The air element has the characteristic of distending. Its function is to cause motion. It is manifested as conveying.[37] This is how they should be given attention by characteristic, and so on. [366]

94. 5. *As to how originated*: among the forty-two components beginning with head hairs shown in the detailed treatment of the earth element, etc., the four consisting of gorge, dung, pus, and urine, are temperature-originated only; the four consisting of tears, sweat, spittle, and snot, are temperature-originated and consciousness-originated only; The fire that cooks what is eaten, etc., is kamma-originated only; in-breath and out-breath are consciousness-originated only; all the rest are of fourfold origination. This is how they should be given attention as to how originated.

95. 6. *As to variety and unity*: there is variety in the specific characteristics, etc., of all the elements; for the characteristic, function, and manifestation, of the earth element is one, and those of the water element, etc., are different. But there is unity in them as materiality, great primary, element, state (*dhamma*), impermanence, etc., notwithstanding the fact that they are various according to [specific] characteristic, etc., and according to origination by kamma and so on.

96. All these elements are 'instances of materiality (*rūpāni*)' because they do not exceed the characteristic of 'being molested (*ruppana*)'. They are 'great primaries (*mahā-bhūta*)' by reason of 'great manifestation', and so on. 'By reason of "great manifestation", and so on' means that these elements

37. '*Abhinīhāra*—conveying': not in this sense in P. T. S. Dict.; '"Conveying" is acting as cause for the successive arising at adjacent locations (*desantaruppatti*) of the conglomeration of elements (*bhūta-saṅghāta*)' (Pm. 363). Elsewhere Pm. (p. 359) says of the air element '"*It blows* (§87): it is stirred; the meaning is that the conglomeration of elements is made to move (go) by its action as cause for successive arising at adjacent locations (points)', and 'Propelling (*samabbhāhana*) is the act of causing the successive-arising-at-adjacent-locations of material groups (*rūpa-kalāpa*)' (p. 362).

are called 'great primaries' for the following reasons, namely, (a) manifestation of greatness, (b) likeness to great creatures (c) great maintenance, (d) great alteration, and (e) because they are great and because they are entities.

97. Herein, (a) *manifestation of greatness*: they are manifested as great both in a continuity that is not clung to (acquired through kamma) and in a continuity that is clung to. For their manifestation of greatness in a continuity that is not clung to is given in the Description of the Recollection of the Buddha in the way beginning:

' Two times a hundred thousand [leagues]
' And then four nahutas as well:
' This earth, this "Bearer of all wealth",
' Has that much thickness, as they tell' (Ch.IV,§41).

And they are manifested on a great scale also in a continuity that is clung to, for instance, in the bodies of fishes, turtles, deities, Dānava demons, and so on. For this is said: 'Bhikkhus, ' there are individual creatures of a hundred leagues in the ' great ocean' (A.iv,207), and so on.

98. (b) *Likeness to great creatures*: just as a magician turns water that is not crystal into crystal, and turns a clod that is not gold into gold, and shows them, and being himself neither a spirit or a bird, shows himself as a spirit or a bird so too, being themselves not blue-black, they turn themselve into blue-black derived materiality, being themselves not yellow . . . not red . . . not white, [367] they turn themselves into white derived materiality and show that. In this way they are'great primaries (*mahā-bhūta*)' in being like the great creatures (*mahā-bhūta*) of a magician.[38]

38. 'A great primary (*maha-bhūta*) is a great wonder (*mahanto abbhuto*) because it shows various unreal things (*abhūta*), various wonders (*abbhuta*) and various marvels (*acchariya*). Or alternatively: there are great wonders (*abbhuta*) here, thus there are magicians. And spirits, etc., are huge (*mahant*) creatures (*bhūta*) owing to being born from them, thus they are great primaries. Or alternatively: this term "great primary" can be regarded as a generic term for all of them. But earth, etc., are great primaries because they deceive, and because, like the huge creatures, their standing place cannot be pointed to. The deception lies in causing the apparent individual essences of blue-black, etc., though they themselves have no such individual essences of blue-black, etc., and it lies in causing the appearance of what has the aspect of woman and man, etc., though they themselves have no such individual essences of woman, man, and so on. Likewise their undemonstrability, since they are not found inside or outside each other though they rely upon each other for support. For if these elements were found inside each other, they would not each perform their particular functions, owing to mutual frustration. And if they were found outside each other, they would be already resolved (separate), and that being so, any description of them as unresolved (inseparable) would be meaningless. So although their standing place is undemonstrable, still each one assists the other by its particular function—the functions of establishing, etc., whereby each becomes a condition for the others as conascence condition and so on' (Pm. 363).

99. And just as, whomsoever the great creatures such as the spirits (*yakkha*) grasp hold of (possess), they have no standing place either inside him or outside him and yet they have no standing independently of him, so too, these elements are not found to stand either inside or outside each other yet they have no standing independently of one another. Thus they are also great primaries (*mahā-bhūta*) in being equal to the great creatures (*mahā-bhūta*) such as the spirits because they have no thinkable standing place [relative to each other].

100. And just as the great creatures known as female spirits (*yakkhinī*) conceal their own fearfulness with a pleasing colour, shape and gesture to deceive beings, so too, these elements conceal each their own characteristic and function classed as hardness, etc., by means of a pleasing skin colour of women's and men's bodies, etc., and pleasing shapes of limbs and pleasing gestures of fingers, toes and eyebrows, and they deceive simple people by concealing their own functions and characteristics beginning with hardness and do not allow their individual essences to be seen. Thus they are great primaries (*mahā-bhūta*) in being equal to the great creatures (*mahā-bhūta*), the female spirits, since they are deceivers.

101. (c) *Great maintenance*: this is because they have to be sustained by the Great Requisities. For these elements are great primaries (*mahā-bhūta*) since they have become (*bhūta*), have occurred, through the means of the food, clothing, etc., which are great (*mahant*) [in importance] because they have to be found every day. Or alternatively, they are great primaries (*mahā-bhūta*) since they are primaries whose maintenance is great.

102. (d) *Great alteration*: the un-clung-to and the clung-to are the [basis of] Great Alterations. Herein, the great alteration of the un-clung-to evidences itself in the emergence of an aeon (see Ch.XIII,§34), and that of the clung-to in the disturbance of the elements [in the body]. For accordingly,

> The conflagration's flame bursts up
> Out of the ground and races higher
> And higher, right to the Brahmā Heaven,
> When the world is burnt up by fire.
>
> A whole world system measuring
> One hundred thousand millions wide
> Subsides, as with its furious waters
> The flood dissolves the world beside.
>
> One hundred thousand million leagues,
> A whole world system's broad extent
> Is rent and scattered, when the world
> Succumbs to the air element.

The bite of Wooden-mouths can make
The body stiff; to all intent,
When roused is its earth element,
It might be gripped by such a snake.

The bite of Rotten-mouths can make
The body rot; to all intent,
When roused its water element,
It might be gripped by such a snake. [368]

The bite of Fiery-mouths can make
The body burn; to all intent,
When roused is its fire element,
It might be gripped by such a snake.

The bite of Dagger-mouths can make
The body burst; to all intent,
When roused is its air element,
It might be gripped by such a snake.

So they are great primaries (*mahā-bhūta*) because they have become (*bhūta*) [the basis of] great (*mahant*) alterations.

103. (c) *Because they are great and because they are entities*: great (*mahant*)' because they need great effort to discern them, and 'entities (*bhūta*=become)' because they are existent; thus they are great primaries (*mahabhūta*) because they are great (*mahā*) and because they are entities (*bhūta*).

This is how all these elements are 'great primaries' by reason of 'great manifestation', and so on.

104. Again, they are elements (*dhātu*) because of bearing (*dhāraṇa*) their own characteristics, because of grasping (*ādāna*) suffering and because of sorting out (*ādhāna*) suffering (see Ch.XV,§19) and because none of them are exempt from the characteristic of being elements. They are states (*dhamma*) owing to bearing (*dhāraṇa*) their own characteristics and owing to their so bearing (*dhāraṇa*) for the length of the moment appropriate to them.[39] They are impermanent in the sense of [liability to] destruction; they are painful in the sense of [causing] terror; they are not self in the sense of having no core [of permanence, and so on]. Thus there is unity of all since all are materiality, great primaries, elements, states, impermanent, and so on.

This is how they should be given attention 'as to variety and unity'.

105. 7. *As to resolution* (*separability*) *and non-resolution* (*inseparability*); they are positionally unresolvable (inseparable) since they always arise together in every single minimal material group consisting of the bare octad and the others;

39. This alludes to the length of duration of a moment of matter's existence, which is described as seventeen times as long as that of consciousness (see VbhA. 25f.).

but they are resolvable (separable) by characteristic. This is how they should be given attention 'as to resolution (separability) and non-resolution (inseparability)'.

106. 8. *As to the similar and dissimilar*: and although they are unresolved (inseparable) in this way, yet the first two are similar in heaviness, and so are the last two in lightness; but [for this reason] the first two are dissimilar to the last two and the last two to the first two. This is how they should be given attention 'as to the similar and dissimilar'.

107. 9. *As to distinction between internal and external*: the internal elements are the [material] support for the physical bases of consciousness, for the kinds of intimation, and for the material faculties. They are associated with postures, and they are of fourfold origination. The external elements are of the opposite kind. This is how they should be given attention 'as to distinction between internal and external'.

108. 10. *As to inclusion*: kamma-originated earth element is included together with the other kamma-originated elements because there is no difference in their origination. Likewise the consciousness-originated is included together with other consciousness-originated elements. This is how they should be given attention 'as to inclusion'.

109. 11. *As to condition*: the earth element, which is held together by water, maintained by fire and distended by air, is a condition for the other three great primaries by acting as their foundation. The water element, which is founded on earth, maintained by fire and distended by air, is a condition for the other three great primaries by acting as their cohesion. The fire element, which is founded on earth, held together by water [369] and distended by air, is a condition for the other three great primaries by acting as their maintaining. The air element, which is founded on earth, held together by water, and maintained by fire, is a condition for the other three great primaries by acting as their distension. This is how they should be given attention 'as to condition'.

110. 12. *As to lack of conscious reaction*: here too the earth element does not know 'I am the earth element' or 'I am a condition by acting as foundation for three great primaries'. And the other three do not know 'The earth element is a condition for us by acting as our foundation'. And similarly in each instance. This is how they should be given attention 'as to lack of conscious reaction'.

111. 13. *As to analysis of conditions*; there are four conditions for the elements, that is to say, kamma, consciousness, nutriment, and temperature.

Herein *kamma* alone is a condition for what is kamma-originated, not consciousness and the rest. And *consciousness*, etc., alone are the respective conditions for what is consciousness-originated, etc., not the others. And *kamma* is the producing condition[40] for what is kamma-originated; it is indirectly decisive-support condition for the rest.[41] *Consciousness* is the producing condition for what is consciousness-originated; it is postnascence condition and presence and non-disappearance conditions for the rest. *Nutriment* is the producing condition for what is nutriment-originated; it is nutriment condition and presence and non-disappearance conditions for the rest. *Temperature* is the producing condition for what is temperature-originated; it is presence and non-disappearance conditions for the rest. A kamma-originated great primary is a condition for a kamma-originated great primary, and also for the consciousness-originated, and so on. Likewise the consciousness-originated and the nutriment originated. A temperature-originated great primary is a condition for a temperature-originated great primary, and for the kamma-originated, and so on (cf. Ch. XX, §27f.).

112. Herein, the kamma-originated earth element is a condition for the other kamma-originated elements both as conascence, mutuality, support, presence, and non-disappearance, conditions and as foundation, but not as producing condition. It is a condition for the other [three] great primaries in a triple continuity (see Ch.XX,§22) as support, presence and non-disappearance, conditions, but not as foundation or producing condition. And here the water element is a condition for the remaining three elements both as conascence, etc., conditions and as cohesion, but not as producing condition. And for the others in a triple continuity it is a condition as support, presence, and non-disappearance, conditions, too, but not as cohesion or producing condition. And the fire element here is a condition for the other three elements both as conascence, etc., conditions and as maintaining, but not as producing condition. And for the others in a triple continuity it is a condition as support, presence, and non-disappearance, conditions too, but not as maintaining or producing condition. And the air element here is a condition for the other three elements [370]

40. 'The term "*producing condition*" refers to causing origination, though as a condition it is actually kamma-condition. For this is said "Profitable and unprofitable volition is a condition, as kamma condition, for resultant aggregates and for materiality due to kamma performed" (Ptn 1.5)' (Pm. 368).

41. '"*For the rest*": for consciousness-originated, and so on. It is indirectly decisive-support condition because in the Patthāna the decisive-support condition has only been given for immaterial dhammas, so there is, directly, no decisive-support condition [in kamma] for material dhammas. However, because of the words "With a person as decisive support" ( ) and "With a grove as decisive support" ( ) in the suttas the decisive-support condition can be indirectly understood according to the suttas in the sense of "absence without" ' (Pm. 368).

both as conascence, etc., conditions and as distension, but not as producing condition. And for the others in a triple continuity it is a condition as support, presence, and non-disappearance, conditions too, but not as distension or producing condition.

The same method applies in the case of the consciousness-originated, the nutriment-originated, and the temperature-originated earth element, and the rest.

113. And when these elements have been made to occur through the influence of the conascence, etc., conditions,

With three in four ways to one due,
And likewise with one due to three;
With two in six ways due to two—
Thus their occurrence comes to be.

114. Taking each one, beginning with earth, there are three others whose occurrence is due to that one, thus with three due to one their occurrence takes place in four ways. Likewise each one, beginning with earth, occurs in dependence on the other three, thus with one due to three their occurrence takes place in four ways. But with the last two dependent on the first two, with the first two dependent on the last two, with the second and fourth dependent on the first and third, with the first and third dependent on the second and fourth, with the second and third dependent on the first and fourth, and with the first and fourth dependent on the second and third, they occur in six ways with two elements due to two.

115. At the time of moving forward and moving backward (M.i 57), the earth-element among these is a condition for pressing. That, seconded by the water element, is a condition for establishing on a foundation. But the water element seconded by the earth element is a condition for lowering down. The fire element seconded by the air element is a condition for lifting up. The air element seconded by the fire element is a condition for shifting forwards and shifting sideways (see Ch.XX, §62f. and MA.,i,160).

This is how they should be given attention 'as to analysis of condition.'

116. As he gives his attention to them 'as to word meaning', etc., in this way the elements become evident to him under each heading. As he again and again adverts and gives attention to them access concentration arises in the way already described. And this concentration too is called 'definition of the four elements' because it arises in one who defines the four elements owing to the influence of his knowledge.

117. This bhikkhu who is devoted to the defining of the four elements immerses himself in voidness and eliminates the perception of living beings. Since he does not entertain

false notions about wild beasts, spirits, ogres, etc., because he has abolished the perception of living beings, he conquers fear and dread and conquers delight and aversion (boredom), he is not exhilarated or depressed[42] by agreeable and disagreeable things, and as one of great understanding, he either ends in the deathless or he is bound for a happy destiny.

Defining the four elements
Is ever the wise man's resort;
The noble meditator lion[43]
Will make this mighty theme his sport.

This is the description of the development of the defining of the four elements [371].

*

[DEVELOPMENT OF CONCENTRATION—CONCLUSION]

118. This completes in all its aspects the commentary on the meaning of the clause 'How should it be developed?' in the set of questions beginning with 'What is concentration?', which was formulated in order to show the method of development of concentration in detail (see Ch.III,§1).

119. This concentration as intended here is twofold, that is to say, access concentration and absorption concentration. Herein, the unification [of mind] in the case of ten meditation subjects and in the consciousness preceding absorption [in the case of the remaining meditation subjects][44] is access concentration. The unification of mind in the case of the remaining meditation subjects is absorption concentration. And so it is developed in two forms with the development of these meditation subjects. Hence it was said above 'This completes in all its aspects, the commentary on the meaning of the clause "How should it be developed?" '

* * *

[THE BENEFITS OF DEVELOPING CONCENTRATION]

120. The question (viii) *WHAT ARE THE BENEFITS OF THE DEVELOPMENT OF CONCENTRATION?* was also asked, however (Ch.III,§1). Herein, the benefits of the development of concentration are fivefold, as a blissful abiding here and now, and so on. For the development of absorption concentration provides the benefit of a blissful abiding here and now for the Arahants with cankers destroyed who develop concentration, thinking 'We shall attain and dwell with unified

42. '*Ugghāta*—exhilarated' and '*nigghāta*—depressed': neither word is in P. T. S. Dict.; Pm. glosses with *ubbilāvitatta* and *dīnabhāvappatti* respectively.
43. Reading *yogivarasīhassa kīḷitaṁ* Cf. Netti '*Sīha-kīḷana*'.
44. The sense demands reading with Pm. *appanāpubbabhāgacittesu* as a single compound.

mind for a whole day'. Hence the Blessed One said: 'But, 'Cunda, it is not these that are called effacement in the Noble 'Ones' discipline; these are called blissful abidings in the 'Noble Ones' discipline' (M.i,40).

121. When ordinary people and Trainers develop it, thinking 'After emerging we shall exercise insight with concentrated consciousness', the development of absorption concentration provides them with the benefit of insight by serving as the proximate cause for insight, and so too does access concentration as a method of arriving at wide open [conditions] in crowded [circumstances].[45] Hence the Blessed One said: 'Bhikkhus, develop concentration; a bhikkhu who is concen-'trated understands correctly' (S.iii,13).

122. But when they have already produced the eight attainments and then, aspiring to the kinds of direct-knowledge described in the way beginning 'Having been one, he becomes many' (Ch.XII,§2), they produce them by entering upon jhana as the basis for direct-knowledge and emerging from it, then the development of absorption concentration provides for them the benefit of the kinds of direct-knowledge, since it becomes the proximate cause for the kinds of direct-knowledge whenever there is an occasion. Hence the Blessed One said: 'He 'attains the ability to be a witness, through realization by 'direct knowledge, of any state realizable by direct knowledge 'to which his mind inclines, whenever there is an occasion' (M.iii,96;A.i,254). [322]

123. When ordinary people have not lost their jhana, and they aspire to rebirth in the Brahmā World thus 'Let us be reborn in the Brahmā World', or even though they do not make the actual aspiration, then the development of absorption concentration provides them with the benefits of an improved form of existence since it ensures that for them. Hence the Blessed One said 'Where do they reappear after developing 'the first jhana limitedly? They reappear in the company 'of the deities of Brahmā's Retinue' (Vbh.424), and so on. And even the development of access concentration ensures an improved form of existence in the happy destinies of the sensual sphere.

124. But when Noble Ones who have already produced the eight attainments develop concentration thinking 'We shall enter upon the attainment of cessation, and by being without consciousness for seven days we shall abide in bliss here and now by reaching the cessation that is nibbana', then the development of absorption concentration provides for them the benefit of cessation. Hence it is said 'Understanding as

45. This is an allusion to M. i, 179, etc.; 'The process of existence in the round of rebirths, which is a very cramped place, is crowded by the defilements of craving and so on' (Pm. 371).

'mastery, owing to. . . sixteen kinds of behaviour of know-'ledge, and to nine kinds of behaviour of concentration, is 'knowledge of the attainment of cessation' (Ps. i, 97; see Ch. XXIII, §18f.).

125. That is how this benefit of the development of concentration is fivefold as a blissful abiding here and now, and so on.

So wise men fail not in devotion
To the pursuit of concentration:
It cleans defiling stains' pollution,[46]
And brings rewards past calculation.

126. And at this point in the Path of Purification, which is taught under the headings of virtue, concentration and understanding in the stanza 'When a wise man, established well in virtue. . .', concentration has been fully explained.

The eleventh chapter concluding 'the Description of Concentration' in the Path of Purification composed for the purpose of gladdening good people.

46. '*Sūdana*—cleaning': not in P. T. S. Dict. see title of Majjhima Nikāya Commentary. Another reading here is *sodhana*.

CHAPTER XII

DESCRIPTION OF DIRECT-KNOWLEDGE— THE SUPERNORMAL POWERS

(*Iddhividha-niddesa*)

[The Benefits of Concentration Continued]

1. [373] It was said above with reference to the mundane kinds of Direct-knowledge that this development of concentration 'provides . . . the benefit of the kinds of direct-knowledge' (Ch.XI,§122). Now in order to perfect those kinds of direct-knowledge the task must be undertaken by a meditator who has reached the fourth jhana in the earth kasina, and so on. And in doing this, not only will this development of concentration have provided benefits in this way, it will also have become more advanced; and when he thus possesses concentration so developed as to have both provided benefits and become more advanced, he will then more easily perfect the development of understanding. So meanwhile we shall deal with the explanation of the kinds of direct-knowledge now.

[The Five Kinds of Direct Knowledge]

2. In order to show the benefits of developing concentration to clansmen whose concentration has reached the fourth jhana, and in order to teach progressively refined Dhamma, five kinds of mundane direct-knowledge have been described by the Blessed One. They are (1) the kinds of Supernormal Power, described in the way beginning 'When his concentrated mind is thus purified, bright, unblemished, rid of defilement, and has become malleable, wieldy, steady, and attained to imperturbability,[1] he directs, he inclines, his mind to the kinds of supernormal power. He wields the various kinds of supernormal power. Having been one, he becomes many, . . .' (D.i,77), the knowledge of the Divine Ear Element, (2) the knowledge of Penetration of Minds, (4) the knowledge of Recollection of Past Life, and (5) the knowledge of the Passing Away and Reappearance of Beings.

[(1) The Kinds of Supernormal Power]

If a meditator wants to begin performing the transformation by supernormal power described as 'Having been one, he

1. '*Āneñja*—imperturbability': a term normally used for the four immaterial states, together with the fourth jhana. See also §16f., and M. Sutta 106.

becomes many', etc., he must achieve the eight attainments in each of the eight kasinas ending with the white kasina. He must also have complete control of his mind in the following fourteen ways: [374] (i) in the order of the kasinas, (ii) in the reverse order of the kasinas, (iii) in the order and reverse order of the kasinas, (iv) in the order of the jhanas, (v) in the reverse order of the jhanas, (vi) in the order and reverse order of the jhanas, (vii) skipping jhanas, (viii) skipping kasinas, (ix) skipping jhanas and kasinas, (x) transposition of factors, (xi) transposition of object, (xii) transposition of factors and object, (xiii) definition of factors, and (xiv) definition of object.

3. But what is 'in the order of the kasinas' here? . . . what is 'definition of object'?

(i) Here a bhikkhu attains jhana in the earth kasina, after that in the water kasina, and so progressing through the eight kasinas, doing so even a hundred times, even a thousand times, in each one. This is called *in the order of the kasinas.* (ii) Attaining them in like manner in reverse order, starting with the white kasina, is called *in the reverse order of the kasinas.* (iii) Attaining them again and again in forward and reverse order, from the earth kasina up to the white kasina and from the white kasina back to the earth kasina, is called *in the order and reverse order of the kasinas.*

4. (iv) Attaining again and again from the first jhana up to the base consisting of neither perception nor non-perception is called *in the order of the jhanas.* (v) Attaining again and again from the base consisting of neither perception nor non-perception back to the first jhana is called *in the reverse order of the jhanas.* (vi) Attaining in forward and reverse order, from the first jhana up to the base consisting of neither perception nor non-perception and from the base consisting of neither perception nor non-perception back to the first jhana is called *in the order and reverse order of the jhanas.*

5. (vii) He skips alternate jhanas without skipping the kasinas in the following way: having first attained the first jhana in the earth kasina, he attains the third jhana in that same kasina, and after that, having removed [the kasina (Ch.X,§6), he attains] the base consisting of boundless space, after that the base consisting of nothingness. This is called *skipping jhanas.* And that based on the water kasina, etc., should be construed similarly. (viii) When he skips alternate kasinas without skipping jhanas in the following way: having attained the first jhana in the earth kasina, he again attains that same jhana in the fire kasina and then in the blue kasina and then in the red kasina, this is called *skipping kasinas.* (ix) When he skips both jhanas and kasinas in the following way: having attained the first jhana in the earth

kasina, he next attains the third in the fire kasina, next the base consisting of boundless space after removing the blue kasina, next the base consisting of nothingness [arrived at] from the red kasina, this is called *skipping jhanas and kasinas.*

6. (x) Attaining the first jhana in the earth kasina [375] and then attaining the others in that same kasina is called *transposition of factors.* (xi) Attaining the first jhana in the earth kasina and then that same jhana in the water kasina . . . in the white kasina is called *transposition of object.* (xii) Transposition of object and factors together takes place in the following way: he attains the first jhana in the earth kasina, the second jhana in the water kasina, the third in the fire kasina, the fourth in the air kasina, the base consisting of boundless space by removing the blue kasina, the base consisting of boundless consciousness [arrived at] from the yellow kasina, the base consisting of nothingness from the red kasina, and the base consisting of neither perception nor non-perception from the white kasina. This is called *transposition of factors and object.*

7. (xiii) The defining of only the jhana factors by defining the first jhana as five-factored, the second as three-factored, the third as two-factored, and likewise the fourth, the base consisting of boundless space . . . and the base consisting of neither perception nor non-perception, is called *definition of factors.* (xiv) Likewise, the defining of only the object as 'This is the earth kasina'. 'This is the water kasina', . . . 'This is the white kasina', is called *definition of object.* Some would also have 'defining of factors and object'; but since that is not given in the Commentaries it is certainly not a heading in the development.

8. It is not possible for a meditator to begin to accomplish transformation by supernormal power unless he has previously completed his development by controlling his mind in these fourteen ways. Now the kasina preliminary work is difficult for a beginner and only one in a hundre[d] or a thousand can do it. The arousing of the sign is difficult for one who has done the preliminary work and only one in a hundred or a thousand can do it. To extend the sign when it has arisen and to reach absorption is difficult and only one in a hundred or a thousand can do it. To tame one's mind in the fourteen ways after reaching absorption is difficult and only one in a hundred or a thousand can do it. The transformation by supernormal power after training one's mind in the fourteen ways is difficult and only one in a hundred or a thousand can do it. Rapid response after attaining transformation is difficult and only one
9. in a hundred or a thousand can do it. Like the Elder Rakkhita who, eight years after his Full Admission to the Order, was in

the midst of thirty-thousand bhikkhus possessing supernormal power who had come to attend upon the sickness of the Elder Mahā-Rohaṇa-Gutta at Therambatthala. [376] His feat is mentioned under the earth kasina (Ch.IV,§135). Seeing his feat, an elder said 'Friends, if Rakkhita had not been there, we should have been put to shame, [It could have been said] "They were unable to protect the Royal Nāga." So we ourselves ought to go about [with our abilities perfected], just as it is proper (for soldiers) to go about with weapons cleaned of stains'. The thirty thousand bhikkhus
10. heeded the elder's advice and achieved rapid response. And helping another after acquiring rapidity in responding is difficult and only one in a hundred or a thousand can do it. Like the elder who gave protection against the rain of embers by creating earth in the sky, when the rain of embers was produced by Māra at the *Giribhaṇḍavahana* offering.[2]

11. It is only in Buddhas, Pacceka Buddhas, Chief Disciples, etc., who have vast previous endeavour behind them, that this transformation by supernormal power and other such special qualities as the Discriminations are brought to success simply with the attainment of Arahantship and without the progressive course of development of the kind just described.

12. So just as when a goldsmith wants to make some kind of ornament, he does so only after making the gold malleable and wieldy by smelting it, etc., and just as when a potter wants to make some kind of vessel, he does so only after making the clay well kneaded and malleable, a beginner too must likewise prepare for the kinds of supernormal powers by controlling his mind in these fourteen ways; and he must do so also by making his mind malleable and wieldy both by attaining under the headings of zeal, consciousness, energy, and inquiry,[3] and by mastery in adverting, and so on. But one who already has the required condition for it owing to practice in previous lives need only prepare himself by acquiring mastery in the fourth jhana in the kasinas.

13. Now the Blessed One showed how the preparation should be done in saying 'When his concentrated mind', and so on. Here is the explanation, which follows the text (see §2).Herein, *he* is a meditator who has attained the fourth jhana. *Thus* signifies the order in which the fourth jhana comes; having obtained the fourth jhana in this order beginning with attaining the first jhana, is what is meant. *Concentrated*: concen-

---

2. '*Giribhaṇḍavahanapūjā*': Pm. (p. 375) says '*Giribhaṇḍavahanapūjā nāma Cetiyagiriṁ ādiṁ katvā sakalad pe samudde ca yāva yojanā mahatī dīpapūjā* (a g. is a name for a great island-offering starting with the Cetiyagiri (Mihintale) and extending over the whole Island and up to a league into the sea)'. Mentioned in AA. commentary to A. Ekanipāta, i, i; MA. ii, 398, and Mahāvaṁsa 34, 81.

3. These are the four headings of the Roads to Power (see §50).

trated by means of the fourth jhana. *Mind*: fine-material-sphere consciousness.

14. But as to the words 'purified', etc., it is *purified* by means of the state of mindfulness purified by equanimity. [377] It is *bright* precisely because it is purified; it is limpid (see A.i,10), is what is meant. It is *unblemished* since the blemishes consisting of greed, etc., are eliminated by the removal of their conditions consisting of bliss, and the rest. It is *rid of defilement* precisely because it is unblemished; for it is by the blemish that the consciousness becomes defiled. It has *become malleable* because it is well developed; it suffers mastery, is what is meant, for consciousness that suffers mastery is called 'malleable'. It is *wieldy* (*kammaniya*) precisely because it is malleable; it suffers being worked (*kammakkhama*), is fit to be worked (*kammayogga*), is what is
15. meant. For a malleable consciousness is wieldy, like well-smelted gold; and it is both of these because it is well developed, according as it is said: 'Bhikkhus, I do not see any one 'thing that, when developed and cultivated, becomes so 'malleable and wieldy as does the mind' (A.i,9).

16. It is *steady* because it is steadied in this purifiedness, and the rest. It is *attained to imperturbability* (*āneñja-ppatta*) precisely because it is steady; it is motionless, without perturbation (*nir-iñjana*), is what is meant. Or alternatively, it is *steady* because steady in its own masterability through malleability and wieldiness, and it is *attained to imperturba-*
17. *bility* because it is reinforced by faith, and so on. For consciousness reinforced by faith is not perturbed by faithlessness; when reinforced by energy, it is not perturbed by idleness; when reinforced by mindfulness, it is not perturbed by negligence; when reinforced by concentration, it is not perturbed by agitation; when reinforced by understanding, it is not perturbed by ignorance; and when illuminated, it is not perturbed by the darkness of defilement. So when it is reinforced by these six states, it is attained to imperturbability.

18. Consciousness possessing these eight factors in this way is susceptible of being directed to the realization by direct-knowledge of states realizable by direct-knowledge.

19. Another method: It is *concentrated* by means of fourth-jhana concentration. It is *purified* by separation from the hindrances. It is *bright* owing to the surmounting of applied thought and the rest. It is *unblemished* owing to absence of evil wishes based on the obtainment of jhana.[4] It is *rid of defilement* owing to the disappearance of the defilements of the mind consisting in covetousness, etc.; and both of these should be understood according to the *Anaṅgaṇa* Sutta (M., Sutta 5) and the *Vattha*

4. I.e. one who wants it to be known that he can practise jhana.

Sutta (M., Sutta 7). It is *become malleable* by masterability. It is *wieldy* by reaching the state of a Road to Power (§50). It is *steady and attained to imperturbability* by reaching the refinement of completed development; the meaning is that according as it has attained imperturbability so it is steady. And the consciousness possessing these eight factors in this way [378] is susceptible of being directed to the realization by direct-knowledge of states realizable by direct-knowledge, since it is the basis, the proximate cause, for them.

20. *He directs, he inclines, his mind to the kinds of supernormal power* (*iddhi-vidha*—lit. kinds of success): here 'success (*iddhi*)' is the success of succeeding (*ijjhana*); in the sense of production, in the sense of obtainment, is what is meant. For what is produced and obtained is called 'successful', according as it is said 'When a mortal desires, if his desire is fulfilled '(*samijjhati*)' (Sn.766), and likewise 'Renunciation succeeds '(*ijjhati*), thus it is a success (*iddhi*) . . . It metamorphoses '(*paṭiharati*) [lust], thus it is a metamorphosis (*pāṭihāriya*)[5] '. . . The Arahant path succeeds, thus it is a success . . . It 'metamorphoses [all defilements], thus it is a metamor-'phosis' (Ps.ii,229).

21. Another method: success is in the sense of succeeding. That is a term for the effectiveness of the means; for effectiveness of the means succeeds with the production of the result intended, according as it is said: 'This householder Citta is 'virtuous and magnanimous. If he should aspire "Let me in 'the future become a Wheel-turning Monarch", being vir-'tuous, he will succeed in his aspiration, because it is puri-'fied' (S.iv,303).

22. Another method: beings succeed by its means, thus it is success. They succeed, thus they are successful; they are enriched, promoted, is what is meant.

That [success (power)] is of ten kinds, according as it is said 'Kinds of success: ten kinds of success', after which it is said further 'What ten kinds of success? Success by resolve, 'success as transformation, success as the mind-made [body], 'success by intervention of knowledge, success by intervention 'of concentration. Noble Ones' success, success born of 'kamma result, success of the meritorious, success through 'the sciences, success in the sense of succeeding due to right 'exertion applied here or there' (Ps.ii,205).

---

5. 'It counter-strikes (*paṭiharati*), thus it is a counter stroke (*pāṭihāriya*—metamorphosis=miracle). What strikes out (*harati*), removes, what is counter to it (*paṭipakkha*) is therefore called counter-striking (*paṭihāriya*), since what is counter-striking strikes out anything counter (*paṭipakkha*) to itself. *Paṭihāriya* (counter-striking) is the same as *pāṭihāriya* (counter-stroke=metamorphosis=miracle)' (Pm. 379).

23. (i) Herein, the success shown in the exposition [of the above summary] thus, 'Normally one, he adverts to him-'self as] many or a hundred or a thousand or a hundred 'thousand; having adverted, he resolves with knowledge '"Let me be many"' (Ps.ii,207), is called *success by resolve* because it is produced by resolving.

24. (ii) That given as follows, 'Having abandoned his normal 'form, he shows [himself in] the form of a boy or the form 'of a serpent . . . or he shows a manifold military array' (Ps.ii,210), is called *success as transformation* because of the abandoning and alteration of the normal form. [379]

25. (iii) That given in this way, 'Here a bhikkhu creates 'out of this body another body possessing visible form, mind-'made' (Ps.ii,210), is called *success as the mind-made* (body) because it occurs as the production of another, mind-made, body inside the body.

26. (iv) A distinction brought about by the influence of knowledge either before the arising of the knowledge or after it or at that moment is called *success by intervention of knowledge*; for this is said: 'The meaning (purpose) as 'abandoning perception of permanence succeeds through 'contemplation of impermanence, thus it is success by 'intervention of knowledge . . . The meaning (purpose) as 'abandoning all defilements succeeds through the Arahant 'path, thus it is success by intervention of knowledge. There 'was success by intervention of knowledge in the venerable 'Bakkula. There was success by intervention of knowledge 'in the venerable Saṅkicca. There was suscess by inter-'vention of knowledge in the venerable Bhūtapāla,' (Ps.ii, 211).

27. Herein, when the venerable Bakkula as an infant was being bathed in the river on an auspicious day, he fell into the stream through the negligence of his nurse. A fish swallowed him and eventually came to the bathing place at Benares. There it was caught by a fisherman and sold to a rich man's wife. The fish interested her, and thinking to cook it herself, she slit it open. When she did so, she saw the child like a golden image, in the fish's stomach. She was overjoyed, thinking 'At last I have got a son'. So the venerable Bakkula's safe survival in a fish's stomach in his last existence is called 'success by intervention of knowledge' because it was brought about by the influence of the Arahant–path knowledge due to be obtained by [him in] that life. But the story should be told in detail (see MA.iv,190).

28. The Elder Saṅkicca's mother died while he was still in her womb. At the time of her cremation she was pierced by stakes and placed on a pyre. The infant received a wound on the corner of his eye from the point of a stake and made a sound.

Then thinking that the child must be alive, they took down the body and opened its belly. They gave the child to the grandmother. Under her care he grew up, and eventually he went forth and reached Arahantship together with the discriminations. So the venerable Saṅkicca's safe survival on the pyre is called 'success by intervention of knowledge' in the way just stated (see DhA.ii,240).

29. The boy Bhūtapāla's father was a poor man in Rājagaha. (380) He went into the forest with a cart to get a load of wood. It was evening when he returned to the city gate. Then his oxen slipped the yoke and escaped into the city. He seated the child beside the cart and went into the city after the oxen. Before he could come out again the gate was closed. The child's safe survival through the three watches of the night outside the city in a place infested by wild beasts and spirits is called 'success by intervention of knowledge' in the way just stated. But the story should be told in detail.

30. (v) A distinction brought about by the influence of serenity either before the concentration or after it or at that moment is called *success by intervention of concentration*, for this is said: 'The meaning (purpose) as abandoning the 'hindrances succeeds by means of the first jhana, thus it is 'success by intervention of concentration . . . The meaning '(purpose) as abandoning the base consisting of nothingness 'succeeds by means of the attainment of the base consisting 'of neither perception nor nor-perception, thus it is success 'by intervention of concentration. There was success by 'intervention of concentration in the venerable Sāriputta . . . 'in the venerable Sañjīva . . . in the venerable Khāṇu-Kon-'dañña . . . in the laywoman dovotee Uttarā . . . in the lay-'woman devotee Sāmāvatī' (Ps.ii,211-12).

31. Herein, while the venerable Sāriputta was living with the Elder Mahā-Moggallāna at Kapotakandarā he was sitting in the open on a moonlight night with his hair newly cut. Then a wicked spirit, though warned by his companion, gave him a blow on the head, the noise of which was like a thunder clap. At the time the blow was given the Elder was absorbed in an attainment; consequently he suffered no harm from the blow. This was success by intervention of concentration in that venerable one. The story is given in the Udāna too (Ud.39).

32. While the Elder Sañjīva was in the attainment of cessation, cowherds, etc., who noticed him thought he was dead. They brought grass and sticks and cowdung and set fire to them. Not even a corner of the Elder's robe was burnt. This was success by intervention of concentration in him because it was brought about by the influence of the serenity occuring in

his successive attainment [of each of the eight jhanas preceding cessation]. But the story is given in the Suttas too (M. i, 333).

33. The Elder Khāṇu-Kondañña was naturally gifted in attainments. He was sitting absorbed in attainment one night in a certain forest. [381] Five hundred robbers came by with stolen booty. Thinking that no one was following them and needing rest, they put the booty down. Believing the Elder was a tree stump, (*khāṇuka*) they piled all the booty on him. The Elder emerged at the predetermined time just as they were about to depart after resting, at the very time in fact when the one who had put his booty down first was picking it up. When they saw the Elder move, they cried out in fear. The Elder said 'Do not be afraid, lay followers; I am a bhikkhu'. They came and paid homage. Such was their confidence in the Elder that they went forth into homelessness, and they eventually reached Arahantship together with the discrimination. The absence here of harm to the Elder, covered as he was by five hundred bundles of goods was success by intervention of concentration (see DhA. ii, 254).

34. The laywoman devotee Uttarā was the daughter of a rich man called Puṇṇaka. A harlot called Sirimā, who was envious of her, poured a basin of hot oil over her head. At that moment Uttarā had attained [jhana in] lovingkindness. The oil ran off her like water on a lotus leaf. This was success by intervention of concentration in her. But the story should be given in detail (see DhA. iii, 310; AA. i. 451).

35. King Udena's chief queen was called Sāmāvatī. The Brahman Māgaṇḍiya, who aspired to elevate his own daughter to the position of chief queen, put a poisonous snake into Sāmāvatī's lute. Then he told the king 'Sāmāvatī wants to kill you, sire. She is carrying a poisonous snake about in her lute'. When the king found it, he was furious. Intending to kill her, he took his bow and aimed a poisoned arrow. Sāmāvatī with her retinue pervaded the king with lovingkindness. The king stood trembling, unable either to shoot the arrow or to put it away. Then the queen said to him 'What is it, Sire, are you tired?'—'Yes, I am tired.'—'Then put down the bow.' The arrow fell at the king's feet. Then the queen advised him 'Sire, one should not hate one who has no hate'. So the king's not daring to release the arrow was success by intervention of concentration in the laywoman Sāmāvatī (see DhA.i,216;AA.i,443).

36. (vi) That which consists in dwelling perceiving the unrepulsive in the repulsive, etc., is called *Noble Ones' success*, according as it is said 'What is Noble Ones' success? Here 'if a bhikkhu should wish "May I dwell perceiving the 'unrepulsive in the repulsive", he dwells perceiving the

1024-O

'unrepulsive in that . . . he dwells in equanimity towards that, 'mindful and fully aware' (Ps.ii,212). [382] This is called 'Noble Ones' success' because it is only produced in Noble
37. Ones who have reached mind mastery. For if a bhikkhu with cankers destroyed possesses this kind of success, then when in the case of a disagreeable object he is practising pervasion with lovingkindness or giving attention to it as elements, he dwells perceiving the unrepulsive; or when in the case of an agreeable object he is practising pervasion with foulness or giving attention to it as impermanent, he dwells perceiving the repulsive. Likewise when in the case of the repulsive and unrepulsive he is practising that same pervasion with lovingkindness or giving attention to it as elements, he dwells perceiving the unrepulsive; and when in the case of the unrepulsive and repulsive he is practising that same pervasion with foulness or giving attention to it as impermanent, he dwells perceiving the repulsive. But when he is exercising the six-factored equanimity in the following way 'On seeing a visible 'object with the eye, he is neither glad nor . . .' (Ps.ii,213), etc., then rejecting both the repulsive and the unrepulsive,
38. he dwells in equanimity, mindful and fully aware. For the meaning of this is expounded in the Paṭisambhidā in the way beginning 'How does he dwell perceiving the unrepulsive 'in the repulsive? In the case of a disagreeable object he 'pervades it with lovingkindness or he treats it as elements' (Ps.ii,212). Thus it is called 'Noble Ones' success' because it is only produced in Noble Ones who have reached mind mastery.

39. (vii) That consisting in travelling through the air in the case of winged birds, etc., is called *success born of kamma result*, according as it is said 'What is success born of kamma result? 'That in all winged birds, in all deities, in some human beings, 'in some inhabitants of states of loss, is success born of 'kamma result' (Ps.ii,213). For here it is the capacity in all winged birds to travel through the air without jhana or insight that is success born of kamma result; and likewise that in all deities, and some human beings, at the beginning of the aeon, and likewise that in some inhabitants of states of loss such as the female spirit Piyaṅkara's mother (see SA.), Uttara's mother (PvA.140), Phussamittā, Dhammaguttā, and so on.

40. (viii) That consisting in travelling through the air, etc., in the case of Wheel-turning Monarchs, etc., is called *success of the meritorious*, according as it is said 'What is success of 'the meritorious? The Wheel-turning Monarch travels through 'the air with his fourfold army, even with his grooms and 'shepherds. The householder Jotika had the success of the 'meritorious. The householder Jaṭilaka had the success of the

'meritorious. [383] The householder Ghosita had the success 'of the meritorious. The householder Meṇḍaka had the success 'of the meritorious. That of the five very meritorious is 'success of the meritorious' (Ps.ii,213). In brief, however, it is the distinction that consists in succeeding when the accumulated merit comes to ripen that is success of the meritorious.

41. A crystal palace and sixty-four wishing trees cleft the earth and sprang into existence for the householder Jotika. That was success of the meritorious in his case (DhA.iv,207). A golden rock of eighty cubits [high] was made for Jatilaka (DhA.iv,216). Ghosita's safe survival when attempts were made in seven places to kill him was success of the meritorious (DhA.i,174). The appearance to Meṇḍaka(=Ram)of rams (*meṇḍaka*) made of the seven gems in a place the size of one *sītā*[6] was success of the meritorious in Meṇḍaka (DhA. iii,364).

42. The 'five very meritorious' are the rich man Meṇḍaka, his wife Candapadumasiri, his son the rich man Dhanañjaya, his daughter-in-law Sumanadevi, and his slave Puṇṇa. When the rich man [Meṇḍaka] washed his head and looked up at the sky, twelve thousand five hundred measures were filled for him with red rice from the sky. When his wife took a nāḷi measure of cooked rice, the food was not used up though she served the whole of Jambudīpa with it. When his son took a purse containing a thousand [ducats (*kahāpana*)] the ducats were not exhausted even though he made gifts to all the inhabitants of Jambudīpa. When his daughter-in-law took a pint (*tumba*) measure of paddy, the grain was not used up even when she shared it out among all the inhabitants of Jambudīpa. When the slave ploughed with a single ploughshare, there were fourteen furrows, seven on each side (see Vin.i, 240;DhA.i,384). This was success of the meritorious in them.

43. (ix) That beginning with travelling through the air in the case of masters of the sciences is *success through the sciences*, according as it is said 'What is success through the sciences? 'Masters of the sciences, having pronounced their scientific 'spells, travel through the air, and they show an elephant in 'space, in the sky . . . and they show a manifold military 'array' (Ps.ii,213).

44. (x) But the succeeding of such and such work through such and such right exertion is *success in the sense of succeeding due to right exertion applied here or there*, according as it is said: 'The meaning (purpose) of abandoning lust succeeds

6. '*Sītā*': not in this sense in P.T.S. Dict.; Pm. (p. 383) says 'It is the path traversed by a ploughshare in ploughing that is called a "*sītā*"' Another reading is *Karīsa* (an area of land).

'through renunciation, thus it is success in the sense of suc- 'ceeding due to right exertion applied here or there . . . The 'meaning (purpose) of abandoning all defilements succeeds 'through the Arahant path, thus it is success in the sense of 'succeeding due to right exertion applied here or there' (Ps.ii, 213). [384] And the text here is similar to the previous text in the illustration of right exertion, in other words, the way. But in the Commentary it is given as follows: 'Any work belonging to a trade such as making a cart assemblage, etc., any medical work, the learning of the three Vedas, the learning of the Three Pitakas, even any work connected with ploughing, sowing, etc.,—the distinction produced by doing such work is success in the sense of succeeding due to right exertion applied here or there'.

45. So, among these ten kinds of success, only (i) success by resolve is actually mentioned in the clause 'kinds of supernormal power (success)' but (ii) success as transformation and (iii) success as the mind-made [body] are needed in this sense as well.

46. (i) *To the kinds of supernormal power* (see §20): to the components of supernormal power, or to the departments of supernormal power. *He directs, he inclines, his mind*: When that bhikkhu's consciousness has become the basis for direct-knowledge in the way already described, he directs the preliminary-work consciousness with the purpose of attaining the kinds of supernormal power, he sends it in the direction of the kinds of supernormal power, leading it away from the kasina as its object. *Inclines*: makes it tend and lean towards the supernormal power to be attained.

47. *He*: the bhikkhu who has done the directing of his mind in this way. *The various*: varied, of different sorts. *Kinds of supernormal power*: departments of supernormal power. *Wields*: *paccānubhoti=paccanubhavati* (alternative form); the meaning is that he makes contact with, realizes, reaches.

48. Now, in order to show that variousness, it is said: 'Having 'been one, [he becomes many; having been many, he becomes 'one. He appears and vanishes. He goes unhindered 'through walls, through enclosures, through mountains, as 'though in open space. He dives in and out of the earth as 'though in water. He goes on unbroken water as though on 'earth. Seated cross-legged he travels in space like a winged 'bird. With his hand he touches and strokes the moon and 'sun so mighty and powerful. He wields bodily mastery 'even as far as the Brahmā World]' (D.i,77).

Herein, *having been one*: having been normally one before giving effect to the supernormal power. *He becomes many*: wanting to walk with many or wanting to do a recital or wanting to ask questions with many, he becomes a hundred or a thousand. But how does he do this? He accomplishes (1) the four planes, (2) the four bases (roads), (3) the eight steps, and (4) the sixteen roots, of supernormal power, and then he (5) resolves with knowledge.

49. 1. Herein, the *four planes* should be understood as the four jhanas; for this has been said by the General of the Dhamma [the Elder Sāriputta]: 'What are the four planes of 'supernormal power? They are the first jhana as the plane 'born of seclusion, the second jhana as the plane of happiness 'and bliss, and third jhana as the plane of equanimity and 'bliss, the fourth jhana as the plain of neither pain nor plea-'sure. These four planes of supernormal power lead to the 'attaining of supernormal power, to the obtaining of super-'normal power, to the transformation due to supernormal 'power, to the majesty[7] of supernormal power, to the mas-'tery of supernormal power, to fearlessness in supernormal 'power' (Ps.ii,205). And he reaches supernormal power by becoming light, malleable and wieldy in body after steeping himself in blissful perception and light perception due to the pervasion of happiness and pervasion of bliss, [385] which is why the first three jhanas should be understood as the accessary plane since they lead to the obtaining of supernormal power in this manner. But the fourth is the natural plane for obtaining supernormal power.

50. 2. The *four bases (roads)* should be understood as the four bases of success (*iddhi-pāda*—roads to power); for this is said: 'What are the four bases (*pāda*—roads) for success '(*iddhi*—power)? Here a bhikkhu develops the basis for 'success (road to power) that possesses both concentration 'due to zeal and the will to strive (endeavour); he develops 'the basis for success (road to power) that possesses both 'concentration due to energy and the will to strive; he deve-'lops the basis for success (road to power) that possesses both 'concentration due to [natural purity of] consciousness and 'the will to strive; he develops the basis for success (road to 'power) that possesses both concentration due to inquiry and 'the will to strive. These four bases (roads) for success '(power) lead to the obtaining of supernormal power (suc-'cess) . . . to the fearlessness due to supernormal power '(success)' (Ps.ii,205).

51. And here the concentration that has zeal as its cause, or has zeal outstanding, is *concentration due to zeal*; this is a term for concentration obtained by giving precedence to zeal consisting in desire to act. Will (formation) as endeavour is *will to strive*; this is a term for the energy of right endeavour

7. '*Visavitā*—majesty': not in P. T. S. Dict.; cf. *passavati*. Pm. (p. 385) glosses with '*iddhiyā vividhānisaṁsa-pasavanāya*'. cf. DhsA. 109; DhsAA. (p. 84) glosses thus '*visavitāyā ti arahatāya*'.

accomplishing its fourfold function (see §53). *Possesses*: is furnished with concentration due to zeal and with the [four] instances of the will to strive.

52. *Road to power* (*basis for success*): The meaning is, the total of consciousness and its remaining concomitants [except the concentration and the will], which are, in the sense of resolve, the road to (basis for) the concentration due to zeal and will to strive associated with the direct-knowledge consciousness, which latter are themselves termed 'power (success)' either by treatment as 'production' (§20) or in the sense of succeeding' (§21) or by treatment in this way, 'beings succeed by its means, thus they are successful; they are enriched, promoted' (§22). For this is said: 'Basis for success '(road to power): it is the feeling aggregate, [perception 'aggregate, formations aggregate, and] consciousness aggre- 'gate, in one so become' (Vbh. 217].

53. Or alternatively: it is arrived at (*pajjate*) by means of that, thus that is a road (*pāda*—basis); it is reached, is the meaning. *Iddhipāda=iddhiyā pāda* (resolution of compound): this is a term for zeal, etc., according as it is said: 'Bhikkhus, if a 'bhikkhu obtains concentration, obtains unification of mind, 'supported by zeal, this is called concentration due to zeal. 'He [awakens zeal] for the non-arising of unarisen evil, un- 'profitable states, [strives, puts forth energy, strains his 'mind and] struggles. [He awakens zeal for the abandoning 'of arisen evil, unprofitable states . . . He awakens zeal for 'the arousing of unarisen profitable states . . . He awakens 'zeal for the maintenance, non-disappearance, increase, 'growth, development and perfection of arisen profitable 'states, strives, puts forth energy, strains his mind and strug- 'gles]. These are called instances of the will to strive. So 'this zeal and this concentration due to zeal and these [four] 'instances of will to strive are called the road to power (basis 'for success) that possesses concentration due to zeal and the 'will to strive' (S.v,268). And the meaning should be under- 'stood in this way in the case of the other roads to power (bases for success).[8]

54. 3. The *eight steps* should be understood as the eight beginning with zeal; for this is said: 'What are the 'eight steps? If a bhikkhu obtains concentration, obtains 'unification of mind, supported by zeal, then the zeal 'is not the concentration; the concentration is not the 'zeal. [386] The zeal is one, the concentration is another. 'If a bhikkhu . . . supported by energy . . . supported by '[natural purity of] consciousness . . . supported by in-

8. Further explanatory details are given in the commentary to the Iddhipāda-Vibhaṅga.

'quiry . . . then the inquiry is not the concentration; the 'concentration is not the inquiry. The inquiry is one, the 'concentration is another. These eight steps to power lead 'to the obtaining of supernormal power (success) . . . to fear-'lessness due to supernormal power (success)' (Ps.ii,205). For here it is the zeal consisting in desire to arouse supernormal power (success), which zeal is joined with concentration, that leads to the obtaining of the supernormal power. Similarly in the case of energy, and so on. That should be understood as the reason why they are called the 'eight steps'.

55. 4. The *sixteen roots*: the mind's unperturbedness[9] should be understood in sixteen modes, for this is said: 'What 'are the sixteen roots of success (power)? Undejected con-'sciousness is not perturbed by indolence, thus it is un-'perturbed.' Unelated consciousness is not perturbed by 'agitation, thus it is unperturbed. Unattracted consciousness 'is not perturbed by greed, thus it is unperturbed. Unrepelled 'consciousness is not perturbed by ill will, thus it is unper-'turbed. Independent consciousness is not perturbed by '[false] view, thus it is unperturbed. Untrammelled con-'sciousness is not perturbed by greed accompanied by zeal, 'thus it is unperturbed. Liberated consciousness is not 'perturbed by greed for sense desires, thus it is unperturbed. 'Unassociated consciousness is not perturbed by defilement, 'thus it is unperturbed. Consciousness rid of barriers is not 'perturbed by the barrier of defilement, thus it is unperturbed. 'Unified consciousness is not perturbed by the defilement of 'variety, thus it is unperturbed. Consciousness reinforced by 'faith is not perturbed by faithlessness, thus it is unperturbed. 'Consciousness reinforced by energy is not perturbed by indo-'lence, thus it is unperturbed. Consciousness reinforced by 'mindfulness is not perturbed by negligence, thus it is un-'perturbed. Consciousness reinforced by concentration is 'not perturbed by agitation, thus it is unperturbed. Con-'sciousness reinforced by understanding is not perturbed by 'ignorance, thus it is unperturbed. Illuminated conscious-'ness is not perturbed by the darkness of ignorance, thus it is 'unperturbed. These sixteen roots of success (power) lead to 'the obtaining of supernormal power (success), . . . to fearless-'ness due to supernormal power (success)' (Ps.ii,206).

56. Of course, this meaning is already established by the words 'When his concentrated mind', etc., too, but it is stated again for the purpose of showing that the first jhana, etc., are the three planes, bases (roads), steps, and roots, of success to supernormal powers). And the first-mentioned method is the one given in the suttas, but this is how it is given in the

9. '*Aneja* (or *aneñja*)—unperturbed': form not in P. T. S. Dict.

Paṭisambhidā. So it is stated again for the purpose of avoiding confusion in each of the two instances.

57. 5. *He resolves with knowledge* (§48): when he has accomplished these things consisting of the planes, bases (roads), steps, and roots, of success (to supernormal power), [387] then he attains jhana as the basis for direct-knowledge and emerges from it. Then if he wants to become a hundred, he does the preliminary work thus 'Let me become a hundred, let me become a hundred', after which he again attains jhana, as basis for direct-knowledge, emerges, and resolves. He becomes a hundred simultaneously with the resolving consciousness. The same method applies in the case of a thousand, and so on. If he does not succeed in this way, he should do the preliminary work again, and attain, emerge, and resolve, a second time. For it is said in the Saṁyutta Commentary that it is allowable to attain once, or twice.

58. Herein, the basic-jhana consciousness has the sign as its object; but the preliminary-work consciousnesses have the hundred as their object or the thousand as their object. And these latter are objects as appearances, not as concepts. The resolving consciousness has likewise the hundred as its object or the thousand as its object. That arises once only, next to change-of-lineage [consciousness], as in the case of absorption consciousness already described (Ch.IV,§78), and it is fine-material-sphere consciousness belonging to the fourth jhana.

59. Now it is said in the Paṭisambhidā 'Normally one, he adverts to [himself as] many or a hundred or a thousand or a hundred thousand; having adverted, he resolves with knowledge "Let me be many". He becomes many, like the venerable Cūḷa-Panthaka' (Ps.ii,207). Here *he adverts* is said with respect only to the preliminary work. *Having adverted, he resolves with knowledge* is said with respect to the knowledge of the direct-knowledge. Consequently, he adverts to many. After that he attains with the last one of the preliminary-work consciousness. After emerging from the attainment, he again adverts thus 'Let me be many', after which he resolves by means of the single [consciousness] belonging to the knowledge of direct-knowledge, which has arisen next to the three, or four, preparatory consciousnesses that have occurred, and which has the name 'resolve' owing to its making the decision. This is how the meaning should be understood here.

60. *Like the venerable Cūḷa-Panthaka* is said in order to point to a bodily witness of this multiple state; but that must be illustrated by the story. There were two brothers, it seems, who were called 'Panthaka (Roadling)' because they were born on a road. The senior of the two was called Mahā-Panthaka.

He went forth into homelessness and reached Arahantship together with the Discriminations. When he had become an Arahant, he made Cūḷa-Panthaka go forth too, and he set him this stanza: [388]

‘As a scented *kokanada* lotus
‘Opens in the morning with its perfume,
‘See the One with Radiant Limbs who glitters[10]
‘Like the Sun s orb blazing in the heavens’
(A.iii,239;S.i,81).

Four months went by, but he could not get it by heart. Then the Elder said ‘You are useless in this dispensation’, and he expelled him from the monastery.

61. At that time the Elder had charge of the allocation of meal [invitations]. Jīvaka approached the Elder, saying ‘Take alms at our house, venerable sir, together with the Blessed One and five hundred bhikkhus’. The Elder consented, saying ‘I accept for all but Cūḷa-Panthaka’. Cūḷa-Panthaka stood weeping at the gate. The Blessed One saw him with the divine eye, and he went to him. ‘Why are you weeping?’ he asked, and he was told what had happened.

62. The Blessed One said ‘No one in my dispensation is called useless for being unable to do a recitation. Do not grieve, bhikkhu’. Taking him by the arm, he led him into the monastery. He created a piece of cloth by supernormal power and gave it to him, saying ‘Now bhikkhu, keep rubbing this and recite over and over again “Removal of dirt, removal of dirt” ’. While doing as he had been told, the cloth became black in colour. What he came to perceive was this: ‘The cloth is clean; there is nothing wrong there. It is this selfhood that is wrong’. He brought his knowledge to bear on the five aggregates, and by increasing insight he reached the neighbourhood of conformity [knowledge] and change-of-lineage [knowledge].

63. Then the Blessed One uttered these illuminative stanzas:

‘Now greed it is, not dust, that we call “dirt”,
‘And “dirt” is just a term in use for greed;
‘This greed the wise reject, and they abide
‘Keeping the Law of him that has no greed.
‘Now hate it is, not dust, that we call “dirt”,
‘ . . .
‘Delusion, too, not dust, that we call “dirt”,
‘And “dirt” is just a term used for delusion;
‘Delusion the wise reject, and they abide
‘Keeping the Law of him without delusion’
(Ndı.505). [389]

10. ‘*Aṅgīrasa*—the One with Radiant Limbs’: one of the epithets for the Buddha. Not in P. T. S. Dict., see A. iii, 239.

When the stanzas were finished, the venerable Cūḷa-Panthaka had at his command the nine Supramundane States attended by the four Discriminations and six kinds of Direct-knowledge.

64. On the following day the Master went to Jīvaka's house together with the community of bhikkhus. Then when the gruel was being given out at the end of the water-offering ceremony,[11] he covered his bowl. Jīvaka asked 'What is it, venerable sir?'—'There is a bhikkhu at the monastery.' He sent a man, telling him 'Go, and return quickly with the Lord'.

65. When the Blessed One had left the monastery,

' Now, having multiplied himself
' Up to a thousand, Panthaka
' Sat in the pleasant mango wood
' Until the time should be announced' (Thag.563).

66. When the man went and saw the monastery all glowing with yellow, he returned and said 'Venerable sir, the monastery is crowded with bhikkhus. I do not know which of them the lord is'. Then the Blessed One said 'Go and catch hold of the hem of the robe of the first one you see; tell him "The Master calls you" and bring him here'. He went and caught hold of the Elder's robe. At once all the creations vanished. The Elder dismissed him saying 'You may go', and when he had finished attending to his bodily needs such as mouth washing, he arrived first and sat down on the seat prepared.

It was with reference to this that it was said 'like the venerable Cūḷa-Panthaka'.

67. The many who were created there were just like the possessor of the supernormal power because they were created without particular specification. Then whatever the possessor of the supernormal powers does, whether he stands, sits, etc., or speaks, keeps silent, etc., they do the same. But if he wants to make them different in appearance, some in the first phase of life, some in the middle phase, and some in the last phase, and similarly some long-haired, some half-shaved, some shaved, some grey-haired, some with lightly dyed robes, some with heavily dyed robes, or expounding phrases, explaining Dhamma, intoning, asking questions, answering questions, cooking dye, sewing and washing robes, etc., or if he wants to make still others of different kinds, he should emerge from the basic jhana, do the preliminary work in the way beginning 'Let there be so many bhikkhus in the first phase of life', etc.; then he should once more attain and emerge, and then resolve. They become of the kinds desired simultaneously with the resolving consciousness.[12]

---

11. Dedication of what is to be given accompanied by pouring water over the hand.

12. '"*They become of the kinds desired*": they become whatever the kinds that were desired: for they come to possess as many varieties in appear-

68. The same method of explanation applied to the clause *having been many, he becomes one*; but there is this difference. After this bhikkhu has thus created a manifold state, then he again thinks 'As one only I will walk about, do a recital, [390] ask a question' or out of fewness of wishes he thinks 'This is a monastery with few bhikkhus. If someone comes, he will wonder "Where have all these bhikkhus who are all alike come from? Surely it will be one of the Elder's feats?" and so he might get to know about me'. Meanwhile wishing 'Let me be one only', he should attain the basic jhana and emerge. Then after doing the preliminary work thus 'Let me be one', he should again attain and emerge and then resolve thus 'Let me be one'. He becomes one simultaneously with the resolving consciousness. But instead of doing this, he can automatically become one again with the lapse of the predetermined time.

69. *He appears and vanishes*: the meaning here is that he causes appearance, causes vanishing. For it is said in the Paṭisambhidā with reference to this: ' "He appears": he is not veiled by ' something, he is not hidden, he is revealed, he is evident. ' "Vanishes": he is veiled by something, he is hidden, he is shut ' away, he is enclosed' (Ps.ii,207).[13]

Now this possessor of supernormal power who wants to make an appearance makes darkness into light, or he makes revealed what is hidden, or he makes what has not come into
70. the visual field come into the visual field. How? If he wants to make himself or another visible even though hidden or at a distance, he emerges from the basic jhana and adverts thus ' Let this that is dark become light' or 'Let this that is hidden be revealed' or 'Let this that has not come into the visual field come into the visual field'. Then he does the preliminary work and resolves in the way already described. It becomes as resolved simultaneously with the resolve. Others then see even when at a distance; and he sees himself too, if he wants to see.

71. But by whom was this miracle formerly performed? By the Blessed One. For when the Blessed One had been invited

---

ance, etc., as it was wished they should have. But although they become manifold in this way by being made the object in different modes of appearance, nevertheless it is only a single resolution consciousness that occurs. This is its power. For it is like the single volition that produces a personality possessed of many different facets (see Ch. XIV, n. 14). And there it is the aspiration to become that is a condition for the differentiation in the kamma; and kamma-result is imponderable. And here too it is the preliminary-work consciousness that should be taken as a condition for the difference. And the field of supernormal power is imponderable too' (Pm. 390).

13. Certain grammatical problems arise about the case of the words '*āvibhāvaṃ*'. etc., both in the sutta passage and (more so) in the Paṭisambhidā passage; they are examined by Pm. (p. 390) but are not renderable into English.

by Cūḷa-Subhaddā and was traversing the seven-league journey between Sāvatthi and Sāketa and with five hundred palanquins[14] created by Vissakamma (see DhA.iii,470), he resolved in suchwise that citizens of Sāketa saw the inhabitants of Sāvatthi and citizens of Sāvatthi saw the inhabitants of Sāketa. And when he had alighted in the centre of the city, he split the earth in two and showed Avīci, and he parted the sky in two and showed the Brahmā World.

72. And this meaning should also be explained by means of the Descent of the Gods (*devorohana*). When the Blessed One, it seems, had performed the Twin Miracle[15] and had liberated eighty-four thousand beings from bonds, he wondered 'Where did the past Enlightened Ones go to when they had finished the Twin Miracle?' He saw that they had gone to the heaven of the Thirty-three. [391] Then he stood with one foot on the surface of the Earth, and placed the second on Mount Yugandhara. Then again he lifted his first foot and set it on the summit of Mount Sineru. He took up the residence for the Rains there on the Red Marble Terrace, and he began his exposition of the Abhidhamma, starting from the beginning, to the deities of ten thousand world-spheres. At the time for wandering for alms he created an artificial Buddha to teach the Dhamma.

73. Meanwhile the Blessed One himself would chew a tooth-stick of *nāgalatā* wood and wash his mouth in Lake Anotatta. Then after collecting alms food among the Uttarakurūs, he would eat it on the shores of that lake. [Each day] the Elder Sāriputta went, there and paid homage to the Blessed One, who told him 'Today I taught this much Dhamma', and he gave him the method. In this way he gave an uninterrupted exposition of the Abhidhamma for three months. Eighty million deities penetrated the Dhamma on hearing it.

74. At the time of the Twin Miracle an assembly gathered that was twelve leagues across. Then saying 'We will disperse when we have seen the Blessed One', they made an encampment and waited there. Anāthapiṇḍika the Less[16] supplied all their needs. People asked the Elder Anuruddha to find out where the Blessed One was. The Elder extended

14. '*Kūṭāgāra*—palanquin': not in this sense in P. T. S. Dict., see story at MA. v, 90, where it is told how 500 of these were made by Sakka's architect Vissakamma for the Buddha to journey through the air in. The same word is also commonly used in the commentaries for the portable structure (catafalque) in which a bier is carried to the pyre. This, built often in the form of a house, is still used now in Ceylon and called *ransivi-ge*. See AA., commentary to A. Tikanipāta 42, and to A. Ekanipāta xx, 38.; also DhA. iii, 470, Not in this sense in P. T. S. Dict.

15. The only book in the Tipitaka to mention the Twin Miracle is the Paṭisambhidāmagga (Ps. i, 53).

16. Anāthapiṇḍika's younger brother (Pm. 391).

light, and with the divine eye he saw where the Blessed One had taken up residence for the Rains. As soon as he saw this, he announced it.

75. They asked the venerable Mahā-Moggallāna to pay homage to the Blessed One. In the midst of the assembly the Elder dived into the earth. Then cleaving Mount Sineru, he emerged at the Perfect One's feet, and he paid homage at the Blessed One's feet. This is what he told the Blessed One: 'Venerable sir, the inhabitants of Jambudīpa pay homage at the Blessed One's feet, and they say "We will disperse when we have seen the Blessed One" '. The Blessed One said 'But, Moggallāna, where is your elder brother, the General of the Dhamma?'—' At the city of Saṅkassa, venerable sir.'—'Moggallāna, those who wish to see me should come tomorrow to the city of Saṅkassa. Tomorrow being the Uposatha Day of the full moon, I shall descend to the city of Saṅkassa for the Mahā-pavāraṇā ceremony'.

76. Saying 'Good, venerable sir', the Elder paid homage to Him of the Ten Powers, and descending by the way he came, he reached the human neighbourhood. And at the time of his going and coming he resolved that people should see it. This, firstly, is the miracle of becoming apparent that the Elder Mahā-Moggallāna performed here. Having arrived thus, he related what had happened, and he said 'Come forth after the morning meal and pay no heed to distance' [thus promising that they would be able to see in spite of the distance].

77. The Blessed One informed Sakka Ruler of Gods 'Tomorrow, O King, I am going to the human world'. The Ruler of Gods [392] commanded Vissakamma 'Good friend, The Blessed One wishes to go to the human world tomorrow. Build three flights of stairs, one of gold, one of silver and one of crystal'. He did so.

78. On the following day the Blessed One stood on the summit of Sineru and surveyed the eastward world element. Many thousands of world-spheres were visible to him as clearly as a single plain. And as the eastward world element, so too he saw the westward, the northward and the southward world elements all clearly visible. And he saw right down to Avīci, and up to the realm of the Highest Gods. That day, it seems, was called the day of the Revelation of Worlds (*loka-vivaraṇa*). Human beings saw deities, and deities saw human beings. And in doing so the human beings did not have to look up or the deities down. They all saw each other face to face.

79. The Blessed One descended by the middle flight of stairs made of crystal; the deities of the six sense-sphere heavens by that on the left side made of gold; and the deities of the Pure Abodes, and the Great Brahmā, by that on the right made of silver. The Ruler of Gods held the bowl and robe. The Great

Brahmā held a three-league-wide white parasol. Suyāma held a yak-tail fan. Five-crest (*Pañcasikhā*) the son of the *gandhabba* descended doing honour to the Blessed One with his bilva-wood lute measuring three quarters of a league. On that day there was no living being present who saw the Blessed One but yearned for enlightenment. This is the miracle of becoming apparent that the Blessed One performed here.

80. Furthermore, in Tambapaṇṇi Island (Ceylon), while the Elder Dhammadinna, resident of Taḷaṅgara, was sitting on the shrine terrace in the Great Monastery of Tissa (*Tissamahāvihāra*) expounding the Apaṇṇaka Sutta, 'Bhikkhus, when a 'bhikkhu possesses three things he enters upon the un-'tarnished way' (A.i,113), he turned his fan face downwards and an opening right down to Avīci appeared. Then he turned it face upwards and an opening right up to the Brahmā World appeared. Having thus aroused fear of hell and longing for the bliss of heaven, the Elder taught the Dhamma. Some became Stream Enterers, some Once-returners, some Non-returners, some Arahants.

81. But one who wants to cause a vanishing makes light into darkness, or he hides what is unhidden, or he makes what has come into the visual field come no more into the visual field. How? If he wants to make himself or another invisible even though unconcealed or nearby, he emerges from the basic jhana and adverts thus, 'Let this light become darkness' or [393] 'Let this that is unhidden be hidden' or 'Let this that has come into the visual field not come into the visual field'. Then he does the preliminary work and resolves in the way already described. It becomes as he has been resolved simultaneously with the resolution. Others do not see even when they are nearby. He too does not see, if he does not want to see.

82. But by whom was this miracle formerly performed? By the Blessed One. For the Blessed One so acted that when the clansman Yasa was sitting beside him, his father did not see him (Vin.i,16). Likewise, after travelling two thousand leagues to meet [king] Mahā-Kappina and establishing him in the fruition of Non-return and his thousand ministers in the fruition of Stream Entry, he so acted that Queen Anojā, who had followed the king with a thousand women attendants and was sitting nearby, did not see the king and his retinue. And when it was asked 'Have you seen the king, venerable sir?', he asked 'But which is better for you, to seek the king or to seek [your] self?' (cf.Vin.i,23). She replied '[My] self, venerable sir'. Then he likewise taught her the Dhamma as she sat there, so that, together with the thousand women attendants, she became established in the fruition of Stream Entry, while the ministers reached the fruition of Non-

return, and the king that of Arahantship (see AA.i,322; DhA.ii,124).

83. Furthermore, this was performed by the Elder Mahinda, who so acted on the day of his arrival in Tambapaṇṇi Island that the king did not see the others who had come with him (see Mahāvaṁsa, i,p.103).

84. Furthermore, all miracles of making evident are called an appearance, and all miracles of making unevident are called a vanishing. Herein, in the miracle of making evident both the supernormal power and the possessor of the supernormal power are displayed. That can be illustrated with the Twin Miracle; for in that both are displayed thus: 'Here the Per-'fect One performs the Twin Miracle, which is not shared 'by disciples. He produces a mass of fire from the upper 'part of his body and a shower of water from the lower part 'of his body . .' (Ps.i,125.) In the case of the miracle of making unevident only the supernormal power is displayed not the possessor of the supernormal power. That can be illustrated by means of the Mahaka Sutta [S.iv,200], and the Brahmanimantanika Sutta (M.i,330). For there it was only the supernormal power of the venerable Mahaka and of the Blessed One respectively that was displayed, not the possessors of the supernormal power, according as it is said:

85. 'When he had sat down at one side, the householder Citta 'said to the venerable Mahaka "Venerable Sir, it would be 'good if the lord would show me a miracle of supernormal 'power belonging to the higher than human state."— '"Then, householder, spread your upper robe out on the 'terrace [394] and scatter[17] a bundle of hay on it."—"Yes, 'venerable sir," the householder replied to the venerable 'Mahaka, and he spread out his upper robe on the terrace 'and scattered a bundle of hay on it. Then the venerable 'Mahaka went into his dwelling and fastened the latch, after 'which he performed a feat of supernormal power such that 'flames came out from the keyhole and from the gaps in the 'fastenings and burned the hay without burning the upper

86. 'robe'[S.iv.290], also according as it is said 'Then, bhikkhus, 'I performed a feat of supernormal power such that Brahmā 'and Brahma's retinue and those attached to Brahmā's 'retinue, might hear my voice and yet not see me, and having 'vanished in this way, I spoke this stanza:

> ' I saw the fear in [all kinds of] becoming.
> ' Including becoming that seeks non-becoming ;
> ' And no becoming do I recommend ;
> ' I cling to no delight therein at all' (M.i,330).

---

17. '*Okāseti*...to scatter': P. T. S. Dict., this ref., gives 'to show', which does not fit the context. Pm. glosses with *pakirati*.

87. *He goes unhindered through walls, through enclosures, through mountains, as though in open space*: here *through walls* is beyond walls ; the yonder side of a wall, is what is meant. So with the rest, And *wall* is a term for the wall of a house; *enclosure* is a wall surrounding a house, monastery (park), village, etc.; *mountain* is a mountain of soil or a mountain of stone. *Unhindered* : not sticking. *As though in open space* : just as if he were in open space.

88. One who wants to go in this way should attain the space-kasina [jhana] and emerge, and then do the preliminary work by adverting to the wall or the enclosure or some such mountain as Sineru or the World-sphere Mountains, and he should resolve. 'Let there be space'. It becomes space only ; it becomes hollow for him if he wants to go down or up; it becomes cleft for him if he wants to penetrate it. He goes through it unhindered.

89. But here the Elder Tipiṭaka Cūḷa-Abhaya said : Friends, what is the use of attaining the space-kasina [jhana]? Does one who wants to create elephants, horses, etc., attain an elephant-kasina jhana or a horse-kasina jhana, and so on? Surely the only standard is mastery in the eight attainments, and after the preliminary work has been done on any kasina, it then becomes whatever he wishes'. The bhikkhus said 'Venerable sir, only the space kasina has been given in the text, so it should certainly be mentioned'.

90. Here is the text: 'He is normally an obtainer of the space-'kasina attainment. He adverts: "Through the wall, through 'the enclosure, through the mountain". [395] Having 'adverted, he resolves with knowledge: "Let there be space". 'There is space. He goes unhindered through the wall, 'through the enclosure, through the mountain. Just as men 'normally not possessed of supernormal power go unhindered 'where there is no obstruction or enclosure, so too this pos-'sessor of supernormal power, by his attaining mental mastery 'goes unhindered through the wall, through the enclosure 'through the mountain, as though in open space' (Ps.ii.208).

91. What if a mountain or a tree is raised in this bhikkhu's way while he is travelling along after resolving; should he attain and resolve again?—There is no harm in that. For attaining and resolving again is like taking the Dependence (see Vin.i.58.ii.274) in the Preceptor's presence. And because this bhikkhu has resolved 'Let there be space' there will be only space there, and because of the power of his first resolve it is impossible that another mountain or tree can have sprung up meanwhile made by temperature. However, if it has been created by another possessor of supernormal power and created first, it prevails; the former must go above or below it.

92. *He dives in and out of the ground* (*paṭhaviyā pi ummujja-nimmujjaṁ*). Here it is rising up out of that is called 'diving out (*ummujja*)' and it is sinking down into that is called 'diving in (*nimmujja*)'. *Ummujja - nimmujjaṁ==ummujjañ ca nimmujjañ ca* (resolution of compound).

One who wants to do this should attain the water-kasina [jhana] and emerge. Then he should do the preliminary work, determining thus 'Let the earth in such an area be water', and he should resolve in the way already described. Simultaneously with the resolve, that much extent of earth according as determined becomes water only. It is there he does the diving in and out.

93. Here is the text: 'He is normally an obtainer of the water-'kasina attainment. He adverts to earth. Having adverted, 'he resolves with knowledge "Let there be water". There is 'water. He does the diving in and out of the earth. Just 'as men normally not possessed of supernormal power do 'diving in and out of water, so this possessor of supernormal 'power, by his attaining mental mastery, does the diving 'in and out of the earth as though in water' (Ps.ii.208).

94. And he does not only diving in and out, but whatever else he wants, such as bathing, drinking, mouth washing, washing of chattels, and so on. And not only water, but there is whatever else (liquid that) he wants, such as ghee, oil, honey, molasses, and so on. When he does the preliminary work, after adverting, thus 'Let there be so much of this and this' and resolves, (396) it becomes as he resolved. If he takes them and fills dishes with them, the ghee is only ghee, the oil, etc., only oil, etc., the water only water. If he wants to be wetted by it, he is wetted, if he does not want to be wetted by it, he is not wetted. And it is only for him that that earth becomes water, not for anyone else. People go on it on foot and in vehicles, etc.. and they do their plouging, etc., there. But if he wishes 'Let it be water for them too', it becomes water for them too. When the time determined has elapsed, all the extent determined, except for water originally present in water pots, ponds, etc., becomes earth again.

95. *On unbroken water*: here water that one sinks into when trodden on is called 'broken', the opposite is called 'unbroken'. But one who wants to go in this way should attain the earth-kasina [jhana] and emerge. Then he should do the preliminary work, determining thus 'Let the water in such an area become earth', and he should resolve in the way already described. Simultaneously with the resolve the water in that place becomes earth. He goes on that.

96. Here is the text: 'He is normally an obtainer of the earth-'kasina attainment. He adverts to water. Having adverted, 'he resolves with knowledge "Let there be earth". There is

'earth. He goes on unbroken water. Just as men normally 'not possessed of supernormal power go on unbroken earth, 'so this possessor of supernormal power, by his attaining of 'mental mastery, goes on unbroken water as if on earth' (Ps.ii.208).

97. And he not only goes, but he adopts whatever posture he wishes. And not only earth, but whatever else [solid that] he wants such as gems, gold, rocks, trees, etc.; he adverts to that and resolves, and it becomes as he resolved. And that water becomes earth only for him; it is water for anyone else. And fishes and turtles and water birds go about there as they like. But if he wishes to make it earth for other people, he does so too. When the time determined has elapsed, it becomes water again.

98. *Seated cross-legged he travels*: he goes seated cross-legged. *Like a winged bird*: like a bird furnished with wings. One who wants to do this should attain the earth kasina and emerge. [937] Then if he wants to go cross-legged, he should do the preliminary work and determine an area the size of a seat for sitting cross-legged on, and he should resolve in the way already described. If he wants to go lying down, he determines an area the size of a bed. If he wants to go on foot, he determines a suitable area the size of a path, and he resolves in the way already described. 'Let it be earth'. Simultaneously with the resolve it becomes earth.

99. Here is the text: "Seated cross-legged he travels in space 'like a winged bird": he is normally an obtainer of the earth-'kasina attainment. He adverts to space. Having adver-'ted, he resolves with knowledge. "Let there be earth". 'There is earth. He travels (walks), stands, sits, and lies 'down, in space, in the sky. Just as men normally not possess-'ed of supernormal power travel (walk), stand, sit, and lie 'down, on earth, so this possessor of supernormal power, by 'his attaining of mental mastery, travels (walks), stands, sits, 'and lies down, in space, in the sky' (Ps.ii.208).

100. And a bhikkhu who wants to travel in space should be an obtainer of the divine eye. Why? On the way there may be mountains, trees, etc., that are temperature-originated, or jealous *Nāgas*, *Suppaṇṇas*, etc., may create them. He will need to be able to see these. But what should be done on seeing them? He should attain the basic jhana and emerge, and then he should do the preliminary work thus 'Let there be space', and resolve.

101. But the Elder [Tipiṭaka Cūḷa-Abhaya] said 'Friends, what is the use of attaining the attainment? Is not his mind concentrated? Hence any area that he has resolved thus "Let it be space" is space'. Though he spoke thus, nevertheless

the matter should be treated as described under the miracle of going unhindered through walls. Moreover he should be an obtainer of the divine eye for the puspose of descending in a secluded place, for if he descends in a public place, in a bathing place, or at a village gate, he is exposed to the multitude. So, seeing with the divine eye, he should avoid a place where there is no open space and descend in an open space.

102. *With his hand he touches and strokes the moon and sun so mighty and powerful*: here the 'might' of the moon and sun should be understood to consist in the fact that they travel at an altitude of forty-two thousand leagues, and their 'power' to consist in their simultaneous illuminating of three [of the four] continents, [398] Or they are 'mighty' because they travel overhead and give light as they do, and they are 'powerful' because of that same might. *He touches*: he seizes, or he touches in one place. *Strokes*: he strokes all over, as it were the surface of a looking-glass.

103. This supernormal power is successful simply through the jhana that is made the basis for direct-knowledge; there is no special kasina attainment here. For this is said in the Paṭi-
'sambhidā: "With his hand . . . so mighty and powerful":
'here this possessor of supernormal power who has attained
'mind mastery . . . adverts to the moon and sun. Having
'adverted, he resolves with knowledge "Let it be within
'hand's reach". It is within hand's reach. Sitting or lying
'down, with his hand he touches, makes contact with,
'strokes, the moon and sun. Just as men normally not posses-
'sed of supernormal power touch, make contact with, stroke,
'some material object within hand's reach, so this possessor
'of supernormal power, by his attaining of mental mastery,
'sitting or lying down, with his hands touches, makes contact
'with, strokes, the moon and sun' (Ps.ii, 298).

104. If he wants to go and touch them, he goes and touches them. But if he wants to touch them here sitting or lying down, he resolves 'Let them be within hand's reach'. Then he either touches them as they stand within hand's reach when they have come by the power of the resolve like palmyra fruits loosed from their stalk, or he does so by enlarging his hand. But when he enlarges his hand, does he enlarge what is clung to or what is not clung to? He enlarges what is not clung to supported by what is clung to.

105. Here the Elder Tipiṭaka Cūḷa-Nāga said 'But, friends, why does what is clung to not become small and big too? When a bhikkhu comes out through a keyhole, does not what is clung to become small? And when he makes his body big, does it not then become big, as in the case of the Elder Mahā-Moggalāna?'.

106. At one time, it seems, when the householder Anāthapiṇḍika had heard the Blessed One preaching the Dhamma, he invited him thus 'Venerable sir, take alms at our house together with five hundred bhikkhus, and then he departed. The Blessed One consented. When the rest of that day and part of the night had passed, he surveyed the ten-thousand-fold world element in the early morning. Then the Royal *Nāga* (Serpent) called Nandopananda came within the range of his knowledge.

107. The Blessed One considered him thus: 'This Royal *Nāga* has come into the range of my knowledge. Has he the potentiality for development?' Then he saw that he had wrong view and no confidence in the Three Jewels.[399] He considered thus 'Who is there that can cure him of his wrong view?' He saw that the Elder Mahā-Moggallāna could. Then when the night had turned to dawn, after he had seen to the needs of the body, he addressed the venerable Ānanda: Ānanda, tell five hundred bhikkhus that the Perfect One is going on a visit to the Gods'.

108. It was on that day that they had got a banqueting place ready for Nandopananda. He was sitting on a divine couch with a divine white parasol held aloft, surrounded by the three kinds of dancers[18] and a retinue of *Nāgas*, and serving the various kinds of food and drink served up in divine vessels. Then the Blessed One so acted that the Royal *Nāga* saw him as he proceeded directly above his canopy in the direction of the divine world of the Thirty-three, accompanied by the five hundred bhikkhus.

109. Then his evil view arose in Nandopananda the Royal *Nāga*: 'There go these bald-headed monks in and out of the realm of the thirty-three directly over my realm. I will not have them scattering the dirt off their feet on our heads'. He got up, and he went to the foot of Sineru. Changing his form, he surrounded it seven times with his coils. Then he spread his hood over the realm of the Thirty-three and made everything there invisible.

110. The venerable Raṭṭhapāla said to the Blessed One 'Venerable sir, standing in this place formerly I used to see Sineru and the Ramparts of Sineru,[19] and the thirty-three, and the Vejayanta Palace, and the flag over the Vejayanta Palace. Venerable sir, what is the cause, what is the reason, why I now see neither Sineru nor . . . the flag over the Vejayanta

---

18. Pm. (p. 394) '*Vadhū-kumāri-kaññā-vatthūhi tividhāhi nāṭakitthīhi*'.

19. ' "*The ramparts of Sineru*": the girdle of Sineru. There are, it seems, four ramparts that encircle Sineru, measuring 5,000 leagues in breadth and width. They were built to protect the realm of the Thirty-three against *Nāgas*, *Garudas*, *Kumbhaṇḍas* and *Yakkhas*. They enclose half of Sineru, it seems' (Pm. 394).

Palace?' —'This Royal *Nāga* called Nandopananda is angry with us, Raṭṭhapāla. He has surrounded Sineru seven times with his coils, and he stands there covering us with his raised hood, making it dark.'— 'I will tame him, venerable sir.' But the Blessed One would not allow it. Then the venerable Bhaddiya and the venerable Rāhula and all the bhikkhus in turn offered to do so, but the Blessed One would not allow it.

111. Last of all the venerable Mahā-Moggallāna said 'I will tame him, venerable sir.' The Blessed One allowed it, saying 'Tame him, Moggallāna'. The Elder abandoned that form and assumed the form of a huge Royal *Nāga*, and he surrounded Nandopananda fourteen times with his coils and raised his hood above the other's hood, and he squeezed him against Sineru. The Royal *Nāga* produced smoke. [400] The Elder said 'There is smoke not only in your body but also in mine', and he produced smoke. The Royal *Nāga's* smoke did not distress the Elder, but the Elder's smoke distressed the Royal *Nāga*. Then the Royal *Nāga* produced flames. The Elder said 'There is fire not only in your body but also in mine', and he produced flames. The Royal *Nāga's* fire did not' distress the Elder, the Elder's fire distressed the Royal *Nāga*.

112. The Royal *Nāga* thought 'He has squeezed me against Sineru, and he has produced both smoke and flames'. Then he asked 'Sir, who are you?'—'I am Moggallāna, Nanda.' —'Venerable sir, resume your proper bhikkhu's state'. The Elder abandoned that form, and he went into his right ear and came out from his left ear; then he went into his left ear and came out from his right ear. Likewise he went into his right nostril and came out from his left nostril; then he went into his left nostril and came out from his right nostril. Then the Royal *Nāga* opened his mouth. The Elder went inside it, and he walked up and down, east and west inside his belly.

113. The Blessed One said 'Moggallāna, Moggallāna, beware; this is a mighty *Nāga*'. The Elder said 'Venerable sir, the four roads to power have been developed by me, repeatedly practised, made the vehicle, made the basis, established, consolidated, and properly undertaken. I can tame not only Nandopananda, venerable sir, but a hundred, a thousand, a hundred thousand Royal *Nāgas* like Nandopananda'.

114. The Royal *Nāga* thought 'When he went in in the first place I did not see him. But now he comes out I shall catch him between my fangs and chew him up'. Then he said 'Venerable sir, come out. Do not keep troubling me by walking up and down inside my belly'. The Elder came out and stood outside. The Royal *Nāga* recognised him, and blew a blast from his nose. The Elder attained the fourth jhana,

and the blast failed to move even a single hair on his body. The other bhikkhus would, it seems, have been able to perform all the miracles up to now, but at this point they could not have attained with so rapid a response, which is why the Blessed One would not allow them to tame the Royal *Nāga*.

115. The Royal *Nāga* thought 'I have been unable to move even a single hair on this monk's body with the blast from my nose. He is a mighty monk.' The Elder abandoned that form, and having assumed the form of a *Supaṇṇa*, he pursued the Royal *Nāga*, demonstrating the *Supaṇṇa*'s blast. [401] The Royal *Nāga* abandoned that form, and having assumed the form of a young brahman, he said 'Venerable sir, I go for refuge to you', and he paid homage at the Elder's feet. The Elder said 'The Master has come, Nanda; come, let us go to him'. So having tamed the Royal *Nāga* and deprived him of his poison, he went with him to the Blessed One's presence.

116. The Royal *Nāga* paid homage to the Blessed One and said 'Venerable sir, I go for refuge to you.' The Blessed One said 'May you be happy, Royal *Nāga*'. Then he went, followed by the Community of Bhikkhus, to Anāthapiṇḍika's house. Anāthapiṇḍika said 'Venerable sir, why have you come so late?'—'There was a battle between Moggallāna and Nandopananda.'—'Who won, venerable sir? Who was defeated?' —'Moggallāna won; Nanda was defeated.' Anāthapiṇḍika said 'Venerable sir, let the Blessed One consent to my providing meals for seven days in a single series, and to my honouring the Elder for seven days'. Then for seven days he accorded great honour to the five hundred bhikkhus with the Enlightened One at their head.

117. So it was with reference to this enlarged form created during this taming of Nandopananda that it was said 'When he makes his body big, does it not then become big, as in the case of the Elder Mahā-Moggallāna?' (§105). Although this was said the bhikkhus observed 'He enlarges only what is not clung to supported by what is clung to'. And only this is correct here.[20]

20. 'Only this is correct because instances of clung to (kammically acquired) materiality do not arise owing to consciousness or to temperature. Or alternatively, clung to is intended as all matter that is bound up with faculties (i.e. 'sentient'), too. And so to take it as enlargement of that is likewise not correct. Consequently enlargement should be understood only in the way stated. Though the clung-to and the un-clung-to occur, as it were, mixed up in a single continuity, they are nevertheless not mixed up in meaning. Herein, just as when a pint measure (*āḷhaka*) of milk is poured into a number of pints of water, though the milk becomes completely mixed up with the water, and is present appreciably in all, it is nevertheless not the milk that has increased there, but only the water. And so too although the clung-to and un-clung-to occur mixed up together, it is nevertheless not the clung-to that is enlarged. It should be taken that it is the consciousness-born

118. And when he has done this, he not only touches the moon and sun, but if he wishes, he makes a footstool [of them] and puts his feet on it, he makes a chair [of them] and sits on it, he makes a bed [of them] and lies on it, he makes a leaning-plank [of them] and leans on it. And as one does, so do others. For even when several hundred thousand bhikkhus do this and each one succeeds, still the motions of the moon and sun and their radiance remain the same. For just as when a thousand saucers are full of water and moon disks are seen in all the saucers, still the moon's motion is normal and so is its radiance. And this miracle resembles that.

119. *Even as far as the Brahmā* World: having made even the Brahmā World the limit. *He wields bodily mastery*: herein, he wields self-mastery in the Brahmā World by means of the body. The meaning of this should be understood according to the text.

Here is the text: '"He wields bodily mastery even as ' far as the Brahmā World": if this possessor of supernormal ' power, having reached mental mastery, wants to go to ' the Brahmā World, though far, he resolves upon nearness, ' "Let it be near". [402] It is near. Though near, he ' resolves upon farness. "Let it be far". Though many ' he resolves upon few "Let there be few". There are ' few. Though few, he resolves upon many "Let there be ' many". There are many. With the divine eye he sees the ' [fine-material] visible form of that Brahmā. With the ' divine ear element he hears the voice of that Brahmā. ' With the knowledge of penetration of minds he understands ' that Brahmā's mind. If this possessor of supernomal ' power, having reached mental mastery, wants to go to the ' Brahmā World with a visible body he converts his mind to ' accord with his body, he resolves his mind to accord with his ' body. Having converted his mind to accord with his body, ' resolved his mind to accord with his body, he arrives at ' blissful (easy) perception and light (quick) perception, and ' he goes to the Brahmā World with a visible body. If this ' possessor of supernormal power, having reached mental ' mastery, wants to go to the Brahmā World with an invisible ' body, he converts his body to accord with his mind, he re- ' solves his body to accord with his mind, Having converted ' his body to accord with his mind, resolved his body to accord ' with his mind, he arrives at blissful (easy) perception and ' light (quick) perception, and he goes to the Brahmā World ' with an invisible body. He creates a [fine material] visible ' form before that Brahmā, mind-made with all its limbs, ' lacking no faculty. If that possessor of supernormal power

matter that is enlarged by the influence of the supernormal power, and the temperature-born is enlarged *pari passu*' (Pm. 395).

'walks up and down, the creation walks up and down there 'too. If that possessor of supernormal power stands, ... 'sits, ... lies down, the creation lies down there too. If that 'possessor of supernormal power produces smoke, ... pro- 'duces flames, ... preaches Dhamma, ... asks a question. ... 'being asked a question, answers, the creation, being asked a 'question, answers, there too. If that possessor of super- 'normal power stands with that Brahmā, converses, enters 'into communication, with that Brahmā, the creation stands 'with that Brahmā there too, converses, enters into com- 'munication, with that Brahmā there too. Whatever that 'possessor of supernormal power does, the creation does the 'same thing' (Ps.ii,209).

120. Herein, *though far, he resolves upon nearness*: having emerged from basic jhana, he adverts to a far-off divine world or to the Brahmā World thus, 'Let it be near'. Having adverted and done the preliminary work, he attains again, and then resolves with knowledge 'Let it be near'. It becomes near. The same method of explanation applies to the other clauses too.

121. Herein, who has taken what was far and made it near? The Blessed One. For when the Blessed One was going to the Divine world after Twin Miracle, he made Yugandhara and Sineru near, and from the earth's surface he set one foot [403] on Yugandhara, and then he set the other on the summit of Sineru.

122. Who else has done it? The Elder Mahā Moggallāna. For when the Elder was leaving Sāvatthi after completing his meal, he abridged the twelve-league crowd and the thirty-league road to the city of Saṅkassa, and he arrived at the same moment.

123. Furthermore, the Elder Cūḷa-Samudda did it as well in Tambapaṇṇi Island. During a time of scarcity, it seems, seven hundred bhikkhus came to the Elder one morning. The Elder thought 'Where can a large community of bhikkus wander for alms?' He saw nowhere at all in Tambapaṇṇi Island, but he saw that it would be possible on the other shore at Pāṭaliputta (Patna). He got the bhikkhus to take their bowls and [outer] robes, and he said 'Come friends, let us go wandering for alms'. Then he abridged the earth and went to Pāṭaliputta. The bhikkhus asked 'What is the city, venerable sir?'.—'It is Pāṭaliputta, friends.'—'Pāṭaliputta is far away, venerable sir.'—'Friends, experienced Elders make what is far near.'—'Where is the ocean (*mahā-samudda*) venerable sir?'—'Friends, did you not cross a blue stream on the way as you came?'—'Yes, venerable sir, but the ocean is vast.'—'Friends, experienced Elders also make what is vast small.'

124. And the Elder Tissadatta did likewise, when he had put on his upper robes after bathing in the evening, and the thought of paying homage at the Great Enlightenment Tree arose in him.

125. Who has taken what was near and made it far? The Blessed One. For although Aṅgulimāla was near to the Blessed One, yet he made him far distant (see M.ii,99).

126. Who has made much little? The Elder Mahā-Kassapa. One feast day at Rājagaha, it seems, there were five hundred girls on their way to enjoy the festival, and they had taken moon cakes with them. They saw the Blessed One but gave him nothing. On their way back, however, they saw the Elder. Thinking 'He is our Elder', they each took a cake and approached the Elder. The Elder took out his bowl and made a single bowlful of them all. The Blessed One had sat down first to await the Elder. The Elder brought them and gave them to the Blessed One.

127. In the story of the rich man Illīsa, however (Jā.i,348; DhA.i,372), the Elder Mahā-Moggallāna made little much. And in the story of Kākavaḷiya the Blessed One did so. The Elder Mahā-Kassapa, it seems. after spending seven days in attainment, stood at the house door of a man in poor circumstances called Kākavaḷiya in order to show favour to the poor. [404] His wife saw the Elder, and she poured into his bowl the unsalted sour gruel that she had cooked for her husband. The Elder took it and placed it in the Blessed One's hand. The Blessed One resolved to make it enough for the Greater Community of Bhikkhus. What was brought in a single bowl became enough for all. And on the seventh day Kākavaḷiya became a rich man.

128. And not only in the case of making little much, but whatever the possessor of supernormal power wishes, whether to make the sweet, unsweet, or the unsweet sweet, etc., is successful for him. For so it was that when the elder Mahā-Anula saw many bhikkhus sitting on the banks of the Gangā River [in Ceylon] eating plain rice, which was all that they had got after doing their alms around, he resolved 'Let Gangā River water be cream of ghee', and he gave a sign to the novices. They fetched it in their vessels and gave it to the Community of Bhikkhus. All of them ate their meal with sweet cream of ghee.

129. *With the divine eye*: remaining here and extending light, he sees the visible form of that Brahmā. And remaining here he also hears the sound of his speech and he understands his mind.

130. *He converts his mind according to his body*: he converts the mind to accord with the material body; taking the consciousness of the basic jhana, he mounts it upon the body, he makes

its going slow to coincide with that of the body; for the body's mode of going is slow.

131. *He arrives at blissful perception and light perception*: he arrives at, enters, makes contact with, reaches, the perception of bliss and perception of lightness that are conascent with the consciousness whose object is the basic jhana. And it is perception associated with equanimity that is called 'perception of bliss'; for equanimity is called 'bliss' since it is peaceful. And that same perception should be understood to be called 'perception of lightness' too because it is liberated from hindrances and from the things that oppose it beginning with applied thought. But when he arrives at that state, his physical body too becomes as light as a tuft of cotton. He goes to the Brahmā World thus with a visible body as light as a tuft of cotton wafted by the wind.

132. As he goes thus, if he wishes, he creates a path in space by means of the earth kasina and goes on foot. If he wishes, he resolves by means of the air kasina that there shall be air, and he goes by air like a tuft of cotton. Moreover the desire to go is the measure here. When there is the desire to go, one who has made his mental resolve in this way goes visibly, carried by the force of the resolution like an arrow shot by an archer. [405]

133. *He converts his body to accord with his mind*: he takes the body and mounts it on the mind. He makes its going swift to coincide with that of the mind; for the mind's mode of going is swift.

He arrives at blissful perception and light perception: he arrives at perception of bliss and perception of lightness that are conascent with the supernormal-power consciousness whose object is the material body. The rest should be understood in the way already described. But here there is only the going of consciousness[21].

---

21. '"*There is only the going of consciousness*": there is only a going that is the same as that of the mind. But how does the body, whose going [being that of matter] is slow, come to have the same going as the mind, which quickly passes? Its going is not the same in all respects; for in the case of converting the mind to comform with the body the mind, does not come to have the same going as the body in all respects. For it is not that the mind then occurs with the moment of a material state, which passess slowly, instead of passing with its own kind of moment, which is what establishes its individual essence. But rather the mind is called "converted to accord with the going of the body" as long as it goes on occuring in a continuity that conforms with body until the desired place is arrived at. This is because its passing occurs parralled with that of the body, whose going is slow, owing to the resolution "Let the mind be like this body". And likewise, it is while the body keeps occurring in suchwise that its arrival at the desired place comes about in only a few quick passes of the mind instead of passing slowly, as in those who have not developed the roads to power—and this mode of occurrence is due to the possession of the perception of

134. When it was asked 'As he goes with an invisible body thus, does he go at the moment of the resolution-consciousness's arising or at the moment of its presence or at the moment of its dissolution?', an elder replied 'He goes in all three moments'.—'But does he go himself, or does he send a creation?—'He does as he pleases. But here it is only the going himself that has been given [in the text].'

135. *Mind-made*: mind made because created by the mind in resolution. *Lacking no faculty*: this refers to the shape of the eye, ear, etc.; but there is no sensitivity in a created visible form.[22] *If the possessor of supernormal power walks up and down, the creation walks up and down there too*, etc., all refers to what a disciple creates; but what the Blessed One creates does whatever the Blessed One does, and it also does other things according to the Blessed One's pleasure.

136. When this possessor of supernormal power, while remaining here sees a visible object with the divine eye, hears a sound with the divine ear element, knows consciousness with the penetration of minds, he does not wield bodily power in doing that. And when, while remaining here, he stands with that Brahmā, converses, enters into communication, with that Brahmā, he does not wield bodily power, in doing that. And when he makes his resolve described in the way beginning 'though far, he resolves upon nearness,' he does not wield bodily power in doing that. And when he goes to the Brahmā World with a visible or an invisible body, he does not wield bodily power in doing that. But when he enters upon the process described in the way beginning 'He creates a visible form before that Brahmā, mind-made', then he wields bodily power in doing that. The rest, however, is said here for the purpose of showing the stage prior to the wielding of the bodily power. This, firstly, is (i) success by resolve (§45).

---

lightness, to say nothing of the resolve "Let this body be like this mind"—that the body is called "converted to accord with the going of the mind," not because it arrives at the desired place in a single consciousness moment. And when taken thus the simile "Just as a strong man might stretch out his bent arm, or bend his outstretched arm" (Vin. i, 5) can be taken literally. And this must be accepted in this way without reserve, otherwise there is conflict with the Suttas, the Adhidhamma and the Commentary, as well as contradiction of natural law (*dhammatā*). "Bhikkus, I see no other one thing that is so quickly transformed as the mind" (A. i, 10)—here it is material states that are referred to by the word "other" because they do not pass quickly. And in the Abhidhamma only matter is called prenascence conditions and only consciousness postnascence condition. And wherever states (*dhamma*) arise, there they dissolve. There is no transmigration to an adjacent location (*desantara-saṅkamana*), nor does the individual essence become other. For it is not possible to effect any alteration of the characteristics of dhammas by force of the roads to power. But it is possible to effect alteration of the mode in which they are present (*bhāva*.)' (Pm.397).

22. 'This should be regarded as implying that there is no sex or life faculty in it either'. (Pm. 398).

137. The difference between (ii) success as transformation, and (iii) success as the mind-made [body] is as follows (see §22 and §45-6).

(ii) One firstly who performs a transformation [406] should resolve upon whatever he chooses from among the things beginning with the appearance of a boy, described as follows: 'He abandons his normal appearance and shows the appear- 'ance of a boy or the appearance of *Nāga* (serpent), or the 'appearance of a *Suppaṇṇa* (winged demon), or the appear- 'ance of an *Asura* (demon), or the appearance of the Ruler '[of Gods] (Indra), or the appearance of some [other sensual 'sphere] deity, or the appearance of a Brahmā, or the appear- 'ance of the sea, or the appearance of a rock, or the appear- 'ance of a lion, or the appearance of a tiger, or the appearance 'of a leopard, or he shows an elephant, or he shows a horse. 'or he shows a chariot, or he shows a foot soldier, or he shows 'a manifold military array' (Ps. ii, 210).

138. And when he resolves he should emerge from the fourth jhana that is the basis for direct-knowledge and has one of the things beginning with the earth kasina as its object, and he should advert to his own appearance as a boy. After adverting and finishing the preliminary work he should attain again and emerge, and he should resolve thus 'Let me be a boy of such and such a type'. Simultaneously with the resolve consciousness he becomes the boy, just as Devadatta did (Vin. ii. 185; DhA. i, 139). This is the method in all instances. But *he shows an elephant,* etc., is said here with respect to showing an elephant, etc., externally. Herein, instead of resolving 'Let me be an elephant', he resolves 'Let there be an elephant'. The same method applies in the case of the horse and the rest.

This is success as transformation.

139. (iii) One who wants to make the mind-made [body] should emerge from the basic jhana and first advert to the body in the way already described, and then he should resolve 'Let it be hollow'. It becomes hollow. Then he adverts to another body inside it, and having done the preliminary work in the way already described, he resolves 'Let there be another body inside it.' Then he draws it out like a reed from its sheath, like a sword from its scabbard, like a snake from its slough. Hence it is said 'Here a bhikkhu creates from this 'body another body possessing visible form, mind-made, 'with all its limbs, lacking no faculty. Just as though a man 'pulled out a reed from its sheath and thought thus: "This 'is the sheath; this is the reed; the sheath is one; the reed is 'another, it was from the sheath that the reed was pulled 'out"' (Ps. ii, 210), and so on. And here, just as the reed, etc., are similar to the sheath, etc., so too the mind-made

visible form is similar to the possessor of supernormal power, and this simile is given in order to show that.

This is success as the mind-made [body].

The twelfth Chapter called 'The Description of the Supernormal Powers' in the Path of Purification composed for the purpose of gladdening good people.

CHAPTER XIII

DESCRIPTION OF DIRECT-KNOWLEDGE— CONCLUSION

(*Abhiññā-niddesa*)

[(2) THE DIVINE EAR ELEMENT].

1. [407] It is now the turn for the description of the Divine Ear Element. Herein, and also in the case of the remaining three kinds of direct-knowledge, the meaning of the passage beginning 'When his concentrated mind...' (D.i,79) should be understood in the way already stated (Ch. XII, §13f.); and in each case we shall only comment on what is different. [The text is as follows: 'He directs, he inclines, his mind to the 'divine ear element. With the divine ear element, which is 'purified and surpasses the human, he hears both kinds of 'sounds, the divine and the human, those that are far as well 'as near' (D.i,79).]

2. Herein, *with the divine ear element*: it is *divine* here because of its similarity to the divine; for deities have as the divine ear element the sensitivity that is produced by kamma consisting in good conduct and is unimpeded by bile, phlegm, blood, etc., and capable of receiving an object even though far off because it is liberated from imperfections. And this ear element consisting in knowledge, which is produced by the power of this bhikkhu's energy in development, is similar to that, so it is 'divine' because it is similar to the divine. Furthermore, it is 'divine' because it is obtained by means of divine abiding and because it has divine abiding as its support. And it is an 'ear element (*sota-dhātu*)' in the sense of hearing (*savana*) and in the sense of being a soulless [element]. Also it is an 'ear element' because it is like the ear element in its performance of an ear element's function. With that divine ear element.

Which is purified: which is quite pure through having no imperfection. *And surpasses the human*: which in the hearing of sounds surpasses, stands beyond, the human ear element by surpassing the human environment.

3. *He hears both kinds of sounds:* he hears the two kinds of sounds. What two? *The divine and the human*; the sounds of deities and of human beings, is what is meant. This should be understood as partially inclusive. *Those that are far as well as near*: what is meant is that he hears sounds that are far off, even in another world-sphere, and those that are

near, even the sounds of the creatures living in his own body. This should be understood as completely inclusive.

4. But how is this [divine ear element] aroused? The bhikkhu [408] should attain jhana as basis for direct-knowledge and emerge. Then with the consciousness belonging to the preliminary-work concentration[1] he should advert first to the gross sounds in the distance normally within range of hearing: the sound in the forest of lions, etc., or in the monastery the sound of a gong, the sound of a drum, the sound of a conch, the sound of recitation by novices and young bhikkhus reciting with full vigour, the sound of their ordinary talk such as 'What, venerable sir?', 'What, friend?', etc., the sound of birds, the sound of wind, the sound of footsteps, the fizzing sound of boiling water, the sound of palm leaves drying in the sun, the sound of ants, and so on. Beginning in this way with quite gross sounds, he should successively advert to more and more subtle sounds. He should give attention to the sound sign of the sounds in the eastern direction, in the western direction, in the northern direction, in southern direction, in the upper direction, in the lower direction, in the eastern intermediate direction, in the western intermediate direction, in the northern intermediate direction, and in the southern intermediate direction. He should give attention to the sound sign of gross and of subtle sounds.[2]

5. These sounds are evident even to his normal consciousness; but they are especially evident to his preliminary-work-concentration consciousness.[3] As he gives his attention to the sound sign in this way, [thinking] 'Now the divine ear element will arise', mind-door adverting arises making one of these sounds its object. When that has ceased, then either four or five implusions impel, the first three, or four, of which are of the sense sphere and are called Preliminary-work, Access, Conformity, and Change-of-lineage, while the fourth, or the fifth, is fine-material-sphere absorption consciousness belonging to the fourth jhana.

---

1. 'With the consciousness belonging to the particular concentration that constitutes the preliminary work. The meaning is: by means of consciousness concentrated with the momentary concentration that occurs in the form of the preliminary work for knowledge of the divine ear element. The ocassion of access for the divine ear element is called preliminary-work consciousness but; that as stated refers to multiple advertings' (Pm. 401).

2. 'The sound sign is the sound itself since it is the cause for the arising of the knowledge. Or the gross-subtle aspect acquired in the way stated is the sound sign' (Pm. 402).

3. 'This is momentary-concentration consciousness, which owing to the fact that the preliminary work contingent upon the sound has been performed, occurs in one who has attained the basic jhana and emerged for the purpose of arousing the divine ear element' (Pm. 402).

6. Herein, it is knowledge arisen together with the absorption consciousness that is called the divine ear element. After that [absorption has been reached, the divine ear element] becomes merged in that ear [of knowledge][4]. When consolidating it, he should extend it by delimiting a single finger-breadth thus 'I will hear sounds within this area', then two finger-breadths, four finger-breadths, eight finger-breadths, a span, a *ratana* (=24 finger-breadths), the interior of the room, the verandah, the building, the surrounding walk, the park belonging to the community, the alms-resort village, the district, and so on up to the [limit of the] world sphere, or even more. This is how he should extend it by delimited stages.

7. One who has reached direct-knowledge in this way hears also by means of direct knowledge without re-entering the basic jhana any sound that has come within the space touched by the basic jhana's object. And in hearing in this way, even if there is an uproar with sounds of conchs, drums, cymbals, etc., right up to the Brahmā World. [409] he can, if he wants to, still define each one thus 'This is the sound of conchs, this is the sound of drums'.

The explanation of the divine ear element is ended.

*

[(3) Penetration of Minds]

8. As to the explanation of knowledge of Penetration of Minds, [the text is as follows: 'He directs, he inclines, his 'mind to the knowledge of penetration of minds. He 'penetrates with his mind the minds of other beings, of 'other persons, and understands them thus: he understands '[the manner of] consciousness affected by greed as affected 'by greed, and understands [the manner of] consciousness 'unaffected by greed as unaffected by greed; he understands 'consciousness affected by hate as affected by hate, and 'consciousness unaffected by hate as unaffected by hate; he 'understands consciousness affected by delusion as affected 'by delusion, and consciousness unaffected by delusion as 'unaffected by delusion; he understands cramped consciousness as cramped, and distracted consciousness as distracted; 'he understands exalted consciousness as exalted, and unexalted consciousness as unexalted; he understands surpassed 'consciousness as surpassed and unsurpassed consciousness 'as unsurpassed; he understands concentrated consciousness

4. ' "*Become merged*": is amalgamated with the divine ear element. He is called an obtainer of divine-ear knowledge as soon as the absorption consciousness has arisen. The meaning is that there is now no further need of development for the purpose' (Pm. 403).

'as concentrated and unconcentrated consciousness as un-'concentrated; he understands the liberated [manner of] 'consciousness as liberated, and the unliberated [manner of] 'consciousness as unliberated' (D.i,79)]. Here, it goes all round (*pariyāti*), thus it is penetration (*pariya*); the meaning is that it delimits (*paricchindati*). The penetration of the heart (*cetaso pariyaṁ*) is 'penetration of minds (*cetopariya*)'. It is penetration of hearts and that is knowledge, thus it is knowledge of penetration of minds (*cetopariyañāṇa*). [He directs his consciousness] to that, is what is meant.

Of other beings: of the rest of beings, himself excluded. *Of other persons*: this has the same meaning as the last, the wording being varied to suit those susceptible of teaching [in another way], and for the sake of elegance of exposition. *With his mind the minds*: with his [manner of] consciousness the [manner of] consciousness of other beings. *Having penetrated* (*paricca*): having delimited all round. *He understands*: he understands them to be of various sorts beginning with that affected by greed.

9. But how is this knowledge to be aroused? That is successfully done through the divine eye, which constitutes its preliminary work. Therefore the bhikkhu should extend light, and he should seek out (*pariyesitabba*) another's [manner of] consciousness by keeping under observation with the divine eye the colour of the blood present with the matter of the physical heart as its support.[5] For when [a manner of] consciousness accompanied by joy is present, the blood is red like a banyan-fig fruit; when [a manner of] consciousness accompanied by grief is present, it is blackish like a rose-apple fruit; when [a manner of] consciousness accompanied by serenity is present, it is clear like sesamum oil. So he should seek out another's [manner of] consciousness by keeping under observation the colour of the blood in the physical heart thus 'This matter is originated by the joy faculty; this is originated by the grief faculty; this is originated by the equanimity faculty' and so consolidate his knowledge of penetration of hearts.

10. It is when it has been consolidated in this way that he can gradually get to understand not only all manner of sense-sphere consciousness but those of fine-material and immaterial consciousness as well by tracing one [manner of] consciousness from another without any more seeing the physical heart's matter. For this is said in the Commentary: 'When he wants to know another's [manner of] consciousness in the immaterial

5. 'The "matter of the heart" is not the heart-basis, but rather it is the heart as the piece of flesh described as resembling a lotus bud in shape outside and like a *kosātakī* fruit inside (Ch. VIII, §111). For the blood mentioned here is to be found with that as its support. But the heart-basis occurs with this blood as its support' (Pm. 403).

1024-P

moods, whose physical-heart matter can he observe? Whose material alteration [originated] by the faculties can he look at? No one's. The province of a possessor of supernormal power is [simply] this, namely, wherever the [manner of] consciousness he adverts to is, there he knows it according to these sixteen classes. But this explanation [by means of the physical heart] is for one who has not [yet] done any interpreting.[6]

11. As regards [*the manner of*] *consciousness affected by greed*, etc., the eight [manners of] consciousness accompanied by greed (see Table II, nos. (22)-(29)) [410] should be understood as [*the manner of*] *consciousness affected by greed.* The remaining profitable and indeterminate [manners of] consciousness in the four planes are *unaffected by greed.* The four, namely, the two consciousnesses accompanied by grief (nos. (30) and (31), and the two consciousnesses [accompanied respectively by] uncertainty (32) and agitation (33) are not included in this dyad, though some elders include them too. It is the two consciousnesses accompanied by grief that are called *consciousness affected by hate.* And all profitable and indeterminate consciousnesses in the four planes are *unaffected by hate.* The remaining ten kinds of unprofitable consciousnesses (nos. (22)-(29) and (32) and (33)) are not included in this dyad, though some elders include them too. *Affected by delusion......unaffected by delusion*: here only the two, namely, that accompanied by uncertainly and that accompanied by agitation, are affected by delusion *simplicitur* [without being accompanied by the other two unprofitable roots]. But [all] the twelve kinds of unprofitable consciousnesses (nos. (22)-(33)) can also be understood as [the manner of] consciousness affected by delusion since delusion is present in all kinds of unprofitable consciousnesses. The rest are *unaffected by delusion.*

12. *Cramped* is that attended by stiffness and torpor. *Distracted* is that attended by agitation. *Exalted* is that of the fine-material and immaterial spheres. *Unexalted* is the rest. *Surpassed* is all that in the three [mundane] planes. *Unsurpassed* is the supramundane. *Concentrated* is that attained to access and that attained to absorption. *Unconcentrated* is that not attained to either. *Liberated* is that attained to any [of the five kinds of] deliverance, that is to say, deliverance by substitution of opposites [through insight], by suppression [through concentration], by cutting off [by means of the path], by tranquillization [by means of fruition], and by renunciation [as nibbana] (see Ps.i,26 under 'abandoning').

6. 'Of one who has not done any interpreting (*abhinivesa*) reckoned as study for direct-knowledge' (Pm. 407). A rather special use of the word *abhinivesa*, perhaps more freely renderable here as 'practice'.

Unliberated is that which has not attained to any of the five kinds of liberation.

So the bhikkhu who has acquired the knowledge of penetration of hearts understands all these [manners of consciousness, namely, the manner of] consciousness affected by greed as affected by greed...[the unliberated manner of] consciousness as unliberated.

*

[(4) Recollection of Past Life]

13. As to the explanation of Knowledge of Recollection of Past Life, [the text is as follows: 'He directs, he inclines, his mind 'to the knowledge of recollection of past life. He recollects 'his manifold past life, that is to say, one birth, two births, 'three births, four births, five births, ten births, twenty 'births, thirty births, forty births, fifty births, a hun-'dred births, a thousand births, a hundred thousand 'births, many aeons of world contraction, many aeons 'of world expansion, many aeons of world contraction 'and expansion; there I was so named, of such a race, 'with such an appearance, such was my food, such my 'experience of pleasure and pain, such the end of my life span; 'and passing away from there, I reappeared elsewhere; and 'there too I was so named, of such a race, with such an appear-'ance, such was my food, such my experience of pleasure and 'pain, such the end of my life span; and passing away from 'there, I reappeared here; thus with its aspects and particu-'lars he recollects his manifold past life' (D.i,81). Herein,] *to the knowledge of recollection of past life* [means] for knowledge concerning recollection of past life. *Past life* is aggregates lived in the past in former births. 'Lived' [in that case means] lived out, undergone, arisen and ceased in one's own [subjective] continuity. Or alternatively, [past life] is mental objects lived [in the past in one's former births]; and 'lived' in that case means lived by living in one's [objective] resort, which has been cognized and delimited by one's own consciousness, or cognized by another's consciousness, too. In the case of recollection of those [past Enlightened Ones] who have broken the cycle, and so on,[7] these last are only accessible to Enlightened Ones. *Recollection of past life*: the mindfulness (memory) by means of which he recollects the past life is the recollection of past life. *Knowledge* is the knowledge associated with that mindfulness. [411] *To the knowledge of recollection of past life*: for the purpose of the knowledge of the recollection of past life in this way; for the attaining, for the reaching, of that knowledge, is what is meant.

7. For the term *chinna-vaṭumaka* (one who has broken the cycle of rebirths) as an epithet of former Buddhas see M. iii, 118.

14. *Manifold*: of many kinds; or that has occurred in many ways. Given in detail, is the meaning.[8] *Past life* is the continuity lived here and there, taking the immediately previous existence as the beginning [and working backwards]. *He recollects*: he recalls it, following it out by the succession of aggregates, or by death and rebirth-linking.

15. There are six kinds of people who recollect this past life. They are: other sectarians, ordinary disciples, Great Disciples, Chief Disciples, Pacceka Buddhas, and Buddhas.

16. Herein, other sectarians recollect only as far back as forty aeons, but not beyond that. Why? Because their understanding is weak for lack of Delimitation of Mind and Matter (see Ch.XVIII). Ordinary disciples recollect as far back as a hundred aeons and as far back as a thousand aeons because their understanding is strong. The eighty Great Disciples recollect as far back as a hundred thousand aeons. The two Chief Disciples recollect as far back as an incalculable age and a hundred thousand aeons. Pacceka Buddhas recollect as far back as two incalculable ages and a hundred thousand aeons. For such is the extent to which they can convey [their minds back respectively]. But there is no limit in the case of Buddhas.

17. Again, other sectarians only recollect the succession of aggregates; they are unable to recollect according [only] to death and rebirth-linking, letting go of the succession of aggregates. They are like the blind in that they are unable to descend upon any place they choose; they go as the blind do without letting go of their sticks. So they recollect without letting go of the succession of aggregates. Ordinary disciples both recollect by means of the succession of aggregates and trace by means of death and rebirth-linking. Likewise the eighty Great Disciples. But the Chief Disciples have nothing to do with the succession of aggregates. When they see the death of one person, they see the rebirth-linking, and again when they see the death of another, they see the rebirth-linking. So they go by tracing through death and rebirth-linking. Likewise Pacceka Buddhas.

18. Buddhas, however, have nothing to do either with succession of aggregates or with tracing through death and rebirth-linking; for whatever instance they choose in many millions of aeons, or more or less, is evident to them. So they go, and so they descend with the lion's descent[9] wherever they want, even skipping over many millions of aeons as though they

---

8. '*Saṁvaṇṇita*—given in detail': Pm. glosses by '*Vitthāritan ti attho*. Not in this meaning in P.T.S. Dict. see prologue verses to the 4 Nikāyas.

9. A commentarial account of the behaviour of lions will be found in the Manorathapūraṇī, commentary to A. Catukkanipāta 33. Pm. says '*Sīhokkamanavasena sīhātipatanavasena ñāṇagatiyā gacchati*' (p. 408).

were an elision in a text. And just as an arrow shot by such a master of archery expert in hair-splitting as Sarabhaṅga (see Jā.v,129) always hits the target without getting held up among trees, creepers, etc., on its way, and so neither gets held up nor misses, so too, since Buddhas go in this way their knowledge does not get held up in intermediate births [412] or miss; without getting held up or missing, it seizes any instance required.

19. Among these beings with recollection of past life, the sectarians' vision of past life seems like the light of a glow-worm, that of ordinary disciples like the light of a candle, that of the Great Disciples like the light of a torch, that of the Chief Disciples like the light of the Morning Star, that of Pacceka Buddhas like the light of the Moon, and that of Buddhas like the glorious Autumn Sun's disk with its thousand rays.

20. Other sectarians see past life as blind men go [tapping] with the point of a stick. Ordinary disciples do so as men who go on a log bridge. The Great Disciples do so as men who go on a footbridge. The Chief Disciples do so as men who go on a cart bridge. Pacceka Buddhas do so as men who go on a main foot-path. And Buddhas do so as men who go on a high road for carts.

21. In this connexion it is the disciples' recollection of past life that is intended. Hence it was said above ' "He recollects": he recollects it, following it out by the succession of aggregates, or by death and rebirth-linking' (§14).

22. So a bhikkhu who is a beginner and wants to recollect in this way should go into solitary retreat on return from his alms round after his meal. Then he should attain the four jhanas in succession and emerge from the fourth jhana as basis for direct-knowledge. He should then advert to his most recent act of sitting down [for this purpose], next, to the preparation of the seat, to the entry into the lodging, to the putting away of the bowl and [outer] robe, to the time of eating, to the time of returning from the village, to the time of wandering for alms in the village, to the time of entering the village, to the time of setting out from the monastery, to the time of paying homage at the shrine terrace and, the Enlightenment-Tree terrace, to the time of washing the bowl, to the time of picking up the bowl, to the things done from the time of picking up the bowl back to the mouth washing, to the things done in the early morning, to the things done in the middle watch, in the first watch. In this way he should advert to all the things done during the whole night and day in reverse order.

23. While this much, however, is evident even to his normal consciousness it is especially evident to his preliminary-work

consciousness. But if anything there is not evident, he should again attain the basic jhana, emerge and advert. By so doing it becomes as evident as when a lamp is lit. And so, in reverse order too, he should advert to the things done on the second day back, and on the third, fourth and fifth day, and in the ten days, and in the fortnight, and as far back as a year.

24. When by these means he adverts to ten years, twenty years, and so on as far back as his own rebirth-linking in this existence, [413] he should advert to the mentality-materiality occurring at the moment of death in the preceding existence; for a wise bhikkhu is able at the first attempt to remove[10] the rebirth-linking and make the mentality-materiality at the death moment his object.

25. But the mentality-materiality in the previous existence has ceased without remainder and another has arisen, and consequently that instance is, as it were, shut away in darkness, and it is hard for one of little understanding to see it. Still he should not give up the task, thinking 'I am unable to remove the rebirth-linking and make the mentality-materiality that occurred at the death moment my object'. On the contrary, he should again and again attain that same basic jhana, and each time he emerges he should advert to that instance.

26. Just as when a strong man is felling a big tree for the purpose of making the peak of a gable, but is unable to fell the big tree with an axe blade blunted by lopping the branches and foliage, still he does not give up the task; on the contrary, he goes to a smithy and has his axe sharpened, after which he returns and continues chopping the tree; and when the axe again gets blunt, he does as before and continues chopping it; and as he goes on chopping it in this way, the tree falls at length, because each time there is no need to chop again what has already been chopped and what has not yet been chopped gets chopped; so too, when he emerges from the basic jhana, instead of adverting to what he has already adverted to he should advert only to the rebirth-linking, and at length he removes the rebirth-linking and makes the mentality-materiality that occurred at the death moment his object. And this meaning should also be illustrated by means of the wood-cutter and the hair-cutter as well.

27. Herein, the knowledge that occurs making its object the period from the last sitting down for this purpose back to the rebirth-linking is not called knowledge of recollection of past life; but it is called preliminary-work-concentration knowledge; and some call it 'knowledge of the past (*atītaṁsa-ñāṇa*)', but that is inappropriate to the fine-material sphere.

---

10. '*Ugghatetvā*': see Ch. X, §6.; the word is obviously used here in the same sense.

However, when this bhikkhu has got back beyond the rebirth-linking, there arises in him mind-door adverting making its object the mentality-materiality that occurred at the death moment. And when that has ceased, then either four or five impulsions impel making that their object too. The first of these, called 'preliminary-work', etc., in the way already described (§5), are of the sense sphere. The last is a fine-material absorption consciousness of the fourth jhana. The knowledge that arises in him then together with that consciousness is what is called 'knowledge of recollection of past life'. It is with the mindfulness (memory) associated with that knowledge that he 'recollects his manifold past life, that is to say one birth, two births,...[414] thus with details and particulars he recollects his manifold past life' (D. i, 81).

28. Herein, *one birth* is the continuity of aggregates included in a single becoming starting with rebirth-linking and ending with death. So too with *two births*, and the rest.

But in the case of *many aeons of world contraction*, etc., it should be understood that the aeon of world contraction is an aeon of diminution and the aeon of world expansion is an

29. aeon of increase. Herein, what supersedes the contraction is included in the contraction since it is rooted in it; and so too what supersedes the expansion is included in the expansion. This being so, it includes what is stated thus, 'Bhikkhus, there, 'are four incalculables of the aeon. What four? The con- 'traction, what supersedes the contraction, the expansion. 'and what supersedes the expansion' (A. ii, 142 abbreviated)

30. Herein, there are three kinds of contraction: contraction due to water, contraction due to fire, and contraction due to air (see M. Sutta 28). Also there are three limits to the contraction: the Ābhassara (Streaming-radiance) Brahmā World, that of the Subhakiṇha (Refulgent-glory), and that of the Vehapphala (Great-fruit). When the aeon contracts owing to fire, all below the Ābhassara [Brahmā World] is burnt up by fire. When it contracts owing to water, it is all dissolved by water up to the Subhakiṇha [Brahmā World]. When it contracts owing to air, it is all demolished by wind up to the Vehapphala [Brahmā World].

31. In breadth it is always one of the Buddha fields that is destroyed. For the Buddha fields are of three kinds, that is, the field of birth, the field of authority, and the field of scope.

Herein, the field of birth is limited by the ten thousand world-spheres that quaked on the Perfect One's taking rebirth-linking, and so on. The field of authority is limited by the hundred thousand million world-spheres where the following safeguards (*paritta*) are efficacious, that is, the *Ratana Sutta* (Sn.p.39), the *Khandha Paritta* (Vin. ii, 109; A. ii, 72), the *Dhajagga Paritta* (S. i, 218), the *Āṭānāṭiya Paritta*

(D.iii,194), and the *Mora Paritta* (Jā.ii,33). The field of scope is boundless, immeasurable: 'As far as he wishes' (A.i,228) it is said. The Perfect One knows anything anywhere that he wishes. So one of these three Buddha fields, that is to say, the field of authority is destroyed. But when that is being destroyed, the field of birth also gets destroyed. And that happens simultaneously; and when it is reconstituted, that happens simultaneously (cf.MA.iv,114).

32. Now it should be understood how its destruction and reconstitution come about thus. On the occasion when the aeon is destroyed by fire, [415] first of all a great cloud heralding the aeon's destruction appears, and there is a great downpour all over the hundred thousand million world-spheres. People are delighted, and they bring out all their seeds and sow them. But when the sprouts have grown enough for an ox to graze, then not a drop of rain falls any more even when asses bray. Rain is withheld from then on. This is what the Blessed One referred to when he said 'Bhikkhus, an occasion 'comes when for many years, for many hundred years, for 'many thousand years, for many hundred thousand years, 'there is no rain' (A.iv,100). Beings that live by rain die and are reborn in the Brahmā World, and so are the deities that live on flowers and fruits.

33. When a long period has passed in this way, the water gives out here and there. Then in due course the fishes and turtles die and are reborn in the Brahmā World, and so are the beings in hell. Some say that the denizens of hell perish there with the appearance of the seventh sun (§41).

Now there is no rebirth in the Brahmā World without jhana; and some of them, being obsessed with the scarcity of food are unable to attain jhana, so how are they reborn there? By means of jhana obtained in the [sense-sphere] divine world.

34. For then the sense-sphere deities called World-marshall (*loka-byūha*) Deities come to know that at the end of a hundred thousand years there will be the emergence of an aeon, and they travel up and down the haunts of men, their heads bared, their hair dishevelled, with piteous faces, mopping their tears with their hands, clothed in dyed cloth, and wearing their dress in great disorder. They make this announcement, 'Good sirs, good sirs, at the end of a hundred thousand years from now there will be the emergence of an aeon. This world will be destroyed. Even the ocean will dry up. This great Earth, and Sineru King of Mountains, will be consumed and destroyed. The destruction of the earth will extend as far as the Brahmā World. Develop lovingkindness, good sirs, develop compassion, gladness, equanimity, good sirs, Care for your mothers, care for your fathers, honour the Elders of your clans'.

35. When human beings and earth deities hear their words, they mostly are filled with a sense of urgency. They become kind to each other and make merit with lovingkindness, etc., and so they are reborn in the divine world. There they eat divine food, and they do the preliminary work on the air kasina and acquire jhana. Others, however, are reborn in a [sense-sphere] divine world through kamma to be experienced in a future life. For there is no being traversing the round of rebirths who is destitute of kamma to be experienced in a future life. They too acquire jhana there in the same way. [416] All are eventually reborn in the Brahmā World by acquiring jhana in a [sense-sphere] divine world in this way.

36. However, at the end of a long period after the withholding of the rain, a second sun appears. And this is described by the Blessed One in the way beginning, 'Bhikkhus, there is the occasion when...' (A.iv,100), and the Sattasuriya Sutta should be given in full. Now when that has appeared, there is no more telling night from day. As one sun sets the other rises. The world is uninterruptedly scorched by the suns. But there is no sun deity in the aeon-destruction sun as there is in the ordinary sun.[11] Now when the ordinary sun is present, thunder clouds and mare's-tail vapours cross the skies. But when the aeon-destruction sun is present, the sky is as blank as the disk of a looking-glass and destitute of clouds and vapour. Beginning with the rivulets the water in all the rivers except the Five Great Rivers[12] dries up.

37. After that, at the end of a long period, a third sun appears. And when that has appeared, the Great Rivers dry up too.

38. After that, at the end of a long period, a fourth sun, appears. and when that has appeared, the Seven Great Lakes in Himalaya, the sources of the great rivers, dry up, that is to say, Sihapapāta, Haṁsapātana, [13] Kannamuṇḍaka, Rathakāra, Aṅotatta, Chaddanta, and Kunāla.

39. After that, at the end of a long period, a fifth sun appears. and when that has appeared, there eventually comes to be not enough water left in the great ocean to wet one finger joint.

40. After that, at the end of a long period, a sixth sun appears. And when that has appeared, the whole world-sphere becomes nothing but vapour, all its moisture being evaporated.

---

11. 'The "*ordinary sun*" is the Sun's divine palace that arose before the emergence of the aeon. But like the other sense-sphere deities at the time of the emergence of the aeon the Sun Deity too produces jhana and reappears in the Brahmā World. But the actual sun's disk becomes brighter and more fiery. Others say that it disappears and another appears in its place' (Pm. 412).

12. The five are the Ganges, Yamunā (Jumma), Sarabhu, Sarassatī, and Mahī (Pm. 412).

13. Haṁsapātana is another name for Maṇḍākinī (Pm.). For seven Great Lakes see A. iv, 101

And the hundred thousand million world-spheres are the same as this one.

41. After that, at the end of a long period, a seventh sun appears. And when that has appeared, the whole world-sphere together with the hundred thousand million other world-spheres catches fire. Even the summits of Sineru, a hundred leagues and more high, crumble and vanish into space. The conflagration mounts up and invades the realm of the Four Kings. When it has burnt up all the golden palaces, the jewelled palaces and the crystal palaces there, it invades the Realm of the Thirty-three. And so it goes right on up to the plane of the first jhana. When it has burnt three [lower] Brahmā Worlds, it stops there at the Ābhassara World. [417] As long as any formed thing (formation) the size of an atom still exists it does not go out; but it goes out when all formed things have been consumed. And like the flame that burns ghee and oil it leaves no ash.

42. The upper space is now all one with the lower space in a vast gloomy darkness. Then at the end of a long period a great cloud arises, and at first it rains gently, and then it rains with ever heavier deluges, like lotus stems, like rods, like pestles, like palm trunks, more and more. And so it pours down upon all the burnt areas in the hundred thousand million world-spheres till they disappear. Then the winds (forces) beneath and all around that water rise up and compact it and round it, like water drops on a lotus leaf. How do they compact the great mass of water? By making gaps; for the wind makes gaps in it here and there.

43. Being thus compressed by the air, compacted and reduced, it gradually subsides. As it sinks, the [lower] Brahmā World reappears in its place, and divine worlds reappear in the places of the four upper divine worlds of the sensual sphere.[14] But when it has sunk to the former earth's level, strong winds (forces) arise and they stop it and hold it stationary, like the water in a water pot when the outlet is plugged. As the fresh water gets used up, the essential humus makes its appearance on it. That possesses colour, smell and taste, like the surface film on milk rice when it dries up.

44. Then the beings that were reborn first in the Brahmā World of Streaming Radiance (Ābhassara) fall from there with the exhaustion of their life span, or when their merit is exhausted, and they reappear here. They are self-luminous and wander in the sky. On eating the essential humus, as is told in the Aggañña Sutta (D.iii,85), they are overcome by craving, and

14. 'At the place where the Yāma Deities are established. The places where the Cātumahārājika and Tāvatimsa heavens become established do not reappear at first because they are connected with the earth' (Pm. 412).

they busy themselves in making lumps of it to eat. Then their self-luminosity vanishes, and it is dark. They are frightened when they see the darkness.

45. Then in order to remove their fears and give them courage, the sun's disk appears full fifty leagues across. They are delighted to see it, thinking 'We have light', and they say 'It has appeared in order to allay our fears and give us courage (*sūrabhāva*), so let it be called "Sun (*suriya*)"'. So they give it the name 'Sun (*suriya*)'. Now when the sun has given light for a day, it sets. Then they are frightened again, thinking 'We have lost the light we had', and they think 'How good if we had another light!'. [418]

46. As if knowing their thought, the moon's disk appears, forty-nine leagues across. On seeing it they are still more delighted, and they say 'It has appeared, seeming as if it knew our desire (*chanda*), so let it be called "Moon (*canda*)"'. So they give it the name 'Moon (*canda*)'.

47. After the appearance of the moon and sun in this way, the stars appear in their constellations. After that, night and day are made known, and, in due course, the month and half month, the season, and the year.

48. On the day the moon and sun appear, the mountains of Sineru, of the World-sphere and of Himalaya appear too. And they appear on the full-moon day of the month of Phagguna (March), neither before nor after. How? Just as, when millet is cooking and bubbles arise, then simultaneously, some parts are domes, some hollow, and some flat, so too, there are mountains in the domed places, seas in the hollow places, and continents (islands) in the flat places.

49. Then as these beings make use of the essential humus, gradually some become handsome and some ugly. The handsome ones despise the ugly ones. Owing to their contempt the essential humus vanishes and an outgrowth from the soil appears. Then that vanishes in the same way and the *badālatā* creeper appears. That too vanishes in the same way and the rice without red powder or husk that ripens without tilling appears, a clean sweet-smelling rice fruit.

50. Then vessels appear. They put the rice into the vessels, which they put on the tops of stones. A flame appears spontaneously and cooks it. The cooked rice resembles jasmine flowers. It has no need of sauces and curries, since it has whatever flavour they want to taste.

51. As soon as they eat this gross food, urine and excrement appear in them. Then wound orifices break open in them to let these things out. The male sex appears in the male, and the female sex in the female. Then the females brood over the males, and the males over the females for a long time. Owing

to this long period of brooding the fever of sense desires arises. After that they practise sexual intercourse.

52. [419] For their [overt] practice of evil they are censured and punished by the wise, and so they build houses for the purpose of concealing the evil. When they live in houses, they eventually fall in with the views of the more lazy, and they make stores of food. As soon as they do that, the rice becomes enclosed in red powder and husks and no longer grows again of itself in the place where it was reaped. They meet together and bemoan the fact, 'Evil has surely made its 'appearance among beings; for formerly we were mind-'made...' (D.iii,90), and all this should be given in full in the way described in the Aggañña Sutta.

53. After that, they set up boundaries. Then some being takes a portion given to another. After he has been twice rebuked, at the third time they come to blows with fists, clods, sticks, and so on. When stealing, censuring, lying, resorting to sticks, etc., have appeared in this way, they meet together, thinking 'Suppose we elect a being who would reprove those who 'should be reproved, censure those who should be censured, 'and banish those who should be banished, and suppose we 'keep him supplied with a portion of the rice?' (D.iii,92).

54. When beings had come to an agreement in this way in this aeon, firstly this Blessed One himself, who was then the Bodhisatta (Being Due to be Enlightened), was the handsomest, the most comely, the most honourable, and was clever and capable of exercising the effort of restraint. They approached him, asked him, and elected him. Since he was recognized (*sammata*) by the majority (*mahā-jana*) he was called Mahā-Sammata. Since he was lord of the fields (*khetta*) he was called Khattiya (warrior noble). Since he promoted others' good (*rañjeti*) righteously and equitably he was a king (*rājā*). This is how he came to be known by these names. For the Bodhisatta himself is the first man concerned in any wonderful innovation in the world. So after the Khattiya circle had been established by making the Bodhisatta the first in this way, the Brahmans and the other castes were founded in due succession.

55. Herein, the period from the time of the great cloud heralding the aeon's destruction up till the ceasing of the flames constitutes one incalculable, and that is called the 'contraction'. That from the ceasing of the flames of the aeon destruction up till the great cloud of rehabilitation, which rains down upon the hundred thousand million world-spheres, constitutes the second incalculable, and that is called 'what supersedes the contraction'. That from the time of the great cloud of rehabilitation up till the appearance of the moon and sun constitutes the third incalculable, and that is called the

'expansion'. That from the appearance of the moon and sun up till [420] the reappearance of the great cloud of the aeon destruction is the fourth incalculable, and that is called 'what supersedes the expansion'. These four incalculables make up one great aeon. This, firstly, is how the destruction by fire and reconstitution should be understood.

56. The occasion when the aeon is destroyed by water should be treated in the way already described beginning 'First of all a great cloud heralding the aeon's destruction appears...' (§32).

57. There is this difference, however. While in the former case a second sun appeared, in this case a great cloud of caustic waters[15] appears. At first it rains very gently, but it goes on to rain with gradually greater deluges, pouring down upon the hundred thousand million world-spheres. As soon as they are touched by the caustic waters the earth, the mountains, etc., melt away, and the waters are supported all round by winds. The waters take possession from the earth up to the plane of the second jhana. When they have dissolved away the three Brahmā Worlds there, they stop at the Subhakiṇha World. As long as any formed thing the size of an atom exists they do not subside; but they suddenly subside and vanish away when all formed things have been overwhelmed by them. All beginning with 'The upper space is all one with the lower space in a vast gloomy darkness...' (§41) is as already described, except that here the world begins its reappearance with the Ābhassara Brahmā World. And beings falling from the Subhakiṇha Brahmā World are reborn in the places beginning Ābhassara Brahmā World.

58. Herein, the period from the time of the great cloud heralding the aeon's destruction up till the ceasing of the aeon-destroying waters constitutes one incalculable. That from the ceasing of the waters up till the great cloud of rehabilitation constitutes the second incalculable. That from the great cloud of rehabilitation...These four incalculables make up one great aeon. This is how the destruction by water and reconstitution should be understood.

59. The occasion when the aeon is destroyed by air should be treated in the way already described beginning with 'first of all a great cloud heralding the aeon's destruction appears ...' (§32).

60. There is this difference, however. While in the first case there was a second sun, here a wind arises in order to destroy the aeon. First of all it lifts up the coarse flue, then the fine flue, then the fine sand, coarse sand, gravel, stones, etc.,

---

15. '*Khārudaka*—caustic waters': the name given to the waters on which the world-spheres rest (see MA.iv,178).

[421] until it lifts up stones as big as a catafalque,[16] and great trees standing in uneven places. They are swept from the earth up into the sky, and instead of falling down again they are broken to bits there and cease to exist.

61. Then eventually wind arises from underneath the great earth and overturns the earth, flinging it into space. The earth splits into fragments measuring a hundred leagues, measuring two, three, four, five hundred leagues, and they are hurled into space too, and there they are broken to bits and cease to exist. The World-sphere Mountains, and Mount Sineru are wrenched up and cast into space, where they crash against each other till they are broken to bits and disappear. In this way it destroys the divine palaces built on the earth [of Mount Sineru] and those built in space, it destroys the six sensual-sphere divine worlds, and it destroys the hundred thousand million world-spheres. Then world-sphere collides with world-sphere, Himalaya Mountain with Himalaya Mountain, Sineru with Sineru, till they are broken to bits and disappear.

62. The wind takes possession from the earth up to the plane of the third jhana. There, after destroying three Brahmā Worlds, it stops at the Vehapphala World. When it has destroyed all formed things in this way, it spends itself too. Then all happens as already described in the way beginning. 'The upper space is all one with the lower space in a vast gloomy darkness...' (§41). But here the world begins its reappearance with the Subhakiṇha Brahmā World. And beings falling from the Vehapphala Brahmā World are reborn in the places beginning with the Subhakiṇha Brahmā World.

63. Herein, the period from the time of the great cloud heralding the aeon's destruction up till the ceasing of the aeon-destroying wind is one incalculable. That from the ceasing of the wind up till the great cloud of rehabilitation is the second incalculable ... These four incalculables make up one great aeon. This is how the destruction by wind and reconstitution should be understood.

64. What is the reason for the world's destruction in this way? The [three] roots of the unprofitable are the reasons. When any one of the roots of the unprofitable becomes conspicuous, the world is destroyed accordingly. When greed is more conspicuous, it is destroyed by fire. When hate is more conspicuous, it is destroyed by water—though some say that it is destroyed by fire when hate is more conspicuous, and by water when greed is more conspicuous—. And when delusion is more conspicuous, it is destroyed by wind.

16. '*Kūṭāgāra*': see Ch. XII, n. 4; here this seems the most likely of the various meanings of the word.

65. Destroyed as it is in this way, it is destroyed for seven turns in succession by fire and the eighth turn by water; then again seven turns by fire and the eighth by water, and when it has been seven times destroyed by water at each eighth [422] turn, it is again destroyed for seven turns by fire. Sixty-three aeons pass in this way. And now the air takes the opportunity to usurp the water's turn for destruction, and in destroying the world it demolishes the Subhakiṇha Brahmā World where the life span is the full sixty-four aeons.

66. Now when a bhikkhu capable of recollecting aeons is recollecting his former life, then of such aeons as these he recollects *many aeons of world contraction, many aeons of world expansion, many aeons of world contraction and expansion.* How? In the way beginning *There I was* ...

Herein *There I was*: in that aeon of contraction I was in that kind of becoming or generation or destiny or station of consciousness or abode of beings or order of beings.

67. *So named*: [such forenames as] Tissa, say, or Phussa. *Of such a race*: [such family names as] Kaccāna, say, or Kassapa. This is said of the recollection of his own name and race (surname) in his past existence. But if he wants to recollect his own appearance at that time, or whether his life was a rough or refined one, or whether pleasure or pain was prevalent, or whether his life span was short or long, he recollects that too. Hence he said *with such an appearance ...such the end of my life span.*

68. Here *with such an appearance* means fair or dark. *Such was my food*: with white rice and meat dishes as food or with windfall fruits as food. *Such my experience of pleasure and pain*: with varied experience of bodily and mental pleasure and pain classed as worldly and unworldly, and so on. *Such the end of my life span*: with such a life span of a century or life span of eighty-four thousand aeons.

69. *And passing away from there, I reappeared elsewhere*: having passed away from that becoming, generation, destiny, station of consciousness, abode of beings or order of beings, I again appeared in that other becoming, generation, destiny, station of consciousness, abode of beings or order of beings. *And there too I was*: then again I was there in that becoming, generation, destiny, station of consciousness, abode of beings or order of beings. *So named*, etc., are as already stated.

70. Furthermore, the words *there I was* refer to the recollection of one who has cast back retrospectively as far as he wishes, and the words *and passing away from there* refer to his reviewing after turning forward again; consequently the words *I appeared elsewhere* can be understood to be said with reference to the place of his reappearance next before his appearance here, which is referred to by the words *I appeared here.* But

the words *there too I was,* etc., [423] are said in order to show the recollection of his name, race, etc., there in the place of his reappearance next before this appearance. *And passing away from there, I reappeared here*: having passed away from that next place of reappearance, I was reborn here in this Khattiya clan or Brahman clan.

71. *Thus*: so *With its aspects and particulars*: with its particulars consisting in name and race; with its aspects consisting in appearance, and so on. For it is by means of name and race that a being is particularized as, say Tissa Kassapa: but his distinctive personality is made known by means of appearance, etc., as dark or fair. So the name and race are the particulars, while the others are the aspects. *He recollects his manifold past life*: the meaning of this is clear.

The explanation of the knowledge of recollection of past life is ended.

[(5) The Divine Eye—Knowledge of Passing Away and Reappearance of Beings]

72. As to the explanation of the knowledge of Passing Away and Reappearance of Beings, [here is the text: 'He directs, 'he inclines, his mind to the knowledge of the passing away 'and reappearance of beings. With the divine eye, which 'is purified and surpasses the human, he sees beings passing 'away and reappearing, inferior and superior, fair and ugly, 'happy or unhappy in their destiny; he understands beings as 'faring according to their deeds: these worthy beings who 'are ill-conducted in body, speech and mind, revilers of Noble 'Ones, wrong in their views, acquirers of kamma due to 'wrong views, have, on the break up of the body, after death, 'appeared in a state of loss, in an unhappy destiny, in perdi-'tion, in hell; but these worthy beings, who are well conduct-'ed in body, speech and mind, not revilers of Noble Ones, 'right in their views, acquirers of kamma due to right view, 'have, on the break up of the body, after death, appeared in 'a happy destiny, in the heavenly world: thus with the divine 'eye, which is purified and surpasses the human, he sees beings 'passing away and reappearing, inferior and superior, fair and 'ugly, happy or unhappy in their destiny; he understands 'beings as faring according to their deeds' (D.i,82). Herein,] '*to the knowledge of the passing away and reappearance*: *cutūpa-'pātañāṇāya=cutiyā ca upapāte ca ñāṇāya* (resolution of 'compound); [the meaning is,] for the kind of knowledge 'by means of which beings' passing away and reappearance is 'known; for knowledge of the divine eye, is what is meant. '*He directs, he inclines, his mind*: he both directs and inclines 'preliminary-work consciousness. *He* is the bhikkhu who does 'the directing of his mind.

73. But as regards *with the divine eye*, etc., it is *divine* because of its similarity to the divine; for deities have as divine eye the sensitivity that is produced by kamma consisting in good conduct and is unimpeded by bile, phlegm, blood, etc., and capable of receiving an object even though far off because it is liberated from imperfections. And this eye, consisting in knowledge, which is produced by the power of this bhikkhu's energy in development is similar to that, so it is 'divine' because it is similar to the divine. Also it is 'divine' because it is obtained by means of divine abiding, and because it has divine abiding as its support. And it is 'divine' because it greatly illuminates by discerning light. And it is 'divine' because it has a great range through seeing visible objects that are behind walls, and so on. All that should be understood according to the science of grammar. It is an *eye* in the sense of seeing. Also it is an *eye* since it is like an eye in its performance of an eye's function. It is *purified* since it is a cause of purification of view, owing to seeing passing away and reappearance.

74. One who sees only passing away and not reappearance assumes the annihilation view; and one who sees only reappearance and not passing away assumes the view that a new being appears. But since one who sees both outstrips that twofold [false] view, that vision of his is therefore a cause for Purification of View. And the Buddhas' sons see both of these. Hence it was said above [424] 'It is "purified" since it is a cause of purification of view, owing to seeing passing away and reappearance'.

75. *It surpasses the human* in the seeing of visible objects by surpassing the human environment. Or it can be understood that it *surpasses the human* in surpassing the human fleshly eye. With that *divine eye, which is purified and superhuman, he sees beings*, he watches beings as men do with the fleshly eye.

76. *Passing away and reappearing*: he cannot see them with the divine eye actually at the death moment or at the moment of reappearance.[17] But it is those who, being on the verge of

---

17. '"*He cannot see them with the divine eye*"—with the knowledge of the divine eye—because of the extreme brevity and extreme subtlety of the material moment in anyone. Moreover it is present materiality that is the object of the divine eye, and that is by prenascence condition. And there is no occurrence of exalted consciousness without adverting and preliminary work. Nor is materiality that is only arising able to serve as object condition, nor that which is dissolving. Therefore it is rightly said that he cannot see with the divine eye materiality at the moments of death and reappearance. If the knowledge of the divine eye has only materiality as its object, then why is it said that he "sees beings"? It is said in this way since it is mainly concerned with instances of materiality in a being's continuity, or because that materiality is a reason for apprehending beings. Some say that this is said according to conventional usage' (Pm. 417).

death, will die now that are intended as 'passing away' and those who have taken rebirth-linking and have just reappeared that are intended by 'reappearing'. What is pointed out is that he sees them as such passing away and reappearing.

77. *Inferior*: despised, disdained, looked down upon, scorned, on account of birth, clan, wealth, etc., because of reaping the outcome of delusion. *Superior*: the opposite of that because of reaping the outcome of non-delusion. *Fair*: having a desirable, agreeable, pleasing appearance because of reaping the outcome of non-hate. *Ugly*: having undesirable, disagreeable, unpleasing appearance because of reaping the outcome of hate; unsightly, ill-favoured, is the meaning. *Happy* in their destiny: gone to a happy destiny; or rich, very wealthy, because of reaping the outcome of non-greed. *Unhappy in their destiny*: gone to an unhappy destiny; or poor with little food and drink because of reaping the outcome of greed.

78. *Faring according to their deeds*: moving on in accordance with whatever deeds (kamma) may have been accumulated. Herein, the function of the divine eye is described by the first expressions beginning with 'passing away'. But the function of knowledge of faring according to deeds is described by this last expression.

79. The order in which that knowledge arises is this. Here a bhikkhu extends light downwards in the direction of hell, and he sees beings in hell undergoing great suffering. That vision is only the divine eye's function. He gives it attention in this way 'After doing what deeds do these beings undergo this suffering?'. Then knowledge that has those deeds as its object arises in him in this way 'It was after doing this'. Likewise he extends light upwards in the direction of the [sensual-sphere] divine world, and he sees beings in the Nandana Grove, the Missaka Grove, the Phārusaka Grove, etc., enjoying great good fortune. That vision also is only the divine eyes' function. He gives attention to it in this way 'After doing what deeds do these beings enjoy this good fortune?'. Then knowledge that has those deeds as its object arises in him in this way 'It was after doing this'. This is what is called Knowledge of Faring According to Deeds.

80. There is no special preliminary work for this. And as in this case, so too in the case of Knowledge of the Future; for these have the divine eye as their basis and their success is dependent on that of the divine eye. [425]

81. As to *ill-conducted in body*, etc., it is bad conduct *duṭṭhu caritaṁ*), or it is corrupted conduct (*duṭṭhaṁ caritaṁ*) because it is rotten with defilements, thus it is ill-conduct (*duccarita*). The ill-conduct comes about by means of the body, or the ill-conduct has arisen due to the body, thus it is ill-conduct

in body. So too with the rest. *Ill-conducted* is endowed with ill-conduct.

82. *Revilers of Noble Ones*: being desirous of harm for Noble Ones consisting of Buddhas, Pacceka Buddhas, and disciples, and also of householders who are Stream Enterers, they revile them with the worst accusations or with denial of their special qualities (see Ud. 44 and M. Sutta 12); they abuse and upbraid them, is what is meant.

83. Herein, it should be understood that when they say. 'They have no asceticism, they are not ascetics', they revile them with the worst accusation; and when they say 'They have no jhana or liberation or path or fruition, etc.', they revile them with denial of their special qualities. And whether done knowingly or unknowingly it is in either case reviling of Noble Ones; it is weightly kamma resembling that of immediate result, and it is an obstacle both to heaven and to the path. But it is remediable.

84. The following story should be understood in order to make this clear. An elder and a young bhikkhu, it seems, wandered for alms in a certain village. At the first house they got only a spoonful of hot gruel. The elder's stomach was paining him with wind. He thought 'This gruel is good for me; I shall drink it before it gets cold'. People brought a wooden stool to the doorstep, and he sat down and drank it. The other was disgusted and remarked 'The old man has let his hunger get the better of him and has done what he should be ashamed to do'. The Elder wandered for alms, and on return to the monastery he asked the young bhikkhu 'Have you any footing in this Dispensation, friend?'—'Yes, venerable sir, I am a Stream Enterer.'—'Then, friend, do not try for the higher paths; one whose cankers are destroyed has been reviled by you.' The young bhikkhu asked for the Elder's forgiveness and was thereby restored to his former state.

85. So one who reviles a Noble One, even if he is one himself, should go to him; if he himself is senior, [426] he should sit down in the squatting position and get his forgiveness in this way 'I have said such and such to the venerable one; may he forgive me'. If he himself is junior, he should pay homage, and sitting in the squatting position and holding out his hands palms together, he should get his forgiveness in this way 'I have said such and such to you, venerable sir; forgive me'. If the other has gone away, he should get his forgiveness either by going to him himself or by sending someone such as a co-resident.

86. 'If he can neither go nor send, he should go to the bhikkhus who live in that monastery, and, sitting down in the squatting position if they are junior, or acting in the way already described if they are senior, he should get forgiveness by saying

'Venerable sirs, I have said such and such to the venerable one named so and so; may that venerable one forgive me'. And this should also be done when he fails to get forgiveness in his presence.

87. If it is a bhikkhu who wanders alone and it cannot be discovered where he is living or where he has gone, he should go to a wise bhikkhu and say 'Venerable sir, I have said such and such to the venerable one named so and so. When I remember it, I am remorseful. What shall I do?'. He should be told 'Think no more about it; the Elder forgives you. Set your mind at rest'. Then he should extend his hands palms together in the direction taken by the Noble One and say 'Forgive me'.

88. If the Noble One has attained the final nibbana, he should go to the place where the bed is, on which he attained the final nibbana, and should go as far as the charnel ground to ask forgiveness. When this has been done, there is no obstruction either to heaven or to the path. He becomes as he was before.

89. *Wrong in their views*: having distorted vision. *Acquirers of kamma due to wrong view*: those who have kamma of the various kinds acquired through wrong view, and also those who incite others to bodily kamma, etc., rooted in wrong view. And here, though reviling of Noble Ones has already been included by the mention of verbal misconduct, and though wrong view has already been included by the mention of mental misconduct, it may be understood, nevertheless, that the two are mentioned again in order to emphasize their great
90. reprehensibility. Reviling Noble Ones is greatly reprehensible because of its resemblance to kamma with immediate result. For this is said 'Sāriputta, just as a bhikkhu possessing virtuous conduct, concentration and understanding could here and now attain final knowledge, so it is in this case, I say; if he does not abandon such talk and such thoughts and renounce such views, he will find himself in hell as surely as if he had been carried off and put there' (M.i, 71).[18] [427]. And there is nothing more reprehensible than wrong view, according as it is said 'Bhikkhus, I do not see any one thing so reprehensible as wrong view' (A. i, 33).

91. *On the break up of the body* on the giving up of the clung-to aggregates. *After death*: in the taking up of the aggregates generated next after that. Or alternatively, *on the break up of the body* is on the interruption of the life faculty, and *after death* is beyond the death consciousness.

92. *A state of loss* and the rest are all only synonyms for hell. Hell is a *state of loss* (*apāya*) because it is removed (*apeta*)

18. In rendering *yathābhataṁ* here in this very idiomatic passage MA. ii, 32 has been consulted.

from the reason (*aya*)[19] known as merit, which is the cause of [attaining] heaven and deliverance; or because of the absence (*abhāva*) of any origin (*āya*) of pleasures. The destiny (*gati*= going), the refuge, of suffering (*dukkha*) is the *unhappy destiny* (*duggati*); or the destiny (*gati*) produced by kamma that is corrupted (*duṭṭha*) by much hate (*dosa*) is an *unhappy destiny* (*duggati*). Those who commit wrongdoings, being separated out (*vivasa*), fall (*nipatanti*) in here, thus it is *perdition* (*vinipāta*); or alternatively, when they are destroyed (*vinassanto*), they fall (*patanti*) in here, all their limbs being broken up, thus it is *perdition* (*vinipāta*). There is no reason (*aya*) reckoned as satisfying here, thus it is *hell* (*niraya*).

93. Or alternatively, the animal generation is indicated by the mention of *states of loss*; for the animal generation is a state of loss because it is removed from the happy destiny; but it is not an unhappy destiny because it allows the existence of Royal *Nāgas* (serpents), who are greatly honoured. The Realm of Ghosts is indicated by the mention of the *unhappy destiny*; for that is both a state of loss and an unhappy destiny because it is removed from the happy destiny and because it is the destiny of suffering; but it is not perdition because it is not a state of perdition such as that of the Asura Demons. The race of Asura Demons is indicated by the mention of *perdition*; for that is both a state of loss and an unhappy destiny in the way already described, and it is called 'perdition' (deprivation) from all opportunities. Hell itself in the various aspects of Avīci, etc., is indicated by the mention of *hell*.

Have...appeared: have gone to; have been reborn there, is the intention.

94. The bright side should be understood in the opposite way. But there is this difference. Here the mention of the *happy destiny* includes the human destiny, and only the divine destiny is included by the mention of *heavenly*. Herein, a good (sundara) destiny (*gati*) is a *happy destiny* (*sugati*). It is the very highest (*suṭṭhu aggo*) in such things as the objective fields comprising visible objects, etc., thus it is *heavenly* (*sagga*). All that is a *world* (*loka*) in the sense of crumbling and disintegrating (*lujjana-palujjana*). This is the word meaning.

Thus with the divine eye, etc., is all a summing-up phrase; the meaning here in brief is this: so with the divine eye...he sees.

95. Now a clansman who is a beginner and wants to see in this way should make sure that the jhana, which has a kasina as its object and is the basis for direct-knowledge, is made in all ways susceptible of his guidance. Then one of these three kasinas, that is to say, the fire kasina, white kasina, [428] or light kasina, should be brought to the neighbourhood [of

19. For the word *aya* see Ch. XVI, §. 17.

the arising of divine-eye knowledge]. He should make this access jhana his resort and stop there to extend [the kasina]; the intention is that absorption should not be aroused here; for if he does induce absorption, then [the kasina] will become the support for basic jhana, but not for the [direct-knowledge] preliminary work. The light kasina is the best of the three. So either that, or one of the others, should be worked up in the way stated in the Description of the Kasinas, and it should be stopped at the level of access and extended there. And the method for extending it should be understood in the way already described there too. It is only what is visible within the area to which the kasina has been extended that can be seen.

96. However, while he is seeing what is visible, the turn of the preliminary work runs out. Thereupon the light disappears. When that has disappeared, he no longer sees what is visible (Cf. M. iii, 158). Then he should again and again attain the basic jhana, emerge and pervade with light. In this way the light gradually gets consolidated till at length it remains in whatever sized area has been delimited by him in this way 'Let there be light here'. Even if he sits watching all day he can still see visible objects.

97. And here there is the simile of the man who set out on a journey by night with a grass torch. Someone set out in a journey by night, it seems, with a grass torch. His torch stopped flaming. Then the even and uneven places were no more evident to him. He stubbed the torch on the ground and it again blazed up. In doing so it gave more light than before. As it went on dying out and flaring up again, eventually the sun rose. When the sun had risen, he thought 'There is no further need of the torch', and he threw it away and went on by daylight.

98. Herein, the kasina light at the time of the preliminary work is like the light of the torch. His no more seeing what is visible when the light has disappeared owing to the turn of the preliminary work running out while he is seeing what is visible is like the man's not seeing the even and uneven places owing to the torch's stopping flaming. His repeated attaining is like the stubbing of the torch. His more powerful pervasion with light by repeating the preliminary work is like the torch's giving more light than before. The strong light's remaining in as large an area as he delimits is like the sun's rising. His seeing even during a whole day what is visible in the strong light after throwing the limited light away is like the man's going on by day after throwing the torch away.

99. Herein, when visible objects that are not within the focus of the bhikkhu's fleshly eye come into the focus of his eye of knowledge—that is to say, visible objects that are inside his

belly, belonging to the heart basis, belonging to what is below the earth's surface, behind walls, mountains and enclosures, or in another world-sphere—[429] and are as if seen with the fleshly eye, then it should be understood that the divine eye has arisen. And only that is capable of seeing the visible objects here, not the preliminary-work consciousnesses.

100. But this is an obstacle for an ordinary man. Why? Because wherever he determines 'Let there be light', it becomes all light, even after penetrating through earth, sea and mountains. Then fear arises in him when he sees the fearful forms of spirits, ogres, etc., there owing to which his mind is distracted and he loses his jhana. So he needs to be careful in seeing what is visible (see M.iii, 158).

101. Here is the order of arising of the divine eye: when mind-door adverting, which has made its object that visible datum of the kind already described, has arisen and ceased, then, making that same visible datum the object, all should be understood in the way already described beginning 'Either four or five impulsions impel ... ' (§5). Here also the [three of four] prior consciousnesses are of the sense sphere and have applied and sustained thought. The last of these consciousnesses, which accomplishes the aim, is of the fine-material sphere belonging to the fourth jhana. Knowledge conascent with that is called 'Knowledge of the Passing Away and Reappearance of Beings' and 'Knowledge of the Divine Eye'.

The explanation of knowledge of passing away and reappearance is ended.

*

[General]

The Helper, Knower of five aggregates,
102. Had these five Direct-knowledges to tell;
When they are known, there are concerning them
These general matters to be known as well.

103. Among these, the divine eye called Knowledge of Passing Away and Reappearance, has two accessary kinds of knowledge, that is to say, Knowledge of the Future and Knowledge of Faring According to Deeds. So these two along with the five beginning with the Kinds of Supernormal Power make seven kinds of direct-knowledge given here.

104. Now in order to avoid confusion about the classification of their objects,

The sage has told four object Triads
By means of which one can infer
Just how these seven different kinds
Of Direct-knowledges occur.

105. Here is the explanation. Four Object Triads have been told by the Greatest of the Sages. What four? The Limited-

object Triad, the Path-object Triad, the Past-object Triad, and the Internal-object Triad.[20]

106. (I) Herein, *Knowledge of Supernormal Power* [430] occurs with respect to seven kinds of object, that is to say, as having a limited or exalted, a past, future or present, and an internal or external, object. How?

When he wants to go with an invisible body after making the body dependent on the mind, and he converts the body to accord with the mind (Ch. XII, §119), and he sets it, mounts it, on the exalted consciousness, then taking it that the [word in the] accusative case is the proper object, it *has a limited*[21] *object* because its object is the material body. When he wants to go with a visible body after making the mind dependent on the body and he converts the mind to accord with the body and sets it, mounts it, on the material body, then taking it that the [word in the] accusative case is the proper object, it *has an exalted object* because its object is the exalted consciousness.

107. But that same consciousness takes what has passed, has ceased, as its object, therefore it *has a past object*. In those who resolve about the future, as in the case of the Elder Mahā-Kassapa in the Great Storing of the Relics, and others, it *has a future object*. When the Elder Mahā-Kassapa was making the Great Relic Store, it seems, he resolved thus 'During the next two hundred and eighteen years in the future let not these perfumes dry up or these flowers wither or these lamps go out', and so it all happened. When the Elder Assagutta saw the Community of Bhikkhus eating dry food in the Vattaniya Lodging he resolved thus 'Let the water pool become cream of curd every day before the meal', and when the water was taken before the meal it was cream of curd; but after the meal there was only the normal water.[22]

---

20. See Abhidhamma *Mātikā* ('Schedule') Dhs. p. 1 f. This consists of 22 sets of triple classifications (*tika*) and 100 sets of double ones (*duka*). The first triad is 'profitable, unprofitable, and [morally] indeterminate' and the first dyad is 'root-cause, not-root-cause'. The Mātikā is used in the Dhammasaṅgaṇī (for which it serves as the basic structure), in the Vibhaṅga (in some of the 'Abhidhamma Sections' and in the 'Questionnaries') and in the Paṭṭhāna. All dhammas are either classifiable according to these triads and dyads, under one of the headings, if the triad of dyad is all-embracing, or are called 'not-so-classifiable (*na-vattabba*)', if the triad or dyad is not. The four triads mentioned here are: no. 13 'Dhammas with a limited object, with an exalted object, with a measureless object'; no. 16 'Dhammas with a path as object, with a path as root-cause, with a path as predominance'; no. 19 'Dhammas with a past object, with a future object, with a present object'; and no. 21 Dhammas with an internal object with an external object, with an internal-external object'.

21. The 'word in the accusative case' is in the first instance 'body', governed by the verb 'converts' (*kāyam pariṇāmeti*); see Pm.

22. Pm. comments 'Although with the words "*These perfumes*", etc., he apprehends present perfumes, etc., nevertheless the object of his resolving consciousness is actually their future materiality that is to

108. At the time of going with an invisible body after making the body dependent on the mind it *has a present object.*

At the time of converting the mind to accord with the body, or the body to accord with the mind, and at the time of creating one's own appearance as a boy, etc., it *has an internal object* because it makes one's own body and mind its object. But at the time of showing elephants, horses, etc., externally it *has an external object.*

This is how, firstly, the kinds of supernormal power should be understood to occur with respect to the seven kinds of object.

109. (2) *Knowledge of the Divine Ear Element* occurs with respect to four kinds of object, that is to say, as having a limited, and a present, and an internal or external, object. How?

Since it makes sound its object and since sound is limited (see Vbh. 74) it therefore has a limited object.[23] But since it occurs only by making existing sound its object it *has a present object.* At the time of hearing sounds in one's own belly it *has an internal object.* At the time of hearing the sounds of others it *has an external object.* [431] This is how the knowledge of the divine ear element should be understood to occur with respect to the four kinds of object.

110. (3) *Knowledge of Penetration of Minds* occurs with respect to eight kinds of object, that is to say, as having a limited, exalted or measureless object, path as object and a past, future or present object, and an external object. How?

At the time of knowing others' sense-sphere consciousness it *has a limited object.* At the time of knowing their fine-material-sphere or immaterial-sphere consciousness it *has an exalted object.* At the time of knowing path an fruition it *has a measureless object.* And here an ordinary man does not know a Stream Enterer's consciousness, nor does a Stream Enterer know a Once-returner's, and so up to the Arahant's consciousness. But an Arahant knows the consciousness of all the others. And each higher one knows the consciousnesses of all those below him. This is the difference to be understood. At the time when it has path consciousness as its object it *has path as object.* But when one knows others' consciousness within the past seven days, or within the future seven days then it *has a past object* and *has a future object* respectively.

---

be associated with the distinction of not drying up. This is because the resolve concerns the future ... "*Cream of curd*": when resolving, his object is the future appearance of curd'.

Vattanīyasenāsana was apparently a monastery in the Vindhya Hills (*Viñjaṭavī*): see Mv. XIX,6, DhsA, 419. The Elders Assagutta and Rohaṇa instructed Kajangala who was sent to convert Menander (Lamotte, Histoire de la Buddhisme Indien, p.440).

23. Cf. also Vbh. 62 and 91.

111. How does it have a present object? 'Present (*paccuppanna*)' is of three kinds, that is to say, present by moment, present by continuity, and present by extent. Herein, what has reached arising (*uppāda*), presence (*ṭhiti*), and dissolution (*bhaṅga*), is *present by moment*. What is included in one or two rounds of continuity is *present by continuity*.

112. Herein, when someone goes to a well-lit place after sitting in the dark, an object is not clear at first: until it becomes clear, one or two rounds of continuity should be understood [to pass] meanwhile. And when he goes into an inner closet after going about in a well-lit place, a visible object is not immediately evident at first until it becomes clear, one or two rounds of continuity should be understood [to pass] meanwhile. When he stands at a distance, although he sees the alterations (movements) of the hands of washermen and the alterations (movements) of the striking of gongs, drums, etc. yet he does not hear the sound at first (see Ch. XIV n.22): until he hears it one or two rounds of continuity should be understood [to pass] meanwhile. This, firstly, is according to the Majjhima Reciters.

113. The Samyutta Reciters, however, say that there are two kinds of continuity, that is to say, material continuity and immaterial continuity: that a material continuity lasts as long as the [muddy] line of water touching the bank when one treads in the water takes to clear,[24] as long as the heat of the body in one who has walked a certain extent takes to die down, as long as the blindness in one who has come from the sunshine into a room does not depart, as long as when, after someone has been giving attention to his meditation subject in a room and then opens the shutters by day and looks out, the dazzling in his eyes does not die down; and that an immaterial continuity consists in two or three rounds of impulsions. Both of these are [according to them] called 'present by continuity'. [432]

114. What is delimited by a single becoming (existence) is called *present by extent*, with reference to which it is said in the *Bhaddekaratta* Sutta 'Friends, the mind and mental objects 'are both what is present. Consciousness is bound by desire 'and greed for what is present. Because consciousness is 'bound by desire and greed he delights in that. When he 'delights in that, then he is vanquished with respect to present 'states' (M. iii, 197).

And here 'present by continuity' is used in the commentaries while 'present by extent' is used in the suttas.

24. Pm. adds 'Some however explain the meaning in this way: It is as long as, when one has stepped on the dry bank with a wet foot, the water line on the foot does not disappear'.

115. Herein, some[25] say that consciousness 'present by moment' is the object of knowledge of penetration of minds. What reason do they give? It is that the consciousness of the possessor of supernormal power and that of the other arise in a single moment. Their simile is this: just as when a handful of flowers is thrown into the air the stalk of one flower is probably struck by the stalk of another, and so too, when with the thought 'I will know another's mind' the mind of a multitude is adverted to as a mass, then the mind of one is probably penetrated by the mind of the other either at the moment of arising or at the moment of presence or at the
116. moment of dissolution. That, however, is rejected in the Commentaries as erroneous, because even if one went on adverting for a hundred or a thousand years, there is never co-presence of the two consciousnesses, that is to say, of that with which he adverts and that [of impulsion] with which he knows, and because the flaw of plurality of objects follows if presence [of the same object] to both adverting and impulsion is not insisted on. What should be understood is that the object is present by continuity and present by extent.

117. Herein, another's consciousness during a time measuring two or three cognitive series with impulsions extending before and after the [strictly] currently existing cognitive series with impulsions, is all called 'present by continuity'. But in the Samyutta Commentary it is said that 'present by extent' should be illustrated by a round of impulsions. That is
118. rightly said. Here is the illustration. The possessor of supernormal power who wants to know another's mind adverts. The adverting [consciousness] makes [the other's consciousness that is] present by moment its object and ceases together with it. After that there are four or five impulsions, of which the last is the supernormal-power consciousness, the rest being of the sense sphere. That same [other's] consciousness, which has ceased, is the object of all these too, and so they do not have different objects because they have an object that is 'present by extent'. And while they have a single object it is only the supernormal-power consciousness that actually knows another's consciousness, not the other's just as in the eye-door it is only eye consciousness that actually sees the
119. visible datum, not the others. So this has a present object in what is present by continuity and what is present by extent. [433] Or since what is present by continuity falls within what is present by extent, it can therefore be understood that it *has a present* object simply in what is present by extent.

It *has an external object* because it has only another's mind as its object.

---

25 The residents of the Abhayagiri Monastery Anurādhapura (Pm.)

This is how knowledge of penetration of minds should be understood to occur with respect to the eight kinds of objects.

120. (4) *Knowledge of Past Life* occurs with respect to eight kinds of object, that is to say, as having a limited, exalted, or measureless object, path as object, a past object, and an internal, external or not-so-classifiable object. How?

At the time of recollecting sense-sphere aggregates it *has a limited object.* At the time of recollecting fine-material-sphere or immaterial-sphere aggregates it *has an exalted object.* At the time of recollecting a path developed, or a fruition realized, in the past either by oneself or by others, it *has a measureless object.* At the time of recollecting a path developed it *has a path as object.* But it invariably *has a past object.*

121. Herein, although Knowledge of Penetration of Minds and Knowledge of Faring According to Deeds also have a past object, still of these two the object of the knowledge of penetration of minds is only consciousness within the past seven days. It knows neither other aggregates nor what is bound up with aggregates, [that is, name, surname, and so on]. It is said indirectly that it has a path as object since it has the consciousness associated with the path as its object. Also the object of Knowledge of Faring According to Deeds is simply past volition. But there is nothing, whether past aggregates or what is bound up with aggregates, that is not the object of Knowledge of Past Life; for that is on a par with Omniscient Knowledge with respect to past aggregates and states bound up with aggregates. This is the difference to be understood here.

122. This is the method according to the Commentaries here. But it is said in the Paṭṭhāna 'Profitable aggregates are a 'condition, as object condition, for knowledge of super- 'normal power, for knowledge of penetration of minds, for 'knowledge of past life, for knowledge of faring accarding to 'deeds, and for knowledge of the future' (PtnI.154), and therefore four aggregates are also the objects of knowledge of penetration of minds and of knowledge of faring according to deeds. And there too profitable and unprofitable [aggregates are the object] of knowledge of faring according to deeds.

123. At the time of recollecting one's own aggregates it *has an internal object.* At the time of recollecting another's aggregates it *has an external object.* At the time of recollecting [the concepts consisting in] name, race (surname) in the way beginning 'In the past there was the Blessed One Vipassin. His mother wạs Bhandumatī. His father was Bhandumant' (see D.ii,6-7), and [the concept consisting in] the sign of earth, etc., it *has a not-so-classifiable* object.

And here the name and race (surname, lineage) must be regarded not as the actual words but as the meaning of the words, which is established by convention and bound up with aggregates. For the actual words [434] are 'limited' since they are included by the sound base, according as it is said: 'The Discrimination of Language has a limited object' (Vbh. 304). Our preference here is this.

This is how the knowledge of past life should be understood to occur with respect to the eight kinds of object.

124. (5) *Knowledge of the Divine Eye* occurs with respect to four kinds of object, that is to say, as having a limited, a present, and an internal or external object. How? Since it makes materiality its object and materiality is limited (see Vbh. 62) it therefore *has a limited object*. Since it occurs only with respect to existing materiality it *has a present object*. At the time of seeing materiality inside one's own belly, etc., it *has an internal object*. At the time of seeing another's materiality it has an external object. This is how the knowledge of the divine eye should be understood to occur with respect to the four kinds of object.

125. (6) *Knowledge of the Future* occurs with respect to eight kinds of object, that is to say, as having a limited or exalted or immeasurable object, a path as object, a future object, and an internal, external, or not-so-classifiable object. How? At the time of knowing this, 'This one will be reborn in the future in the sense sphere', it *has a limited object*. At the time of knowing 'He will be reborn in the fine-material or immaterial sphere' it *has an exalted object*. At the time of knowing 'He will develop the path, he will realize fruition' it *has an immeasurable object*. At the time of knowing 'He will develop the path' it *has a path as object* too. But it invariably *has a future object*.

126. Herein, although Knowledge of Penetration of Minds has a future object too, nevertheless its object is then only future consciousness that is within seven days; for it knows neither any other aggregate nor what is bound up with aggregates. But there is nothing in the future, as described under the knowledge of past life (§121), that is not an object of Knowledge of the Future.

127. At the time of knowing 'I shall be reborn there' it *has an internal object*. At the time of knowing 'So-and-so will be reborn there' it *has an external object*. *But at the time of* knowing name and race (surname) in the way beginning 'In 'the future the Blessed One Metteyya will arise. His father 'will be the Brahman Subrahmā. His mother will be the 'Brahmani Brahmavatī' (see D.iii,76) it has a not-so-classifiable object in the way described under knowledge of past life (§ 123).

This is how the knowledge of the future should be understood.

128. (7) *Knowledge of Faring According to Deeds* occurs with respect to five kinds of object, that is to say, as having a limited or exalted, a past, and an internal or external object. How? At the time of knowing sense-sphere kamma (deeds) it *has a limited object.* [435] At the time of knowing fine-material-sphere or immaterial-sphere kamma it *has an exalted object.* Since it knows only what is past it *has a past object.* At the time of knowing one's own kamma it *has an internal object.* At the time of knowing another's kamma it *has an external object.* This is how the knowledge of Faring According to Deeds should be understood to occur with respect to the five kinds of object.

129. And when [the knowledge] described here both as 'having an internal object' and 'having an external object' knows [these objects] now internally and now externally, it is then said that it *has an internal-external object* as well.

The thirteenth chapter concluding 'The Description of Direct-knowledge' in the Path of Purification composed for the purpose of Gladdening good people.